# JESUS
## AND THE LAW OF ATTRACTION

Do you want to improve your life, attain total happiness, treat an illness, increase your finances, find true love, or heal a relationship? God gave us the means to achieve all of these things and more, and Jesus gave us the key to unlocking the divine formula!

In his bestselling book, *Jesus and the Law of Attraction*, Bible scholar and spiritual educator Lochlainn Seabrook has provided us with a comprehensive, one-of-a-kind guide that will forever alter the way you view Christ and His earthly mission, while giving you the power to transform your life on every level.

A treasure trove of invaluable spiritual knowledge, dug from the archives of the Ancient Wisdom and Jesus' secret teachings.

# ☙ THE LOCHLAINN SEABROOK COLLECTION ☙

Everything You Were Taught About the Civil War is Wrong, Ask a Southerner!
Everything You Were Taught About American Slavery is Wrong, Ask a Southerner!
Confederate Flag Facts: What Every American Should Know About Dixie's Southern Cross
Give This Book to a Yankee! A Southern Guide to the Civil War For Northerners
Honest Jeff and Dishonest Abe: A Southern Children's Guide to the Civil War
Confederacy 101: Amazing Facts You Never Knew About America's Oldest Political Tradition
Slavery 101: Amazing Facts You Never Knew About America's "Peculiar Institution"
The Great Yankee Coverup: What the North Doesn't Want You to Know About Lincoln's War!
Confederate Blood and Treasure: An Interview With Lochlainn Seabrook
A Rebel Born: A Defense of Nathan Bedford Forrest - Confederate General, American Legend (winner of the 2011
        Jefferson Davis Historical Gold Medal)
A Rebel Born: The Screenplay
Nathan Bedford Forrest: Southern Hero, American Patriot - Honoring a Confederate Icon and the Old South
The Quotable Nathan Bedford Forrest: Selections From the Writings and Speeches of the Confederacy's Most Brilliant
        Cavalryman
Give 'Em Hell Boys! The Complete Military Correspondence of Nathan Bedford Forrest
Forrest! 99 Reasons to Love Nathan Bedford Forrest
Saddle, Sword, and Gun: A Biography of Nathan Bedford Forrest For Teens
Nathan Bedford Forrest and the Battle of Fort Pillow: Yankee Myth, Confederate Fact
Nathan Bedford Forrest and the Ku Klux Klan: Yankee Myth, Confederate Fact
Nathan Bedford Forrest and African-Americans: Yankee Myth, Confederate Fact
The Quotable Jefferson Davis: Selections From the Writings and Speeches of the Confederacy's First President
The Quotable Alexander H. Stephens: Selections From the Writings and Speeches of the Confederacy's First Vice
        President
The Alexander H. Stephens Reader: Excerpts From the Works of a Confederate Founding Father
The Quotable Robert E. Lee: Selections From the Writings and Speeches of the South's Most Beloved Civil War General
The Old Rebel: Robert E. Lee As He Was Seen By His Contemporaries
The Articles of Confederation Explained: A Clause-by-Clause Study of America's First Constitution
The Constitution of the Confederate States of America Explained: A Clause-by-Clause Study of the South's Magna Carta
The Quotable Stonewall Jackson: Selections From the Writings and Speeches of the South's Most Famous General
Abraham Lincoln: The Southern View - Demythologizing America's Sixteenth President
The Unquotable Abraham Lincoln: The President's Quotes They Don't Want You To Know!
Lincolnology: The Real Abraham Lincoln Revealed in His Own Words - A Study of Lincoln's Suppressed, Misinterpreted,
        and Forgotten Writings and Speeches
The Great Impersonator! 99 Reasons to Dislike Abraham Lincoln
The Quotable Edward A. Pollard: Selections From the Writings of the Confederacy's Greatest Defender
Encyclopedia of the Battle of Franklin - A Comprehensive Guide to the Conflict that Changed the Civil War
Carnton Plantation Ghost Stories: True Tales of the Unexplained from Tennessee's Most Haunted Civil War House!
The McGavocks of Carnton Plantation: A Southern History - Celebrating One of Dixie's Most Noble Confederate
        Families and Their Tennessee Home
Jesus and the Law of Attraction: The Bible-Based Guide to Creating Perfect Health, Wealth, and Happiness Following
        Christ's Simple Formula
The Bible and the Law of Attraction: 99 Teachings of Jesus, the Apostles, and the Prophets
Christ Is All and In All: Rediscovering Your Divine Nature and the Kingdom Within
Jesus and the Gospel of Q: Christ's Pre-Christian Teachings As Recorded in the New Testament
Seabrook's Bible Dictionary of Traditional and Mystical Christian Doctrines
The Way of Holiness: The Story of Religion and Myth From the Cave Bear Cult to Christianity
Christmas Before Christianity: How the Birthday of the "Sun" Became the Birthday of the "Son"
Autobiography of a Non-Yogi: A Scientist's Journey From Hinduism to Christianity (with Amitava Dasgupta)
Britannia Rules: Goddess-Worship in Ancient Anglo-Celtic Society - An Academic Look at the United Kingdom's
        Matricentric Spiritual Past
The Book of Kelle: An Introduction to Goddess-Worship and the Great Celtic Mother-Goddess Kelle, Original Blessed
        Lady of Ireland
The Goddess Dictionary of Words and Phrases: Introducing a New Core Vocabulary for the Women's Spirituality
        Movement
Princess Diana: Modern Day Moon-Goddess - A Psychoanalytical and Mythological Look at Diana Spencer's Life,
        Marriage, and Death (with Dr. Jane Goldberg)
Aphrodite's Trade: The Hidden History of Prostitution Unveiled
UFOs and Aliens: The Complete Guidebook
The Caudills: An Etymological, Ethnological, and Genealogical Study - Exploring the Name and National Origins of a
        European-American Family
The Blakeneys: An Etymological, Ethnological, and Genealogical Study - Uncovering the Mysterious Origins of the
        Blakeney Family and Name

*Five-Star Books & Gifts From the Heart of the American South*

# SeaRavenPress.com

# JESUS

## AND THE LAW OF ATTRACTION

The Bible-Based Guide to Creating Perfect Health,
Wealth, and Happiness Following Christ's Simple Formula

# Lochlainn Seabrook

JEFFERSON DAVIS HISTORICAL GOLD MEDAL WINNER

*Foreword by Dannion Brinkley*

SEA RAVEN PRESS, NASHVILLE, TENNESSEE, USA

# JESUS AND THE LAW OF ATTRACTION

Published by
Sea Raven Press, Cassidy Ravensdale, President
PO Box 1484, Spring Hill, Tennessee 37174-1484 USA
SeaRavenPress.com • searavenpress@gmail.com

1ˢᵗ SRP paperback edition (978-0-9858632-5-8): September 2013
1ˢᵗ SRP hardcover edition: February 2016

ISBN: 978-1-943737-29-1 (hardcover)
Library of Congress Control Number: 2013939626

Jesus and the Law of Attraction: The Bible-Based Guide to Creating Perfect Health, Wealth, and Happiness Following Christ's Simple Formula, by Lochlainn Seabrook. Foreword by Dannion Brinkley. Includes endnotes.

*Front & back cover design & art, book design, layout, & interior art by Lochlainn Seabrook.*
*All images, graphic design, graphic art, & illustrations copyright © Lochlainn Seabrook.*
*Front cover image: "Christ Pantokrator," 12ᵗʰ-Century apse mosaic, Cefalù Cathedral, Cefalù, Sicily, Italy*
*Cover photography, image manipulation, graphic design, & graphic artwork © Lochlainn Seabrook.*
*All other photos, images, & artwork © Lochlainn Seabrook. All quotes are public domain.*

The views on Jesus and the Bible documented in this book *are* those of the publisher.

The paper used in this book is acid-free and lignin-free. It has been certified by the Sustainable Forestry Initiative and the Forest Stewardship Council and meets all ANSI standards for archival quality paper.

**All are thrice spirit-blessed who read this little book.**

PRINTED & MANUFACTURED IN OCCUPIED TENNESSEE, FORMER CONFEDERATE STATES OF AMERICA

# Dedication

To the Sun of Righteousness.

Malachi 4:2

# Epigraph

"Therefore I say unto you, what things soever ye desire, when ye pray, believe that ye receive them, and ye shall have them." — Jesus

# CONTENTS

# List of Illustrations

Photo © Lochlainn Seabrook

# Notes to the Reader

✠ As the twenty-seven books of the New Testament clearly reveal, Jesus' approach to the Kingdom of God and His corresponding teachings on the Law of Attraction were purely mystical, that is, psychological. He never once, for example, unambiguously and openly defines either subject,[1] and instead speaks of them in parables, metaphors, allegories, and symbols,[2] many which were so arcane that neither His Disciples or even His own inner circle of private initiates, the Twelve Apostles, could understand them.[3]

Because one cannot comprehend spiritual esoterica, like the Lord's teachings on the Law of Attraction, through a literal reading of the New Testament, out of necessity I have approached this topic using a mystical exegesis as well. To make Jesus' words as understandable as possible, I often give, for example, both the outer (literal) and inner (spiritual) meaning of His statements, based on, in particular, the traditional principles of mystical Christianity, the ancient Christian mystery schools, and those of some of the earliest known followers of the Christ, the pre-Christian Gnostics.

To further aid those who are new to Jesus' mystical "secret teachings," I have included a glossary of primitive Christianity's most commonly used occultic words and phrases.

✠ All canonical Bible passages are from the King James Version (KJV), unless otherwise noted. As a result, my readings and interpretations may differ from those found in other versions. Because of this, I highly recommend the use of the KJV in combination with *Jesus and the Law of Attraction*. Note that I use the KJV, not because it is the first "authorized" Bible (it is the third), or because it is the first English Bible (it is the seventh), but because it is still the one best known to the general public.

✠ While I have retained the original text of the KJV, I have divided long Bible passages into paragraphs suited to modern readers (these often differ from the standard biblical divisions).

✠ Though many of the Bible's books are pseudepigraphical (that is, their authors are unknown or, more often, are falsely attributed), for simplicity's sake I use the authors ascribed by Christian tradition.

✠ There are some 50,000 Christian denominations, sects, factions, churches, societies, schisms, communities, and cults in the world today. This book is not associated with any of them. What it *is* associated with are the original and authentic teachings of Jesus as they appear in the New Testament.

Many if not most of these teachings derive from the Gospel of Q (from the German word *quelle*, "source"), a now lost document (though mentioned by 2nd-Century Bishop Papias of Hierapolis,[4] and also Paul)[5] containing the shared earliest oral traditions surrounding Jesus' sayings—which were liberally used by Matthew and Luke, and to some extent Mark, before it finally disappeared.[6] Thus, the Synoptic Gospels contain precious remnants of the Lord's actual thoughts and words.

As paleographic evidence shows, the Gospel of Q, of course, predates the four canonical Gospels, with the earliest "layer" (known as Q1) probably being recorded as early as the 30s (shortly after Jesus' death), Q2 being composed sometime in the 40s and 50s, and Q3 written as late as the year 75.

The Gospel of Q does not mention or delve into the life of Jesus, His birth, baptism, messiahship, the Last Supper, His trial, crucifixion, transfiguration, resurrection, or ascension. Its earliest layer also contains no apocalyptic warnings, no martyrological dogma, no complex theodicies, no salvific creeds, no named apostles, and no rules or instructions on how to organize and maintain the community of Q (which authored Q)—or any future type of "church" for that matter. Rather, as one would expect from the earliest followers of the Master (who were not "Christians" and never thought of themselves as such), Q centers not on Jesus, but on Jesus' *teachings*, one of the most important which included His life-saving, life-altering doctrines on the Law of Attraction, the focus of this book.

Other Jesuine teachings from the Gospel of Q that are found in the New Testament are the Lord's Prayer, the Golden Rule, the Beatitudes, and many of His parables, such as those concerning the all-important Kingdom of God, or what I term "the Realm of Divine Mind."[7]

For those who are interested, another important source for Jesus' original and authentic teachings is the Gnostic Christians' Gospel of Thomas (which could itself be a version of the Gospel of Q),[8] another "sayings gospel," some of whose sibylline doctrines can be found in the writings of early Christian mystics.[9]

✠ Though, as promised in the subtitle, this is indeed a (canonical) Bible-based work, at times I have found it either needful or of interest to quote agrapha: the Lord's noncanonical words; that is, His statements recorded in sources outside the Bible. In many cases, quoting agrapha is necessary to fill in the gapping holes left by the heavy often error-filled editing of the New Testament by ancient ecclesiastical priests, scribes, and copyists.

✠ All quotations from Levi H. Dowling's *The Aquarian Gospel of Jesus the Christ* are from the 1911 edition, and are thus in the public domain. This book is cited in the main text as the Aquarian Gospel and in my endnotes as AGJC, followed by the chapters and verses.

✠ All italics within quotes are mine.

✠ Bracketed words within quotes contain my comments and corrections.

✠ In order to get the most out of this book, I recommend the following.
   • Whatever your personal beliefs or background, read with an open and inquisitive mind, that is, as a "little child," in the words of Jesus.[10] With the clutter of preconceived notions, beliefs, and ideas out of the way, you will be able to absorb the maximum amount of new knowledge. You can only harvest from these teachings what the soil of your mind has been prepared to plant.
   • After reading this book, give yourself time to metabolize it mentally and spiritually. Then reread it. As your consciousness elevates, second, third, and even fourth readings will reveal more and more about the "pearl of great price,"[11] "the revelation of the mystery, which was kept secret since the world began," as Paul called it.[12]
   Following these two suggestions will give you the fullest understanding of Jesus' doctrines on the Law of Attraction. The more you comprehend, the more benefits you will derive from *Jesus and the Law of Attraction*.

✠ To those Christians who may question the validity of the teachings in this book, please keep in mind that nearly all of them are taken directly from the canonical Bible (KJV). Additionally, to prove them true or false, you must first try them out. Follow the instructions provided, then apply the teachings to your daily life and judge the outcome for yourself. These doctrines are from Jesus after all, the Master Teacher,[13] Psychologist,[14] and Physician[15] who said, "by their fruits [results] ye shall know them."[16]

✠ The principles offered in this book work only by faith. Thus, because the results depend on the individual, no guarantees are made or implied—except the spiritual-scientific one preached by Jesus: your life is the direct result of what you think, say, and do.[17]

✠ Bless the world by sharing the doctrines in *Jesus and the Law of Attraction* with your family members, friends, neighbors, and coworkers who want to hear the Word of God. Being eternal, the Word is still very much alive, and is ready to work miracles in the lives of all those who are prepared to receive it.[18]

The "Crown of Life" awaits all those who believe; that is, those who have faith in the unseen powers of the Father, and who closely follow Jesus' teachings on the Law of Attraction.

# To Skeptics & Nonbelievers

here are those scientifically-minded skeptics who may regard this entire book, based on the title alone, as "pseudoscience," as lacking a scientific basis. I am familiar with this approach and, as one with a background in not only religion but in science as well, I accept it, for it is one of the jobs of science to disprove unscientific theories.

However, as I show, Jesus' teachings on the Law of Attraction *are* scientific, for in the outer branches of science (quantum mechanics) and religion (mysticism), the laws of physics and the laws of God merge, becoming unified. Thus Jesus' doctrines turn Christianity from a supernatural faith into a scientific one.

As I see it, when it comes to the Law of Attraction the real problem with skeptics is that few if any have truly tested it. They simply reject the idea outright because it does not fit into their (usually rigidly orthodox) worldview. As such, they consider the Law unworthy of study, the same attitude that has long prevailed among scientists concerning ghosts, UFOs, Bigfoot, the Loch Ness Monster, ESP, angels, fairies, miracles, and countless other so-called "paranormal" phenomena.

Since it is one of science's primary tasks to explore the unknown, since science is meant to be an open-ended search for the truth, and since it is the duty of science to uncover the facts no matter what they turn out to be, I consider such scientists to be not only scientifically irresponsible, but unscientific.

What can one say, for example, about scientists who dismiss even the placebo effect, which has been repeatedly demonstrated in every home, hospital, and laboratory, and which is one of the most obvious proofs of the power of the Divine Mind (which Jesus called the "Father")? This is false science masquerading as true science.[19]

This unscientific skepticism is especially hard to justify in light of the mind-bending discoveries now coming from fields like quantum physics, which reveal, for instance, that the known laws of physics do not exist in the center of black holes, that there are subatomic particles that travel faster than the speed of light (disproving Einstein's 1905 theory of special relativity); that subatomic particles of energy—no matter how far apart they are separated—can communicate with one another *instantly*; and that neutrinos (a subatomic particle that contains a small amount of mass) can pass undetected and unaffected through matter, even over long distances.

And let us not forget the Copenhagen Interpretation (a 1920s explanation of quantum mechanics), which, in simple terms, shows that even down to the subatomic level, the beliefs, perceptions, and expectations of scientists determine the outcome of their experiments. In other words, biological and even nonbiological material responds to human thought, and furthermore, can be altered by thought to accord with the thinker's intentions. Why? Because, as I will show, thought is spiritual energy, the most powerful force in the Universe.

As it turns out, that Holy Grail of science, the "Standard Model of Physics," is not so "standard" after all.

The reality is that those who disbelieve in the Law of Attraction, whether they are scientists or religionists, will never be able to prove or disprove it. Why? Because skepticism prevents the Law from working favorably. As my readers will learn from this very book, one of the most important elements of working with the Law of Attraction is perfect faith, unwavering belief. According to Jesus Himself, it is not a case of "seeing is believing," it is a case of "believing is seeing." For while under scientific law the physical (condition) is the cause and the mind (thought) is the effect, under God's Law the mind (thought) is the cause and the physical (condition) is the effect.

It is not simply scientific or religious skepticism that is dangerous to the advancement of humanity. It is *close-minded* skepticism, whether an atheist or a believer. For the members of today's "Skeptics Club" are merely modern science's version of the ancient "scribes and Pharisees"—the world's revered but spiritually unenlightened mainstream authorities—who Jesus so vociferously condemned.[20]

Let skeptics, whatever their worldview and belief system, keep this Law of Attraction statement by Einstein in mind: "Your imagination is your preview of life's coming attractions."[21] Like Jesus and thousands of other intelligent and spiritually advanced individuals (see Appendix A), the famed German physicist understood that the Law of Attraction is at the root, not only of human life, but of every aspect of the Universe down to the smallest quark.

Finally, let us not forget that there was a day in the not so distant past when science scoffed at reports of rocks falling from the sky, of gigantic hairy ape men, and of sixty foot long sea monsters. But this unscientific arrogance quickly turned to humility when meteorites, gorillas, and giant squid turned out to be all too real!

One day mainstream science will come to accept Jesus' teachings on the Law of Attraction as well, and then, as Victorian Transcendentalist Ralph Waldo Emerson once intimated, our science books will be written by men and women of God, not of universities.[22]

# THE SEABROOK TRINITY
## YOUR INNER MENTAL TRIAD
### A Key to Jesus' Teachings on the Law of Attraction

*By Lochlainn Seabrook*

---

## THE SUPERCONSCIOUS MIND
*Mind (that is, Spirit) / Mental / The Creator / Power / Thought*
### THE SOURCE / THE ONE

- The "Father" or "God" in patriarchal religions
- The "Mother" or "Goddess" in matriarchal religions
- The "I AM" or "Divine Mind" in mystical religions
- The "Unified Field," "Laws of Physics," or "Nature" in science
- Located at the Crown Chakra (top of head)

Keywords: Androgynous, Light, Perfection, Omnipresent, Omnipotent, Omniscient, Omniactive, Manifestation, Materialization, Universal, Infinite, Eternal

---

## THE CONSCIOUS MIND
*Body / Physical / The Thinker / The Master / Wisdom / Word*

- The "Son" or the "Lord" in patriarchal religions
- The "Sun" in matriarchal religions
- The "Christ," "Logos," "Higher Self," or "Spiritual Law" in mystical religions

Located at the Third Eye Chakra (forehead); correlates with the left side of the brain, which governs the right side of the body. Logical, sequential, analytical, objective, finite.

Keywords: Masculine, Day, Knowledge, Earthly, Ideas, Facts, Science

---

## THE SUBCONSCIOUS MIND
*Soul / Spiritual / The Communicator / The Servant / Love / Action*

- The "Holy Spirit," "Holy Ghost," or "Comforter" in patriarchal religions
- The "Moon" or "Goddess" (of Wisdom) in matriarchal religions

Located in the regions of the Solar Plexus Chakra (just above the naval) and Heart Chakra (chest); correlates with the right side of the brain, which governs the left side of the body. Emotional, random, intuitive, subjective, infinite.

Keywords: Feminine, Night, Belief, Heavenly, Expression, Symbols, Spirituality

# Psalms 91
To be read once a day

"He that dwelleth in the secret place of the most High shall abide under the shadow of the Almighty. I will say of the Lord, he is my refuge and my fortress: my God; in him will I trust. Surely he shall deliver thee from the snare of the fowler, and from the noisome pestilence. He shall cover thee with his feathers, and under his wings shalt thou trust: his truth shall be thy shield and buckler. Thou shalt not be afraid for the terror by night; nor for the arrow that flieth by day; nor for the pestilence that walketh in darkness; nor for the destruction that wasteth at noonday. A thousand shall fall at thy side, and ten thousand at thy right hand; but it shall not come nigh thee. Only with thine eyes shalt thou behold and see the reward of the wicked. *Because thou hast made the Lord, which is my refuge, even the most High, thy habitation; there shall no evil befall thee, neither shall any plague come nigh thy dwelling. For he shall give his angels charge over thee, to keep thee in all thy ways.* They shall bear thee up in their hands, lest thou dash thy foot against a stone. Thou shalt tread upon the lion and adder: the young lion and the dragon shalt thou trample under feet. Because he hath set his love upon me, therefore will I deliver him: I will set him on high, because he hath known my name. He shall call upon me, and I will answer him: I will be with him in trouble; I will deliver him, and honour him. With long life will I satisfy him, and shew him my salvation."[23]

# FOREWORD

Next to being a former Marine, nothing in my life makes me prouder than my Southern heritage. Being a son of Dixie, raised in South Carolina by loving parents deeply ingrained in the Southern religious tradition, was more than enough to make me question the workings of God when I was struck by lightning. Well, I was not simply struck by lightning; I was struck, and killed for 28 minutes by that fiery bolt of wrath from the heavens. I phrase it this way because in the scriptures lightning and thunder are referred to as tokens of God's wrath.

Once I came across this biblical interpretation, I made it my mission to learn all I could about the life and times of Jesus, and the mysteries of the Divine. I've never been a very patient man so much to my dismay it took me nearly four years to recover completely from the devastating damage the lightning's immense electrical force inflicted upon my physical, mental and emotional being. There were days I thought I would not survive. Nevertheless, by the grace of God, survive I did. And through those years of recovery I was given ample time to read everything I could get my hands on about the teachings and miracles of Jesus.

Since that time, I have written three bestselling books on my one death and two subsequent near-death experiences. I've shared my story with audiences worldwide, as I have dedicated my life to helping other people understand and find comfort in the spiritual reality I experienced when I was what we call, dead. I had no pulse, heartbeat or respiration by the time I reached the hospital so, my body was covered with a sheet and set aside in an empty room, because the emergency room was so busy that night. Yet, I can tell you without a moment's hesitation that I never felt more alive than I was during the time I traveled down the now famous tunnel, and into the bright and beautiful Light standing guard at the entrance, to the heavenly realms.

Honestly, people ask me all the time if, during my time on the other side, I saw Jesus. And the answer is, no . . . I did not. Nor did I see any of my dearly departed relatives. Instead, I was embraced by the Spirit of Love, as I had never before experienced it. Yet, through the majestic command of Lochlainn's words, in *Jesus and the Law of Attraction*, I was given a rare opportunity to reminisce over those first breathtaking moments of love and inspiration I experienced on the other side, way back in 1975.

I don't know if Lochlainn has ever had a near-death experience, but he certainly writes with the profound authority of someone who has. After authoring more than thirty books, on a wide variety of magnificent subjects, his research and literary genius reveal themselves, for all to enjoy. What I enjoyed most about this book is his amazing ability to seamlessly combine the religious teachings of Jesus, and the metaphysical interpretation of the Universal Law of Attraction. The way in which Lochlainn constructs this spiritual perspective opens our minds and our hearts to a broader viewpoint of the way the Divine operates.

By making a point of truly absorbing and utilizing the information being offered in this remarkable book, you will undoubtedly find greater inspiration, imagination, intuition and revelation—all of which are intended to help you lead a more meaningful, rewarding and joyous life. We are living in a time when the lines of separation between religion and spirituality are passing away. The interfaith marriage of Divine Law and interpretive practices, such as those set down in this book, are now bringing us into a reality of authentic connectedness—a deeper connectedness to one another and to the Divine Spirit. Moreover, Lochlainn is empowering us with the understanding that we are more in control of our lives, and of our destiny, than we ever believed possible.

If used as a personal guidebook, to help you properly align Immutable Universal Law with Christ Consciousness, *Jesus and the Law of Attraction* will be one of the most important books you will ever need. In closing, I can find no better words than these written by Lochlainn himself:

> "Once you have been introduced to Jesus' teachings on the Law of Attraction, you are to keep your Inner Light, the Universal Self, the Christ Within, alive at all times. Follow Jesus' advice and keep your spiritual 'Candle Within' burning brightly day and night."

> *"Stay strong in your faith."*

Dannion Brinkley
September 5, 2013

# PREFACE

## "Behold, I Shew You a Mystery"[24]

I have been working with Jesus' teachings on the Law of Attraction for over forty years. To say that my life has been deeply touched and affected by them would be a vast understatement. For I have seen numerous "miracles" take place, such as the complete disappearance of so-called "terminal" illnesses, the total transformation of individuals, marriages, and families, and stunning positive and negative occurrences (for the Law works in both directions) involving real estate, vehicles, business, and money.

I have not only experienced my own "miracles" using the Law—stunning both the medical establishment and the Church—I have witnessed a thousand other smaller ones with my own eyes as well, events that orthodox scientists said were "inconceivable," that the traditional clergy declared "unthinkable," and which mainstream doctors told me was "impossible." I ignored them all, and instead took Jesus' Law of Attraction statement literally, that "with God all things are possible."[25] And He is right!

Yes, based on faith as well as countless personal experiences, I am a true believer, and I could not be otherwise. As such, rest assured that I would not have written this book unless I had seen God's Law in action.

It is my prayer that the revelations of the "deep things of God"[26] unveiled herein will, as with Paul, cause the "scales" to fall from your spiritual eyes,[27] and that those who were once spiritually "blind" will be able to "see" the Lord and the Law of Attraction in an entirely new light, allowing them, in turn, to experience an entirely new way of life.[28]

Truly blessed are those who have the "ears to hear"[29] the momentous message that this little work contains.[30] For within it will be found "things which have been kept secret from the foundation of the world";[31] suppressed esoteric doctrines from Jesus' "Everlasting Gospel"[32] and His "Hidden Wisdom of God in a mystery,"[33] that the Indwelling Father[34] wants to share with all of His children—including you![35]

Read carefully, with an open heart and mind, and "Christ shall give thee light."[36] With this light you, dear reader, will discover the literal keys to the Kingdom of God,[37] what I call "the Realm of Divine Mind," where anything can become reality.[38] Truly, I offer this work to you, that your

> "hearts might be comforted, being knit together in love, and unto all riches of the full assurance of understanding, to the acknowledgment of the mystery of God, and of the Father, and of Christ; in whom are hid all the treasures of wisdom and knowledge."[39]

Do not worry about understanding everything in your first reading. Even the greatest Law of Attraction masters spend years studying these doctrines. Just open the book and begin, knowing that you will be guided by the Holy Spirit,[40] that the Truth will be revealed to you by the "Father which is in heaven,"[41] and that ultimately you will receive the specific lessons you need for your current life situation and level of spiritual consciousness.[42]

Those who are spiritually "slumbering,"[43] that is, those who are new to the secret mysteries of the Lord's inner teachings (including the Law of Attraction), may at first find it difficult to understand or accept the Jesuine principles I discuss. To them Paul says: "It is high time to awake out of sleep."[44]

Conversely, those who are spiritually "alert," that is, those who are open to, or who are already familiar with, the Law of Attraction, *will* more easily understand and embrace the teachings found here. To these Jesus would have said: "You are not far from the Kingdom of God."[45]

Those in the latter group, those with receptive hearts and open minds—that is, they who "become as little children"—will certainly "enter into the Kingdom of Heaven."[46] As such, they are personally invited by Jesus to enjoy the rich rewards that come from practicing the Law of Attraction (part of His "Gospel of the Kingdom"),[47] working with the Universal Divine Mind (the "Father which is secret"),[48] and creating perfect health, wealth, and happiness while here on earth (the "Kingdom within"):[49]

"Come, ye blessed of my Father, inherit the kingdom prepared for you from the foundation of the world."[50]

May this book "give unto you the spirit of wisdom [Sophia] and revelation in the knowledge [Gnosis] of God."[51] May it start you on the path to claiming your divine inheritance[52]—the key to understanding Jesus' teachings on the Law of Attraction—which will provide you and your loved ones with an eternity of perfect health, wealth, and happiness.[53]

Do not hesitate, for "all things are for your sake."[54] Just as God delights in working in you,[55] He purposefully chose to make the Universe and everything in it[56] so that He could experience the "good pleasure" of giving it all to you.[57] Therefore, it truly all belongs to you,[58] "an inheritance incorruptible, and undefiled, and that fadeth not away, reserved in heaven for you"![59]

Lochlainn Seabrook
Franklin, Williamson County, Tennessee, USA
*Soli Deo Gloria*
God-written, Autumnal Equinox, 2013

Jesus blessing children. To work with the Law of Attraction most efficiently, the Lord taught that we must become as "little children," which allows us access to the mysterious Kingdom of God that "is within you."

# 1

# YOU ARE DIVINE!

> "Death and life are in the power of the tongue: and they that love it shall eat the fruit thereof."[60]

## THE CHRISTIAN SECRET OF THE AGES

**WHAT IF I WERE TO** tell you that you are a god or goddess, and that because of this you have unlimited powers to create perfect health, wealth, love, peace, and happiness?

And what if I were to tell you that there is a simple formula for creating your perfect life, your own Garden of Eden, your own personal land of "milk and honey,"[61] that is both spiritually- and scientifically-based; a formula that, if followed correctly, will allow you to perform "miracles" even greater than those performed by Jesus?

My fellow Christians would undoubtedly accuse me of blasphemy, while skeptics would declare me mentally unstable.

But what if I were to tell you that these ideas come not from me, but from the man upon whom the entire Christian religion was built: Jesus! Yes, it was He who said that each of us is a divine being with the ability to control the circumstances of our lives in every area.

## JESUS' OWN WORDS

Since this is indeed a Bible-based book, let us establish where in the Good Book the Lord makes these claims. The first is in the Gospel of John:

> Jesus answered them, "Is it not written in your law, 'I [God] said, Ye are gods?'"[62]

The second is also in John:

> "Verily, verily, I [Jesus] say unto you, he that believeth on me, the works that I do shall he do also; and greater works than these shall he do . . ."[63]

Is it really possible that Jesus said that we are each deities in our own right, with the divine power to do even "greater works" than he did? Yes, these are Jesus' own words, taken directly from the canonical book of John.

## JESUS' SOURCES

Careful readers will note that Jesus says: "Is it not written in your law, 'I said, "Ye are gods?"'" What does he mean "written in your law"?

He is referring to the Law of Moses; that is, the ancient Hebrew doctrines found in the first five books of what Christians view as part of the Old Testament, and which Jews call the Torah.

In other words, the idea that each one of us is a god is not original to Jesus. It was known to countless ancient biblical prophets, philosophers, and writers who lived centuries even millennia before Jesus. Let us look at some of these early passages for a moment.

In the book of Genesis, according to Moses, it is written:

> "And the Lord God said, 'Behold, the man [Adam] is become as one of us . . .'"[64]

This concept is found in other Old Testament books as well, such as Psalms, the book which Jesus cites above:

> "I have said, 'Ye are gods; and all of you are children of the most High.'"[65]

Here is how this doctrine appears in the book of Isaiah:

> "Shew the things that are to come hereafter, that we may know that ye are gods . . ."[66]

## A PREHISTORIC CONCEPT

According to Western religious tradition, Genesis was written nearly 3,400 years ago, or around 1400 B.C.; Psalms (actually a collection of poems) was written between 3,200 and 2,500 years ago, or between 1,200 and 500 B.C.; and Isaiah was written about 2,700 years ago, or around 700 B.C.

These ancient Hebrew concepts, of course, derive from even older religions and philosophies, many dating back to the very dawn of recorded history some 8,000 years ago, and even beyond into the prehistoric era.

It is clear then that the idea that we have a divine nature has been an integral part of human spirituality from the very beginning of our existence, extending all the way up through nearly every known society and religion, from ancient Egypt to modern America; from Hinduism, Wicca, Judaism, and Buddhism, to Zoroastrianism, Jainism, Druidry, and Christianity.[67]

Despite its noble and ancient history, the idea that we are each deities in our own right greatly upset people in Jesus' day. And it is still upsetting people today. Indeed, it was this very doctrine that caused some, even among Jesus' friends, to say that He was possessed by a demon, and that He was insane.[68] And it was this very teaching that caused the Jews to rise up in anger against Him, and which ultimately led to His crucifixion.[69]

As we are about to see, however, this prejudice against Jesus was truly unwarranted, for not only does the Old Testament substantiate this particular teaching, but science does as well.

DEBUNKING ORTHODOX SCRIPTURE TWISTING
Even though, along with Jesus, we are not supposed to consider it "robbery to be equal with God,"[70] there are some in the formalistic Christian community—I am speaking specifically of the self-proclaimed "defenders of the faith"—who maintain that the Master did not mean what He said when He declared that "we are all gods and goddesses in our own right."[71] To counter this they will tell you that only Jesus possesses both a human nature and a separate divine nature in one (a Catholic doctrine known as "hypostatic union"), and that because of this He could have only used the word "gods" (in the Bible from the Greek word *theos*) to mean "human rulers," such as magistrates or judges.

It is true that "human rulers" is one of the many meanings of *theos*. But is this what Jesus really meant when He said we humans are "gods"? Since establishing the truth about this word is essential to the topic of this book, let us examine Jesus' statement in context.

Here is the entire scriptural scene as recorded in the King James Version. I have included the word *theos* to show where it is used in the original Greek text:

And it was at Jerusalem the feast of the dedication, and it was winter. And Jesus walked in the temple in Solomon's porch.

Then came the Jews round about him, and said unto him, "How long dost thou make us to doubt? If thou be the Christ, tell us plainly." Jesus answered them, "I told you, and ye believed not: the works that I do in my Father's name, they bear witness of me. But ye believe not, because ye are not of my sheep, as I said unto you. My sheep hear my voice, and I know them, and they follow me: and I give unto them eternal life; and they shall never perish, neither shall any man pluck them out of my hand. My Father, which gave them me, is greater than all; and no man is able to pluck them out of my Father's hand. *I and my Father are one.*"

Then the Jews took up stones again to stone him. Jesus answered them, "Many good works have I shewed you from my Father; for which of those works do ye stone me?" The Jews answered him, saying, "*For a good work we stone thee not; but for blasphemy; and because that thou, being a man, makest thyself God* [*theos*]." Jesus answered them, "Is it not written in your law, 'I said, Ye are gods [*theos*]?' If he called them gods [*theos*], unto whom the word of God [*theos*] came, and the scripture cannot be broken; Say ye of him, whom the Father hath sanctified, and sent into the world, 'Thou blasphemest'; because I said, 'I am the Son of God [*theos*]'? If I do not the works of my Father, believe me not. But if I do, though ye believe not me, believe the works: that ye may know, and believe, that *the Father is in me, and I in him.*"

Therefore they sought again to take him: but he escaped out of their hand, and went away again beyond Jordan into the place where John at first baptized; and there he abode.[72]

If Jesus was using the word *theos* to mean "human rulers," here is how his exchange with the Jewish officials would read:

"Many good works have I shewed you from my Father; for which of those works do ye stone me?" The Jews answered him, saying, "For a good work we stone thee not; but for blasphemy; and because that thou, being a man, makest thyself God." Jesus answered them, "Is it not written in your law, 'I said, Ye are human rulers?' If he called them human rulers, unto whom the word of God came, and the scripture cannot be broken; Say ye of him, whom the Father hath sanctified, and sent into the world, 'Thou blasphemest'; because I said, I am the Son of God?[73]

Obviously, using the formalistic translation, Jesus' words become nonsensical; especially considering the overt fact that if one calls himself a "human ruler," it is not blasphemy. The Pharisees would have only considered Jesus' statement blasphemous if He had used the word "gods" to mean "deities," that is, divine beings. It is self-evident then that this is exactly what He meant.[74]

## THE "CHRIST IN YOU"

In support of the Lord's statement, the Bible offers many other passages that speak of our divine nature.[75] Here is part of the prayer Jesus uttered following the Last Supper. As He clearly states, His petition concerns not just the Twelve Apostles, but *all* believers:

> "Neither pray I for these alone, but for them also which shall believe on me through their word; *That they all may be one; as thou, Father, art in me, and I in thee, that they also may be one in us:* that the world may believe that thou hast sent me. *And the glory [powers] which thou gavest me I have given them; that they may be one, even as we are one: I in them, and thou in me, that they may be made perfect in one;* and that the world may know that thou hast sent me, and hast loved them, as thou hast loved me. . ."[76]

Plainly, Jesus is asserting that He and the Father are one, that we in turn are one with He and the Father, and that He has given us the same "glory," "perfection," and "love" that the Father has given Him.

Paul was well aware of our divinity, calling each one of us "an heir of God through Christ,"[77] after which he says: "Christ [will] be formed" *within* all believers.[78] He also makes this remarkable statement, declaring that "Christ is in all":

> "And [we] have put on the new man [attained a new level of consciousness by defeating our Lower Self], which is renewed in knowledge [Gnosis] after the image of him [God] that created him [Christ]: Where there is neither Greek nor Jew, circumcision or uncircumcision, Barbarian, Scythian, bond nor free: but *Christ is all, and in all.*"[79]

Paul is obviously not speaking here of the religiopolitical title Christ ("anointed"), which—because they were considered divine—was given to all early Jewish kings and Pagan emperors,[80] and some lower ranked religious authorities as well.[81] Nor was he speaking of Mary's human son, "Jesus Christ."[82] He is referring to "*the* Christ,"[83] that is, the great

Indwelling Christ,[84] or what he called the "Christ in you,"[85] the same Christ which Paul says "was also in Jesus."[86] It is the same Christ which John referred to as "the true Light which lighteth every man that cometh into the world,"[87] for the Inner Christ is universal,[88] and thus lived before Jesus[89] as the preexistent "Lord of Lords, King of the Ages."[90]

Solomon described it this way: "The spirit of man is the candle of the Lord."[91] This divine "candle" is the Christ Within, your Higher Self, which was totally realized and perfected in the figure of our Lord Jesus, whose countenance, John said, was "as the sun,"[92] and whom Malachi foretold as the "Sun of Righteousness."[93]

The Sun being an archetypal symbol of spiritual enlightenment (known in the East as nirvana or samadhi), Jesus was often portrayed in ancient Christian art as the Greek Pagan Sun-god Helios, soaring through the heavens in his fiery chariot.[94] Thus in the book of Revelation Jesus is equated with the astrological star sign Leo (the lion), which is ruled by the sun.[95]

Mystically, the effulgent "sunlight" of Jesus is the light of Christ, which exists as a potentiality within each one of us. Jesus said: "Believe in the light, that ye may be the children of light,"[96] while Paul wrote: "Awake thou that sleepest, and arise from the dead, and Christ shall give thee light."[97] The inner meaning:

> "It is time to awaken from your spiritual torpor, and come up out of the coffin of dead religion. Allow the Indwelling Christ to enlighten your mind with the Truth."[98]

Here is another passage from Paul, this one from his letter to the Colossians:

> "I am made a minister, according to the dispensation of God which is given to me for you, to fulfil the word of God; even the mystery which hath been hid from ages and from generations, but now is made manifest to his saints: To whom God would make known what is the riches of the glory of this mystery among the Gentiles [nonbelievers]; which is *Christ in you*, the hope of glory."[99]

Here is the inner meaning:

> "God ordained me to spread a message, a secret that has been concealed from the beginning of time until now. The secret is this:

Christ is not outside of you, He is inside of you. And because you are one with Christ, and because Christ is one with God, you too are one with God and therefore possess the glorious powers of God."[100]

## WE ARE SONS OF GODS

John tells us that we are made "sons of God"[101] merely from the enormous "love the Father hath bestowed upon us."[102] Paul goes as far as to say that anyone who is "led by the Spirit of God, they are the sons of God."[103] Are you led by God's Spirit? If so, you are a Son or Daughter of God, divine inside and out!

Are you loved by God? Absolutely. For you are His child, made to perfection in His image.[104] Do you believe? Then you are a Son of God! Paul likened our "sonship" to "spiritual adoption":

". . . we, when we were children, were in bondage under the elements of the world: but when the fulness of the time was come, God sent forth his Son, made of a woman, made under the law, to redeem them that were under the law, that we might receive the adoption of sons. And because ye are sons, God hath sent forth the Spirit of his Son into your hearts, crying, 'Abba, Father.' *Wherefore thou art no more a servant, but a son; and if a son, then an heir of God through Christ.*"[105]

In the Acts of Paul and Thecla, Paul makes this comment:

"Blessed are those who follow the teachings of Jesus, for they shall be called the sons of the Most High."[106]

Jesus gives a lucid explanation of the "sons of God" concept in the Aquarian Gospel:

"When man comes to himself and comprehends the fact that he is son of God, and knows that *in himself lies all the powers of God*, he is a master mind and all the elements will hear his voice and gladly do his will. Two sturdy asses bind the will of man; their names are Fear and Unbelief. When these are caught and turned aside, the will of man will know no bounds; then man has but to speak and it is done."[107]

The Gospel of John states unequivocally that whoever believes "on the name" of Jesus automatically becomes a "son of God," or Christ:[108]

> "But as many as received him, *to them gave he power to become the sons of God*, even to them that believe on his name."[109]

In "receiving Him" we are sanctified with the "oil of gladness" by the Father,[110] giving us, like Jesus, possession of the Indwelling Christ,[111] anointed into Christhood by God Himself.[112] And just as it was said about both Melchizedek and the Lord,[113] as Sons of God we are eternal, unborn, deathless spirits:

> "Without father, without mother, without descent, having neither beginning of days, nor end of life; but made like unto the Son of God . . ."[114]

No more perfect description of the World-Christ, the Universal Indwelling Christ that lives within each one of us,[115] has ever been written,[116] for the *Christos* is none other than Spiritual Law, Divine Law—which includes the Law of Attraction. Here we have Jesus' true Gospel, what He called "the Gospel of the Kingdom,"[117] and it was for this very reason that the Apostle John gave Christ Himself the mystical title: "the Everlasting Gospel."[118]

Whether male or female, the book of Genesis tells us, we are exact duplicates of God, for during the Creation of the Universe

> God said, "Let us *make man in our image*, after our likeness" . . . So *God created man in his own image, in the image of God created he him; male and female* created he them.[119]

The pre-Christian Pagan Roman poet Ovid was familiar with the true meaning of this scripture, which resulted in his famous statement: *Est deus in nobis* ("God is in us").

## WE PERFECTLY MIRROR THE IMAGE OF GOD

Paul later sustained this fact, avowing that we have all been "anointed," that is, christed,[120] and so now "the Truth of Christ is *in* us"[121]—for you were literally born with the "Son in you."[122] John declared the same thing: all believers "have an unction [christing] from the Holy One."[123] More to the point, since the "Christ is formed *in* you,"[124] He dwells in you, and because "Christ is the image of God,"[125] we must have been sculpted in the same image—for we are exact representations of the Father.[126] Thus, we perfectly reflect His glory, or as Paul put it:

> "But *we all*, with open face beholding as in a glass the glory of the Lord, *are changed into the same image* from glory to glory, even as by the Spirit of the Lord."[127]

Since we are *all* exact copies of God, like perfect reflections in a looking glass Paul says, we need not search outside ourselves for proof of God, as so many individuals mistakenly do. You yourself are godly throughout every cell, for *the Christ is you, your true self!* This is why Jesus said:

> "If any man shall say unto you, 'Lo, here is Christ,' or 'there'; believe it not."[128]

If this seems like a foreign concept to you, take heart. Even many of the Master's closest and most spiritually mature initiates could not grasp this fact. The following exchange took place, for example, between Jesus and His Apostles. As He so often did, Jesus is speaking here as the Universal Indwelling Christ[129] that exists within each one of us:[130]

> Philip saith unto him, "Lord, shew us the Father, and it sufficeth us." Jesus saith unto him, "Have I been so long time with you, and yet hast thou not known me, Philip? *he that hath seen me hath seen the Father*; and how sayest thou then, 'Shew us the Father'? Believest thou not that *I am in the Father, and the Father in me? the words that I speak unto you I speak not of myself: but the Father that dwelleth in me, he doeth the works.* Believe me that *I am in the Father, and the Father in me*: or else believe me for the very works' sake."[131]

This is Jesus' typically mystical way of saying that we are one with the Divine Mind, which He referred to as the "Father." And the part of us that makes us one with Him is the Indwelling Christ, our Higher Self, our incorporeal true self!

Indeed, our physical bodies, though they are like mud pots, jars of clay,[132] mere "earthen vessels," they are filled with an amazing spiritual "treasure":[133] the life energy of the Christ Within which is "made manifest in our mortal flesh."[134] This is why Jesus taught that we should not call anyone "master" (that is, teacher), for there is only one, and that teacher is the Indwelling Christ.[135]

## "CHRIST IN US, THE HOPE OF GLORY"

The Psalmist tells us that we were made "a little lower than the gods," then crowned with divine "glory and honour,"[136] while Paul goes even further, saying that "we shall judge angels."[137] In the book of Jeremiah, God gives Himself the title: "The Lord Our Righteousness."[138] What does this mean? God does not call Himself "The Lord *My* Righteousness." He uses the word "our," which refers to us, His children. This is a not so arcane allusion, of course, to our true nature, our divine nature,[139] which Paul referred to as: "Christ *in* us, the hope of glory."[140]

"Know ye not your own selves, how that Jesus Christ is *in* you?" asked the Thirteenth Apostle.[141] Indeed, it is the universality of the Christ Within[142] that enables us to be "crucified"[143] and "raised up" alongside the resurrected Jesus.[144] If we did not possess the same Inner Christ that the Lord did, this would not be possible.

This is why Paul made this extraordinary comment, one you will seldom hear discussed from the pulpit: "God revealed His son *in* me."[145] Now we are fellow human beings with Paul. If the "son" (the Christ) is in him, then He is in us as well. Of course He is. For the Interior Christ is both universal[146] and immortal![147]

Is this blasphemy? Absolutely not. It is ordained scripture! And by ignoring it we thwart the divine program that God has for us, a wondrous plan that we will be discussing in great detail throughout this book.

## THE GREAT I AM

Arguably the most obvious biblical references to our personal godhood are to be found in the book of Psalms and the book of Exodus. In the former the Father declares: "Be still, and know that *I am God*."[148] In the latter Moses asks God what His name is, and God gives this answer:

> "*I AM THAT I AM* . . . Thus shalt thou say unto the children of Israel, *I AM* hath sent me unto you."[149]

The Divine "I AM" spoken of here is what the Old Testament writers call "Jehovah" and what the New Testament writers call "Christ." In other words, the great I AM is our authentic inner nature, our Divine Nature;[150] it is the real you and me, our genuine self. Moses, one of the great ancient practitioners of the Law of Attraction, understood his oneness with the Father, for he used the phrase "I AM" to identify himself with God when He appeared to the prophet from inside a burning bush:

> "And when the Lord saw that Moses turned aside to see, God called unto him out of the midst of the bush, and said, 'Moses, Moses.' And Moses said, 'Here *I am*.'"[151]

Paul too was well versed in the use of this divine mystical name, saying:

> "But by the grace of God *I am what I am*[152] . . . [Thus] I beseech you, be as *I am*; for *I am* as ye are."[153]

The I AM is spelled Aum or Om in Hinduism, Amam in Hebrew, Hum in Tibetan, Amon in ancient Egyptian texts, and Amen in mainstream Christianity (all mean "faithful"), and it is represented by the creative Logos or the Word in Gnostic Christianity[154] and as Sol-Om-On in Kabbalah.[155] Thus John the Apostle used it cryptically in the Greek word "Om-ega" (that is, Omega),[156] even employing it as a noun: "*The* Amen, the faithful and true witness, the beginning of the creation of God."[157] This is why Pliny referred to the I AM as *Artifex Omnium Natura*: the "Architect of the Universe."

The great I AM is your essence. Though it is within you, it is the end all and be all of everything, for it is a piece of God Himself. It is that aspect of you that answers when someone asks you who are you are: "I am (your name)." It is that which stares back at you from behind your eyes when you look in a mirror, just as Paul said.[158]

## THE I AM IS YOUR HIGHER SELF

The I AM is not your Ego, your false self, your human self, your Lower Self—which will perish with your material body (for "all flesh is grass").[159] It is your eternal God-Nature, your lucent Divine Self, your immortal God-Self, the "Christ that is formed in us,"[160] that is "in all of us,"[161] as Paul put it. It is that spiritual part of you which God "created in his own image":[162] the *perfect* you!

It is your Higher Self, your Divine Self, the incorporeal Supreme Self, the mystics' Cosmic Man, the Hindus' "Atman," Paul's "inner man"[163] or "inward man,"[164] Peter's "hidden man of the heart,"[165] Luke's "Holy One,"[166] Daniel's "Ancient of Days";[167] it is that part of you that was never born and will never die, and which is "the same yesterday, and to day, and for ever."[168]  For the Indwelling "Christ abideth for ever."[169]

The I AM is one more common term for the Immortal Indwelling Christ that lies at the core of us all,[170] and which Jesus, like other ancient spiritual teachers, often used to announce His divinity to others: "I AM he," he once told a group of startled Pharisees, who then "fell to the ground."[171] Here is another revealing exchange He had with this rigidly religious Jewish sect:

> Again the high priest asked him, and said unto him, "Art thou *the Christ*, the Son of the Blessed?" And Jesus said, "*I am . . .*"[172]

Jesus used the mystical I AM title repeatedly.  Some other examples:

"I AM from above."[173]
"I AM the bread of life."[174]
"I AM the door of the sheep."[175]
"I AM the good shepherd."[176]
"I AM the light of the world."[177]
"I AM he that liveth."[178]
"I AM Master and Lord."[179]
"I AM meek and lowly in heart."[180]
"I AM a king."[181]
"I AM the way, the truth, and the life."[182]
"I AM the true vine."[183]
"I AM the Christ."[184]

In mystical Christianity, the "I am" the Master speaks of here is not Himself, His personal Ego, the human being known as Jesus; but rather (as the last example reveals) "*the* Christ" that dwells within, which being universal,[185] exists in each one of us as our Higher Self.[186]  Sadly, this doctrine, which is known in one form or another in every religion, is the same one that the Jews in Jesus' day called "blasphemy,"[187] and in Paul's day "heresy,"[188] and which many uninformed Christian authorities today still think of as an impious sacrilege.

Being an expression of God, of the Divine Mind, the Indwelling Christ or great I AM is the power of thought incarnate in Man.  It is "the Word [thought] made flesh."[189]  Thus the 17th-Century French philosopher René Descartes said: "I think, therefore I AM."

## WE ARE ALL "ABRAHAMS"

Being unlimited, boundless, and ubiquitous, the Inner Christ, of course, existed prior to the birth of Jesus, as He Himself admitted.[190] The Lord, in His usual mystical way, explained it like this: "Before Abraham was, I AM."[191]

The magnificent import of this statement can be seen in the occult fact that Abraham's birth name was Abram,[192] which means "exalted Father." The "Father" is the Divine Mind, the Great Cosmic Spirit, the Cosmic Intellect, or what the ancient Egyptians knew as "Father Mind" or "Supreme Mind." The Sanskrit word for this, the immanent and infinite "One Absolute Reality," is Brahman. Thus Abram was the ancient Hebrew version of the Hindu Brahman: "a Brahman," in fact, who was later renamed A-Brahman, that is, Abraham[193]—whose name means "Father of a multitude," the "multitude" being everything in the Universe.[194]

This scripture ties in perfectly with several others in the Gospel of John. Again, speaking as the Indwelling Christ, His Higher Self, Jesus says to the Pharisees, who represent the human Ego, or on a broader scale, the Lower Self of humanity:

> "Ye are from beneath; I am from above: ye are of this world; I am not of this world. I said therefore unto you, that ye shall die in your sins: for if ye believe not that I am he, ye shall die in your sins. . . . I have many things to say and to judge of you: but he that sent me is true; and I speak to the world those things which I have heard of him." They understood not that he spake to them of the Father. Then said Jesus unto them, "When ye have lifted up the Son of man, then shall ye know that I am he, and that I do nothing of myself; but as my Father hath taught me, I speak these things.[195]

The inner meaning:

> "You act out of your Lower Selves; I act out of my Higher Self; you are religious; I am spiritual; therefore I say that if you do not believe in the Universal I AM that I AM, you will suffer due to your disbelief." . . . The Pharisees did not understand that Jesus was talking about the Divine Mind, so He said to them: "When you honor the Son of Man, the human Jesus, you will realize that I AM that I AM; and that I do nothing for my own honor; but only those things that the Divine Mind has directed me to say and do."[196]

Here, as He so often did, Jesus is telling us that the Universal Indwelling

Christ[197] is one with the Father ("I AM"),[198] that is, with Divine Mind;[199] for, as Paul taught, Christ possesses the full nature of God.[200]

Now if, as the Master asserted, "I and my Father are one,"[201] and we are one with Christ[202]—in fact, He is *in* us[203] and we are *in* Him[204]—then we humans are also one with the Father,[205] and can therefore be nothing less than gods and goddesses ourselves.[206] For Christ and the Father are one and the same, and we are one with both![207]

By definition there is only a single "One": one Source, one Substance, one Fire, one Mind, one Brahman, one God over all, be they Christian, Jew, or Pagan[208]—and we are all one with it.[209] Why is there only one ultimate Source, one God? For the same reason we have only one heart: it would be impossible to synchronize two hearts. The second would always be slightly out of alignment with the first, disrupting the entire system.

And so it is with the God of our Universe, a word that derives from the Latin *uni*, meaning "one" or "single." The Father Himself said:

> "I am the Lord: that is my name: and my glory will I not give to another, neither my praise to graven images."[210]

There can be only one, and that "one" is the "living God,"[211] who has expressed Himself in us as the Indwelling Christ.[212] It is this, the Christ Within, who Paul described as

> "*the image of the invisible God, the firstborn of every creature*: for by him were all things created, that are in heaven, and that are in earth, visible and invisible, whether they be thrones, or dominions, or principalities, or powers: *all things were created by him, and for him: and he is before all things, and by him all things consist.*"[213]

Because we are one with the One, just as Zen Buddhism holds that we are each a Buddha, Jesus taught that each one of us is *a Brahman*; that is, we are each an "Abraham," whose real self is the immortal Christ that has always existed and will always exist.[214]

This doctrine is not peculiar to Christianity. In fact, it is preached around the world in every major faith. For example, just as the Old Testament prophets said we are all deities,[215] just as Jesus said we are all gods,[216] just as Paul said we are all "sons of Gods,"[217] "one in Christ,"[218] and just as God Himself said that we are all immortal supernatural beings,[219] the

Hindus too teach that we are all what they refer to as "avatars": sparks of divinity that have descended from Heaven to incarnate into mortal bodies.

## WHY YOU ARE AN INDIVIDUALIZATION OF GOD

Jesus phrased it this way: "He that hath seen me hath seen the Father."[220] The inner meaning: "He that has realized his union with the Indwelling Christ has realized his oneness with the Divine Mind."[221] Paul referred to this mystically as "winning Christ,"[222] while the Hebraist asserted that the spiritually mature will become "partakers of his holiness."[223] Now you will understand the true significance of this statement by God, the Divine Mind: "I AM holy."[224]

Now you can also say, along with the Psalmist, "I AM holy,"[225] for the real you is a piece of the Father, and He is truly holy. This means that we too, not just Jesus, possess a hypostatic nature in which both our human and divine aspects are one.[226] For like the Lord, in each of us "dwelleth all the fulness of the Godhead bodily," making us *complete in Him.*"[227]

Yes, we are all one within, one with the Cosmos, and one with each other, for God Himself is one.[228] Being ageless, timeless, and boundless, however, He could not know Himself. In order to do so, He had to individuate Himself as finite matter. This He did by creating earthly life, which means that each one of us is a thought of the Divine Mind, or in biblical terminology, a "child of God." We are all an aspect of the immeasurable, inexhaustible, everlasting Father, who is expressing Himself through us. You are, in other words, the infinite consciousness of God, the Great and Limitless I AM![229]

The Victorian English biologist Herbert Spencer described God and our relationship to Him this way:

> "God is infinite intelligence, infinitely diversified through infinite time and infinite space, manifesting through an infinitude of everlasting individualities."

Here is this same concept in the words of Jesus:

> "I am in my Father, and ye in me, and I in you."[230]

## THE CHURCH FATHERS ON THEOSIS

Though many modern Christian authorities reject Jesus' doctrine of theosis—that is, God's deification of humanity—a number of early Church

Fathers heartily embraced this, the great Master Secret, imparted by our Lord some 2,000 years ago. Here is what one of them, the 3rd-Century theologian Hippolytus of Rome, had to say about it:

> "For *thou hast become God*: for whatever sufferings thou didst undergo while being a man, these He gave to thee, because thou wast of mortal mould, but whatever it is consistent with God to impart, these God has promised to bestow upon thee, because *thou hast been deified, and begotten unto immortality*. This constitutes the import of the proverb, 'Know thyself'; that is, *discover God within thyself, for He has formed thee after His own image*. For with the knowledge of self is conjoined the being an object of God's knowledge, for *thou art called by the Deity Himself*."[231]

Likewise, the estimable 4th-Century theologian, Saint Augustine, wrote:

> "And *we indeed recognize in ourselves the image of God*, that is, of the supreme Trinity, an image which, though it be not equal to God, or rather, though it be very far removed from Him,—being neither co-eternal, nor, to say all in a word, consubstantial with Him,—is *yet nearer to Him in nature than any other of His works, and is destined to be yet restored, that it may bear a still closer resemblance. For we both are, and know that we are, and delight in our being, and our knowledge of it*."[232]

Citing 2 Peter 1:4, Athanasius, the 4th-Century Bishop of Alexandria, said this about the divinization of human beings:

> "He [Jesus] has become Man, *that He might deify us in Himself*, and He has been born of a woman, and begotten of a Virgin, in order to transfer to Himself our erring generation, and *that we may become henceforth a holy race, and 'partakers of the Divine Nature,'* as blessed Peter wrote."[233]

The 4th-Century Archbishop of Constantinople, Gregory of Nazianzus, explained theosis this way:

> "For He [Jesus] whom you now treat with contempt was once above you. He who is now Man was once the Uncompounded. What He was He continued to be; what He was not He took to Himself. In the beginning He was, uncaused; for what is the Cause of God? But afterwards for a cause He was born. And that cause

was that you might be saved, who insult Him and despise His Godhead, because of this, that He took upon Him your denser nature, having converse with flesh by means of Mind. While *His inferior Nature, the Humanity, became God, because it was united to God,* and became One Person because the Higher Nature prevailed . . . *in order that I too might be made God so far as He is made Man.*"

Based on Jesus' teaching that we are gods,[234] the 2nd-Century theologian, Clement of Alexandria, left us this instruction on Divine Man:

". . . and they [humans] are called by the appellation of gods, being *destined to sit on thrones with the other gods* that have been first put in their places by the Savior."

The 4th-Century Bishop of Nyssa, Saint Gregory, wrote:

"This is the safest way to protect the good things you enjoy: realize how much your Creator has honored you above all other creatures. He did not make the heavens in His image, nor the moon, the sun, the beauty of the stars, nor anything else which surpasses all understanding. *You alone are a similitude of eternal beauty, a vessel of happiness, a mirror image of the True Light. And if you look at Him, you will become what He is, imitating Him who shines within you, whose glory is reflected in your purity. Nothing in all of creation can equal your grandeur.* All the heavens can fit in the palm of God's hand. . . . And though He is so great, *you can wholly embrace Him: He dwells within you. He pervades your entire being.*"

In his massive work, *Summa Theologica*, the 13th-Century Italian saint and theologian Thomas Aquinas made this comment:

". . . when it is said that 'God was made Man,' the making is taken to be terminated in the human nature. Hence, *properly speaking, this is true: 'God was made Man.'*"[235]

Can Jesus, the Apostles, the Old Testament prophets, and the Church Fathers, even God Himself, all be wrong about a spiritual doctrine that has existed since the beginning of historical records among all people, in all societies, in all religions, right up and into modern times? Here is what the 19th-Century American poet Walt Whitman had to say about God in Man:

"Divine am I inside and out, and I make holy whatever I touch or am touch'd from."[236]

## WE ARE WHAT JESUS SAID WE ARE

We have now firmly established that, despite all the tortured scripture twisting that John 10:34 has undergone by the unenlightened, Jesus meant exactly what he said: we are all divine beings, possessing all of the qualities and powers of a supernatural deity. Speaking as the Indwelling Christ, this is precisely what Jesus meant when He said to God (Divine Mind) that "everything I have is yours and everything you have is mine."[237] Or as Paul put it:

> "The Spirit itself beareth witness with our spirit, that we are the children of God: and if children, then heirs; heirs of God, and joint-heirs with Christ; if so be that we suffer with him, that we may be also *glorified together*."[238]

This is Paul's way of expressing what Jesus said decades earlier, plainly and simply: "You are gods"![239]

# 2

# YOUR DIVINE POWER

> "A good man out of the good treasure of his
> heart bringeth forth that which is good; and an
> evil man out of the evil treasure of his heart
> bringeth forth that which is evil: for of the
> abundance of the heart his mouth speaketh."[240]

## THE MOST POWERFUL FORCE IN THE UNIVERSE

**ACCORDING TO JESUS AND MANY** ancient Bible authorities, every man is a god and every woman is a goddess, imbued with the same supernatural qualities as God the Father. Shakespeare too understood this. Here is how he phrased it in his famous play *Hamlet*:

> "What a piece of work is a man, how noble in reason, how infinite
> in faculties, in form and moving how express and admirable, in
> action how like an angel, in apprehension how like a god!"

Yes, you are divine. I am divine. Everyone on earth has a "divine spark" that God instilled in us, linking us one to the other.

Look at it this way: if God were a vine, we would each be a branch on that vine.[241] If God were an ocean, we would each be a drop of water in that ocean. To paraphrase the great astronomer Carl Sagan, we humans are God Stuff.[242] And in fact, God is the Universe, and we are each an atom in that Universe. We are truly all one, spiritually and vibrationally connected by the invisible threads of God Stuff. Of this oneness Emerson wrote:

> ". . . the universe is represented in every one of its particles.
> Everything in nature contains all the powers of nature. Everything
> is made of one hidden stuff. . . . The world globes itself in a drop
> of dew. The microscope cannot find the animalcule which is less

perfect for being little. Eyes, ears, taste, smell, motion, resistance, appetite, and organs of reproduction that take hold on eternity,—all find room to consist in the small creature. . . . The true doctrine of omnipresence is that God appears with all His parts in every moss and cobweb. . . . Thus is the universe alive."[243]

But, some will ask, how can all be God and God be all when around us we see so much misery, disease, violence, corruption, and death? If we are all gods, why is the world filled with such negativity, sorrow, and darkness?

The reason is simple: most people are not aware of their divine nature.[244] Even most of those who are do not realize the wonderful power they possess within themselves due to their divinity. And so they misuse it.

Just what is this power?

It is the power of thought!

Now thought is a numinous force, a divine energy. So you see, thinking is not actually a mental activity, it is a spiritual activity!

Thought, in fact, is the omnipotent, omnipresent, omniscient, omniactive, omnific, circumambient, universal force that is embodied in what we call "God" and what Hermes Trismegistus called "All-Father Mind," for as the early Gnostic Christians taught, "God is all mind."[245] Also known as the Sovereign Mind or Divine Mind, It/He/She thus has unlimited capabilities to think anything into being, as Job observed of the Father:

> "I know that thou canst do every thing, and that no thought can be withholden from thee."[246]

Indeed, Divine Mind is the creative energy that formed you, your parents, your ancestors, the home you live in, the clothes you wear, the foods you eat, the appliances you use, and the beliefs and opinions you hold.

And where does thought come from? It begins as a desire in our mind, then this desire becomes a belief, which, if focused on long enough, becomes a thing. Here is an example.

A painter wants to share a particular viewpoint with others. This is his mental desire. This desire leads to an idea for a painting. The idea for the painting initiates the thought of what he must do to achieve this, and this thought initiates the painting process—which is creative. Finally, the painting is completed, manifesting on the material plane as a physical object.

All artistic works come into being in this exact same manner; not only paintings, but every book, poem, photograph, article, song, and film that has ever been made or ever will be made.

Actually, there is nothing that does not begin with a thought, for we live in a Mind-based Universe. Everything is born of a mental desire, which becomes an idea, and which then grows into a thought. It was this same force that brought plants, animals, mountains, rivers, forests, and even our planet, our solar system, and the stars, into being as well.

Thought then is the most powerful force in our Universe, which is itself a product of thought: God's thought!

## HOW GOD THOUGHT THE UNIVERSE INTO BEING

The importance of thought can be seen in the Bible: the first three chapters of the first book, Genesis, are completely dedicated to the story of how God made "heaven and earth" utilizing the creative power of thought. How did he do it? God used what the Apostle John labels the "Logos," or the Word:

> "In the beginning was the Word, and the Word was with God, and the Word was God."[247]

The psychological or inner meaning of the Greek word *logos*, which John revealingly referred to as the "Logos of Life,"[248] is "the mental faculty of thinking," that is, thought! Thus God brought the entire Universe into being using thought alone, which is why the Hebraist said that "the worlds were framed by the word of God";[249] and it is why he affirmed that "God upholds all things by the word of his power."[250] Let us review John's scripture with this new knowledge:

> "In the beginning was Thought, and Thought was with God, and Thought was God."[251]

So thought is literally God and God is literally thought, and this thought, the Logos, "abides" within each one of us.[252] For the Word is Christ[253] and Christ is the true self, the Higher Self, of every human being.[254]

Since you are a divine being, a god yourself, a portion of God in fact, you are equipped with the same thought power as the Father, the very One who created our Universe and everything in it.[255] Thus you possess the same potential as God to create anything you desire. And you create what you desire by using the power of your mind, or to paraphrase Paul, "the word of your power."[256] In essence, *with your word you make your world!*[257]

Thought is the God-Power of your God-Self, which is why it is the law that everything must conform to thought. Thus, in the ancient Gnostic Christian work called the Dialogue of the Savior, Jesus says: "The light of the physical body is the mind."[258]

The Apostle Peter described our oneness with the Father,[259] and the powers that go along with our divine nature,[260] like this:

> "Grace and peace be multiplied unto you through the knowledge [Gnosis] of God, and of Jesus our Lord [the Indwelling Christ], according as *his divine power hath given unto us all things that pertain unto life and godliness*, through the knowledge [Gnosis] of him that hath called us to glory and virtue: whereby are given unto us exceeding great and precious promises: *that by these ye might be partakers of the divine nature . . .*"[261]

Yes, we are all "partakers of the divine nature"; we all literally share in the holiness of God, the supernatural powers of Divine Mind.[262]

According to the Bible, this aspect of ourselves, known to Christians around the world as the "Indwelling Christ,"[263] is so all-powerful, so godlike, that we have dominion over everything on earth, both animate and so-called "inanimate":

> And God said, "Let us make man in our image, after our likeness: and let them have dominion over the fish of the sea, and over the fowl of the air, and over the cattle, and over all the earth, and over every creeping thing that creepeth upon the earth." . . . And God blessed them [humans], and God said unto them, "Be fruitful, and multiply, and replenish the earth, and subdue it: and have dominion over the fish of the sea, and over the fowl of the air, and over every living thing that moveth upon the earth."[264]

## THE THREE MINDS: OUR INNER COSMIC TRINITY

Scientists tell us that we have two minds, the Conscious Mind and the Subconscious Mind, which perform symbiotically to maintain our health and regulate our daily lives. This is all true, up to a point.

Jesus tells us that there is also a third mind, however, one He called the "Father," which today we know as the Superconscious Mind. The Lord also tells us that these three minds, working in conjunction, go far beyond mere biology. They extend into the realm of psychology, a word that literally translates as "the science of the Soul."

Together, in fact, this mental triad forms the greatest power in the

Universe: the "supernatural" power of thought called the Divine Mind, known in ancient Egypt as the god Thoth ("incarnated thought"), and later to Christians as the "Logos" or the "Word." In His usual mystical way, here is how Jesus referred to our Inner Cosmic Trinity:

> "If any man serve me [Conscious Mind], let him follow me; and where I AM, there shall also my servant [Subconscious Mind] be: if any man serve me, him will my Father [Superconscious Mind] honour."[265]

Paul referred to the Universal Triad Within in this manner:

> "The grace of the Lord Jesus Christ [Conscious Mind], and the love of God [Superconscious Mind], and the communion of the Holy Ghost [Subconscious Mind], be with you all."[266]

Here is John's description of our Interior Trinity:

> "For there are three that bear record in heaven, the Father [God, Superconscious Mind], the Word [Christ, Conscious Mind], and the Holy Ghost [the Holy Spirit, Subconscious Mind]: and these three are one."[267]

Yes, "these three are one," and we call this one mind the "Divine Mind"! It is this group, the "Father," the "Son," and the "Holy Spirit"—our Holy Inner Trinity—that Paul mystically referred to as "the invisible things" of the "Godhead."[268]

How do these three minds work together?

Simply stated, ideas are generated in the Conscious Mind. These ideas are passed onto the Subconscious Mind as thoughts. The Subconscious Mind then sets about turning these thoughts into physical reality, which are then drawn from the Superconscious Mind, where everything already exists. Paul made several fascinating statements on this topic:

> "The head of every man is Christ [the Conscious Mind]," while "the head of Christ is God [Superconscious Mind]."[269]

> "But to us there is but one God, the Father, of whom are all things, and we in him; and one Lord Jesus Christ, by whom are all things, and we by him."[270]

The inner meaning of the latter:

> "There is only one Divine Mind. However, it is made up of several parts: the Superconscious Mind, *from* which all things manifest, and the Conscious Mind, *by* which all things manifest."[271]

Here is another way of looking at it. If our Inner Mental Triad was a computer, the Conscious Mind would be the keyboard, the Subconscious Mind would be the CPU (Central Processing Unit), and the Superconscious Mind would be the monitor.

To get a better understanding of how these three minds work within the Law of Attraction, let us look at them more closely.

THE CONSCIOUS MIND

The Conscious Mind, a physical part of our brain that remains behind after so-called "death," is not part of the real you, your God-Self. It is an intellectual machine that collects information through our five senses. From this information it learns to make decisions that it feels will help keep us alive and healthy. As an observational mechanism that reasons and judges, it is a tool that helps insure our survival.

The Conscious Mind is finite, has no memory, can think only one thought at a time, goes dormant when we sleep, and controls our voluntary muscle system, always carefully analyzing situations and offering rational decisions for what actions we should take from moment to moment.

Despite its simplistic "security alarm" programming, the Conscious Mind plays an enormous role within the Law of Attraction: not only is it the primary method by which we communicate with God, from it are generated our thoughts, the very ones that are passed into the Subconscious Mind to begin the manifestation process. Thus, as we are about to see, our happiness, our state of health, our relationships, our bank accounts, every circumstance and aspect of our lives, all depend on the types of thoughts we create in our Conscious Minds.

Spiritually the Conscious Mind corresponds to the "Son" or "Logos" in patriarchal religions, and the "Sun" in mystical religions. In the Bible the Conscious Mind is personified by Jesus, who is referred to variously as "Master,"[272] "Lord,"[273] the "Christ,"[274] and the "Sun of Righteousness."[275] Metaphysically the Conscious Mind represents our speech, the "Word." As we progress, you will soon understand why the Lord, speaking as the Indwelling Christ or Conscious Mind, made this celebrated statement!

"I am the way, the truth, and the life: no man cometh unto the Father, but by me."[276]

## THE SUBCONSCIOUS MIND

The Subconscious Mind, the spiritual aspect of our brain, is not mind in the way we normally think of it. It was given its name for good reason: it is not conscious, but rather it blindly operates "behind the scenes" at a level below consciousness. Doing what?

Biologically speaking, it is wired to our autonomic nervous system and other involuntary bodily functions, diligently guarding our health by regulating our immune system, circulation, heartbeat, breathing, digestion, elimination, glands, hormones, reflexive muscle movement, cellular regeneration, and responses to sensory signals like hunger and pain.

The Subconscious is always awake, even during deepest sleep, unconsciousness, and trance states. It is where our memories are stored; it is the part of our brain that activates when we forget how to spell a word. And yet, it does not reason or think on its own. What it does do is completely accept, record, and store, without question or discrimination, whatever is suggested to it by the Conscious Mind.

While these unconscious processes are all vital to our survival and even to the Law of Attraction, it is its second function that we are most interested in at the moment.

Spiritually speaking, the Subconscious Mind operates as a rigidly obedient servant that helps transform your thoughts and beliefs into material form. In fact, this is its only nonphysical function: it is your very own supernatural "PA" (personal assistant), whose sole purpose is to do your bidding, turning whatever you believe into living Truth, that is, physical reality. And here we have one of the mystical Christian meanings behind the phrase "the Word was made flesh."[277]

You are probably familiar with the Arabian tale called *Aladdin's Lamp*, in which the lamp's genie must do whatever its owner wishes. This story is based on ancient knowledge of the Subconscious Mind, which operates in exactly the same way. Thus, your Subconscious Mind is your personal genie, fashioned by God to aid you in creating your perfect life *right now*.

The Subconscious Mind (electrically negative) is nearly the opposite of the Conscious Mind (electrically positive), which is why these two energy polarities work so well together. While the Conscious Mind functions by perception, the Subconscious Mind functions by suggestion. While the

Conscious Mind is purely objective, the Subconscious Mind is purely subjective. While the Conscious Mind is finite, the Subconscious Mind is infinite. The Conscious Mind is mortal, the Subconscious Mind is immortal. The Conscious Mind is inductive, the Subconscious Mind is deductive. The Conscious Mind evaluates and judges, the Subconscious Mind is completely noncritical and neutral. Indeed, it is not only incapable of judgment, it has no need to judge, for this task is performed by the Conscious Mind.

On a spiritual level all the Subconscious does is record and then create whatever is suggested to it by the Conscious Mind, impartially, fairly, and 100 percent accurately every time. How does it do this?

Though much of the Subconscious remains a mystery, what is certain is that it has access to the complete catalog of every piece of knowledge and wisdom of the entire Universe.[278] In other words, it knows everything and has unlimited power. Thus, it is just as easy for the Subconscious Mind to completely cure a "terminal" disease as it is to heal a cut finger, and it is just as effortless for it to manifest a million dollars as it is to materialize one penny, for truly, as Peter said: "One day is with the Lord as a thousand years, and a thousand years as one day."[279]

Spiritually the Subconscious Mind is feminine and corresponds to the "Holy Spirit"[280] in patriarchal religions, and the "Moon" in mystical religions. Around the Mediterranean and the Black Sea, she began as Sophia, the Pagan goddess of Wisdom, whose sacred symbols—for example, the dove, the crescent moon, and the stars—were often borrowed by early Christian theologians, writers, and mythographers.[281] At Istanbul, Turkey, the great 6th-Century Byzantine cathedral, Hagia Sophia ("Holy Wisdom"), still stands as a testament to the goddess' enduring popularity in the region.

As ancient religious teachers often ordained their followers by breathing on them (a practice known as insufflation), and as the Greek word *pneuma* ("spirit" or "ghost") can also mean "wind," the Holy Spirit is more correctly known as the "Breath of Life,"[282] or the "Holy Breath." This is almost certainly the name Jesus knew it by, as the Gospel of John intimates.[283]

In the Bible the Subconscious Mind is also personified as the "Holy Ghost,"[284] the "Comforter,"[285] and the archetypal figure of the "servant."[286] Paul rightly called himself a "servant of Christ,"[287] meaning the Subconscious Mind (the Holy Spirit) is a subordinate assistant to the Conscious Mind (Jesus). The biblical phrases "servant of the Lord"[288] and "servant of God"[289] have the same meaning. Metaphysically, the Subconscious Mind represents mental action, as well as our physical deeds.

This always obedient mental servant, which lives within all of us,[290] obeys every dominant command of the Conscious Mind. "Command ye me," saith the Father;[291] "thy will be done," saith the Son.[292]

## THE SUPERCONSCIOUS MIND

The Superconscious Mind is the ultimate Source of everything. It is the unlimited celestial storehouse where God maintains the spiritual counterparts of everything on the physical plane, and in particular, all of our earthly desires. It has been rightly called the "Akashic Record," the divine depository, where all of our thoughts, words, and actions are written down and stored for eternity, and from whence they may be retrieved at any time! Jesus was referring to the Superconscious Mind when He said: "All things are delivered unto me of my Father."[293]

Paul described it as containing "all spiritual blessings."[294] This is because all things already exist there, including all possible realities. It is, in other words, not only the "First Cause," it is the entire Universe itself, seen and unseen, past, present, and future—"the Alpha and Omega, the beginning and the end, the first and the last."[295] It is, as Paul noted, the substance in which "we live, and move, and have our being."[296] Everything on the material plane has its start in the Superconscious, which is why mystics refer to it as "the One." Hence, Jesus declared:

> "A man can receive nothing, except it be given him from heaven."[297]

God is not called omnipresent for nothing. He truly is present in all things. And because we are physically and spiritually a part of the Superconscious Mind, all humans, indeed, all things, are one, profoundly connected at the deepest material and divine levels, making "heaven and earth one."[298]

As we will see, this is one of the reasons the Lord asked us to "love thy neighbor as thyself."[299] Your neighbor *is* yourself, "for we are members one of another";[300] or as Paul put it in cosmic terms, "we are one body in Christ."[301] Thus, whatever you think about your neighbor, you are thinking about yourself. Whatever you say about him or her, you are saying about yourself. Whatever you do to him or her, you are doing to yourself.

The Superconscious Mind is not directly connected to the Conscious Mind. Instead, the two are tied together by the Subconscious Mind, which acts as a communications link between them. We think a thought in the Conscious Mind, which it passes onto the Subconscious Mind. If it is a persistent thought or desire that is made with conviction, the Subconscious Mind turns it into a belief. When faith is combined with this belief, it is supercharged by the Subconscious, which sends it onto the Superconscious Mind. Because this thought is already a reality there, the Superconscious merely has to allow physical manifestation to occur. This is what I call *the Law of Attraction, God in action!*

Spiritually the Superconscious Mind corresponds to the "Father" or "God" in patriarchal religions, and "Mother" or "Goddess" in matriarchal religions. Biblical writers refer to it as the Lord, Jehovah, Elohim, or Yahweh; Hindus call it Brahman (or Brahma, depending on one's view); mystical Jews call it the Book of God's Remembrance; mystical Christians call it Supreme Intelligence, Universal Mind, the Book of Life,[302] or, as mentioned, the Akasha ("primary substance").[303] Scientists have their own names for it, of course: the Unified Field, the Laws of Physics, or Nature.

Jesus said that the Superconscious Mind (God) is "Spirit." Not "*the* Spirit," or "*a* Spirit," but simply "Spirit";[304] that is, the one substance that makes up everything in the Universe. Metaphysically, the Superconscious Mind represents thinking, our thoughts.

Spencer called this particular mind the "Infinite and Eternal Energy":

> "Amid all the mysteries by which we are surrounded, nothing is more certain than that we are ever in the presence of an Infinite and Eternal Energy from which all things proceed."

## "THE MIND OF CHRIST"

In mystical Christianity the combined power of these three phases of mind—the Conscious, Subconscious, and Superconscious—is known as the Divine Mind, that is, God. Spiritually connected to it is the Christ, also known as the Christ Within, or the Indwelling Christ,[305] the eternal "high priest"[306] of our personal "church within,"[307] which the Hebraist called the one and only true church, made by the hands of God, not man.[308]

We all possess an unborn, uncreated, immortal, indestructible Inner Christ that has existed since the beginning of time:[309] it is our Higher Self, the deific human, God in Man,[310] "for every man is God made flesh."[311] This is what Jesus, speaking as the Indwelling Christ, meant when He said the following to his seventy Disciples:

"He that heareth you heareth me; and he that despiseth you despiseth me; and he that despiseth me despiseth him that sent me."[312]

In fact, it is the Christ Within which makes us humans divine. Each one of us is a literal individualization of God (Divine Mind), for we have all been created in God's image, perfectly reflecting His glory and power.[313] Thus, the great 13th-Century mystical poet Rumi wrote:

"I looked in temples, churches, and mosques. But I found the divine in my heart."

Paul would have agreed, for according to him, we are each an "anointed" Christ,[314] exact duplicates of the Father.[315] In 1838 Emerson made the following comments in an address before Harvard's Divinity School:

"Jesus Christ belonged to the true race of prophets. He saw with open eye the mystery of the soul. Drawn by its severe harmony, ravished with its beauty, he lived in it, and had his being there. Alone in all history, he estimated the greatness of man. One man was true to what is in you and me. He saw that God incarnates himself in man, and evermore goes forth anew to take possession of his world. He said, in this jubilee of sublime emotion, 'I am divine. Through me, God acts; through me, speaks. Would you see God, see me; or, see thee, when thou also thinkest as I now think.'"

Now you know the answer to the riddle: why has no man ever seen God? It is because, as the Apostle John correctly observed, God dwelleth not outside of us, "God dwelleth in us."[316]

Those who come to this realization, of our oneness, our at-one-ment, with the "Creator,"[317] have achieved what has been variously known as "God Realization," "Abraham Consciousness," "Moses Consciousness," "Buddha Consciousness," "Cosmic Consciousness," "Krishna Consciousness," "Christ Consciousness," or as Paul named it, "the mind of Christ."[318] It was Jesus' high, pure, spiritual state of consciousness that the Thirteenth Apostle was referring to when he said: "Arm yourselves with the same mind."[319]

From the mystical Christian point of view, through the attainment of Christ Consciousness we personally experience the Inner Parousia, the spiritual "Second Coming of the Christ" within[320] (which is why "of that day and that hour knoweth no man, no, not the angels which are in heaven, neither the Son, but the Father").[321] By following Jesus' teachings, in particular those pertaining to the Law of Attraction, you become a "Son of God," just as Jesus promised,[322] and all things that you decree "shall be established unto thee."[323] Here is how God Himself addressed His earthly devotees:

> "I will *dwell in them*, and *walk in them*; and I will be their God, and they shall be my people. . . . And [I] will be a Father unto you, and ye shall be my sons and daughters," saith the Lord Almighty.[324]

Now because the Universal Christ[325] is imbued with "all the fulness of the Godhead bodily,"[326] and because you have the Indwelling Christ,[327] it is clear that you too possess all the powers of the Godhead![328] For we are "complete in him, which is the head of all principality and power."[329] Paul had a wonderful way of describing this reality:

> "Let this mind be in you, which was also in Christ Jesus: who, being in the form of God, thought it not robbery to be equal with God."[330]

How plain the meaning of Paul's statement is: we are supposed to think like Jesus did, namely, that we are "equal with God"! Reread it until you grasp this simple but world-altering truth.

In the Aquarian Gospel, Jesus elaborates on this topic:

> "All men are sons of God and if they live a holy life they always are at home with God. They see and understand the works of God, and in his sacred name they can perform these works. . . . The virtues of the heavens are in God's hands, and every loyal son may use these virtues and these powers. Man is the delegate of God to do his will on earth, and man can heal the sick, control the spirits of the air, and raise the dead.
>
> "Because I have the power to do these things is nothing strange. All men may gain the power to do these things; but they must conquer all the passions of the lower self; and they can conquer if they will. So *man is God on earth*, and he who honors God must honor man; for God and man are one, as father and the child are one."[331]

A BASIC ANALOGY
Here is an alternate way of looking at how the Father, the Divine Mind, works within us and through us.

Let us say you want to purchase a paintbrush from a warehouse store. You walk in and place your order with the salesperson at the counter. She goes back to the warehouse, retrieves your paintbrush, and brings it to the front counter. You pay her and leave.

In this parable you symbolize the Conscious Mind, the paintbrush symbolizes your thought-desire, the salesperson symbolizes the Subconscious Mind, the warehouse symbolizes the Superconscious Mind, and the money symbolizes faith. Here is how Jesus, speaking as the Indwelling Christ, encapsulated the entire process: "All things are delivered to me of my Father."[332]

PROOF OF THE SUBCONSCIOUS MIND'S SPIRITUAL POWER
Though the existence of the Conscious Mind has been well established by science, many people are not nearly as familiar with our other mind, the Subconscious. Because it is both so powerful *and* mysterious, there is tremendous curiosity about it, leading many to ask: is there scientific evidence for the Subconscious Mind's amazing, seemingly supernatural abilities?

As we will see, the obvious answer is that proof comes from using the Law of Attraction, which *always* generates wonderful even miraculous results—if used correctly. This shows the power of the Subconscious Mind in action, a power that never fails and always materially reproduces our mental desires exactly.[333]

Everyday evidence of the power of the Subconscious Mind is plentiful and easy to find, ranging from ESP, mental telepathy, precognition, psychometry, clairgustance, second sight, astral projection, pyrokinesis, bilocation, levitation, mediumship, automatic writing, and clairvoyance, to clairsentience, retrocognition, remote viewing, channeling, divination, psychokinesis, apportation, postdiction, clairalience, aura reading, telekinesis, scrying, faith healing, premonition, and clairaudience.[334]

As Jesus so dramatically proved, all of these phenomena are possible because we earthly "Sons" share a divine connection with the heavenly "Father," the Unified Field, which makes up the substance of every particle in the Universe. Indeed, there is only one power, and that power is of God;[335] and there is only one Source, one Energy, one God[336]—and we are all one with it and it is one with all of us.[337] "For," as Paul commented,

". . . of him, and through him, and to him, are all things: to whom be glory for ever. Amen."[338]

Divine Mind's intelligence permeates everything, even what we wrongly call "inanimate" objects. Because of this, every object is sentient on one level or another. In other words, every rock, every grain of sand, every atom, is alive with the divine intelligence of the One Great Spirit! Truly, as Jesus taught: "God is not the God of the dead, but of the living,"[339] for nothing is truly dead, for nothing can truly "die."

Of this infinite substance, the Universal Mind, Emerson once said:

> "There is one mind common to all individual men. Every man is an inlet to the same and to all of the same. He that is once admitted to the right of reason is made a freeman of the whole estate. What Plato has thought, he may think; what a saint has felt, he may feel; what at any time has befallen any man, he can understand. Who hath access to this universal mind is a party to all that is or can be done, for this is the only and sovereign agent."

In the Upanishads, the Hindus' "Secret Doctrine," we find this beautiful scripture:

> "And he who beholds all beings in the Self, and the Self in all beings, he never turns away from it. When to a man who understands, the Self has become all things, what sorrow, what trouble can there be to him who once beheld that unity?"

As mentioned earlier, here is how Jesus, in His always succinct manner, stated the same eternal principle. He is speaking as the Indwelling Christ:

> "I am in my Father, and ye in me, and I in you."[340]

In plain language Jesus is saying that the Indwelling Christ is in the Divine Mind, the Divine Mind is in the Indwelling Christ, and both are in us!

THE PLACEBO EFFECT

The placebo effect is no doubt the most commonly known evidence for the power of the Subconscious Mind, or what the Lord variously referred to as the "Holy Spirit,"[341] the "Holy Ghost," or the "Comforter."[342]

Let us say we have an unwell person who, like nearly all sick individuals, has caused her own illness through wrong-thinking. Her doctors have pronounced her "incurable," which only means that since mainstream medicine has run out of options, her cure must come from within herself—not that she is truly "incurable."

I tell her I have a pill that will heal her. What I do not tell her is that this pill is made only of sugar and water. The idea of my "cure-all pill" is taken into her Conscious Mind and completely accepted. It is now a belief. This belief passes into her Subconscious Mind as a thought. Her Subconscious then unquestioningly begins to reprogram and strengthen her immune system, after which the Superconscious Mind begins physically manifesting her belief. In a few days she is all better and doctors pronounce it a "miracle."

Yet, just as there is no such thing as an "accident," there is no such thing as a "miracle," for everything that we experience is operating under the strict scientific principles of the Law of Attraction.

For those who have never worked with the power of thought and the Law of Attraction, and so doubt even the placebo effect, we have an even stronger piece of evidence: hypnosis.

HYPNOSIS
We will remember that the always wide awake Subconscious Mind takes its orders from the Conscious Mind. During hypnosis the hypnotist puts the Conscious Mind to sleep temporarily. In doing so he takes over the role of the Conscious Mind, which allows him to directly address the Subconscious. He becomes the Conscious Mind, so to speak, and the Subconscious Mind being "unconscious," does not know the difference.

As the "Conscious Mind," the hypnotist can now plant any suggestion he desires into the Subconscious. For example, he can tell it that the individual's left leg has no feeling below the knee. The person's Subconscious, which controls pain response, dutifully shuts off all physical sensation in the lower left leg. If desired, doctors could then perform any operation they wanted on that part of the person's body, even amputation, without anesthetics. Here we have illustrated the tremendous power of the Subconscious, revealed through hypnosis.

This is proof positive of the Subconscious Mind's fantastic ability, which, when combined with the Conscious and Superconscious Minds, can transform spiritual energy (thought) into physical reality. This is the divine power that God has given to each one of us via our divine nature.[343] It is the power that enables us to alter our circumstances and create perfect health, wealth, and happiness in the here and now, just, as we have seen, as the Apostle Peter guaranteed:

> "According as his divine power hath given unto us all things that pertain unto life and godliness, through the knowledge of him that hath called us to glory and virtue: whereby are given unto us exceeding great and precious promises: that by these *ye might be partakers of the divine nature*, having escaped the corruption that is in the world through lust."[344]

Truly, Paul said in his letter to the Laodiceans, "it is God who worketh in you."[345] And it is because of this very fact that we are "partakers of his holiness,"[346] that is, sharers in His divine powers.

Even if He was not kneeling, as He is in this scene, Jesus was in an almost constant state of prayer during His daily ministry. Luke mentions that on one occasion the Lord "went out into a mountain to pray, and continued all night in prayer to God." Paul said that we should "pray without ceasing." Why was prayer so important to Jesus and the Apostles? Because prayer is a type of affirmation, one in which we are in direct mental, that is, spiritual, communication with the Divine Mind—which Jesus called the "Father." Prayer, in fact, is one of the methods He said we are to use to work in conjunction with the Law of Attraction, as this scripture from Matthew illustrates: "And all things, whatsoever ye shall ask in prayer, believing, ye shall receive."

# 3

# DEFINING THE LAW

"Thou shalt also decree a thing, and it shall be
established unto thee: and the light shall shine
upon thy ways."[347]

THE POWER OF THOUGHT

**WE HAVE SEEN THAT JESUS** told us we are divine beings, gods
and goddesses, and that along with this, God has given each one of
us a truly divine gift: the power of thought. We have seen that this
gift is generated within our two minds, the Conscious and the Subconscious,
and that working together with the Superconscious Mind, they transform
our mental desires into physical reality.

Now it is time to see how the power of thought relates to the Law
of Attraction, what Paul called "the revelation of the mystery, which was
kept secret since the world began . . ."[348]

THE LAW ON THE PHYSICAL PLANE

What is the Law of Attraction? It is a scientific rule, created by God, that
operates according to the Universe's most basic principle: *like attracts like.*
This law, which forms the very foundation of our entire physical dimension
(and, as we will see, the spiritual dimension as well), can be observed in the
smallest known particles all the way up to the largest known objects in the
Universe.

At the atomic level, an atom is like a tiny solar system: its nucleus,
composed of protons and neutrons, is encircled by a "cloud" of orbiting
electrons. Physicists tell us that these elementary particles are held together
by the "strong nuclear force." But what is the strong nuclear force?
According to scientists it is one of the four basic forces in Nature, the other
three being the weak nuclear force, gravity, and electromagnetism.

Science knows these as the "four fundamental forces," while scientifically minded Christians call them aspects of the Law of Attraction. Since there is only one universal law, cause, principle, and power operating behind everything, these phrases have the same meaning *and* the same source, and that source is what Jesus called the "Father."

The planet we live on also gives evidence of the Law of Attraction: earth's gravitational pull not only keeps us all glued firmly to the ground, but it also holds both our satellites and our moon in perfect space orbit.

The Sun maintains earth and the other planets in orbit throughout our solar system. Our solar system is part of the Milky Way galaxy, at whose center is a massive black hole. Its gravity, which is so strong that not even light can escape it (hence the name black hole), keeps some 100 billion stars rotating around it.

Our galaxy, the Milky Way, is in turn part of a larger entity called a galaxy cluster, which can contain hundreds even thousands of galaxies. The largest known gravitationally bound objects in our universe, galaxy clusters are held together not only by the masses of huge clouds of hot gas that fill the space between the galaxies, but by a mysterious and as yet unidentified "something" called "dark matter"—which makes up about 25 percent of our isotropic Universe.

Galaxy clusters are often found inside of something even larger: a cluster of clusters called a galaxy supercluster. A galaxy supercluster is a chain-like neighborhood of a dozen or so galaxy clusters, some spanning 300 million light years in diameter, that are irregularly distributed across space into still larger supercluster complexes called walls, sheets, and filaments. There are literally millions of superclusters in the visible Universe, objects so prominent that they were alluded to some 2,800 years ago in the book of Isaiah.[349]

Astronomers believe that at least 90 percent of all galaxies are located in superclusters, and ours, the Milky Way Galaxy, is one of them. The supercluster we are in, called the Virgo Supercluster, is composed of over 1 million galaxies and about 2,000 galaxy clusters, and is around 110 million light years across.

Meanwhile our galaxy, in fact, our entire supercluster, the Virgo Supercluster, is being pulled at millions of miles an hour toward a mysterious massive region of space called the Great Attractor, a "gravity anomaly" some 220 million light years away in the direction of the constellation Centaurus.

What does all of this mean? Physically speaking, behind the

smallest known atomic particles to the largest known astronomical objects, lies the Law of Attraction!

## THE LAW ON THE SPIRITUAL PLANE

Now here is the magic. Matter is not really "solid" as we think of it, but is in fact energy vibrating at a certain frequency: a rock is just a super condensed mass of atomic particles after all. So if you were as small as an atom, you could pass right through it. This means that because mass is really just energy, the two are actually one and the same thing. That is, there is no such thing as "solid matter" as we know it. There is only *invisible* energy that appears *visible* to our physical eyes because it is vibrating so slowly.

"Everything in life is vibration," Einstein correctly observed. Lao Tzu, the great ancient Chinese philosopher, put it this way:

> "These two things, the spiritual and the material, though we call them by different names, in their origin are one and the same. This sameness is a mystery—the mystery of mysteries. It is the gate of all spirituality."

In other words, this book you are holding, the seat you are sitting on, the location you are sitting in, even your own body, are not really physical. They are merely visible forms of invisible energy, which for practical reasons we label "physical." Understand this and you have entered through "the gate of all spirituality"!

What is energy? Scientists like to break it down into various subforms, such as kinetic energy, light energy, electrical energy, heat energy, mechanical energy, and potential energy. But despite centuries of study and testing, they still do not know where energy comes from or what it is exactly. There are plenty of theories and opinions, but the ultimate source of energy remains a mystery—to science.

Christianity, however, knows the answer: energy is created by Mind and therefore is Mind, Divine Mind! Paul, for example, mystically identified energy as the "One God and Father of all, who is above all, and through all, and in you all."[350] He is, as Zechariah said, the "Lord of Hosts,"[351] that is, the "Authority Over All Powers";[352] the Father who

> "stretcheth forth the heavens, and layeth the foundation of the earth, and *formeth the spirit of man within him*."[353]

This correlates with the book of Genesis: "In the beginning God created the heaven and the earth,"[354] that is, everything.

The inner meaning of this statement is this: "God" is the Universal Divine Mind, "heaven" is the spirit plane, and "earth" is the physical plane. And here is the part of the Gospel, the "Good News," that Jesus spoke of; and as the topic of this book, it is what we are most interested in: the Law of Attraction does not merely operate on the physical plane, from subatomic particles to galactic superclusters. Since physical mass and energy are the same thing, it also functions on the spiritual plane as well. In other words, it works from within your own heart.

The biblical Greek word for heart is *kardia*, the mystical meaning which is, not surprisingly, "Divine Mind": the mental fountain of all thought and desire. Likewise, the biblical Hebrew word for heart is *leb* (*lev*), whose occult meaning is: "Universal Mind," the seat of thinking. So the same all-powerful law that keeps the planets in orbit is also available to you, right here and now. As American mystic and founder of the Unity Church Charles Fillmore once declared: "Divine Mind is the one and only reality."

Victorian author Prentice Mulford, one of the founders of the New Thought movement, had this to say about what he termed "Supreme Mind" or "Supreme Wisdom," and which Jesus called the "Father":

> "A Supreme Power and Wisdom governs the Universe. The Supreme Mind [that is, Divine Mind] is measureless, and pervades endless space. The Supreme Wisdom, Power and Intelligence is in everything that exists from the atom to the planet.
>
> "The Supreme Power and Wisdom is more than in everything. The Supreme Mind is everything. The Supreme Mind is every atom of the mountain, the sea, the tree, the bird, the animal, the man, the woman. The Supreme Wisdom cannot be understood by man or by beings superior to man. But man will gladly receive the Supreme thought and wisdom, and let it work for happiness through him, caring not to fathom its mystery."

# 4

# AS ABOVE, SO BELOW

"A fool's mouth is his destruction, and his lips
are the snare of his soul."[355]

BELIEVING MAKES IT TRUE

**S**INCE MASS AND ENERGY ARE one—that is, the physical and the spiritual are merely two qualities of the same source (God)—whatever is formed on the divine level (mind) must manifest on the material level (body). And since, as the books of Genesis and John teach, thought (Spirit) is the First Cause and creation (Physical) is the secondary effect,[356] and because God has given each one of us the irrevocable gift[357] of Divine Thought, it only follows that *whatever we think must eventually become true for us*, for everything is Spirit and Spirit is Mind.

This is why, after all, Jesus did not answer when Pilate asked him, "what is truth?"[358] There is no one personal truth that applies to all, for the only thing that can be true to us as individuals is that which we believe to be true. If someone else does not believe your truth, then it is not true for them. However, it is still true for you.

How can this be so?

THOUGHTS ARE THINGS

It is because thoughts must become things. In fact, thoughts are things! This is the inescapable spiritual law of God, one that is as ironclad as any physical law of science, including mathematics, gravity, and electricity. Why? Because they all derive from the same source: Divine Mind, the "Father."

Here is another way of looking at it. Scientists refer to the power behind the Universe as "Nature"; Jesus calls it God. Scientists refer to the foundation of Nature as "physics"; Jesus calls it God. Scientists refer to the numerical underpinnings of physics as "mathematics"; Jesus calls them God.

Scientists call the building blocks of the physical plane "matter"; Jesus calls them God. The labels are interchangeable depending on our perspective, be it spiritual or scientific. However, they all mean the same thing because they are all one and the same, despite our insistence on labeling them.

"WHATSOEVER YE SHALL BIND ON EARTH"
The ancient esoteric Christian teaching "as above, so below" now makes perfect sense. For whatever thought is formed in the mind ("above") is created on the physical ("below"). Or to put it another way, just as water always flows downhill, spiritual energy (thought) always flows from the invisible down to the visible.

As part of His teachings on the Law of Attraction, Jesus commented on this particular aspect in the "Lord's Prayer," instructing us to pray as follows:

> "Our Father which art in heaven, hallowed be thy name. Thy kingdom come. Thy will be done, as in heaven, so in earth."[359]

Here is the inner meaning of this scripture:

> The Divine Mind (the "Father") that is located in my spiritual center ("heaven") is sacred. Through this mind, my perfect life ("kingdom") will manifest on the physical plane. For the Law is that whatever is commanded on the spiritual level ("heaven") will be brought forth on the physical level ("earth").[360]

In the Gospel of Matthew, Jesus spells out the Law in no uncertain terms:

> "Verily I say unto you, whatsoever ye shall bind on earth shall be bound in heaven: and whatsoever ye shall loose on earth shall be loosed in heaven. Again I say unto you, that if two of you shall agree on earth as touching any thing that they shall ask, it shall be done for them of my Father which is in heaven."[361]

According to our Lord this amazing spiritual power is one of the great "Keys to the Kingdom of Heaven," which He gave to Peter:

> "And I will give unto thee the keys of the kingdom of heaven: and whatsoever thou shalt bind on earth shall be bound in heaven: and whatsoever thou shalt loose on earth shall be loosed in heaven."[362]

## BUDDHA & SOLOMON ON THE LAW OF ATTRACTION

Like Jesus, Buddha also possessed the Law of Attraction "keys of the kingdom." Here is what the esteemed Asian teacher said about the Law in the Dhammapada:

> "All that we are is the result of what we have thought: it is founded on our thoughts, it is made up of our thoughts. If a man speaks or acts with an evil thought, pain follows him, as the wheel follows the foot of the ox that draws the carriage. . . . If a man speaks or acts with a pure thought, happiness follows him, like a shadow that never leaves him. . . . It is good to tame the mind, which is difficult to hold in and flighty, rushing wherever it listeth; a tamed mind brings happiness. Let the wise man guard his thoughts, for they are difficult to perceive, very artful, and they rush wherever they list: thoughts well guarded bring happiness.
>
> "Those who bridle their mind . . . will be free from the bonds of Mara [illusion, Satan]. If a man's thoughts are unsteady, if he does not know the true law, if his peace of mind is troubled, his knowledge will never be perfect. If a man's thoughts are not dissipated . . . then there is no fear for him while he is watchful. . . . Whatever a hater may do to a hater, or an enemy to an enemy, a wrongly-directed mind will do us greater mischief. Not a mother, not a father will do so much, nor any other relative; a well-directed mind will do us greater service."

In the book of Proverbs, King Solomon perfectly captured the entire Law of Attraction in one of the most beautifully written, most potent scriptures of all time:

> "For as a man thinketh in his heart, so is he."[363]

Again, mystically speaking, the "heart" is the Divine Mind. This, the Mental Law, is the Divine Power you were given by God as an integral aspect of your God-Self. So here we have the entire Law of Attraction in eleven words, direct from the Bible itself! In modern English, it is ten words:

> "As you think, so you and your life will be."[364]

Commit this statement to memory. Study it, and understand it. Repeat it often, and live it. It is one of the "Keys to the Kingdom of Heaven"![365]

# 5

# THE
# TWO-EDGED SWORD

"A man's heart deviseth his way: but the Lord
directeth his steps."[366]

## THE CREATIVE POWER OF YOUR THOUGHTS

**JESUS TAUGHT US THAT AS** divine beings we possess the most
resplendent force in the Universe: the power of thought, which is the
power of God! This gives each one of us, as it does God Himself, the
ability to create both good and evil. For since thoughts are creative, it is
only logical that good thoughts create good things, while bad thoughts create
bad things. Hence, in the book of Isaiah, God the Father (Divine Mind)
says:

> "I form the light, and create darkness: I make peace, and create
> evil: I the Lord do all these things."[367]

In the Aquarian Gospel Jesus states it this way:

> "All nature is subservient to the will of man, and evil men, as well
> as good, have all the powers of mind, and may control the
> elements."[368]

The 17th-Century English scholar and poet John Milton was also
well aware of this incredible two-edged power:

> "The mind in itself and in its own place, can make a hell out of

heaven or a heaven out of hell."

Jesus' brother, James the Just, understood the potentially dangerous dual power of the mind, and how this colossal force can be used for good or evil through our words and deeds:

> ". . . the tongue is a little member [body part], and boasteth great things. Behold, how great a matter a little fire kindleth! And the tongue is a fire, a world of iniquity: so is the tongue among our members, that it defileth the whole body, and setteth on fire the course of nature; and it is set on fire of hell. For every kind of beasts, and of birds, and of serpents, and of things in the sea, is tamed, and hath been tamed of mankind: but the tongue can no man tame; it is an unruly evil, full of deadly poison.
>
> "Therewith bless we God, even the Father; and therewith curse we men, which are made after the similitude of God. Out of the same mouth proceedeth blessing and cursing. My brethren, these things ought not so to be. Doth a fountain send forth at the same place sweet water and bitter? Can the fig tree, my brethren, bear olive berries? either a vine, figs? so can no fountain both yield salt water and fresh. Who is a wise man and endued with knowledge among you? let him shew out of a good conversation his works with meekness of wisdom. But if ye have bitter envying and strife in your hearts, glory not, and lie not against the truth.
>
> "This wisdom descendeth not from above, but is earthly, sensual, devilish. For where envying and strife is, there is confusion and every evil work. But the wisdom that is from above is first pure, then peaceable, gentle, and easy to be intreated, full of mercy and good fruits, without partiality, and without hypocrisy. And the fruit of righteousness is sown in peace of them that make peace."[369]

The Jewish forerunners of Jesus and James also had full knowledge of what I call the "sword of thought," whose blade is sharpened on both edges. This is from the apocryphal Testaments of the Twelve Patriarchs:

> "Sow good things in your souls, that ye may find them in your life. But if ye sow evil things, ye shall reap every trouble and affliction."[370]

Hindus too have long known about the amazing powers of thoughts and words, and their ability to "cut both ways"—which is why sacred Hindu scripture teaches that one must be extremely careful about what comes out of one's mind and mouth. According to the Taittiriya Upanishad, our divine mental powers have three manifestations or *gunas*: they can "create, preserve, or destroy." This idea is so important in Hinduism that it has been personified in the faith's pre-Christian Holy Trinity; three all-powerful gods known collectively as Trimurti, and individually as Brahma the Creator, Vishnu the Preserver, and Shiva the Destroyer.

The author of Hebrews depicted the two-edged sword of thought like this:

> "For the word of God is quick, and powerful, and sharper than any twoedged sword, piercing even to the dividing asunder of soul and spirit, and of the joints and marrow, and is a discerner of the thoughts and intents of the heart."[371]

Here is John the Revelator's description of the Indwelling Christ:

> "And he had in his right hand seven stars: and out of his mouth went a sharp twoedged sword: and his countenance was as the sun shineth in his strength."[372]

## WHY YOU ARE FREE TO CHOOSE

As an extension of God, the Universal Mind, you contain a "piece of God," one aspect of which you know as your Subconscious Mind. And it is this, your inner Subconscious Mind, not an outer God, that is the all-powerful creator of your daily experiences. This is as it should be, for God gave you your Subconscious Mind on purpose. Why?

Being a fair-minded God,[373] He wants you to have total freedom to make anything you want of your life, good or bad, positive or negative, wonderful or horrible, productive or destructive. The Indwelling Christ "hath made us free"[374] through "our liberty which we have in Christ Jesus,"[375] for "where the Spirit of the Lord is, there is liberty."[376] This means that you have complete licence to create and live any kind of life you desire.

There is no one and no thing that can impede you in any way but yourself. This is "the Truth in Christ,"[377] the most astounding Truth in the Universe. Only when you understand and accept it will you fully appreciate this amazing freedom. It is the same freedom Jesus promised us when he said:

"And ye shall know the truth, and the truth shall make you free."[378]

Jesus was called "the Nazarene,"[379] from the word *nazara*, "the Truth."[380] So you have been set free by the literal embodiment of the Truth, revealed by the One whose teachings on the Law of Attraction have altered the world!

We humans, of course, are not the only creatures on earth who have access to the Law of Attraction.[381] Every living thing is a creation of and is connected to the Sovereign Mind, the Divine Mind. The difference is that animals, lacking complete self-awareness, act out of instinct. Only humans are truly self-conscious and have the divine capacity to control their thoughts, and in turn their conditions. Here is how the 19th-Century New England educator Amos Bronson Alcott put it:

> "Thought means life, since those who do not think [that is, the lower animals] . . . do not live in any high or real sense. Thinking makes the man."

This indeed is why the Father gave us the godlike power to dominate "every living thing":

> "Be fruitful, and multiply, and replenish the earth, and subdue it: and have dominion over the fish of the sea, and over the fowl of the air, and over every living thing that moveth upon the earth."[382]

The question facing each one of us everyday is this: what will I do with this wonderful power and freedom God has given me? Will I use the Law of Attraction wisely or unwisely?

Is not the answer obvious? God thinks so. Here is what He said:

> "Behold, I set before you this day a blessing and a curse; a blessing, if ye obey the commandments of the Lord your God, which I command you this day: and a curse, if ye will not obey the commandments of the Lord your God . . ."[383]

The "commandments of the Lord your God" include, of course, the Father's rules regarding the Law of Attraction, which we will be discussing in detail shortly.

THE MAGNIFICENT POWER OF THE MIND OF GOD WITHIN
Einstein recognized the Law of Attraction, which is why he once

commented: "Coincidence is God's way of remaining anonymous." Thus, if you are serious about working positively with the Law of Attraction, you must reject the false ideas of "luck," "destiny," "coincidence," "chance," "accidents," "predestination," "fortune," "serendipity," "fate," "kismet," and "happenstance."

As the author of your own reality, you intentionally or unintentionally attract, create, and form every event, condition, experience, and circumstance that comes into your life, both good and bad. Like God, you form your own light and you create your own darkness; you make your own peace and you create your own evil.[384] Your Conscious and Subconscious Minds, the divine powers of your God-Self, do "all these things."[385]

If your life is not going as you wish, you must begin by changing your thoughts, for you truly are the captain of your own ship, the creator of your own personality, life, and fate. Change the direction of your thoughts, and everything else will follow. Consider the words of the 18th-Century German writer Johann Wolfgang von Goethe:

> "Life is a quarry, out of which we are to mold and chisel and complete a character."

The Divine Mind within you[386] is so powerful that there is nothing it cannot accomplish. It knows all and therefore can do all.[387] This is why, as we will see, we should never question it as we work with the Law of Attraction, for the Divine Mind is far more powerful than anything on the physical plane.

When athletes, for instance, practice *mentally* for an upcoming game, they perform better than athletes who practice *physically*. Drinkers who think alcohol is good for them often have less health problems than reluctant teetotalers. And happy individuals who eat junk food are actually healthier than unhappy people who eat natural foods.

These are just a few examples of the "workshop of the mind,"[388] your mental laboratory, that magnificent power of the mind of the God who "dwells in you" and "walks in you"![389]

Jesus tells us that He did not come to judge humanity, but to save humanity, which He did, in part, by leaving us His amazing teachings on the Law of Attraction. One of these teachings concerns tolerance, as He shows here in the famous scene at Jacob's Well in Samaria, where the Lord refuses to condemn an immoral woman. Instead, He offers her the water of "everlasting life," that is, the lifesaving knowledge that we are each the creators of our own reality.

# 6

# WHY JESUS TAUGHT THE LAW IN PARABLES

"Keep thy heart with all diligence; for out of it
are the issues of life."[390]

## JESUS & "THE MYSTERIES OF THE KINGDOM OF GOD"

**WITH SUCH AN ENORMOUS FORCE** at each person's disposal,
is it any wonder that ancient teachers of the Law of Attraction
were very careful about who they shared it with, that great
"mystery which was kept secret since the world began"?[391] This is why, in
fact, Jesus taught the masses in parables, saving His "inner teachings" for His
close circle of handpicked neophytes. "The wise can understand; the foolish
have no need to know," Jesus states in the Aquarian Gospel,[392] a statement
supported by the recently discovered Secret Gospel of Mark.

In a 17th-Century copy of a letter penned by Clement of Alexandria,
the 2nd-Century Church Father mentions that Mark composed a "more
spiritual" covert version of his public (canonical) Gospel,[393] one that contains
the "hierophantic [esoteric] teachings of the Lord," which are to be read
"only to those who are being initiated into the great mysteries."[394]

Some believe that this centuries old document may not be
genuine. But even if it is not, we still have proof that Jesus headed a secret
initiatic school in which He imparted "hierophantic" knowledge to his closest
associates. How do we know this? Because He Himself says so in the New

Testament. Here are the Lord's own words from Luke:

> And he said [to the Apostles], "Unto you it is given to know the mysteries of the kingdom of God: but to others [the masses] in parables; that seeing they might not see, and hearing they might not understand."[395]

Some of the more important "mysteries" Jesus is talking about concern the Divine Mind, the power of thought, and the Law of Attraction, all which you can use to create your own "kingdom of God," that is, your our ideal life in the here and now.

HOW JESUS PROTECTED THE LAW FROM BEING MISUSED

Jesus considered the knowledge of these teachings so incredibly powerful that they could be hazardous in the wrong hands. Clement—who was well aware of the Master's esoteric doctrines—understood, saying that he would not share these secret teachings with strangers, the "Profane," as he called them, for it would be like giving a sword to a child.[396]

This is precisely why Jesus taught the Law to those he considered spiritually mature, such as the Apostles, directly and openly, but he taught it to the multitudes in an arcane manner, in this case in parables: imaginative allegorical stories that relay deep spiritual and moral concepts through symbols, figures, words, images, ideas, myths, numbers, and emblems. Thus canonical Mark says:

> "And with many such parables spake he the word unto them [the spiritually immature masses], as they were able to hear it [that is, according to their level of spiritual evolvement]. But without a parable spake he not unto them: and when they were alone, he expounded all things [openly] to his [spiritually mature] disciples."[397]

In the Aquarian Gospel Jesus explains that some are too spiritually undeveloped to understand the deeper meanings of many of His teachings, and so He must teach them using allegorical tales or parables:

> Now, his disciples were beside him in the boat, and Thomas asked, "Why do you speak in parables?" And Jesus said, "My words, like every master's words, are dual in their sense. To you [advanced spiritual initiates] who know the language of the soul, my words have meanings far too deep for other men to comprehend. The

other sense of what I say is all the multitude [spiritual beginners]
can understand; these [outer] words are food for them; the inner
thoughts are food for you. Let every one reach forth and take the
food that he is ready to receive."[398]

But, as Jesus was well knew, not even the Apostles, His inner secret
circle of twelve initiates, were spiritually mature enough to be able to
understand everything about the "mysteries." This is why, in the Gospel of
John, He tells them: "I have yet many things to say unto you, but ye cannot
bear them now."[399]

Parabolic teaching was a common practice among the ancient
mystery schools of the Roman Empire, and Jesus was only one of many early
Law of Attraction teachers who used it. In fact, parabolization has been
employed by spiritual teachers around the world for millennia. Here, for
instance, is passage from the Hindus' Mundaka Upanishad:

> "Let the truth of Brahman [God] be taught only to those who obey
> his law, who are devoted to him, and who are pure in heart."

## THE THREE SPIRITUAL LANGUAGES OF THE BIBLE

We have seen that the Law of Attraction is a powerful double-edged sword
that can benefit us or hurt us, and that it was for this very reason that Jesus
was careful who He revealed it to. There is further evidence for these facts
in the Good Book, however. Not just in the secret methods by which Jesus
and other biblical figures taught the Law, but also as revealed in the cryptic
manner in which the Bible itself was written. First a little background.

As part of the ancient program to protect the "mysteries of the
Kingdom of God" from being used for evil purposes, the Bible was written
in three languages. I am not speaking of the linguistic languages Hebrew,
Aramaic, and Greek. I am referring to the three spiritual languages:

1) *The Exoteric Language:* This forms the outer, obvious, verbatim,
and literal meanings of the Bible's many words and phrases. It is meant for
the general public; the masses of the spiritually unevolved; the uninitiated
or the unenlightened; that is, those in the beginning levels, kindergarten
through fifth grades, of Spiritual School. They have no real awareness, and
thus no true understanding, of what Jesus called "the mysteries of the
Kingdom of God."[400] This class makes up the vast majority of the orthodox
branches, denominations, and cults of Christianity, and are the ones most
likely to abuse the sacred "mysteries."

Members of this group are usually regular church goers and place great emphasis on accepted mainstream doctrine. Thus, they maintain, we are born in sin, only Jesus' death can save us, and God is a corporeal, transcendent, anthropomorphic deity who lives outside of us, and whose "Kingdom" exists only in the Afterlife. Jesus Himself is the one and only Son of God, the personal savior of Christian believers, who came to earth to die on the cross for our sins. These individuals know Him as "Jesus Christ."[401] Spirituality is a foreign concept. Religion, religious duties, religious rules, religious rituals are the main concerns in life. There is an "us versus them" bunker mentality. There is only one true religion, one pathway to Heaven: Christianity (and often only through their particular denomination).

Likewise, this group accepts the scriptural hermeneutics (interpretations) of their clergy and catechists, usually without question. As biblicists, when they do read the Bible, it is literally, never probing beneath the surface. The spiritual life is lived solely from the outside in, and spiritual knowledge is absorbed from exterior sources.

2) *The Mesoteric Language:* This forms the middle, partially veiled meanings of the Bible's many words and phrases. It is meant for those who have begun to grasp the mysteries of the Kingdom of God, but are not yet able to put them into practice. These are the incompletely evolved, who correlate with what we call Middle School, the sixth through ninth grades of Spiritual School. They have some understanding and some knowledge of the mysteries of the Kingdom of God, but are not yet ready to graduate, as more "inner work" needs to be done.

This class, which makes up only a small percent of the laity, attends church sporadically and is considered to be "falling away" from the faith by the more orthodox, literal-minded Exoteric Language group. At the same time, these individuals are starting to realize that other religions may also have merit, and begin to take an interest in non-Christian belief systems. With the realization that Jesus was a man (as Luke, John, and the author of Hebrews tell us),[402] and that "Christ" is not a surname but a title (though one with deep metaphysical meaning), they know the Lord as "Jesus *the* Christ"—the same appellation by which the Lord knew Himself.[403]

Members of this group may enjoy reading and studying the inner meanings of the Bible, but are not advanced enough to begin actually living these principles yet. They have begun to seriously question if not completely reject the literalistic, formalistic, scriptural interpretations of their clergy and religious teachers. The spiritual life is lived both from the outside in and the inside out, and spiritual knowledge is absorbed from both external sources (books, teachers, etc.) and internal sources (self-reflection, meditation, etc.).

3) *The Esoteric Language:* This forms the inner, cryptic, allegorical, and symbolic meanings of the Bible's many words and phrases, that is, their *true* meaning. It is meant for those who have advanced to the highest levels of spirituality and who have full understanding and use of the mysteries of the Kingdom of God. These are the "initiated," the "enlightened"; that is, those in the upper final levels, tenth through twelfth grades, of Spiritual School. This class makes up a tiny minority of the Christian faith, probably less than 1 percent.

Essentially mystical, these individuals easily recognize the Indwelling Christ[404] and perceive themselves and God as one and the same.[405] Indeed, they see God in everyone and everything. The Kingdom of God is here and now, in this lifetime, as Jesus affirmed,[406] and as gods and goddesses ourselves, we possess the same powers as the Father.[407]

The idea of original sin is rejected and our innate perfection,[408] as creatures made "complete"[409] in the pure image of the perfect God,[410] is acknowledged and accepted. Jesus is seen as the world's premier example of the fully enlightened Ideal Man, a "pattern for the sons of men,"[411] sent to earth to remind us of our divine nature,[412] our oneness with the Father,[413] and to show us that what He achieved we can also achieve.[414] For due to the Indwelling Christ,[415] we are all sons of Gods, just as Paul and John taught.[416]

This high consciousness group fully understands the spiritual import and gnomic connotations behind the names "Jesus Christ" and "Jesus the Christ," and so does not take them literally, as the previous two groups do. They perceive the word Christ to be a mystical title ("anointed"), representing the Higher Self that exists within each one of us—meaning that we are each a Christ in our own right, as the Bible reveals.[417]

Known in mystical Christianity as the "Indwelling Christ," or "Christ Within," the Christ has always existed and always will, for it is eternal and universal[418] it is the real you, the immortal you, the divine you. As such, the preexistent Christ lived before Jesus,[419] a fact that He Himself openly teaches in the Gospel of Matthew:

> While the Pharisees were gathered together, Jesus asked them, saying, "what think ye of Christ? whose son is he?" They say unto him, "the Son of David." He saith unto them, "how then doth David in spirit call him 'Lord,' saying, 'the Lord said unto my Lord, sit thou on my right hand, till I make thine enemies thy

footstool?'[420] If David then call him Lord, how is he his son?" And no man was able to answer him a word, neither durst any man from that day forth ask him any more questions.[421]

Transdenominational and ecumenically oriented, this group recognizes the unity of all religions, seeing the all-embracing nature of spirituality wherever and however it manifests in the world. Thus, respecting all faiths, non-Christian religions are acknowledged as other pathways to the Almighty—for spiritually speaking, this group maintains, "all roads lead to Rome."[422] They do not, in other words, confuse the messenger with the message, as the orthodox do.

These individuals have usually lost the need to attend church, and have rejected nearly all of the so-called "traditional" interpretations of the Bible as well as the authority of the clergy. Avid readers of the Bible, they grasp the full meaning of the biblical teachings that Jesus, Paul, and others purposefully concealed from the formalistic.

Members of this group are seen by institutional Christians as "apostates," "the faithless," "mystics," "New Agers," and even "atheists." However, though they are now essentially nonreligious, they are the most *spiritual* of the three groups. For them, the external trappings of religion, so important to the orthodox, have lost all meaning and importance. The spiritual life is lived purely from the inside out, and spiritual knowledge is absorbed only from one internal source: the Higher Self (self-knowledge, self-realization, self-illumination).

## THE THREE SPIRITUAL EDUCATIONAL LEVELS OF THE CHURCH

Observing these three naturally occurring gradations of spiritual awareness among the masses, the ancient pre-Christian mystery schools divided their educational system into three levels of spiritual attainment, a concept that was adopted by the new Christian Church in the 1st Century. These were, starting from the lowest or least spiritually mature and moving upward:

1) The Beginners (initiates), or the *Somatics* (that is, the "Bodies").
2) The Progressing (intermediates), or the *Psychics* (that is, the "Souls").
3) The Perfect (advanced), or the *Pneumatics* (that is, the "Spirituals").[423]

These three degrees, which correspond exactly with the three spiritual languages of the Bible (Exoteric, Mesoteric, and Esoteric) as described above, were known in the early Christian Church by other names as well, including: 1) the Auditors, the Material, or the Purification; 2) the Catechumens, the Initiation, or the Intellectual; and 3) the Faithful, the Accomplishment, or the Spiritual.[424]

For those who may doubt these facts, we have the written testimony of the following early Church Fathers, all who openly discussed the existence of the Christian mysteries and the three-degree Christian school. Along with Bishop Clements, there was: Saint Chrysostom, Tertullian, Origen, Bishop Archelaus of Cascara, Bishop Cyril of Jerusalem, Saint Basil, Saint Gregory of Nazianzus, Saint Ambrose, Saint Augustine, Saint Cyril of Alexandria, and Bishop Theodoret of Cyropolis, among many others. Ancient Pagans too, like Roman attorney Minucius Felix, noted the early Christian practice of a three-tiered initiation process into what Paul referred to, in the Pagan tradition, as the "Mysteries of God."[425]

## PAUL & THE "HIDDEN WISDOM"

This three-level educational system was adopted by early Christian teachers, such as Paul, because they understood that we are all in different spiritual grades in "Earth School." As such, Jesus' doctrines must be taught in a different manner to each of the three grades, just as we do with children of different ages. As Paul states mystically to his followers at Corinth, Greece:

> "There is one glory of the sun [the Perfect], and another glory of the moon [the Progressing], and another glory of the stars [the Beginners]: for one star differeth from another star in glory."[426]

Paul uses the word "glory" here to mean spiritual awareness. Thus, he taught what he called the "hidden wisdom,"[427] or the "deep things of God,"[428] to these three groups using the Exoteric, Mesoteric, and Esoteric methods; or as he put it: "in the spirit [we] speaketh mysteries."[429]

The Thirteenth Apostle, who revealingly refers to himself as one of the "stewards of the mysteries of God,"[430] refers openly to all three groups in this same letter, as we will now see. Note that Paul calls his most advanced followers the "Perfect" or the "Spiritual," his intermediate followers the "Natural," and his beginner followers the "Carnal" or the "Babes."

This part of his letter to the Corinthians is addressed to the latter, the spiritually immature, who had earlier asked Paul why he used different language when instructing the various groups of his followers:

"Howbeit we speak wisdom among them that are *perfect* [the Advanced]: yet not the wisdom of this world, nor of the princes of this world, that come to nought: but *we speak the wisdom of God in a mystery*, even *the hidden wisdom*, which God ordained before the world unto our glory: which none of the princes of this world knew: for had they known it, they would not have crucified the Lord of glory.

"But as it is written, 'eye hath not seen, nor ear heard, neither have entered into the heart of man, the things which God hath prepared for them that love him.' But *God hath revealed them unto us by his Spirit*: for the Spirit searcheth all things, yea, *the deep things of God*. For what man knoweth the things of a man, save the spirit of man which is in him? even so the things of God knoweth no man, but the Spirit of God.

"Now we have received, not the spirit of the world, but the spirit which is of God; that we might know the things that are freely given to us of God. Which things also we speak, not in the words which man's wisdom teacheth, but which the Holy Ghost teacheth; comparing spiritual things with spiritual. But the *natural* man [the Intermediates] receiveth not the things of the Spirit of God: for they are foolishness unto him: neither can he know them, because they are [that is, can only be] spiritually discerned.

"But he that is *spiritual* [the Advanced] judgeth all things, yet he himself is judged of no man. For who hath known the mind of the Lord, that he may instruct him? But *we have the mind of Christ* [Christ Consciousness]. And I, brethren, could not speak unto you as unto *spiritual* [the Advanced], but as unto *carnal* [the Beginners], even as unto *babes* in Christ.

"I have fed you with milk [elementary exoteric doctrines], and not with meat [advanced esoteric doctrines]: for hitherto ye were not able to bear it, neither yet now are ye able. For ye are yet *carnal* [unenlightened]: for whereas there is among you envying, and strife, and divisions, are ye not *carnal* [spiritually immature] and walk as men?"[431]

It is especially telling that Paul's use of the word mystery here (in Greek *musterion*) refers not to an unknown riddle, the common definition, but to "a secret teaching confided only to the initiated."

It is also interesting to note that some of the Christian Perfect (Pneumatics) at Corinth began to see themselves as spiritual royalty, spiritual "kings," as they called themselves, far above and beyond the uninitiated, that is, the Beginners (Somatics). Because of this haughty attitude, in his letter Paul had to remind them to be careful of succumbing to pride.[432]

## JESUS & HIS ADVANCED INITIATES
Of this particular group, the Perfect, Jesus made numerous comments as well. Among them:

> "Be ye therefore *perfect*, even as your Father which is in heaven is *perfect*."[433]

> "If thou wilt be *perfect*, go and sell that thou hast, and give to the poor, and thou shalt have treasure in heaven: and come and follow me."[434]

> "I in them, and thou in me, that they may be made *perfect* in one; and that the world may know that thou hast sent me, and hast loved them, as thou hast loved me."[435]

> "The disciple is not above his master: but every one that is *perfect* shall be as his master."[436]

The inner meaning of this last passage:

> "My Beginner (initiate) and my Progressing (intermediate) students have not yet attained my degree of spiritual maturity; however, my Perfect (advanced) students have. They are now just like me."[437]

In the understandably famous Gospel of Thomas we find this interesting exchange between Peter and our Lord:

> Simon Peter said to Him, "Let Mary leave us, for women [used here as a symbol of the Somatics or unenlightened class] are not worthy of Life." Jesus said, "I myself shall lead her in order to make her male [a symbol of the Pneumatics or enlightened class], so that she too may become a living spirit resembling you males [the Perfect]. For every woman [spiritual beginner] who will make herself male [spiritual expert] will enter the Kingdom of Heaven."[438]

In the Gospel of Thomas the Contender, when Thomas asks Jesus a question about a specific teaching, the Lord gives the following answer regarding the spiritually mature, that is, the Perfect:

"Thomas, you are referring to the doctrine of *the perfect*. And if you want to become *perfect*, you will follow it."[439]

## PAUL ENCOURAGES HIS INITIATES TO ATTAIN THE PERFECT
Paul too encouraged his lower ranked followers to reach for the highest degree of his esoteric brotherhood, the Perfect.  Here are a few examples:

"For we are glad, when we are weak, and ye are strong: and this also we wish, even your *perfection*. . . . Finally, brethren, farewell. Be *perfect*, be of good comfort, be of one mind, live in peace; and the God of love and peace shall be with you."[440]

"Till we all come in the unity of the faith, and of the knowledge of the Son of God, unto a *perfect* man, unto the measure of the stature of the fulness of Christ."[441]

"Not as though I had already attained, either were already *perfect*: but I follow after, if that I may apprehend that for which also I am apprehended of Christ Jesus."[442]

"Let us therefore, as many as be *perfect*, be thus minded: and if in any thing ye be otherwise minded, God shall reveal even this unto you."[443]

"Whom we preach, warning every man, and teaching every man in all wisdom; that we may present every man *perfect* in Christ Jesus."[444]

"Epaphras, who is one of you, a servant of Christ, saluteth you, always labouring fervently for you in prayers, that ye may stand *perfect* and complete in all the will of God."[445]

"That the man of God may be *perfect*, throughly furnished unto all good works."[446]

"God having provided some better thing for us, that they without us should not be made *perfect*."[447]

## JAMES & PETER COMMENT ON THE PERFECT
Here is what Jesus' brother, James the Just, said about the most advanced spiritual class, the Perfect:

"But let patience have her *perfect* work, that ye may be *perfect* and entire, wanting nothing."[448]

"For in many things we offend all. If any man offend not in word, the same is a *perfect* man, and able also to bridle the whole body."[449]

The Apostle Peter recognized the Perfect group as well:

"But the God of all grace, who hath called us unto his eternal glory by Christ Jesus, after that ye have suffered a while, make you *perfect*, stablish, strengthen, settle you."[450]

In the book of Hebrews we find these passages concerning the spiritual progress of Jesus' followers, encouraging them not to fall back down to the lower levels of spiritual school:

". . . let us go on unto *perfection*; not laying again the foundation of repentance from dead works, and of faith toward God, of the doctrine of baptisms, and of laying on of hands, and of resurrection of the dead, and of eternal judgment. And this will we do, if God permit. For it is impossible for those who were *once enlightened*, and have tasted of the heavenly gift [the Law of Attraction], and were made partakers of the Holy Ghost, and have tasted the good word of God, and the powers of the world to come, if they shall fall away, to renew them again unto repentance; seeing they crucify to themselves the Son of God afresh, and put him to an open shame."[451]

THE ANCIENT WISDOM: THE GOSPEL OF THE INNER CHRIST
"The hidden wisdom of God in a mystery" that Paul speaks of above refers to Jesus' secret teachings on the Universal Divine Mind, the Law of Attraction, and Man's oneness with God.[452] It is, Paul declares,

"the mystery of God, and of the Father, and of Christ; in whom are hid all the treasures of wisdom and knowledge."[453]

The Bible itself bears witness to Paul's statement, for the vast majority of Jesus' parables were about the mysterious treasure-filled "Kingdom of God." The "Kingdom," for example, is mentioned 119 times in the four canonical Gospels, but the word "atonement" does not appear even once. Based on this fact alone, it is clear which doctrine Jesus considered the most important.

Paul would have agreed, which is why he preached about the salvific benefit of living according to the Gospel of the Indwelling Christ:

> "For I am not ashamed of *the gospel of [the Indwelling] Christ*: for it is the power of God unto salvation to every one that believeth; to the Jew first, and also to the Greek [non-Jews]. For therein is the righteousness of God revealed from faith to faith: as it is written, 'The just shall live by faith.'"[454]

## PAUL CALLS THE OT STORIES "ALLEGORIES" & "JEWISH FABLES"

These same sacred truths—known collectively as the "Ancient Wisdom," or biblically, as the "mystery which hath been hid from ages and from generations"[455]—were also concealed in the Old Testament under layers of arcane language, symbolism, parables, folklore, myth, and allegories.

Thus Paul, like most other early Christian teachers of the Law of Attraction, taught that many of the Old Testament stories are not literal, true-life historical events.[456] Rather, they are he said, "Jewish fables,"[457] spiritual "allegories" meant to hide ancient occult knowledge and wisdom concerning powerful sacred doctrines, like the Law of Attraction, from the uninitiated.[458] (Peter preached the same doctrine, noting, for example, that the waters of Noah's flood symbolized baptism.)[459]

For Paul, the "uninitiated" were those who were not part of his secret brotherhood,[460] and those who did not adhere to his own personal gospel.[461] As such, those Christian biblicists who take such tales literally, according to Paul, are committing a grave sin. Why? Because the literal (outer) meaning is merely a literary device to hide the true (inner) meaning from the spiritually immature, and it is this inner meaning that we are meant to try and discover and understand. As the saint himself asserted: "The letter killeth, but the spirit giveth life."[462] The true believer lives, he continued, according to the heart, not according to a strict literal interpretation of religious law:[463]

> "But now we are delivered from the law, that being dead wherein we were held; that we should serve in *newness of spirit*, and not in the *oldness of the letter*."[464]

## THE CODED LANGUAGE OF JESUS & PAUL

We should not be surprised to learn that Jesus too taught the "mysteries of the Kingdom of God" using the three-tier system of the ancient mystery schools. Many times throughout the Gospels He speaks of employing the Exoteric method, mainly through parables, to teach the masses (the uninitiated), while using the Esoteric method to educate His Apostles (the advanced),[465] and sometimes His Disciples (the intermediates). According to Matthew it was to the latter group, for example, that He addressed His celebrated Sermon on the Mount, not to the general public.[466]

The question is why did Jesus, Paul, and the teachers of countless other early Christian secret brotherhoods, Jewish rabbinical schools, and Pagan mystery cults use the three spiritual languages to teach inner and outer doctrines, such as the Law of Attraction, to their three-tiered followers, the Beginners, the Progressing, and the Perfect?

First, concerning Jesus specifically. He had many enemies (mainly religiously strict Jews, such as the Pharisees)—whom He referred to as "the children of the wicked one"[467]—who wanted to trick Him into saying something blasphemous, illegal, or treasonous. Though the Master often spoke openly and boldly, even in the midst of His critics, there were times when He felt it was best to protect Himself, His followers, and especially His inner teachings from those who would do them harm. After all, when the unenlightened try to teach arcane spiritual principles, the teacher and his students, not to mention the sacred doctrines themselves, all fall further and further away from the Truth.

It was to protect both the Word and Himself from these types of dangers that Jesus relied on parabolic language. Other ancient spiritual teachers, such as Paul, had similar reasons for speaking selectively, esoterically, and even secretly to those "as they were able to hear it."[468]

Second, ancient religious teachers believed that if their spiritually immature and uninitiated aspirants (the Beginners), along with the unilluminated masses, were to get hold of the "hidden wisdom"—powerful Law of Attraction principles that enable one to alter physical reality—they might abuse or misuse this very special and formidable power of God, perhaps even for evil purposes.

Because of this, sacred information was taught to them in a coded language, the Esoteric language, so that they could only grasp the outer meaning of the secret "principles of the oracles of God."[469] Those who were more spiritually evolved, such as the Progressing class, would glean what they could, while the upper class, the Perfect, would have full access[470] to these oracles, the "hidden wisdom" (inner meaning), due to their enlightened state.[471] Speaking to the "babes" (the Beginners) among his followers, Paul phrased the situation like this:

"Of whom we have many things to say, and hard to be uttered, seeing ye are dull of hearing [spiritually immature]. For when for the time ye ought to be teachers [advanced initiates], ye have need that one teach you again which be the first principles of the oracles of God [divine secrets of the Father]; and are become such as have need of milk [basic spiritual teachings], and not of strong meat [advanced spiritual teachings].

"For every one that useth milk is unskilful in the word of righteousness: for he is a babe [a Beginner]. But strong meat belongeth to them that are of full age [the Perfect], even those who by reason of use have their senses exercised to discern both good and evil [the Progressing or Intermediates]. Therefore leaving the principles of the doctrine of [the Indwelling] Christ, let us go on unto *perfection* [that is, work toward the highest spiritual level, the Perfect]; not laying again the foundation of repentance from dead works, and of faith toward God . . ."[472]

Again, note that the author speaks of the simple doctrines he teaches to his Beginners as "milk" for "a babe," and the more complex ones he teaches to his advanced students, the Perfect, those who are of "full age," as "strong meat."

## JESUS ADDRESSES HIS SECRET INNER CIRCLE

Jesus goes into great detail replying to the following question put to Him by His Disciples: why do you withhold the mysteries from the outer circle (the masses), but teach them to your inner circle (the Disciples)? they asked. Here is the story as told by Mark:

And when he was alone, they that were about him with the twelve [Apostles, or advanced initiates] asked of him the parable. And he said unto them, "Unto you it is given to know the mystery of the kingdom of God: but unto them that are without, all these things are done in parables: that seeing they may see, and not perceive; and hearing they may hear, and not understand; lest at any time they should be converted, and their sins should be forgiven them."[473]

Matthew goes into more detail in his account:

And the disciples came, and said unto him, "Why speakest thou unto them [the multitudes] in parables?" He answered and said unto them, "Because it is given unto you to know the mysteries of the kingdom of heaven, but to them it is not given. For whosoever hath, to him shall be given, and he shall have more abundance: but whosoever hath not, from him shall be taken away even that he hath. Therefore speak I to them in parables: because they seeing see not; and hearing they hear not, neither do they understand. And in them is fulfilled the prophecy of Esaias, which saith,

'By hearing ye shall hear, and shall not understand; and seeing ye shall see, and shall not perceive: for this people's heart is waxed gross, and their ears are dull of hearing, and their eyes they have closed; lest at any time they should see with their eyes, and hear with their ears, and should understand with their heart, and should be converted, and I should heal them.'[474]

"But blessed are your [inner] eyes, for they see [deep spiritual things]: and your [inner] ears, for they hear [deep spiritual things]. For verily I say unto you, that many prophets and righteous men have desired to see those things which ye see, and have not seen them; and to hear those things which ye hear, and have not heard them."[475]

Jesus then uses a parable to describe the three groups He teaches using the standard mystery school technique:

"Hear ye therefore the parable of the sower. When any one heareth the word of the kingdom, and understandeth it not, then cometh the wicked one, and catcheth away that which was sown in his heart. This is he which received seed by the way side. But he that received the seed into stony places, the same is he that heareth the word, and anon with joy receiveth it; Yet hath he not root in himself, but dureth for a while: for when tribulation or persecution ariseth because of the word, by and by he is offended. He also that received seed among the thorns is he that heareth the word; and the care of this world, and the deceitfulness of riches, choke the word, and he becometh unfruitful. But he that received seed into the good ground is he that heareth the word, and understandeth it; which also beareth fruit, and bringeth forth, some an hundredfold, some sixty, some thirty."[476]

Now let us reread these passages stripped of Jesus' coded language, so that everything will be made plain:

> The Disciples came to Jesus and asked him: "Why do you teach the masses using allegories?" Jesus replied: "Because I have chosen you, my closest and spiritually mature followers, to understand the secret teachings of the Law of Attraction, while the masses have not been chosen because, being spiritually immature, they are not ready, posing a danger to themselves and society. For those who already comprehend and practice the Law of Attraction always receive more abundance, while those who know nothing about the Law of Attraction, and so do not practice it, from them more and more is taken away, even what little they have to begin with.
>
> "This is why I teach to the masses using allegories; because even though they can see with their physical eyes, they cannot see with their spiritual eyes; and even though they can hear with their physical ears, they cannot hear with their spiritual ears. And so they are incapable of truly understanding anything about the Law of Attraction. It is these very people, the uninitiated masses, that have fulfilled the prophecy of Isaiah:
>
>> 'Though listening through physical ears you hear, you will not understand; and though looking through physical eyes you see, you will not perceive: For the masses' subconscious minds have been struck dumb, and their ears are blocked off, and their eyes are closed; otherwise they might have to see with their spiritual eyes and hear with their spiritual ears; then comprehending through the Divine Mind, they would be transformed into spiritually mature individuals, and I would then be able to heal them.'
>
> "But Disciples, my spiritually mature followers, you should be very happy because you are able to see with your spiritual eyes and hear with your spiritual ears. I tell you truly that many of the most important, powerful, and admirable men in history have longed to be able to see spiritually like you, but were unable to, and to hear spiritually like you, but could not.
>
> "Let me explain further by telling you the allegory of the farmer and the three levels or degrees of spiritual awareness.
>
> "The third or lowest level is comprised of the Beginner or *Somatic* (the 'Body'), a completely unenlightened person. He is so spiritually immature that he is not even open to hearing about

the Law of Attraction. If you try to teach it to him, he will not be able to understand it. For Satan—that is, his Ego—will negate the positive thoughts that you have tried to plant in his Subconscious Mind, making him feel unworthy of happiness, health, and abundance. This is like the farmer who sows his crop seeds on a hard dry road instead of on moist black soil: there will be no growth.

"The second or middle level is made up of the Progressing or the *Psychic* (the 'Soul'), a semi-enlightened person. He is open to hearing about the Law of Attraction, and will even be happy to learn about it. But being a spiritually intermediate, he is not deeply grounded in spiritual truth. So when the first stressful event comes along in his life, he loses his faith and forgets the teaching. This is like the farmer who sows his crop seeds on rocky soil: the seeds try to grow but cannot take root. Similarly we have the man who at first seems to understand the teaching of the Law, but is soon seduced away by the false promises of materialism. This is like the farmer who sows his crop seeds amid thorns: they suffocate the seedlings before they can sprout, making them unfertile.

"The first or highest degree is formed around the Perfect or the *Pneumatic* individual (the 'Spiritual'). This man is fully spiritually mature and thus fully spiritually receptive. As such, when he hears about the Law of Attraction for the first time, he understands it immediately, for it is not learned from a book, but from the Higher Self (self-knowledge or Gnosis). He accepts it and begins to practice it. He soon starts manifesting his invisible desires on the visible plane. This is like the farmer who sows his crop seeds on healthy, fertile, freshly tilled soil: his harvest will be thirty, sixty, even 100 times what he originally planted."[477]

Thus spoke the Master of Galilee to his band of privately initiated followers, a group that included an even deeper inner circle of "secret Disciples" comprised of individuals like Joseph of Arimathea.[478]

JAMES, JOHN, & PETER: JESUS' MOST SECRET INNER CIRCLE
The early Gnostic Christians—one group who wrote an entire text in honor of the Pneumatics or Perfect called: "The Thunder: Perfect Mind"[479]—held that the Apostles James (mystically, judgment and the Conscious Mind), John (love and the Superconscious Mind), and Peter (faith and the Subconscious Mind) were the only ones Jesus considered spiritually mature enough to be able to comprehend the most deeply occult secrets of what he revealingly called, not "the Gospel of Jesus Christ," but "the Gospel of the

Kingdom"[480]—a timeless arcane philosophy so fascinating that even "angels desire to look into it."[481]

This view is not "heterodox" as some would have us believe. Rather it is orthodox, for it is confirmed by the canonical Gospels themselves.[482] Additionally, Clement of Alexandria, according to Eusebius, corroborates it in a 2nd-Century document, saying:

> "After His resurrection, the Lord transmitted the [Sacred] Gnosis to James the Just, and John and Peter. They then passed it on to the other Apostles, who then gave it to the Seventy, one of whom was Barnabas."[483]

In short, parables were necessary in Jesus' day, and are still necessary in our day, because, as the Aquarian Gospel states:

> "Man is not far enough advanced to live by faith; he cannot comprehend the things his eyes see not, he yet is [a] child, and during all the coming age he must be taught by pictures, symbols, rites, and forms. His God must be a human God; he cannot see a God by faith. And then he cannot rule himself; the king must rule; the man must serve."[484]

Those who want to practice the Law of Attraction productively, however, must become the opposite and strive to be Perfect.[485] That is, they must learn to live by faith,[486] learn to spiritually comprehend things that their physical eyes cannot see,[487] and learn to trust in the "eternal, immortal, invisible" God of Jesus[488] rather than the visible "human" God of modern Pagan Christianity.[489] Only then can we come to realize what Jesus taught us we truly are: kings of our own personal Inner Realm,[490] that magical but real place that the Lord called the "Kingdom Within,"[491] and which He preached as "the Gospel of the Kingdom."[492]

Jesus welcomes everyone into the Kingdom of God, for everyone is eligible, including non-Christians and even nonbelievers. The only requirement is that one must be "born again" spiritually that is, psychologically and take on the consciousness of a "little child"—which Paul called "the mind of Christ" and which Christian mystics call "Christ Consciousness." As it forms the very foundation of Jesus' central message (that all humans possess a divine spark known as the "Indwelling Christ"), His teachings focused almost solely on the Kingdom of God. The importance of this doctrine lies in the fact that it is much easier to practice the Law of Attraction when one has entered the Kingdom, for inside of it our divine powers are greatly enhanced while the laws of physics are greatly diminished. Outside the Kingdom, however, our divine powers are not nearly as strong, while material laws have full sway over us. Though all are invited into the Kingdom, few will choose to accept. As the Lord Himself said: "For many are called, but few are chosen."

# 7

# UNDERSTANDING
# THE LAW

## Part 1

"A man's belly shall be satisfied with the fruit
of his mouth; and with the increase of his lips
shall he be filled."[493]

## CONNECTING WITH GOD RIGHT NOW

OW CAN WE MAKE PERSONAL use of the Law of Attraction, the most powerful force in the Universe? How do we take a scientific law that lies at the foundation of everything from atoms to galaxies and make it work for us on an everyday level?

We connect with God, the omnipotent, immanent, invisible force behind the Law of Attraction.[494] And how do we connect with God? Through thought! Thought is the electrical conduit that links us to the Almighty, to the Source of all Creation. It joins the invisible with the visible, bridges the gap between the spiritual and the physical, and spans the chasm between heaven and earth.

It works this way because the Subconscious Mind is that piece of Himself that God placed in each one of us. This is the incorporeal Supreme Self, your God-Self, which the Father "created in his own image,"[495] and which He imbued with the same extraordinary power that He possesses: the power of creation! Paul said that because of this, we reflect God's glory mirror-like, "as in a glass."[496]

Now since like attracts like, God responds to whatever comes out of your Subconscious Mind, and, in turn, your Subconscious Mind responds to whatever comes out of God. If you have a need, you send this thought out to the Father, and He returns it to you fulfilled. It is the Law of Action (thought) and Reaction (manifestation) accomplished, and it is always exact: what you think now you will receive later.

It is like an alternating circuit of electricity, with God being the positive (spiritual) charge and you being the negative (material) charge: your thought closes the electrical switch, forming a complete circuit between you and the Father, between the natural and the supernatural. The flowing of this "electricity" is the magical creative energy that, as gods and goddesses,[497] each one of us possesses, as Peter said, "through the Gnosis of the Indwelling Christ."[498]

God Himself perfectly describes this "electrical" Law of Attraction principle in the book of Isaiah:

> "So shall my word be that goeth forth out of my mouth: it shall not return unto me void, but it shall accomplish that which I please, and it shall prosper in the thing whereto I sent it."[499]

Here is the inner meaning of this important scripture as spoken by the Father, the Divine Mind. Read it as if it is coming from the real you, that is, your God-Self:

> "My thoughts are magnetic, and therefore always attract identical patterns back to themselves, as physical manifestations. Therefore, my thoughts can never return empty. They must always bring me back that which I desire, materializing in the form of my personal circumstances, conditions, events, and experiences."[500]

## THE LAW OF REPULSION

An often overlooked aspect of the Law of Attraction is its opposite: the Law of Repulsion. *If like attracts like, then like must repulse unlike.* What does this mean for us on an individual level!

It means that if you are thinking negative, ugly, discordant, destructive thoughts, you are actually driving away the physical manifestation of their opposites: positive, beautiful, harmonious, constructive circumstances, experiences, and conditions! Conversely, if you are thinking positive, beautiful, harmonious, constructive thoughts, you are driving away the physical manifestation of their opposites: negative, ugly, discordant, destructive circumstances, experiences, and conditions.

Why is this?

Our Universe is a reciprocal Universe: *whatever is sent out is received back, laden with corresponding vibrational energy*. Furthermore, it is designed to be all-inclusive: because the Law of Attraction is at its foundation, *it does not exclude anything*.

This is why the Universe has no filter, and why there is no judgment. Whether positive or negative, productive or destructive, beneficial or detrimental, all thoughts are received by the Divine Mind as is. More importantly, whether you desire something or do not want something, if you think about it long enough, if you truly concentrate on it, it is included on the list of what your Subconscious Mind is going to materialize.[501]

So the more you dwell on the things about your life that you dislike, the more of this you attract, while simultaneously repelling the very things you want. The more you dwell on the things about your life that you like, the more of this you attract, while simultaneously repelling the things you do not want.

"He that hath ears to hear, let him hear."[502] For if you understand this, you are in possession of one of the greatest "keys" to the Kingdom of Heaven,[503] that great "mystery of God."[504] Apply this key to your daily life and you wield unlimited power to create your own circumstances.[505]

Now you know "the hidden wisdom of God in a mystery" that Paul referred to,[506] and which Jesus called one of "the mysteries of the Kingdom of God."[507] Now you know "the mystery of the faith,"[508] "the mystery of God, and of the Father, and of Christ; in whom are hid all the treasures of wisdom [Sophia] and knowledge [Gnosis]."[509] Now you know the true inner meaning of Paul's statement: "O the depth of the riches of the Sophia and Gnosis of the Divine Mind!"[510]

Now you also know why Jesus "made known unto us the mystery of his will."[511] You "understand my knowledge in the mystery of Christ,"[512] a "great mystery"[513] unveiled personally to me, as with Paul, by the revelation of Christ Himself;[514] "the mystery, which from the beginning of the world hath been hid in God, who created all things by Jesus Christ."[515]

Now you are aware of "the mystery of Christ" that Paul and his followers preached;[516] you now know how this, the most powerful force in the known Universe, works for and against humanity on a personal level. That force is the Law of Attraction, and when you use it properly you are united with the Father and He is united with you![517]

## THE FATHER HEARS EVERY PRAYER

Every sincere thought you think is immediately listened to by God, the Universal Divine Mind, and acted upon. This is what is meant by the old adage: "God answers every prayer," for according to the Bible, He does.[518] In Jeremiah we find this wonderful passage:

> "Call unto me, and I will answer thee, and shew thee great and mighty things, which thou knowest not."[519]

Knowing this, whatever the circumstance, do not allow fear into the temple of your mind. You are never truly and completely alone.[520] God is always with you,[521] always listening to your prayers,[522] always answering your prayers,[523] twenty-four hours a day, seven days a week. "I am the Lord their God, and will hear them," saith the Father.[524] To those of you who have been taught that the thought-seeds you plant in the prayer-field cannot be "harvested" until sometime in the future, Jesus made this figurative comment:

> "Lift up your eyes, and look on the fields; for they are white already to harvest."[525]

The only reason some of you may not be aware of this truth is that until now you have not fully understood how God and prayer work.

## UNDERSTANDING THE TRUE NATURE OF GOD

If you are like most people, you were probably taught that God is an enormous, all-powerful deity sitting on a great golden throne somewhere up in Heaven. While it is admitted that He loves His children, He is usually portrayed as a grumpy, overly critical, short-tempered old man, who sports a beard and long hair, wears a crown and a robe, and holds a scepter or trident in one hand.

Being God of the Universe, he has little time or inclination to deal with our puny personal problems down here on earth. He has more important things to do, such as organizing great armies of angels, judging sinners, rewarding saints, listening to the heavenly choir sing, and hurling thunderbolts at Satan.

Actually, this is not the God of Jesus at all, and therefore it is not the true *Christian* God. In fact, the description above is of the *Pagan* God, which some of the more overly imaginative Old Testament writers borrowed from, among others, ancient Mesopotamian, Egyptian, Phoenician, Akkadian, Hittite, Indian, Persian, Babylonian, Ugarite, Sumerian, Roman, and Greek mythology.

As was the custom at the time, nearly all of the primary male deities of early societies and religions were portrayed in the same way. Several of these ancient "father-gods" or "sky-gods," in particular the Egyptian Ra, the Greek Zeus, the Indian Vishnu, the Roman Jupiter, and the Canaanite Baal, were used as models upon which the Old Testament version of God was patterned—as ancient statues of these old deities clearly show.[526] Indeed, according to God Himself, He was at one time literally known as "Baal" by His Hebrew followers:

> "And it shall be at that day," saith the Lord, "that thou shalt . . . call me no more Baal."[527]

So deeply was the Pagan concept of the Father embedded among the ancient Hebrews that they also knew Him as both the Pagan deity El Elyon (the name of a Canaanite city-god)[528] and as the Pagan deity El Shaddai (the name of a Semitic mountain-goddess).[529]

Jesus did away with this idolatry, this ancient Pagan, carnalized, anthropomorphic view of an angry, violent, transcendent, corporeal God sitting imperiously on His heavenly throne;[530] the heartless "man of war" of the book of Exodus,[531] who cruelly ordered the death penalty for such minor things as gathering sticks[532] or kindling a fire on the Sabbath Day,[533] for eating leavened bread during Passover,[534] and for promiscuity,[535] blasphemy,[536] and heresy.[537]

Jesus completely overturned the Old Testament notion of the tempestuous "Lord" who sanctioned or even commanded the wholesale slaughter of children and even entire nations;[538] the ever-demanding "jealous God"[539] who bellows, blusters, and threatens His way through the pages of such books as Micah, Nahum, Habakkuk, and Zephaniah.[540]

## JESUS PREACHED AN INVISIBLE GOD MADE OF PURE SPIRIT

In place of this human-fabricated Hebrew Zeus,[541] Jesus declared once and for all that "God is Spirit." In other words, He is not a physical deity, He is simply the entire Universe and everything in it.[542] Thus, Jesus said:

> ". . . the Father himself, which hath sent me, hath borne witness of me. Ye have neither heard his voice at any time, nor seen his

shape."[543]

"No man hath seen God at any time; the only begotten Son [that is, the Indwelling Christ], which is in the bosom of the Father, he hath declared him."[544]

Only those who have entered the Kingdom of God have actually "seen" God. For since "God" is the Divine Mind, we can only "see" Him through our spiritual (non-physical) eyes, just as Jesus taught:

"Not that any man hath seen the Father, save he which is of God, he hath seen the Father."[545]

John echoed the views of our Lord, reaffirming that God lives inside of those who are loving:

"No man hath seen God at any time. If we love one another, God dwelleth in us, and his love is perfected in us."[546]

In the Gnostic Christian text known as the Apocryphon of John, Jesus rightly says that what men call "God" is actually "the invisible Spirit, and it is not right to view him as a god."[547]

Let us note here that Jesus was not against Pagan gods because there is something inherently evil about them, as so many modern Christian authorities teach. After all, each ancient god and goddess was merely a symbol, a personification, of one of the many universal divine principles, the same ones that are taught to this day in both the mainstream and the mystical branches of the Christian Church, and in every other religion in fact.

No, Jesus was against praying to manmade deities because it is a waste of our time. Why? Because being mythological, there is no one to hear us! The divinities of Paganism, having been fabricated by the imagination of Man, are truly nothing but lifeless "graven images."[548] Of them Jesus has this to say in the Aquarian Gospel:

"These gods possess no ears to hear, no eyes to see, no heart to sympathize, no power to save. . . these gods are made of air, and clothed with shadows of a thought."[549]

Hence the Lord always refers to the Pagans' God as "the God of the dead," and the true God, Divine Mind, as "the God of the living."[550] Jesus explains in the following account from Mark:

> Then come unto him [Jesus] the Sadducees, which say there is no
> resurrection; and they asked him, saying, "Master, Moses wrote
> unto us, 'If a man's brother die, and leave his wife behind him, and
> leave no children, that his brother should take his wife, and raise up
> seed unto his brother.' Now there were seven brethren: and the
> first took a wife, and dying left no seed. And the second took her,
> and died, neither left he any seed: and the third likewise. And the
> seven had her, and left no seed: last of all the woman died also. In
> the resurrection therefore, when they shall rise, whose wife shall
> she be of them? for the seven had her to wife."
>
> And Jesus answering said unto them, "Do ye not
> therefore err, because ye know not the scriptures, neither the
> power of God? For when they shall rise from the dead, they
> neither marry, nor are given in marriage; but are as the angels
> which are in heaven. And as touching the dead, that they rise: have
> ye not read in the book of Moses, how in the bush God spake unto
> him, saying, 'I am the God of Abraham, and the God of Isaac, and
> the God of Jacob'? He is not the God of the dead, but the God of
> the living: ye therefore do greatly err."[551]

Yes, just as Jesus teaches, God is pneumamorphic; that is, He is
Spirit,[552] and a part of this Spirit lives within you.[553] This is why individuals
who have near-death experiences never actually "see" God during their
temporary journeys to Heaven. Instead, as they themselves testify, they
"feel" Him as an all-encompassing sensation of pure love that fills every atom
of the Universe. He truly is, Paul said, "the invisible God[554] . . . whom no
man hath seen, nor can see,"[555] and who "dwelleth not in temples made with
hands."[556] Where does He dwell then? He lives within your "inner
church,"[557] "the true tabernacle of faith, constructed by the Lord, not
man."[558]

WORSHIPING THE FATHER IN SPIRIT
Though He preached an omnipresent, immanent, circumambient, and
unseeable God, Jesus knew that future teachers would fall back into idolatry
and try to anthropomorphize both the invisible spiritual Father[559] and the
invisible Indwelling Christ[560]—just as they did in His day. He admonished
His followers to watch out for these types of men and the "false Christs," or
humanlike saviors, that they would extol to the masses. They will try to
deceive even the most spiritually advanced souls with this erroneous

doctrine, He warned.[561]

But be not led astray, He continued, for even as God is Spirit, God's realm, the Kingdom of Heaven, is also invisible, for it is "within you,"[562] that is, the "kingdom is within the soul."[563] However, the day will come when all will recognize their oneness with the Divine Mind, and their own divine nature will shine forth.[564] It will be at that time, Jesus said, that "the true worshippers shall worship the Father in spirit and in truth: for the Father seeketh such to worship him."[565]

## PAUL AT MARS' HILL

Paul, following Jesus' teachings, also felt strongly about this topic, as he noted during his famous Mars' Hill Sermon. Here is Luke's description of the Apostle's speech, in which he discusses the ancient Pagan, and now modern mainstream Christian, idea of a literal, material, humanlike God:

> Then Paul stood in the midst of Mars' hill, and said, "Ye men of Athens, I perceive that in all things ye are too superstitious. For as I passed by, and beheld your devotions, I found an altar with this inscription, 'To the Unknown God.' Whom therefore ye ignorantly worship, him declare I unto you. God that made the world and all things therein, seeing that he is Lord of heaven and earth, *dwelleth not in temples made with hands; neither is worshipped with men's hands*, as though he needed any thing, seeing he giveth to all life, and breath, and all things; and hath made of one blood all nations of men for to dwell on all the face of the earth, and hath determined the times before appointed, and the bounds of their habitation; that they should seek the Lord, if haply they might feel after him, and find him, though *he be not far from every one of us*: for *in him we live, and move, and have our being*; as certain also of your own poets have said, for we are also his offspring. Forasmuch then as we are the offspring of God, *we ought not to think that the Godhead is like unto gold, or silver, or stone, graven by art and man's device*."[566]

U.S. President Thomas Jefferson also had firm opinions on this subject, as he wrote in 1823:

> ". . . the reformation of these blasphemous attributes [that is, of the Pagan idea of a humanlike Supreme Being], and substitution of those more worthy, pure, and sublime [that is, that God is simply Spirit], seems to have been the chief object of Jesus in His discourses to the Jews; and His doctrine of the cosmogony of the world is very clearly laid down in the three first verses of the first

chapter of John, in these words . . . which truly translated mean, 'In the beginning God existed, and reason (or mind) was with God, and that mind was God. This was in the beginning with God. All things were created by it, and without it was made not one thing which was made.' Yet this text, so plainly declaring the doctrine of Jesus, that the world was created by the Supreme, Intelligent Being, has been perverted by modern Christians . . ."

The point is that God, being Spirit, not only dwells *outside* of you, for—as we have seen—He is everything,[567] but He dwells *within* you as well,[568] as your Higher Self, as your God-Self, as the Indwelling Christ[569] "which lighteth every man."[570] For as believers we are "changed into the image of the glory of the Lord,"[571] and literally "bear the image of the heavenly,"[572] perfectly reflecting God's glory "as in a mirror."[573] We even rule over our own inner spiritual monarchy, the "Kingdom of God" or "Kingdom of Heaven."[574] Here is how Jesus described this momentous doctrine in the Gospel of Luke:

> "The kingdom of God cometh not with observation: neither shall they say, 'Lo here!' or, 'lo there!' for, behold, *the kingdom of God is within you.*"[575]

For, as Paul said:

> "the kingdom of God is not meat and drink [that is, physical]; but righteousness, and peace, and joy in the Holy Ghost [that is, spiritual, mental]."[576]

Concerning agrapha, in the Gnostic Christian Gospel of Thomas (which predates Paul's letters) Jesus phrases it this way:

> "If those who lead you say to you, 'See, the kingdom is in the sky,' then the birds of the sky will precede you. If they say to you, 'It is in the sea,' then the fish will precede you. Rather, *the kingdom is inside of you, and it is outside of you.* When you come to know yourselves [that is, your true self, the Indwelling Christ], then you will become known, and you will realize that it is *you who are the sons of the living father* [Divine Mind]. But if you will not know yourselves, you dwell in poverty [spiritual impoverishment] and it is you who are that poverty."[577]

In another section of Thomas, Jesus has this discussion with some of His followers:

> His disciples said to Him, "When will the Kingdom come?" Jesus said, "It will not come by waiting for it. It will not be a matter of saying 'Here it is' or 'There it is.' Rather, *the Kingdom of the Father is spread out upon the earth, and men do not see it.*"[578]

In his *Refutation of All Heresies*, the early orthodox Church Father Hippolytus of Rome noted, with distaste, that Gnostic Christians taught that the Kingdom of Heaven is to "be sought for *within* a man."[579] And contrary to Christian tradition, but according to our Lord Himself, so it is![580]

## THE "KINGDOM" IS PSYCHOLOGICAL HARMONY

What is your life, your personal inner "kingdom," like right now? Good, bad, or in between, it is all the result of your past thoughts. What are you thinking right now? Whatever that thought is, it is creating your future. For your Subconscious Mind, the literal Mind of God within you,[581] is constantly working to "make your word flesh,"[582] that is, to physically manifest your most predominant thoughts and prayers (desires). Indeed, this is its only spiritual function: to materially create what it is you most hunger for in your heart.

We all have a mental image of our ideal life, one of harmony, happiness, and prosperity; a life that we yearn to create while we are here on earth. But did you know that this psychological ideal is identical to the pure state of consciousness that Jesus calls the "Kingdom of God" or "Kingdom of Heaven"? And are you aware that the power to enter and live in this Kingdom is already within you, materializing your desires every moment of everyday in exact accord with whatever you are thinking at the moment?[583] Is that not wonderful, magical, and amazing?

Just think: you can create anything you want with your thoughts alone, just as God (whom scientists call "Nature" or the "laws of physics") created the entire Universe and everything in it by thought alone. And yet most people are creating the opposite of what they really want!

## THE MASS MIND

One of the main causes of this unfortunate situation is what is called the "mass mind" (also known as "race mind"): the everyday consciousness of society, where all of the combined memories of humanity are stored. The mass mind includes the beliefs, ideas, dogmas, thoughts, traditions, opinions, doctrines, feelings, rumors, concerns, and fears of our families, our religion, our schools, our neighbors, our coworkers, and the media (TV, radio, magazines, the Internet, etc.).

Mass mind tells us, for example, that life is "survival of the fittest," "making money is difficult," "rich people are lucky," "the poor are unfortunate," and that aging, illness, poverty, crime, loneliness, war, lack, failure, suffering, toil, disasters, starvation, fear, limitation, accidents, debt, evil, sin, ignorance, and misery are "inherent components of human existence."

Our daily lives are bombarded with such false manmade ideas from all sides, particularly from TV, where, for instance, commercials about endless (mostly nonexistent) diseases—and the medications that allegedly "cure" them—predominate. Newspapers, social media, and the nightly news, with their focus on the shocking, the violent, the unattractive, and the horrible, fill our every waking hour with displays of the worst aspects of human behavior, reinforcing our already negative view of humanity, life, and the world.

Our Conscious Minds absorb these gloomy messages from the mass mind, and, if we are exposed to them long enough, they are sent onto our Subconscious Minds, where, if we choose to accept them, they become beliefs. The Subconscious Mind then passes these beliefs onto the Superconscious Mind (God), which allows them to become physical reality. The largely negative ideas that began in the mass mind, are now part of our personal lives, effecting our finances, our health, and our happiness, as well as our overall circumstances, conditions, environment, daily experiences, and even our entire future. However, as Law of Attraction authority Emerson points out:

> "The good news is that the moment you decide that what you know is more important than what you have been taught to believe, you will have shifted gears in your quest for abundance. Success comes from within, not from without."

The Apostle John was well aware of the dangers of listening to the mass mind, which is why he emphasized to the early Church that the entire material world operates under the reign of Satan (the human Ego).[584] Thus, he left us this warning:

"Love not the world, neither the things that are in the world. If any man love the world, the love of the Father is not in him. For all that is in the world, the lust of the flesh, and the lust of the eyes, and the pride of life, is not of the Father, but is of the world. And the world passeth away, and the lust thereof: but he that doeth the will of God abideth for ever."[585]

Here is the inner meaning of John's words:

"Do not allow yourself to get caught up in the physical plane, or even in worldly things. You cannot be attached to this earthly place and be attached to the Divine Mind at the same time. Most of what comes from the mass mind—such as the titillation of the physical desires of the Lower Self, and our silly self-important ideas concerning pride and honor—are not products of the Divine Mind; they are products of the human mind, the Ego. All of these things are meaningless, and the people who pursue them will never find true happiness on earth. But those who follow the Gospel of the Indwelling Christ will find happiness both here and in the Afterlife."[586]

Not everything that comes from the mass mind is negative, and therefore erroneous, of course. But the vast majority of it is, and it is this particular material that you must be careful of. Why? Because it is fabricated by Satan (the biblical name for the human mind or Ego), the opposite of God (the biblical name for the Divine Mind). Though at first it may seem impossible to conquer the negative effects of the mass mind, do not be discouraged. Jesus overcame the false and destructive beliefs of the World Ego,[587] and so can you, for He left us specific instructions on what to do.[588]

SAY "YES" TO THE GOOD, "NO" TO THE BAD
Here is one of the Lord's most practical suggestions on how to deal with the mass mind: "Let your communication be, 'Yea, yea; Nay, nay': for whatsoever is more than these cometh of evil."[589]

What is Jesus saying here?

Simply this: when confronted with the everyday consciousness of society, mass mind, say "yes" to any and all thoughts, concepts, beliefs, and ideas that are godly; that is, that are good, wholesome, positive, cheering, and uplifting. Say "no" to any and all thoughts, concepts, beliefs, and ideas that are ungodly; that is, that are bad, unwholesome, negative, depressing, and demoralizing. For positive thoughts are always true, and are therefore health-, happiness-, and wealth-inducing, while negative thoughts are always false, and are therefore health-, happiness-, and wealth-reducing.

When watching TV, for example, how does one differentiate between what is true or false? As you watch and listen, ask yourself this question: "Is this something that I would want manifesting as a physical reality in my life?" If it is not, change the channel immediately.

This rule, in fact, applies to every life situation, including what goes into and what comes out of your mind. Instantly "switch" your mental channel if you find yourself thinking about something that you do not want to be a part of your future. You cannot afford to let destructive and incorrect thoughts, ideas, concepts, and beliefs loose in your Conscious Mind. If you listen to, absorb, or accept the negative beliefs and opinions of the mass mind, you are courting disaster, actually inviting adversity into your life. In Jesus' words, the mass mind is like a corpse (death), which we must leave to the vultures (the spiritually immature).[590]

How true. So if you are serious about turning your dreams into reality, the thousands of false beliefs that you have picked from the mass mind since your birth must all be unlearned, and ultimately erased, from your Conscious Mind. These must be replaced with childlike (innocent and pure) thoughts, ideas, and beliefs that are positive, true, health-giving, and happiness-producing.

As we will see, this is an integral part of the process of being "born again," the major consciousness change Jesus requires of us.[591] In being "born again," we symbolically start life anew and psychologically become as "little children."[592] It is only this pure state of mind, Christ Consciousness, Paul's "mind of Christ,"[593] that allows us entrance into the Kingdom of God (harmony, bliss, perfection),[594] where all of our desires become physical reality.[595] Changing your thoughts will change everything, including your life, for, as the Hindus say, "God's nature itself is bliss."[596] Thus those who attune themselves to the Father will experience all of the divine joy that is God!

ANYONE IS CAPABLE OF CHANGE AT ANY TIME

While we are on the topic of personal transformation, let me make an important point here: do not accept the mass mind myth that "people never change." This is false and has prevented many individuals from entering the Kingdom of Heaven. Being psychologically and spiritually "born again" is effortless if you believe it is effortless. Millions have believed just that, and have altered themselves and their lives for the better.

The Law of Attraction brings to you what you believe. So believe change is easy and light and it will be, just as Jesus promised.[597] Here is the Father's guarantee:

> "Then will I sprinkle clean water upon you, and ye shall be clean . . . A new heart also will I give you, and a new spirit will I put within you: and I will take away the stony heart out of your flesh, and I will give you an heart of flesh."[598]

Follow Jesus' simple teachings on the Law of Attraction, and "it shall be done unto you"![599]

Jesus referred to Himself as "the good shepherd who giveth his life for his sheep," while Peter called Him "the Shepherd of your souls." And yet He was also portrayed as the innocent, humble, all-giving *Agnus Dei*, or as John the Baptist described him, the "Lamb of God." For Jesus devoted His entire ministry, even sacrificing His life, to teach Mankind "the hidden wisdom" of God, "the revelation of the mystery which was kept secret since the world began": your real self, the Christ, the great I AM, is in the Father, you are in the Christ, and the Christ is in you. The Universal Indwelling Christ is indeed pure, gentle, and magnanimous, for it is one with the Divine Mind. Because of this, you have access to the same supernatural powers as the Father, enabling you to use the Law of Attraction to shape your current environment, conditions, circumstances, and even your destiny in the Afterlife.

# 8

# UNDERSTANDING
# THE LAW
## Part 2

"O Lord, I cried unto thee, and thou hast
healed me."[600]

## THE POWER OF GOD WORKS BOTH WAYS

LONG WITH YOUR FORMIDABLE DIVINE power to think
things into physical reality comes a great truth, one that you may
have already begun to consider.

The divine aspect of you, your Subconscious Mind, was known by
the early Jews as the "Ancient of Days"[601] and the "Sun of Righteousness,"[602]
and by the earliest Christians as the Indwelling Christ[603] or Divine Mind,[604]
because it contains all the powers of God Himself. These include the ability
to create or destroy, to produce health or sickness, to make good or evil,
light or darkness.[605]

In other words, you and you alone are responsible for everything
that has ever occurred in your life, from the seemingly tiniest experiences
to the greatest events. You have attracted it all. For the Universal
Subconscious Mind within you does not differentiate between positive and
negative thoughts. It does not judge you. It does not tell you what it thinks
you should say or do. It has no critical powers at all. Spiritually speaking,
it is merely an obedient servant, created for one task only: to physically
manifest your thoughts; and it will work to manifest them whether they are
righteous or evil, beneficial or harmful.

This is what Jesus was referring to when He said that the Father "shall reward every man according to his works [that is, thoughts, words, and deeds]."[606]  We are each always receiving back exactly what we are sending out in the way of thought, speech, and action.  In biblical parlance: He that doeth right shall receive for the right which he hath done.

> "But he that doeth wrong shall receive for the wrong which he hath done: and [with Divine Mind] there is no respect of persons."[607]

Paul stated it this way: "Every man shall bear his own [karmic] burden."[608]

This means, of course, that you must carefully guard your mind against thinking thoughts that you do not want to become real, for according to the quantum physics behind the Law of Attraction, *like attracts like*: no matter what you are thinking, the Divine Mind within you will almost immediately begin to draw more of that to you.  Thus if you think a constructive thought ("God"), your Subconscious Mind will start the process of bringing life-affirming circumstances to you, creating for you a "Heaven" on earth.  But if you think a destructive thought ("Satan"), it will start the process of bringing life-negating circumstances to you, making for you a "Hell" on earth.

It is not concerned with whether what you are thinking will work for you or against you.  Your Subconscious Mind knows only how to create physical reality from what you give it, no matter who or what you are, prince or pauper, saint or sinner.  This is why that renowned enemy of the Apostles, the Gnostic Christian leader Simon Magus, was able to perform all of the same miracles as Peter, including healings, levitation, and exorcisms.[609]

Here we have answered one of life's greatest mysteries: why do bad things happen to good people, and why do good things happen to bad people?  Jesus explained it this way:

> "[The Father] maketh his sun to rise on the evil and on the good, and sendeth rain on the just and on the unjust."[610]

The inner meaning:

> "Both immoral people and moral people can use the Divine Mind however they wish, to produce negative or positive conditions in their lives."[611]

Now that you know your thoughts become things, and that you can choose what comes out of your mind, you must be extremely careful what you think about!

## THE IMPORTANCE OF POSITIVE THINKING

Let us say you grew up in an abusive home, or you suffered some form of trauma as an adult. Your thoughts are probably quite often negative and depressing. Even if you know that these thoughts are unhealthy for you, because you are thinking them, they are being sent to your Subconscious Mind, which quickly goes to work creating more reasons for you to feel pessimistic about yourself and your life.

Let us say you grew up in a religion that taught that because you were born in "original sin" you are a sinner, that human nature is inherently evil, and that you are an "imperfect" being who is constantly battling with the Devil for control of your soul. The Law of Attraction then, which is always serving you, is constantly creating more reasons for you to feel like a miserable sinner, inevitably leading you down the road to poverty, ill health, and ruin.

Is this really what you want? Is this really how God and Jesus intended for you to live out your life? As we will see, the answer is a resounding no!

How much better it would be for you to think positively about yourself, about your life, your body, your marriage, your parents, your children, your neighbors, your relationships, your home, your job, your finances, your future. For you will then be consciously and correctly putting the Law of Attraction to work for you in a wholesome and productive manner; one that will build you up, increase your happiness, strengthen your relationships, and create perfect health and ever increasing financial abundance.

This method, right-thinking, is what the Psalmist mystically called "dwelling in the secret place of the most High":

> "He that dwelleth in the secret place of the most High shall abide under the shadow of the Almighty."[612]

The inner meaning:

> "He or she that continually thinks positively elevates their consciousness to the highest level. Here they will find that the

Divine Mind not only protects them from all harm, but brings to them unending goodness in the form of their ideal life."[613]

Since God is all good things, to indulge in wrong-thinking is to disrespect the Divine Mind, which wants the best for us. To think poorly of yourself is to negate your positive thoughts and oppose God's life plan for you: perfect health, wealth, and happiness! Opposing the Father is futile anyway, for He does not change to suit us, or for any other reason.[614] He is truly "the same yesterday, and to day, and for ever."[615]

HEIRS OF THE PROMISE

So it is we who must align ourselves with God and His intentions, and we do this by thinking only uplifting, beautiful, high consciousness thoughts. In this way we attract more of the same into our lives and fulfill God's promise, which He never breaks.[616] What is that promise?

If you attune your thoughts to your Higher Self (the real you, the Indwelling Christ,[617] the Great I AM),[618] then you become a coheir (copartner) with God (the Universal Divine Mind),[619] who will care for you, protect you, feed you, clothe you, and nurture you, as well as make all of your dreams come true. This is the promised heirship, the "hope we have as an anchor of the soul, both sure and stedfast."[620]

Now you know why God has always been seen as our "divine parent," and called either the "Father" or the "Mother" from ancient times right into the present day. We are indeed "the children of [the] promise,"[621] "heirs of [the] promise,"[622] which Paul described like this:

"And if ye be Christ's, then are ye Abraham's seed, and heirs according to the promise."[623]

The inner meaning:

"If you think Christlike thoughts, then you become a spiritual descendant of the Divine, and you will be given all of the powers of God."[624]

Great indeed is "the mystery of godliness,"[625] "which can neither be defined by any words, nor conceived by the mind."[626]

Paul also noted that those who are spiritually immature are *servants* of God. But when we achieve spiritual maturity, we become *Sons* of God,[627] "an heir of God through Christ."[628] Here is what the Thirteenth Apostle had to say about our coheirship, our copartnership, with God:

> ". . . we are the children of God: and if children, then heirs; heirs of God, and joint-heirs with Christ . . ."[629]

In other words, we are "children of God,"[630] of Divine Mind, because we are the thoughts of Divine Mind, and as thought-creations of the Divine Mind, we inherit all of the dignity, inner peace, beauty, and power of both the Indwelling Christ[631] and the Indwelling Father.[632] In turn, this entitles us to have anything we desire, for as His spiritual offspring we deserve only the best in life. And we deserve the best because we are inheritors of God and His divine kingdom. In Paul's words: "Ye are Christ's; and Christ is God's."[633]

Now, because the Indwelling Christ has always existed,[634] our coheirship with Him was foreordained before the beginning of time, as Paul commented:

> "[Christ,] in whom also we have obtained an inheritance, being predestinated according to the purpose of him who worketh all things after the counsel of his own will . . ."[635]

In the book of Acts Peter says that we share in the "Everlasting Covenant" which God sealed with His people thousands of years ago,[636] assuring everyone of the Father's blessing:

> "Ye are the children of the prophets, and of the covenant which God made with our fathers, saying unto Abraham, and in thy seed shall all the kindreds of the earth be blessed."[637]

God Himself said:

> "And I will bring them, and they shall dwell in the midst of Jerusalem [an ancient mystical symbol of a mental state of peace, prosperity, and harmony]: and they shall be my people, and I will be their God, in truth and in righteousness."[638]

## THE IMPORTANCE OF BEING SINGLE-MINDED

The book of Isaiah provides this wonderful scripture for those who have or are experiencing abuse, trauma, or any other kind of extreme difficulty:

"The voice of him that crieth in the wilderness, 'prepare ye the way of the Lord, make straight in the desert a highway for our God. Every valley shall be exalted, and every mountain and hill shall be made low: and the crooked shall be made straight, and the rough places plain.'"[639]

The inner meaning:

When we keep our minds focused on the things of God, the "wilderness" (disorder) in our lives is cleared away, our "valleys" (sadness) are raised up, our "mountains and hills" (problems) are leveled, our "crooked" (evil) ways are destroyed, and our "rough" patches (complications) are eliminated, allowing a "straight highway" (direct connection) to the Father, who will provide all we need for our healing, health, welfare, and happiness.[640]

Knowing this, which way are you going to think from now on? Positively or negatively? Spiritually or materially? "Choose you this day whom you will serve."[641] It must be one or the other, for "a double minded man is unstable in all his ways."[642] You cannot devote yourself to both your Higher Divine Self (the Son, the Sun, the Christ) and your Lower Human Self (the Ego, the Devil, Satan) at the same time. Why? Because dualism does not work with Divine Mind, with God, for He is "one Lord."[643] Paul said,

". . . with the mind [Higher Self] I myself serve the law of God; but with the flesh [Lower Self] the law of sin. . . . For to be carnally minded [to live out of the Lower Self] is death; but to be spiritually minded [to live out of the Higher Self] is life and peace."[644]

Jesus phrased it this way:

"No man can serve two masters: for either he will hate the one, and love the other; or else he will hold to the one, and despise the other. Ye cannot serve God [Higher Self] and mammon [Lower Self]."[645]

Paul also made these comments:

". . . for what fellowship hath righteousness with unrighteousness? and what communion hath light with darkness? And what concord hath Christ [Higher Self] with Belial [Lower Self]? or what part hath he that believeth with an infidel [nonbeliever]?"[646]

"For the flesh [Lower Self] lusteth against the Spirit [Higher Self], and the Spirit against the flesh: and these are contrary the one to the other."[647]

In essence, for the Law of Attraction to work in your favor, your brain-mind (Lower Self) must be in accord, in union, with your heart-mind (Higher Self). If your Subconscious Mind has been programmed with thoughts of negativity, you cannot hope to get healthy, even if that is what you are desiring in your Conscious Mind. Consciously wanting to have financial security will do you no good if subconsciously you do not believe you are worthy of being wealthy. Wanting the best for yourself while thinking the worst of yourself will never result in anything but problems and complications.

So the two must work in unison: the Conscious Mind must be suggesting positive thoughts to a clear, clean, open, childlike Subconscious Mind, unhampered by negative programming, evil thoughts, and memories of past traumas. Then and only then can Divine Mind respond to your affirmations and prayers; or in biblical parlance: "open rivers in high places, and fountains in the midst of the valleys . . . [and] make the wilderness a pool of water, and the dry land springs of water."[648]

## THE "PEARL OF GREAT PRICE"
You would not be reading this book if you did not want to improve your life. So I am sure that from now on you are going to work on learning to focus only on positive thoughts, uplifting ideas, constructive beliefs, and cheerful memories. Keep your thinking on the affirmative side. Knowing that it is obediently working to physically manifest your beliefs and ideas, always send your Subconscious the highest, purest, most noble and godly thoughts.

Paul, that great practitioner of the Law of Attraction, understood the power of the Subconscious Mind and the importance of right-thinking, which is why he said this:

"Whatsoever things are true, whatsoever things are honest, whatsoever things are just, whatsoever things are pure, whatsoever things are lovely, whatsoever things are of good report; if there be any virtue, and if there be any praise, think on these things."[649]

This is not to gloss over those who suffer from childhood trauma, addictions, and other types of serious mental and physical ailments, and may thus find it difficult to follow Paul's admonition. God understands what you have been through.

At the same time, however, He has given you a "pearl of great price,"[650] your Subconscious Mind, which you can use in conjunction with the Law of Attraction to heal yourself. Like the Psalmist then, you can always "lift up mine eyes unto the hills (Subconscious Mind), from whence cometh my help."[651]

Yes, as we will be discussing, because Divine Mind knows how to do anything it is asked, you can completely heal any mental, emotional, psychological, or physical disease using the power of thought and the Law. Indeed, this is one of the many reasons God gave us these gifts! Algernon Sidney, the great 17th-Century English libertarian, was right: "God truly helps those who help themselves."

Here is another way to look at it. We can only progress in life in accordance to what we are thinking. If our thinking is up, our lives will go up. If our thinking is down, like a sinking ship our lives will go down with it. Victorian British Prime Minister Benjamin Disraeli was a student of the Law of Attraction:

> "Nurture your mind with great thoughts, for you will never go any higher than you think."

Knowing this truth, Paul gave us the following good advice:

> "And we beseech you, brethren, to know [respect] them which labour among you, and are over you in the Lord [fellow believers], and admonish [teach] you; and to esteem them very highly in love for their work's sake. And be at peace among yourselves. Now we exhort you, brethren, warn them that are unruly [lazy and disorderly], comfort the feebleminded, support the weak, be patient toward all men. See that none render evil for evil unto any man; but ever follow that which is good, both among yourselves, and to all men [that is, follow the Golden Rule]. Rejoice evermore [always be happy]. Pray without ceasing [stay in constant communication with the Divine Mind].
>
> In every thing give thanks [be grateful for your many blessings]: for this is the will of God in Christ Jesus concerning you [that is, this is how the Divine Mind and the Indwelling Christ work together for you]. Quench not the Spirit [that is, do not impede

godly things]. Despise not prophesyings [that is, do not denigrate the psychic gifts of others]. Prove all things [test things out for yourself]; hold fast that which is good [be righteous]. Abstain from all appearance of evil [ignore evil]. And the very God of peace sanctify you wholly; and I pray God your whole spirit and soul and body be preserved blameless unto the coming of our Lord Jesus Christ [the realization of the Indwelling Christ]."[652]

## THE LAW OF ATTRACTION MADE EASY
Let us always keep in mind that the Law of Attraction is an impersonal scientific principle that reproduces in physical form exactly what you are thinking, believing, and feeling. And since each thought has its own frequency, you are always attracting like frequencies into your life.

Here is the simplest way to look it. If you want to be happy, you must send out happy frequencies in the form of happy thoughts. If you want to be healthy, you must send out healthy frequencies in the form of healthy thoughts. If you want to be wealthy, you must send out wealthy frequencies in the form of wealthy thoughts. If you want more abundance in your life, you must send out an abundance frequency in the form of abundant thoughts.

On the other hand, if you want to be unhappy, you must send out unhappy frequencies in the form of unhappy thoughts. If you want to be unhealthy, you must send out unhealthy frequencies in the form of unhealthy thoughts. If you want to be poor, you must send out poverty frequencies in the form of thoughts of impoverishment. If you want less abundance in your life, you must send out shortage frequencies in the form of thoughts of lack. You now have a new appreciation for the old saying: "Be careful what you wish for. You are sure to get it!"

Because of the way the Law works, you are always attracting whatever your predominant thoughts are, while at the same time repulsing their opposites. Learn to cultivate the type of consciousness that matches what you want. If, for instance, you want material security, develop within yourself wealth consciousness, prosperity consciousness, money consciousness, and abundance consciousness. Eat, think, talk, and sleep affluence with complete confidence, as if you already have it.

If you are in poverty, however, and continue to visualize yourself poor, you will continue to be, and wealth will flee from you like a fog before the sun. That is the Law. Divine Mind (God) always outpictures in exact duplication what you think, believe, say, and feel, whether it is holy or unholy, or whether it is favorable or detrimental to you.

You are always calling into being what it is you are thinking about. Nothing could be easier to understand, and no concept could be easier to begin implementing into your life: with your word you make your world.[653] This is why Jesus said:

> "Take my yoke upon you, and learn of me; for I am meek and lowly in heart: and ye shall find rest unto your souls. For my yoke is easy, and my burden is light."[654]

Just as the seed of an oak tree can only grow into an oak tree, and the seed of a cactus can only grow into a cactus, your thoughts can only grow into their own kind. Paul was keenly aware of how this aspect of the Law of Attraction functions; that the thought-seeds you plant in your mental garden, the Subconscious Mind, whether positive or negative, will bring about a like-minded harvest in the form of your outer circumstances and experiences:

> "Be not deceived; God is not mocked: for *whatsoever a man soweth, that shall he also reap.* For he that soweth to his flesh shall of the flesh reap corruption; but he that soweth to the Spirit shall of the Spirit reap life everlasting."[655]

The inner meaning:

> "Do not fool yourself. This is serious; God is not to be scoffed at: whatever thoughts you think will come back to you in physical form. In other words, those thoughts that come from the Lower Self (Ego, Satan) will bring unhappiness, illness, and poverty; but those thoughts that come from the Higher Self (the Christ, the Son) will manifest in your life as joy, health, and wealth."[656]

This, the Law of Attraction, is God's most basic and most important principle, one that thoroughly permeates the Bible from the first page of the book of Genesis to the last page of the book of Revelation. This makes the Bible, in fact, the world's greatest self-help guide to living the good life!

## THE CHRISTIAN LAW OF KARMA

Do you see now why Jesus placed so much importance on how you think, speak, believe, and behave? The *cause* you create always produces an *effect* ("karma" in Buddhism and Hinduism), and this effect, be it positive or negative, will touch every aspect of your life—no matter who you are. Here is how Paul phrased it:

> "Knowing that whatsoever good thing any man doeth, the same shall he receive of the Lord, whether he be bond or free."[657]

This is why Paul stressed that we work on continually summoning positive feelings, such as "love, joy, peace, longsuffering, gentleness, goodness, faith, meekness, [and] temperance."[658] If we flood our beings with these types of uplifting emotions, we not only draw more of them to ourselves, but we imbue everyone around us with them as well.

Now think about this profound Zen-like fact for a moment: *cause and effect are one and the same.* The thought is the result and the result is the thought; the creator is the creation and the creation is the creator. Once you understand this, you will see that it is for our own good, and for no other reason, that Jesus gave us specific rules or "commandments" to follow. Truly, as Emerson said, "Man is what he thinks all day long." Jesus, the ultimate master of the Law of Attraction, understands this, and so provided us with a set of simple guidelines on how to think properly "all day long."

Let us be clear: following Jesus' commandments is not a strict moralistic system forced upon us by a cruel God. It is the Father's way of guiding us toward learning to think positively, constructively, and wisely, for all is mind and mind is all! Christianity is not the only religion that embraces this concept. In fact, nearly every faith on earth teaches it. Here is how the Hindus put it: "Happiness, harmony, and health have their origins in faith and piety."[659]

You may have been taught otherwise, but the fact is that Jesus is not a sadistic disciplinarian. He did not command that we love our neighbor and constrain ourselves from judging others so that He could punish us when we failed, for as He Himself said:

> ". . . the Son of man is not come to destroy men's lives, but to save them."[660]

Jesus' teachings are eternal, God-formed Law of Attraction principles, impersonal but sacred doctrines that are meant to help us grow spiritually[661] and create the best lives possible for ourselves; universal cosmic laws intended to increase our happiness and allow us to manifest our dreams, our ideal world, our own personal inner "Kingdom of Heaven" here on earth.

Thus when Jesus says that we should forgive others, it is not simply because he said so; so that as good Christians we can avoid roasting in Hell until the end of time. It is because by being forgiving, others will be forgiving toward us, making our lives more enjoyable and our bodies and minds healthier.

Here is how Jesus phrased this particular Law of Attraction doctrine in the Gospel of Matthew:

> "For if ye forgive men their trespasses, your heavenly Father will also forgive you: but if ye forgive not men their trespasses, neither will your Father forgive your trespasses."[662]

> "So likewise shall my heavenly Father do also unto you, if ye from your hearts forgive not every one his brother their trespasses."[663]

Jesus in the Gospel of Mark:

> "And when ye stand praying, forgive, if ye have ought against any: that your Father also which is in heaven may forgive you your trespasses. But if ye do not forgive, neither will your Father which is in heaven forgive your trespasses."[664]

In the Gospel of Luke, Jesus gives his simplest yet most complete and understandable exposition on this specific aspect of the Law:

> "Judge not, and ye shall not be judged: condemn not, and ye shall not be condemned: forgive, and ye shall be forgiven."[665]

Who is it that is going to judge, condemn, and forgive you? It is your "heavenly Father," the Lord, Jehovah, or Yahweh, which is identical to the Universal Divine Mind, the Indwelling Christ,[666] the Great I AM presence within. And what is the Great I AM? It is the Supreme Self, the Higher Self, your God-Self, which was named after the image it was created in: the omnific life-force and Source of All, God.[667]

If you harshly and unfairly judge others, your "final judgment" will not be "eternal damnation" in the Afterlife. It is the suffering you will experience right here on earth as others harshly and unfairly judge you in return. How easy it is to avoid this misery by being nonjudgmental and forgiving toward others.

## THE LAW IS SCIENTIFICALLY & SPIRITUALLY PRECISE

The Law of Attraction is so scientifically accurate that it is actually mathematically exact: we get back precisely what we give out, all the time, no exceptions. You cannot escape the Law of Divine Mind. Here is how Jesus articulated it in the Gospel of Matthew:

> "For with what judgment ye judge, ye shall be judged: and with what measure ye mete, it shall be measured to you again."[668]

In the Gospel of Mark:

> And he said unto them, "Take heed what ye hear: with what measure ye mete, it shall be measured to you: and unto you that hear shall more be given."[669]

In the Gospel of Luke:

> "Give, and it shall be given unto you; good measure, pressed down, and shaken together, and running over, shall men give into your bosom. For with the same measure that ye mete withal it shall be measured to you again."[670]

Paul stated this Law of Attraction principle this way:

> "Whatsoever ye do, do it heartily, as to the Lord, and not unto men; knowing that of the Lord ye shall receive the reward of the inheritance: for ye serve the Lord Christ. But he that doeth wrong shall receive for the wrong which he hath done: and there is no respect of persons [Divine Mind makes no distinction between saint and sinner, and so they are treated the same]."[671]

Emerson, one of many 19th-Century experts on the Law of Attraction, wrote:

> "All things are moral. . . . Justice is not postponed. A perfect equality adjusts its balance in all parts of life. The dice of God are always loaded [that is, nothing is "random"]. The world looks like a multiplication table, or a mathematical equation, which, turn it

> how you will, balances itself. Take what figure you will, its exact
> value, nor more nor less, still returns to you. Every secret is told,
> every crime is punished, every virtue rewarded, every wrong
> redressed, in silence and certainty."

This is what our Lord meant when He said:

> "For there is nothing covered, that shall not be revealed; neither
> hid, that shall not be known."[672]

So you see, if you understand and work with the Law of Attraction
in a positive and productive manner, it always operates for you, not against
you. Not only is this a scientific truth, it is Jesus' guarantee!

## WHY YOU SHOULD FOLLOW THE TEN COMMANDMENTS

Just as that great work of enlightenment, the Bible, is the ultimate Law of
Attraction guide, the core of the Good Book, the Ten Commandments, are
the ultimate Law of Attraction principles, created not, as so many churches
today teach, to force you to behave a certain way out of fear of punishment.
They were formulated to benefit you, to help you grow spiritually;[673] that
is, to help you find and follow your bliss. This is, in fact, exactly what God
promised us:

> "For I the Lord thy God will hold thy right hand, saying unto thee,
> Fear not; I will help thee."[674]

Now let us examine these ten famous instructions for a moment,
and using the new spiritual knowledge (Gnosis) and wisdom (Sophia) God
has given us,[675] their true inner meaning will be unveiled:

1st Commandment: "I AM the Lord thy God. Thou shalt have no other gods
before me": you and the Great I AM presence within you,[676] the
Indwelling Christ,[677] are one and the same: God. There is only *one*
Source,[678] and you are created in its image,[679] which is why you
reflect its image "as in a mirror."[680]

2nd Commandment: "Thou shalt not make unto thee any graven image":
God is Spirit and so should be worshiped in Spirit.[681]

3rd Commandment: "Thou shalt not take the name of the Lord thy God in
vain": speak respectfully of the Source of all,[682] for that which
comes out of your mouth is the result of thought, and thought is the

one and only, all-powerful, physical manifestation force. (Consider this: each time we speak God's name, even profanely, we are summoning Him. Thus, we only want to do this from a consciousness of love and reverence.)

4th Commandment: "Remember the sabbath day, to keep it holy": set aside one day a week to focus solely on godly things and honor the Source, with which you are coheir.[683]

5th Commandment: "Honour thy father and thy mother": strive to create and maintain peace in your family of origin.[684] (If for some reason this is not possible, for the sake of your spiritual growth, bless all and move forward with your life.)[685]

6th Commandment: "Thou shalt not kill": what you sow you shall reap. All of the misery created by this heinous act against God will follow you,[686] for spiritually speaking the life you take is actually your own.[687] As the Aquarian Gospel states: "Woe to the cruel and relentless man; he is himself the victim of his deeds. The evil he would do to other men rebounds; the scourger is the scourged."[688]

7th Commandment: "Thou shalt not commit adultery": respect the sacrality of marital relationships, and yours will be respected as well.[689]

8th Commandment: "Thou shalt not steal": what you take from others will be exactly taken from you in one form or another.[690]

9th Commandment: "Thou shalt not bear false witness": if you lie, gossip, give false testimony in court, or spread erroneous rumors, the same will be done to you.[691]

10th Commandment: "Thou shalt not covet": when the Law of Attraction is used correctly, there is more than enough for all, thus there is no need to compete with, encroach on, or envy others. You must, and can, harmlessly draw in your own good.[692]

The importance of following these ancient Law of Attraction principles, all which predate both Judaism and Christianity, will become increasingly clear in subsequent chapters.

Jesus' Disciples (His close followers, as opposed to the Twelve Apostles) listen intently while He instructs them from a boat anchored off the shore of the Sea of Galilee. What is He teaching them? It could have only been one thing, what the Lord Himself called, not "the Gospel of Jesus Christ," but "the Gospel of the Kingdom." Though over the centuries both the orthodox Catholic and Protestant Churches have done their best to conceal this doctrine from the laity, Christian mystics have kept "the Secret" alive for those "who have ears to hear": the Gospel of the Kingdom concerns Jesus' teachings on our divine nature, our divine powers, and the Law of Attraction. "You are gods," the Master tells us, "and whoever becomes one with the Indwelling Christ can perform even greater miracles than I have. Simply ask and you shall receive."

# 9

# JESUS & THE
# LAW OF ATTRACTION

"Then they cry unto the Lord in their trouble,
and he saveth them out of their distresses. He
sent his word, and healed them, and delivered
them from their destructions."[693]

## THINKING IS OUR TRUE OCCUPATION

WE HAVE STUDIED JESUS' TEACHING, part of what he termed "the Gospel of the Kingdom,"[694] that each one of us is a divine being, created in the exact image of God. We have seen that as gods and goddesses we have been given a very special and irrevocable gift:[695] the creative power of thought. We now understand that there is only *one* force fueling the entire Universe from top to bottom:[696] "God, the Father, of whom are all things, and we in him."[697] And because of this, that which is created in the mental is also perfectly duplicated in the physical.

Because we are in God and God is in us,[698] our Inner Divine Mind has unlimited creative power, one that is actively working every second of everyday. Thus, whatever you are thinking you are attracting, whatever you are feeling you are magnetizing, whatever you assume you are enlarging, whatever you accept you are increasing, whatever you are desiring you are magnifying, and whatever you believe with all your heart is gravitating toward you—right now.

All things are created by thought through the Sovereign Mind, the Divine Mind, for, as has been rightly said, thinking—that is, the "Father's business"—is the one and only true occupation of life. And indeed, it is because of this that God the Father gave us complete control over our thoughts.

Look at it this way. If you do not consciously control your thinking, the Law of Averages takes over by default, and you become subject to whatever you are currently absorbing from the mass mind. The only thing that can possibly result from this is personal havoc, tragedy, hardship, failure, confusion, pain, and what the world ignorantly refers to as "misfortune"!

Thus, it behooves you to take total command over what goes in and out of your Conscious Mind (Indwelling Christ, the Higher Self), or as Paul stated it, you must "bring into captivity every thought to the obedience of Christ."[699] For you have no more important task than to think and to think correctly, to work with the Divine Mind (the "Father") in pursuit of the realization of your dreams and desires. This is your actual job, your real work, your true business in life.

Jesus understood this, even at a young age. When His concerned parents discovered the lost twelve year old at the local Jewish Temple, they questioned Him concerning His whereabouts, to which He gave this tart reply:

> "How is it that ye sought me? wist ye not that I must be about my Father's business?"[700]

## THE KEY TO UNDERSTANDING JESUS

Now let us look at the Master's own personal teachings regarding the Law of Attraction. So that the Law could be understood by all people whatever their level of spirituality maturity, Jesus gave us many different versions, each requiring varying degrees of spiritual understanding. So we will begin with the most basic ones, those which contain "the simplicity that is in Christ."[701]

In the mystical Christian tradition, the key to understanding Jesus and the inner (true) meaning of His teachings is this: in most cases, when the Lord uses the words "I," "me," "my," and "mine," He is not referring personally to Himself, Jesus, the *physical* (human) son of Joseph and Mary.[702] He is speaking of the *spiritual* (divine) Universal Christ,[703] or God-Self, within all of us, the common practice of all the great spiritual teachers throughout history.

This entity is also called the Indwelling Christ,[704] the "inner man,"[705] the "inward man,"[706] the "hidden man of the heart,"[707] the "true Light,"[708] the "Ancient of Days,"[709] or the Great I AM Presence within;[710] in other words, it is our Higher Self, the "high priest"[711] of our own personal God-made "church within"[712]—the one and only "true tabernacle"[713]—with its "Twelve Apostles" (that is, our Twelve Spiritual Mental Powers).[714] This, the real you, is what makes you an individualization of God.

It is this, the Immortal Universal Christ Within,[715] that the Master was referring to when He said:

> "All power is given unto me in heaven and in earth . . . and, lo, I am with you alway[s], even unto the end of the world. Amen."[716]

JESUS AND THE LAW: THE BEGINNER'S TEACHINGS
In the Gospel of John, Jesus makes this simple but potent statement:

> ". . . *ask, and ye shall receive*, that your joy may be full."[717]

The inner meaning of this, translated into modern English, is:

> "Whatever you desire in your mind will come to pass, in order that you are as happy as possible."[718]

Just in case this statement was not plain enough, Jesus added this clarification:

> "Verily, verily, I say unto you, *whatsoever ye shall ask the Father in my name, he will give it you*."[719]

Here the inner meaning is this:

> "Truly, truly, I am telling you, that you can have anything you want. All you have to do is imprint ['ask'] the desire in the Divine Mind ['the Father'] on behalf of the Indwelling Christ ['in my name'], and you will have it."[720]

Here is another slightly more complex statement by Jesus regarding the power of the Divine Mind and the Law of Attraction:

> "And I say unto you, ask, and it shall be given you; seek, and ye shall find; knock, and it shall be opened unto you. For *every one that asketh receiveth; and he that seeketh findeth; and to him that knocketh it shall be opened*. If a son shall ask bread of any of you that is a father, will he give him a stone? or if he ask a fish, will he for a fish give

him a serpent? Or if he shall ask an egg, will he offer him a scorpion? If ye then, being evil, know how to give good gifts unto your children: how much more shall your heavenly Father give the Holy Spirit to them that ask him?"[721]

The inner meaning:

"Whatever you ask of the Divine Mind (the Father), it will be given to you. Whatever you want, it will provide it for you. Whatever your questions, it will answer them for you. For whatever you ask for you will get; anything you seek you will find; knock on the door of the Divine Mind, and it will open for you. If your son asked you for some bread, would you give him a rock? Or if he asked you for a fish, would you give him a snake? Or if he asked you for an egg, would you give him a scorpion? If you, despite being spiritually immature, know exactly what to give your children, do you not realize how much more the Father, Divine Mind, will give through the Subconscious Minds of those who ask?"[722]

## JESUS AND THE LAW: INTERMEDIATE TEACHINGS

The following scriptures from the Jesuine arcanum are slightly more complex, beginning with this one from the Gospel of John:

"And *whatsoever ye shall ask in my name, that will I do*, that the Father may be glorified in the Son. *If ye shall ask any thing in my name, I will do it.*"[723]

The inner meaning:

"Whatever it is that you want, simply ask the Divine Mind for it in the name of the Indwelling Christ, and it will respond to your request as if it is from the Indwelling Christ. This shows honor and respect for both the Christ Within and the Universal Mind. Thus, no matter what you ask for in the name of the Indwelling Christ, Divine Mind will always receive it as a direct command from the Christ Himself, and it will be granted to you."[724]

The following is also from John. Again, Jesus is speaking here as the Universal Indwelling Christ:[725]

"Ye have not chosen me, but I have chosen you, and ordained you, that ye should go and bring forth fruit, and that your fruit should remain: that *whatsoever ye shall ask of the Father in my name, he may give it you.*"[726]

The inner meaning:

"You think you have selected the Indwelling Christ, but it is not true. It has selected you, and invested you with all the powers of the Father, Divine Mind, so that you will be able to think anything you desire into existence, forever. Remember, whatever you want, simply ask Divine Mind in the name of the Christ Within, and it will be manifested for you."[727]

Another passage from the Gospel of John:

"If ye abide in me, and my words abide in you, *ye shall ask what ye will, and it shall be done unto you.*"[728]

The inner meaning:

"If you stay focused on your oneness with the Indwelling Christ, and follow My spiritual teachings, you will be able to ask for anything you like and it will be given to you by Divine Mind."[729]

The following passage, from the Gospel of Matthew, cites a fascinating occurrence:

Now in the morning as he [Jesus] returned into the city, he hungered. And when he saw a fig tree in the way, he came to it, and found nothing thereon, but leaves only, and said unto it, "Let no fruit grow on thee henceforward for ever." And presently the fig tree withered away. And when the disciples saw it, they marvelled, saying, "How soon is the fig tree withered away!"

Jesus answered and said unto them, "Verily I say unto you, if ye have faith, and doubt not, ye shall not only do this which is done to the fig tree, but also if ye shall say unto this mountain, 'be thou removed, and be thou cast into the sea'; it shall be done. And *all things, whatsoever ye shall ask in prayer, believing, ye shall receive.*"[730]

There is no doubt with His degree of faith that Jesus could move a mountain into the ocean if He so desired! However, the "mountain" He is referring to here is not a real one. It is a symbol of the "mountain" of daily troubles we sometimes face. Here is another example from Matthew:

> "If ye have faith as a grain of mustard seed, ye shall say unto this
> mountain, 'Remove hence to yonder place'; and it shall remove;
> and *nothing shall be impossible unto you.*"[731]

Yes, Jesus' "mountain" represents human problems. Read the above passages from Matthew again with this new understanding, and further your enlightenment. You will see that nothing is hopeless, no problem is too big, when you have pure faith behind you. And it only takes a tiny amount of faith to change your life, as little as a mustard seed!

Now we know what Paul meant when he said that we can transform our conditions by "holding the mystery of the faith in a pure conscience."[732] Everything, whether physical, spiritual, emotional, or psychological must conform to the omnipotent power of the Law of Attraction. That is God's promise, and it is fulfilled by faith and by faith alone.[733]

## JESUS AND THE LAW: ADVANCED TEACHINGS

Let us now look at the third and most spiritually advanced level of Jesus' Law of Attraction teachings. He made the following statements in the Gospel of John:

> "I am the true vine, and my Father is the husbandman. Every
> branch in me that beareth not fruit he taketh away: and every
> branch that beareth fruit, he purgeth it, that it may bring forth
> more fruit. Now ye are clean through the word which I have
> spoken unto you. *Abide in me, and I in you.* As the branch cannot
> bear fruit of itself, except it abide in the vine; no more can ye,
> except ye *abide in me.* I am the vine, ye are the branches: He that
> *abideth in me, and I in him,* the same bringeth forth much fruit: for
> without me ye can do nothing. If a man abide not in me, he is cast
> forth as a branch, and is withered; and men gather them, and cast
> them into the fire, and they are burned. *If ye abide in me, and my
> words abide in you, ye shall ask what ye will, and it shall be done unto
> you.*"[734]

Here is the inner meaning. It is an allegory of how you (your Higher Self), the Father (Divine Mind), and the Law of Attraction can work together to manifest your desires:

> "The Great I Am, the Indwelling Christ, is like a grapevine, while

the Divine Mind (God, the Father, Unified Field) is like the farmer. The farmer cuts off and throws away any branches (unenlightened humans) that do not strive to produce healthy grapes (positive physical manifestations); but those branches that do (strive to realize their oneness with the Christ and the Father), he will keep and prune (strengthen) so that they produce more grapes. Those who have heard and embraced My Word, their branches have already been pruned (they are already enlightened). To those I say, continue to accept the fact that you live within Christ just as Christ lives within you.

"Here is another way of looking at it: the 'grapevine' (Indwelling Christ) symbolizes humanity's Higher Self, the 'branches' symbolize humanity's Lower Self. And remember: just as a branch cannot produce healthy grapes unless it is attached to the grapevine, your Lower Self cannot physically manifest your thought-desires unless it is attached to the Higher Self. Those who live out of their Lower Self alone will experience poverty, sickness, and unhappiness. But if you live out of your Higher Self, the Christ Within, you can ask for whatever you want and it will be given to you on the material plane by Divine Mind."[735]

Another one of Jesus' more complex teachings on the Law comes from the Gospel of Matthew:

"Verily I say unto you, whatsoever ye shall bind on earth shall be bound in heaven: and whatsoever ye shall loose on earth shall be loosed in heaven. Again I say unto you, that if two of you shall agree on earth as touching any thing that they shall ask, it shall be done for them of my Father which is in heaven."[736]

The inner meaning:

"I am telling you truly that anything you declare real on the physical plane will be declared real on the spiritual plane, and anything you declare false on the physical plane will be declared false on the spiritual plane. I repeat, *anything* two of you want materially, just ask the Divine Mind and it will be given to you."[737]

The Gospel of Matthew also provides us with the following stunning Law of Attraction formula, given by Jesus to His Disciples during the Sermon on the Mount:

". . . take no thought, saying, 'What shall we eat?' or, 'What shall we drink?' or, 'Wherewithal shall we be clothed?' . . . for your heavenly Father knoweth that ye have need of all these things. But seek ye first the kingdom of God, and his righteousness; and all these things shall be added unto you."[738]

The inner meaning:

"If you are currently short on the essentials of life, and are wondering how you will be able to afford to eat, drink, and clothe yourself, do not worry. The Divine Mind knows exactly what you need. All you have to do is focus on things that make you happy, and think godly thoughts as well; then everything you desire will be taken care of for you."[739]

Jesus' most advanced yet simply worded Law of Attraction formula is from the Gospel of Mark:

"What things soever ye desire, when ye pray, believe that ye receive them, and ye shall have them."[740]

The inner meaning:

"When you affirm your desires to the Divine Mind, fully believe that it has already manifested them for you, and they will become a physical reality."[741]

Reread this statement until you have memorized it and fully understand it, for this is part of "the stone which the builders (of the mainstream Christian Church) rejected," but which is actually the cornerstone of Jesus' entire teaching,[742] what He called "the Gospel of the Kingdom."[743]

JESUS & THE LAW OUTSIDE THE FOUR GOSPELS
In the first book of John, the Apostle states Jesus' teaching on the Law of Attraction like this:

"And whatsoever we ask, we receive of him, because we keep his commandments, and do those things that are pleasing in his sight."[744]

Also from the first book of John:

*"These things have I written unto you that believe on the name of the Son of God; that ye may know that ye have eternal life, and that ye may believe on the name of the Son of God. And this is the confidence that we have in him, that, if we ask any thing according to his will, he heareth us: and if we know that he hear us, whatsoever we ask, we know that we have the petitions that we desired of him."*[745]

Jesus' brother James the Just had this to say concerning the power of faith, the Law of Attraction, and Divine Mind:

*"If any of you lack wisdom, let him ask of God [Divine Mind], that giveth to all men liberally, and upbraideth not; and it shall be given him. But let him ask in faith, nothing wavering. For he that wavereth is like a wave of the sea driven with the wind and tossed. For let not that man [who lacks faith] think that he shall receive any thing of the Lord [Divine Mind]."*[746]

James addressed those believers who were not getting results using the Law, reprimanding them for not approaching it correctly:

*"Ye ask, and receive not, because ye ask amiss, that ye may consume it upon your lusts."*[747]

The inner meaning:

*"You ask the Divine Mind for your desires but get no results because you have the wrong motives. You only want your desires fulfilled so you can use them for your own pleasure."*[748]

Paul was also an expert on the Law of Attraction, paring it down to this elemental but famous expression:

*"Whatsoever a man soweth that shall he also reap."*[749]

The inner meaning:

*"Whatever thoughts you think, words you say, or actions you perform will manifest on the physical plane."*[750]

Below, the Thirteenth Apostle uses the example of charity and generosity, stating that, according to the Law, those with a kind heart will be rewarded by Divine Mind with "all sufficiency in all things":

> "But this I say, he which soweth sparingly shall reap also sparingly; and he which soweth bountifully shall reap also bountifully. Every man according as he purposeth in his heart, so let him give; not grudgingly, or of necessity: for God loveth a cheerful giver. *And God is able to make all grace abound toward you; that ye, always having all sufficiency in all things, may abound to every good work.* (As it is written, He hath dispersed abroad; he hath given to the poor: his righteousness remaineth for ever. Now he that ministereth seed to the sower both minister bread for your food, and multiply your seed sown, and increase the fruits of your righteousness;) *being enriched in every thing to all bountifulness,* which causeth through us thanksgiving to God. For the administration of *this service not only supplieth the want of the saints, but is abundant also by many thanksgivings unto God.*"[751]

The so-called "Pseudepigrapha" (falsely ascribed works) also speak of Jesus' teaching on the Law. This passage is from a letter by the early Church Father Ignatius to Bishop Polycarp, both followers of the Apostle John:

> "And as for those [things] that are not seen, pray to God that he would reveal them unto thee, that so thou mayest be wanting in nothing, but mayest abound in every gift."[752]

The Old Testament too contains hundreds if not thousands of Law of Attraction teachings and statements, many which are quoted at the beginning of each chapter in this book. Here is another, this one from the book of Numbers:

> "As truly as I live," saith the Lord, "as ye have spoken in mine ears, so will I do to you."[753]

These beautiful Law of Attraction passages are from Deuteronomy:

> "[If you] shalt obey his voice according to all that I command thee this day, thou and thy children, with all thine heart, and with all thy soul; . . . then the Lord thy God will . . . have compassion upon thee . . . and he will do thee good."[754]

In Psalms we find these ancient Law of Attraction principles:

"Trust in the Lord, and do good; so shalt thou dwell in the land, and verily thou shalt be fed. *Delight thyself also in the Lord; and he shall give thee the desires of thine heart. Commit thy way unto the Lord; trust also in him; and he shall bring it to pass.* . . . Rest in the Lord, and wait patiently for him. . . . Cease from anger, and forsake wrath: fret not thyself in any wise to do evil. . . . But the meek shall inherit the earth; and shall delight themselves in the abundance of peace. . . but the Lord upholdeth the righteous. The Lord knoweth the days of the upright: and their inheritance shall be for ever.

". . . For such as be blessed of him shall inherit the earth; . . . *The steps of a good man are ordered by the Lord*: and he delighteth in his way. Though he fall, he shall not be utterly cast down: for the Lord upholdeth him with his hand. I have been young, and now am old; yet have I not seen the righteous forsaken, nor his seed begging bread. He is ever merciful, and lendeth; and his seed is blessed. Depart from evil, and do good; and dwell for evermore. *For the Lord loveth judgment, and forsaketh not his saints; they are preserved for ever* . . . The righteous shall inherit the land, and dwell therein for ever."[755]

Of course, as we have seen, the most famous Law of Attraction doctrine in the entire Bible comes from the Old Testament's book of Proverbs:

"For as a man thinketh in his heart, so is he."[756]

This is arguably the clearest articulation of the Law of Attraction ever written, and it is well worth memorizing, practicing, and sharing with others. Jesus did exactly that, and changed the world!

Jesus walking on the Sea of Galilee during a storm, while His frightened Apostles watch His approach from the safety of their fishing boat. As with modern day skeptics and nonbelievers, they did not understand the meaning behind this "miracle." Jesus was demonstrating the simple principle behind the Law of Attraction: we can easily dominate the laws of physics—*if we believe we can*, for under the Law what we believe becomes true for us. With pure faith in the Indwelling Christ we can do anything, including altering biology and expanding and compressing time, utterly transforming our conditions, environment, and experiences. Those who understand *and* believe this will certainly "receive a full reward." For, according to the Lord's Law of Attraction teachings: "If thou canst believe, all things are possible to him that believeth."

# 10

# WORKING WITH CHRIST'S SIMPLE FORMULA

"Whoso keepth his mouth and his tongue
keepeth his soul from troubles."[757]

## THE HUMAN RADIO

**JESUS' FORMULA FOR USING THE** Law of Attraction is so elementary that it can be broken down into three primary steps: *conceive*, *believe*, and *receive*.  All three are necessary for the Law to function, so an understanding of each step is vital for anyone wanting to work with the Law successfully.  Before we examine these stages, however, we need to know how the "electrical" aspects of the mind operate.

We humans have often rightfully been compared to a radio.  But we are not simply like a radio; we *are* radios, both scientifically and spiritually!  Here is how it works.

Following in the path of Jesus, the earliest Christians were ardent practitioners of the Law of Attraction, and taught that mental thought, spiritual belief, and physical manifestation are symbolized in the concept of the Holy Trinity, in the following order, the Son, the Holy Spirit, and the Father:

1) Our thoughts spring from desires conceived in the *Conscious Mind*, the "Thinker" of our mental trinity.  (In mystical Christianity the Conscious Mind is synonymous with the "Son," "Sun," or "Master.")

2) Our most dominant thoughts are received by the *Subconscious Mind*, the "Communicator" of our mental trinity, and turned into beliefs. (In mystical Christianity the Subconscious Mind is synonymous with the "Holy Spirit," "Holy Ghost," "Servant," "Paraclete," or "Comforter.")

3) The *Superconscious Mind*, the "Creator" of our mental trinity, then picks up the transmission signal of these beliefs, transforms them into physical reality, and broadcasts them back to us as our daily experiences. (In mystical Christianity the Superconscious Mind is synonymous with the "Father.")

Together these three minds form the Divine Mind,[758] our Inner Trinity, the Great I AM,[759] known by scientists as the "Unified Field." This massive realm of consciousness is eternal and infinite in all directions, and everything from the smallest particles to the largest objects in the Universe are a part of it. "It" is none other than God, Hermes' "All-Father Mind," which is why the ancient Gnostic Christians taught that "God is all mind."[760] Now within God all things are truly unified, for God Himself is one and we, due to the Indwelling Christ,[761] are one with Him.[762]

John the Apostle said that Christ lives "in the bosom of the Father," and yet the Father has never been seen by any man.[763] Why? Because He, God, is not a manlike deity, as so many of us have been taught; rather He is the very substance of the Universe. According to the Bible, we are in union not only with Him,[764] but also with Christ,[765] the Logos or Word,[766] the Holy Spirit,[767] and the Comforter,[768] and they in turn are in union with us. Understand this. It is the Universal Truth that our spirits unendingly seek!

God, the Divine Mind, is like a great body of water, and we are like molecules of $H_2O$ in that water: when a pebble is thrown in, its ripples spread out over the entire expanse, impacting everything in their path. After touching an object, the ripples reverse, returning to their original source—the point where the pebble originally met the water's surface.

What does this mean for you on a personal level, as a practitioner of the Law of Attraction? It means that whatever you think, say, or do affects everything and everyone else on this planet and beyond, and that these actions will all be returned to you in kind!

You may not notice the impact you are having on the Universe, or even the way in which it is reflecting your thoughts and deeds back to you. But rest assured that this is occurring, for you are a human radio, designed by God to transmit and receive: every single thought, word, and deed that comes from you is being broadcast, listened to, and recorded for all time, affecting everything around you on some level.[769] Here is how Buddha phrased it:

> "We are what we think. All that we are arises with our thoughts. With our thoughts, we make the world."

In the Aquarian Gospel, Jesus says:

> "The universal God is one, yet he is more than one; all things are God; all things are one. By the sweet breaths of God all life is bound in one; so if you touch a fiber of a living thing you send a thrill from [the] center to the outer bounds of life. And when you crush beneath your foot the meanest worm, you shake the throne of God, and cause the sword of right to tremble in its sheath."[770]

Members of the Jainist religion have taken this message to heart, which is why, to avoid accidently stepping on insects, they often carefully sweep the path in front of them as they walk. Jains know that even our most seemingly trivial actions and thoughts are world-altering. Every moment of everyday our behavior, no matter how insignificant it may seem to us, is literally helping to create and shape the Universe!

THOUGHTS ARE THINGS
The reason the Law of Attraction works is because thoughts are literal things. Sensors attached to the scalp can detect the brain's activity, oscillations which show up on a monitor screen as waveforms. These brainwaves (the more commonly known which are called Beta, Alpha, Theta, and Delta waves) are the result of the activity of millions of cells in the brain known as neurons, which communicate to one another electrically (and also chemically).

Neurons accomplish this by regulating a small amount of voltage through an "electrically excitable membrane," neural information that is processed, then transmitted to other neurons. These particular types of nerve cells are actually classified according to their electrophysiological traits, or firing rates.

What does all of this tell us?

Thoughts are things, thoughts are creators, thoughts are builders, imbued with a divine magnetism that draws everything in that is like the thoughts themselves. Operating in the invisible (spiritual) as electric waveforms, thoughts have the full capacity to manifest in the visible (physical) as material objects. For everything, from the book you are now holding, to the Universe itself, began as a thought frequency in the Divine Mind of God, becoming "the Word made flesh."[771]

This means that you are the sum total of every thought you have ever had up until this moment. You cannot be anything that you have not thought, and since there is no limitation to what you can think, there is no limitation to what you can create. That is the Lord's great Truth.[772] It is what the Old Testament prophets called one of God's "secrets of wisdom,"[773] one of the great sacred mysteries "which have been kept secret from the foundation of the world"![774]

## THE WORLD'S GREAT THINKERS ON THE POWER OF THOUGHT

Jesus is in good company when it comes to His views on the principle of spiritual reciprocity. Here are a few modern examples of what some of the world's most noted intellectuals have to say about "the Secret"—what we know now as the power of thought and the Law of Attraction:

> "Garner up pleasant thoughts in your mind, for pleasant thoughts make pleasant lives." — John Wilkins

> "Spiritual force is stronger than material; thoughts rule the world." — Emerson

> "Temples have their sacred images; and we see what influence they have always had over a great part of mankind; but, in truth, the ideas and images in men's minds are the invisible powers that constantly govern them; and to these they all pay universally a ready submission." — Jonathan Edwards

> "If, instead of a gem or even a flower, we could cast the gift of a lovely thought into the heart of a friend, that would be giving as the angels give." — George Macdonald

> "What we are afraid to do before men, we should be afraid to think before God. Bad thoughts are worse enemies than lions and tigers; for we can keep out of the way of wild beasts, but bad thoughts win their way everywhere. The cup that is full will hold no more; keep your hearts full of good thoughts, that bad thoughts may find no room to enter. Every one must see and feel, that bad thoughts quickly ripen into bad actions; and that, if the latter only are forbidden, and the former left free, all morality will soon be at an end." — Bishop Beilby Porteus

"Man being made a reasonable, and so a thinking creature, there is nothing more worthy of his being, than the right direction and employment of his thoughts, since upon this depend both his usefulness to the public, and his own present and future benefit in all respects." — William Penn

"Guard well thy thoughts; our thoughts are heard in Heaven." — Edward Young

"The key to every man is his thought." — Emerson

"All that a man does outwardly is but the expression and completion of his inward thought. To work effectually, he must think clearly; to act nobly, he must think nobly. Intellectual force is a principal element of the soul's life, and should be proposed by every man as the principal end of his being." — William Ellery Channing

"Thoughts, even more than overt acts, reveal character." — W. S. Plumer

"A vivid thought brings the power to paint it; and in proportion to the depth of its source is the force of its projection." — Emerson

"Good thoughts are blessed guests, and should be heartily welcomed, well fed, and much sought after. Like rose leaves, they give out a sweet smell if laid up in the jar of memory." — Charles Haddon Spurgeon

"'Give me,' said Herder to his son, as he lay in the parched weariness of his last illness, 'give me a great thought, that I may quicken myself with it.'" — Jean Paul Richter

"Secret study, silent thought, is, after all, the mightiest agent in human affairs." — William Ellery Channing

"When God lets loose the great thinker on this planet, then all things are at risk. . . .There is not a piece of science, but its flank may be turned to-morrow; nor any literary reputation, nor the so-called eternal names of fame, that may not be revised and condemned." — Emerson

"To believe in the heroic makes heroes." — Benjamin Disraeli

"Our thoughts are epochs in our lives; all else is but as a journal of the winds that blow while we are here." — Henry David Thoreau

"Thought means life, since those who do not think do not live in any high or real sense. Thinking makes the man." — Amos Bronson Alcott

"Thought is the seed of action; but action is as much its second form as thought is its first. It rises in thought, to the end that it may be uttered and acted. Always in proportion to the depth of its sense does it knock importunately at the gates of the soul, to be spoken, to be done." — Emerson

"A thought embodied and embrained in fit words walks the earth a living being." — Edwin Percy Whipple

"It is the habitual thought that frames itself into our life. It affects us even more than our intimate social relations do. Our confidential friends have not so much to do in shaping our lives as thoughts have which we harbor." — J. W. Teal

"There is no thought in any mind, but it quickly tends to convert itself into a power, and organizes a huge instrumentality of means." — Emerson

"An arrow may fly through the air and leave no trace; but an ill thought leaves a trail like a serpent. The old thoughts never die; immortal dreams outlive their dreamers . . . no thought once formed and uttered ever can expire." — Charles Mackay

These are truly exceptional words to live by!

Let us now look at how we can use the amazing knowledge of the power of thought in conjunction with the Law of Attraction.

## STEP ONE: CONCEPTION

The first step to working with the Law is to think a thought. This step we call "conceive." We are not talking about mundane thoughts, however, like what to wear to work today, or what to have for dinner tonight. Divine Mind overlooks these, as it should. If it manifested the 80,000 thoughts each one of us has everyday the world would descend into complete chaos.

So Divine Mind has a selection process: it recognizes only those thoughts which are strongest; that is, the thoughts that dominate our

Conscious Minds, those which we think of most often. Remember that the Subconscious Mind does not judge our thoughts in any way. It only pays attention to the habitual thoughts sent to it by the Conscious Mind. It then immediately sends them onto the Superconscious Mind, to be turned into material form.

"Gird up the loins of your mind and be sober," said the Apostle Peter.[775] That is, control your thoughts; be careful what you allow into our Conscious Mind. And make your dominant thoughts positive! Create a clear image and make it focused and simple, for without a strong vision you cannot grow or move forward.[776]

## IMAGINATION IS A GIFT FROM GOD

Use your imagination, another one of God's many dazzling gifts to humanity, to think up anything you want. There are no limitations!

If you want better health, for example, think about wellness. Imagine yourself being completely healthy. If you want a boyfriend, girlfriend, husband, or wife, think of your ideal mate. Imagine the two of you together. If you want a better job with better pay, think of the perfect occupational setting. See yourself working at this job, and the happiness you are getting from receiving a higher income.

## WHY YOU SHOULD AVOID THE NEGATIVE

If you want peace, joy, and abundance, do not spend your valuable time looking at images, photos, TV programs, videos, or movies that you consider displeasing, upsetting, or offensive. Stay away from writings that are pessimistic, malicious, or harmful. Do not associate with individuals or groups who paint the world in a dismal or hopeless light, or who cause pain or injury to others. Why?

Because as you are responding emotionally to these images and ideas, you are attracting their like back into your life as your personal experiences. As you continue to concentrate on such things, your circumstances can only deteriorate, for that is the nature of the Law of Attraction. Instead, focus on pictures, literature, and ideas that are pleasing, calming, agreeable, helpful, and uplifting. This ensures that your life will be filled with positive experiences, which will in turn automatically begin to improve your conditions.

## ALWAYS FOCUS ON WHAT YOU WANT

Likewise, never ever think about what you do not have, what you do not want; never dwell on lack, the negative, the unseemly, or the worst case scenario. If you focus on the politician you do not want in office, for example, you are helping him get elected. Instead, concentrate solely on the candidate you favor.

If you worry about the so-called "shortage" of food in the world, you are both contributing to the problem and enlarging it. Instead, put your attention on our planet's amazing overabundance of fruit, vegetables, and meat products.

If you are anti-racism, you are only aiding in the creation of more bigotry and prejudice. Instead, put your energy into spreading the ideas of tolerance and racial harmony.

On a more personal level, if you live in fear of illness, danger, failure, or financial troubles, you automatically attract them into your life. Instead, focus on health, safety, success, and prosperity.

If you are seriously interested in change, either personally or globally, always concentrate on what you want, not on what you do not want. Send out only positive thoughts, and always imagine what you desire in the present tense, thinking, speaking, and acting as if it has already occurred, as if you have already received it.

Focus on the wonderful feelings that will result from your dreams coming true. Nurture these feelings, and know that believing causes your feelings to materialize: "Commit thy works unto the Lord, and thy thoughts shall be established."[777] If you are struggling with belief and faith, simply pretend that these positive emotions are real, for Divine Mind does not differentiate between reality and fantasy. Everything is fact to "thy Father which is in secret."[778]

MONITOR YOUR FEELINGS

If you are ever wondering whether what you are feeling is in tune with the Divine Mind or not, ask yourself this question: is what I am feeling something I would want manifested in my life as a physical reality? If the answer is yes, continue on. If no, you must immediately alter your feelings, thoughts, and emotions to those that put you back into proper spiritual alignment with what you want. This is usually simply a matter of thinking thoughts or doing things that make you happy—which is why the admonition "be of good cheer" appears in the Bible so often.[779]

Your feelings are indeed an accurate guide to whether you are on the correct vibrational frequency or not: the better you are feeling, the clearer your "radio transmission" is to the Divine Mind. If you are feeling depressed, angry, or confused, your mental link to the Father is greatly weakened. You want a clean, clear, strong "signal" going out to God, so monitor your feelings and emotions at all times. Paul wisely said:

> "Be ye angry, and sin not [that is, if you are angry with someone, do not be vengeful]: let not the sun go down upon your wrath [never go to sleep upset]: neither give place to the devil [Ego]. Let no corrupt [unspiritual] communication proceed out of your mouth, but that which is good to the use of edifying, that it may minister grace [positive vibrations] unto the hearers. . . . Let all bitterness, and wrath, and anger, and clamour, and evil speaking, be put away from you, with all malice: and be ye kind one to another, tenderhearted, forgiving one another, even as God for Christ's sake hath forgiven you. Be ye therefore followers of God, as dear children; and walk in love . . ."[780]

Because your feelings follow your thoughts, monitoring your feelings is all-important when working with the Law. Following Paul's advice helps keep them on a positive track.

ENTHUSIASM IS GODLY

If you are concerned about how your new business is going to do, for instance, *feel* your way into spiritual oneness with Divine Mind by staying positive. Keep your excitement up,[781] for enthusiasm is a divine gift from the Father, and is actually one of the major components in the Law of Attraction. Indeed, the word enthuse derives from the Greek phrase *en theos*, meaning "in God." To feel enthusiasm about your affirmations then is putting to positive use the divine power of your Indwelling Christ.[782] So be in God: be enthusiastic!

Imagine that your new business is already a success, with customers and money flowing in abundance. Sense the amazing joy that comes from being a successful wealthy entrepreneur. Get excited, put emotion into your thoughts, and expect only good things.

This is important because the Law of Attraction stipulates that the stronger the thought, and the more feeling behind it, the sooner it is recognized by God, and the sooner and more powerfully He reacts to it. It is the cosmic version of "the squeaky wheel gets the grease." (We will be discussing different methods for increasing the potency of your thoughts in the next chapter.)

## PUT POWER, INTENSITY, & ENERGY INTO YOUR THOUGHTS

In short, the more intense your thought, the more focus you put on it, the more you meditate on it, the more you repeat it mentally or verbally, the more powerful the emotion behind it, then the more intensity, focus, emotion, power, and speed God responds with.

It works this way because the Law of Attraction is an immutable scientific principle that, like electricity, works both ways: from you to God and back.[783] For you are the negative (physical) charge and God is the positive (spiritual) charge. Your dominant thoughts create a complete circuit between these two polarities, which activates the creative force of the Divine Mind.

## THE "ELECTRICAL" CIRCUIT BETWEEN GOD & MAN

Whatever it is you want, your positive feelings combined with your prevailing positive thoughts will summon the entire Universe to your bidding! Now read the following verse from the book of Isaiah with your spiritual eyes, and be amazed:

> Thus saith the Lord, the Holy One of Israel, and his Maker, "Ask me of things to come concerning my sons, and concerning the work of my hands *command ye me.*"[784]

These are the actual words of God the Father!

How many times have you been told to "obey God's commandments"? But has anyone ever told you that God said that we can dictate our desires to Him as well? "Command ye me" saith the Lord of Hosts! In fact, this is the only way to complete the "electrical" circuit between us and God: He asks us to follow His suggestions, and if we do so we get to suggest things to Him in return. This is what I call the Law of Attraction, God in action!

## STEP TWO: BELIEVE

We will recall that Jesus said that if we seek the Kingdom of God first, all our needs would be provided for.[785] But there is another important reason we should seek to enter into God's Kingdom: *it is far easier to work with the Law of Attraction from within this awesome mental realm than outside of it.*

Some mistakenly believe, however, that once inside we only need repeat various mantras, affirmations, and prayers. But entering the Kingdom so that we can use the Law to our advantage is not just a matter of repeating various phrases. As Paul said: "For the kingdom of God is not in word, but in power."[786] The spiritual "power" he is referring to is activated by all-consuming belief. Thus phase two of the Law of Attraction is called "believe."

FAITH IN GOD, NOT RELIGION

Belief is really another word for faith. But the "faith" we are discussing throughout this book is not what people commonly think of as *religious* faith, belief in the doctrines of one's church. The faith we are concentrating on is total *spiritual* trust in the one true God (the invisible Divine Mind)[787]—which is exactly what Jesus taught[788]—and just as importantly, the scientific laws that the Father has placed at our disposal, laws specifically tailored to help us improve our lives. Paul referred to this as having "faith in the operation of God."[789]

We cannot possibly hope to understand this type of spiritual trust intellectually. It is simply part of "the mystery of the faith."[790] Nonetheless, this impenetrable enigma is elegantly described in the book of Hebrews as follows. True faith is

> "the substance of things hoped for, the evidence of things not seen. . . . Through faith we understand that the worlds were framed by the word of God, so that things which are seen were not made of things which do appear."[791]

This kind of faith is, in fact, the very foundation of the Law of Attraction, for, using the mind alone, you must manifest on the physical plane that which does not yet exist on the physical plane. To do this requires that you see things not as they are, but as you want them to be; that you firmly believe that what is, is not, and that what is not, is.

DO NOT JUDGE ACCORDING TO PHYSICAL APPEARANCE

This is vital, because trusting our five physical senses can be extremely misleading. For example, looking up at the night sky, our eyes tell us that the stars are moving across the heavens, and so Man thought for thousands of years. Today, however, we know that it is not the stars that are moving, it is the earth turning on its axis. By the same token, to properly work with the Law of Attraction, we must learn to see beyond the physical and into the spiritual.

This is how the Indwelling Christ views things,[792] and as you raise your consciousness you will too, for you are not your body, mind, or Ego. You are your Higher Self, the Christ Within.[793] God does not judge according to the visible, the physical,[794] and neither should we. "Do ye look on things after the outward appearance?," asked Paul.[795] Here is Jesus' answer:

> "Judge not according to the appearance, but judge righteous judgment."[796]

## "ALL THINGS ARE POSSIBLE TO HIM THAT BELIEVETH"

Training yourself to see and believe in what does not yet exist on the physical is the supreme test of your faith, a power so important that Paul said that everything else is meaningless in comparison.[797] Here is an example of this type of faith, one that Peter rightly described as "being much more precious than of gold."[798]

When Jesus raised Lazarus from the dead, He did not claim the "miracle" as His own. He gave full credit to the amazing belief of Lazarus' sister Martha, saying:

> "Said I not unto thee, that, if thou wouldest believe, thou shouldest see the glory of God?"[799]

If this type of powerful all-consuming faith can bring the dead back to life, it is obvious that it can be used to manifest any desire we have!

Though most will never hear the following words preached from their church pulpit, this statement is so important, let us commit it to memory. Jesus is speaking here to a father who has asked the Master to cast out an "evil spirit" that had taken possession of his son. In response, Jesus says to the man:

> "If thou canst believe, all things are possible to him that believeth."[800]

The father did believe, and the demon left his son's body—immediately!

It is interesting to note that earlier the father had asked some of Jesus' Disciples (followers) to help cure his son, but they had been unable to. Upon hearing this, Jesus turned to both the father and His Disciples and called them "faithless," proving yet once again that according to the Lord, unyielding faith, implacable belief, is the key to working with the Law of

Attraction.[801]

The faith of Lazarus' sister Martha (in the story above) is an example of the high state of spiritual consciousness we must have in order to successfully communicate with the Father. Here is how India's famed spiritual leader Mahatma Gandhi described it:

> "Faith is nothing but a living, wide-awake consciousness of God within. He who has achieved that faith wants nothing. . . . I am a man of faith. My reliance is solely on God."

## WHY PETER COULD NOT WALK ON WATER

Pertaining to faith and working with the Law of Attraction, here is an example of what *not* to do. According to Matthew, when Jesus invited Peter to walk on the water to Him, Peter was half way across when he made the mistake of gazing down at the waves. Seeing the actual "appearance" of the sea, he lost all confidence and began to sink. As Jesus reached out his hand to save the Apostle, He said: "O thou of little faith, wherefore didst thou doubt?"[802] In Luke's account of the incident, Jesus puts it even more bluntly: "Where is your faith?," He asks His skeptical follower.[803]

The moral? Do not judge according to appearance; do not focus on what is going on *outside* of you, but rather put your faith in what is going on *inside* of you; in other words, on your thoughts. For in God's realm, the Kingdom of Heaven, it is thought, not physical reality, that is the only true power.

## THERE IS ONLY ONE REALITY: MIND!

While the Human Mind makes a distinction between what it considers reality and illusion, fortunately for us the Divine Mind does not recognize this difference. It only acknowledges thought. Einstein understood, saying: "Reality is merely an illusion, albeit a very persistent one." To God there is only one reality, and that reality is Mind!

Brain research indeed shows, for example, that *simply imagining a white rose causes the same basic reactions in our brain that would occur if we were actually looking at a real white rose.* In terms of the Law of Attraction, this means that even if what you want is not yet "real" on the physical level, if you merely think it in your Conscious Mind, God accepts this thought as reality, and proceeds to materialize it on the earth plane.[804]

God never responds to what is. He responds to what you are thinking; or more precisely, to the mental and emotional vibrations you are putting out. "As above, so below."[805]

God sees things very differently than we do. Earth-based science tells us that the condition is always the cause and that thought is always the effect. Thus, to the scientist, physical objects are seen as the source of all power, while thought is completely powerless. With God, however, it is the opposite: thought is always the cause and the condition is always the effect. Thus, to the believer, thought is the source of all power, while physical objects are completely powerless.

Strange as it may seem after reading this, God's law of physics and man's law of physics are actually one and the same. It is just that most of our scientists have not figured this out yet!

Since the Law always gives us what we believe, not what is, to manifest our desires we must, as the book of Hebrews affirms, have complete faith "in the evidence of things not seen."[806] Or as Paul put it, we must learn to "*calleth those things which be not as though they were.*"[807]

Ignore your physical reality and focus only on what you want, believing that it is yours already. For in spiritual reality your desires belong to you as soon as you think of them. All you need to do is call them into physical existence through the Law of Attraction.

Be not concerned for your life, needs, or wants. Turn to the Christ Within, exemplified in our Lord Jesus, and all will be provided, just as the Master states:

> And Jesus said unto them, "I am the bread of life: he that cometh to me shall never hunger; and he that believeth on me shall never thirst."[808]

Worry, doubt, and fear (Satan) are the arch enemies of the Law of Attraction (God), so banish them from your heart and mind now and forever.[809] Instead, give your faith fully to the Father saying, "Lord, I believe," and it will be done unto you![810]

STEP THREE: RECEPTION
The third phase of working with the Law of Attraction deals with acquiring the results of our affirmations. So this step is called "receive." Many teachers of the Law maintain that our participation is not required during this period; that the only real work we must do is during steps one and two.

I believe, however, that the manner in which we receive the "gifts of the Holy Ghost"[811] is just as important as the thoughts we think and the level of faith we have.

## ALLOW DIVINE MIND TO WORK IN ITS OWN MANNER

First, while waiting to receive our abundance, we must cast off all preconceived ideas about how it is to come about, and allow God to work His magic in secret, in his own time and way.[812] If we make specific demands on the Divine Mind as to the hows, whens, wheres, and whys, we are showing the opposite of faith; we are showing fear and mistrust. For the Universal Mind always *gives* to us freely, not because we demand it.[813] As Jesus said: "It is your Father's good pleasure to *give* you the kingdom."[814]

Consider this: if someone asked you to do something for them, but then showed no faith in your ability to accomplish the task, this lack of support would undermine your enthusiasm, jeopardizing the entire scheme. And so it is with the Sovereign Mind, the Divine Mind, which operates according to our degree of faith.

Eliminate all doubt, stipulate no conditions, ask no questions. Leave this entire part of the manifestation process completely up to God. Never doubt or challenge the Father![815] For He is all-wise,[816] and knows far better that we ever could, how, when, where, and why to materialize our desires. Stand back and *allow* the natural process of the Law to work in its own way, and your word (thoughts) will surely be made flesh (materialize).[817]

## GOD'S PSYCHIC COMMUNICATION SYSTEM

During the reception phase make sure you are open to your sixth sense, the psychic side of your being, the small quiet "inner voice," for this is one of the many ways our responsive God answers our prayers and affirmations. In fact, inspiration, intuition, imagination, epiphanies, revelations, visions, and dreams are all part of the marvelous communication system of the Father, allowing Divine Mind to speak to us directly in a language that is God's and God's alone. Your imagination, as one example, is so powerful that it can create happiness or misery, good health or sickness, prosperity or impoverishment. So use it wisely!

The Bible contains numerous illustrations of psychic forms of communication. Though men like Daniel, for instance, were given the specific power to interpret "visions and dreams,"[818] the truth is that "all flesh" has been given the ability to prognosticate, "dream dreams," and "see visions."[819] Since we are all prophets (that is, possess psychic abilities), this means that you are just as capable of receiving extrasensory ideas, impressions, and instructions from God as Daniel, or any modern psychic medium for that matter. Emerson once said:

> "There is guidance for each of us, and by lowly [inner] listening, we shall hear the right word."

If you "receive" a notion—no matter how unusual—through your intuitive sense, pay attention to it; follow up on it. This could be the Father's method of responding to your affirmation, for God indeed "moves in mysterious ways, His wonders to perform." Here is what He tells us in the book of Numbers:

> "Hear now my words: if there be a prophet among you, I the Lord will make myself known unto him in a vision, and will speak unto him in a dream."[820]

## GRATITUDE

Lastly, to maximize your receiving, keep yourself in a perpetual state of gratitude, "giving thanks always for all things unto God."[821] No matter how difficult your life may be right now, you have much to be thankful for. To be filled with feelings of dislike for your current situation will only draw more of the same.

Follow Paul's example. "I have learned," he wrote to the converts at Philippi (modern day Greece), "in whatsoever state I am, therewith to be content."[822] Or as the book of Hebrews puts it:

> ". . . be content with such things as ye have: for he [God, Divine Mind] hath said, 'I will never leave thee, nor forsake thee.'"[823]

Count your blessings and thank the Father for them as often as you can. Bestselling motivational author Louise Hay starts each morning by thanking her bed for a good night's sleep. Nothing is too small to be grateful for. Acknowledge everything you love as a divine gift and magnetize more of the same into your life.[824] Here is how the Psalmist phrased it:

> "Let us come before his presence with thanksgiving, and make a joyful noise unto him with psalms."[825]

Gratitude should be practiced not only during the reception phase, but everyday of your life. The Law of Attraction will not only send you more of what you are thankful for, but more things to be thankful for:

> "Being enriched in every thing to all bountifulness, which causeth through us thanksgiving to God."[826]

We all like to be appreciated, and God, the Divine Mind, is no exception. This is particularly true when we are cocreating with Him under the Law of Attraction.[827] So follow Paul's advice:

> "Be careful for [that is, be anxious about] nothing; but in every thing by prayer and supplication with thanksgiving let your requests be made known unto God."[828]

Our job during the receiving period is simple: it is to be patient, allowing, open, and thankful, while surrendering our egotistical notions. "The servant of the Lord must not strive," said Paul.[829] Simply keep your faith strong so that you will "inherit the promises" of God.[830] Expect a wonderful outcome, and the Father will "give you an expected end."[831] But do not focus on the details of your affirmations, as this could cause doubts and fears (Satan)—the enemy of Divine Mind (God). There is no need to push the river. Just let go and let God!

THE "GROWING PAINS" PHASE

During the initial stages of working with the Law of Attraction, some people find that things seem to go in the opposite direction of what they are affirming. For example, someone trying to heal themselves of an illness may feel worse; someone who is struggling financially may find themselves with less money; someone who is trying to buy a house may lose a number of bids in quick succession.

It is important to realize that this is merely the "growing pains" phase in the process, and as such is both necessary and temporary. It is necessary because as our consciousness is changing to adapt to our new way of thinking, the old encrusted patterns of thinking must break off and fall away. Just like a snake shedding its old skin, there may be some momentary irritation, discomfort we may experience as a "setback."

Additionally, from the perspective of our new higher level of spiritual consciousness, our old lives and relationships, our old conditions and circumstances, our old thoughts and daily patterns, will now probably feel unpleasant to us. This is a natural reaction, and should not be resisted.

Those who experience this disconcerting stage and do not understand it, are likely to become discouraged and give up. Do not let this happen to you! God gave us this promise:

> "And the Lord, he it is that doth go before thee; he will be with thee, he will not fail thee, neither forsake thee: fear not, neither be dismayed."[832]

Once you have been introduced to Jesus' teachings on the Law of Attraction, you are to keep your Inner Light, the Universal Self, the Christ Within,[833] alive at all times. Follow Jesus' recommendation and keep your spiritual "Candle Within" burning brightly day and night:

> "No man, when he hath lighted a candle, putteth it in a secret place, neither under a bushel, but on a candlestick, that they which come in may see the light."[834]

Stay strong in your faith.[835] Keep at your affirmations. Be patient with God, who has always been patient with you.[836] In a short amount of time—after the necessary spiritual changes have taken place within you—this phase will pass, and you will quickly move onto the next one.

If you lose your faith at this stage you will only attract more of what you are feeling: depression and frustration! For the Law of Attraction is not only working on your *past* thoughts, it is also closely following your *current* thoughts, beliefs, and feelings, trying to manifest the strongest ones into the physical.

Continue to believe, and keep your expectations high. Predict complete victory for yourself. Plan on receiving your "expected end."[837] Know without any doubt that the externalization of your desires is on its way. Thus our Lord truly said: "He that shall endure unto the end, the same shall be saved."[838]

THE TIME DELAY

How long does it take the Law of Attraction to manifest our affirmations? The answer is that there is no clear cut answer. Divine Mind works in accordance with our level of faith: generally speaking, the clearer and stronger our belief, the faster the response.[839]

The Egoless Jesus was able to effect instant healings (such as when

He reattached the severed ear of a Jewish servant)[840] and instant manifestations of physical objects (such as when He made a coin appear in the mouth of a freshly caught fish),[841] because He was perfectly attuned to His oneness with the Father. His faith was so great that he could control any aspect of the material plane, including the weather.[842]

Through the Father (Divine Mind), Jesus also had the ability to instantly summon 72,000 angels,[843] as well as bend the laws of physics to his mental commands. The latter power He proved when He turned water into wine,[844] fed 5,000 people with five loaves of bread,[845] and walked across the surface of the Sea of Galilee.[846] Even the winds and the oceans obeyed the Lord![847] This is why, speaking as the Indwelling Christ, He said:

"All power is given unto me in heaven and in earth."[848]

And here is a clue to "the Secret" that has been withheld from us by those who control society, politics, religion, and education: the Secret is literally that *the Secret is not outside of you, it is inside of you.* As Jesus says to the Apostles in the Gnostic Christian document known as the Dialogue of the Savior:

"I am telling you that what you are looking for is inside of you."[849]

And what is the great secret that is "inside of you"? Since you also possess the Indwelling Christ—for it is your incorporeal true self, the indestructible immortal you—you also possess, in potential, the same divine powers Jesus had, including the ability to attract whatever you want into your life!

Do you have the perfect faith of Jesus? Do you have a total awareness of your oneness with God? If you do, there is no reason your desires cannot materialize immediately, just as Jesus' did.[850] In fact, He promised that we would not only have the same abilities as He, but that we would perform even greater works than He did.[851] "Become better than I," Jesus encourages the Twelve Apostles in the Apocryphon of James.[852]

The reality is, however, that even though those of us who have faith in the Indwelling Christ[853] are both clothed in Him and one with Him,[854] most of us are not at Jesus' level of spiritual evolution yet. After all, He was given the title Christ for good reason. The word Christ, meaning "anointed" or "coronated," is from the ancient Chaldean word for the sun, *chris*—the sun (that is, light) being the ancient archetypal symbol of enlightenment: the complete knowledge and understanding of our personal Christhood, "our

light and our salvation."[855] Or as the celebrated Indian teacher Paramahansa
Yogananda affirmed:

> "Self-realization is the complete and assured knowledge that we do
> not need to strive for oneness with God, for we are already one
> with Him."[856]

## THE ENLIGHTENED ONES

Just as our Lord assured us there would be, thousands, perhaps millions, of
others are living on earth right now who are operating at very high states of
consciousness, near to, level with, or even above that of Jesus.[857] These
individuals, known variously as masters, ascended masters, self-realized
masters, superbeings, saints, prophets, enlightened ones, sages, adepts,
divine lights, paramuktas, master-minds, man-gods, God-men, rishis,
swamis, gurus, superminds, illumined ones, illumined souls, illumined
masters, yogis, yogi-Christs, siddhas, and avatars, have perfected the Law
of Attraction to the point where their desires manifest instantly, or
sometimes even before they consciously think them—"for your Father
knoweth what things ye have need of, before ye ask him."[858]

These pure consciousness people pass their days flowing from one
joy and success to another, their lives moving in perfect harmony, unruffled
by things such as health problems, relationship issues, or financial
difficulties. To such masters of time and space, everyday is perfect, for they
have truly realized one of God's greatest Law of Attraction truths, as found
in the book of Isaiah:

> "And it shall come to pass, that before they call, I will answer; and
> while they are yet speaking, I will hear."[859]

If you persist in the correct practice of the Law of Attraction, you too can
one day attain this level of spiritual maturity.[860] In fact, God wants and
expects you to!

For obvious reasons, however, this book is not intended for this
group. It was written for beginners and intermediates on the path toward
union with God, who know little or nothing about the Law of Attraction,
and who have not yet discovered their own Inner Christ. For those of us
who fall into this category (the other 99 percent of humanity), we can
expect a time delay.

THE RESULTS OF UNRESTRAINED THOUGHT

As much as we might not like it (for we all want our desires to be fulfilled as soon as possible), the time delay is actually important for those who are not yet masters of the Law. One reason is that not having a thorough understanding, unwanted incidents are likely to occur. Take the following example.

Let us assume that God did not create a time delay in the Law of Attraction, so that everything we thought came into being instantly. What would happen if you were sitting at your dinner table one evening and began intensely thinking about a blue whale? The time delay gives us a period of reflection so that we can truly focus in on what it is we want. This avoids the problems that would ensue from uncontrolled and chaotic thinking.

CLEANSING THE MIND OF OLD BELIEFS

Even if you feel you have properly prepared *and* that you are correctly affirming your desires, your manifestations may still be taking longer than you would like. Why?

In this case we are usually blocking our incoming good due to old negative thought patterns that are still buried in our Subconscious Mind. These mental "weeds" must be yanked out by the roots, so that the "soil" of the Subconscious is cleared and ready for the spiritual "planting" of positive "seeds" (thoughts).

Doing affirmations is one of the best methods there is for "weeding" out your mental garden; that is, for overriding and deleting the old destructive mental programs, while replacing them with new healthy ones. So the sooner you begin the better. But because this cleansing process requires time (the duration of which will be different for each individual), it will also slow down the manifestation of your desires. This is natural and is to be expected.

OVER INTELLECTUALIZING THE LAW OF ATTRACTION

Two words of caution.

First, anyone can start affirming at any time. But keep in mind that while Jesus' teachings on the Law are outwardly quite simple, there is a right and a wrong way to go about conceiving, believing, and receiving. Thus, carefully studying and understanding the doctrines in this book will save you time, energy, and frustration later on.

Second, while study is vitally important, do not over analyze the intellectual side of the Law. The academic pursuit of spirituality can inevitably lead to vain conceit and false pride, as we find among some Christian "authorities" today. These inveterate self-aggrandizers, who have repeatedly dissected every passage and parsed every word in the Bible, have become delirious with too much education.[861] As Paul noted disdainfully of this often haughty group, despite always having their noses buried in scripture, they are "never able to come to the knowledge of the truth."[862]

TAKE YOUR TIME

Let us also keep in mind that the principles which make up the Law of Attraction were fine-tuned over thousands of years by some of the most spiritually advanced individuals who have ever lived. Along with Jesus these would include Buddha, Zoroaster, Julian of Norwich, Lao Tzu, Plato, Saint Germaine, Joan of Arc, Sri Mahvatar Babaji, Hildegard of Bingen, Gandhi, and Emanuel Swedenborg, among thousands of others. You cannot hope to learn and comprehend such a body of knowledge all in one sitting.

I myself have been studying Jesus' teachings on the Law for many decades, and am still learning new things everyday. Despite the fact that the Lord Himself patiently instructed the Twelve Apostles for three years, many of them still struggled to understand His teachings right up to the day of His crucifixion.[863]

Take your time, study, pray, and practice. Due to the many ingrained false beliefs you have absorbed during your life from the mass mind, you will undoubtedly need to read this book several times before it all begins to make sense (a practice I heartily encourage). Eventually, everything will become second nature to you, and the time between your affirmations and your manifestations will decrease.

BE OPEN, ALLOWING, & PATIENT

There is one more reason that God instituted a time delay: although the Universal Mind likes efficiency and can work at any rate of speed, because it is dealing with our earthly laws of physics, in many cases it takes earthly time to line everything up in our favor.

For instance, let us say you want to sell your house. God already knows who is going to purchase it, when, and for how much. The "problem" is that your buyer has not yet been approved for a mortgage, is trying to put together a down payment, and, to complicate matters, is about to get married. God will easily sort all of this out so that everyone benefits. It is obvious, however, that it is not going to happen instantly.

So do not fret over the "when." Put it out of your mind, stick to your Law of Attraction program, and be patient.[864]  The 18th-Century French cosmologist Count de Buffon put it like this:

> "Never think that God's delays are God's denials.  Hold on, hold fast, hold out.  Patience is genius."

In the end, if materializing our desires requires extra time, the Divine Mind will take it.  It may be that He is simply testing us, to see how sincere our belief is before He grants our wishes.  Either way, only God knows when it is the correct moment, and so forbearance becomes a virtue.  For "to every thing there is a season, and a time to every purpose under the heaven."[865]

Enjoy this period between affirming and receiving.  And rest assured that *your manifestation will occur at the exact time it is supposed to, and always in wonderful ways that are far beyond anything you asked for, imagined, or hoped for.*  I know, because it has happened to me and thousands of others in just this fashion!

So do not rush God.  The Father knows best!

# 11

# AFFIRMATIONS
## Part 1

"The mouth of a righteous man is a well of life."[866]

## YOUR LIFE IS WHAT YOU THINK ABOUT MOST

𝕿HE LAW OF ATTRACTION IS always working, and you are always working with the Law of Attraction, either consciously or unconsciously, either positively or negatively. Everything you have ever experienced has been, and everything you will experience in the future will be, the result of your most persistent thoughts, your most deeply cherished beliefs, and your most heartfelt emotions.[867]

You are always molding physical reality. Not directly, but by what you mentally focus on most often. The ancient Egyptian Church Father, Origen of Alexandria, understood the Law. I have concluded, he stated,

"that the position of every created being is the result of his own work and his own motives."

There is no escape from the Law. It is always exact, for God purposefully made it that way. It is His irrevocable,[868] indescribable gift to you:[869] the gift of total freedom to make of your life what you will.[870] Being a just and loving God, He has given us complete licence to sculpt our own fate—without His interference.[871] This is just one of the many benefits we derive from the freedom we have in the Indwelling Christ,[872] for "where the Spirit of the Lord is, there is liberty."[873]

There is no such thing as unjustness, inequality, or inequity in your life, and there cannot be; for you are "running your own show." You cannot get any fairer than that! Once you grasp this, you will see that there is indeed perfect justice in the Universe, and the seemingly strange words of Buddha—in which he speaks of our physical world with all of both its wonders and horrors—will make complete sense:

"All things are perfect just as they are."

This is so because Divine Mind is always perfectly outpicturing the thoughts our Conscious Minds are sending to our Subconscious Minds, good or bad. Your life is exactly what you are thinking, and the world is exactly what we are all thinking!

## AS A GOD YOU ARE RESPONSIBLE FOR YOUR OWN LIFE

Your so-called "destiny" is completely up to you, not God. If you have a negative experience, God did not bring it about. You did. If you have a positive experience, God did not bring it about. You did. God is not creating your daily life, you are. You always get to choose your own circumstances, your own experiences, your own life, your own future. Does this seem cruel? Hardly. It shows just how much God loves you!

Do you realize that He has made you the author, editor, illustrator, designer, and publisher of your own Book of Life?[874] Here is another way of looking at it: you are the scriptwriter, producer, director, casting director, editor, and actor in your own biographical movie. And with every thought you have, you are writing a new scene. *You* are truly "making it all up as you go along"!

This unending self-creative process continues even after you fall "asleep" at night (that is, when your Conscious Mind goes dormant) and the God Within you,[875] your always wide awake Subconscious Mind, takes over and begins "dreaming." As it turns out, "dreams" are actually a series of short, original, but *very real* nightly "movies" written and produced by you, for the daily purpose of rejuvenating your spirit—which, by the end of each day, has become deenergized by life on the physical plane.[876] This is why in the purely mental (that is, spiritual) world of your "dreams," you are always playing the lead role: as a god or goddess,[877] you are always the creator of your experiences, even when you are asleep!

Yes, when Jesus said that you are a deity—an individual expression of the Father—he meant it.[878] How joyous and freeing a thought this is.

But with it comes a stark reality: everything is completely up to you, for you are the high priest[879] of your own church within;[880] you are the

CEO of your own spiritual company; you are the president of your own interior country; you are the king or queen of your own inner kingdom. Along with this prestigious position of power comes the honor-bound duty to assume personal responsibility for everything that occurs in your life. You cannot have one without the other.

## IT IS NEVER TOO LATE TO CHANGE

Now the Father's devotion to us, and to our personal freedom, is so strong that He literally calls us "sons of God."[881] We are His children, genuine members of the family of God for all time.[882] Thus, nothing, not even death, can disunite us from this bond. This is true love, is it not? Paul said:

> "For I am persuaded, that neither death, nor life, nor angels, nor principalities, nor powers, nor things present, nor things to come, nor height, nor depth, nor any other creature, shall be able to separate us from the love of God . . ."[883]

It is because of God's eternal and inseparable love for you, His child, along with the amazing liberty He has granted you, that you are never too old, too sick, too poor, or too far gone to change the course of your health, your finances, your relationships, your occupation, or any other situation in your life. What you do with yourself, how you chart your destiny, is always up to you, whatever your physical age. God loves His latecomers, His "Prodigal Sons,"[884] just as much if not more than those who have never strayed from the straight and narrow Way.[885]

## BEGINNING WITH AFFIRMATIONS

Obviously, we want to the use the Law of Attraction for positive things, to improve our lives, our health, our relationships, our finances, our living situation. One of the most powerful methods for achieving this is the daily use of affirmations. Along with visualization, prayer, and meditation, it is one of the best ways to connect with God, communicate with the Divine Mind, focus and strengthen our desires, and move things along toward the physical manifestation of our dreams.

Remember: God speaks to us through the mind. Therefore it is through the mind that we must speak back to Him. For "by thought, not words, the heart is carried up to God, where it is blest."[886]

DESIRE IS GOOD

Affirmations are the natural and spontaneous outgrowth of desire. We begin affirming what we like and what we want at an early age, even in infancy, with rudimentary facial expressions and various hand gestures and sounds. As we grow older our wants become more complex, and by adulthood our desires are at their peak intensity. Our entire lives are permeated with wishes, needs, and cravings. Even the Zen Buddhist monk desires something: to have no desires.

Yet, many of us have been trained to think of desire in the negative, as something unpleasant. Why? Because wanting something that you do not seem to be able to have is painful. But now that you know about Jesus' teachings on the Law of Attraction, it is time to reconsider this view!

Our English word desire comes from the Latin *desiderare*, meaning "of the stars." When we want something badly enough we "wish upon a star." Here is the real inner meaning of desire, however: star is from the Latin *stella*, which is identical to *aster*, the Greek word for star. Aster is related to the word astral, which is from the Greek word *astron*, meaning "of or related to the stars." In mystical Christianity the astral plane is the spiritual abode of the angels of God, the powerful light beings who respond to *all* of our desires, positive or negative.[887]

But there is an even more profound meaning of the word desire: our desires are literally made up of star matter, or what I call God Stuff. This tells us that desire is one of the Father's many incredible endowments to man and womankind. New Thought author Wallace Wattles once said: "Desire is a manifestation of power," and so it is: God's power!

Desire is what spurns new thoughts and new ideas; it is what motivates us, pushes us into new directions, onward and upward to the next step in our lives. It is the fuel that thrusts us forward in our development as ever evolving souls, which is why God gave us this particular emotion to begin with: desire is a tool that we use, consciously or unconsciously, for our spiritual betterment. And the Father, the Divine Mind, is right there ready and waiting to assist you in fulfilling your desire.

All you have to do is clarify it and bring it into sharp focus, thereby turning it into a crystalline thought. Then take this thought and put all of your faith behind it, firmly believing that it is yours, that it is already accomplished. Then, as discussed in the previous chapter, simply "let go and let God."

## DEFINING AN AFFIRMATION

What is an affirmation? It is the positive assertion of something, a thought, an idea, a wish, a need, a hope, a desire. Its opposite is the negation: a doubtful or destructive repudiation of something.

Many of us are so used to expressing negations throughout our daily lives that we scarcely give it any thought. Little wonder that we have relationship, health, and financial problems! Train yourself to express only positive thoughts, to affirm every good thing around you, and watch every aspect of your life begin to improve immediately.

## AFFIRMATION CREATION

There are countless numbers of books on affirmations, many which provide hundreds even thousands of positive statements for every possible use. And although I give examples throughout this book, I highly recommend making your own. There is nothing more powerful than a self-created affirmation, for only you know what you really want and how you want to communicate this desire to the Father.

Here now are some guidelines for forming your personal affirmations.

## RULE ONE: CLARITY

The first rule of affirmation creation is to always make them clear and precise. Just like we humans, the Universal Intelligence loves clarity and brevity. In the case of affirmations, being definitive makes our desires easier for God to deal with. In other words, it allows the Divine Mind to work more efficiently in manifesting what we want.

While you can create and repeat as many affirmations as you like, make each individual affirmation brief. Keep wording to a minimum. Break long sentences up into smaller more concise statements. This will help increase the power and intelligibility of your affirmations.

## RULE TWO: HERE & NOW

The second rule is to always put your affirmations in the present moment, in the present tense. In the Kingdom of Heaven there is no time as we know it here on earth. The past, present, and future all occur at the same time on the spirit plane. Thus God and His angels are always working for us in the *present moment*, where all power resides, never in the past or in the future.

An affirmation such as "I'm going to be happy soon," is forthcoming, a time period that God does not recognize, thus it can never come true. Your happiness will always lay just out of reach, exactly as you are imaging it.

God is a "now" God, which is what Jesus meant when he said: "The kingdom of heaven *is* at hand,"[888] and "theirs *is* the kingdom of heaven."[889] And it is what Paul meant when he said: "The Lord *is* at hand."[890] Yet many people make the mistake of procrastinating, of putting off their good until an unforseen future time—which never arrives! Jesus, finding this same attitude among His Disciples, said to them:

> "Say not ye, 'There are yet four months, and then cometh harvest'? behold, I say unto you, lift up your eyes, and look on the fields; for they are white already to harvest."[891]

In other words, what you are thinking *right now* is working its way back to you *right now*, so there is no time to lose if you want to create the ideal life for yourself! This makes this very moment incredibly important to both your present and your future happiness, health, and prosperity. Here is how the Father stated this Law of Attraction concept in the book of Deuteronomy:

> "And thou shalt . . . obey [follow] the voice of the Lord [Divine Mind], and do all his commandments which I command thee this day. And the Lord thy God will make thee plenteous [prosperous] in every work of thine hand, in the fruit of thy body, and in the fruit of thy cattle, and in the fruit of thy land, for good: for the Lord will . . . rejoice over thee for good . . . [but only] if thou shalt hearken unto the voice of the Lord thy God, to keep his commandments . . . and [only] if thou turn unto the Lord thy God with all thine heart, and with all thy soul [that is, think positively all the time].
>
> "For *this commandment which I command thee this day, it is not hidden from thee, neither is it far off. It is not in heaven, that thou shouldest say, 'Who shall go up for us to heaven, and bring it unto us, that we may hear it, and do it?' Neither is it beyond the sea, that thou shouldest say, 'Who shall go over the sea for us, and bring it unto us, that we may hear it, and do it?' But the word is very nigh unto thee, in thy mouth, and in thy heart [that is, it is within you], that thou mayest do it.*
>
> "See, I [Divine Mind] have set before thee this day [the choice between] life and good, and death and evil; in that I command thee this day to love the Lord thy God, to walk in his ways, and to keep his commandments and his statutes and his judgments [that is, engage in right-thinking], that thou mayest live

and multiply: and the Lord thy God shall bless thee in the land whither thou goest to possess it."[892]

Yes, God has given you the mental (spiritual) power to begin changing your life right now, and that power is within you right now. So this is the perfect time to start. Do not procrastinate. Indeed, the Father, who is always concerned about your well-being, wants you to have what you need right now, not tomorrow, a month from now, or next year. Here is how the writer of Proverbs phrased it: "Hope deferred maketh the heart sick: but when the desire cometh, it is a tree of life."[893]

And what is the "Tree of Life"? It is an ancient archetypal symbol of the divine manifestation of paradisiacal happiness, health, and prosperity![894]

RULE THREE: THE GREAT I AM

The third rule is to start your affirmations with the words "I am" whenever possible. God told Moses that his name is "I AM,"[895] and that is exactly what it means: according to both God and Jesus, "ye are gods," for the real you, that part of your being that introduces you to new people as "I am" so-and-so, is a literal manifestation of God.[896]

When you use the phrase "I am" in a sentence, you are speaking with the Almighty's most potent supernatural expression: the voice of the Supreme Self, your God-Self, the Universal Divine Mind, the Great I AM, the original sacred name of God. "This is my name for ever," the Father declared, "and this is my memorial unto all generations."[897]

By using God's sacred name, I AM, in our affirmations, we are not only connecting with Him, we are realizing our oneness with Him, while tapping into the greatest force in the Universe: the power of Divine Mind. For the words "I AM" not only link the physical to the spiritual, they contain the actual sacred word-power of God: the Aum (or Om) of the Hindus, the Amam of the early Jews, the Amon of the ancient Egyptians, the Om-ega of Gnostic Christians, and the Amen of ecclesiastical Christianity. Thus, when we utter the words "I am" we tap into this super creative power, allowing us to transform anything we like, even biology.

This is just what Jesus meant when He said: "Before Abraham was, I AM."[898] By claiming His at-one-ment with the Father, by acknowledging His eternal God-Self, He aligned Himself with Divine Mind, thereby gaining the right to use all the powers of the Godhead. This allowed the God-tuned Jesus to heal the sick, give sight to the blind, give hearing to the deaf, cast out devils, cleanse lepers, and raise the dead.[899]

As a "son of God," you are entitled to all of these same divine powers as well.[900] You too have access to the ineffable, beginningless, imperishable Father through the everlasting Indwelling Christ.[901]

## RULE FOUR: NEGATIVE WORDS

The fourth rule for working with affirmations is to avoid using words and phrases that negate. These include: "do not," "is not," "cannot," "should not," "will not," "are not," "must not," "never," and of course "not." This is because the Divine Mind tends to overlook this type of grammar, and instead zeroes in on the subject of the sentence.

If you say, for example, "I will not have an accident today," the Divine Mind reads this as "I will have an accident today," because it is focusing on the subject ("accident") while ignoring the words "will not." A better way to say this would be: "I am safe and protected today."

If you say "I don't want to be unhappy," the Divine Mind centers on the subject ("unhappy") and interprets the sentence like this: "I want to be unhappy." Instead say: "I am happy."

Because of this characteristic of the Universal Intelligence, it is also highly recommended that you do not use negative verbs, nouns, and adjectives such as "hate," "pain," "miserable," "illness," and "jealous." If you create an affirmation like "I am no longer sick," the Divine Mind processes it as: "I am sick." Instead say: "I am healthy." Do not say "I won't be poor ever again." Instead say it positively: "I always have more money than I need." These are meant to be *affirmations* (life-affirming sayings) after all.

## RULE FIVE: TOTAL FAITH

The fifth and final rule is to express your affirmations with complete conviction and total faith. Faith, without which the world would be nothing,[902] is the foundation of the entire Law of Attraction. Why?

For God to manifest our affirmations on the physical plane, we must be able to see our desires as having already been accomplished. If we focus on the fact that we do not yet have what we want, the Law will only attract more feelings of lack. Ignore the appearance of things and see only what you want as having already been accomplished.[903]

To do this you must disregard what your *five outer senses* are telling you through your Conscious Mind (physical reality), and concentrate only on what your *one inner sense* is telling you through your Subconscious Mind (spiritual reality).[904] This is what God does,[905] and being an expression of

God[906] we must too if we expect the Law to bring us our desired results.

Christian minister Charles Capps likes to use the example of an elevator: if you are on the basement floor you are not going to push the basement floor button. If you do, you will not go anywhere. If you want to get off the basement level, you need to push a button for one of the floors above you. This situation requires you to look past your present circumstance and see the future as you want it to be.

Working with the Law of Attraction is no different. For it to operate in your favor, disregard where you are and instead look to where you want to go—just as if you are using an elevator. This is the meaning of faith: being able to perfectly visualize the invisible, while ignoring the visible; being able to believe that what we do not yet have, we have, and what is, is not. For *the Divine Mind gives us what we believe to be true and real, not what is true and real.*

EXAMPLES OF AFFIRMATIONS

What does a proper affirmation look like? Let us take the topic of money, for instance. Do you want increased financial security? Then some appropriate affirmations would be: "I am wealthy," "I am affluent," "I am financially independent." Notice that these affirmations comply with our first three rules: they are clear, they are set in the present tense, and they each begin with God's name, "I AM."[907]

Let us look at another example, this one concerning physical well-being: "I am healthy"; "I am in perfect health"; "I am radiant and alive with God's healing love." Again, our affirmations are definitive, in the moment, and use the power of the Father's original secret name.

Here is one more. Let us assume you want a new home, but you have not even started looking for it yet. You do not want to say: "Someday I'll have the home of my dreams." This is vague, set in the future, and does not use the sacred I AM. Instead, it should read something like this: "I am in love with my beautiful new home in Nashville, Tennessee." Or, "I am the proud and happy owner of a wonderful new home in Dallas, Texas."

Always tell God exactly what you want in the most precise manner possible, and *as if you already have it.* Use the voice of your God-Self to intensify its force, then add perfect faith (belief) to activate the Law of Attraction's powers of physical manifestation.

Naturally, not every affirmation has to be like the ones above. In fact, I encourage you to create your affirmations as personally and uniquely as possible. There are no restrictions on what you can think up. Although you should always be clear, there are some situations that do not require you to speak in the present tense or use the I AM phrase.

For instance, if you have an upcoming meeting, you can program it ahead of time to turn out the way you want: "My meeting is going to go smoothly, and all sides will come away satisfied." Plan your day ahead this way: "Today is going to be a fantastic day and everything is going to flow in my favor."

Have a school exam coming up? Say this: "I will have perfect recall and breeze through the test." Going on a long road trip? Use this affirmation, or one like it: "Me and my family are completely protected and will arrive safely at our destination."

To add extra force to your affirmations, end them with this phrase: "It is done." This seals your thoughts with a powerful statement that has long been employed by the spiritually enlightened to more fully emphasize their desires to the Divine Mind.[908] Meaning "so be it," it is used in the same sense as the word "amen" (which you can also use), and so relates to the Father your approval or confirmation of your affirmations.[909]

## EXPRESSING AFFIRMATIONS MENTALLY
An affirmation can be conveyed in a number of different ways. The most obvious and common method is *mentally*. The greatest benefit to repeating affirmations over and over silently to yourself is that they can be done anytime, anywhere.

## EXPRESSING AFFIRMATIONS VERBALLY
The second most common way to use affirmations is to *speak* them out loud. This method is perfect for when you are getting ready for work, driving in your car, waiting at a traffic light, sitting in a hunting blind, any situation in which you are alone and noise is not a factor (if it is, you can always whisper your affirmations).

To make them easier to remember, turn your affirmations into rhymes. To make them more fun, create melodies and sing them as songs. To add spiritual impact, turn them into mantras or chants, as Paul's followers did.[910]

One way to increase the intensity of your verbal affirmations is to say them out loud in front of a mirror. Repeat your affirmations while staring directly at yourself. What is that light emanating from behind your eyes? Where is that twinkle in your pupils coming from? Who is that looking back at you?

It is the "true Light" of the Indwelling Christ[911] "which lighteth every man"![912] It is your God-Self,[913] the Great I AM,[914] which was created by the Father in His own image.[915] According to Jesus, those who believe in this Divine Light become eternal "Children of Light,"[916] for the Law of Attraction stipulates that what you believe becomes true for you.

Do you believe?

## EXPRESSING AFFIRMATIONS LITERARILY

The third method is to *write* out your affirmations. I recommend using a notebook or journal to record them in. Develop a routine, such as writing out your affirmations first thing each morning and last thing each night before going to sleep. Try writing a letter to yourself, clearly and firmly stating your desires and expectations. Another method for deeply programing your Subconscious Mind is to create a "wish list" of all the things you want.

Also try this: write or type your affirmations on pieces of paper and stick them up around your home. Kitchen cupboards, bathroom mirrors, and closet doors are just a few of the places where you are most likely to see and read your posts. You can also put them up around your workspace and on the dashboard of your car or truck, anywhere you can think of. The goal is to make your affirmations such a familiar and comfortable part of your everyday life, that repeating them eventually becomes second nature.

## EXPRESSING AFFIRMATIONS VISUALLY

The fourth method is to *visualize* your affirmations. Visualizing entails "seeing" what you want in your mind's eye. Go window shopping, for example, and see yourself purchasing the things you want and need. See yourself paying for these items, taking them home, and unpacking them. See yourself using them. Feel the pleasure and happiness they bring you.

Experiment with setting up a "visualization board": a cork bulletin board onto which you pin pictures of your desires. Hang it in a place where you will see it often. Another method is to create a "vision box": a container into which you place images of your wants and needs. Anything that helps implant and reinforce your Subconscious Mind with your thoughts will work. You are only limited by your imagination.

The important aspect here is to "see" your desires as being real now, as having already been manifested in the physical. Imagine being with your ideal mate *now*, living in your dream home *now*, working at the perfect job *now*, driving your favorite car *now*.

Remember that God always works through the Law of Attraction in the present moment. If you visualize something as having not occurred yet, it will always remain in the future. Heed the advice of the early Gnostic Christians, who taught that "what thou see, thou shall become."[917]

## DOUBLE YOUR AFFIRMATION POWER
According to Jesus, if you have a mate, partner, spouse, family member, or friend who is willing to do affirmations with you, your Law of Attraction prayers will have extra force:

> "Again I say unto you, that if two of you shall agree on earth as touching *any thing that they shall ask, it shall be done for them* of my Father which is in heaven."[918]

All of the affirmation methods we have discussed, including this one, work because each of them uses repetition to program your Subconscious Mind with your innermost desires.[919] Repeatedly writing the same thing, for example, forms microscopic memory pathways in your brain, permanently imprinting its neurons with your affirmations.

The physical brain, of course, is directly wired to our spiritual brain, the Divine Mind, and it is through this link that God is listening to everything we think, say, and write.[920] Now the Father, the inventor of the Law of Attraction, said: "Every man's word shall be his burden."[921] This means that as divine mental creators, we are each responsible for our own lives. So make sure that all of your thoughts, words, and writings count!

## BACK UP YOUR WORDS WITH POSITIVE EMOTION
It is important to understand, however, that Divine Mind is not just reacting to the words of our affirmations. It is also reacting to what we are feeling as we think, speak, write, or visualize our affirmations.

So remember to imbue your thought-desires with the correct feelings, emotions that match what you want. When our mental vibrations line up with our emotional vibrations, we are tapped into the awesome, timeless, limitless power of the Father, where anything and everything is possible.[922]

Something is only impossible if you choose to believe it is.[923] Otherwise, there are no limits to what you can create because you are an individualization of God,[924] and God is unlimited![925]

RULES REGARDING THE LAW OF ATTRACTION

While the Law of Attraction is, like the law of gravity, a hard and fast rule, when it comes to actually doing your affirmations there are few hard and fast rules.

How often should you do them? Some repeat them only once in the morning and once at night. Others have a set time they put aside for doing affirmations, such as five, ten, or fifteen minutes a day. Still others do affirmations every chance they get, throughout the entire day, right up to the moment they fall asleep; then they start over the moment they wake up.

I personally recommend the last method for most people, particularly beginners. Why? Because our Subconscious Minds carry so many negative and false beliefs, absorbed from the mass mind, that over time these tend to undermine and counteract our positive affirmations. These old erroneous beliefs must be eradicated completely before our new wholesome thoughts can become a permanent part of our Subconscious.

The most efficient way to do this is by continually reciting our affirmations. Positive thoughts are a thousand times more powerful than negative ones, and will eventually drive them out, just as Paul said: "Be not overcome of evil, but overcome evil with good."[926]

Jesus' frantic parents, Joseph and Mary, discover their missing twelve year old son at the Temple in Jerusalem interacting with a group of Jewish scholars. According to Luke, "all that heard him were astonished at his understanding and answers." When Mary asked Him why He had disappeared, the young Jesus replied crisply: "I am out doing my Father's business." What did Jesus mean by this? Not even His own parents understood His answer. But we do: the "Father" is Jesus' code word for the Divine Mind, that part of our nature that is an actual extension of God, and which gives us unlimited power to fashion our own circumstances, experiences, and conditions, even our own fate. The Father's "business" is thinking, or more precisely, using the power of thought to mold and sculpt our daily lives. For as the enlightened youngster well knew, thinking is life's only real occupation, for Mind is God and God is Mind. Eighteen "silent" years later—a "lost" period during which, according to reliable sources, Jesus traveled throughout India, Tibet, Iran, Assyria, Egypt, and Greece—the now thirty year old prophet, healer, and teacher extraordinaire would begin His true earthly mission: preaching what He referred to as "the Gospel of the Kingdom," which included His secret doctrines on our at-one-ment with the Father, human divinity, the power of thought, and the Law of Attraction.

# 12

# AFFIRMATIONS
## Part 2

"The Lord will perfect that which concerneth me: thy mercy, O Lord, endureth for ever."[927]

## AFFIRMING TO THE FATHER IN SECRET

**W**HEN WE FIRST LEARN OF the "glad tidings," or Good News, about the inner Kingdom and the Law of Attraction,[928] our immediate instinct is to share it with others, particularly our family members and close friends. However, Jesus offered us a warning about this:

"But thou, when thou prayest, enter into thy closet, and when thou hast shut thy door, pray to thy Father which is in secret."[929]

Here is the inner meaning of this scripture:

"When doing your affirmations, do it within the confines of your own mind; go into your personal 'mental room' and close the 'door.' This is the private abode of the Divine Mind, the Father."[930]

Paul said something similar:

"For our conversation is in heaven; from whence also we look for the Saviour, the Lord Jesus Christ."[931]

The inner meaning:

"Hold your personal discussions with the Father within your Higher

Self, the same place where you will find your saving grace, the Indwelling Christ."[932]

In essence, Jesus and Paul are not only telling us to keep our prayers (affirmations) to ourselves, but our knowledge of and interest in the Law of Attraction as well. Why?

To begin with, the Father within us[933] dwells in secret and "sees" in secret.[934] Because of this He likes to work in secret as well. Then, as Jesus tell us,

"thy Father, which seeth in secret, shall reward thee openly."[935]

The inner meaning:

"Divine Mind, which perceives you telepathically, will manifest in the physical all that you pray for in the spiritual."[936]

Who are we to seek entrance into the inner sanctum of the Holy of Holies, that "most holy place," where the Divine Mind labors for humanity in absolute stillness, peace, silence, and secrecy? Here is what the Father Himself says about respecting His "holy place":

"And they shall not come near unto me, to do the office of a priest unto me, nor to come near to any of my holy things, in the most holy place . . ."[937]

Our sacred regard for the Father and His sacred spiritual workshop, His mental laboratory (the Subconscious Mind), is thus paramount.

What does all of this mean in plain English? Simply this: do not interfere. Do not stress, fuss, fret, predict, or intellectualize.[938] Do not try to steer the outcome in the direction you want. Your desires are in the most capable hands in the Universe. Trust and allow. Do you think you know more than our omniscient God? "Fear not, believe only," said Jesus![939]

The second reason our Lord advises that we do our affirmations and prayer in private is because a skeptic could easily jeopardize our entire Law of Attraction program by inserting doubts into our minds. Absolute incessant faith is necessary for the Law to work, therefore you cannot afford to let a single thought of disbelief creep in. Depending on the degree of uncertainty introduced, this can only delay the good you have coming to you.

Only speak about the Law with others who you already know share your views, and who you positively know will be receptive. There are many who are not yet ready to hear Jesus' teachings on the Law of Attraction and the Divine Mind. They will discover it in their own way when the time is right.

Metaphysically, this is what Paul meant when he asked his followers to avoid associating with the "wicked," that is, nonbelievers: he did not want their faith jeopardized by "doubting Thomases."[940] Jesus too counseled us not to share what is sacred, personal, and private with those who might not appreciate it:

"Give not that which is holy unto the dogs."[941]

The Master even told us what could happen if we share the "secret sayings" concerning the Law of Attraction with the wrong people, even close family members, some who may not be prepared for it:

"The father shall be divided against the son, and the son against the father; the mother against the daughter, and the daughter against the mother; the mother in law against her daughter in law, and the daughter in law against her mother in law."[942]

However, the Lord urged believers to remain faithful to the Indwelling Christ and to His teachings, including those on the Law of Attraction, saying:

"He that loveth father or mother more than me is not worthy of me: and he that loveth son or daughter more than me is not worthy of me."[943]

The third and final reason we want to keep our Law of Attraction work private is because we do not want to dilute the power of our affirmations. By discussing our spiritual activities with others, particularly those who are not spiritually mature, we reduce the energetic force of what we are trying to accomplish. The wetter gunpowder gets, the less effective it is. We want our spiritual "gunpowder" to be as potent as possible. So keep it "dry": keep your affirmational work to yourself.

The overall lesson? If you want to show respect for the Father, if you want to prevent doubts from undermining your faith in the Law, and if you want to keep peace with your family and friends, "pray in secret"!

YES GOD ANSWERS EVERY SINCERE PRAYER!
What kinds of things can you affirm through the power of thought?

There is no limitation. You can affirm anything from preparing a successful meal to healing a disease; from insuring a good night's sleep to living a long life; from programming a safe drive to work to protecting your family, home, and business; from mending a broken relationship to increasing your finances; from losing weight to gaining confidence. Whatever it is, your Subconscious Mind will always seek to create in the visible that which is given to it in the invisible. That is why ancient Gnostic and Hellenistic Christians made these cryptic but now understandable observations:

> "Whatever is currently on the inside of you is what you will soon see on the outside of you."[944]

> "Every single thing that is visible is an exact reproduction of that which is concealed."[945]

Let us keep in mind that affirmations are received as prayers by God, and that He has promised to answer every sincere prayer. Notice that I say every *sincere* prayer. We think some 80,000 thoughts a day, many hundreds of these which are desires. Even though the Divine Mind has unlimited power, it would be senseless for it to try and manifest every thought-desire we have. How does it know which ones to respond to and which ones to ignore?

The answer is that the Universal Mind focuses only on our most prevailing and earnest thoughts, while allowing sporadic and trivial thoughts to go unnoticed. This is why repeating our affirmations throughout the day is so important: this allows God to differentiate between what is important to us and what is not.

"Pray without ceasing," said Paul,[946] "praying always with all prayer and supplication in the Spirit."[947] "Men ought always to pray, and not to faint," said Jesus.[948] The "Lord over all is rich unto all that call upon him,"[949] "for the eyes of the Lord are over the righteous, and his ears are open unto their prayers."[950]

WHY SOME PRAYERS SEEM TO GO UNANSWERED
"But," some will protest, "I have prayed many times and received no response from God. Even in my darkest most desperate moments, when I

have cried out to the Father in prayer, nothing good happened. Things only got worse! How do you explain this?"

Popular pastor Joel Osteen once said that "God is not moved by our tears," and this is true. The Father does not respond to begging or demands; He is not impressed by our sadness; He is not affected by our problems. In fact, He is unmoved by anything manmade, including violence, suffering, misfortune, poverty, and sickness. What is He moved by then?

According to our Lord and His teachings on the Law of Attraction, God is moved by our thoughts! For the Father is an inward God, a spiritual God, a cosmic God, an immanent God, the unemotional pneumamorphic God of Jesus,[951] not an outward God, a physical God, a personal God, a transcendent God, the emotional anthropomorphic God of modern day Pagan Christianity.[952] As such, He patterns His responses to us based on what is going on *inside* of us, not what is going on *outside* of us. This is *true* compassion, which is why Paul referred to the Divine Mind as "the Father of mercies."[953]

Those who claim that God does not answer their prayers do not understand that He *is* actually responding. What He is responding to, however, is not the words of our prayers, but the thoughts behind the words of our prayers. How could it be otherwise, for the "Father that dwelleth within you"[954] is purely psychological;[955] or as the Gnostic Christians say: "God is all mind"![956] His response to our prayers then is in strict accordance with His promise to us, that we always reap (receive) physically what we sow (think) mentally.[957]

Thus, asking something positive of God while the mind is flooded with negative, sad, angry, or frustrated thoughts, will only push us further into the hole of hopelessness and despair. As a divine thinking magnet, we can only attract to ourselves that which matches our predominant thoughts. This is why such prayers seem to go unanswered, and it is why things sometimes seem to remain unchanged, or even deteriorate after we pray: God is always giving us what is in our "heart" (Subconscious Mind), not what is in our "head" (Conscious Mind).

Make sure that when you pray your mind is projecting what you want (happiness, health, prosperity), not what you do not want (sadness, sickness, poverty), for God always responds to the thoughts behind your prayers exactly. Let us recall the main tenet of the Law of Attraction: God gives us back what we think and only what we think, for thought is the principle way in which we communicate with Him, the Divine Mind. Here is how Emerson articulated it:

When success exalts thy lot,
God for thy virtue lays a plot:
And all thy life is for thy own,
Then for mankind's instruction shown;
And though thy knees were never bent,
To Heaven thy hourly prayers are sent,
And whether formed for good or ill,
Are registered and answered still.

## BIBLICAL PROOF THAT GOD RESPONDS TO US

As Emerson asserts, and as the Bible itself amply testifies, God is listening to you right now, sifting through your thoughts, searching for the sincerest, most intense, faith-filled prayers and affirmations to reply to, as the following examples illustrate.

Let us start with our Lord. As He was preparing to raise Lazarus from the dead, He looked upward and said:

> "Father, I thank thee that thou hast heard me. And I knew that *thou hearest me always . . .*"[958]

If God "always hears" Jesus, we know that He also always hears us as well, for Jesus and we are both one with the Father.[959]

In the book of Psalms we find this lovely passage:

> "Delight thyself also in the Lord; and *he shall give thee the desires of thine heart.* Commit thy way unto the Lord; trust also in him; and *he shall bring it to pass.*"[960]

The book of Isaiah relates this declaration from the Father:

> "And it shall come to pass, that before they call, *I will answer*; and while they are still speaking, *I will hear*,"[961]

This passage is also from Isaiah:

> "Thou shalt weep no more: he will be very gracious unto thee at the voice of thy cry; when he shall hear it, *he will answer thee.*"[962]

From the book of 2 Chronicles:

> "If my people, which are called by my name, shall humble

themselves, and pray, and seek my face [presence], and turn from
their wicked [egotistical] ways, then *I will hear [them] from heaven,
and will forgive their sin* [mistakes], *and will heal their land.*"[963]

From the book of Job:

"Thou shalt make thy prayer unto him, and *he shall hear thee.*"[964]

From the book of Jeremiah:

"For I know the thoughts that I think toward you," saith the Lord,
"thoughts of peace, and not of evil, *to give you an expected end.* Then
shall ye call upon me, and ye shall go and pray unto me, and *I will
hearken unto you.* And ye shall seek me, and find me, when ye shall
search for me with all your heart."[965]

Also from Jeremiah:

Thus saith the Lord the maker thereof, the Lord that formed it, to
establish it; the Lord is his name; "Call unto me, and *I will answer
thee*, and shew thee great and mighty things, which thou knowest
not."[966]

The Gnostic-minded Apostle John certainly understood the Father,
the Christ Mind, the Law of Attraction, and the power of prayer:

"And this is the confidence that we have in him, that, if we ask any
thing according to his will, *he heareth us*: and if we know that he
hear us, whatsoever we ask, we know that we have the petitions
that we desired of him."[967]

Here is another scripture from Isaiah, one that reveals the mystical
name of the One listening to and answering our affirmational prayers: it is
the Source of All, the Great I AM, the Divine Mind embodied in us as our
God-Self:[968]

"Then shalt thou call, and *the Lord shall answer*; thou shalt cry, and
he shall say, 'Here *I am*.'"[969]

Paul had this to say about using prayer-affirmations and the Law of
Attraction:

"Be careful for nothing [that is, worry about nothing]; but in every thing by prayer and supplication with thanksgiving let your requests be made known unto God."[970]

Emerson once wrote about "the Secret," that our "thought is law" and our "speech is thunder":

"The secret which every intellectual man quickly learns—that beyond the energies of his possessed and conscious intellect he is capable of a new energy (as of intellect doubled upon itself), by abandonment of the nature of things; that beside his privacy of power as an individual man, there is a great public power upon which he can draw, by unlocking, at all risks, his human doors, and suffering the ethereal tides to roll and circulate through him; then he is caught up into the life of the universe, *his speech is thunder*, *his thought is law*, and his words are universally intelligible to plants and animals."

British poet Alfred Tennyson understood these precepts as well. Here is what he said on this topic in the 1860s:

"Speak thou to Him *for He hears*, and Spirit with Spirit may meet.
"Closer is He than breathing, and nearer than hands and feet."

In the Aquarian Gospel, the Lord left us with these marvelous instructions on how to tap into the Law of Attraction through prayer:

And Jesus said, "The answer to your prayer may not appear in fulness in a little time. Be not discouraged; pray again and then again, for *God will hear*. . . . Behold, I say to you, ask firmly and you shall receive; seek trustingly and you shall find; knock earnestly, the door will open up. All things are yours, and when you ask, not as a begging man would ask, but as a child, you shall be satisfied.

"A son may ask his father for a loaf of bread; the father will not give to him a stone; or he may ask him for a fish; he will not give a crab; or he may ask him for an egg; the father will not give a pebble from the brook. Behold, if men of flesh know how to give abundantly to children of the flesh, will not your heavenly Father give abundantly to you when you shall pray?"[971]

GUARD THE ENTRANCE OF YOUR MIND
Having established that God answers every genuine prayer, we must

remember to carefully guard our thoughts. This is one of the most important principles when working with the Law of Attraction: *do not* allow any dark, negative, or pessimistic thoughts to enter past the gate of your Conscious Mind: the Indwelling Christ, your Higher Self. What if one manages to slip in on occasion? Simply immediately replace it with a light, positive, optimistic thought. Paul wisely advised that we "bring into captivity every thought to the obedience of Christ."[972]

This new way of thinking is not always easy for beginners, for it requires enormous discipline and mental self-control, which, for most people, takes time to develop. But as practice makes perfect, if one persists in right-thinking long enough, it will become a habit, and the self-destructive tendency toward wrong-thinking will begin to fade. Eventually, when you have a negative thought, it will feel alien and uncomfortable. At that point you will know that you are well on your way to conquering your old negative thinking patterns.[973]

## THE LAW REQUIRES MENTAL & SPIRITUAL DISCIPLINE

The spiritual and psychological work needed to properly use the Law of Attraction is why, after all, Jesus' closest followers were called "Disciples": this word derives from the word *discipline*, meaning "training through enforced obedience in accordance with a set system of rules." To become a disciple of Jesus then[974]—that is, to begin living by and through the Indwelling Christ (your Higher Self)—indeed takes self-discipline.

## THE WAY OF THE ONLY BEGOTTEN SON

Follow what spiritual teachers, including Jesus, have long called "the Way" (ongoing positive thoughts, words, and deeds),[975] for the only route to the Father (Divine Mind) is through the Indwelling Christ[976] (personified in Jesus). We can do nothing on our own.

This is indeed "the Way, the Truth, and the Life," and as the "Son," or Indwelling Christ, tells us, "no man cometh unto the Father, but by me,"[977] that is, the Conscious Mind. Hence the meaning behind the Christ's mystical title, "the Only Begotten Son of God":[978] we each have only one Conscious Mind (an "Only Begotten Son"), and it is only through it that we can connect to its "Father": the Divine Mind ("God").

Staying on "the Way of the Lord" builds up your spiritual momentum,[979] so that eventually, to your amazement, you will find that you are no longer thinking negatively; that only positive thoughts flow through your mind.

When you finally achieve this perfect balance between your Conscious Mind (the Masculine Principle) and your Subconscious Mind (the Feminine Principle),[980] your mental powers will be so disciplined and strong that it will be impossible for any kind of negativity to enter past the gates of your personal spiritual realm, the "Kingdom Within."[981] You will have achieved one of the most important aspects of the Law of Attraction: absolute mental self-control,[982] which early Christians knew as "the Way of the Light."[983]

## MASTERING RIGHT-THINKING THROUGH PRACTICE

Jesus expects us to be masters of our thoughts, emotions, and actions, and the Holy Spirit empowers us to do just that.[984] Here is how He described the mental balance we are to attain:

> "Behold, I send you forth as sheep in the midst of wolves: be ye therefore wise as serpents, and harmless as doves."[985]

The inner meaning:

> "If you live through the Indwelling Christ, you will be a minority, a believer dwelling in the midst of a majority of nonbelievers, many of them hostile to the Truth; to alleviate any danger to yourself, you must be as crafty as a warrior, and as inoffensive as a pacifist."[986]

Does this seem impossible? It is not. Practice, practice, practice!

## USING THE LAW WISELY

Right-thinking is especially important because the Universal Divine Mind is not concerned with *why* you want something; whether it is good or bad, positive or negative; whether it benefits you or hurts you. It does not judge you, your affirmations, or your motivations. Yes, it will even make your worst fears come true if that is what you think about the most, just as the 18th-Century French philosopher Voltaire wrote:

> "The longer we dwell on our misfortunes, the greater is their power to harm us."

And let us not forget the cry of Job, who focused so intently on his worries that they manifested on the physical plane:

"For the thing which I greatly feared is come upon me, and that which I was afraid of is come unto me."[987]

Thus, because of the way it works, only the very foolish would knowingly use the Law of Attraction for destructive purposes, to hurt others, for example; for this would merely attract more of the same into their own lives. In her beautiful 1888 poem, "Secret Thoughts," here is how the Victorian poet Ella Wheeler Wilcox phrased our mental two-edged sword:[988]

I hold it true that thoughts are things,
Endowed with bodies, breath, and wings,
And that we send them forth to fill,
The world with good results—or ill.

That which we call our secret thought,
Speeds to the earth's remotest spot,
And leaves its blessings or its woes,
Like tracks behind it as it goes.

It is God's law. Remember it,
In your still chamber as you sit.
With thoughts you would not dare have known,
And yet make comrades when alone.

These thoughts have life; and they will fly,
And leave their impress by-and-by,
Like some marsh breeze, whose poisoned breath,
Breathes into homes its fevered breath.

And after you have quite forgot,
Or all outgrown some vanished thought,
Back to your mind to make its home,
A dove or raven, it will come.

Then let your secret thoughts be fair;
They have a vital part and share,
In shaping worlds and molding fate,
God's system is so intricate.

So while Divine Mind does not evaluate the motives behind our affirmations, we ourselves need to be careful to use our thought-power only for good. The pages of history are replete with examples of imprudent men and women who misused the Law of Attraction, only to find themselves the victims of their own greed, cruelty, lusts, and stupidity. Now we can more fully understand God's admonition: if we use the Law wisely our lives will be "blessed"; if we use the Law foolishly our lives will be "cursed."[989]

Paul made a similar statement: "Neither give place to the devil."[990] This means that we should not allow our Ego, our Lower Self, to control us. We must control it. The moral?

Keep your thoughts and affirmations positive. The Law is unbreakable and gives you back what you send out.[991] Always use the Divine Mind for good, to improve, to increase, to benefit, to heal, for productive ends.

## THE LAW & THE GOLDEN RULE

Jesus spelled out this "Golden Rule" aspect of the Law of Attraction in the Gospel of Matthew:

> "Therefore all things whatsoever ye would that men should do to you, do ye even so to them: for this is the law . . ."[992]

To those who follow this commandment, to think only positive, say only good, and do only right, God made this promise:

> "Thou lovest righteousness, and hatest wickedness: therefore God, thy God, hath anointed thee with the oil of gladness above thy fellows."[993]

Like every other passage in the Bible the "oil of gladness" is interpreted differently by different people. Why? Because we are all in different stages of spiritual development. How ever you personally choose to define it, you can be sure that it includes this meaning: if you live righteously, God has pledged to anoint (bless) you with happiness.

Simply put, if we engage in right-thinking the Divine Mind will respond to our affirmations with righteous rewards!

Even before He was officially Paganized by Constantine the Great and the Catholic Church, Jesus, "the Light of the World," began to be associated with contemporary Pagan solar-deities, such as Apollo, Sol, Helios, and Phoebus. This was due in part to Malachi's reference to the coming Messiah as the "Sun of Righteousness," as well as the fusion of Jesus with the ever popular Pagan sun-god Mithras, whose birthday fell on December 25, whose holy day was held on "Sun's Day" (that is, Sunday), and whose Twelve Disciples were linked with the twelve astrological star-signs of the Zodiac. Following in this tradition, in the above illustration, entitled *Sol Justitiae* ("Sun of Justice"), Medieval German artist and Catholic Albrecht Dürer (1471-1528) has portrayed Jesus as a Pagan sun-god who mercilessly judges the deeds of mankind. The Lord, who condemned idolatry of any kind, particularly of Himself, would have been horrified at such a depiction. Dürer's Jesus is seated upon a lion, symbol of the astrological star-sign Leo, ruled by the sun—inspired by the Apostle John's Paganesque reference to Jesus as "the Lion of the tribe of Juda." The Church's shocking transformation of Jesus—from Son-God to Sun-God—helped smooth the transition of the Roman Empire from Paganism to Christianity, and aided the clergy in converting millions of "heretics" after Paganism was banned by the religious totalitarian, Theodosius I. The Christian emperor, who began issuing a series of harsh anti-Pagan edicts in the year 381, executed all those who violated his new laws, symbolized in Jesus' raised sword, a "godly instrument of death" (and symbol of a ray of sunshine), under which untold thousands cruelly perished.

# 13

# ENTERING THE KINGDOM OF GOD

## Part 1

"The mouth of the upright shall deliver them."[994]

THE KINGDOM OF GOD IS OPEN TO ALL

**THOUGH IN THE PAST THE** Law of Attraction was only made known to the wealthy and the powerful, who paid large sums of money to learn its secrets, this was never God's intention. He has always wanted the Law to be available to every human being, including the lowliest, poorest, and least spiritually mature among us.

He wants every single person—no matter what their religion, color, or nationality—to know about and have access to this amazing power, the power to create your own circumstances, conditions, environment, surroundings, and experiences, the power to create your own destiny![995] Hence Peter's words: "God is no respecter of persons."[996] When it comes to the Law of Attraction, the Father does not favor one over another, so you have as much right to understand it and use it as anyone else. The power that was once accessible only to kings and queens is now available to you![997]

One of the aspects of what Jesus called "entering into the Kingdom of God,"[998] that is, the "attaining the Consciousness of Divine Mind," is working with the Law of Attraction. Our Lord declared that all men and women are invited to participate. Thus, He compared the Kingdom of God (in Greek, *Basileia tou Theou*) to a wedding feast in which the king tells his servants:

"Go ye therefore into the highways, and as many as ye shall find, bid to the marriage."[999]

In another passage Jesus states:

"And I say unto you, that many shall come from the east and west, and shall sit down with Abraham, and Isaac, and Jacob, in the kingdom of heaven."[1000]

Paul too reminded us that the Father has openly called all of His children to share in His Kingdom and in His "glory" (divine powers):

"As ye know how we exhorted and comforted and charged every one of you, as a father doth his children, that ye would walk worthy of God, who hath called you unto his kingdom and glory."[1001]

### SEEK THE KINGDOM & ABUNDANCE IS YOURS

Jesus promised us that those who enter the Kingdom of God and correctly practice the Law of Attraction, will be able to live carefree lives filled with abundance, health, and happiness; lives without worry, fear, hunger, or poverty. Peter put it this way: "Cast all your cares upon God, for he careth for you."[1002]

In the Gospel of Judas, Jesus calls this high level of consciousness—which we know as the Kingdom of God or Heaven—a "great and boundless realm." It is the "secret place of the most High" mentioned in the Old Testament, and those who "dwell" here "shall abide under the shadow of the Almighty," where "no evil shall befall them."[1003] Here is how the Psalmist phrased it:

"The Lord [God the Father, Divine Mind] is my shepherd; I shall not want. He maketh me to lie down in green pastures: he leadeth me beside the still waters. He restoreth my soul: he leadeth me in the paths of righteousness for his name's sake. Yea, though I walk through the valley of the shadow of death, I will fear no evil: for thou art with me; thy rod and thy staff they comfort me. Thou preparest a table before me in the presence of mine enemies: thou anointest my head with oil; my cup runneth over. Surely goodness and mercy shall follow me all the days of my life: and I will dwell in the house of the Lord for ever."[1004]

Yes, if you "dwell in the house of the Lord" (the Kingdom of

Heaven) you shall "not want," you shall "fear no evil," your "cup will runneth over," all of your desires will come true, and you will want for nothing. As Paul said:

> "God hath not given us the spirit of fear; but of power, and of love, and of a sound mind."[1005]

This "sound mind" is the Divine Mind, which is always outwardly expressing our most dominant inner thoughts. Consider the words of Jesus:

> "Therefore I say unto you, take no thought for your life, what ye shall eat, or what ye shall drink; nor yet for your body, what ye shall put on. Is not the life more than meat, and the body than raiment? Behold the fowls of the air: for they sow not, neither do they reap, nor gather into barns; yet your heavenly Father feedeth them. Are ye not much better than they? Which of you by taking thought can add one cubit unto his stature?
>
> "And why take ye thought for raiment? Consider the lilies of the field, how they grow; they toil not, neither do they spin: and yet I say unto you, that even Solomon in all his glory was not arrayed like one of these. Wherefore, if God so clothe the grass of the field, which to day is, and to morrow is cast into the oven, shall he not much more clothe you, O ye of little faith?
>
> "Therefore take no thought, saying, 'what shall we eat?' or, 'what shall we drink?' or, 'wherewithal shall we be clothed?' (For after all these things do the Gentiles [nonbelievers] seek:) for your heavenly Father knoweth that ye have need of all these things. But *seek ye first the kingdom of God, and his righteousness; and all these things shall be added unto you.*"[1006]

What a pledge Jesus has made to us! When we "enter" the Kingdom of God, the realm of Divine Mind, we realize not only our personal divinity and oneness with God, but our amazing divine powers as well; powers that enable us to create any kind of life we want for ourselves and for our loved ones. We discover, in fact, that our Higher Self, our Divine Self, the Indwelling Christ,[1007] makes us the king[1008] of our own personal kingdom within![1009]

This is due to the fact that when we are operating out of this inner realm, our divine powers are fully activated. Thus, it is at this time that not only do we have maximum spiritual control over our physical lives (health, wealth, happiness, etc.), but the physical plane has the least effect upon us in return.

Think about this for a moment. Now you understand why Jesus preached what He called "the Gospel of the Kingdom,"[1010] instead of "the Gospel of Jesus Christ" (which was preached only by those who came after Him);[1011] now you know why His focus was always on the "Father" (Divine Mind)[1012] and the "Son" (the Indwelling Christ),[1013] rather than on Himself as the human Jesus;[1014] now you see why He asked us to "obey" His commandments:[1015] this grants us entrance into the here-and-now Kingdom of Heaven,[1016] where anything and everything is possible through thought alone![1017] As Peter commented,

> ". . . for if ye do these things, ye shall never fall: for so an entrance shall be ministered unto you abundantly into the everlasting kingdom of our Lord and Saviour Jesus Christ."[1018]

This is why Paul says that due to our union with the Indwelling Christ, we are "enriched" in all things.[1019]

In the Aquarian Gospel the Lord further elucidates upon this topic:

> The news spread through the city and along the shore that Judah's king had come, and multitudes drew near to press his hand. And Jesus said, "I cannot show the king, unless you see with eyes of soul, because the kingdom of the king is in the soul. And every soul a kingdom is. There is a king for every man. This king is love, and when this love becomes the greatest power in life, it is the Christ; so Christ is king. And every one may have this Christ dwell in his soul, as Christ dwells in my soul."[1020]

## THE INNER JOURNEY

Although everyone is invited to the "feast" of the Kingdom of God, only a handful will actually attend, for "many are called, but few are chosen."[1021] The truth is, as Jesus stated, that not even being a Christian will necessarily grant one entrance into the Kingdom:

> "Not every one that saith unto me, 'Lord, Lord,' shall enter into the kingdom of heaven; but he that doeth the will of my Father which is in heaven. Many will say to me in that day, 'Lord, Lord, have we not prophesied in thy name? and in thy name have cast out devils? and in thy name done many wonderful works?' And then will I profess unto them, 'I never knew you: depart from me, ye that work iniquity.'"[1022]

Indeed, not only did the Master say that individuals from both the East (that is, Pagans) and the West (Christians) would one day sit down together in the Kingdom of Heaven,[1023] but the lowest outcasts of society would enter it before the literal minded, overly strict, intolerant, prejudiced, judgmental, formalistic "Pharisees" of Christianity.[1024]

The reason for this is that entering the Kingdom of God (realizing our at-one-ment with God) is an intensely personal journey that requires one to undergo a radical transformation of personality, one that awakens the spiritual conscious from its unconscious slumber.

To put it another way, it is a highly private, individualistic endeavor, requiring diligence, sacrifice, and dedication to a new way of thinking, a new way of acting, a new way of speaking; in truth, an entirely new way of life. This is what Paul meant when he said that "we must through much tribulation enter into the kingdom of God."[1025]

This refining process is what separates the wheat (the dedicated) from the chaff (the insincere), proving ourselves worthy of entrance into this most sacred realm[1026]—one that was so important to Jesus that He dedicated the majority of His teachings to it.[1027]

Indeed, totally giving up one's old life to the Great I AM Presence within[1028] is the only way to attain the Kingdom and realize our divinity. It is the equivalent of an inner revolution of body, mind, and spirit, in which our former unspiritual life (which was led by the Ego or "Satan") is "killed" off, replaced by a brand new life in Christ (led by the Divine Mind or "God").

In mystical Christianity this transition is symbolized in the image of the crucifixion of the selfish atheistic "I," the Ego, on the cross: we figuratively "kill off" our old egocentric life and its leader the Human Mind, and substitute it with a spiritcentric life headed by the Divine Mind.[1029] Psychologically, this is what Jesus meant by the following:

> "Whosoever will come after me, let him deny himself, and take up his cross, and follow me. For whosoever will save his [ego-centered] life shall lose it; but whosoever shall lose his [ego-centered] life for my sake and the gospel's [of the Kingdom of God], the same shall save it. For what shall it profit a man, if he shall gain the whole world [materially], and lose his own soul [that is, lose touch with his own Indwelling Christ]?"[1030]

If you are serious about entering the Kingdom of God, the Realm of Divine Mind, you must follow the Indwelling Christ.[1031] This means forfeiting your former Ego-guided life for a new Spirit-led life; for the vain, shallow, dualistic Ego (which sees itself as being separate from God) is little more than conceit and narcissism, the opposite of the all-giving Father. "Vanity of vanities, saith the preacher; all is vanity."[1032]

In his second letter, the Apostle Peter clearly lays out the requirements for entrance into the "everlasting" Inner Kingdom:

> ". . . giving all diligence, add to your faith virtue; and to virtue knowledge; and to knowledge temperance; and to temperance patience; and to patience godliness; and to godliness brotherly kindness; and to brotherly kindness charity. For if these things be in you, and abound, they make you that ye shall neither be barren nor unfruitful in the knowledge [Gnosis] of our Lord Jesus Christ. But he that lacketh these things is [spiritually] blind, and cannot see afar off, and hath forgotten that *he was purged from his old sins.* Wherefore . . . rather, brethren, give diligence to make your calling and election sure: for if ye do these things, ye shall never fall: for so *an entrance shall be ministered unto you abundantly into the everlasting kingdom of our Lord and Saviour Jesus Christ.*"[1033]

Peter tells us that to gain entrance we must strive for the pristine state of consciousness possessed by Jesus Himself: Abraham Consciousness, Moses Consciousness, Cosmic Consciousness, or Christ Consciousness,[1034] a state which *anyone* can attain—if he or she is willing to work at it—due to the Universal Christ Within.[1035]

ONENESS WITH THE "CHRIST WHO LIVETH IN US"
Listen closely. This is the key to your light (enlightenment) and your salvation (well-being).[1036] We must give ourselves over entirely to the Indwelling Christ, our Divine Author and Perfecter,[1037] and we begin this process by "crucifying" (dissolving) the Ego (which Paul called "the flesh"),[1038] a spiritual act that Zen Buddhists refer to as the "great death." As Paul did, we must nail our "I" to the cross[1039] before we can recognize the "Christ who liveth in us."[1040] This is what the Thirteenth Apostle meant when he made the following mystical statement:

> "For to me to live is Christ, and to die is gain."[1041]

The inner meaning:

"To me life is the Indwelling Christ, my Higher Self; thus the death of its opposite, my Lower Self, my Ego, is a victory."[1042]

To "live and die in Christ" requires a complete renewal of the mind, or what Jesus referred to as being spiritually "born again": the "death" of our old consciousness—called the "old man" by Paul[1043]—and the "birth" of a new consciousness—called the "new man" by Paul.[1044] Why is this necessary?

The world around us does not change itself to suit us. We must change ourselves to suit God, Divine Mind! In his letter to the Romans, here is how the Thirteenth Apostle explained it:

> "And *be not conformed to this world* [mass mind]: but *be ye transformed by the renewing of your mind*, that ye may prove what is that good, and acceptable, and perfect, will of God."[1045]

Once we have "renewed our mind" by the "crucifixion" of our Lower Self on the spiritual cross, that part of us "dies." We have truly "overcome the Wicked One," as John put it.[1046] Our Higher Self is then "risen" and brought under the protection of the Divine Mind. Thus, Barnabas gave us this mystical statement: "Blessed are they who put their trust in the cross."[1047]

Here is how Paul phrased this concept in the flowery language of my cousin, the Medieval King James:

> "If ye then be risen with Christ, seek those things which are above, where Christ sitteth on the right hand of God. Set your affection on things above [on the Higher Self], not on things on the earth [on the Lower Self]. For ye [your Egos] are dead, and your life is hid with [the Indwelling] Christ in God [Divine Mind]."[1048]

Isaiah gave us this message about mental renewal, also contrasting the Lower Self with the Higher Self:

> "Seek ye the Lord [Divine Mind] while he may be found, call ye upon him while he is near: let the wicked forsake his way, and the unrighteous man his thoughts: and let him return unto the Lord, and he will have mercy upon him; and to our God, for he will abundantly pardon. 'For my [the Higher Self's] thoughts are not your [the Lower Self's] thoughts, neither are your ways my ways,' saith the Lord. 'For as the heavens are higher than the earth, so are

my ways higher than your ways, and my thoughts than your thoughts.'"[1049]

## THE PROBLEM WITH THE EGO

Until we have achieved total Christ Consciousness, we must renew our mind on a daily basis. Why? In great part, this is due to our old negative programming, harmful ideas instilled in our minds over many years by the mass mind. These destructive beliefs, stored in our Subconscious, have become so deeply embedded that only by repeated effort (right-thinking, right-speaking, and right action)[1050] can we eliminate them.[1051]

But there is another reason we need to refresh our minds everyday, as well: the persistent and stubborn nature of the Ego. Our Ego cannot imagine earthly life without itself, for being "Satanic" it is self-centered, self-assertive, self-absorbed, and self-interested, and being dualistic it perceives itself as an independent god in its own right—completely separate from God the Father.

Being innately irresponsible, our Ego cannot tolerate the idea that we are responsible for everything that happens to us. Seeing itself as pitiable, isolated, downtrodden, sad, and contemptible, it feels unworthy of all the good things in life, such as perfect health, wealth, and happiness. Perceiving itself as inadequate, guilt-ridden, insecure, and pessimistic, it fabricates feelings of low self-esteem in order to confirm its own poor self image.

Knowing that it is mortal and that it will pass into nothingness when our God-Self sheds our physical body,[1052] our Ego fears death above all. Finally, and most damaging to us, there is the Ego's belief that being tiny, weak, powerless, and insignificant, it must utterly reject Jesus' teaching that we are gods, with access to all of the same powers as the Father.[1053]

So our Ego-Self, our human spirit, fights our God-Self, the Holy Spirit, at every turn, constantly struggling to combat Divine principles, Divine teachings, Divine Truth, putting as much distance between itself and the Almighty as possible. This is the true meaning of Paul's often misunderstood statement:

"For the wages of sin is death, but the gift of God is eternal life through Jesus Christ our Lord."[1054]

The inner meaning:

"The 'payment' we receive for wrong thought, wrong speech, and wrong action—that is, living from out of the Lower Self or Ego—is separation from the Divine Mind. But those who live from out of the Indwelling Christ—that is, the Higher Self—are rewarded with permanent oneness with the Divine Mind, where anything and everything is possible."[1055]

It is little wonder that the ancients referred to the powerful and voracious human Ego esoterically as the "Devil," "Satan," "Lucifer," and the "Adversary." It represents the "bad guy" in the archetypal battle between good and evil, light and darkness, that is at the heart of so many books, films, plays, TV shows, poems, operas, computer games, and songs.

Paul often spoke of this eternal conflict between the Ego/Lower Self, or what he called the "outward man," and the Christ/Higher Self, or what he termed the "inward man":[1056]

"For I know that in me (that is, in my flesh [Lower Self],) dwelleth no good thing: for to will is present with me; but how to perform that which is good I find not. For the good that I would I do not: but the evil which I would not, that I do. Now if I do that I would not, it is no more I that do it, but sin that dwelleth in me. I find then a law, that, when I would do good, evil is present with me.

"For I delight in the law of God after the *inward man* [Higher Self]: but I see another law in my members [body], warring against the law of my mind [Conscious Mind], and bringing me into captivity to the law of sin which is in my members. O wretched man that I am! who shall deliver me from the body of this death [that is, spiritual separation from Divine Mind]? I thank God through Jesus Christ our Lord [that is, for the Indwelling Christ or Higher Self]. So then with the mind [Conscious Mind] I myself serve the law of God [Divine Mind]; but with the flesh [Ego/Lower Self] the law of sin [wrong-thinking]."[1057]

With your new understanding of the human Ego, read the following statement by Peter:

"Be sober, be vigilant; because your adversary the devil, as a roaring lion, walketh about, seeking whom he may devour."[1058]

Acclaimed motivational author and speaker Dr. Wayne Dyer teaches that Ego is an acronym for "Edging God out," and he is correct. And it is for this reason that we must "crucify" it everyday, pushing back the human (the "outward man") to make way for the divine ("inward man").

## PUTTING NEW WINE INTO NEW BOTTLES

Now you know what Paul meant when he said "in Jesus Christ our Lord, I die daily,"[1059] and "for thy sake we are killed all the day long."[1060] Indeed, as the Lower Self (connected with our physical body) decreases in power, the Higher Self (connected with our spiritual body) increases in power, as the saint tells us in his second letter to the Corinthians:

> "For which cause we faint not; but though our outward man perish, yet the inward man is renewed day by day."[1061]

And in his letter to his followers at Ephesus, Paul says:

> "That ye put off concerning the former conversation the old man [the old consciousness of your Lower Self], which is corrupt according to the deceitful lusts; and be renewed in the spirit of your mind ["the Mind of Christ"]; and that ye put on the new man [the new consciousness of your Higher Self], which after God [Divine Mind] is created in righteousness and true holiness."[1062]

In order to gain membership into the Kingdom, you must not only "renew your mind" and "put on the new man" that is created in God's image,[1063] you must also be willing to leave behind everyone who is not ready to embark on their own inner journey. But whoever accepts you, also accepts the Holy Christ Within, and whoever accepts the Holy Christ Within accepts the Father, Divine Mind, as well. So saith our Lord Jesus, who, as He so often did, speaks here as the Indwelling Christ:

> "Whosoever therefore shall confess me [the Indwelling Christ] before men, him will I confess also before my Father which is in heaven [Divine Mind]. But whosoever shall deny me before men, him will I also deny before my Father which is in heaven. Think not that I am come to send peace on earth: I came not to send peace, but a sword. For I am come to set a man at variance against his father, and the daughter against her mother, and the daughter in law against her mother in law. And a man's foes shall be they of his own household.
>
> "He that loveth father or mother more than me is not worthy of me [the Indwelling Christ]: and he that loveth son or daughter more than me is not worthy of me. And he that taketh

not his cross [does not crucify his Ego], and followeth after me, is not worthy of me [will never achieve oneness with the Christ Within].

"He that findeth his life shall lose it [he who tries to preserve his Ego will be miserable]: and he that loseth his life for my sake shall find it [he who "kills" his Ego for the purpose of attaining "the mind of Christ" will be happy]. He that receiveth [accepts] you receiveth me, and he that receiveth me receiveth him that sent me [God, Divine Mind]."[1064]

As Jesus notes, this process of violently overthrowing the Ego, the "old man," the old ways of thinking, in order to enter the Kingdom was actually well-known at one time, particularly during the 1st Century, the period in which He lived on earth:

"And from the days of John the Baptist until now the kingdom of heaven suffereth violence, and the violent take it by force."[1065]

Still, this type of complete crisis of consciousness, that is, "putting on the new man," is necessary for entrance into the Kingdom, as Jesus states:

"No man putteth a piece of new cloth unto an old garment, for that which is put in to fill it up taketh from the garment, and the rent is made worse. Neither do men put new wine into old bottles: else the bottles break, and the wine runneth out, and the bottles perish: but they put new wine into new bottles, and both are preserved."[1066]

The inner meaning:

"No sane person tries to fit a new concept into an outdated belief system, for it will only weaken the belief system further. Or put another way, a low consciousness thought cannot be contained in a high consciousness mind, and a high consciousness thought cannot be contained in a low consciousness mind. In other words, in order to enter the Kingdom of Divine Mind, one must become spiritually enlightened, which requires discarding the old unspiritual ways of thinking."[1067]

In the Aquarian Gospel Jesus puts it this way:

"Old wine may be preserved in ancient skins; but new wine calls
for bottles new. This spirit-truth I bring is to this generation new,
and if we put it in the ancient skins of [fundamentalist, orthodox]
Jewish forms, lo, it will all be lost. It must expand; the ancient
bottles cannot yield and they would burst. Behold the kingdom of
the Christ! it is as old as God himself, and yet it is as new as
morning sun; it only can contain the truth of God."[1068]

## NONCONFORMITY & THE KINGDOM OF HEAVEN

Of course, not everyone is interested in putting "new wine into new
bottles," of forcefully overturning their Ego, their old patterns of thinking,
their entire worldview. When one embarks on the road less traveled, the
individual path to Godhood, it takes a fearless and totally committed
nonconformist, one who understands that this lonely and sometimes perilous
inner journey leads to a paradise of splendor and unfathomable rewards.
For:

"Eye hath not seen, nor ear heard, neither have entered into the
heart of man, the things which God hath prepared for them that
love him."[1069]

Who then would not look forward to drinking the "new wine" with Jesus in
the Father's Kingdom?[1070]

Sadly, as is the case today, in Jesus' time many Christians were
conformists who much preferred being part of a collective group, one in
which they could remain spiritually unconscious, while their pastor
interpreted scripture for them and told them what to think, what to say, and
what to do.

Thus, though Jesus invited everyone to enter the Kingdom of God
and discover the stunning self-creative powers of the Law of Attraction for
themselves, very few take Him up on the offer. Fear, apathy, the mass
mind, and the herd mentality make it much easier for the average Christian
to remain part of his church group instead of striking out on his own—which
is what Jesus and the Kingdom require. "Be not conformed to this world,"
said Paul.[1071] For when it comes to the Spirit, conformity is death,
individualism is life! One of our most enlightened Transcendentalists, Ralph
Waldo Emerson, wrote:

"Do not go where the path may lead, go instead where there is no
path and leave a trail."

GOD LOVES INDIVIDUALS!

If you want to please God, care not what others think. Do not imitate anyone, ignore societal trends. Instead, think for yourself, develop your own style, your own philosophies, your own views. You are here to discover yourself, your divinity, and to forge your own road toward oneness with God, whatever you image Him/Her/It to be. New Thought leader Prentice Mulford once said:

> "In the spiritual life every person is his or her own discoverer, and you need not grieve if your discoveries are not believed by others."

Jesus was the world's ultimate independent thinker and nonconformist, one who not only refused to be squeezed into the rigid mold of either traditional religion or society, but who taught that each person is a completely unique god or goddess,[1072] imbued with their own divine powers.[1073] No wonder both His conformist critics and even His close friends thought He was a madman, possessed by the Devil![1074]

Jesus dealt with the social consequences of His nonconformity by spending as much time in solitude as He could, away from the bustling towns, far from the madding crowds and the needy crush of His many followers.[1075] Here is how the Master answered the question: should we conform to religion and society or not?

> "Enter ye in at the strait gate: for wide is the gate, and broad is the way, that leadeth to destruction, and many there be which go in thereat: Because strait is the gate, and narrow is the way, which leadeth unto life, and few there be that find it."[1076]

The modern inner interpretation:

> "There are two gates before you: one leading to the Kingdom of Heaven, the other to the Kingdom of Hell. Which one will you choose? I am asking you to choose the gate to the Kingdom of Heaven. But few of you will do so, for the entranceway to the Kingdom of Heaven is narrow and uncomfortable, and its pathway is cluttered with obstacles; meaning that in order to get in, you will have to undergo an inner and sometimes painful personal trial that completely changes your consciousness. Thus, most of you will choose the gate to the Kingdom of Hell, because its entranceway is wide and its pathway is open and clear; meaning that, because there is no change of consciousness required, it is much easier to get in.

> But be forewarned: the comfortable path to the Kingdom of Hell
> leads to personal misery!"[1077]

The gate of the Kingdom of Heaven is so narrow that we must go through single file, one person at a time. Yet the gate of the Kingdom of Hell is so wide that an entire group of people can go through at once. The former gate is for individualists and nonconformists, the latter gate is for groups and conformists!

## WHO IS MOST LIKELY TO ENTER THE KINGDOM OF GOD?

It is precisely because of the difficultly of entering the Kingdom of Heaven that the poor, the downtrodden, the sick, the humble, the simple, the modest, the uneducated, the traumatized, the undesirable, the inferior, the injured, the unrighteous, the unpopular, the lonely, and the pariahs of society are most likely to seek entrance. They have much less to lose and much more to gain than the rich, the powerful, the healthy, the self-sufficient, the righteous, the educated, and the popular members of society. Thus Jesus said:

> "Blessed are the poor in spirit: for theirs is the kingdom of heaven.
> . . . Blessed are they which are persecuted for righteousness' sake:
> for theirs is the kingdom of heaven."[1078]

The Lord was very well aware that the lowliest would enter the Kingdom of God before the most honored of society (in Jesus' day, the fundamentalist Pharisees):

> Jesus saith unto them, "Verily I say unto you, that the publicans [tax collectors] and the harlots [sex workers] go into the kingdom of God before you."[1079]

Indeed, God's radical Kingdom turns the normal world upside down:

> "But many that are first shall be last; and the last shall be first."[1080]

For preaching the truth about theosis, that is, the doctrine of God in Man, a teaching from what He referred to as "the Gospel of the Kingdom," Jesus was called a "blasphemer" and a "heretic," and put to death by the Sanhedrin at Jerusalem under the auspices of the reluctant Pagan procurator of Judea, Pontius Pilate. Just as with so many modern Christians, Jews, and Pagans today, Jesus' ancient enemies could not understand that His "Kingdom" was not physical. It was spiritual, that is mental; a state of consciousness that Paul knew as "the mind of Christ." Those who delve into this mystical doctrine—and understand it and practice it—will receive all the benefits of the Law of Attraction, or what Paul called "the reward of the inheritance": a life of freedom, joy, abundance, and health, just as the Lord promised.

# 14

# ENTERING THE KINGDOM OF GOD
## Part 2

"For ever, O Lord, thy word is settled in heaven. Thy faithfulness is unto all generations: thou hast established the earth, and it abideth."[1081]

## THE KINGDOM WITHIN

IT IS CLEAR THAT THE Father, Divine Mind, did not create His kingdom, the Kingdom of God, for groups, churches, or religions. And it is for this very fact that you will never hear this truth being advocated from the pulpit at Sunday School!

Yet, Paul understood this truth, which is why he preached against the formation of "strife [partisanship], seditions [divisions], and heresies [following the beliefs of the Ego/Satan]," assuring us that "they which do such things shall not inherit the kingdom of God."[1082]

Just as importantly, the Kingdom is not understandable through the intellect,[1083] it is not set in the future, and it is not located anywhere on the physical plane, as we have been wrongly taught. The Kingdom of God was designed strictly for the individual, it exists in the here and now, and it must be discovered through self-reflection. Why? Because, as Jesus said:

"The Kingdom of God is *within* you."[1084]

Little wonder that the Kingdom goes completely unnoticed by most people: like God Himself, it is immanent and invisible.[1085] It is so seemingly inconsequential, even to many Christian authorities, that Jesus compared it to two of the world's smallest and most humble objects, a mustard seed and a grain of bread yeast:

> "Unto what is the kingdom of God like? and whereunto shall I resemble it? It is like a grain of mustard seed, which a man took, and cast into his garden; and it grew, and waxed a great tree; and the fowls of the air lodged in the branches of it. . . . Whereunto shall I liken the kingdom of God? It is like leaven [yeast], which a woman took and hid in three measures of meal, till the whole was leavened."[1086]

Though, because it is not perceptible to human eyes the Kingdom seems insignificant to many, Jesus teaches us that it is so important that we are to try and obtain it before and above all other things: "Seek ye first the kingdom of God."[1087] And here, according to the Master, is why:

> "Verily I say unto you, there is no man that hath left house, or parents, or brethren, or wife, or children, for the kingdom of God's sake, who shall not receive manifold more in this present time, and in the world to come life everlasting."[1088]

## REQUIREMENTS FOR ENTRANCE
The reality is that as simple as following the Law of Attraction is, Jesus said that we must inwardly transform ourselves in order to enter the Realm of Divine Mind and successfully manifest our affirmations:

> "Verily, verily, I say unto thee, except a man be born again, he cannot see the kingdom of God."[1089]

What does it mean to be "born again"? Jesus answered the question in the following cryptic manner:

> "Verily I say unto you, except ye be converted, and become as little children, ye shall not enter into the kingdom of heaven."[1090]

What did He mean by this, and why is "becoming as little children" vital to working with the Law of Attraction?

## CHURCHIANITY VS. CHRISTIANITY

Everyday society, known as mass mind, has programmed us with a host of negative beliefs. "Money doesn't grow on trees," "to the victor go the spoils," "it's a dog-eat-dog world," and "life is not a bowl of cherries," are just a few of the damaging sayings that most of us been exposed to. Many religiocentric Christian churches have contributed greatly as well by forcing us to abandon independent thinking for group thought, self-revelation for authoritarian doctrine, and high self-esteem for low self-esteem.

In many cases we have been asked to substitute Jesus' teachings for manmade teachings, fabricated or mistranslated concepts that are not found in the Bible[1091]—further weakening the laity's already poor biblical literacy rate.[1092]  Sadly, often these false teachings have nothing to do with spirituality (the entire focus of Jesus' teachings) and everything to do with Church finances, membership, and politics.

Perhaps worst of all, many bibliolatrous clergymen and women assert that every word in the Good Book must be accepted literally, including obviously mythological stories that even Paul said were meant to be read symbolically, that is as "allegories," not historical fact.[1093]

Along with this, much of institutional Christianity has become little more than "Churchianity," with all of the emphasis on traditionally accepted religious rules, regulations, formalities, ceremonies, pomp, instruction, rites, and customs.  Here, God is not "within" us, as Jesus taught in His "Gospel of the Kingdom,"[1094] but dwells externally in some far off region of space, only answering our prayers if and when we obey the rules of our particular church.  Here also the symbols of scripture are approached noetically and studied intellectually, but the original spiritual meaning behind them is completely ignored, thus leaving a spiritual void in the heart and soul.

Mainstream Christianity's rule-based approach to religion goes completely against Jesus' teachings, not only on the Law of Attraction, but concerning spirituality as a whole.  As Paul said to his followers at Galatia, it is not by "works" that we achieve at-one-ment (perfect union) with God, it is through "faith" (belief) in the Indwelling Christ:

> "Knowing that a man is not justified by the works of the law, but by the faith of Jesus Christ, even we have believed in Jesus Christ, that we might be justified by the faith of Christ, and not by the works of the law: for by the works of the law shall no flesh be justified."[1095]

The academic, literalized, formalized, Paganesque conception of Christianity has left many people emotionally jaded, intellectually asleep, and spiritually dead,[1096] for our modern day Christian "Pharisees" honor Jesus with words only, but their hearts are far from Him. They have "made the word of God of none effect through their tradition . . . teaching for doctrines the commandments of men" instead of the Father's.[1097] Paul said of the Pharisees of his own day:

> "For they being ignorant of God's righteousness, and going about to establish their own righteousness, have not submitted themselves unto the righteousness of God."[1098]

This, along with the cynical, know-it-all attitude of so many believers today, is scarcely recognizable as spiritual let alone Christian. Einstein commented on this type of person when he said:

> "The intuitive mind [Subconscious Mind] is a sacred gift and the rational mind is a faithful servant [Conscious Mind]. We have created a society that honors the servant and has forgotten the gift."

Yes, the Pharisees of Jesus' day are still alive and well in the Christian Church, and the spiritually "blind" men and women who follow them will, as the Lord said, all fall into the same ditch together.[1099]

THE PHARISEES
Who were the Pharisees? A strict Jewish sect that flourished in the Roman Empire, they focused almost solely on the externals of religion rather than on the internals of spirituality. Thus, while they earnestly followed every rule in detail and knew every religious regulation by heart, they were deficient in the truly important things of God: love, compassion, and faith.[1100]

They taught that striving to be moral and righteous through obedience to manmade religious doctrines leads to happiness, health, and prosperity. But the truth is that following churchly regulations alone never achieves anything except confusion and unhappiness, which is why Jesus was so against the formulaic, literalistic, fundamentalist, paint-by-numbers approach to spirituality. Due to the Law of Attraction, only right-thinking, positive thinking, creative thinking, faithful thinking, can produce the life that we really want, and this is totally lacking in the censorious pseudorighteousness of the Pharisaic style religion!

Several Bible stories are instructive.

Whenever Jesus healed on the Jewish Sabbath (Saturday), the Pharisees viciously attacked Him, threatening to take His life for breaking Holy Law. Jesus ignored both the rule and its inflexible enforcers, rightly saying: "My Father works continuously, and so must I."[1101] On another occasion, when Jesus' hungry Disciples plucked ears of corn from a field on the Sabbath, the Pharisees grew angry, saying:

> "Behold, thy disciples do that which is not lawful to do upon the sabbath day." But he [Jesus] said unto them, "Have ye not read what David did, when he was an hungred, and they that were with him; how he entered into the house of God [the Jerusalem Temple], and did eat the [special sacramental] shewbread, which was not lawful for him to eat, neither for them which were with him, but only for the priests?
>
> "Or have ye not read in the law, how that on the sabbath days the priests in the temple profane the sabbath, and are blameless? But I say unto you, that in this place is one greater than the temple. But if ye had known what this [Old Testament scripture] meaneth, 'I will have mercy, and not sacrifice,' ye would not have condemned the guiltless. For the Son of man [the human being] is Lord even of the sabbath day."[1102]

In the Gospel of Matthew, Jesus phrased the problem with the Pharisees this way:

> "Woe unto you, scribes [the Pharisees' scripture copyists] and Pharisees, hypocrites! for ye pay tithe of mint and anise and cummin, and have omitted the weightier matters of the law [namely], judgment, mercy, and faith: these ought ye to have done, and not to leave the other undone."[1103]

In the Aquarian Gospel Jesus makes a similar comment:

> "He who hearkens unto God and keeps his law and does his will on earth, shall rule with Christ. The scribes and Pharisees regard the *letter* of the law; they cannot comprehend the *spirit* of the law; . . . It is not what man does that gives him right to enter through the gates; his pass word is his character and his desire is his character. The letter of the law deals with the acts of man; the spirit of the law takes note of his desires."[1104]

In the same book we find this fascinating story, in which the Lord once again upbraids the overly ritualistic Pharisees:

A company of scribes and Pharisees came from Jerusalem to learn wherein the power of Jesus lay. But when they learned that he and his disciples heeded not the custom of the Jews, regarding washing of the hands before they ate, they were amazed. And Jesus said, "Hypocrisy is queen among you scribes and Pharisees. . . . You men who pose as men of God, and still reject the laws of God and teach the laws of men, stand forth and tell [us] when God gave unto men the ceremonial laws that you observe; and tell these people how the spirit life is sullied if one washes not before he eats."

His critics answered not, and then he said, "Hear me, you men of Israel! Defilement is a creature of the heart. The carnal mind lays hold of thought, and makes a monstrous bride; this bride is sin; sin is a creature of the mind. That which defiles a man is not the food he eats. The bread and fish and other things we eat, are simply cups to carry to the cells of flesh material for the building of the human house, and when their work is done as refuse they are cast away. The life of plant and flesh that goes to build the human house is never food for soul. The spirit does not feed upon the carcasses of animal, or plant.

"God feeds the soul direct from heaven; the bread of life comes from above. The air we breathe is charged with Holy Breath, and he who wills may take this Holy Breath. The soul discriminates, and he who wants the life of Christ may breathe it in. According to your faith so let it be. Man is not a part of his abiding place [physical body]; the house is not the man. The lower world builds up the house of flesh, and keeps it in repair; the higher world provides the bread of spirit life. The loveliest lilies grow from stagnant ponds and filthiest muck. The law of flesh demands that one should keep the body clean. The law of spirit calls for purity in thought and word and deed."[1105]

Jesus gives His most famous and fiery anti-Pharisee sermon in the Gospel of Matthew:

Then spake Jesus to the multitude, and to his disciples, saying, "The scribes and the Pharisees sit in Moses' seat: all therefore whatsoever they bid you observe, that observe and do; but do not ye after their works: for they say, and do not. For they bind heavy burdens and grievous to be borne, and lay them on men's shoulders; but they themselves will not move them with one of their fingers. But all their works they do for to be seen of men: they make broad their phylacteries, and enlarge the borders of their garments, and love the uppermost rooms at feasts, and the chief seats in the synagogues, and greetings in the markets, and to be called of men, 'Rabbi, Rabbi.'

"But be not ye called Rabbi: for one is your Master, even [the Indwelling] Christ; and all ye are brethren. And call no man your father upon the earth: for one is your Father [Divine Mind], which is in heaven. Neither be ye called masters: for one is your Master, even Christ. But he that is greatest among you shall be your servant. And whosoever shall exalt himself shall be abased; and he that shall humble himself shall be exalted.

"But woe unto you, scribes and Pharisees, hypocrites! for ye shut up the kingdom of heaven against men: for ye neither go in yourselves, neither suffer ye them that are entering to go in. Woe unto you, scribes and Pharisees, hypocrites! for ye devour widows' houses, and for a pretence make long prayer: therefore ye shall receive the greater damnation. Woe unto you, scribes and Pharisees, hypocrites! for ye compass sea and land to make one proselyte, and when he is made, ye make him twofold more the child of hell than yourselves.

"Woe unto you, ye blind guides, which say, 'Whosoever shall swear by the temple, it is nothing; but whosoever shall swear by the gold of the temple, he is a debtor!' Ye fools and blind: for whether is greater, the gold, or the temple that sanctifieth the gold? And, whosoever shall swear by the altar, it is nothing; but whosoever sweareth by the gift that is upon it, he is guilty. Ye fools and blind: for whether is greater, the gift, or the altar that sanctifieth the gift?

"Whoso therefore shall swear by the altar, sweareth by it, and by all things thereon. And whoso shall swear by the temple, sweareth by it, and by him that dwelleth therein. And he that shall swear by heaven, sweareth by the throne of God, and by him that sitteth thereon. . . . Ye blind guides, which strain at a gnat [in your drinks], and swallow a camel.

"Woe unto you, scribes and Pharisees, hypocrites! for ye make clean the outside of the cup and of the platter, but within they are full of extortion and excess. Thou blind Pharisee, cleanse first that which is within the cup and platter, that the outside of them may be clean also. Woe unto you, scribes and Pharisees, hypocrites! for ye are like unto whited sepulchres, which indeed appear beautiful outward, but are within full of dead men's bones, and of all uncleanness. Even so ye also outwardly appear righteous unto men, but within ye are full of hypocrisy and iniquity.

"Woe unto you, scribes and Pharisees, hypocrites! because ye build the tombs of the prophets, and garnish the sepulchres of the righteous, and say, 'If we had been in the days of our fathers, we would not have been partakers with them in the blood of the prophets.' Wherefore ye be witnesses unto yourselves, that ye are the children of them which killed the prophets. Fill ye up then the measure of your fathers. Ye serpents, ye generation of vipers, how can ye escape the damnation of hell?

"Wherefore, behold, I send unto you prophets, and wise men, and scribes: and some of them ye shall kill and crucify; and some of them shall ye scourge in your synagogues, and persecute them from city to city: that upon you may come all the righteous blood shed upon the earth, from the blood of righteous Abel unto the blood of Zacharias son of Barachias, whom ye slew between the temple and the altar.

"Verily I say unto you, all these things shall come upon this generation. O Jerusalem, Jerusalem, thou that killest the prophets, and stonest them which are sent unto thee, how often would I have gathered thy children together, even as a hen gathereth her chickens under her wings, and ye would not! Behold, your house is left unto you desolate."[1106]

As the following passages from the Aquarian Gospel show, Jesus' unsparing attack on the Pharisees was so severe that it made Peter afraid for his Master's life:

And Peter said, "Lord, what you said today has grievously offended scribe and Pharisee." And Jesus said, "These scribes and Pharisees are not the scions of the tree of life; *they are not plants of God; they are the plants of men*, and every foreign plant shall be plucked up. Let all these men alone; they are blind guides; they lead a multitude of people who are blind. The leaders and the led together walk; together they will fall into the yawning pits."[1107]

## SPIRITUALITY VS. RELIGIOSITY

It is clear from these stories and parables that as a result of their overly structured belief system, the ancient Jewish Pharisees were religious rather than spiritual, Self-righteous rather than God-righteous. Along with this, they emphasized the letter of the Law over the spirit of the Law, reason over intuition, intellect over self-awareness, form over substance, Ego over selflessness, and the personal, physical, transcendent, anthropomorphic God of the Old Testament over the impersonal, incorporeal, immanent, pneumamorphic God of Jesus.

They, like so many Christians today, had fallen under the spell of idolatry.[1108] They had "imagined a vain thing,"[1109] and worshiped a "dumb idol,"[1110] a "god wrought out by hands of man."[1111] And yet the Master told us:

> "God is Spirit: and they that worship him must worship him in spirit and in truth."[1112]

Unlike many modern Christians, this is precisely what the earliest Christians did: "We . . . worship God in spirit," said Paul.[1113] Hence, he taught his followers this important truth:

> "Forasmuch then as we are the offspring of God, we ought not to think that the Godhead is like unto gold, or silver, or stone, graven by art and man's device."[1114]

As for the Pharisaic literalization of the Good Book, a biblicistic practice more popular now than ever before, Paul said that God

> "hath made us able ministers of the new testament; not of the letter, but of the spirit: for *the letter killeth, but the spirit giveth life.*"[1115]

And it was the Victorian American clergyman Henry Ward Beecher who once proclaimed:

> "Whoever believes that churches, or books, or institutions, or customs, are more valuable than men is a Pharisee."

## SPIRITUAL JESUS VS. THE RELIGIOUS PHARISEES

It is little wonder that the *religious* Pharisees opposed the *spiritual* Jesus, or that he opposed them in return: Jesus represented the Kingdom of God (the Realm of Divine Mind) while the Pharisees represented the Kingdom of Satan (the Realm of Human Mind, or Ego).[1116]

This is why Paul rightly called those who belonged to the latter kingdom spiritual "castaways,"[1117] it is why John called them "children of the devil,"[1118] and it is why Peter referred to them as "beguiling unstable souls," "wells without water," and "clouds that are carried with a tempest."[1119]

As we have just seen, Jesus did not spare the fundamentalist

Pharisees either, often referring to them by a myriad of derogatory names and phrases, including: "hypocrites," "fools," "blind guides," "serpents," "whited sepulchres," "generation of vipers," and "children of the Devil," among other things.[1120] Of such overly strict religionists, Paul made this observation:

> "Having the understanding darkened, being alienated from the life of God through the ignorance that is in them, because of the blindness of their heart . . ."[1121]

Another group of scriptures from the Aquarian Gospel is illuminating. Here Jesus issues a warning to His followers concerning the manmade rules-obsessed Pharisees and their rigid unspiritual approach to God:

> "Be on your guard; the leaven [false ideas] of the Pharisees [that is, any and all formalistic religionists] is being thrown in every measure of the meal of life. It is a poison that will taint whatever it may touch; and it will blight the soul as sure as fumes of the Diabolos [the Devil]; it is hypocrisy. The Pharisees seem fair in speech, but they are diabolical in heart. And then they seem to think that thought is something they can lock within themselves. They do not seem to know that every thought and wish is photographed and then preserved within the Book of Life to be revealed at any time the masters will.
>
> "That which is thought, or wished, or done in darkest night shall be proclaimed in brightest day; that which is whispered in the ear within the secret place shall be made known upon the streets. And in the judgment day when all the books are opened up, these men, and every other man, shall be a-judged, not by what they've said or done, but by the way in which they used the thoughts of God, and how the ethers of eternal love were made to serve; for men may make these ethers serve the carnal self, or serve the holy self within."[1122]

## THE KINGDOM OF GOD VS. THE KINGDOM OF SATAN

In the following passages Paul highlights the differences between the Kingdom of God and the Kingdom of Satan, emphasizing the fact that those who enter into the latter "shall not inherit" the former:

> "For the flesh [Lower Self] lusteth against the Spirit [Higher Self], and the Spirit against the flesh: and these are contrary the one to

the other: so that ye cannot do the things that ye would. But if ye
be led of the Spirit, ye are not under the [obsolete] law [of Moses].

"Now the works of the flesh [Lower Self] are manifest,
which are these; adultery, fornication, uncleanness, lasciviousness,
idolatry, sorcery, hatred, variance, emulations, wrath, strife,
seditions, heresies, envyings, murders, drunkenness, revellings,
and such like: of the which I tell you before, as I have also told you
in time past, that *they which do such things shall not inherit the kingdom
of God.*

"But *the fruit of the Spirit* [Higher Self] *is love, joy, peace,
longsuffering, gentleness, goodness, faith, meekness, temperance*: against
such there is no law. And they that are [the Indwelling] Christ's
have crucified the flesh [the Ego] with the affections and lusts. If
we live in the Spirit, let us also walk in the Spirit. Let us not be
desirous of vain glory, provoking one another, envying one
another."[1123]

What is important here is that Jesus taught that if we think like the
vain, formalistic, glory-loving Pharisees, we cannot "enter the Kingdom of
Heaven," for our minds will be too encrusted with preconceived religious
notions to fully grasp the many highly spiritual, and often radical, aspects of
the Law of Attraction. In the Gospel of Matthew, Jesus was very clear on
this point:

"For I say unto you, that *except your righteousness shall exceed the
righteousness of the scribes and Pharisees, ye shall in no case enter into the
kingdom of heaven.*"[1124]

Here is the inner meaning of this scripture:

"I am telling you that unless your thinking surpasses the narrow,
formalized, materialistic thinking of those who call themselves
'traditional Christians,' you will in no way be able to enter the
Realm of the Divine Mind and work efficiently with the Law of
Attraction."[1125]

This is why the Master made the following comment in Luke:

"I thank thee, O Father, Lord of heaven and earth, that thou hast
hid these things from the [so-called] wise and prudent [that is, the
people regarded as 'religious authorities'], and hast revealed them
unto babes [those with open, receptive, childlike minds]: even so,

Father; for so it seemed good in thy sight."[1126]

Jesus noted that the wealthy will also tend to have trouble entering the Kingdom. Not because they are affluent, but because a man or woman with material riches is more likely to become too focused on affairs of the physical rather than the spiritual:[1127]

> "Children, how hard is it for them that trust in riches to enter into the kingdom of God! It is easier for a camel to go through the eye of a needle, than for a rich man to enter into the kingdom of God."[1128]

## THE CHILDLIKE MIND

The solution to overcoming the unbending Pharisaic mindset, Jesus said, is to psychologically restore our minds to that of a child,[1129] or what Zen Buddhists call "beginner's mind." For a child's mind is much like our Higher Self, our Divine Self, our Indwelling Christ,[1130] Luke's the "Holy One,"[1131] the Hindus' "Paramatma": it is naturally pure, selfless, open, guilt-free, flexible, guileless, humble, loving, trusting, and enthusiastic. Why? Because children have not yet been mentally sullied by worldly society, by atheistic science, or by dogmatic manmade religion.

False human-invented notions like shortage, famine, illness, poverty, and warfare, are incomprehensible to children. They see only good and think only good. Furthermore, they are so innocent to the ways of the adult world with all of its fictitious preconceived ideas, that they are completely lacking any kind of mental limitations. The word "impossible" does not yet exist in their vocabulary. Being newly arrived from Heaven, where anything is possible through thought alone, a child simply *knows* that whatever he believes is fact. He has not yet been taught otherwise by his parents, school, church, or society.

This is why there is really no such thing as "pretend" to a child. To a youngster, playing make-believe is actually playing real-believe, for whatever he thinks is real or is told is real, is real to him. Mass mind has not yet imbued his Conscious Mind with any sense of mental restriction; nor has it saturated it with the herd mentality, with group-think, with politics, or religion. Thus, the untainted child is a true individualist, a born freethinker, always deciding what is best for himself independently and without self-limitation; always learning and growing without placing any psychic regulations on himself.

A child is indeed a natural "disciple" of God, and in the purest definition of the word: "pupil," "student," "learner." This is precisely why Jesus referred to His followers, not as Christians (a disparaging title first appended to them by the Pagans at Antioch),[1132] but as "disciples."[1133] For one cannot truly follow in Jesus' footsteps without being an eternal student; that is, without having the open, inquisitive, ever expanding mind of "a little child," without which entrance into the Inner Kingdom is barred.[1134] Thus the Lord makes these comments in the Aquarian Gospel:

> Now Jesus heard the twelve [Apostles] dispute among themselves. The spirit of the carnal self [Ego] was moving in their hearts, and they were questioning among themselves who was the greatest in the sight of God and man. And Jesus said, "You men, for shame! the greatest is the servant of the rest."
>
> And then he called to him a little child; he took it in his arms and said, "The greatest is the little child, and if you would be great at all you must become as is this child in innocence, in truth, in purity in life. Great men scorn not the little things of earth; he who regards and honors such a child, regards and honors me, and he who scorns a child, scorn[s] me. If you would enter through the kingdom gate you must be humble as this little child.
>
> "Hear me, you men, this child, as every other child, has one to plead its cause before the throne of God. You scorn it at your peril, men, for lo, I say, its counterpart beholds the face of God at every moment, every day. And hear me once again, he who shall cause a little one to stumble and to fall is marked, accursed; and it were better far if he had drowned himself."[1135]

## THE ADULT MIND

Now contrast the childlike mind with the adult mind, which is much more likely to operate at the level of the Lower Self, the false self, the Hindus' "Jivatma," which Paul called the "outward man,"[1136] and which the Apostle John mystically referred to as "the beast that was, and is not, and yet is."[1137] Having been exposed to decades of low consciousness thought, the adult mind tends to be spiritually contaminated, selfish, closed, inflexible, guileful, unloving, mistrusting, and cynical. A mind like this is severely limited, and therefore cannot think beyond what it has been taught by the mass mind.

The adult mind laughs at games of make-believe, scoffs at anything that cannot be experienced by the five senses. It firmly embraces such false ideas as shortage, famine, illness, crime, privation, and warfare. It easily succumbs to the herd mentality, and likes nothing better than to form cliques, groups, societies, organizations, political bodies, and religions with like-minded people. In the adult world independent thinking is discouraged and individualism is often regarded with something between mild bemusement and outright fear and disdain.

Which do you think is more likely to have success with the Law of Attraction, the child's mind or the adult's mind?

THE IMPORTANCE OF BEING CHILDLIKE

The answer is obvious: the open childlike mind allows God to work with us; the closed adult mind forces God to work against us. Our mind, in fact, is like a garden hose: it functions most efficiently when it is open and free-flowing, the equivalent of a childlike mind. But bend the hose and put a kink in it, and you have blocked the movement of the water, the equivalent of the jaded adult mind.

This is precisely why Peter asked his followers to cast off their adult minds and replace them with that of infants:

> "Wherefore laying aside all malice, and all guile, and hypocrisies, and envies, and all evil speakings, as newborn babes, desire the sincere milk of the word, that ye may grow thereby: if so be ye have tasted that the Lord is gracious."[1138]

The early Christians who wrote the outstanding Gnostic document, The Thunder: Perfect Mind, made a similar if more esoteric statement: "Advance into childhood," they proclaimed![1139]

Because the Kingdom of God is a holy place of complete purity, it is easy to understand why Jesus said we must regain the spiritual mind and conscience of a child before we can enter: a child's mind is completely lacking in the "impurities" of the average adult mind and conscience, for "to spirit everything is clean."[1140] This is what Paul meant when he said:

> "Unto the pure all things are pure: but unto them that are defiled and unbelieving is nothing pure; but even their mind and conscience is defiled."[1141]

In the Aquarian Gospel Jesus put it this way: Abraham Consciousness, Moses Consciousness, Cosmic Consciousness, Buddha Consciousness, Chrishna Consciousness, Christ Consciousness, or the "mind of Christ,"[1142] whatever name we choose to give it,

> "sleeps in every soul, and cannot be awakened till the Holy Breath
> [Holy Spirit] becomes a welcome guest. This Holy Breath knocks
> at the door of every soul, but cannot enter in until the will of man
> throws wide the door. There is no power in intellect to turn the
> key; philosophy and science both have toiled to get a glimpse
> behind the veil; but they have failed. *The secret spring that throws ajar*
> *the door of soul is touched by nothing else than purity in life, by prayer and*
> *holy thought.*"[1143]

It is only the childlike mind, in both children and adults, that can create the
"purity in life" that Jesus speaks of.

Attaining "beginner's mind," the childlike mind, is so important that
our Lord gave us these admonitions in the Gospel of Matthew:

> And Jesus called a little child unto him, and set him in the midst of
> them, and said, "Verily I say unto you, except ye be converted, and
> become as little children, ye shall not enter into the kingdom of
> heaven. Whosoever therefore shall humble himself as this little
> child, the same is greatest in the kingdom of heaven.
> 
> "And whoso shall receive one such little child in my name
> receiveth me. But whoso shall offend one of these little ones which
> believe in me, it were better for him that a millstone were hanged
> about his neck, and that he were drowned in the depth of the sea.
> . . . Take heed that ye despise not one of these little ones; for I say
> unto you, that in heaven their angels [spiritual helpers] do always
> behold the face of my Father [Divine Mind] which is in heaven.
> 
> "For the Son of man is come to save that which was lost.
> How think ye? if a man have an hundred sheep, and one of them be
> gone astray, doth he not leave the ninety and nine, and goeth into
> the mountains, and seeketh that which is gone astray? And if so be
> that he find it, verily I say unto you, he rejoiceth more of that
> sheep, than of the ninety and nine which went not astray. Even so
> it is not the will of your Father which is in heaven, that one of these
> little ones should perish."[1144]

## JESUS WANTS US TO BE FREETHINKING INDIVIDUALS

The childlike mind is also inherently individualistic, an extremely important
attribute, for as we have seen, the group-oriented adult mind is not allowed
entrance into the Kingdom of God. The "gate" is only wide enough to allow
one person through at a time, eliminating "membership" to organizations,

cults, sects, and religions altogether. Thus, only those individuals who have cast off the herd mentality and learned to think and make decisions for themselves are granted access to the Kingdom Within.[1145]

A middle man is not needed for us to connect to God. In fact, the Father prefers direct one-on-one communication with us. This is, after all, why He made the "Way" to His Kingdom difficult and the "gate" at the entrance narrow![1146]

Why is individualism so vital to Jesus' teaching on the Law of Attraction?

God does not dwell within groups of people, organizations, or religions. He dwells within individuals. Thus, in order to copartner with each one of us on the physical plane,[1147] He has to individuate Himself into each one of us. This makes each human being divine in his or her our own right, a personal and unique expression or individualization of the Almighty; the literal embodiment of the Supreme Being on earth. This is why, in fact, Jesus quoted the Old Testament, saying: "You are gods."[1148]

## THE ONE UNFORGIVABLE SIN

This means that speaking out against our individuality, our uniqueness, or anyone else's, is speaking out against our divinity, our Godship, our Indwelling Christ, the very life spark that vivifies us,[1149] and which gives us access to the Divine Mind (the Father).[1150]

Another name for our divine nature[1151] is the Holy Ghost, or "Comforter Within."[1152] Here is what Jesus said about denying the third member of the Godhead:

> "Wherefore I say unto you, all manner of sin and blasphemy shall be forgiven unto men: but the blasphemy against the Holy Ghost shall not be forgiven unto men. And whosoever speaketh a word against the Son of man, it shall be forgiven him: but whosoever speaketh against the Holy Ghost, it shall not be forgiven him, neither in this world, neither in the world to come."[1153]

Jesus is unambiguous: those who blaspheme against Him will be exempted,[1154] but those who blaspheme against the Holy Ghost will be held accountable. Jesus placed our inner divine nature[1155] higher up on the spiritual scale than Himself!

What is the inner meaning of these scriptures? Jesus (the Son of Man) represents the Conscious Mind ("Master"), the mind of the group.

The Holy Ghost (Holy Spirit) represents the Subconscious Mind ("Servant"), the mind of the individual. It is a forgivable sin to disrespect the Conscious Mind, for merely being the *mortal* aspect of man's brain, its sole spiritual task is to think. But to disrespect the Subconscious Mind is unforgivable, for the Subconscious Mind is the *eternal* aspect of man's brain, whose sole spiritual task is to create!

It is, in other words, our Divine Nature, our God-Self, the very essence of the Creator, the Father, individualized in us.[1156] Because of this, if we dishonor it in anyway through wrong-thinking, we only attract more of the same into our lives. Hence, Jesus' warning.

The moral? Respect your individuality, as well as the individuality of others. Ignore the negative thinking trends of the mass mind, for those who follow it "like sheep have gone astray."[1157] Instead, learn to think for yourself! The great German philosopher Arthur Schopenhauer once wrote:

> "We may divide thinkers into those who think for themselves, and those who think through others. The latter are the rule, and the former the exception. The first are original thinkers in a double sense . . . . It is from them only that the world learns wisdom. For only the light which we have kindled in ourselves can illuminate others."

## ONLY THE SOLITARY CAN ENTER THE KINGDOM

Thinking for yourself illuminates the world because you are operating from your real self, the Christ, which is in us all.[1158] Just as importantly, the freethinker honors his divinity, respects the true God Within.[1159] This is the authentic meaning of the phrase "fear the Lord"[1160] or "fear God"[1161] (fear being used here in the Medieval English sense of "respect" or "honor").

Jesus had this to say about the importance of being a freethinking nonconformist like Himself:

> "If any man come to me, and hate not his father, and mother, and wife, and children, and brethren, and sisters, yea, and his own life also, he cannot be my disciple."[1162]

The inner meaning:

> "If one wants to enter the Kingdom Within, he must be willing to think entirely for himself, even ignoring the social and religious beliefs of his entire family and all of his relations; even going as far

as rejecting his own Ego desires; otherwise he will never achieve oneness with the Indwelling Christ."[1163]

In the Gospel of Thomas, Jesus phrases this concept more starkly:

"There are many people standing outside the door of the Kingdom. But *only the solitary will be allowed to enter the chamber of enlightenment.*"[1164]

## YE MUST BE BORN ANEW

There are no clear cut, systematized instructions in the Bible for how an adult is to recover the individualistic mind of a child. We must work it out for ourselves, for it is one of the great psychological "mysteries of the Kingdom of God" that Jesus taught.[1165] In other words, it is a deeply spiritual, intuitive process that cannot be learned via sermons, books, or by any other external means. From our human perspective here on earth, hidden by the veil that separates us from Heaven, we truly "see through a glass, darkly."[1166]

Yet, we know this much: since the Kingdom is within us,[1167] the solution to the riddle must be found within us as well, through inner self-knowledge, or "Gnosis," as some of the first Christians called it.[1168] Paul referred to it as that which "passeth [outer] knowledge."[1169] It is from this, the inner "Divine Library," that Jesus attained His knowledge,[1170] and it is why Paul said that you must "work out your own salvation."[1171] For God made it impossible for us to understand Him, know Him, or become one with Him based on either group knowledge or our own limited human knowledge.[1172]

Remember: while *religion* is an outer group-oriented experience, *spirituality* is an inner individual-oriented one.[1173] Paul, one of the earliest mystical Christians, said:

"But let every man prove his own [spiritual] work, and then shall he have rejoicing *in himself alone*, and not in another."[1174]

The ever enigmatic Jesus did leave us one sibylline clue about being "reborn," however. Let us look once more at the following passage, focusing on the word "again":

"Verily, verily, I say unto thee, except a man be born *again*, he cannot see the kingdom of God."[1175]

The original Greek word here is *anothen*, which is traditionally translated as "again." But another meaning for *anothen* is "anew," so the sentence could also read:

> "Verily, verily, I say unto thee, except a man be born anew [mentally], he cannot enter the Realm of Divine Mind."[1176]

This provides a psychological sense, getting us closer to the truth.

The most accurate translation of *anothen*, however, is "from above, from a higher place." The sentence would then read:

> "Verily, verily, I say unto thee, except a man be born from above, he cannot enter the Realm of Divine Mind."[1177]

The phrase "from above" is an arcane Christian reference to the Higher Self, the immortal preexistent Indwelling Christ[1178] that lived before Jesus.[1179] It is the "true Light,"[1180] the "hidden man of the heart,"[1181] the "Ancient of Days,"[1182] the "inner man,"[1183] the "inward man,"[1184] symbolized in Hinduism by the Crown Chakra (Paul called it the "incorruptible crown,"[1185] Peter called it the "crown of glory"),[1186] which lies within every one of us, and which makes our word flesh; that is, manifests our desires in the physical.[1187]

So Jesus is saying that our inner transformation toward becoming more mentally childlike can be achieved by focusing on the Christ Presence Within, the Great I AM.[1188] The most advantageous way of doing this is by imitating Christ through righteous living, righteous thought, righteous words, and righteous action. This would include prayer,[1189] affirmations,[1190] meditation,[1191] fasting,[1192] studying the Word of God (any sacred scripture),[1193] and intoning or chanting the holy names of God,[1194] along with developing such characteristics as unconditional love,[1195] charitableness,[1196] nonviolence,[1197] tolerance,[1198] and generosity[1199] toward others.[1200]

Whatsoever ye do unto others, ye do unto yourself.[1201] Thus being philanthropic, for instance, causes others to be philanthropic toward you. This is what Jesus meant when He said "it is more blessed to give than to receive."[1202] This is just one example out of thousands illustrating how we can harness the Law of Attraction to work for us instead of against us.

In short, by following Jesus' commandments, "ye are complete in Him";[1203] that is, you become in tune with your real self, your God-Self, while achieving atonement (at-one-ment) with the Universal Mind, which has its earthly counterpart in the mind of a child. As our consciousness rises to the level of the Divine Child Within, we make ourselves suitable to "enter the Kingdom of God," which in turn makes it easier and more fulfilling to work with the Law of Attraction.

Now you know why Jesus placed so much significance on entering the Kingdom of God, why He preached almost nothing else: He wants us to be happy and live the most fulfilling lives we can. Now you know why He mentions the word "salvation" only once in the entire New Testament (and then not in relation to Himself);[1204] why He never mentions "atonement"; why His enlightened followers preached the doctrine of Universal Salvation;[1205] and why the phrase "original sin" is missing from the Bible altogether.[1206]

You now know why the word "kingdom" appears 150 times in the New Testament and why nearly all of Jesus' parables are about the Kingdom of God. Most importantly, now you know why, unlike His posthumous followers, Jesus preached "the Gospel of the Kingdom"[1207] rather than "the Gospel of Jesus Christ,"[1208] a teaching so intriguing, so deep, so holy, that even "the angels desire to look into it"![1209]

Jesus giving His famed address, the Sermon on the Mount, to His Disciples (followers). The Sermon (portions of which Jesus took directly from the 1st-Century B.C. book known as the Testaments of the Twelve Patriarchs—later banned by the Church as "apocrypha") must be genuine, for unlike many other words attributed to the Master, much of it is recorded in the Gospel of Q, our earliest known record of Jesus' authentic sayings. The Sermon contains the Eight Beatitudes, which may have been loosely patterned on Buddha's much older doctrine known as the Eightfold Path. If it is true that Jesus traveled through (and studied in) Tibet during His "lost" eighteen years, He would have been quite familiar with Buddha's teachings. The Lord's celebrated speech contains many of His most important Law of Attraction teachings, and is therefore worthy of close study, memorization, and daily practice.

# 15

# LOVE

"A man shall be satisfied with good by the fruit
of his mouth."[1210]

## LOVE IS THE FOUNDATION OF THE UNIVERSE

**THE BASIS OF THE ENTIRE** Universe is love, for the Creator, Divine Mind, is itself love. Thus the very substance of our physical being, atoms, is made from love with love, while our soul, our Higher Self, what the Hindu calls Atma, is love in pure form. How is this possible?

Because, as Jesus taught, the Universal Inner Christ,[1211] our Indwelling Christ,[1212] that which we refer to in ourselves as I AM,[1213] is in fact God, and "God is love."[1214] This means that the "Christ in you"[1215] is universal love and that "universal love is king."[1216]

According to Paul, "this mystery" is God's great secret,[1217] the veritable "mystery of Christ,"[1218] the eternal enigma of the ages: Christ, who possesses the nature of God,[1219] is not outside of us. He is *within* us,[1220] governing our inner church as our Higher Self,[1221] and because of this we have the same powers He does.[1222] For He is "the true Light which lighteth every man that cometh into the world."[1223] Understanding this, Paul said, is the key to the treasure of all spiritual knowledge and wisdom,[1224] including the Law of Attraction. This is what Jesus was referring to when He made the following mystical comment:

"I have meat [food] to eat that ye know not of."[1225]

Paul referred to this esoteric food as "spiritual meat" and "spiritual drink."[1226]

With love as the bedrock of the Universe, it is only natural that it is the most powerful emotion in the world, and that we are born with an inherent need to experience this emotion, both in giving it to others and receiving it from others.

Love is indeed our natural state, for love is all around us and within us. It permeates the Universe down to the most infinitesimal subatomic particle. In fact, anything that is not love is an illusion created by the human Ego (Satan), for, as Paul also noted, "we live, and move, and have our being" in love.[1227]

## WHY JESUS WAS SO CONCERNED WITH LOVE

Not surprisingly, love turns out to be central to both Jesus' Law of Attraction teachings and to His message about our at-one-ment with the Father.[1228] Why? To answer this question we must take a brief detour back into the ancient world.

Pre-Christian Pagan religions, as well as ancient Judaism, recognized the Masculine Principle (men) and the Feminine Principle (women), and so worshiped both a supreme Father-God and a supreme Mother-Goddess. In ancient Egypt, for example, there was Ra and his wife Isis; in Mesopotamia there was Tammuz and Ishtar; in the Celtic nations there was Daghda and Danu; in India there was Brahma and Saraswati; in Scandinavia there was Odin and Frigga; in ancient Greece there was Zeus and Hera; in Rome there was Jupiter and Juno; and among the Hebrews there was Yahweh (Jehovah) and his wife Ashtoreth (Asherah).[1229]

Up until about 1000 B.C., ancient Jews, such as the henotheistic Israelite King Solomon, unabashedly worshiped both Yahweh and Ashtoreth.[1230] This gender-balanced godhead, found in nearly every religion from at least 6000 B.C. onward, was disturbed shortly thereafter, however, by a sweeping social movement known as the Patriarchal Takeover.[1231]

According to both the archaeological record and ancient myth, it was at this time that men began to take increasing control of society, politics, and religion, as can be seen, for example, in the often violent conflicts among the early Jews between patriarchal god-worshiping androcentrists (such as Elijah) and matriarchal goddess-worshiping gynocentrists (such as Jezebel).[1232]

Opposing the growing male-dominant clergy was the Judean Queen Maachah, who fought to revive goddess-worship and reinstate Ashtoreth into the Hebrew religion.[1233] Another early goddess-worshiping Semitic feminist was the Judean Queen Athaliah, who, like Jezebel,[1234] was ruthlessly murdered for her attempt to restore female spirituality.[1235]

Despite this female-based revolution, ultimately the goddess-worshipers' resistance was put down, and by around 900 B.C., among the Jews at least, the Patriarchal Takeover of what would become Judaism was nearly complete.[1236] Jewish goddess-worship, and the loose polytheism that went along with it, was destroyed, ousted and replaced by harsh monotheistic doctrines, by-the-letter rituals, and androcentric customs.[1237]

So great was Ashtoreth's obliteration that by the time of Jesus' birth some 900 years later, the patriarchalized Jewish masses knew almost nothing of their once great Mother-Goddess.[1238] Even the Pagan Romans had started to subordinate Juno to Jupiter, and everywhere religious misogyny began to prevail among the now more male-dominant faiths and sects.[1239]

The eradication of goddess-worship from religion, however, created a major problem: one of the most important attributes of the Female Principle (represented by the Great Mother-Goddess) is love, symbolized by the heart (Subconscious Mind). With the removal of the Divine Feminine, love and its many feminine liberal correlates, such as spirituality, kindness, charity, compassion, emotion, intuition, forbearance, sympathy, clemency, tenderness, sensitivity, empathy, freedom, mercy, philanthropy, leniency, self-knowledge (Gnosis), indulgence, individualism, patience, forgiveness, generosity, altruism, and tolerance, were also denigrated.

These were superseded by the Male Principle and its more masculine conservative concerns, such as orthodoxy, religiosity, physicality, toughness, tyranny, aggression, convention, mercilessness, strictness, opposition, enmity, apathy, remorselessness, church-knowledge, impatience, obedience, submission, cruelty, greed, callousness, punishment, prejudice, and intolerance.

Above all, the new all-male, politically-oriented priesthood instituted a policy of intellectualizing spirituality and formalizing religious doctrine, the intellect being symbolized by the brain (Conscious Mind). All of this was in marked contrast to the more relaxed approach to religion taken by the earlier family-oriented Goddess-worshipers.[1240]

Jesus, the literal human embodiment of love, saw this great imbalance, this indiscriminate cleansing of the Female Principle from religion, as a momentous spiritual tragedy, and after His spiritual awakening (mystically symbolized by a descending "dove")[1241] He immediately set out to correct it. Not by trying to reintroduce Goddess-worship, but by working to reinstate the qualities of the Divine Feminine, whose chief characteristic is love.

This, in fact, was the very first thing the Lord did after His baptism in the Jordan River: during His first major public discourse, the Sermon on the Mount, His primary theme was love.[1242]  For the rest of His life, the intuitive, pacifistic, "feminine" Jesus was opposed, as we have seen, by the intellectual, aggressive, "masculine" Pharisees, who placed rules and regulations above love, mercy, and kindness.

The like-minded descendants of these religious formalists are the same ones who apotheosized, politicized, dogmatized, deified, fetishized, mythicized, idolatrized, and Paganized Jesus after His death, suppressed His secret teachings on the Law of Attraction,[1243] then officially declared Him a Savior-God—for the first time—at the Council of Nicaea in the year 325.[1244]  (For more on this topic, see Appendix B.)

JESUS ON THE LAW OF LOVE
In the Gospel of Matthew—as part of His goal to restore the gapping hole left in religion by the overthrow of the Divine Feminine—Jesus tells us that love is the foundation of the entire Law.  As the only spiritual teacher who focused so intently on love at the time, this was quite unique.  Many considered Jesus' message of love a "radical teaching," particularly the always overly intellectual Pharisees.  As Jesus was preaching one day,

> one of them [Pharisees], which was a lawyer, asked him a question, tempting him, and saying, "Master, which is the great commandment in the law?" Jesus said unto him, "'Thou shalt *love* the Lord thy God with all thy heart, and with all thy soul, and with all thy mind.' This is the first and great commandment. And the second is like unto it, 'Thou shalt *love* thy neighbour as thyself.' *On these two commandments hang all the law and the prophets.*"[1245]

Love of God (Divine Mind), love of our true self (the Indwelling Christ), and love of our neighbor (a spiritual extension of our self),[1246] puts us on the path toward entering the Kingdom of God, as Jesus says in Mark:

> And one of the scribes came, and having heard them reasoning together, and perceiving that he had answered them well, asked him [Jesus], "Which is the first commandment of all?" And Jesus answered him, "The first of all the commandments is, 'Hear, O Israel; the Lord our God is one Lord: and thou shalt *love* the Lord thy God with all thy heart, and with all thy soul, and with all thy mind, and with all thy strength': this is the first commandment. And the second is like, namely this, 'Thou shalt *love* thy neighbour as thyself.' There is none other commandment greater than these."
> And the scribe said unto him, "Well, Master, thou hast

said the truth: for there is one God; and there is none other but he: and to love him with all the heart, and with all the understanding, and with all the soul, and with all the strength, and to love his neighbour as himself, is more than all whole burnt offerings and sacrifices." And when Jesus saw that he answered discreetly, he said unto him, "*Thou art not far from the kingdom of God.*"[1247]

As we have seen, gaining entrance into God's Kingdom is vital to understanding how to work with the Law of Attraction in an efficient and productive manner. And the love of our self is our passage in, for love connects and ties everything together as one.[1248]

I am not speaking of the narcissistic love of the Lower Self (Ego) that we so often see paraded in vulgar fashion in society. I am speaking of the eternal love of the Higher Self, the Great I AM Presence within;[1249] the unborn, preexistent, indestructible, uncreated, immortal Indwelling Christ that was never born and will never die.[1250] In the Aquarian Gospel, Jesus says:

"There are two selfs; the higher and the lower self. The higher self is human spirit clothed with soul, made in the form of God. The lower self, the carnal self, the body of desires, is a reflection of the higher self, distorted by the murky ethers of the flesh. The lower self is an illusion, and will pass away; the higher self is God in man, and will not pass away. The higher self is the embodiment of truth; the lower self is truth reversed, and so is falsehood manifest.

"The higher self is justice, mercy, love and right; the lower self is what the higher self is not. The lower self breeds hatred, slander, lewdness, murders, theft, and everything that harms; the higher self is mother of the virtues and the harmonies of life. The lower self is rich in promises, but poor in blessedness and peace; it offers pleasure, joy and satisfying gains; but gives unrest and misery and death. It gives men apples that are lovely to the eye and pleasant to the smell; their cores are full of bitterness and gall.

"If you would ask me what to study I would say, yourselves; and when you well had studied them, and then would ask me what to study next, I would reply, yourselves. He who knows well his lower self, knows the illusions of the world, knows of the things that pass away; and he who knows his higher self, knows God; knows well the things that cannot pass away. Thrice blessed is the man who has made purity and love his very own; he has been ransomed from the perils of the lower self and is himself his higher self."[1251]

This is why all happiness, all health, all prosperity, all healing, begins with loving yourself, your Higher Self!

In the Gospel of Thomas, Jesus, speaking as the Higher Self or Indwelling Christ, says:

> "Those who get close to me are close to the fire of enlightenment, but those who are far from me are nowhere near the kingdom."[1252]

What is Jesus saying here?  Knowledge and acceptance of your Divine Self is the cure-all for every problem and ill, for without self-love there can be no true belief, no faith, no hope, and no charity.  Why?  Because your Higher Self is an individualization of God, a veritable piece of the Almighty.  Knowing then that you are one with God who is perfect, you can never again hurt, undermine, devalue, mistreat, abuse, or belittle yourself.  For lack of self-love means lack of love for God, and lack of love for God means lack of love for yourself.[1253]

By the same token, you can never again allow anyone to knowingly hurt and abuse you, for due to your divine nature[1254] you are holy,[1255] and your mental, physical, and spiritual energies are like "pearls of great price."[1256]  Would you give three pearls worth $1 million each to a wild animal?  Here is how Jesus phrased it:

> "Give not that which is holy unto the dogs, neither cast ye your pearls before swine, lest they trample them under their feet, and turn again and rend you."[1257]

Due to the Law of Attraction, if you treat yourself with love, kindness, and respect, others will too.  If you do not, you will be "trampled under their feet."

Love spiritually connects us to the Divine Mind, which is why love transforms and heals, why it is the ultimate soothing balm of the body, mind, and soul.  Read the following cosmic words from the Gospel of John carefully, and embrace them.  Jesus is speaking as the Indwelling Christ (using the word "me") in reference to the Divine Mind ("my Father"):

> "If a man love me, he will keep my words: and my Father will love him, and we will come unto him, and make our abode with him."[1258]

Another amazing promise made to us by the world master of space and time!

USING LOVE & THE LAW OF ATTRACTION

Being at the foundation of everything, love plays a major role in the workings of the Law of Attraction. By being loving we are broadcasting a truly holy vibration, the highest spiritual vibration known, and the Universe is sending this vibration back to us in the form of more love from others and more things to love in our lives.

Would you like to increase the effect of your love so that the power of the Law of Attraction is doubled? Do you want to improve every aspect of your life beginning right now? Here is how:

- Love your (higher) self unconditionally.
- Only think loving thoughts about yourself.
- Only say loving things about yourself.
- Only do loving things to and for yourself.
- Forgive yourself (as God has forgiven you)[1259] for everything you have ever done in the past that may have gone against the Holy Spirit.[1260]
- Accept yourself exactly as you are.
- Acknowledge that you are special, unique, needed, loved, and wanted.[1261]
- Be kind to yourself in every way.
- Be tolerant, patient, and understanding with yourself.
- Think only helpful, positive, and productive thoughts about yourself.
- Say only helpful, positive, and productive things about yourself.
- Bless yourself everyday, whenever you think of it.
- Completely love and respect your *spirit* by cultivating uplifting beliefs, ideas, and opinions. Your spirit is your God-Self,[1262] the Indwelling Christ,[1263] who rules as a "king"[1264] over your inner Kingdom of Heaven,[1265] and which, being immortal, never dies, and has existed from the beginning of time.[1266]
- Completely love and respect your *mind* by thinking positively and by "feeding" it nourishing and edifying information. Think Christlike thoughts[1267] and your mind will become Christ's.[1268] This is part of the "great mystery of godliness" that Paul spoke of.[1269]
- Completely love and respect your *body* and all of its organs, structures, and cells; nurture it, pamper it, and, as mentioned, always say and think positive things about it. Your body is the physical temple of the Father,[1270] the "temple of the living God,"[1271] who dwells within you.[1272] Its cells are each filled with the actual divine intelligence of God, and will respond in kind to your thoughts.[1273] So think good thoughts!

By this point you must be aware that your happiness is integrally tied to the world around you, for what you send out vibrationally always returns to you.[1274] So apply these same rules to the rest of humanity:

• Love everyone and everything unconditionally.[1275]
• Only think loving thoughts about others.
• Only say loving things about others.
• Only do loving things to and for others.[1276]
• Forgive anyone who has ever caused you pain. Not just once, but as many times as they hurt you.[1277]
• Accept everyone exactly as they are. (This is one of the greatest gifts you can give someone, and it will completely transform your relationships!)[1278]
• Acknowledge that everyone is special, unique, needed, loved, and wanted, for every man and woman contains the same "true Light" you do: that of the Indwelling Christ.[1279]
• Be kind to others always, and in every situation.[1280]
• Be tolerant, patient, and understanding with others.[1281]
• Think only helpful, positive, and productive thoughts about others.[1282]
• Say only helpful, positive, and productive things to others.[1283]
• Send out a silent blessing to the entire world every chance you get. Yes, even those who have brought suffering into your life.[1284]
• Always respect the spirits, minds, and bodies of all living creatures, and in all ways. For what you do returns to you.[1285]
• In summation, "love one another with a pure heart fervently,"[1286] and you will experience the Kingdom of Heaven within![1287]

To maintain your happiness once you have achieved it, avoid the following at all costs:

• Negativity toward others in any form: thought, word, or action.[1288] As Peter put it, "lay aside all malice, and all guile, and hypocrisies, and envies, and all evil speakings."[1289]
• Criticism of any kind, of yourself and everyone else.[1290]
• Overwork, late nights, unhealthy habits and lifestyle in general.[1291]
• Jealousy, envy, or resentment toward others.[1292]
• Responding negatively to insults (instead, ignore them as Jesus did,[1293] or better yet, "pay back" with a blessing, as He recommended).[1294]
• Unnecessary judgment of others in any way.[1295]

- Worry or fear of others.[1296]
- Seeking to hurt, ruin, or take advantage of others.[1297]
- Arguments, quibbling, and foolish discussions, particularly over religion and the Bible.[1298]
- Purposeful aggression or violence of any kind towards others.[1299]
- Racism, sexism, ageism, lookism, and all of the other negative "isms."[1300]

When contemplating this list, remember the wise words of Saint Ignatius: "Where there is division and wrath, God dwelleth not."[1301]

If you desire God's presence in your life, be holy in everything you do, for God Himself is holy.[1302] Do not show favoritism,[1303] for God does not.[1304] Instead, respect and honor everyone,[1305] for all are equal in the eyes of God.[1306] Practice these things, and by the Law of Attraction, you will draw all that is sacred, blessed, and beautiful.[1307]

In short, "love the truth and peace" and your life will be filled with joy and prosperity.[1308] Jesus was not called the Prince of Peace,[1309] the "very God of Peace,"[1310] for no reason, nor was he referred to as "the true God,"[1311] the same God who is made of pure love,[1312] without good cause. Following the Master's teachings brings not only inner and outer peace, but unending love into our lives. That is the Law!

## THE IMPORTANCE OF FOLLOWING THESE RULES

The reason we want to comply with these rules is simple: how you deal with others is the way God will deal with you.[1313] Or to put it in modern parlance, doing things that make others happy draws good things back to you, making you happy as well. For whatever we think, say, or do is magnetized back to us by the Law of Attraction. If you judge someone harshly, others will begin to judge you harshly. If you criticize someone, others will criticize you.[1314] On the other hand, if you treat others fairly, you will be treated fairly.

Everything operates under the Law of Attraction, which like all of the other laws of physics, is perfectly just, changeless, and unbreakable.[1315] So always let your words be affirming and cheerful; or as the writer of Proverbs so beautifully phrased it, let them be "like apples of gold in pictures of silver."[1316]

Jesus, the ultimate Lord of the Law of Attraction, understands human nature perfectly, which is why He said the following:

"Judge not, that ye be not judged. For with what judgment ye

judge, ye shall be judged: and with what measure ye mete, it shall
be measured to you again.  And why beholdest thou the mote
[sliver] that is in thy brother's eye, but considerest not the beam
[log] that is in thine own eye?  Or how wilt thou say to thy brother,
'Let me pull out the mote out of thine eye'; and, behold, a beam is
in thine own eye?  Thou hypocrite, first cast out the beam out of
thine own eye; and then shalt thou see clearly to cast out the mote
out of thy brother's eye."[1317]

## BEING LOVING IS FOR OUR OWN GOOD

The Sovereign Mind, the Divine Mind, which is listening to you twenty-
fours a day,[1318] is constantly working to send you back the materialization of
your most prominent thoughts,[1319] your deepest held beliefs, and your
strongest emotions.[1320]  Thus, following these rules is for our own good, not
to please a conceited, personal, vengeful, corporeal, anthropomorphic God
who exists only in the imaginations of the founders and followers of Pagan
Christianity.

Was such a "molten (metal) God,"[1321] a "dumb idol,"[1322] a "graven
image,"[1323] a "vain thing,"[1324] ever preached by our Lord?[1325]   Never!
Instead, He taught that the Father (Divine Mind) is pure Spirit, and thus
must be worshiped in Spirit.[1326]  For the true God is the "*living* God" of
Jesus,[1327] who dwells continually in the heart and soul of every believer;[1328]
the opposite of the *dead* God who is worshiped by Pagan Christians only at
church on Sundays.[1329]

Here is what Jesus, the "Shepherd and Bishop of our souls,"[1330] says
on the subject of our relationship with the Father:

"What man is there of you, whom if his son ask bread, will he give
him a stone?  Or if he ask a fish, will he give him a serpent?  If ye
then, being evil [that is, susceptible to wrongdoing], know how to
give good gifts unto your children, how much more shall your
Father which is in heaven give good things to them that ask
him?"[1331]

The "Father" Jesus describes here is a loving, forgiving, tolerant divine
parent, not the tumultuous, temperamental, punitive, Paganesque God of
the Old Testament, who was patterned on the Roman Jupiter and the Greek
Zeus.[1332]

As the world's greatest teacher on the Law of Attraction, Jesus'
commandments concerning love now make perfect sense.  This is from the

Gospel of Matthew:

> "Ye have heard that it hath been said, 'Thou shalt love thy neighbour, and hate thine enemy.' But I say unto you, love your enemies, bless them that curse you, do good to them that hate you, and pray for them which despitefully use you, and persecute you; that ye may be the children of your Father which is in heaven: for he maketh his sun to rise on the evil and on the good, and sendeth rain on the just and on the unjust. For if ye love them which love you, what reward have ye? do not even the publicans [tax collectors] the same? And if ye salute your brethren only, what do ye more than others? do not even the publicans so?"[1333]

The following sensational passage is from one of the works favored by early Gnostic Christians: the Gnostic- and Essene-flavored Gospel of John. Read closely these canonical words of the Lord speaking as the Indwelling Christ!

> "At that day [of enlightenment] ye shall know that *I am in my Father, and ye in me, and I in you.* He that hath [understands] my commandments, and keepeth them, he it is that loveth me: and he that loveth me shall be loved of my Father, and *I will love him, and will manifest myself to him.*"
>
> Judas saith unto him, not Iscariot, "Lord, how is it that thou wilt manifest thyself unto us, and not unto the world?" Jesus answered and said unto him, "*If a man love me, he will keep my words: and my Father will love him, and we will come unto him, and make our abode with him.* He that loveth me not keepeth not my sayings: and the word which ye hear is not mine, but the Father's which sent me."[1334]

In the following Law of Attraction passages, also from John, Jesus clearly states that by obeying His commandments on love, whatever we ask the Father (Divine Mind) in His name, will be given to us:

> "As the Father hath loved me, so have I loved you: continue ye in my love. If ye keep my commandments, ye shall abide in my love; even as I have kept my Father's commandments, and abide in his love. These things have I spoken unto you, that my joy might remain in you, and *that your joy might be full.* This is my commandment, that ye love one another, as I have loved you. Greater love hath no man than this, that a man lay down his life for his friends.

> "Ye are my friends, *if* ye do whatsoever I command you.
> Henceforth I call you not 'servants'; for the servant knoweth not
> what his lord doeth: but I have called you 'friends'; for all things
> that I have heard of my Father I have made known unto you. Ye
> have not chosen me, but I have chosen you, and ordained you, that
> ye should go and bring forth fruit, and that your fruit should
> remain: that *whatsoever ye shall ask of the Father in my name, he may*
> *give it you.* These things I command you, that ye love one
> another."[1335]

Paul's opinion of the importance of love is found in his first letter
to the Corinthians:

> "Though I speak with the tongues of men and of angels, and have
> not love, I am become as sounding brass, or a tinkling cymbal. And
> though I have the gift of prophecy, and understand all mysteries,
> and all knowledge; and though I have all faith, so that I could
> remove mountains, and have not love, I am nothing. And though
> I bestow all my goods to feed the poor, and though I give my body
> to be burned, and have not love, it profiteth me nothing.
>      "Charity suffereth long, and is kind; love envieth not;
> love vaunteth not itself, is not puffed up, doth not behave itself
> unseemly, seeketh not her own, is not easily provoked, thinketh no
> evil; Rejoiceth not in iniquity, but rejoiceth in the truth; Beareth all
> things, believeth all things, hopeth all things, endureth all things.
> Love never faileth . . . And now abideth faith, hope, love, these
> three; but *the greatest of these is love.*"[1336]

Paul also reinforced Jesus' commandment about loving the self:

> "For all the law is fulfilled in one word, even in this; 'Thou shalt
> love thy neighbour *as thyself.*'"[1337]

## LOVING YOURSELF IS LOVING GOD

Why did Jesus and Paul place so much emphasis on loving ourselves, that is,
our Higher Self?

For one thing, your Higher Self, your Divine Self, is the real you,
which is Spirit. And this Spirit is made of the same sacred substance as God,
whom Jesus said is Spirit.[1338]

Why are both made from the same divine material? Because all
Spirit is one and that Spirit is God, also known as the Indwelling Christ,[1339]
or the Great I AM.[1340] Does this mean that God is Man? No![1341] God is

all,[1342] and we are individual expressions of God, who dwells within us.[1343]

Thus, to love your Higher Self (as opposed to your Lower Self, or Ego) is to love God, and to love God is to love your Higher Self. This is why Jesus said that the two most important commandments are to love God "with all thy heart, and with all thy soul, and with all thy mind,"[1344] and to "love thy neighbor as thyself."[1345] The latter commandment is especially significant, because just as you are an individualization of God, so too is your neighbor—and both literally and figuratively, *everyone* is your neighbor!

Now read the following teaching from Matthew, spoken by Jesus to His Disciples, with this new knowledge:

> "When the Son of man shall come in his glory, and all the holy angels with him, then shall he sit upon the throne of his glory: and before him shall be gathered all nations: and he shall separate them one from another, as a shepherd divideth his sheep from the goats: and he shall set the sheep on his right hand [both symbolic of the righteous], but the goats on the left [both symbolic of the wrong-doers].
>
> "Then shall the King say unto them on his right hand, 'Come, ye blessed of my Father, inherit the kingdom prepared for you from the foundation of the world: for I was an hungred, and ye gave me meat: I was thirsty, and ye gave me drink: I was a stranger, and ye took me in: naked, and ye clothed me: I was sick, and ye visited me: I was in prison, and ye came unto me.'
>
> "Then shall the righteous answer him, saying, 'Lord, when saw we thee an hungred, and fed thee? or thirsty, and gave thee drink? When saw we thee a stranger, and took thee in? or naked, and clothed thee? Or when saw we thee sick, or in prison, and came unto thee?' And the King shall answer and say unto them, 'Verily I say unto you, inasmuch as ye have done it unto one of the least of these my brethren, ye have done it unto me.'
>
> "Then shall he say also unto them on the left hand, 'Depart from me, ye cursed, into everlasting fire, prepared for the devil and his angels: for I was an hungred, and ye gave me no meat: I was thirsty, and ye gave me no drink: I was a stranger, and ye took me not in: naked, and ye clothed me not: sick, and in prison, and ye visited me not.'
>
> "Then shall they also answer him, saying, 'Lord, when saw we thee an hungred, or athirst, or a stranger, or naked, or sick, or in prison, and did not minister unto thee?' Then shall he answer them, saying, 'Verily I say unto you, inasmuch as ye did it not to one of the least of these, ye did it not to me.' And these shall go away into everlasting punishment: but the righteous into life

eternal."[1346]

Paul taught that all ten of the Ten Commandments could be summed up under one law, the Law of Love:

> "Owe no man any thing, but to love one another: for he that loveth another hath fulfilled the law. For this, 'Thou shalt not commit adultery, Thou shalt not kill, Thou shalt not steal, Thou shalt not bear false witness, Thou shalt not covet'; and if there be any other commandment, it is briefly comprehended in this saying, namely, 'Thou shalt love thy neighbour as thyself.' Love worketh no ill to his neighbour: therefore *love is the fulfilling of the law*."[1347]

## GOD PLACED YOU ON EARTH FOR A PURPOSE

Do you want to know how important you are, not only to the world, but to God? Look at yourself in the mirror. There is only one of you, and God intentionally made you that way. Even if you are an identical twin or triplet, you each have different fingerprints, revealing your deep spiritual uniqueness.

You may not feel loved or needed at this moment, but know that you are, otherwise you would not be on earth.[1348] God placed you here to fulfill an important mission,[1349] a vital task, one that you must learn on your own, and with the help of the Holy Spirit—which He gave to us partly for this very purpose: self discovery.[1350]

The idea that one must uncover and learn about one's true self is an idea as old as Mankind. Some 1,500 years ago, for instance, Socrates taught that the most important thing in life is to "know thyself." A similar doctrine was found not only among the ancient Gnostic Christians (whose very name comes from the Greek word *gnosis*, meaning "knowledge" of the self), but also among the early Jesus communities who wrote the books of the New Testament.[1351]

But what "self" are we talking about?

It is your real self, the Indwelling Christ,[1352] and it is your awareness of it that will enable you to see that you are the only one on this planet who can fulfill your specific mission, and that you will not leave here until it is complete.[1353] Emerson understood. Here is how he phrased it:

> "I am an organ of God and God hath need of me where I am, otherwise I would not be here."

Naturally, our Lord had something important to say about self-esteem and self-worth as well:

> "And I say unto you my friends, be not afraid of them that kill the body, and after that have no more that they can do. But I will forewarn you whom ye shall fear: fear him [God, that is, Divine Mind], which after he hath killed hath power to cast into hell; yea, I say unto you, fear him [respect and revere Him]. Are not five sparrows sold for two farthings [pennies], and not one of them is forgotten before God? But even the very hairs of your head are all numbered. Fear not therefore: ye are of more value than many sparrows."[1354]

The esoteric meaning here is clear: we respect the Divine Mind (God) by thinking only positive, uplifting, loving thoughts. If we disrespect it by thinking negative, gloomy, hateful thoughts, we will reap what we have sown by attracting trouble, pain, and complications into our lives (being "cast into hell"). To avoid this, begin by loving yourself, the Indwelling Christ, which is far more valuable to God than anything else.

SPIRITUAL SELFISHNESS

Many of us have been taught that we must put others *above* ourselves, that we should love others *before* ourselves. This view, however, which I call "spiritual altruism," contradicts Jesus' commandment on love. And who would know better than the Master Psychologist, the one who taught what I refer to as "spiritual psychology," the same one who Isaiah revealingly calls "Counsellor"?[1355]

Counselor Jesus understands that if we do not love, honor, and respect ourselves, then we cannot truly love, honor, and respect others. He understands that love of the Higher Self creates a harmonious vibration in the mind-body-spirit complex, which produces health, happiness, and prosperity in our lives. After all, how can we be of service to others if we are not healthy, happy, and prosperous ourselves? This being true, it is our spiritual responsibility to work with Divine Mind to achieve all three.

Put another way, if you yourself are unhealthy, how can you help heal someone who has a disease? If you yourself are unhappy, how can you console someone who is dispirited? If you yourself are not prosperous, how can you aid someone who is poor?

Jesus' approach to love of self is known as "spiritual selfishness," for under His law it all begins with *you*. In fact, spiritually speaking, you are the center of the Universe, for everything in creation was made just for you! According to the Bible, everything, including the world, everything present and everything to come, even life itself, "all are yours";[1356] "all things are for your sake," said Paul.[1357]

Understanding this profound truth means taking good care of yourself, your Higher Self. When you do, under the promise of the Law, God will take good care of you in return. And with the Divine Mind tending to you, you will be so strong, so joyous, and so well-situated that there will be nothing you cannot do!

LOVING YOURSELF THROUGH THE LAW

Here is how to work with the Law of Attraction to engender a true and total love for yourself:

• Create affirmations of love for yourself and repeat them throughout the day.
• Visualize yourself as you want yourself to be, not as you are. Keep this new image in your mind at all times. "What thou see [mentally], thou shall become [physically]."[1358]
• Always be kind to yourself; indulge yourself; think thoughts that make you cheerful, do things that make you happy, spend time with people who you enjoy, eat foods that make you feel good, paint the rooms in your house in colors that please you, put up pictures that delight you, listen to music that you love, adopt the pet you have always wanted (animals of all kinds are wonderful healers!), attend a concert or play, treat yourself to a massage, lay on the beach, take a bike ride, go for a walk in the woods, climb a mountain, visit a museum. Whatever it is you like, do it. In the Gospel of Thomas, Jesus phrased this important Law of Attraction principle this way: "Never do what you hate to do."[1359] In other words, concentrate on feeling good and everything else will follow![1360]

Remember, even if you have severe depression, addictions, illness, or trauma of any kind, you can start now, on your own, to begin to love yourself and rebuild your life into what you want it to be, and what you have always known it should be. Love heals all, and "God is love,"[1361] therefore being loving engenders a godly healing. This is a biblical truth![1362]

Truly, there is nothing that is impossible for the Mind of God, the Mind of Christ that is within you,[1363] just as ancient Christian mystics taught:[1364] the famous acronym, INRI, actually stands for *In Nobis Regnat Iesus* ("Within Us Jesus Reigns").[1365] The Indwelling Christ knows everything,[1366] including how to deal with every one of your difficulties.[1367] Realizing this fact alone will bring you happiness. How wonderful. Paul understood:

> "I can do all things through Christ which strengtheneth me."[1368]

According to Jesus' teachings on the Law of Attraction, the better you feel about yourself, the healthier you will be. The healthier you are, the happier you will be. The happier you are, the more abundance you draw into your life. The more of all three of these you have, the more of a blessing you can be to others. It is that simple! Memorize these stupendous words from the book of Proverbs, and live them:

> "For as a man thinketh in his heart, so is he."[1369]

YOU ARE PERFECT!
There are those who are spiritually immature, and who thus misunderstand the word "sin" as it is written in the New Testament. They do not have the inner spiritual "eyes to see" that the word sin merely means "to miss the mark"—that is, make a mistake, or religiously speaking, commit an error, a trespass, or an offence against what we know to be right. And not realizing that the concept of "original sin" is a fabrication of the early Catholic Church, they believe that we are all born "tainted with corruption." This group will tell you that because you were "born in sin," you are "imperfect."

You listen to such false non-biblical beliefs at your peril. In fact, these inaccurate teachings are not only anti-Christian, they are part of what has always caused so much misery, ill health, and poverty in the world.

As all of the Apostles did, Peter knew that we are all "made perfect," that is, born perfect, due to the Indwelling Christ, which itself is perfect,[1370] and which, because it is universal,[1371] dwells within us all as our Higher Self, our God-Self:[1372]

> "But the *God* of all grace, who hath called us unto his eternal glory by *Christ* Jesus, after that ye have suffered a while, *make you perfect*, stablish, strengthen, settle you."[1373]

One cannot be "made perfect" if he does not already have the seeds of perfection within him. Paul too noted that the redeeming sacrifice of the Christ "forever perfected" all genuine believers.[1374] Such statements expose the great lie being taught in so many churches today.

Jesus went much further than either Paul or Peter, stating that the only thing that prevents us from realizing our spiritual flawlessness is the proper knowledge. This is why he established the truth once and for all with the following powerfully clear statement:

> "*Be ye therefore perfect, even as your Father which is in heaven is perfect.*"[1375]

Jesus would not and could not tell us to "be perfect" if He did not know that we *are* perfect. How can you "*be* perfect" if you are not already perfect? He is telling you and me, in other words, to realize our innate perfection. In doing so, Jesus compares us to our "Father in heaven," the Divine Mind, the Great I AM Presence within,[1376] who is indeed perfect.[1377] Paul too was well aware of our innate spiritual perfection, so magnificently fulfilled in the Christ, for "ye are complete [that is, perfect] in him."[1378]

Now, not only did Jesus say that you are one with the Father,[1379] but the Bible says that the Father is actually your Higher Self, the real you, the supernal you, your deific side, God in Man.[1380] You literally reflect His glory exactly, "as in a mirror."[1381] Thus, created in the Father's image, you cannot be anything but perfect.[1382] And so you are, "for every man is God made flesh"![1383]

The reason you think you are not is because you think you are not, and this comes from thinking thoughts of imperfection, and from listening to those who preach anti-Jesus doctrine. The Law of Attraction makes what you believe come true, so you must think thoughts of perfection, beauty, and wholeness in order to be perfect, beautiful, and whole! This is what Jesus did. "Go, and do thou likewise."[1384]

Jesus summed up the importance of love in the following passage, which highlights the total oneness and complete perfection of you, me, the Indwelling Christ, the Father, and the Divine Mind:

> "*I in them, and thou in me, that they may be made perfect in one*; and that the world may know that thou hast sent me, and hast loved them, as thou hast loved me."[1385]

Believe this "with all your heart, and with all your soul, and with all your mind," and it will become real for you. Be strong and stay focused on doing good things and saying good things, and you will attract more good.[1386] In the Aquarian Gospel, Jesus says:

> "He who loves not the [Indwelling] Christ, which is the love of God, before all else, can never gain the prize of spirit consciousness."[1387]

Yes, love is the true panacea for every problem, for every illness, for every difficulty. Realize your innate perfection and start loving yourself—and everyone and everything else—this very minute. Then watch your life begin to transform. You could do nothing better than to start with this sage biblical advice: say everything *in* love,[1388] and do everything *with* love![1389]

The Ascension of Jesus, that is, His bodily rise into the realm of Spirit.
While the actual event appears to have had little importance to the New
Testament writers (for example, neither Matthew or authentic Mark
mention it, Paul and Peter give only one vague reference each, and Luke
says no one witnessed it), it is of great importance to us. For it is
symbolic of the Soul achieving final union with the Divine, an exaltation
that we will all experience one day. As Paul said, God "will have all men
to be saved." But in truth, your salvation comes not from God.
According to the teachings of the Lord, it comes from how you think,
speak, and act while on earth; in other words, on how you use the Law
of Attraction. The wise use it spiritually by always thinking, speaking,
and behaving in positive and loving ways. They understand the mystical
words of Jesus, that God "shall reward every man according to his
works." They have learned the lesson that Paul taught about the
unbreakable Law of Attraction: "Whatsoever a man soweth, that shall
he also reap." God gave us a set of rules on how to best use the Law
to ensure our salvation and ascension: the Ten Commandments and the
Eight Beatitudes. Follow them in spirit, and when it is your time, like the
Master, you too will ascend directly into eternal at-one-ment with the
"Father," Jesus' name for the Divine Mind.

# 16

# HAPPINESS

"He that keepeth his mouth keepeth his life."[1390]

## WHAT IS HAPPINESS?

**APPINESS IS NOT MERELY THE** absence of unhappiness, as cynics believe. Happiness is an intentional state of consciousness that comes from thinking happy thoughts. Happy thoughts stem from being loving, and love is God.[1391] Therefore, if you love God and the things of God, you will create happiness for yourself. Disregard God and the things of God, and you will create unhappiness for yourself.[1392] This is not religion, it is science. It is a universal law, and those who understand it,[1393] and those who follow it to the letter, will find happiness.[1394]

Atheists, skeptics, and agnostics will counter by saying that true happiness is possible without believing in God. And I would agree, *if* we are talking about the personal, corporeal, transcendent, anthropomorphic God of institutional Christianity, for this is a false deity, a "vain thing," built upon the sky-gods of ancient Pagan mythology.[1395] But it is not possible to be happy if we disregard the genuine living God,[1396] and that is the impersonal, invisible, immanent, spiritual I AM, the great universal creative energy that scientists call the "Unified Field."[1397] Why is this not possible?

Part of the Great I AM exists within you and that part is, in fact, your Higher Self, your Divine Self, which makes you an individualization of God.[1398] This is why that which makes you happy is that which makes God happy, and that which makes God happy is that which makes you happy.

## UNDERSTANDING VIRTUE & REWARD, SIN & PUNISHMENT

Here is the inner meaning of this concept: when you do something that creates unhappiness in the world around you, by the Law of Attraction you are also making God, your Higher Self, unhappy. This error in judgment is what the New Testament writers called, in Greek, *hamartia*, meaning "to miss the mark," a word translated by medieval Christian scribes as *synne*, or in modern English, "sin." And so we have the inner (true) meaning of the phrase to "sin against God": *a violation of Spiritual Law.*

Because "sin" goes against the Supreme Self, the Higher Self, your incorporeal God-Self, you feel guilt, which generates unhappiness. And so we have the inner meaning of the phrase "God punishes you for bad behavior": *violating Spiritual Law leads to detrimental consequences.*

But the opposite is also true: when you do something that creates happiness in the world around you, you are also making God, your Higher Self, happy. Because this virtuous act is in accord with your God-Self, you feel pleasure, which generates happiness. And so we have the inner (true) meaning of the phrase "God rewards you for good behavior": *obeying Spiritual Law leads to beneficial consequences.*

It is pure science no matter how you look at it, for the realm of the Mind (psychology, the "study of the Soul") and Spirit are one and the same, which is why Christian mystic Paul said:

"God will render to every man according to his deeds."[1399]

The inner meaning:

"Divine Mind gives back to every person exactly what he or she puts out in the form of thoughts, words, and actions."[1400]

Yes, whatever label we "human radios" choose to put on "God," the outcome of our thoughts, words, and actions will always be identical to the income of thoughts, words, and actions: we are always "receiving" happiness or unhappiness depending on what spiritual vibrations we decide to "broadcast" out to the Universe. Buddha declared the following truth:

"*All that we are is the result of what we have thought.* If one speaks or acts with an evil thought ['sin'], pain ['punishment'] follows that person. If one speaks or acts with a pure thought [righteousness], happiness [bliss] follows that person, like a shadow that never leaves him or her. *The mind is everything. What we think we become.*"

This is why we must choose our thoughts carefully: when it comes to what you think, be deliberate. Be selective. Be intentional. Develop mental self-control. For you cannot benefit from the Law of Attraction if you allow the Law of Averages to govern your thoughts!

Remember, the Conscious Mind (the Christ) is the Master of the Subconscious Mind (the Servant). But *you* are the master of the Conscious Mind. If you let it master you, it will quickly sink down to the level of the mass mind, and trouble will surely ensue. So follow Paul's advice, and bend every thought "to the obedience of Christ."[1401] This is virtuous thinking, righteous thinking.

## EVIL & THE DEVIL ARE MANMADE CREATIONS

While we are on the topics of happiness and sin, this is the ideal place to discuss the Devil ("demon"), or Lucifer ("bringer of light") or Satan ("adversary"), as he is also known.

There are many today who believe that "evil is a real force" and that "the Devil is a living breathing entity." There are people who even claim to have heard or seen Satan—and I have no reason to doubt them. But the truth is that these experiences and ideas are only real to such individuals *because* they believe in them! People who sincerely do not believe in evil or the Devil at the Subconscious level never experience either. How can this be?

Evil does not exist outside of us. It is an illusion created by the human mind, or Ego, and once firmly accepted, the Subconscious Mind sets about turning it into physical reality. Thus those who believe in evil, experience it. Those who do not believe in it, do not experience it.

Paul, for example, assured us that while there are in fact dark forces, they are not physical in origin. They are spiritual—that is mental, which is why his solutions to the problem of evil are so often couched in militaristic metaphors and symbols involving psychology. Here, for example, is what he wrote to his followers at Ephesus:

> "My brethren, be strong in the Lord, and in the power of his might. Put on the whole *armour of God* [Divine Mind], that ye may be able to stand against the wiles [tricks] of the devil [human Ego]. For *we wrestle not against flesh and blood, but against principalities, against powers, against the rulers of the darkness of* this world, *against spiritual wickedness* [psychological evildoing] *in high places* [in the mind].
> "Wherefore take unto you the whole *armour of God,* that ye may be able to withstand in the evil day, and having done all, to stand. Stand therefore, having your *loins girt about with truth,* and having on the *breastplate of righteousness*; and your *feet shod with the*

*preparation of the gospel of peace*; above all, taking the *shield of faith*, wherewith ye shall be able to quench all the fiery darts [thoughts] of the wicked [malicious and unenlightened]. And take the *helmet of salvation*, and the *sword of the Spirit*, which is the *word of God [Divine Mind]*: praying always with all *prayer* and supplication *in the Spirit.*"[1402]

In the Aquarian Gospel, Jesus gives us the plain truth about the so-called "Devil":

"The devil and the burning fires are both the works of man, and none can put the fires out and dissipate the evil one, but man who made them both."[1403]

This fact is precisely why the ancients created the famous "Three Wise Monkeys" in the postures of "see no evil, hear no evil, speak no evil."[1404] Because evil is a manmade illusion, if you refuse to see it, hear it, or speak it, it will not come into your experience. Disbelieve in evil and it will disappear from your life. Conversely, believe in goodness and it will appear in your life, just as Paul said:

". . . yet I would have you [be] wise unto [that is, aware of] that which is good, and simple [unaware] concerning evil."[1405]

On the other hand, those who believe they can see evil, *will* see evil things. Those who believe they can hear evil, *will* hear evil things. Those who believe they can speak evil, *will* speak evil things. And seeing, hearing, and speaking evil things only attracts all three into your life. It is that simple, for the Law of Attraction is mathematically precise.

The beauty of the Law is that the choice is always ours. However, those who choose to believe in a manmade Devil must consider the words of Jesus and Paul. Both long ago asserted that "the ruler of this world," that is, Satan, is now nonexistent, for he was "cast out" and "destroyed" due to the Lord's crucifixion.[1406] In turn, having revoked the Law of Moses,[1407] Jesus' death freed humanity from sin,[1408] "saving" the righteous[1409] "by the sacrifice of himself."[1410]

THE BIBLE'S NAME FOR THE HUMAN EGO
Now what is the human Ego? It is our modern term for the ancient biblical figure known as Satan! As such, it is true that the Devil does indeed "tempt"

us and even "cause" us to sin. However, we are not talking about a real demon. We are talking about our own Lower Self, our Ego, which, in the spiritual sense, is utterly self-centered, dualistic, and atheistic. This is the same psychological archetype that Paul called the "old man," which he said we are to "put off" or "crucify."[1411]

What significance does this have for those of us who are interested in Jesus and the Law of Attraction?

Those who want to protect themselves and their loved ones from evil, from the Devil, need only ignore these human-invented concepts. Strip them of their power by disregarding them completely, and you will never be bothered by them. Evil comes not from without. It comes from within, from within our own minds, our Egos. The human "I," the Ego, in turn derives its ideas from the mass mind, from ignorance, from self-loathing, and from error-filled religious teachings.

There is nothing evil that will hurt you but your own thoughts of evil. There is no Devil that can harm you but your own belief in the Devil. Both words are similar in spelling and meaning, and both are false. Release these ideas back to where they came from: the "hell" of the mass mind. *The only things that can come into your life are those which you invite by consistent thought!*

This is why we are not to blame either the Devil or God if we succumb to temptation, to evil thoughts, words, or deeds, for, as Paul stated: "There hath no temptation taken you but such as is common to man."[1412] In short, as human beings we are personally responsible for all that we experience. Thus James the Just wrote:

> "Blessed is the man that endureth temptation: for when he is tried, he shall receive the crown of life [Christ or Cosmic Consciousness], which the Lord hath promised to them that love him. *Let no man say when he is tempted, 'I am tempted of God':* for God cannot be tempted with evil, neither tempteth he any man: but *every man is tempted, when he is drawn away of [by] his own lust, and enticed.*"[1413]

So fear not, worry not, doubt not, anguish not.[1414] Believe only in God, whose name gives us the word "good." That is, believe only in things that are positive, beautiful, and elevating. Know with all of your being that you are safe, secure, protected, loved, guided, and guarded. Rest assured that by believing this, the Divine Mind (the "Father") behind the Law of Attraction will protect you from all harm, all danger, all injury, and that the concepts of "evil" and "Satan" will eventually vanish from your life like the erroneous fabricated fantasies they are. Let us heed the wisdom of the book of Proverbs:

> "In all thy ways acknowledge him [God, Divine Mind], and he shall direct thy paths."[1415]

## THE LORD'S VIEW OF EVIL

Does Jesus have anything specific to say about evil? Absolutely, and here is His entire view: "Resist not evil."[1416] Why? Because, as the noted Swiss psychiatrist Carl Jung pointed out: "What you resists persists."

The Master of Galilee understands that when we defy evil, we are recognizing it as an actual reality, and anything we consider "real," we believe in. This belief activates the Law of Attraction, which immediately sets about turning evil into a physical manifestation. By doing this we solicit evil, we literally invite it into our lives; then we become a part of it and it becomes a part of us. This is what Jesus meant when He made the following metaphorical statement:

> "For all they that take the sword shall perish with the sword."[1417]

The "sword" here refers to both a real sword and an emblematic one; the latter one which symbolizes hate, revengefulness, malice, hostility, enmity, vindictiveness, ruthlessness, criticism, sexism, ageism, racism, cynicism, and every other negative emotion. Thus, if we do not wish to "perish with the sword" of negativity, we must rid our minds, hearts, and lives of negative thoughts, concepts, words, and actions. Do as Paul suggested:

> "In malice be ye children, but in understanding be men."[1418]

The inner meaning:

> "When it comes to evil, be innocent, be oblivious, but in understanding evil, be wise, be vigilant."[1419]

## CAST OUT THE CONCEPT OF "HATE"

Let us take the word hate as an example. Being negative in nature, it is innately harmful physically, mentally, and spiritually. Therefore, this is a word that should never be used for anything or anyone, for once we think it, speak it, or act it out, it begins its unerring path back to us in the form of problems, havoc, and eventual disaster.

New Thought author Charles F. Haanel uses the example of the great 19th-Century thinkers Ralph Waldo Emerson and Thomas Carlyle. The former concentrated on his loves, and so reaped a life of tranquility, ease, and balance. The latter focused on his hatreds, and so created a life of conflict, struggle, and confusion. Which would you prefer, the life of Emerson or the life of Carlyle? God gave you the choice!

RETURNING GOOD FOR EVIL

To improve our lives on every level and bring happiness, we must first remove all evil from our minds. To do so, do not resist it. Simply refuse to acknowledge it. If someone hurts you, for instance, let it go immediately. Allow our Father in Heaven to avenge the wrongs of others, just as He promised He would.[1420] For Divine Mind is a self "consuming fire" when it is harnessed for unrighteousness (wrong-thinking).[1421]

Embracing evil, believing in evil, even merely recognizing evil as a "reality," causes it to gravitate toward you by the Law of Attraction. To live a life free of evil, one in which you and your loved ones are fully protected, follow Jesus' timeless Law of Attraction teachings:

> "Ye have heard that it hath been said, 'an eye for an eye, and a tooth for a tooth' [known as the *lex talionis*, or 'law of retaliation']: But I say unto you, that ye *resist not evil*: but whosoever shall smite thee on thy right cheek, turn to him the other also. And if any man will sue at the law, and take away thy coat, let him have thy cloke also.
>
> "And whosoever shall compel thee to go a mile, go with him twain. Give to him that asketh thee, and from him that would borrow of thee turn not thou away. Ye have heard that it hath been said, 'thou shalt love thy neighbour, and hate thine enemy.' But I say unto you, love your enemies, bless them that curse you, do good to them that hate you, and pray for them which despitefully use you, and persecute you; that ye may be the children of your Father which is in heaven: for he maketh his sun to rise on the evil and on the good, and sendeth rain on the just and on the unjust.
>
> "For if ye love them which love you, what reward have ye? do not even the publicans [tax collectors] the same? And if ye salute your brethren only, what do ye more than others? do not even the publicans so? Be ye therefore perfect, even as your Father

which is in heaven is perfect."[1422]

## EVIL: THE MANMADE MYTH!

At first these doctrines may seem difficult to put into practice—but only to those who do not understand how the Law of Attraction works. Actually, just as it is far easier to think positively than negatively, it is far easier to follow Jesus' teachings than to suffer the consequences of not following them! In the Aquarian Gospel, the Lord makes these comments:

> "Men seek salvation from an evil that they deem a living monster of the nether world; and they have gods that are but demons in disguise; all powerful, yet full of jealousy and hate and lust; whose favors must be bought with costly sacrifice of fruits, and of the lives of birds, and animals, and human kind. And yet these gods possess no ears to hear, no eyes to see, no heart to sympathize, no power to save.
>
> "This evil is a myth; these gods are made of air, and clothed with shadows of a thought. The only devil from which men must be redeemed is self, the lower self. If man would find his devil he must look within; his name is self. If man would find his savior he must look within; and when the demon self has been dethroned the savior, Love, will be exalted to the throne of power. The David of the light is Purity, who slays the strong Goliath of the dark, and seats the savior, Love, upon the throne."[1423]

## FREEING YOURSELF FROM EVIL

The most effortless method for avoiding evil then is to fill yourself with love, for as Paul said, pure love does not believe in, accept, or acknowledge evil.[1424] Another method is to keep yourself focused on the Christ Within,[1425] for, being perfect,[1426] it too does not recognize evil, sin, immorality, wickedness, or any other form of iniquity.[1427]

The very idea of evil itself is nothing but an illusionary ball and chain created by unenlightened Man and Woman. Thus in the Aquarian Gospel Jesus says:

> "The chains that bind men to the carcasses of earth are forged in fancy's shop; are made of air, and welded in illusion's fires."[1428]

To free yourself from your own "chains," keep your mind on godly things. By the Law, devilish things must and will disappear from your experience, and "illusion's fires" will be permanently extinguished.

To be happy, think happy thoughts, for these are of God (Divine Mind, the Christ). To be unhappy, think unhappy thoughts, for these are of the Devil (Human Mind, the Ego). In truth, there is no "adversary" but your own Ego, your Lower Self, and that is something you have complete control over. For as a Son of God,[1429] your Indwelling Christ[1430] has instant, constant, full access to the complete powers of the all-knowing, all-wise Father.[1431]

HAPPINESS OR UNHAPPINESS: THE CHOICE IS YOURS

How marvelous this is: through the judicious use of the Law of Attraction, you get to decide what to bring into your daily experience! You no longer have to be a *victim* of circumstance. You can be the *victor* of circumstance! You can determine what kind of day you are going to have, even what kind of life you are going to have, by changing your thoughts.

Just think, your entire future is in your hands, not other people's, not fate's, not even God's! Joyous thoughts bring a nonstop banquet of delicious rewards, as the book of Proverbs promises:

> "All the days of the afflicted are evil: but he that is of a merry heart [mind] hath a continual feast."[1432]

According to the Law of Attraction, happy thoughts attract more things to be happy about, and unhappy thoughts attract more things to be unhappy about. Which do you want? It is always up to you. Consider the words of the famed ancient Roman Emperor Marcus Aurelius:

> "The happiness of your life depends upon the quality of your thoughts."

What is more, happiness not only creates more happiness, it also generates health and abundance, while unhappiness not only creates more unhappiness, it also generates ill health and lack. Knowing these truths, it behooves you to do everything you can to think things that not only make you happy, but others as well. Now you know why Jesus and the Apostles were so fond of the phrase "be of good cheer,"[1433] and why Paul preached this injunction: "Rejoice evermore."[1434]

FOLLOWING YOUR BLISS

In conjunction with the Law of Attraction, here are a few ways to bring more happiness into your life. Some of these suggestions seem obvious. But actually, that is why many of us never consider them:

• *Think* about things that make you happy. Your Conscious Mind can only hold one thought at a time. So make it a positive one!
• *Say* things that make you happy. When in the company of others, use words that uplift the spirit.
• *Do* things that make you happy. Make a list of all the things you enjoy doing, then work through it, checking them as you go. When you are done, add more happiness-inducing activities to your list.

Here is how the noted American mythologist Joseph Campbell put it: "Follow your bliss." Think, say, and do things that make you feel good about yourself and the world. Make your home beautiful, and fill it with things that bring you joy. Wear clothes that you love, go to places that you love, spend time with people you love.

If you feel good, you are attracting more that will make you feel good. Feeling good makes you think good thoughts, and thinking good thoughts makes you feel good. Thus the book of Proverbs says:

> "A merry heart [mind] maketh a cheerful countenance: but by sorrow of the heart [mind] the spirit is broken."[1435]

If a thought comes into your mind that makes you unhappy, replace it right away with a happy one. Get back on a frequency of positivity. This sends out vibrations of happiness that, by the Law of Attraction, *must* come back to you in kind.

Keep this up. At some point it will become a habit. Then eventually you will not even think unhappy thoughts anymore. Like always attracts like, good or bad. Now that you understand these precepts, put them into practice and watch the blessings flow. Harken to the straightforward words of Jesus:

> "If ye know these things, happy are ye if ye do them."[1436]

# 17

# RELATIONSHIPS

"The lips of the wise shall preserve them."[1437]

## SOCIABLE MAN & WOMAN

**WE ARE THE MOST SOCIAL** of all the world's creatures. Other people are integral to every aspect of our lives, from family, friends, and school, to work, entertainment, and religion. The very core of our personal lives revolves around the relationships we have with the rest of humanity. Thus, when any one of these is not working, our lives can go into crisis.

Some of you reading this now may have an unproductive, unhealthy, or even toxic relationship with someone that you would like to rectify. Maybe you want to strengthen an already wonderful relationship. Or perhaps you are seeking a new relationship. Jesus' teachings on the Law of Attraction can help remedy all of these situations.

## HEAL A BROKEN RELATIONSHIP

What follows are simple instructions on repairing a damaged relationship with someone using the Law. Obviously, an exception to these rules would be someone who has abused you or is abusing you. In that case, you must decide whether or not to bring in outside assistance.

Either way, if you have enough faith, you can still use the Law of Attraction (alone or in conjunction with other modalities) to make positive changes in your own life—for all things are possible with God,[1438] who promises to always comfort those who are downcast![1439]

To begin with, start with yourself by doing the following inner work:

• Forgive the other person completely for any real or imagined hurts.[1440]

This means letting go of the past and moving forward.[1441]
- Accept the other person completely, good, bad, and everything else.[1442] This means no criticism, no complaints, no accusations about anything that has already transpired.[1443]  Release all of your yesterdays.  You cannot change them now.  They no longer exist.
- Give the other person unconditional love.  This means no demands on that person or your relationship with them.[1444]

If the person you are involved with is also willing to practice these suggestions, and continue on with them indefinitely, so much the better.

Once you have gone through this list and checked each one of them off, you can begin using the Law of Attraction to make the necessary changes:

- Create affirmations for how you want the relationship to be right now.  Example: "We have a beautiful healthy relationship that is fulfilling to both of us."
- Mentally repeat, and also write out, your affirmations on a daily basis.  Another example: "Our relationship is getting better and better everyday."
- Create visualizations that depict the relationship functioning happily and productively.  See the two of you communicating, relating, and sharing in a mutually loving and respectful manner.

Again, if possible, try to do work on these points together.  If that is impractical, please know and believe that miracles can still come from your inner work alone.

Either way, *always* make choices which you feel are appropriate for your situation.

STRENGTHEN AN EXISTING HEALTHY RELATIONSHIP
Follow these Law of Attraction principles to fortify any relationships you have that are already functional and healthy.  Everyday:

- Bless the other person.
- Bless the past, present, and future of this relationship.
- Be grateful for this relationship.
- Continue to accept, trust, nurture, support, and love the other person.  Whatever the two of you are doing, it is working!

- Create affirmations that acknowledge the beauty, strength, and mutually fulfilling aspects of the relationship. Example: "We have a wonderful relationship that is improving everyday."
- Create visualizations that portray the relationship continuing to function healthfully and create ongoing happiness.

## FINDING A NEW FRIEND OR ROMANTIC MATE

If you would like to draw new friendships or a romantic partner into your life, do the following:

- Create affirmations of your potential friend or love match as if they are already in your life. Examples: "I love my new best friend." "I am so blessed to have found my soul mate."
- Create visualizations that paint a mental picture of your ideal friend or partner. See them in your life. Make a mental movie of what you want to come about. See the two of you enjoying your time together. In your mind's eye, portray every scenario that you can think of to fully impress the Divine Mind with your desires.

## REMINDERS

As always, state your affirmations in the present tense, as if your desire has already occurred. You can say these to yourself, write them down, or say them out loud; or a combination of all three. Repeat them at least twice a day, more if possible. For Divine Mind will immediately get to work outpicturing any desire you convey once it sees that it is coming from a consistent and persistent thought.[1445]

Part of Jesus' teachings on the Law of Attraction states that you must affirm (pray) in private. So keep your affirmations and visualizations to yourself, or, if you deem it appropriate, just between you and your partner.[1446] You do not want to dilute the energy of your affirmations, or invite doubt and ridicule from others. This is between you and God (Divine Mind).

Remember that you must always take full responsibility for your life: if you are in an unhealthy relationship, you attracted it. If you are in a healthy relationship, you attracted it. If you are alone, you attracted it. If your life is full of friends and family, you attracted it.

This is not my teaching. It is an ancient biblical teaching, one based on even older Law of Attraction doctrines dating back thousands of years.[1447] Jesus understood and accepted these time-tested principles,[1448] and if you do as well, you will be able to "move mountains"![1449] Assuming responsibility for your experiences reempowers you, allowing you to regain your divine abilities. This puts the most powerful force in the Universe, the power of thought, back into your hands, right where God always intended it to be.

When you are one with your incorruptible Indwelling Christ, you have access to His unlimited wisdom.[1450] Use this wisdom to work with the Law of Attraction wisely. When you do, Jesus promises that you will no longer be a slave of your conditions. Instead, you will be the master of your conditions![1451]

A NOTE ON CHILDREN

One of our most important relationships is with our children. If you have children, or are planning on having them, pass along the ultimate family inheritance by teaching them about the Law of Attraction. Think of how different your life would be today if your own parents had instilled these amazing principles in you at an early age!

If you pay attention to your children's thoughts now, you will not have to worry about their behavior later. So give them the power to create happy, healthy, prosperous lives using Jesus' Law of Attraction doctrines, and when they are older they will bless you everyday God sends.

GOD FULFILLS YOUR AFFIRMATIONS IN HIS OWN TIME & WAY

If, over time, you feel that your Law of Attraction work concerning relationships (or any other area of your life) is not bearing the fruit you expected, generally speaking this can be attributed to one of three factors:

1) Cause: You are not applying the Law of Attraction principles properly. Solution: Reread this book and make sure you completely understand the Law as taught by Jesus.

2) Cause: You have not given the Divine Mind, God, enough time to manifest your desires. Solution: Let go of any preconceived ideas and expectations you may have. Keep at your affirmations and be patient. Do not give up on the Law, ever!

3) Cause: God is purposefully leading you in a new direction, one that will yield results so wonderful that you cannot begin to fathom them at this moment.[1452] Solution: Trust in the Lord![1453]

This anonymous 15th-Century painting of God (center), Jesus (right), and the Virgin Mary (left), portrays something that has never existed in all of human history, except in the minds of the uneducated and spiritually immature. God the Father on his heavenly throne. This anthropomorphic view of the Supreme Being as a humanlike ruler is, in fact, purely Pagan in origin, and was adopted by Old Testament writers from a wide assortment of sky-gods and "heavenly fathers" (such as Ra, Baal, Vishnu, Jupiter, and Zeus) venerated throughout ancient Egypt, Mesopotamia, Greece, Rome, Phoenicia, Persia, and India. From here the idea was absorbed into what I call modern Pagan Christianity, where it remains to this day, misleading one generation of mainstream Christians after another. As is clear from the New Testament, Jesus overturned this childish mythological image of God, this erroneous idolatry of a manmade Supreme Being, rightly calling it the "God of the dead." In its place He preached an "invisible God," the true God, whom He referred to as the "God of the Living," declaring once and for all that "God is Spirit, and they that worship him must worship him in spirit." Spirit being another word for mind, the early Gnostic Christians wrote: "God is all mind." Hence, today we know the "Father" as the Divine Mind, that aspect of the Law of Attraction which makes "all things possible with God."

# 18

# WORK

"A wholesome tongue is a tree of life: but perverseness therein is a breach in the spirit."[1454]

## YOU ATTRACT YOUR OCCUPATION

**W**HAT WE DO TO EARN a living is one of the most important aspects of human existence. Naturally then, our "job," whatever it may be, is central to our happiness, health, and prosperity. Each person has their own vital role to play on the world stage, for spiritually speaking, *all* occupations are of equal importance, from the lower rungs on the ladder to the higher ones, from a company's janitor to its CEO. God, who judges all men equally (for He is "no respecter of persons"),[1455] certainly sees no difference between them, and since we are extensions of God, neither should we, for in Spirit there is none.[1456] We are all "one body in [the Indwelling] Christ."[1457]

The old saying, "do what you love and you will never work a day in your life," is true. So if you love your job, you have created this through the Law of Attraction, and congratulations are in order.

On the other hand, if you detest your job, you have also created this through the Law of Attraction—though no doubt unconsciously. The wonderful thing is, you now have the knowledge to use the Law *consciously* to better your situation. In fact, that urge you feel to find a more suitable job is God's way of saying: "I AM here to do your bidding. Believe and I will make it so."[1458] What we want also wants us; what we are attracting is also attracting us. This is what it means to copartner with the Divine, to be "partakers of Christ,"[1459] to "labor" with God,[1460] to share in His holiness.[1461]

AFFIRMING YOUR DREAM JOB

If you want a job, or if you want a better job to replace your current one, you need not compete and struggle to find it. Begin by planting the request in your Subconscious Mind, then use the following Law of Attraction techniques to magnetize the ideal situation into your life:

• Create affirmations about the job you would like. Examples: "Finding a new job is easy. I am surrounded by great opportunities." "My new job is perfectly suited to me and I am enjoying it."
• Every morning and every evening, write out your thought-desires. Spell out the details of your dream job.
• Create visualizations in which you see yourself doing what you love, earning the money you want.

By affirming what you want, you are telling Divine Mind what to "make flesh";[1462] that is, what to materialize, for you. By writing out what you want, you are imprinting the Divine Mind with your needs. By visualizing what you want, you are giving Divine Mind an exact diagram of your desire.[1463]

YOUR ROLE AS GOD'S "BUSINESS PARTNER"

Since you are a copartner with God, your spiritual "business partner," you cannot simply sit and wait for your future employer to contact you. You are in spiritual "business" with the Father, so you must do your share of the work to make the "business" successful.

In this case this means doing what you can to track down the job you are looking for: search the papers, make the calls, fill out the applications, attend the interviews. As you go about your job search, the Holy Spirit will lead you to exactly what you are looking for using inspiration, intuition, and so-called "coincidences."

Anticipate a great outcome, knowing that every minute the Divine Mind is powerfully working for you, steadily, silently, and unseen. Look forward to the "expected end" that God has promised you,[1464] but keep your expectations realizable so that He can work His wonders efficiently. In other words, although the Father can create anything for us, it would not be realistic for someone who dropped out of high school to expect to procure a job as a physician. Affirm and visualize a job that is achievable for you now. You can work on upgrading your qualifications in the future if that is what you desire.

JOINING THE EVER SWELLING RANKS OF THE SELF-EMPLOYED
Do not discount the possibility that your next job could be one of your own creation. Thousands of individuals and families start their own businesses each year, and, in fact, this group makes up the largest category of small businesses in the U.S. If you are open to this idea, or actually want to be self-employed, do your affirmations accordingly, then listen to your "inner voice." This is the voice of God speaking to you, guiding you toward the perfect business concept in fulfillment of your specific needs.

BE PERSISTENT & THINK BIG!
Persevere in the direction of your desire following Jesus' Law of Attraction principles and you will "receive the promise";[1465] that is, you will attract the right situation, the right ideas, and the right people into your life, all at the right time, enabling you to achieve the goals you have planted in your Subconscious Mind.[1466]

Repeat after Jesus:

"And I, if I be lifted up . . . will draw all men unto me."[1467]

God is big. So think big!

# 19

# ABUNDANCE

"The tongue of the wise useth knowledge aright."[1468]

## THE UNIVERSAL ABUNDANCE

**GOD IS PURE ABUNDANCE! ALL** around us we see proof of this, for as the Bible says, "in Him all fullness dwells."[1469] Every square inch of our planet is covered with the creations of the Divine Mind, even our biggest cities. Everything is born in the mind of God, from dirt, sand, and rocks to grass, bushes, and trees. This includes all "manmade" structures as well, from common everyday items to the tallest skyscrapers. The world you see around you is God's world, filled to the brim and overflowing with His "unsearchable riches."[1470]

Drive out from the city and into the country. There you will see the clearest evidence of God's abundance: wild grass and flowers grow right up to the edge of the road, packed so tightly you cannot see the soil beneath. No human planted these. God did! Towering over these green carpets are forests made up of thousands of species of trees, sprouting up in rampant profusion as far as the eye can see. We have all seen grass, flowers, and even trees springing up from cracks in the middle of highways and freeways, another witness to the Father's exuberant expression of superabundance.

The night sky is filled with trillions of stars that continue in every direction, far beyond the capacity of our most powerful telescopes, while under our oceans millions of species of fish and marine plants form a living cornucopia, a veritable "sea of life." Even a teaspoon of pond water contains thousands of microscopic organisms, each one pulsating with the Divine Life Force.

And God has not rested from His original Creation: not only are some 20,000 formerly unknown species of plants and animals still being discovered each year, but God's evolutionary process continues, everyday creating new varieties of flora and fauna. This is why we will never be able to discover and name every organism on earth: the living God (Divine Mind)[1471] never stops creating, and the unlimited plenitude of His Creation will always be far ahead of anything scientists can count and catalog.[1472]

Here is how the book of Genesis describes the overabundance of God's Creation:

> And God said, "Let the waters bring forth *abundantly* the moving creature that hath life, and fowl that may fly above the earth in the open firmament of heaven." And God created great whales, and every living creature that moveth, which the waters brought forth *abundantly*, after their kind, and every winged fowl after his kind: and *God saw that it was good.*[1473]

To those who have the "(inner) eyes to see" and the "(inner) ears to hear,"[1474] all of this is evidence of the natural wealth that the Father lovingly bestows on His world everyday. The Father Himself calls this amazing earthly richness "good"!

WEALTH & POVERTY

If God is this generous with Nature, He is far more generous with His human children. In fact, as part of His plan for us here on earth, we have been designed to live abundantly, for abundance is our natural state. Deprivation and lack are illusions of the mass mind: we create poverty because we believe in it, because society teaches it and focuses on it. When you reject the phantom of shortage and privation, and instead believe in limitless abundance, you begin to draw God's natural wealth into your life. Then you only need to labor as often or as seldom as you believe you need to, and you will be as rich as you think you can be![1475]

Those who teach that living in poverty is "godly" in the sight of the Father, and that being poor is beneficial because it "humbles" us, have not only misread their Bibles, they have become blind to one of God's most important principles: abundance and wealth are part of our spiritual birthright. Emerson once rightly said:

> "*Man was born to be rich*, or grows rich by the use of his faculties, by the union of thought with nature [that is, God]."

Some 1,900 years earlier, Jesus guaranteed that those who realize the reality of the Indwelling Christ will have "access" to "all" that the Father has:[1476]

> "All that the Father giveth me shall come to me; and him that cometh to me I will in no wise cast out."[1477]

> "All things that the Father hath are mine: therefore said I, that 'he shall take of mine, and shall shew it unto you.'"[1478]

In modern language Jesus is saying that the Superconscious Mind (the "Father") will grant us anything we want through our Conscious Mind (the "Son"). Paul said the same thing:

> "If God be for us, who can be against us? He that spared not his own Son, but delivered him up for us all, how shall he not with him also *freely give us all things?*"[1479]

God has promised to "freely give us all things"! Why would He want it any other way? As human parents we deny nothing to our children that we can possibly give them. Our Divine Parent is no different, except for one thing: being unlimited, God can provide us with anything, including all of our heart's desires.[1480] This is how much the Father loves us.[1481]

In the Lord's parable of the Prodigal Son, the father is a symbol of God and his two sons are symbols of humanity. When the elder son complains about the festive homecoming held in honor of the return of his wayward younger brother, the father lovingly tells him: "Son, thou art ever with me, and all that I have is thine."[1482]

Think about this statement the next time you are feeling in any way impoverished. It is God's personal reminder to you that as your Divine Parent, His abundance is already yours in Heaven.[1483] To bring it into the physical, you need only have perfect faith in the spiritual; belief without the slightest doubt. Victorian New Thought authority Prentice Mulford wrote:

> "The Supreme Power [Divine Mind, the Father] has us in its charge, as it has the suns and endless systems of worlds in space. As we grow more to recognize this sublime and exhaustless wisdom, we shall learn more and more to demand that wisdom draw it to ourselves, make it a part of ourselves, and thereby be ever making ourselves newer and newer. This means ever perfecting health, greater and greater power to enjoy all that exists, gradual transition into a higher state of being and the development of powers we do

not now realize as belonging to us.

"We are the limited yet ever growing parts and expressions of the Supreme Never Ending Whole. It is the destiny of all in time to see their relation to the Supreme and also to see that the straight and narrow path to ever-increasing happiness is a perfect trust and dependence on the Supreme for the all round symmetrical wisdom and idea which we individually cannot originate.

"Let us then daily demand faith, for faith is power to believe and power to see that all things are parts of the Infinite Spirit of God, that all things have good or God in them, and that all things when recognized by us as parts of God must work for our good."

Mulford is entirely correct. If you agree, you must reject the false teachings of privation and want!

Let us read the words of the Master from Galilee for ourselves. Here is what Jesus says in the Gospel of Luke:

"Fear not, little flock; for *it is your Father's good pleasure to give you the kingdom.*"[1484]

The "kingdom" Jesus is speaking of is the Kingdom of God, a heavenly realm, not just in the Afterlife, but one that also exists right here and now.[1485] It is your own heaven on earth—your personal "promised land,"[1486] your private "land flowing with milk and honey"[1487]—given to you by divine right as an "heir of God through Christ."[1488] In the Aquarian Gospel our Lord explains the Kingdom of Heaven in this manner:

". . . heaven is not far away; and it is not a place of metes and bounds, is not a country to be reached; *it is a state of mind.* God never made a heaven for man; he never made a hell; we are creators and we make our own. Now, cease to seek for heaven in the sky; just open up the windows of your hearts, and, like a flood of light, a heaven will come and bring a boundless joy; then toil will be no cruel task."[1489]

Jesus says that it is the "good pleasure" of the Divine Mind, the Father, to "give you the kingdom"; that is, whatever you want![1490] Now consider His words as recorded by the Apostle John:

> "I am come that they might have *life*, and that they might have it
> more *abundantly*."[1491]

The word life here is from the Greek word *zoe*, meaning "the absolute
fullness of life." The word abundantly is from the Greek word *perissos*,
meaning "beyond measure," "exceeding," "extraordinary," "surpassing" all
that has come before it. Yes, Jesus wants you to live an abundant life, not
only spiritually, but also materially, as He Himself did. For you truly are
"the apple of His eye."[1492]

In his third epistle John made the following comment:

> "Beloved, I wish above all things that thou mayest prosper and be
> in health, even as thy soul prospereth."[1493]

Where did John get such notions? They could only have come from the man
I call, in Greek, *Iesous Trismegistus*: "Thrice-Greatest Jesus," for He was the
world's most enlightened teacher, powerful healer, and insightful prophet!
He was also the world's greatest Law of Attraction educator, and it was
under Him, the Holy Nazarene,[1494] that John served for three years.[1495]

## JESUS WAS A MILLIONAIRE, SPIRITUALLY & MATERIALLY!

Jesus spent nearly every minute of those last three years of His life preaching
not "the Gospel of Jesus,"[1496] but what He called "the Gospel of the
Kingdom,"[1497] that is, "the Good News about the Divine Mind." How did
He manage to survive without working at His regular job as a carpenter?[1498]
We can only assume that He was financially independent, for He could
manifest money just as easily as He manifested bread and fish for the
multitudes.[1499] In fact, on at least one known occasion He did exactly
that.[1500]

Jesus and the Apostles, in fact, possessed so much money that they
needed a treasurer[1501] and paid taxes,[1502] and from what the Bible tells us,
most of the Apostles were married,[1503] and thus were obviously
homeowners and landowners as well.[1504]

Where did Jesus and the Apostles' enormous wealth come from?
They did not work—they were always out "freely" healing[1505] and preaching
"the Gospel of the Kingdom"[1506]—and so did not generate an income. And
if our Lord was truly a homeless itinerant, a wandering Jewish mendicant,
as many Christian churches today teach, how is it that He so easily mingled
with the haughty upperclass of Roman society,[1507] self-important Pagans who

normally turned up their noses at both religious mystics and Jews?[1508]
It is true that Jesus said:

> "The foxes have holes, and the birds of the air have nests; but the
> Son of man hath not where to lay his head."[1509]

But this was just His cryptic response to a potential follower who had asked
Him if he could become one of His Disciples. Here is the inner meaning of
Jesus' reply:

> "You can follow me. But keep in mind that those who are God-
> realized or enlightened, that is, are aware of their Divine
> Nature,[1510] dwell in the spiritual Kingdom Within,[1511] not in a
> physical organized church."[1512]

This is why, after all, during his vision of the World Beyond, John the
Revelator saw "no temple" in the heavenly city of New Jerusalem.[1513]
Jesus could materialize anything, and so why not financial wealth
to make His life, and the lives of His Apostles and family members, more
comfortable and enjoyable? Indeed, money easily flowed to Him from all
sides, which, due to the Law of Attraction, only drew more affluence,
mainly from His many supporters from across the Near East. These ranged
from those on the lower echelons of society, such as Mary Magdalene[1514] and
her all-female priesthood,[1515] to the super rich from among Jesus "secret
Disciples,"[1516] one of the better known being Joseph of Arimathea, an
influential member of the local Sanhedrin:[1517]

> "When the even [night] was come, there came a rich man of
> Arimathaea, named Joseph, who also himself was Jesus' disciple.
> . ."[1518]

If Jesus had close associations with such men, we have every reason
to believe that He Himself was materially well off, just as the Thirteenth
Apostle said: "He was rich,"[1519] Paul bluntly remarked to his followers, and
"God shall supply all your need[s] according to his riches in glory by Christ
Jesus"![1520]
Thus, like wealthy people around the world, we can only assume
that the Lord too lived in a large beautiful home, probably in Capernaum.[1521]
In the Gospel of John, Jesus makes this statement:

"In my Father's house are many mansions: if it were not so, I would have told you. I go to prepare a place for you."[1522]

Those who have had near-death experiences tell us that Heaven is indeed filled, as far as the eye can see, with huge sprawling estates of every description! So let us take Jesus' words literally for a moment. If He is preparing mansions for us in the Afterworld, during His life here on earth He could have easily purchased or even manifested His own. The Aquarian Gospel, in fact, corroborates my theory:

"In Cana Jesus tarried not; he went his way with his disciples to Capernaum, where *he secured a spacious house* where, with his mother, he could live; where his disciples might repair to hear the Word. He called the men who had confessed their faith in him to meet him *in his home*, which *his disciples called, 'The school of Christ'* . . . *[where they] were taught the secret things of God.*"[1523]

Were the passages referring to Jesus' own personal mansion, "the School of Christ," taken out of the Bible by the early orthodox Church? It is possible, for there is not a single *original complete* Gospel manuscript in existence to refer to. All we have are highly annotated, edited, and "corrected" partial copies of partial copies, rewritten hundreds of years *after* Jesus' Ascension, by ecclesiastical priests who did not want the "secret sayings" of the real Jesus to be known.[1524]

Still, obvious vestiges of the Master's teachings on abundance and the Law of Attraction remain throughout the New Testament. Here, for example, is one of them, this one by Paul:

"And God is able to make all grace abound toward you; that *ye, always having all sufficiency in all things*, may abound to every good work."[1525]

"Always having all sufficiency in all things." What a grand promise this is to us, the "heirs of God's kingdom," that is, those of us who are "rich in faith" and love the Cosmic Christ[1526] which is in us all.[1527] And because God cannot lie, we know that this promise is true.[1528]

## ALL WEALTH ORIGINATES IN GOD!

As a diligent student of the Old Testament, Jesus had good reason for preaching abundance: as we are about to see, many of the Near East's most celebrated pre-Christian spiritual teachers were extremely wealthy. Where did their great affluence come from? Not from scrimping and saving, not from clever business ideas, not from powerful business connections, not even from hard work and the "sweat of their faces."[1529]

*All* wealth derives from only one source, and that source is God the Father, the Divine Mind, as the following scriptures testify. Let us begin with a passage from the book of Deuteronomy:

> "But thou shalt *remember the Lord thy God: for it is he that giveth thee power to get wealth*, that he may establish his covenant which he sware unto thy fathers, as it is this day."[1530]

From the same book:

> "*The Lord shall open unto thee his good treasure*, the heaven to give the rain unto thy land in his season, and to bless all the work of thine hand: and thou shalt lend unto many nations, and thou shalt not borrow."[1531]

This is from the book of 1 Chronicles:

> "*Both riches and honour come of thee* [God], and thou reignest over all; and in thine hand is power and might; and in thine hand it is to make great, and to give strength unto all. Now therefore, our God, we thank thee, and praise thy glorious name."[1532]

The book of Hosea relates this statement from God:

> ". . . I gave her [Israel] corn, and wine, and oil, and *multiplied her silver and gold . . .*"[1533]

From the book of Psalms:

> "Let *the Lord* be magnified, *which hath pleasure in the prosperity of his servant.*"[1534]

The following two passages are from the book of Ecclesiastes:

> ". . . every man should eat and drink, and *enjoy the good of all his labour, it is the gift of God.*"[1535]

*"Every man also to whom God hath given riches and wealth*, and hath given him power to eat thereof, and to take his portion, and to rejoice in his labour; *this is the gift of God."*[1536]

## COMBINING MATERIAL WEALTH WITH SPIRITUAL AWARENESS

The "preacher" who wrote Ecclesiastes repeats an eternal truth that was also well-known to Jesus: the "riches and wealth" we receive from our labors are "good" because they are a "gift of God." And if wealth is from the Father, it means that abundance is our natural state!

This being true, we must disabuse ourselves of the traditional Christian idea that "poverty is good, wealth is bad." For, as Ezra asserts, "both riches and honor come from God."[1537] In the book of Haggai, God Himself declares that all the silver and gold in the world is His.[1538] Now since we are His children, His literal heirs,[1539] this wealth belongs to us as well. "For all things are yours," declared Paul![1540]

It is true that Paul once made this greatly misunderstood comment:

"For the love of money is the root of all evil: which while some coveted after, they have erred from the faith, and pierced themselves through with many sorrows."[1541]

He does not say "money is the root of all evil," however. He says *"love* of money is the root of all evil." Jesus made a similar statement:

"Children, how hard is it for them that trust in riches to enter into the kingdom of God! It is easier for a camel [rope] to go through the eye of a needle, than for a rich man to enter into the kingdom of God."[1542]

Again, Jesus does not say that riches themselves are what make it hard for a man or woman to enter the Kingdom of God. He says "trust in riches," that is, an overemphasis on material wealth, is what makes it difficult. This is because the materialistic individual tends to lose sight of spiritual things. This is what John meant when he said:

"Love not the world, neither the things that are in the world. If any man love the world, the love of the Father is not in him. For all that is in the world, the lust of the flesh, and the lust of the eyes, and the pride of life, is not of the Father, but is of the world."[1543]

The book of Deuteronomy states the problem this way:

> "And when thy herds and thy flocks multiply, and thy silver and thy gold is multiplied, and all that thou hast is multiplied; then thine heart be lifted up, and thou forget the Lord thy God, which brought thee forth out of the land of Egypt, from the house of bondage."[1544]

And in the book of Psalms we find this passage:

> ". . . if riches increase, set not your heart upon them."[1545]

What the Father really wants for us is to have both material abundance *and* spiritual awareness. When these are in balance, there is nothing that can prevent us from entering the Kingdom of God and inheriting Christ's "incomprehensible wealth"[1546] and the endless "riches of his glory"![1547]

## AFFLUENCE IN THE OLD TESTAMENT

Indeed, many good and righteous biblical figures were wealthy, among them: Abraham, Isaac, Jacob, Esau, Barzillai the Gileadite, David, Solomon, Jehoshaphat, Hezekiah, and Job, to name but a few. The following passages, for example, are from the book of Genesis:

> "Abram [Abraham] went up out of Egypt, he, and his wife, and all that he had, and Lot with him, into the south. And *Abram was very rich in cattle, in silver, and in gold.*"[1548]

> "Then Isaac sowed in that land, and *received in the same year an hundredfold: and the Lord blessed him.* And the man waxed great, and went forward, and grew until he became very great: for he had possession of flocks, and possession of herds, and great store of servants: and the Philistines envied him."[1549]

> "And the man [Jacob] *increased exceedingly*, and had much cattle, and maidservants, and menservants, and camels, and asses."[1550]

> "And Esau took his wives, and his sons, and his daughters, and all the persons of his house, and his cattle, and all his beasts, and all his substance, which he had got in the land of Canaan; and went into the country from the face of his brother Jacob. For *their riches were*

*more than that they might dwell together*; and the land wherein they were strangers could not bear them because of their cattle."[1551]

In the book of 2 Samuel we find these words:

"And Barzillai the Gileadite came down from Rogelim, and went over Jordan with the king, to conduct him over Jordan. Now Barzillai was a very aged man, even fourscore years old: and *he had provided the king of [with] sustenance while he lay at Mahanaim; for he was a very great [rich] man.*"[1552]

The following is from the book of 1 Chronicles:

Thus David the son of Jesse reigned over all Israel. And the time that he reigned over Israel was forty years; seven years reigned he in Hebron, and thirty and three years reigned he in Jerusalem. And he died in a good old age, *full of days, riches, and honour . . .*"[1553]

From 2 Chronicles:

"Then Solomon came from his journey to the high place that was at Gibeon to Jerusalem, from before the tabernacle of the congregation, and reigned over Israel. And Solomon gathered chariots and horsemen: and he had a thousand and four hundred chariots, and twelve thousand horsemen, which he placed in the chariot cities, and with the king at Jerusalem. And *the king made silver and gold at Jerusalem as plenteous as stones*, and cedar trees made he as the sycomore trees that are in *the vale for abundance.*"[1554]

Also from 2 Chronicles:

"And the Lord was with Jehoshaphat, because he walked in the first ways of his father David, and sought not unto Baalim; . . . Therefore the Lord stablished the kingdom in his hand; and all Judah brought to Jehoshaphat presents; and *he had riches and honour in abundance.*"[1555]

Again, from 2 Chronicles:

"And *Hezekiah had exceeding much riches and honour:* and he made himself treasuries for silver, and for gold, and for precious stones, and for spices, and for shields, and for *all manner of pleasant jewels;*

storehouses also for the *increase* of corn, and wine, and oil; and stalls for *all manner of beasts, and cotes for flocks.* Moreover he provided him cities, and possessions of flocks and herds *in abundance*: for *God had given him substance very much.*"[1556]

From the book of Job:

> "There was a man in the land of Uz, whose name was Job; and that man was perfect and upright, and one that feared [respected] God, and eschewed evil. And there were born unto him seven sons and three daughters. His substance also was seven thousand sheep, and three thousand camels, and five hundred yoke of oxen, and five hundred she asses, and a very great household; so that *this man was the greatest [richest] of all the men of the east.*"[1557]

From the book of Proverbs:

> "*The blessing of the Lord, it maketh rich*, and he addeth no sorrow with it."[1558]

From the book of Psalms:

> "*They shall prosper* that love thee. Peace be within thy walls, and *prosperity within thy palaces.*"[1559]

## JESUS' MANY WEALTHY FOLLOWERS

We have seen that Jesus and the Apostles were wealthy too, as were many of the Master's Disciples and everyday followers. These included not only Joseph of Arimathaea,[1560] but Zacchaeus,[1561] the young ruler,[1562] and various groups of female devotees.[1563]

Jesus' posthumous proteges, such as Paul, also had numerous affluent followers, among them: Aquila and Priscilla,[1564] Narcissus,[1565] the Ethiopian treasurer,[1566] Nympha,[1567] Cornelius the centurion,[1568] Aristobulus,[1569] Lydia,[1570] Gaius,[1571] Onesiphorus,[1572] Stephanas,[1573] Ananias and Sapphira,[1574] Barnabas,[1575] and Philemon,[1576] along with a wide assortment of other unnamed individuals in the early Church as well.[1577]

The Jesus community at Phillipi, which included Lydia (above), was particularly solvent, as Paul noted:

> "Now ye Philippians know also, that in the beginning of the gospel, when I departed from Macedonia, no church communicated with

me as concerning giving and receiving, but ye only. For even in Thessalonica ye sent once and again unto my necessity. Not because I desire a gift: but I desire fruit that may abound to your account. But I have all, and abound: I am full, having received of Epaphroditus the things which were sent from you, an odour of a sweet smell, a sacrifice acceptable, wellpleasing to God."[1578]

Indeed, so great was the financial prosperity of the entire Jesus Community of the 1st Century, Luke wrote, that "neither was there any among them that lacked."[1579]

ONLY DIVINE MIND CAN "FILL YOUR BARN WITH PLENTY"
It is plain that riches, money, affluence, physical possessions, whatever term we want to apply to material abundance, is *always* a positive force in our lives if it is attained honestly and used wisely.

With it we not only benefit ourselves and our families, but those less fortunate than us; that is, those who have not yet learned to use the Law of Attraction to materially improve their lives. We might even go as far as to say that one of Man's most useful qualities is wealth, for with it he can and does change lives, and even the world itself.

We must always remember, however, that all abundance originates in Divine Mind, for as the Gospel of Mary asserts: "Wherever your mind is, there you will find the riches."[1580] Divine Mind, the Father, God, as the book of Deuteronomy states, is the only one who can "giveth thee power to get wealth."[1581]

This, what the Hindus call "Divine Wealth," is the true and only Source of all riches, and it is to this Source we must turn if we want to claim our rightful inheritance in the Kingdom of God.[1582] Here is how the book of Proverbs characterizes it:

"Honour the Lord [Divine Mind]. . . so shall thy barns be filled with plenty, and thy presses shall burst out with new wine."[1583]

"Let these sayings sink down into your ears,"[1584] and your "floors shall be full of wheat, and your presses shall overflow with wine and oil"![1585]

Addressing Him as "Good Master," a rich young ruler has asked Jesus how he may obtain eternal life, to which the Lord replies: "Why do you call me 'good'? There is none good but God." Despite this self-deflecting comment (just one of many which He made), and despite Jesus' constant pronouncement that we are all, like Him, gods imbued with a divine nature, the ancient Ecclesia (the early Catholic Church) chose to follow the Pagan tradition of apotheosization, turning the Prince of Peace into "the *only* begotten Son of God"—contradicting the teaching not only of Jesus Himself, but of the Apostles John and Paul as well (see e.g., John 1:12; 10:34; Romans 8:14). The Paganization of Jesus is clear from objective historical and paleographic studies. It is obvious that the Lord never spoke of Himself as the "Son of God," for this phrase appears nowhere in the earliest record of His sayings, the Gospel of Q (where He refers to Himself only as the "Son of Man," the common Aramaic term for a human being; see e.g., Ezekiel 2:1). Other examples of what I call "divinity passages" were also later intentionally added by the Church to the books of the New Testament, scriptures such as Acts 8:37 and 1 John 5:7—both which are absent from the Codex Sinaiticus (written around A.D. 340). To make Jesus' Paganesque deification official, the doctrine of Jesus' Godhood was formally declared at the Council of Nicaea in the year 325. Up until that time, the Christian masses had assumed that Jesus, though He possessed a divine nature like the rest of humanity, was simply a great teacher, healer, and prophet, a view still held to this day by many Jews, Unitarians, and Universalists around the world. This certainly seems to have been Jesus' own view of Himself as well, as an unbiased study of the historical record will reveal. But whether one accepts Jesus as an enlightened human being or as God's "only begotten Son," the truth of His amazing Law of Attraction teachings, a part of what He called "the Gospel of the Kingdom," remains the same.

# 20

# MONEY

"No weapon that is formed against thee shall prosper; and every tongue that shall rise against thee in judgment thou shalt condemn. This is the heritage of the servants of the Lord, and their righteousness is of me," saith the Lord.[1586]

## WEALTH IS AVAILABLE TO BOTH THE IDLE & THE INDUSTRIOUS

**W**E HAVE ESTABLISHED THAT ABUNDANCE is good, that it is a gift from God, and that it is therefore our natural state. Balanced with spiritual values, abundance helps us manifest all of our earthly desires in the here and now (the Kingdom of God). What we need to look at next is how to draw it into our lives using Jesus' teachings on the Law of Attraction.

First, it is important to understand where money comes from. Many of the richest people in the world expend very little energy attaining and maintaining their wealth, while many of the poorest individuals work night and day and never get ahead. Some of the most immoral people earn vast sums of money, while many of the most righteous struggle daily to make ends meet. How do we explain these seeming dichotomies?

As was discussed in the previous chapter, the answer is that money does not come from hard work, long hours, perspiration, and personal sacrifice, nor does it come from trying to be angelic, or following the often manmade rules of one's church. Money comes from the Source, from God, in response to *what you think*, no matter who you are or what your personal way of life is. This is precisely what God Himself said:

"[You will succeed] *not by might, nor by power, but by my spirit,*" saith the Lord of hosts. "[You will then be able to say:] 'Who art thou,

O great mountain?' [and it] . . . shalt become a plain . . ."[1587]

In his letter to Timothy, Paul put it this way:

> "[Do not] trust in uncertain [material] riches, but in *the living God, who giveth us richly all things to enjoy.*"[1588]

Thus, good hardworking people who want to be rich, but continually think thoughts of lack and want, believe in poverty, and feel poor, will never become wealthy. They will only draw more impoverishment to themselves. On the other hand, wicked lazy people who want to be millionaires, and continually think thoughts of abundance and plenty, believe only in affluence, and feel rich, will become wealthy. This is the Law of Attraction, God in action!

This is what is meant by the Bible passage: "The Lord maketh poor, and maketh rich."[1589] Divine Mind is behind everything, answering the call of your thoughts, whether they be thoughts of wealth or thoughts of poverty, and whether the thinker is a saint or a sinner. For God is "no respecter of persons."[1590] All thoughts are received without favoritism and judged by the Father using the same criteria, according to the same standard, no matter who is thinking them.[1591]

If you throw a boomerang into the air, due to the laws of physics it will circle back to you. The Law of Attraction is no different. Whoever you are, whatever you are focusing your thoughts on, whatever your deepest convictions, whatever you are feeling, will come back to you in the shape of your circumstances, conditions, events, environment, and experiences. Thus the 17th-Century founder of the Quakers, Christian mystic George Fox, wrote:

> ". . . every one of thine own words shall be thy burden, and they shall come home upon thee, and be crammed into thee again; and, in the day of thy judgment, the witness within thee shall answer."

## MONEY IS ENERGY

Fox understood that thoughts are things; or to be more precise, that *thoughts are energy, spiritual energy*, and *thinking is a spiritual activity*, one that can be scientifically validated. As we have noted, the electric waveforms they produce can even be seen on machines, such as electroencephalographs (EEG). When we think, we are actually sending vibrating waveforms out into the Universe. Because of the scientific law "like attracts like," as they move through space and time, these waveforms seek out other waveforms with matching frequencies.

Once joined together, they begin their return trip to you, now doubled, or even tripled or quadrupled, in size and power. This is the start of the manifestation of your thoughts on the physical plane, as well as the fulfillment of God's promise to you:

> "For as the rain cometh down, and the snow from heaven, and returneth not thither, but watereth the earth, and maketh it bring forth and bud, that it may give seed to the sower, and bread to the eater: so shall *my word [thought] be that goeth forth out of my mouth [mind]: it shall not return unto me void, but it shall accomplish that which I please, and it shall prosper in the thing whereto I sent it.*"[1592]

With this understanding of the attracting power of thought, it is now clear why thoughts of lack only draw more lack, and why thoughts of wealth only draw more wealth. *Your word is constantly creating your world;*[1593] or in simple terms, you are what you think. Therefore your health is what you think it is, your experiences match your beliefs, and your life corresponds with what you feel. So too with your finances: they are what you think, believe, and feel they are, for the energy of your thoughts, beliefs, and feelings are constantly attracting their like back to you from the surrounding Universe.

Money, as with everything else, is just energy vibrating at a certain rate. If you want more of it, you must think positive thoughts about it in order to match its vibratory rate. If you want to be a millionaire, for instance, you must think, talk, and act like a millionaire. The Law must eventually physically manifest your thoughts of prosperity, for the creative aspect of your mind, the Subconscious, is your lifelong servant. And its only spiritual job is to obey your commands by drawing down from the Superconscious Mind whatever you claim. From that moment on it is yours forever after by divine fiat.

On the other hand, if you think of money as "filthy lucre,"[1594] believe that poverty is the fate of most people, and feel that the rich are merely "lucky," you are sending out a negative vibration about money that will continue to keep you in dire straits. Now that you know how the Law of Attraction works, would it not be far better to embrace the positive teachings the Bible gives us concerning wealth, such as this from the insightful author of Ecclesiastes: "Money answereth all things"![1595]

FALSE VIEWS OF MONEY
Obviously money in and of itself is neither good or evil. Like fire, it is a form of energy that can be harnessed for constructive use or destructive use. Wise people use money for good only, and because of this they view it as a positive force. This attracts a constant and ever increasing stream of money to them, eliminating the fear, worry, and hardship experienced by people who think of money as something negative.

Those who hold this false view, that money is somehow "evil," not only ignore scripture to the contrary, but are also usually those who do not have enough of it and do not know how to procure more, or those who are extremely wealthy and are ashamed of their affluence. This second group, seeing the enormous amount of poverty in the world, think "there is not enough to go around." In order to "level the playing field," they vigorously oppose ideas like capitalism while promoting political systems like socialism and communism—along with the notion that the rich must be heavily taxed so that their wealth can be spread out evenly among the lower classes.

All of this is wrong-thinking based on the false beliefs of the mass mind!

As we are about to see, in God's Universe there is far more than enough to go around. The poor are only poor because they have been taught to believe in poverty by the mass mind, by their parents, school, society, and religion. The Law of Attraction takes our beliefs literally, outpicturing in the visible what we think in the invisible. And so a poor mind produces a poor bank account.

In short, the difference between the homeless man and the wealthy man all comes down to the thoughts they each think. Look at someone's health, finances, relationships, and living situation, and you are looking at that person's innermost thoughts in physical manifestation.

Now if every single person on earth practiced the Law positively, deprivation and want would disappear and everyone would be wealthy, everyone would have more than they need. Yet even then, the Father's storehouse would still overflow with an excess of superabundance!

When one works *with* the Law of Attraction (health, wealth, and happiness) instead of *against* it (disease, poverty, and misery), there is no need for competition to begin with, and the so-called "dog eat dog" world reveals itself to be what it really is: just another illusion of the mass mind. This is because positive use of the Law means entering the Kingdom of

Heaven, where the riches of God are beyond measure, where extravagant surplus is the norm, where plenitude knows no end. It is a plane of consciousness where your divine powers are at their fullest, and where you are least affected by physical forces!

With your own personal wealth stream now at your disposal, there is no need to impinge on anyone else, nor compete against others for jobs, position, or salary. In fact, if you try to compete with others you are only hurting yourself and wasting time, for your only rival is your own negative thinking, your thoughts of lack, of debt, of limitation.

Each individual can manifest his or her own abundance just as you have manifested yours,[1596] for, based on our thoughts and beliefs, we all have equal access to the Kingdom of God, what I call the Realm of Divine Mind.[1597] Jesus teaches us that through the Law of Attraction, we can go from being competitors to creators, with each person receiving exactly what he or she believes in.

The lesson? Do not compete. Create!

Capitalism then is not a negative system that promotes financial inequality, as many maintain. It merely highlights the financial inequality that naturally results from how individuals use or misuse the Law of Attraction. Become a cocreator with God[1598]—who always "worketh in you"[1599]—and leave the rat race of competition, greed, and jealousy behind!

The Psalmist, an ardent practitioner of the Law of Attraction, gave us this wonderful pro-wealth affirmation, which we should repeat "all the day long":

> "Say continually, 'Let *the Lord* be magnified, which *hath pleasure in the prosperity of his servant*.' And my tongue shall speak of thy righteousness and of thy praise all the day long."[1600]

## MONEY IS WHAT YOU THINK IT IS

Those with anti-money beliefs like to quote the Bible to buttress their negative opinion of wealth. And they have plenty to choose from, for the Good Book contains dozens of scriptures that appear to cast wealth in a bad light.

However, on a close and accurate reading, none specifically say that money itself is evil. The gist of these particular biblical writers is always that it is rank materialism—namely the love of money without spiritual awareness—that is evil. This is an enormous and important difference, and Jesus agreed, saying:

> "Lay not up for yourselves treasures upon earth, where moth and rust doth corrupt, and where thieves break through and steal: but lay up for yourselves treasures in heaven, where neither moth nor rust doth corrupt, and where thieves do not break through nor steal: for where your treasure is, there will your heart be also."[1601]

As mentioned, even the most famous anti-wealth passage in the entire Bible has been misread and therefore misunderstood. Paul never said: "Money is the root of all evil." His exact words were:

> "For *the love of money* is the root of all evil: which while some coveted after, they have erred from the faith, and pierced themselves through with many sorrows."[1602]

The inner meaning:

> "An obsession with money to the exclusion of everything else goes against the Father. Nearly all of those who do this stray from the Path of God and lose their spiritual values, creating countless problems for themselves."[1603]

If you are poor and wish to remain so, or if you have money and wish to create poverty for yourself, by all means continue to view money in a negative light, and continue to study and misinterpret the Bible's many seemingly anti-money passages. However, keep in mind that not only is this approach to money both unscientific and unspiritual—and therefore self-destructive—it goes completely contrary to Jesus' teachings on the Law of Attraction.

If you want financial security and abundance, ignore the naysayers and focus on all of the good things that money, when used wisely, produces. Let us be honest: you cannot create a quality life without money, and you are of little service to the world if you yourself are poor, hungry, and malnourished. Emerson taught that we are all "born to be rich," while bestselling Law of Attraction educator Bob Proctor maintains that it is actually our obligation to become wealthy. And Jesus would agree, as His own words testify:

> "I am come that they might have life, and *that they might have it more abundantly*."[1604]

The inner meaning:

> "Your Indwelling Christ exists to allow you to obtain the absolute most out of life, and that you might obtain it beyond measure."[1605]

## SPIRITUAL AND MATERIAL "BREAD"

Jesus, that great teacher of the Law of Attraction, understood that money, like all things, comes only through the Divine Mind,[1606] the Christ Within, the Great I AM.[1607] Because we all possess an Indwelling Christ,[1608] we can change our financial circumstances whenever we want. We have only to access the Christ Within, our Higher Self, and this we do through thought.

If we repeatedly send our Subconscious Mind the proper thoughts regarding money, it must respond accordingly by manifesting our own personal "bread from heaven," both spiritual and material bread. Thus, speaking as the Great I AM, the Inner Christ, Divine Law, Jesus said:

> "Labour not for the meat which perisheth, but for that meat which endureth unto everlasting life, which the Son of man shall give unto you: for him hath God the Father sealed. . . . Our fathers did eat manna in the desert; as it is written, 'He gave them *bread from heaven* to eat.' . . . Verily, verily, I say unto you, Moses gave you not that *bread from heaven*; but my Father giveth you the true *bread from heaven*. For the *bread of God* is he which cometh down from heaven, and giveth life unto the world. . . .
>
> "*I am* the bread of life: he that cometh to me shall never hunger; and he that believeth on me shall never thirst. . . . *I am* that bread of life. Your fathers did eat manna in the wilderness, and are dead. This is the bread which cometh down from heaven, that a man may eat thereof, and not die. *I am* the living bread which came down from heaven: if any man eat of this bread, he shall live for ever . . ."[1609]

When we partake of the "living bread" of the Indwelling Christ, we not only receive spiritual fulfillment, we will be materially fulfilled as well. Indeed, "eating" the "true bread from heaven" (that is, recognizing your oneness with the Universal Christ Within)[1610] allows you to easily increase the amount of "bread" (money) in your life. This is done by communicating this need from your Indwelling Christ (Conscious Mind) to the Holy Spirit (Subconscious Mind). The Holy Spirit then requests it from the Father (Superconscious Mind), and, as the Lord promised us, "thy will be done, as in heaven, so in earth."[1611] Study closely these words from the Master:

"All that the Father giveth me shall come to me; him that cometh to me I will in no wise cast out."[1612]

## GOD'S ENDLESS SUPPLY OF ABUNDANCE

God, the Divine Mind, is infinite and eternal in all ways and in all directions. Therefore He has no limitations and His bounteous blessings are inexhaustible, for in Him "all fullness dwells."[1613] Because you are an individualization of God,[1614] you are an "heir" to God's Kingdom,[1615] with full recourse to His limitless supply of both spiritual and material treasures.[1616] This is what the Psalmist was referring to when he said: "The Lord is my shepherd; I shall not want";[1617] and "my cup runneth over."[1618]

To demean monetary wealth in particular then is to demean God, for God is all, including everything from a lowly penny to a $100,000 bill.[1619] Who are we to degrade the things of God, let alone God Himself? Who are we to try and constrain the Mind of God? Hear the words of the Father:

> "Prove me now herewith," saith the Lord of hosts, "if I will not *open you the windows of heaven*, and *pour you out a blessing, that there shall not be room enough to receive it.*"[1620]

What a generous God we have, the same "One Source" that scientists call "Nature." And because He approaches us holistically, He knows that we cannot have complete happiness without mental, spiritual, and physical fulfillment. Thus the limitless Father has placed no limits on you. Instead, He wants you to have whatever you want, so that your happiness will be complete. And He will even "open the windows of heaven" for you to make this happen! Jesus said precisely the same thing:

> "Whatsoever ye shall ask the Father in my name, *he will give it you.* . . . ask, and ye shall receive, that your joy may be full."[1621]

No plainer words have ever been spoken: Christ (Divine Law) wants you to be happy, and the Father (Divine Mind) is willing to give you whatever you desire to make it so. Just follow the Lord's simple instructions, and you too will soon see what it means to have your "cup runneth over"!

THE KEYS TO THE KINGDOM

To accomplish this the Father has offered you the literal keys to the Kingdom of God, the keys of life and death, of Heaven and Hell.[1622]  And what are those "keys"?  Among them are His Law of Attraction principles, encapsulated in Jesus' simple three-part formula:

> "What things soever ye desire, when ye pray, believe that ye receive them, and ye shall have them."[1623]

If we break this statement down into its three natural components, we can more clearly see the Lord's mystical "recipe" for improving not only your financial situation, but any area of your life:

1) *Conceive*: create, clarify, and affirm (pray for) your desire.
2) *Believe*: know completely that your desire will come true.
3) *Receive*: let go and let God manifest your desire.

Now read the Master's words again:

> "What things soever ye desire [conceive], when ye pray, believe that ye receive them [believe], and ye shall have them [receive]."[1624]

There is no mistaking the meaning here: when you conceive, believe, and receive, you will achieve!  Thus Paul's deeply mystical comment: "I have planted, Apollos watered; but God gave the increase."[1625]  The inner meaning:

> "The Conscious Mind plants the seed-thought, the Subconscious Mind nurtures it, and the Superconscious Mind manifests it on the physical plane."[1626]

Jesus wants you to know that His Kingdom, the Kingdom of God, is within you,[1627] and that the power to rule this inner land comes from the "Father that dwelleth within you,"[1628] for "God is all mind."[1629]  Therefore, abundance must start from within you as well, for by both divine and natural law anything physical has to begin on the mental plane.

Yes, it is true that some effort is always required in order to earn our keep,[1630] for copartnering with God is a form of labor.[1631]  But the abundant riches we want and need in order to create true happiness originate in thought, and in the beliefs and feelings that flow from them, not in "blood, sweat, and tears." For "God shall supply all your need[s] according to his riches in glory by Christ Jesus."[1632] As our Lord Himself said, whatever your desires are: "Seek ye first the kingdom of God, and his righteousness; and *all these things shall be added unto you.*"[1633]

To "seek the Kingdom of God" means to follow God's commandments, and in simplest terms, to "follow God's commandments" means to think positively, feel positively, speak positively, and act positively. And here we find the true meaning of Paul's commandment: "Give yourself to God."[1634] We must reject all thoughts of lack; refuse to believe in poverty; ignore all feelings of deprivation. These are illusions created by Satan (human Ego) out of ignorance stemming from the limited consciousness of mass mind.

Jesus places no limits on your desires, no restrictions on how many material possessions you can own, how big your home should be, how successful you can be, how much money you can have in your bank account. He does not say, "*some* things shall be added unto you." His exact words are: "*all* things shall be added unto you."

CLAIMING YOUR DIVINE INHERITANCE
And all things *will* be given to you by the Supreme Intelligence, if you will only apply Jesus' teaching on the Law to your own life!

Focus only on what you want, not on what you have. Center your attention on how you want your life to be, not on how it actually is. For the Universal Mind sees no difference between physical reality and spiritual reality. It always responds to what you are spiritually thinking about as if it is physically real. Thus, concentrate on your desires, believe with full expectation,[1635] give thanks,[1636] and release it all to God, Divine Mind.

Here is how New Thought authority Wallace Wattles put it in the early 1900s:

> "The men and women who practice the [Law of Attraction correctly] . . . will certainly get rich; and *the riches they receive will be in exact proportion to the definiteness of their vision, the fixity of their purpose, the steadiness of their faith, and the depth of their gratitude.*"

Money begets money, so the more of it you acquire, the more of it is drawn to you. The attractive force of money is so powerful that banks will not loan you money if you are indigent, but they will happily lend you all you need if you are wealthy. Celebrities attract money simply by virtue of appearing successful, whether they actually are or not. And did you know that a $1,000 bill can fetch up to $2,000 at auction?

Birds of a feather do indeed flock together, which is why wealth likes wealth and poverty likes poverty. For your Inner Trinity is always attracting more of what you are thinking (Christ, Conscious Mind), more of what you are doing (Holy Ghost, Subconscious Mind), and more of what you have already manifested (God, Superconscious Mind). This makes the statement that "the rich get richer and the poor get poorer" absolutely true. But please keep in mind that the law that makes one man affluent is the same law that makes another man insolvent. The only real difference between rich and poor is the manner of thought!

Focus on this then: money is attracted to money, and it will be attracted to you too if you respect it and develop a prosperity consciousness. What we want also wants us in return; what we are attracted to is also attracted to us; what we need also needs us. If you think, believe, and feel positively about money, it will be drawn to you like a magnet from God's unlimited supply of abundance.

You deserve to be wealthy, not only spiritually but also materially. And so does everyone else. This is why you should *always desire the same thing for others that you desire for yourself.* Picture everyone being perfectly wealthy, healthy, and happy, and your positive loving imagery will return to you tenfold, and in ways which you cannot now imagine.[1637]

"Serve the Lord Christ [the Indwelling Christ] and ye shall receive the reward of your inheritance," said Paul.[1638] So go ahead and claim your divine estate now by aligning with the vibration of wealth. It is already yours in the invisible, and always was.[1639] Claiming it, using Jesus' Law of Attraction doctrines, brings it into the physical at the proper time according to the all-knowing wisdom of the "Father that dwelleth within you."[1640] This is what I call "Wealthcare," and it costs you nothing but a little daily mental discipline!

Heed the words of the Divine Mind as recorded in Psalms:

> "Blessed is the man that walketh not in the counsel of the ungodly, nor standeth in the way of sinners, nor sitteth in the seat of the scornful. But his delight is in the law of the Lord; and in his law doth he meditate day and night. And he shall be like a tree planted by the rivers of water, that bringeth forth his fruit in his season; his leaf also shall not wither; *and whatsoever he doeth shall prosper.*"[1641]

Jesus using the Law of Attraction to raise Lazarus from the dead. Like all biblical stories, this one too is amenable to mystical interpretation. Lazarus represents the soul that is asleep to the truth of our divine nature. Jesus represents the I AM, the Higher Self, the Universal Indwelling Christ, that awakens the somnolent Lower Self to the knowledge of its divinity. Lazarus' tomb represents the incarceration of Man by the false thoughts of the mass mind. The stone (right) that blocks the entrance to the tomb is a symbol of the human Ego, which hinders spiritual growth by cutting us off from God, Divine Mind, the "Father." Lazarus' sister Martha (foreground) symbolizes the faith that is necessary to overcome the Ego and mass mind, in order to reawaken the soul from its deathlike slumber back into God Consciousness.

# 21

# HEALTH

"Pleasant words are as an honeycomb, sweet
to the soul, and health to the bones."[1642]

## OUR HEALTH IS WHAT WE BELIEVE IT IS

**ECAUSE HEALTH (EASE) IS OUR** natural state, ill health (disease) is both unnatural and unnecessary, for it is always the result of
wrong-thinking. This is due to the Law of Attraction, a two-edged
sword that, as we have seen, cuts both ways,[1643] for like, good or bad,
attracts like.

Thus, all disease is manmade, or more to the point, self-made. We
bring on our own health problems by thinking negatively, mainly about
ourselves, but also about the world around us. Nearly every disease, in fact,
can be traced to either self-hatred or to our general negative beliefs, or
more often, to both. Conversely, healthy people love themselves and have
positive beliefs about life. In short, what you believe in your heart becomes
true for you in your world. Whatever you are experiencing right now is
merely the manifestation of what you have been thinking about yourself!

Did you know, for example, that cigarette smokers who believe
smoking is not bad for them have less health problems than smokers who do?
Did you know that self-loving people have less diseases from eating
"unhealthy" foods than self-loathing people do who eat "healthy" foods?

Did you know that there are happy people who eat whatever they
want and live into their hundreds, while there are unhappy people who are
meticulous about their diets who only live into their fifties and sixties? Did
you know that there are individuals who take vitamin supplements and
exercise religiously everyday, but who die in their twenties and thirties?
Did you know that both Jesus and Paul taught that a strict diet and physical
exercise are unnecessary, if not completely useless?[1644]

How do we explain these facts? How did comedian George Burns live to be 100 while drinking a shot of whiskey and smoking a dozen cigars everyday for seventy years? All of this goes against what mainstream medicine teaches us.

The answer is elegantly simple: God, working through the Law of Attraction, always gives us what we believe! If we believe that nothing can harm us and that our lifestyle is a healthy one, we too can live into our 100s, just like optimist Mr. Burns. Here, for example, is one of the centenarian's more famous quotes:

> "Age to me means nothing. I can't get old; I'm working. I was old when I was twenty-one and out of work. As long as you're working, you stay young. When I'm in front of an audience, all that love and vitality sweeps over me and I forget my age."

Burns' positive attitude was one of the things that allowed the beloved entertainer to remain youthful well into old age. He kept his focus on life-nurturing thoughts rather than on life-depriving thoughts. Like Jesus, Burns lived according to the wise man's creed: "God is not the God of the dead, but of the living."[1645]

JESUS ON HEALTH & DIET

Jesus certainly felt strongly about this topic. As He did on every other subject, He brilliantly summarized His entire doctrine on physical health in one concise sentence:

> "Not that which goeth into the mouth defileth a man; but that which cometh out of the mouth, this defileth a man."[1646]

Here is the Lord's statement in biblical context, from the Gospel of Matthew:

> Then came to Jesus scribes and Pharisees, which were of Jerusalem, saying, "Why do thy disciples transgress the tradition of the elders? for they wash not their hands when they eat bread." But he answered and said unto them . . . "Ye hypocrites, well did Esaias [Isaiah] prophesy of you, saying, 'This people draweth nigh unto me with their mouth, and honoureth me with their lips; but their heart is far from me. But in vain they do worship me, teaching for doctrines the commandments of men.'"
> And he called the multitude, and said unto them, "Hear,

and understand: not that which goeth into the mouth defileth a man; but that which cometh out of the mouth, this defileth a man." Then came his disciples, and said unto him, "Knowest thou that the Pharisees were offended, after they heard this saying?" But he answered and said, "Every plant, which my heavenly Father hath not planted, shall be rooted up. Let them alone: they be blind leaders of the blind. And if the blind lead the blind, both shall fall into the ditch."

Then answered Peter and said unto him, "Declare unto us this parable." And Jesus said, "Are ye also yet without understanding? Do not ye yet understand, that whatsoever entereth in at the mouth goeth into the belly, and is cast out into the draught? But those things which proceed out of the mouth come forth *from the heart*; and they defile the man. For out of the heart proceed evil thoughts, murders, adulteries, fornications, thefts, false witness, blasphemies: these are the things which defile a man: but to eat with unwashen hands defileth not a man."[1647]

The Aquarian Gospel gives this version, in which Jesus addresses the Apostles' confusion over the parable:

> "Do you not yet perceive that what a man takes in his mouth defiles him not? His food goes not into his soul; it is material for flesh and bone and brawn. *To spirit everything is clean.* That which defiles a man wells up from carnal thoughts; and carnal thoughts spring from the heart, and generate a host of evil things. From out the heart comes murders, thefts and foolishness. All selfish acts and sensual deeds spring *from the heart*. [Thus to] . . . eat with unwashed hands does not defile the man."[1648]

According to Jesus, it is what comes out of our "hearts"—in Greek, the *kardia*; that is, the mind, the mental fountain of thought and desire—that causes disease, not what goes into our mouths. "It is the mind that produces negative (evil) thoughts; these are the things which pollute and sicken us, not what we eat," the Master is saying.[1649]

Following the example of his teacher, Paul made this declaration:

> "Now the Spirit speaketh expressly, that in the latter times some shall depart from the faith, giving heed to seducing spirits, and doctrines of devils; speaking lies in hypocrisy; having their conscience seared with a hot iron; forbidding to marry, and commanding to abstain from meats [that is, specific foods], which God hath created to be received with thanksgiving of them which

> believe and know the truth. For every creature of God is good [to eat], and nothing to be refused, if it be received with thanksgiving: for it is sanctified by the word of God and prayer."[1650]

Also from Paul:

> "For meat destroy not the work of God. All things indeed are pure; but it is evil for that man who eateth with offence."[1651]

The inner meaning:

> "There is no food that can hurt you, for all things are pure in and of themselves. But if one believes a food is harmful, then it will harm him."[1652]

Again, from Paul:

> "But meat commendeth us not to God: for neither, if we eat, are we the better; neither, if we eat not, are we the worse."[1653]

The inner meaning:

> "Food cannot make us more spiritual or less spiritual. There is nothing to be gained by eating a specific food, and there is nothing to lose by not eating a specific food."[1654]

The spiritual belief that our physical diet is relatively unimportant is also reflected in Jesus' statement that "man does not live by bread alone, but by every word that proceedeth out of the mouth of God,"[1655] and by Paul's conviction that we should "nourish ourselves up in the words of faith and of good doctrine."[1656] The book of Hebrews echoes these sentiments:

> "[Concerning diet, be] not carried about with divers and strange doctrines. For it is a good thing that the heart [Subconscious Mind] be established with grace; not with meats [foods], which have not profited them that have been occupied therein."[1657]

## DO YOU HAVE THE FAITH OF JESUS?

As simple as Jesus' health doctrine is, there is a catch to it, one that is mystically embedded in the teaching itself: yes, if you love yourself, are happy and kind, think positive thoughts about everything you eat, you can put whatever you want into your body, including "any deadly thing," and "it shall not hurt you."[1658] But for this to be truly successful, you must believe, with 100 percent certainty, that what you are eating and drinking is good for you.[1659] In other words, you must have the faith of Jesus Himself to make this law work in your favor.

Yet, we must honestly acknowledge that there are very few of us who have the perfect faith of Jesus. We want it, we may be striving for it, we might even be near it—but we do not yet have it. Most of us are simply not spiritually mature or evolved enough to be at His level; the level of perfect enlightenment, perfect Christhood, perfect at-one-ment with God. We have the potential to be, as Jesus Himself repeatedly pointed out,[1660] but the reality is that the majority of us are not there yet.[1661]

What does this mean as far as health?

It means that those of us who do not have perfect faith must watch what we eat and treat our bodies and minds with the greatest care and respect. Paul commented on this situation:

> "For one believeth that he may eat all things: another, who is weak, eateth herbs. . . . I know, and am persuaded by the Lord Jesus, that there is nothing unclean of itself: but to him that esteemeth any thing to be unclean, to him it is unclean."[1662]

In plain English, here is what Paul is saying:

> "According to the power of the mind and the Law of Attraction, anyone who totally believes that all foods are good for him can eat anything. But for those who do not have this high level of faith, it is better that they watch their diet and restrict it solely to "health foods," such as vegetables. As for myself, I *do* have the level of faith of Jesus, and therefore I know that foods are not healthy or unhealthy in and of themselves. But for those who believe that a certain food is unhealthy, for them that food will have an unhealthy effect on their bodies, so they must monitor their diets until their faith increases to the level where they can eat anything they want."[1663]

Having established that most of us do not have the degree of faith of Jesus or Paul, and so must be mindful of our lifestyles and diets, let us now turn to increasing and maintaining our health through God's "unspeakable gift" to us:[1664] the Law of Attraction.

## YOUR BODY IS GOD'S TEMPLE

Your body is not just a lowly disposable physical vehicle carrying your soul and spirit around here on earth, as some ancient Gnostic Christians once taught. Since you are an extension of God, the individualization of God on the material plane,[1665] it is only natural that your God-Self has been supplied with a home equal to its divinity; a sacred abode; a temple, in fact. That temple is your physical body. Here is how Paul put it:

> "Know ye not that *ye are the temple of God*, and that *the Spirit of God dwelleth in you*? If any man defile the temple of God, him shall God destroy; for *the temple of God is holy, which temple ye are*."[1666]

Here is the inner meaning:

> "Do you not understand that because a piece of God lives inside of you, your body is the holy abode of God, the Divine Mind? Now if you dishonor this sacred edifice by wrong thoughts and wrong living, the negativity produced by these transgressions will cause the Divine Mind to create disease in your bodily temple."[1667]

Because "ye are the temple of the living God,"[1668] the Father has truly "come to his temple,"[1669] and so we must serve Him in the proper manner. The way we do this, that is, create optimum health, is by using a holistic approach, which means a combination of healthful foods, healthful thoughts, and a healthful lifestyle. Again, consider the words of Paul:

> "What? know ye not that *your body is the temple of the Holy Ghost which is in you*, which ye have of God, and ye are not your own? For ye are bought with a price: therefore *glorify God in your body, and in your spirit, which are God's*."[1670]

## YOU ARE EVERLASTING IN THE EVERLASTING FATHER

With the Bible as our foundation, let us look at this ancient concept through a mystical Christian lens for a moment.

Yes, your material vessel is the Holy Dwelling Place of the "everlasting Father,"[1671] the "everlasting king,"[1672] our "everlasting light";[1673] the same One who has "everlasting dominion"[1674] over His "everlasting kingdom."[1675] He is the "everlasting God,"[1676] and He has sealed with us an "everlasting covenant,"[1677] built on an "everlasting foundation"[1678] of "everlasting life,"[1679] "everlasting love,"[1680] "everlasting joy,"[1681] and "everlasting salvation"[1682] in the "everlasting gospel" of Christ (Divine Law).[1683]

So honor, adore, and praise Him. "Ye are God's building,"[1684] the veritable "body of Christ"![1685]

## RESPECTING YOUR BODILY TEMPLE THROUGH NATURAL FOODS

For those of us who do not yet have the faith and spiritual maturity of Jesus, eating foods that are healthful is *always* a good thing. I am speaking here of natural organic foods, all which have the most nutrients and the least amount of toxins of any other type of food.

Not only are natural foods perfect for everyone and all ages, but if you are currently ill and trying to heal, they are especially important, for they have curative and nutritive properties completely missing from unnatural, processed, prepackaged, inorganic foods. As we are about to see, natural foods *give* to your body, thereby increasing your health; unnatural foods *steal* from your body, thereby decreasing your health.

A natural foods diet does not necessarily mean a vegetarian diet. Organic meats, eggs, and dairy products are now widely available in stores and, of course, animals procured through hunting and fishing are always organic (and have the added benefit of being naturally lean).

Since this book is about Jesus and the Law of Attraction and not diet, and since diet is such an individual preference (because we are all unique creations of God, there is no one diet that is right for everyone),[1686] I need not get into detail here, other than to impart to you one important recommendation: the closer we come to eating the way our 19th-Century ancestors ate, the better. This means avoiding pre-made, packaged foods (and all of the modern chemicals, additives, dyes, and other poisons they contain) whenever possible, and instead focusing on natural, organic, whole foods.

Preparing your own foods, often from scratch as our forebears did, will bring a new level of fun, enjoyment, and educational value into your home that many of you have probably never experienced before. Stick to a 19th-Century diet and you cannot go wrong: it will bring your family closer together and increase everyone's happiness and health!

## THE IMPORTANCE OF BODY PH

Having briefly discussed food, diet, and nutrition, let us now look at why natural foods are so important. If you are ill, or just want to maintain your present state of health, this is an especially vital section.

Progressive scientists have discovered that the human body functions best when it has the correct pH balance; that is, the proper equilibrium between alkalinity and acidity. Our bodies normally automatically regulate their pH through, for example, the kidneys and the lungs. However, there are a number of things that we ourselves do that greatly affect our body pH, and which can offset the delicate balance to one side or the other. The result can mean perfect health or perfect sickness.

The pH scale ranges from 0 to 14. From our body's point of view, 0 to 6.9 would be acidic; 7 is neutral; and 7.1 to 14 is alkaline. This is because the ideal pH range for our bodies is between 7.35 and 7.45, slightly alkaline. When our blood pH goes above or drops below these two numbers, illness and even death can result. As mentioned, we ourselves play a role in whether our bodies are alkaline or acidic, whether we are healthy or sick, and here is how.

Every food has its own level of alkaline-forming properties or acid-forming properties. Generally speaking, raw, natural, whole, organic foods are more alkaline (healthy), while pre-cooked, pre-made, processed, inorganic foods are more acidic (unhealthy, or at least, less healthy).

More precisely, fruits, vegetables, seeds, and herbs are mainly alkaline, and so are health-producing; while grains (breads, pasta, pastries, etc.), all meats (including fish), dairy (milk, cheese, eggs, etc.), coffee, soda pop, sugar, tobacco products, alcohol, chemicals (food dyes, food additives, artificial sweeteners, auto exhaust, air and water pollution, etc.), and medications (pharmaceuticals) are acidic, and so are disease-producing.

This does not mean, however, that acid foods are always bad for you. In fact, your body needs some acidity to function properly. Here is how it breaks down: to maintain proper health, your diet should be 70 percent alkaline-producing foods, 30 percent acid-producing foods. For those who are ill, the diet should be at least 80 percent alkaline and 20 percent acid.

## THE VITAL CHEMICAL: OXYGEN

The most essential thing you need to know about body pH and diet is this: the critical ingredient to optimum health is *oxygen*. Its importance can be seen in a simple fact: you can live for weeks without food, days without water, but only a few minutes without oxygen.

Now here is the key: the more acidic a food is the *less* oxygen it contains. The more alkaline a food is the *more* oxygen it contains.[1687]

Because of its low oxygen content, a diet high in acid (grains, dairy, meats, and refined foods) chokes off the body's natural cleansing processes and interferes with the immune system, both which are instrumental in helping us maintain health, fight off illnesses, and recover from disease. With the body in a "polluted" state and our physical defenses weakened, the result can be anything from the common cold, increased blood pressure, and insulin problems, to heart trouble, osteoporosis, and cancer.

Conversely, because of its high oxygen content, a diet high in alkalinity (fruits, seeds, herbs, vegetables, and unrefined foods) accelerates the body's natural cleansing processes and fortifies the immune system, greatly increasing our ability to fight off illnesses and quickly recover from disease. The result is excellent health maintenance and heightened protection against every type of sickness. Now you know the ancient wisdom behind your mother's mealtime decree: "Eat your vegetables"!

EARLY CHRISTIAN VEGETARIANS
The Bible itself recommends an alkaline heavy diet, even vegetarianism, as can be seen from the following scriptures:

> And God said, "Behold, I have given you every herb bearing seed, which is upon the face of all the earth, and every tree, in the which is the fruit of a tree yielding seed; to you it shall be for meat."[1688]

> "Better is a dinner of herbs where love is, than a stalled ox and hatred therewith."[1689]

According to both the Bible and the ancient Jewish historian Josephus, John the Baptist was a vegetarian,[1690] while the *Clementine Homilies* and *Recognitions* (by Saint Clement I) portray the Apostle Peter as abstaining from meat. Clement of Alexandria said that the Apostle Matthew did not eat flesh, and in Eusebius' *History of the Church*, Jesus' brother James the Just is depicted as a vegetarian.

As we have seen, Paul often recommended a vegetarian diet to his followers,[1691] and the great Gnostic Christian teacher Mani once said that he became a vegetarian because the Lord had been one. Indeed, the Essene Gospel of Peace portrays Jesus as an intransigent vegetarian, one who believed that the meat of slaughtered animals is toxic to the body—for, as He teaches in this particular document, just as we become what we think, we also become what we eat.

The point here is that, even though the canonical Gospels portray Jesus as a meat eater (in this case, fish),[1692] vegetarianism has a long and celebrated history in the Christian Church, for the health and spiritual reasons which I have discussed above.[1693]

## LET YOUR FOOD BE YOUR MEDICINE!

I have barely scratched the surface of this important topic. However, the basic premise is this: a predominately alkaline diet is health-producing; a predominately acidic diet is ill health-producing. Use the above lists to create the most nutritional and tasty meals you can, and watch your health begin to improve overnight.

While they may look appetizing and taste good, for those who are not yet at the spiritual level of Jesus, processed foods can rob the body of vital nutrients. But do not worry. God provided us with a delicious natural food for every nutritional requirement as well as a wholesome natural remedy for every ailment. Remember the words of Hippocrates the Father of Medicine: "Let your food be your medicine, and your medicine be your food." Or as Ezekiel put it:

> "And by the river upon the bank thereof, on this side and on that side, shall grow all trees for meat [food], whose leaf shall not fade, neither shall the fruit thereof be consumed: it shall bring forth new fruit according to his months, because their waters they issued out of the sanctuary: and *the fruit thereof shall be for meat [food], and the leaf thereof for medicine.*"[1694]

Having received only a few hours of nutritional training at medical school, the average mainstream doctor may not be able to fully answer all of your questions concerning body pH and diet. If you really want to go deep into this area, I would suggest consulting an "alternative" medical practitioner. Do your own reading and research as well. Either way, be proactive. No one will ever care about your health as much as you do!

## THE IMPORTANCE OF MIND PH

The subject of body pH is vital for another reason, one integrally tied to the topic of this book: Jesus and the "workshop of the mind."[1695]

Yes, for those of us who do not have the perfect faith of the Lord, the type of foods we eat have a profound impact on our health. But as He taught us, the mind is the most powerful force in the Universe,[1696] much more powerful than what we put into our bodies.[1697] So we should not be surprised to learn that our thoughts actually have an effect on our body pH as well. This is what I call "mind pH."

The easiest way to understand mind pH is to correlate the alkaline/acid scale with the different types of thoughts, states of consciousness, and emotional responses that are available to us.

First, *all positive thoughts, feelings, and actions have an alkaline effect on our bodies.* These include: love, happiness, kindness, peace, generosity, humor, prosperity, compassion, balance, joy, hope, dignity, honesty, respect, comfort, appreciation, tranquility, activity, health, abundance, euphoria, tolerance, goodness, encouragement, bliss, cooperation, beauty, cheerfulness, gentleness, empathy, friendliness, excitement, harmony, approval, judiciousness, light heartedness, exuberance, heroism, gracefulness, pleasantness, selflessness, purpose, elation, confidence, exhilaration, graciousness, satisfaction, relaxation, praise, helpfulness, trust, mercy, success, thankfulness, interest, faith, strength, enthusiasm, goodwill, wonder, modesty, temperance, positivity, flexibility, supportiveness, honorableness, spirit, fortunateness, recognition, loyalty, freedom, tenderness, receptivity, security, acceptance, reliability, wealth, understanding, productivity, jubilation, patience, thoughtfulness, nobility, passion, fulfillment, purity, ecstasy, serenity, admiration, contentment, courage, and forgiveness.

Second, *all negative thoughts, feelings, and actions have an acidic effect on our bodies.* These include: hatred, anger, fear, jealousy, resentment, guilt, helplessness, stress, worry, confusion, humiliation, boredom, uncertainty, exhaustion, immodesty, tension, disrespect, rejection, hurt, dread, loneliness, regret, chaos, indulgence, failure, abandonment, violence, selfishness, heavy heartedness, bitterness, ugliness, fatigue, disapproval, weakness, pride, dishonor, fatigue, sadness, dissatisfaction, negativity, mercilessness, dishonesty, pressure, intolerance, disinterest, purposelessness, distrust, unfriendliness, remorse, sickness, disloyalty, inadequacy, impurity, victimization, cruelty, betrayal, emptiness, tyranny, self-will, discord, inflexibility, anxiety, cowardice, doubt, lack, discouragement, insecurity, racism, sexism, ageism, lookism, pain, dullness, revenge, frustration, loss, imbalance, irritation, manipulation, discomfort, shame, intimidation, deception, neglect, grief, impatience, disappointment, and hopelessness.

Look over these two lists carefully. Which one seems more like you? If you are a "negative thinker" with a tendency to focus on things on the negative list, go to work right now retraining your Conscious Mind to select thoughts, feelings, and emotions from the positive list. Any time a negative thought comes into your mind, immediately replace it with a positive one.

How important is this? Very! Whenever you think or hold a negative thought or emotion, you are increasing the acidity of your body, which *decreases* the oxygen in your cells. Over time this can have a devastating impact on your physical being, which can result in all manner of health problems, some that can even lead to death. Yes, you can kill yourself with your own thoughts!

On the other hand, every time you think or hold a positive thought or emotion, you are increasing the alkalinity of your body, which *increases* the oxygen in your cells. Oxygen is the "life force" of God and Nature. Therefore as it floods your system, it cleanses away impurities, bringing health, strength, and happiness in its wake. It is true: you can lengthen your life by thinking wholesome thoughts!

THE MIND-BODY CONNECTION
Now let us consider the famous words of Hippocrates, the "Father of Medicine":

> "If someone wishes for good health, one must first ask oneself if he is ready to do away with the reasons for his illness. Only then is it possible to help him."

This rule is such an integral aspect of the Law of Attraction, that it has been known for thousands of years. In fact, this idea was systematized long ago by the advanced teachers of the ancient mystery schools, who well understood the mind-body connection.

Today psychologists call physical problems caused by the mind "psychosomatic" disorders, meaning "mind-body" ailments, or more literally, "spirit-body" ailments (*psyche* is the Greek word for the "soul"). A few of the most commonly recognized of these are hives, shingles, and depression.

But according to our Lord, *all* illnesses are psychosomatic, for everything in the Universe begins on the mental plane, starting off as a thought! Even mainstream medicine now grudgingly admits that 80 percent of all diseases stem from the mind. Someday, however, it will be forced to openly acknowledge what Jesus openly taught 2,000 years ago: 100 percent of all physical ailments are rooted in the mental, for the body ("Jesus") and the mind (the "Father") are one.[1698] Therefore, what you reap in the mental, you sow in the physical—it is that simple.[1699]

Let us look at some of the more common maladies and their mental causes, while acknowledging that although the foundation of all disease is stress—brought on by improper thinking, speaking, acting, and lifestyle—each sickness has its own specific mental association:

Accidents: self-punishment.
Arm Problems: fear of embracing an issue.
Arthritis: weak self-image.
Asthma: "out of breath" from overdoing it.
Breast Problems: toxic emotions; lack of self-love.
Burns: anger turned on the self.
Cancer: self-hatred, as well as guilt, grief, and remorse. (Will localize in
      the organ or region of the body where there are the most
      unresolved psychological and emotional issues.)[1700]
Common Cold: a congested mind.
Cuts: self-anger.
Diabetes: fear of enjoying life.
Digestive Problems: fear of assimilating life.
Ear Problems: fear of hearing the truth.
Eye Problems: fear of seeing (facing) an issue.
Foot Problems: fear of moving forward.
Hand Problems: fear of taking hold of life or an issue.
Headache: feeling over-pressured.
Heart Problems: lack of self-love.
Leg Problems: fear of standing up for yourself.
Obesity: masking unresolved pain and fear.
Reproductive Problems: negating one's masculinity or femininity.
Skin Problems: repressed emotions.

These particular mind-body connections are only meant to be general in nature. Yet, they hold the hidden key to the healings, treatments, remedies, and cures for every illness: it is *always* the Christ Within that heals you, for spiritually speaking there is really only one disease, and that disease is negative thinking! As such, no illness should ever be seen as "incurable," or as a sign of "inevitable death," and I believe that one day these types of medical pronouncements will be considered "malpractice."

It is true, from a scientific viewpoint, that diseases can have a myriad of contributing factors. However, as mentioned, all stem from stress in one form or another. And the only reason we stress ourselves is because we do not love ourselves properly, and the only reason we do not love ourselves properly is due to wrong-thinking, which biblical writers call an "abomination," that is, sin.[1701]

Thus, as Jesus' teachings on the Law of Attraction tell us, *all illnesses are merely our body's "red warning flags," alerting us that we are in a state of mental imbalance*. Correct the equilibrium of the mind (that is, eliminate the "sin") and the equilibrium of the body (health) returns.

In the beautiful florid language of old, here is how Malachi phrased it:

> "But unto you that fear my name shall the Sun of righteousness arise with healing in his wings; and ye shall go forth, and grow up as calves of the stall."[1702]

The inner meaning:

> "If you respect the Divine Mind, you will find the Indwelling Christ filling you with healing energy, like the warm rays of the sun. And you will be as joyful as calves cavorting in the field."[1703]

Do you have any doubts about the healing power of your divine nature,[1704] the Indwelling Christ?[1705] Doubt not. Instead believe, and become "partakers of His holiness."[1706] Jesus Himself said that anyone can become a "Sun/Son of Righteousness" through right-thinking, right-speaking, and right-living:[1707]

> "Then shall the righteous shine forth as the sun in the kingdom of their Father. Who hath ears to hear, let him hear."[1708]

## HEALTHY THOUGHTS CREATE HEALTHY MINDS & BODIES

We all want good health mentally and physically. Obviously, to attain this we must think healthy thoughts. That is the Law. Break the Law by thinking negative thoughts, and we pay the consequences. Obey the Law by thinking positive thoughts, and we reap the benefits. Or as the Apostle John put it: "Every one that doeth righteousness is born of God";[1709] that is, those who learn to think positively will be protected by the Father (Divine Mind), just as an earthly parent watches over his child.

Because our thoughts control our state of health, the benefits of right-thinking go far beyond what many realize.

Our thinking directly affects how we talk and how we behave. And how we talk and behave, just as with what we think, greatly affects our health. For example, those who think positive thoughts are more apt to say positive things and perform positive deeds, and as modern science has revealed, these have a corresponding positive effect on our well-being.

Did you know, for instance, that merely witnessing an act of kindness, such as seeing someone help an elderly man cross the street, positively alters your biology? This powerful health effect is doubled when we ourselves are performing the act of kindness. Researchers have discovered that being kind to others, as just one example, increases one's life span, reduces pain and stress, boosts energy, creates happiness, and even improves the cardiovascular system by releasing oxytocin, a brain chemical that lowers blood pressure.

The opposite is also true too, of course. Thinking negative thoughts, along with witnessing or performing acts of cruelty, shortens our lives, increases pain and stress, lowers energy, creates unhappiness, and prevents the release of oxytocin. This is why what we think, what we see in public, what we listen to on the radio, what we watch on TV, what we read in newspapers and magazines, what we choose to view or post on the Internet, all have such an enormous impact on our health.

We will recall from Chapter Two that our Subconscious Mind (in the Bible, mystically referred to as the "Servant") oversees our autonomic nervous system and regulates our immune system, breathing, heartbeat, digestion, circulation, hormones, elimination, glands, and cellular regeneration. And what is it that oversees and regulates our Subconscious Mind? It is the Conscious Mind (in the Bible, mystically referred to as the "Master"), that aspect of us that interfaces with the world and absorbs or rejects what it experiences through the five senses.

Knowing this, if you are serious about your health, decide right now that from this moment on you will control your thoughts, watch your words, mind your actions, and monitor what you see and hear. Remember, as a human radio you are always transmitting, and through these vibrational transmissions you are attracting like and repulsing unlike. So keep your mental transmissions at the highest frequency possible by thinking positive, loving, kind, generous, merciful thoughts![1710]

Now if you are one of those whose glass of life is half full, if you are one of those who dwells on the negative, who is critical of others, who always sees the worst in the world around them, is it any wonder that you could be experiencing health issues? If you believe that you are a "wretched evildoer" who was "born in sin," that your body is innately "corrupt," and that you are in a constant battle with "Satan," knowing what you now know about Jesus and the Law of Attraction, can it be a surprise that you may be ill?

Can you not see that we invite in both the good and the bad, lightness and darkness, happiness and misery, health and sickness?

Start anew by reeducating your Conscious Mind to focus only on the good in both yourself and in others, so that your Subconscious Mind will send health-giving signals to your body's cells and organs. See the positive in everything. This attracts what you want and drives away that which you do not want. Just as an unclean house attracts vermin and more dirt, so an unkempt mind attracts problems and more mental refuse. As Jesus esoterically states in the Aquarian Gospel:

> "If you will keep your mind fully occupied with good, the evil spirits cannot find a place to stay."[1711]

Concentrate on an image of yourself as being perfect in mind and body, for in Spirit you already are.[1712] Repeat your affirmations and practice your visualizations day and night, until thinking healthy positive thoughts becomes a habit. The sooner you do this—and the more faith you have and the stronger your belief in the power of the mind and the Law of Attraction—the faster you will get results.

You were not born a negative thinker. You taught yourself to think this way over a period of many years. Just as you taught yourself to think negatively, you can and must re-teach yourself to think positively. Incorporate an alkaline diet with alkaline thoughts and you have an unbeatable combination that will maintain perfect health and stave off disease for the rest of your life!

Now you understand why Paul gave us this delightful admonition:

> ". . . whatsoever things are true, whatsoever things are honest, whatsoever things are just, whatsoever things are pure, whatsoever things are lovely, whatsoever things are of good report; if there be any virtue, and if there be any praise, think on these things."[1713]

Paul did not say "consider these things," "study these things," or "discuss these things." He said "*think* on these things." With his vast knowledge of the Law of Attraction, he was well aware that thinking is the most important thing we do, and that what we think about can change our lives for the better or for the worse.

HEALTHY LIFESTYLE
For those of us who are not at Jesus' level of spiritual mastership, there is one other aspect of our holistic approach to health that we must consider, and that is our physical lifestyle. Since we have already covered healthful eating and healthful thinking, here we will focus on the role of physical exercise specifically.

The mass mind teaches that we need daily exercise for optimum health. But according to Jesus, we only need to exercise if we believe we do! This conforms perfectly with the Law of Attraction, for the Divine Mind makes true what we believe to be true.

Paul certainly gave exercise little value, for he did not believe it had any! Here is what he said on the topic:

> "But refuse profane and old wives' fables [pertaining to physical exercise], and exercise thyself rather unto godliness [that is, spiritually]. For bodily exercise profiteth little: but godliness is profitable unto all things, having promise of the life that now is, and of that which is to come. This is a faithful saying and worthy of all acceptation."[1714]

Here is what we can derive from Paul's advice. For those who truly believe that a daily workout (such as walking, swimming, or jogging) has no health benefits, there will be no health benefits, and engaging in it would be a waste of time. For those who do believe in the health benefits of working out, however, some form of daily exercise is vitally important. Again, the reason for this is the Law of Attraction: whatever we hold as real becomes real for us.

The problem is that we have all been so inculcated by the mass mind to believe that working out is vital to our health, even if you consciously believe exercise is valueless, your Subconscious Mind (where all of your beliefs are stored) is still holding the belief that some form of daily exercise is good and necessary.

Now, as mentioned, the Subconscious Mind controls your mental, spiritual, and physical health. So unless you are operating out of the same high consciousness as Jesus (what mystics call Chrishna Consciousness, Christ Consciousness, or "the mind of Christ"),[1715] you cannot afford to ignore the health risks of not getting some daily physical exercise. In other words, most of those reading this book will gain from working out.

Talk to a health professional about the type of exercise that is right for you, and enjoy the time you spend improving and maintaining your health. Just getting outside will increase your feeling of well-being: the sounds, smells, and sights of Nature are relaxing, fresh air supplies vital oxygen to the body, and (morning or late afternoon) sunshine provides Vitamin D3, an invaluable nutrient that is difficult to get from other sources. As you exercise, believe fully that it is benefitting you. And it will!

It is common practice to use the phrase "Jesus healed the sick." However, a close reading of the New Testament reveals the opposite: it is always the patient who heals himself or herself. Before the healing, Jesus would ask His subject if he or she believed that they could be cured. If the answer was "yes," He proceeded to pronounce the Word of God over them and the healing would take place. Afterward, our Egoless Lord was always careful to tell his subject: "*Thy faith* hath made thee whole." Jesus, the greatest practitioner of the Law of Attraction the world has ever known, understood that it is not an outer power that heals. It is an inner power, and that inner power is the faith of the sufferer. When the Master encountered the father with a sick son, He told the desperate man: "If thou canst believe, all things are possible to him that believeth." To this the father replied through his tears: "Lord, I believe; help thou mine unbelief," and the boy was instantly healed. As Jesus taught us, if you are ill, you need look no further than within, to the power of your own faith, to effect a complete and permanent healing.

# 22

# HEALING DIS-EASE

"I create the fruit of the lips; peace, peace to
him that is far off, and to him that is near,"
saith the Lord; "and I will heal him."[1716]

## YOU WERE BORN TO BE HEALTHY

**D**ID YOU KNOW THAT PERFECT health is the norm? This is
because you are a manifestation of God, and God is perfect in every
way. In fact, in God's Universe, the world of Spirit, there is no
such thing as sickness or ill health. Disease is an illusion thought up in the
mind of humanity here on earth. There is no other source it could possibly
come from.

Thus, if you are not in perfect health, it is because, in some way or
another, your thoughts, beliefs, and feelings are going against the goodness
and reality of God. This is why Hindus wisely teach that "the physical body
is literally constructed and maintained by the mind." And it is why I say that
all disease is manmade, self-made.

This is not unscientific "New Age hocus pocus." One of our
greatest scientists, Albert Einstein, once reaffirmed the great truth that Jesus
taught 2,000 years ago: "Thoughts influence the body," declared the eminent
doctor. So, if you have an illness you want to eliminate, you must first
realize that since you created it by thought, you can un-create it by thought.
In the Aquarian Gospel, after the Lord heals a woman who is near death, the
following remarkable conversation ensues:

> Her kindred were astonished and they said to her, "How were you
> healed?" And she replied, "I do not know; I simply asked the man
> of God in thought [that is, telepathically] for healing power, and in
> a moment I was well." The people said, "The gods have surely
> come to earth; for man has not the power to heal by thought." But

Jesus said, "*The greatest power in heaven and earth is thought.* God made the universe by thought; he paints the lily and the rose with thought. Why think it strange that I should send a healing thought and change the ethers of disease and death to those of health and life?"[1717]

Jesus knows the Truth: God's body is perfect and always healthy. Since you are a part of that body,[1718] yours should be too, for God designed it to be perfectly healthy.[1719] If it is not, it can only be due to your thoughts, for you are always thinking your way to either health or sickness.

If you are unhealthy then, your immediate task is to change what you are thinking; alter your thoughts so that they align with the Source, the immanent,[1720] the invisible,[1721] the eternal[1722] Spirit[1723] who created you, your cells, organs, ligaments, glands, bones, muscles, and limbs, and gave you the Breath of Life[1724]—just as God-tuned Jesus gave the Breath of Life to His Disciples.[1725]

All of these bodily structures, down to the tiniest cell, have their own built-in super intelligence, each one programmed by God for perfect health; each one designed to maintain itself in healthy times, and heal itself in unhealthy times. Yes, your body's cells are smarter than any physician, for they are imbued with the infinite knowledge of the Father Himself (Divine Mind)! Thus, in the book of Jeremiah we read:

"For I will restore health unto thee, and I will heal thee of thy wounds," saith the Lord.[1726]

A NEW BODY EVERY YEAR

Here is incontestable proof that your mind controls your health.

Scientists like Dr. Deepak Chopra have determined that it takes about a year for every cell in the human body to be replaced. Some, like the cells on your stomach wall, are replaced every four days; your skin cells are replaced every month; your liver cells every six weeks; and your bones, one of the longest lasting types of cells, are replaced every three months.

Now let us say a woman has a disease of the liver that has lasted thirty weeks. How can this be if her body is giving her a brand new liver every six weeks? It is because she is thinking thoughts of her disease, focusing on her disease, talking about her disease, reading about her disease, looking at pictures of her disease, discussing the symptoms of her disease. She may also be thinking negative thoughts about herself and others. All of this violates Jesus' teachings on the Law of Attraction.

Once she takes her mind off ill health and general negativity and places it back on perfect health and positivity (self-love) where it belongs, the super-intelligence of her liver's cells will respond to her Subconscious Mind's new "command." The result of her now improved thinking is inevitable: she will have a perfectly healthy liver within the next six weeks—the length of time it takes her body to regenerate an entirely new one.[1727] How can this be?

The body *always* responds with perfect scientific precision to our predominant thoughts. Always. There are no exceptions. This is why it is so important to develop a *permanent* attitude of positivity, belief, trust, and faith. The Father Himself (Divine Mind) said: "Behold, I make all things new,"[1728] and this is exactly what He will do with your body, mind, and soul if you follow His instructions, for according to Jesus, your Indwelling Christ has "power over all flesh."[1729] Now this is a claim that no doctor could ever make!

YOU CAN HEAL ANY DISEASE!

How fortunate we are: the Father has given us the tools to recapture and maintain our health if and when it fails us. We discussed some of these in the previous chapter on health, but as this chapter is devoted to healing, let us look at the instruments God gave us for this specific purpose.

First, rest assured that because of our divine nature[1730] and the powerful laws God has placed at our disposal, we are "partakers in His holiness."[1731] Thus, no disease, no ailment, no physical, mental, or emotional problem is too big for God. In fact, as a Christian writing a book on Jesus, I am going to invoke my First Amendment rights guaranteeing freedom of speech and religion, to tell you something that few doctors want you to know: since all diseases are caused by the mind, all diseases can be cured by the mind. Yes, *all* diseases!

And here is the simple spiritual truth: if you believe this with all your heart, it will become true for you. If you do not believe this, it will not become true for you. That is the Law. God's Law![1732]

Consider this: as depicted in the New Testament, the majority of Jesus' miracles have to do with physical healings (all "which are performed without the use of medicines and herbs"),[1733] and on a number of occasions some of these included literally raising people from the dead. Do you find this incredible, unbelievable? Paul asked: "Why should it be thought a thing incredible with you, that God should raise the dead?"[1734]

Why indeed, for Jesus said that we could and would perform even greater "works" than He did.[1735] Furthermore, He declared that those who are "least in the kingdom of heaven" would have greater powers than John the Baptist[1736]—the man who the Lord literally describes as Elijah reborn.[1737] According to Jesus, you have divine abilities that are even more substantial than those possessed by one of the greatest of the Old Testament prophets!

Let us look at this more closely for a moment.

In Chapter Sixteen of the Gospel of Mark, verses nine through twenty were added much later by a priestly interpolator (we know this because they do not appear in the oldest known New Testament manuscripts, such as the Codex Sinaiticus). However, because this nameless clergyman was quite spiritually advanced, he had a true understanding of Jesus and His primary message, that *we are all gods with divine powers.*[1738]

This makes these particular artificially inserted passages even more interesting than if they were original. For they portray not the traditional mainstream Christian version of Jesus (the apocalyptic, political Messiah), but the true Jesus of history (a master teacher, prophet, and healer), as depicted in the earliest record of our Lord: the pre-New Testament document called the Gospel of Q, referred to by Papias, the noted 2nd-Century Bishop of Hierapolis,[1739] and also by Paul.[1740]

In Mark's appended passages, Jesus appears to his Disciples after His Resurrection. Not to talk to them about sin, penance, atonement, communion, the Eucharist, the priesthood, confession, prayer, Mass, the Liturgy, Reconciliation, unction, ordination, the Bible, Christianity, or even religion. What He wanted to talk to them about was faith, the Law of Attraction, and healing! Here is "Mark's" account:

> And Jesus said unto them . . . "*these signs shall follow them that believe*; in my name shall they cast out devils; they shall speak with new tongues; they shall take up serpents; and if they drink any deadly thing, it shall not hurt them; they shall lay hands on the sick, and they shall recover." So then after the Lord had spoken unto them, he was received up into heaven, and sat on the right hand of God. And they went forth, and preached every where, the Lord working with them, and confirming *the word* with signs following. *Amen.*[1741]

"The word" here is what Paul called "the Word of faith":[1742] the power to heal and "perform miracles" according to the faith of the individual and his or her belief in Jesus' Law of Attraction principles.[1743] And, as we have learned, the word "amen" is the Near Eastern version of the universal Aum or Om: the Great I AM, the sacred power-name of God.

Here we have an indication of how important these doctrines truly were to Jesus, for even after His death and resurrection, "Mark" says, Jesus remained on earth for a short time, so that he could continue to work with His followers to preach the Gospel of the Kingdom of God and heal the sick (both physically and spiritually).[1744] In the book of Acts, Luke confirms the Lord's post-resurrection work, saying:

> "The former treatise have I made, O Theophilus, of all that Jesus began both to do and teach, until the day in which he was taken up, after that he through the Holy Ghost had given commandments unto the apostles whom he had chosen: to whom also he shewed himself alive after his passion by many infallible proofs, *being seen of them forty days, and speaking of the things pertaining to the kingdom of God.*"[1745]

As the Kingdom of God is a divine inner state of consciousness[1746] that we have rule over[1747] when we attain what Paul called "the mind of Christ,"[1748] is there any doubt from this that Jesus' primary message was about the Universal Indwelling Christ[1749] and the Law of Attraction?[1750] And in turn is there any doubt that any and all illnesses can not only be prevented, but successfully treated as well, no matter how severe, no matter what the diagnosis?

And how does the healing take place? In using the ever present power of the Laws of the Mind, Love, and Attraction, we become cocreators with the Almighty, the Superconscious Mind, in which "all things are possible."[1751] In this way "we are labourers together with God," as Paul phrased it.[1752]

Your Higher Self,[1753] your Indwelling Christ,[1754] your "mind of Christ,"[1755] has no limitations. Only the ones you create through wrong-thinking. Otherwise it possesses infinite knowledge, wisdom, and power to do for you whatever you ask of it. This "it" is the "Spirit of God" that Jesus speaks of, and it has the power to do anything, including "cast out devils" (that is, treat any ailment).[1756]

Believe this with all your heart and mind and, like Paul, you too will be able to "do all things through Christ which strengtheneth me,"[1757] for ultimately all things come from the Father—Sovereign Mind, Divine

Mind.[1758]  If you understand this, you are well on your way to achieving perfect health, for faith is at the root of the Law, and the Law is God.[1759] Shakespeare correctly observed: "Our remedies in ourselves do lie, which we ascribe to Heaven."

THERE IS ONLY ONE TRUE HEALER!
In India these principles have been known for aeons.  Here is what one early Hindu healer had to say on the art of healing:

> "The laws of nature are the laws of health, and he who lives according to these laws is never sick.  Transgression of these laws is sin, and he who sins is sick.  He who obeys the laws, maintains an equilibrium in all his parts, and thus insures true harmony; and harmony is health, while discord is disease.  That which produces harmony in all the parts of man is medicine, insuring health.  The body is a harpsichord, and when its strings are too relaxed, or are too tense, the instrument is out of tune, the man is sick.  Now, everything in nature has been made to meet the wants of man; so everything is found in medical arcanes [secrets].  And when the harpsichord of man is out of tune the vast expanse of nature may be searched for remedy; there is a cure for every ailment of the flesh. *Of course the will of man is remedy supreme; and by the vigorous exercise of will, man may make tense a chord that is relaxed, or may relax one that is too tense, and thus may heal himself.  When man has reached the place where he has faith in God, in nature and himself, he knows the Word of power; his word is balm for every wound, is cure for all the ills of life.*"[1760]

Notice that the art of healing according to the Hindus and the art of healing according to Jesus are identical.  How can this be?  It is because, as Paul noted at Mars' Hill, there is only One Source, One Fire, One Power, One God, One Healing Energy, and it lies within all people, no matter what their religion, nationality, or race![1761]  Thus saith the Father:

> "Behold, I will bring it [that is, my people] health and cure, and I will cure them, and will reveal unto them the abundance of peace and truth."[1762]

God's revealed "abundance of peace and truth" is the real all-healing "Balm of Gilead"[1763] that humanity has long sought.  It is not physical, it is spiritual. Therefore it works on and in anyone, healing any condition.  Spirit has spoken: *disease is ignorance, therefore the cure is knowledge*!

The great American inventor, Thomas Edison, clearly understood the true path to health:

> "Medicine is played out. Every new discovery of bacteria shows us all the more convincingly that we have been wrong, and that the millions of tons of stuff [pharmaceutical drugs] we have taken were all useless. *The doctor of the future will give no medicine, but will instruct his patient in the care of the human frame; in diet and the cause and prevention of disease.* Surgery, diet, antiseptics— these three are the vital things of the future in the preservation of the health of humanity. There were never so many able, active minds at work on the problem of disease as now; and all their discoveries are ending in the simple truth—that you can't improve on Nature."

Earthly medicine is indeed limited in its powers.

But there is one healer that has no limitations whatsoever: Edison called it "Nature," the ancient Jews called it "Yahweh," the ancient Romans called it "Jupiter," the ancient Greeks called it "Zeus,"[1764] Paul called it the "invisible God,"[1765] Jesus called it the "Father,"[1766] and we call it the "Divine Mind."

Yet the label we place on it is unimportant. What *is* important is the knowledge that this all-healing spiritual power is omnipresent, omniscient, omnipotent, and omniactive, and because of this it exists within each one of us.[1767] In fact, as Jesus declared, you and the Divine Mind are one,[1768] for God Himself put His spirit in you![1769]

Let us look now at the details of how mental (spiritual) healing works using Jesus' teachings on the Law of Attraction.

## YOUR FAITH WILL MAKE YOU WHOLE

Even the most casual Bible reader will have noticed that when Jesus healed someone, He never took personal credit for it; He never said, "*I* have healed you." Quite the opposite. He said "*you* have healed yourself," always attributing the "miracle" to *the faith of His patients.* Not even the Apostles attributed Jesus' healings to Him, for they understood how the Law of Attraction works.[1770]

Here are several examples. The first is from the Gospel of Matthew:

> And when Jesus departed thence, two blind men followed him, crying, and saying, "Thou Son of David, have mercy on us." And

> when he was come into the house, the blind men came to him: and
> Jesus saith unto them, *"Believe ye* that I am able to do this?" They
> said unto him, "Yea, Lord." Then touched he their eyes, saying,
> *"According to your faith be it unto you."* And their eyes were
> opened.[1771]

Note that before the healing takes place, Jesus asks the men if they believe "He" will be able to cure them. The two men were not aware, of course, that the actual healing power would come, not from Jesus, but from their own faith in the Law of Attraction. Knowing this, the Lord needed to hear from them that they "believed" before He began. Thus, afterward He says to them: "It is due to *your faith* that your sight has been restored."

Another account from Matthew:

> Then Jesus went thence, and departed into the coasts of Tyre and
> Sidon. And, behold, a woman of Canaan came out of the same
> coasts, and cried unto him, saying, "Have mercy on me, O Lord,
> thou Son of David; my daughter is grievously vexed with a devil."
> But he answered her not a word. And his disciples came and
> besought him, saying, "Send her away; for she crieth after us." But
> he answered and said, "I am not sent but unto the lost sheep of the
> house of Israel."
>
> Then came she and worshipped him, saying, "Lord, help
> me." But he answered and said, "It is not meet [right] to take the
> children's bread, and to cast it to dogs." And she said, "Truth,
> Lord: yet the dogs eat of the crumbs which fall from their masters'
> table." Then Jesus answered and said unto her, "O woman, *great
> is thy faith: be it unto thee even as thou wilt.*" And her daughter was
> made whole from that very hour.[1772]

What an amazing statement Jesus makes to the woman from Canaan! In modern English:

> "Woman, *your belief in the unseen* is very powerful. Because of this,
> your mental desire has manifested instantly on the material plane.
> Your daughter is now healed, thanks to *your faith*."[1773]

In the Gospel of Mark we find this intriguing story of a woman who heals herself using only her own pure faith. An objective reading reveals that Jesus plays no role in the cure whatsoever:

> And a certain woman, which had an issue of blood twelve years,

and had suffered many things of many physicians, and had spent all that she had, and was nothing bettered, but rather grew worse, when she had heard of Jesus, came in the press [crowd] behind, and touched his garment. For she said [to herself], "*If I may touch but his clothes, I shall be whole.*" And straightway the fountain of her blood was dried up; and she felt in her body that *she was healed* of that plague.

And Jesus, immediately knowing in himself that virtue [spiritual strength] had gone out of him, turned him about in the press, and said, "Who touched my clothes?" And his disciples said unto him, "Thou seest the multitude thronging thee, and sayest thou, 'Who touched me?'" And he looked round about to see her that had done this thing. But the woman fearing and trembling, knowing what was done in her, came and fell down before him, and told him all the truth. And he said unto her, "Daughter, *thy faith hath made thee whole*; go in peace, and be whole of thy plague."[1774]

Again, here the patient does not realize that it is not Jesus who drives the sickness out of her body. It is her own belief in the healing power of the "invisible God."[1775] In truth, she could have touched any object and, believing, she would have been cured, as Jesus Himself suggests: "*Your own belief* has healed you."

From the Gospel of Luke:

And it came to pass, that, when Jesus was returned, the people gladly received him: for they were all waiting for him. And, behold, there came a man named Jairus, and he was a ruler of the synagogue: and he fell down at Jesus' feet, and besought him that he would come into his house: for he had one only daughter, about twelve years of age, and she lay a dying. . . .

While he yet spake, there cometh one from the ruler of the synagogue's house, saying to him, "Thy daughter is dead; trouble not the Master." But when Jesus heard it, he answered him, saying, "*Fear not: believe only, and she shall be made whole.*" And when he came into the house, he suffered no man to go in, save Peter, and James, and John [Jesus' innermost secret circle of initiates], and the father and the mother of the maiden. And all wept, and bewailed her: but he said, "Weep not; she is not dead, but sleepeth." And they laughed him to scorn, knowing that she was dead.

And he put them all out, and took her by the hand, and called, saying, "Maid, arise." And her spirit came [back into her body] again, and she arose straightway: and he commanded to give her meat [a meal]. And her parents were astonished: but he charged them that they should tell no man what was done.[1776]

Notice Jesus' powerful statement to Jairus, the girl's father: "*Fear not: believe only*, and she shall be made whole"!

Here is another account, this one from the Gospel of Mark, illustrating the power of self-faith:

> And they came to Jericho: and as he [Jesus] went out of Jericho with his disciples and a great number of people, blind Bartimaeus, the son of Timaeus, sat by the highway side begging. And when he heard that it was Jesus of Nazareth, he began to cry out, and say, "Jesus, thou Son of David, have mercy on me." And many charged him that he should hold his peace: but he cried the more a great deal, "Thou Son of David, have mercy on me."
>
> And Jesus stood still, and commanded him to be called. And they call the blind man, saying unto him, "Be of good comfort, rise; he calleth thee." And he, casting away his garment, rose, and came to Jesus. And Jesus answered and said unto him, "What wilt thou that I should do unto thee?" The blind man said unto him, "Lord, that I might receive my sight." And Jesus said unto him, "Go thy way; *thy faith hath made thee whole*." And immediately he received his sight, and followed Jesus in the way.[1777]

From the Gospel of Luke:

> And as he [Jesus] entered into a certain village, there met him ten men that were lepers, which stood afar off: and they lifted up their voices, and said, "Jesus, Master, have mercy on us." And when he saw them, he said unto them, "Go shew yourselves unto the priests." And it came to pass, that, as they went, they were cleansed.
>
> And one of them, when he saw that he was healed, turned back, and with a loud voice glorified God, and fell down on his face at his feet, giving him thanks: and he was a Samaritan. And Jesus answering said, "Were there not ten cleansed? but where are the [other] nine? There are not found that returned to give glory to God, save this stranger." And he said unto him, "Arise, go thy way: *thy faith hath made thee whole*."[1778]

Another story from Matthew:

> And when Jesus was entered into Capernaum, there came unto him a centurion, beseeching him, and saying, "Lord, my servant lieth at home sick of the palsy, grievously tormented." And Jesus saith unto him, "I will come and heal him." The centurion answered and said, "Lord, I am not worthy that thou shouldest come under my roof: but *speak the word only, and my servant shall be healed.* For I am a man under authority, having soldiers under me: and I say to this man, 'go,' and he goeth; and to another, 'come,' and he cometh; and to my servant, 'do this,' and he doeth it."
>
> When Jesus heard it, he marvelled, and said to them that followed, "Verily I say unto you, *I have not found so great faith, no, not in Israel. . . .*" And Jesus said unto the centurion, "Go thy way; and *as thou hast believed, so be it done unto thee.*" And his servant was healed in the selfsame hour.[1779]

There are two important facts that we need to look at concerning this particular anecdote. First, Jesus states unequivocally that it was the centurion's faith that caused the healing of his servant: "As thou hast believed, so be it done unto thee." Why is this? It is because, according to the Law of Attraction, what you believe becomes true for you. We can clearly see here how the power of the mind and the Law work together to manifest healings.

Second, Jesus declares that this Pagan military official had more faith than any Christian or Jew He had ever met. This proves that God is indeed, "no respecter of persons,"[1780] that one need not be a Christian or even a believer to work with the Law of Attraction, and that mental healing can be done by anyone, on anyone, anytime, anywhere, and under any conditions! It all depends on the sufferer's degree of belief.

Your own personal faith is so vital to curing yourself that without it not even Jesus could heal you. Here is irrefutable evidence from the Gospel of Matthew:

> And when he [Jesus] was come into his own country, he taught them in their synagogue, insomuch that they were astonished, and said, "Whence hath this man this wisdom, and these mighty works?" Is not this the carpenter's son? is not his mother called Mary? and his brethren, James, and Joses, and Simon, and Judas? And his sisters, are they not all with us? Whence then hath this man [learned] all these things?" And they were offended in him. But Jesus said unto them, "A prophet is not without honour, save in his own country, and in his own house." *And he did not many mighty works there because of their unbelief.*[1781]

Jesus' neighbors did not believe that someone they knew so well could heal the sick. And so, without their faith, He could not. Thus, on this particular occasion He was restricted mainly to teaching. Mark phrased the event this way:

> "*And he could there do no mighty work, save that he laid his hands upon a few sick folk, and healed them.* And he marvelled because of their unbelief. And he went round about the villages, teaching."[1782]

Not even the Gospel can be absorbed without faith, as the writer of the book of Hebrews attests:

> "For unto us [Christians] was the gospel preached, as well as unto them [unbelievers]: but the word preached did not profit them, *not being mixed with faith in them that heard it.*"[1783]

The reason for this is that the Divine Mind can only act through our faith. If we lack true belief, we short-circuit our connection to God. Thus, we have the Hebraist's mystical statement:

> "Without faith it is impossible to please him: for he that cometh to God must believe that he is, and that he is a rewarder of them that diligently seek him."[1784]

The Gospel of Mark contains the following wonderful story of how faith (absolute unquestioning belief) and healing through the Father (Divine Mind) operate in unison for our greater good:

> And when he [Jesus] came to his disciples, he saw a great multitude about them, and the scribes [Jewish copyists and scriptural experts] questioning with them. And straightway all the people, when they beheld him, were greatly amazed, and running to him saluted him.
> And he asked the scribes, "What question ye with them?" And one of the multitude answered and said, "Master, I have brought unto thee my son, which hath a dumb spirit; and wheresoever he taketh him, he teareth him: and he foameth, and gnasheth with his teeth, and pineth away: and I spake to thy disciples that they should cast him out; and they could not."
> He answereth him, and saith, "O faithless generation, how long shall I be with you? how long shall I suffer you? bring him unto me." And they brought him unto him: and when he saw him, straightway the spirit tare [convulsed] him; and he fell on the

ground, and wallowed foaming.

And he asked his father, "How long is it ago since this came unto him?" And he said, "Of a child. And ofttimes it hath cast him into the fire, and into the waters, to destroy him: but if thou canst do any thing, have compassion on us, and help us."

Jesus said unto him, "*If thou canst believe, all things are possible to him that believeth*." And straightway the father of the child cried out, and said with tears, "Lord, I believe; help thou mine unbelief."

When Jesus saw that the people came running together, he rebuked the foul spirit, saying unto him, "Thou dumb and deaf spirit, I charge thee, come out of him, and enter no more into him." And the spirit cried, and rent him sore, and came out of him: and he was as one dead; insomuch that many said, "He is dead." But Jesus took him by the hand, and lifted him up; and he arose.[1785]

Let us imprint these extraordinary words of the Master in our memory for all time, for they embody the very essence of the Law of Attraction: "*If thou canst believe, all things are possible to him that believeth*"!

Paul too found that he had no power to heal on his own. Healing could only take place *according to the faith of his subjects*. This account, for instance, is from the book of Acts:

And there sat a certain man at Lystra, impotent in his feet, being a cripple from his mother's womb, who never had walked: the same heard Paul speak: who stedfastly beholding him, and *perceiving that he had faith to be healed*, said with a loud voice, "Stand upright on thy feet." And he leaped and walked. And when the people saw what Paul had done, they lifted up their voices, saying in the speech of Lycaonia, "the gods are come down to us in the likeness of men."[1786]

Many mistook the "middleman," Paul, as the healer, even considering him a deity! It is clear from these passages, however, that Paul did not perform the healing. He merely acted as a spiritual conduit for the crippled man's own powerful belief, as Luke himself states: "He had faith to be healed."

Matthew gives us the following famous chronicle of Jesus and the fig tree, illustrating once again the Lord's teaching on the power of faith and how it works with the mind and the Law of Attraction:

Now in the morning as he [Jesus] returned into the city, he

hungered. And when he saw a fig tree in the way, he came to it, and found nothing thereon, but leaves only, and said unto it, "Let no fruit grow on thee henceforward for ever." And presently the fig tree withered away. And when the disciples saw it, they marvelled, saying, "How soon is the fig tree withered away!"

Jesus answered and said unto them, "Verily I say unto you, *If ye have faith, and doubt not,* ye shall not only do this which is done to the fig tree, but also if ye shall say unto this mountain, 'Be thou removed,' and be thou cast into the sea; it shall be done. And *all things, whatsoever ye shall ask in prayer, believing, ye shall receive.*"[1787]

Let us now read and understand the inner meaning of this story in modern English:

In the morning, when Jesus came back to Bethany, He felt hungry and went off to find something to eat. He came upon a fig tree alongside the road and, finding it barren, He cursed it, saying "you will never bear fruit again." The fig tree immediately withered away. When the Apostles saw this miracle, they were amazed, asking, "Lord, how did you make the fig tree shrivel up and die so quickly?"

Jesus replied: "I tell you truly, if you believe in something with all your heart and soul, and do not doubt for one second, you will not only be able to do exactly what I did to this fig tree, but you will be able to say to a mountain, 'I now remove you and throw you into the sea,' and it will be done. In fact, *anything* you ask for in prayer will be given to you—provided you believe with 100 percent faith that it is yours already."[1788]

Reread this last sentence again and again, until you have fully absorbed it. It is the entire Law of Attraction in just a few words, set forth in a way that could only come from the God-tuned mind of one who is perfectly enlightened, perfectly aligned with the Indwelling Christ.[1789]

HEALING THROUGH CHRIST'S ATONEMENT
For those who are in need of a healing, and who like their religion less mystical and more literal, we have the following scripture in which it is said that Jesus

healed all that were sick: that it might be fulfilled which was spoken by Esaias [Isaiah] the prophet, saying, "Himself took our infirmities, and bare our sicknesses."[1790]

In other words, we are promised mental, emotional, and physical healing through the atonement of the Christ, as the book of Isaiah testifies:

> "But he was wounded for our transgressions, he was bruised for our iniquities: the chastisement of our peace was upon him; and *with his stripes we are healed.*"[1791]

No matter how you personally choose to view the power of spiritual healing, rest assured that your "infirmities" can be healed anytime, anywhere, through Jesus—the full human embodiment of the perfection of the Indwelling Christ. The only ingredient you need to add to the mix is your own faith. It is this powerful belief in the Divine Mind that gives us the true meaning of the word atonement: At-One-Ment.

Notice that Isaiah does not say "with his stripes *we will be* healed." He says "with his stripes *we are* healed"! He is speaking in the present tense, just as Jesus teaches us to do through His Law of Attraction doctrines. Memorize this scripture, repeat it to yourself, and believe. Allow the Indwelling Christ to give you the healing that is yours by divine right.

Focus on what you want to happen, knowing that it has already occurred. Recognize that you are healed, declare it, accept it, and receive it. Give Jesus your full faith and let the healing power of the Christ Within[1792] give you back the perfect health that, as a Son of God[1793] and an heir to the Kingdom,[1794] is yours and always has been yours![1795]

## A WORD ON SIN, HEALTH, & HEALING

The following story, from the Gospel of John, provides yet another example in which Jesus relies, not on His own powers, but on the patient's personal faith to effect a complete and instant healing:

> After this there was a feast of the Jews; and Jesus went up to Jerusalem. Now there is at Jerusalem by the sheep market a pool, which is called in the Hebrew tongue Bethesda, having five porches. In these lay a great multitude of impotent [sick] folk, of blind, halt, withered, waiting for the moving of the water. For an angel went down at a certain season into the pool, and troubled the water: whosoever then first after the troubling of the water stepped in was made whole of whatsoever disease he had.
> And a certain man was there, which had an infirmity

thirty and eight years. When Jesus saw him lie [lying there], and knew that he had been now a long time in that case, he saith unto him, "Wilt thou be made whole?" The impotent man answered him, "Sir, I have no man, when the water is troubled, to put me into the pool: but while I am coming, another steppeth down before me."

Jesus saith unto him, "Rise, take up thy bed, and walk." And immediately the man was made whole, and took up his bed, and walked: and on the same day was the sabbath. The Jews therefore said unto him that was cured, "It is the sabbath day: it is not lawful for thee to carry thy bed." He answered them, "He that made me whole, the same said unto me, 'Take up thy bed, and walk.'" Then asked they him, "What man is that which said unto thee, 'Take up thy bed, and walk?'" And he that was healed wist not who it was: for Jesus had conveyed himself away [dematerialized], a multitude being in that place.

Afterward Jesus findeth him in the temple, and said unto him, "Behold, thou art made whole: sin no more, lest a worse thing come unto thee." The man departed, and told the Jews that it was Jesus, which had made him whole.[1796]

Jesus adds a statement here that is lacking in many of his other healings. He tells his patient to "sin no more, lest a worse thing come unto thee." Since the word sin is very much misunderstood, and in fact is regularly misused by many Christians, let us pause to examine it more closely in relation to health and healing. For there is a connection, but it is not the one taught by institutional Christianity.

The modern English word sin derives from the Old English *synne*, a medieval archer's term for "missing the mark," "failure to hit the bull's-eye," or "overshooting the target." When King James' scribes translated the New Testament from Greek into English in the early 1600s, *synne* was the closest word they could find to match the original Greek word *hamartia*, which also means "to miss the mark." Over time, *synne* was modernized into the current spelling, sin.

Unfortunately, along with the early Catholic Church's Paganization of Jesus[1797] and its outrageous tampering with the books that would one day become the New Testament,[1798] the meaning of the word sin was transformed as well. Originally indicating merely a spiritual error in judgement, the Church altered sin to mean "a moral transgression against God that can result in eternal damnation in Hell."

The fact is that this definition is a manmade one!

Can we really believe that the Father created us in His perfect image,[1799] then placed us here on earth—knowing full well that we would sin (indulge in wrong-thinking)—only to punish us for all time?[1800]

The idea is preposterous, and as such goes against not only the true meaning of the word sin, it also squarely opposes Jesus' teachings on the Law of Attraction. According to the Master, it is our own personal faith that dissolves our sins (mistakes), not an external anthropomorphic God, the idolatrous "vain thing" of the heathen,[1801] a "god wrought out by hands of man."[1802] Indeed, Jesus taught that our sins can be completely nullified simply by asking God for forgiveness,[1803] and by renewing our faith in the Father.[1804] The Lord's brother, James the Just, preached a similar method:

> "*The prayer of faith* shall save the sick, and the Lord shall raise him up; and *if he have committed sins, they shall be forgiven him.*"[1805]

The *Aquarian Gospel* version of the above story sheds additional light on our powers of self-healing and the topic of sin:

> A flowing spring that people called the Healing Fount, was near Persepolis. And all the people thought that at a certain time of year their deity came down and gave a virtue [healing power] to the waters of the fount, and that the sick who then would plunge into the fount and wash would be made whole. About the fount a multitude of people were in waiting for the Holy One to come and potentize the waters of the fount. The blind, the lame, the deaf, the dumb, and those obsessed were there.
>
> And Jesus, standing in the midst of them, exclaimed [in amazement], "Behold the spring of life! These waters that will fail [that is, they have no inherent healing powers] are honored as the special blessing of your God. From whence do healing virtues come? Why is your God so partial [stingy] with his gifts? Why does he bless this spring today, and then tomorrow take his blessings all away? A deity of power could fill these waters full of healing virtue every day. Hear me, you sick, disconsolate: The virtue of this fount is not a special gift of God. Faith is the healing power of every drop of all the waters of this spring. *He who believes with all his heart that he will be made whole by washing in this fount will be made whole when he has washed; and he may wash at any time. Let every one who has this faith in God and in himself plunge in these waters now and wash.*"
>
> And many of the people plunged into the crystal fount; and they were healed. And then there was a rush, for all the people

were inspired with faith, and each one strove to be among the first to wash, lest all the virtue be absorbed.

And Jesus saw a little child, weak, faint and helpless, sitting all alone beyond the surging crowd; and there was none to help her to the fount. And Jesus said, "My little one, why do you sit and wait? Why not arise and hasten to the fount and wash, and be made well?"

The child replied, "I need not haste; the blessings of my Father in the sky are measured not in tiny cups; they never fail; their virtues are the same forevermore. When these whose faith is weak must haste to wash for fear their faith will fail, have all been cured, these waters will be just as powerful for me. Then I can go and stay a long, long time within the blessed waters of the spring."

And Jesus said, "Behold a master soul! She came to earth to teach to men the power of faith." And then he lifted up the child and said, "*Why wait for anything? The very air we breathe is filled with balm of life. Breathe in this balm of life in faith and be made whole.*" The child breathed in the balm of life *in faith*, and she was well.

The people marveled much at what they heard and saw; they said, "This man must surely be the god of health made flesh" [that is, the Greek deity Asclepius]. And Jesus said, "The fount of life is not a little pool; it is as wide as are the spaces of the heavens. *The waters of the fount are love; the potency is faith, and he who plunges deep into the living springs, in living faith, may wash away his guilt and be made whole, and freed from sin.*"[1806]

Now let us look at another example of this Jesuine teaching. This particular one is from the Gospel of Luke:

And one of the Pharisees desired him that he would eat with him. And he went into the Pharisee's house, and sat down to meat. And, behold, a woman in the city, which was a sinner, when she knew that Jesus sat at meat in the Pharisee's house, brought an alabaster box of ointment, and stood at his feet behind him weeping, and began to wash his feet with tears, and did wipe them with the hairs of her head, and kissed his feet, and anointed them with the ointment.

Now when the Pharisee which had bidden him saw it, he spake within himself, saying, "This man, if he were a prophet, would have known who and what manner of woman this is that toucheth him: for she is a sinner." And Jesus answering said unto him, "Simon, I have somewhat to say unto thee." And he saith, "Master, say on." "There was a certain creditor which had two debtors: the one owed five hundred pence, and the other fifty.

And when they had nothing to pay, he frankly forgave them both. Tell me therefore, which of them will love him most?" Simon answered and said, "I suppose that he, to whom he forgave most." And he said unto him, "Thou hast rightly judged."

And he turned to the woman, and said unto Simon, "Seest thou this woman? I entered into thine house, thou gavest me no water for my feet: but she hath washed my feet with tears, and wiped them with the hairs of her head. Thou gavest me no kiss: but this woman since the time I came in hath not ceased to kiss my feet. My head with oil thou didst not anoint: but this woman hath anointed my feet with ointment. Wherefore I say unto thee, *her sins, which are many, are forgiven; for she loved much*: but to whom little is forgiven, the same loveth little."

And he said unto her, "Thy sins are forgiven." And they that sat at meat with him began to say within themselves, "Who is this that forgiveth sins also?" And he said to the woman, "*Thy faith hath saved thee*; go in peace."[1807]

According to self-selected "defenders of the faith" and formalistic orthodox Christians (symbolized in the New Testament by the Pharisees), the idea that anyone but God can forgive us for our sins is "blasphemy."[1808] So where did Jesus get this "heretical" concept from, the soteriological notion that we can absolve our own sins?[1809]

The answer is that God has given us full responsibility for our lives, good and bad, and this must include the ability to free ourselves from our own errors, from our own negative histories. As we have seen, as divine beings, as individualizations of God, we have the divine power to create and eradicate good and to create and eradicate bad.[1810]

LIVING SIN-FREE

Jesus understands that it cannot be otherwise, for we are always operating under the dynamic Law of Attraction, one of God's most magnificent gifts to humanity. This is why, in the Gospel of Luke, the Master Himself admits that there are people who do not need to repent of anything. They are sinless and therefore sin-free.[1811]

These are the 1 percent of fully enlightened men and women on earth (at any given time), who are using the Law of Attraction properly, positively, and constructively. Paul made note of such individuals as well. They are those who are "dead unto sin": because they live under the law of faith instead of works, sin has no dominion over them.[1812] As the saint declared, those who are able to live this way are indeed "made free from sin.[1813] . . . For whosoever shall call upon the name of the Lord [that is, be Christlike] shall be saved."[1814]

## LOVE DISSOLVES SIN

The "sinful" woman in the above story filled her heart with love for God and godly things, positive thoughts that were so powerful they attracted an instant "cleansing" of her past. Her pure intense love, in fact, made her one with God (at-one-ment). Having changed her thoughts from evil (negative) to righteous (positive), she raised herself from "sinner" to "saint," which is why Jesus said to her: "*Your* faith has saved you."

He did not say: "*My* faith has saved you," for not even His own tremendous personal belief could redeem her. She was her own and only salvation, saved through the power of love, which, according to the book of Proverbs, blots out "*all* of our sins" (past mistakes).[1815] In the Lord's own words: "her sins, which are many, are forgiven; *for she loved much.*"[1816]

## HOW GOD & CHRIST MYSTICALLY SAVE US FROM SIN

And here we find a great spiritual truth occultly concealed behind the Lord's teaching on faith, love, and sin: Jesus tells us that it is love that dissolves our transgressions. Now we know from John that God is love.[1817] Therefore, from this perspective, it is God who redeems us from our sins—a personage whom the formal branch of the Christian Church calls "Jehovah," and whom the mystical branch calls the "Divine Mind."

And yet God has individualized Himself within each one of us[1818] as what Jesus called "the Father which is in secret,"[1819] and as what Paul called the "Christ in you,"[1820] that is, the Indwelling Christ.[1821] Therefore it is also both formalistically and spiritually true that it is Christ who forgives our sins.

Whatever labels we choose for Spirit, God, the Father, the Christ, the Holy Ghost, the Comforter, or love, are all mystically one,[1822] and all have the power to eradicate sin; that is, our past wrongdoings.

## THE CLEANSING POWER OF LOVE, FAITH, & RIGHTEOUSNESS

John the Baptist came to earth, in part, to teach this same lesson on the power of love and the annulment of sin: "Purify your hearts by love and righteousness and you shall be forgiven,"[1823] for our "sins are washed away by purity in life," he exclaims in the Aquarian Gospel.[1824]

If we take Jesus' parable of the Prodigal Son literally, we learn that our "sins against heaven" are not held against us by Father if we but return to Him with love and humility.[1825] All that is truly required of us, according to the Lord, is to ask God for forgiveness, the very act which then emancipates us from the shackles of our past mistakes.[1826]

Paul taught that we are purified of sin by "by faith,"[1827] by belief in Jesus' true Gospel, "the Gospel of the Kingdom,"[1828] or what I call the Good News of the Realm of Divine Mind. This is why, when speaking of quarrelsome, heretical members of the Church, Paul used the Greek word *autokatakritos*, meaning that such corrupt and sinful individuals are "self-condemned."[1829] Why is this important?

If we have the power to condemn ourselves *for* our sins, then we must have the power to absolve ourselves *from* our sins, and indeed we do, just as John preached. According to the Apostle, if we merely "walk in the Light of Christ" He will "cleanseth us from *all* sin."[1830]

SAVING YOURSELF THROUGH RIGHT-THINKING
Let us look at another example in which a "sinner" saves himself, this one also from Luke:

> And it came to pass, that as he [Jesus] was come nigh unto Jericho, a certain blind man sat by the way side begging: and hearing the multitude pass by, he asked what it meant. And they told him, that Jesus of Nazareth passeth by. And he cried, saying, "Jesus, thou Son of David, have mercy on me." And they which went before rebuked him, that he should hold his peace: but he cried so much the more, "Thou Son of David, have mercy on me."
>
> And Jesus stood, and commanded him to be brought unto him: and when he was come near, he asked him, saying, "What wilt thou that I shall do unto thee?" And he said, "Lord, that I may receive my sight." And Jesus said unto him, "Receive thy sight: *thy faith hath saved thee.*" And immediately he received his sight, and followed him, glorifying God: and all the people, when they saw it, gave praise unto God.[1831]

How does this work? How do we, like this blind beggar, "save" ourselves from sin?

According to the Master's own teaching on the Law of Attraction, if one views himself as a "wretched sinner," a doctrine taught by some early Jews and Christians, he only attracts more misery, more reasons to think he is a terrible person. This attitude of self-loathing always brings disaster into one's life in the shape of unhappiness, depression, poverty, and, of course, illness. Thus, by believing that "I am a sinner," one indeed becomes a sinner, in turn summoning all of the negative vibrations and experiences that go along with the unredeemed life!

This type of thinking goes against God's most important commandment: to love Him with all of our heart, soul, strength, and mind.[1832] For having been made in His image,[1833] we are one with God,[1834] beautifully reflecting His glory "as in a mirror."[1835] Therefore to degrade God is to degrade ourselves, our Higher Selves, and vice versa.

The "sin" Jesus spoke to the lame man about (in the Gospel of John) is obvious then. He knew that the man's physical problems were caused by error-filled thoughts. Such thoughts cause us to "miss the mark" when it comes to God's inescapable spiritual laws. Faith-filled thoughts, however, cancel out our "sins," realign us with the Father, and "save" us from a hell of our own making, both here and, as we will see, in the Afterlife. For "heaven and . . . hell are not above, around, below, but in . . ."[1836] Thus, as Jesus put it in the plainest language: "Your faith saves you from the problems your negative thoughts attract to you, including all physical ailments."

This makes perfect sense does it not? In the end, so saith Luke, all will be "saved,"[1837] for, according to Paul, the Father is a God who is "rich in mercy," and whose salvific grace is simply His irrevocable "gift"[1838] to us.[1839] Thus, the Holy Spirit washes clean and completely renews all those who believe.[1840] Jesus went one step further. Speaking to Paul as the Indwelling Christ, he said: *"My loving kindness is all you need."*[1841]

DEFINING SIN

What is sin then? The Lord's brother James the Just defined it this way: it means to "err from the truth."[1842] Simply put, to sin means incorrect thinking, improper beliefs, and negative feelings, all which inevitably lead to a host of other difficulties. This gives us the inner meaning of Jesus' final statement to the healed man: "Now that you are all better, do not think negative thoughts anymore, for you will create even worse problems for yourself."[1843] Jesus left his patient with a gift even greater than the healing itself: His teaching on the Law of Attraction!

God loves us all unconditionally and only wants the best for us,[1844] which is why He made positive thoughts and positive deeds a thousand times more powerful than negative ones, even giving good thoughts and actions the ability to vibrationally "cancel" out our bad thoughts and actions.[1845] For the purpose of divine "punishment" is not to make us suffer, as so many churches today teach, but to help us grow and learn on our spiritual journey toward realizing our oneness with God.

Paul goes even further, saying that the Bible was "written for our learning," not to ensnare us[1846]—and I agree. Recognizing our at-one-ment with the Father (God-realization) and learning to express His attributes is, to me, our main purpose here on earth, and it is the best way I know of to glorify Him.[1847]

Our mistakes and the painful consequences that often accompany them are, in fact, part of the self-correcting system that God designed for us: errors ("sin") merely mean that we have momentarily fallen off our spiritual path; our spiritual "wheels" have gone off the road and we must correct our steering; we have temporarily lost our direction in the "wilderness" of human life.[1848] To get back on "the Way of the Lord"[1849] we must "repent," which means acknowledging our sins (mistakes) and making a commitment to never repeat them again. "For godly sorrow worketh repentance to salvation not to be repented of."[1850]

A "sinner" then is one who is not yet spiritually illuminated; who has not yet allowed the Word of God to enter into him and enlighten him;[1851] one who is not yet aware of his or her God-Self, the Christ Within.[1852]

God does not punish us. We punish ourselves through our own misunderstanding, ignorance, and self-loathing, and through embracing negative manmade ideas.[1853] If you believe in regret, self-mortification, and self-humiliation, you will experience them, for the Subconscious Mind must materialize your most predominant thoughts and beliefs. When we realize our inner perfection, and that this perfection is God Himself, however, we will no longer have any need to chastise, penalize, and criticize ourselves—or others.[1854]

Because of this, it is a "sin" to even dwell on our past sins, to carry them around with us, focus on them, talk about them, cruelly flagellate ourselves over them. By the Law of Attraction, regret only brings more to feel regretful about.

Jesus vehemently taught against the destructive ideas of remorse and focusing on sin, which is so prevalent in today's Christian churches! Once you realize your error and replace it with the correct thought, belief, or action, your "sin" is permanently absolved, and you need never think about it again. Truly, by "the law of the Spirit of life in Christ Jesus,"[1855] the Indwelling Christ,[1856] you are "made free from sin," just as Paul testified.[1857]

This is as it should be, for this perfectly correlates with the Master's teaching on sin. After healing his followers (according to their own faith),

He did not condemn them. Instead He made comments such as "thy sins are forgiven,"[1858] "thy faith hath saved thee,"[1859] and "thy sins be forgiven thee."[1860]

When he encountered the woman "taken in adultery," He did not denounce, damn, or excoriate her as the pseudorighteous fundamentalist Pharisees did.[1861] Quite the opposite. After asking her indicters to let the sinless among them cast the first stone, each one turned and slowly walked away.[1862] He then said to her:

> "Woman, where are those thine accusers? hath no man condemned thee? Neither do I condemn thee: go, and sin no more."[1863]

Jesus' yoke is truly "easy," and His burden is truly "light"![1864]

God knows that wretchedness, sickness, and deprivation are "sins" of our own creation. They are manmade, by the human Ego (Satan), and are therefore self-produced illusions. On the other hand, God wants us to experience abundance in all areas of our lives.[1865] Indeed, contrary to the un-Christian, un-biblical, outdated definition of sin, Jesus commanded that we love ourselves as we love our neighbor.[1866] One cannot love one's self and hate one's self simultaneously,[1867] for "a double minded man is unstable in all his ways."[1868]

When we occasionally stray from the "straight and narrow path" on our journey toward at-one-ment with God,[1869] we are like the archer in an archery competition who fails to hit the bull's-eye: we have "missed the mark" and must try again. Any "punishment" that results from our "sin" comes from us, from the disappointment our Higher Self feels over "missing the mark," not from an angry vengeful God. The Divine Mind itself tells us that it "will abundantly pardon" all those who "return unto the Lord"[1870] and follow "the Way of Holiness";[1871] that is, engage in right-thinking, right-speaking, and right action.[1872]

In simple terms, we have transgressed a scientific law, and the outcome is uncomfortable, just as it would be if we foolishly put our finger on a hot stove. The resulting burn is not a supernatural deity punishing us. We have merely violated ("sinned against") the first law of thermodynamics, and the consequence is painful ("punishment"). Thus we have Paul's mystical statement:

> "We have had [biological] fathers of our flesh which corrected us, and we gave them reverence: shall we not much rather be in

subjection unto the Father of spirits [that is, Divine Mind], and live? For they [our earthly fathers] verily for a few days chastened us after their own pleasure; but he [God] *for our profit*, that we might be partakers of his holiness."[1873]

How true this is. Rome was not built in a day, and we cannot achieve Christhood in one day either. Our mistakes ("sins") give us time to learn who we really are on our journey to at-one-ment with Spirit. The education that comes from our "sins," from our mistakes and failures, is, of course, their very purpose. As Jesus states in the Aquarian Gospel:

> "The greatest lessons that are learned in life come through the failures that are made."[1874]

In the end, the true mystical definition of sin is living purely out of the Ego and the concomitant renunciation of the Father, the denial of God—a state of consciousness that the mass mind calls "atheism." For by disuniting ourselves from Divine Mind, we are disconnecting from the Holy One, the Supreme Being, the Sacred Source of not only our own personal lives, but of the entire Universe. Without the Divine Mind working on our behalf, what do we have? As Jesus said, there is only one true and unforgivable "sin against God": the denial of Spirit.[1875]

## GOD'S SALVATION

Let us keep in mind that the "God" in question is not the rancorous, unforgiving Hebrew "Father" of the Old Testament, who was patterned on the capricious and egocentric sky-gods of ancient Pagandom. "Sin" is an error committed against the authentic Christian God of the New Testament, against the loving and forgiving God of Jesus: the God-Self within, the Supreme Self, the incorporeal Divine Self, the Indwelling Christ, the Higher Self.[1876]

For it is this aspect of ourselves—which Peter called the "hidden man of the heart,"[1877] which Daniel knew as the "Ancient of Days,"[1878] and which Paul referred to as the "inward man"[1879]—that forms the foundation of each and every one of us.[1880] Now read these passages from the book of Proverbs with your newly opened "inner" eyes:

> "My son, despise not the chastening of the Lord; neither be weary of his correction: for *whom the Lord loveth he correcteth*; even as a father the son in whom he delighteth."[1881]

This God, the true God of Jesus, is pure love,[1882] and "he be not far from every one of us," for "in him we live, and move, and have our being."[1883] Being pure love, God seeks not to punish us, for He would then merely be punishing Himself. What He does seek is our "salvation," that is, our well-being, and this, contrary to the manmade teachings of many Christian preachers, He lovingly promised to "all flesh."[1884] And how do we find salvation?

> ". . . man is saved when he has reached deific life; when he and God are one."[1885]

Here we have the inner meaning of the name of the Lord: literally speaking, Jesus means "God is salvation." But mystically it means "the Indwelling Christ delivers, absolves, and redeems you from your mistakes against Spirit." It is our atonement, our at-one-ment with the Father,[1886] our realization of our divine nature,[1887] that crucifies the human Ego (our "old man," "the flesh," the Lower Self, "Satan")[1888] and releases us from the karmic wheel of sin![1889]

## THE SECRET TO MENTAL HEALING

As far as ill health is concerned, what can we learn from the amazing New Testament stories we have reviewed of self-faith, self-belief, the power of the mind, and Jesus' instantaneous healings—which the Hindu revealingly calls "instant beneficence"?

Simply this: any individual can heal himself or herself of any disease, and anyone can aid in healing someone else of any disease. Particularly empowered are groups, whose numbers can intensify God's healing power and fortify the sufferer's faith. The secret is to "turn away from sin" (that is, stop thinking negatively), and have complete faith in the power of the Divine Mind. James the Just wrote:

> "Is any sick among you? . . . the prayer of *faith shall save the sick*, and the Lord shall raise him up; and *if he have committed sins, they shall be forgiven him*. . . . Pray one for another, that *ye may be healed*. The effectual fervent prayer of a righteous man availeth much."[1890]

Yes, "faith shall save the sick," for we have been given the "gifts of healing" by the Holy Spirit![1891]

Jesus revealed the secret of mental healing to his followers some

2,000 years ago: healing takes place according to the degree of faith, the intensity of belief, of the person being healed. And since the level of faith we can attain has no limitations, the outcome of our faith also has no limitations, as the Master Himself taught:

> "*If thou canst believe, all things are possible to him that believeth.*"[1892]

Now what is faith? This word has been so overused and so misused that many of us no longer know what it really means. We know that its opposite is doubt, and in our increasingly atheistic and humanistic world, this is something of which there is no shortage.

Jesus had to deal with the doubting Thomases of the Mediterranean region on a daily basis. Amazed at their lack of spirituality and the depth of their skepticism, He would often exclaim to them: "Except ye see signs [that is, miracles] and wonders, ye will not believe."[1893] This is truly the converse of faith, which, as we have seen, Paul defined like this:

> "Now faith is the substance of things hoped for, *the evidence of things not seen*. . . . Through faith we understand that the worlds were framed by *the word of God*, so that *things which are seen were not made of things which do appear*."[1894]

In modern English, Paul is saying:

> "Faith is the total and complete belief that what we desire has already physically manifested, even though we cannot yet see it with our physical eyes. Faith teaches us that just as God created the Universe from nothing through the power of thought, whatever appears on the physical (visible) plane is due to the action of Divine Mind on the spiritual (invisible) plane."[1895]

And here is how true mental healing takes place. The patient must make a firm decision that he deserves to be healed, and that his healing is guaranteed. He must completely believe, in fact, that he is *already* healed. This powerful belief then vibrationally attracts a regeneration of the affected body parts. Why? Because according to the Law of Attraction, *you attract what you believe*. If you believe that your body is in perfect health, that your illness has disappeared, and that the "sick" cells have been replaced with healthy cells, then it must be.

Be happy and worry not! Consider this wisdom from the book of

Proverbs:

> "*A merry heart doeth good like a medicine*: but a broken spirit drieth the
> bones."[1896]

If you desire a "merry heart," you must let go of the ideas of "sin,"
"hellfire," and "damnation." These childish manmade ideas were invented
by the early Church to control the masses through fear. If you believe in
them, the Law of Attraction states that you will invite them into your life
and be consumed by them. This is not what you want for yourself, and it is
not what God or Jesus wants for you either!

To be happy and healthy, think only thoughts of well-being and it
will be so; speak only words of beauty, perfection, and love, and your body
will be transformed into their likeness, for as the Bible tells us, "the tongue
of the wise is health."[1897] The Father declared that the Word of God is Law
and that His Law cannot be broken:

> "*Thou shalt . . . decree a thing, and it shall be established unto thee*: and
> the light shall shine upon thy ways."[1898]

If you want perfect health then, you must "decree" it in your
Conscious Mind (the "Son," the "Master"). This "establishes" your desire in
your Subconscious Mind (the "Holy Spirit," the "Servant"), after which the
Superconscious Mind ("God," the "Father") physically manifests it for you.
Your healing will occur in correlation to your degree of belief, just as Jesus
promised us: "According to your faith be it unto you."[1899] Truly, as the Lord
affirms in the Aquarian Gospel:

> "*The fount of health is in your soul*; it has a door locked fast; *the key is
> faith*; and *every one can have this key and may unlock the door and plunge
> into the healing fount and be made whole* "[1900]

BEGIN YOUR HEALING NOW!
To start your healing this instant, use the following universal healing
declaration: "God is healing me now. I AM healed." Repeat this decree as
often as you can. Believe it completely, then simply allow the Father to
perform His "magic" on you. Here are the personal instructions of God,
Divine Mind, from the book of Exodus:

"If thou wilt diligently hearken to the voice of the Lord thy God, and wilt do that which is right in his sight, and wilt give ear to his commandments, and keep all his statutes, I will put none of these diseases upon thee, which I have brought upon the Egyptians [a symbol of nonbelievers]: for *I am the Lord that healeth thee.*"[1901]

It is this simple: follow the tenets of the Indwelling Christ, the Great I AM Within,[1902] and you will receive all the fruits of the Holy Spirit: "love, joy, peace, longsuffering, gentleness, goodness, faith, meekness, temperance,"[1903] and of course, perfect health. Long ago the sagacious Solomon wrote:

"Be not wise in thine own eyes: fear the Lord, and depart from evil. It shall be health to thy navel, and marrow to thy bones."[1904]

The inner meaning:

"Do not be a know-it-all. Respect the Divine Mind and learn to think, speak, and act positively at all times. You will be rewarded with health all the days of your life."[1905]

Do you receive it? If you do, you will harvest one-hundred times what you have sown![1906]

Judas Iscariot, Jesus' treasurer, betrays the Lord in the Garden of Gethsemane for thirty pieces of silver. Even here, during this world-altering act of disloyalty and treachery, Jesus uses the moment to teach the Law of Attraction. When an angry Peter impetuously cuts off the ear of Malchus, the servant of a Jewish high priest who was standing nearby, Jesus touches the victim's wound and immediately heals him. Since we possess the same divine nature (the Indwelling Christ) as Jesus, such power ("glory") is available to all of us through following the Lord's teachings on the Law of Attraction. If used correctly, this awesome faith-based power enables us to physically manifest whatever we desire, including instant and complete healings of any ailment, just as Jesus taught—and demonstrated.

# 23

# JESUS' ULTIMATE CANCER TREATMENT

"Then shall thy light break forth as the morning, and thine health shall spring forth speedily: and thy righteousness shall go before thee; the glory of the Lord shall be thy rereward [harvest]."[1907]

## THERE IS A CURE!

IN ORDER TO BETTER UNDERSTAND how health, disease, and healing are affected by the Law of Attraction, let us take cancer as an example, which, for reasons that will become clear, I refer to as "C." Since nearly one out of every two people (48 percent) in the U.S. has gotten "C" or will get it, this particular ailment serves as an ideal illustration of how nearly all diseases are created and how they can be cured using Jesus' Law of Attraction principles.

Yes I said it: "C" can be cured! I know because I have seen it with my own eyes, and so have thousands of others. And in this chapter you will learn the cure for yourself. For the sake of simplicity and practicality, I will address the reader here as if he or she has "C."

## THE PHYSICAL & MENTAL CAUSES OF "C"

If you ask the average mainstream doctor how one gets "C," you will invariably be told that "no one knows," or just as likely, "it seems to be hereditary." From a spiritual perspective, both of these answers are wrong, and are therefore a deception on humanity.

All diseases begin in the mind, usually as a lack of self-love, or to be more specific, self-hatred. This disgust with the Self leads the individual to do things that he would not ordinarily do if he admired and respected himself, such as think negative thoughts, eat an unhealthy diet, avoid exercise, fresh air, and sunlight, overwork, live recklessly, try to hurt others, argue with family members, hold grudges, refuse to forgive, and seek revenge for past wrongs.

The behavioral list of the self-hater is endless, for self-hatred stems from the always vain and atheistic Ego (the "Devil" or "Satan" of the Bible), which is innately self-centered, separates us from God, and whose needs and demands can never be satisfied. The results of living purely by the Ego are always destructive!

As we learned in the previous chapter, *negativity* in any form, whether mental (wrong thoughts) or physical (wrong foods), creates an overly acidic condition in the body. An acidic human body can be compared to a small body of water whose fresh-flowing source is cut off: deprived of the life-giving oxygen contained in its source stream, as the pond sits, it begins to stagnate and ferment, creating more and more poisons within itself. Finally it becomes so toxic that all life within it is driven out. The pond is now nothing but thick brown sludge, completely devoid of the spark of life.

But if we were to turn its source stream back on, the pond would immediately begin receiving fresh oxygen, which cleanses, renews, purifies, and heals. The toxins in its waters would be destroyed and flushed out, and insects, fish, amphibians, and birds would return, restoring the cycle of life to the entire system. The pond becomes healthy and whole once again.

If you have "C," this is the perfect analogy of what is happening in your body.

The materialists around you (be they family members, friends, or mainstream medical practitioners) have probably already informed you that the cause of your condition is unknown, or that you inherited it from a parent or ancestor. He or she is also likely to have told you that you only have a few treatment options, that none of these offer a guarantee, and that even if any of them work, your life span will only be extended for a few years at best.

WHAT JESUS SAID ABOUT DIS-EASE

Now hear this: *all* of these statements go completely against what the world's greatest spiritualists teach, including our Lord Jesus!

According to the personal Law of Attraction doctrines of the Eternal Physician[1908] (Jesus' Greek name, *Iesous*, means "the Healer"), we are responsible for everything that happens to us. As such, we create our own health and our own ill health. So if we have "C," it is our own doing, for, according to God's promise to us,[1909] our word (thought) always becomes flesh (materializes in the physical).[1910]

This is not bad news. It is just one aspect of Jesus' "Good News" for humanity. In fact, once you grasp and accept this truth—this vital aspect of His authentic Gospel, the "Gospel of the Kingdom,"[1911] the Realm of Divine Mind—you will realize that it is one of the greatest, most indescribable gifts you will ever receive![1912]

Why is this part of the "glad tidings," the "Good News" of Jesus Christ? Because *what you create with your mind, you can un-create with your mind.* Since "C" is, like nearly all diseases, self-made, you can unmake it just as easily as you made it to begin with!

Remember, you are in a copartnership with God,[1913] and God is the totality of the Superconscious Mind (the "Father"), the Conscious Mind (the "Son," or the "Word"), and the Subconscious Mind (the "Holy Ghost"), our sacred inner trinity.[1914] When these three minds combine to work in unison, they form the most powerful force in the Universe, attracting to us our heart's most inner desires. And since the Law of Attraction is both a spiritual and a scientific law, it cannot be violated.

We have been told over and over that there is no cure for "C." Indeed, there are numerous multimillion dollar organizations whose researchers do nothing but seek a cure. Many of these institutions have been in existence for decades and have spent untold billions of dollars. Yet no cure has been found, and the type of cure they are looking for will never be found. Why?

Because they are looking for an *external* cure. Since all disease begins within the individual, the cure must be sought *internally*, in the mind!

Thus, there are really only two features of "C" that we need be concerned with: first, the thoughts of the mind (the mental aspect); and second the results of these thoughts, which have manifested in the body as "C" (the physical aspect).

As noted, this chapter assumes that the reader has "C." However, even if you do not have it, this chapter will benefit you, because you will learn how to avoid creating it, and almost every other type of disease as well.

## THE MENTAL CURE FOR "C"

According to the Law of Attraction, whatever you believe becomes true for you. So, technically speaking, you can heal yourself of "C" in almost any manner you choose.

If you believe that reading books by Mark Twain, for example, will eliminate "C" from you body, by all means, read Twain's books. If you believe that listening to Beethoven's symphonies will permanently wipe "C" from your cells, then listen to Beethoven's symphonies. If you believe that watching John Wayne movies will destroy "C," then watch them, because they will. Believe and it will be so!

Dodie Osteen, mother of the popular Texas preacher Joel Osteen, cured herself of "C" by reciting forty specific verses from the Bible over and over. The Word of God is the Father's own personal medicine, and it reveals the magical power of the Divine Mind at work!

## MEDITATION

Anything that relieves tension and stress is good for treating "C," and for disease in general, for stress is at the *physical* root of all ailments. An ideal form of stress relief is meditation, which has the double benefit of healing the body while elevating the consciousness.

The Western form of meditation is easy and requires no investment in education or equipment: simply sit or lie in a comfortable position for fifteen minutes. During this time concentrate solely on your breathing. Hundreds of thoughts will float across the "screen" of your mind. Let them pass. Stayed focused on the sensation of your breath going in and out, which is being powered by the Divine Mind.

What is happening is that for the five, ten, or fifteen minutes that you are meditating, you are not purposefully generating any thoughts. Those that do arise originate by themselves, then disappear just as quickly. Your task is merely to observe them without judgment, reaction, or attachment, as they stream through your consciousness. Eventually a feeling of transcendent peace will come over you.

During this stillness, known by mystics as "the Silence," you are strengthening your connection to your God-Self, the Great I AM Presence Within, fulfilling God's biblical commandment: "Be still, and know that I AM God."[1915]

During meditation we indeed come very close to the Divine. James the Just said: "Draw nigh to God, and he will draw nigh to you,"[1916] which matches Paul's affirmation: "The Lord is at hand."[1917] Thus, meditation is the perfect time to reintroduce ourselves to Him, as is written in the book of Job:

> "*Acquaint now thyself with him, and be at peace: thereby good shall come unto thee.* Receive, I pray thee, the law from his mouth, and lay up his words in thine heart."[1918]

Elevating your consciousness through communing with God in the Silence will help you heal yourself of any mental and physical disorder, while making it easier to work with the Law of Attraction. For when we meditate, the Divine Mind (the "Lord") is in its most natural state (the "Holy Temple"), just as the book of Habakkuk states:

> "But the Lord is in his holy temple: let all the earth keep silence before him."[1919]

From the book of Zechariah:

> "Be silent, O all flesh, before the Lord: for he is raised up out of his holy habitation."[1920]

The modern West has also long been aware of the healing attributes of the Silence, as English philosopher and founder of Pennsylvania, William Penn, observed:

> "True silence is the rest of the mind, and is to the spirit what sleep is to the body, nourishment and refreshment."

In the Aquarian Gospel, Jesus elucidates on the topic of the Silence. Meditation, he says, heals us because it reconnects us with the One Source:

> "There is a Silence where the soul may meet its God, and there the fount of wisdom is, and all who enter are immersed in light, and filled with wisdom, love and power.
> "... The Silence is not circumscribed; is not a place closed in with wall, or rocky steeps, nor guarded by the sword of man. Men carry with them all the time the secret place where they may meet their God. It matters not where men abide, on mountain

top, in deepest vale, in marts of trade, or in the quiet home; they may at once, at any time, fling wide the door, and find the Silence, find the house of God; it is within the soul.

"One may not be so much disturbed by noise of business, and the words and thoughts of men if he goes all alone into the valley or the mountain pass. And when life's heavy load is pressing hard, it is far better to go out and seek a quiet place to pray and meditate.

"The Silence is the kingdom of the soul which is not seen by human eyes. When in the Silence, phantom forms may flit before the mind; but they are all subservient to the will; the master soul may speak and they are gone.

"If you would find this Silence of the soul you must yourself prepare the way. None but the pure in heart may enter here. And you must lay aside all tenseness of the mind, all business cares, all fears, all doubts and troubled thoughts. Your human will must be absorbed by the divine; then you will come into a consciousness of holiness."[1921]

It is in this Holy Silence that you will discover the "perfect peace" of God,[1922] an inner serenity "which passeth all understanding."[1923] Then and only then will the meaning of the words of the Master Psychologist become apparent:

> "Peace I leave with you, my peace I give unto you: not as the world giveth, give I unto you. Let not your heart be troubled, neither let it be afraid."[1924]

Is it any wonder that Jesus often journeyed into the "wilderness" by Himself to take in the Silence, sometimes for as long as forty days?[1925]

ONE OF THE BEST MEDICINES
One of the most potent mental cures for "C" is laughter! Scientific studies show that laughing relieves pain, lowers stress hormones, strengthens the immune system, relaxes muscles, boosts energy, and releases a cascade of feel-good brain chemicals into the body known as endorphins. Even smiling discharges endorphins, increasing our sense of well-being, improving our mood, easing tension, and creating feelings of optimism, joy, and hope. No wonder humor is so healing!

To reinforce and speed up your healing, I recommend reading funny books, watching funny movies, and doing fun things with your family and friends. Because humor is a positive emotion, it also has an alkaline-aerobic effect on the body. If there are two things "C" does not like, it is happiness and oxygen!

Journalist and author Norman Cousins was afflicted with a life threatening ailment but was able to heal himself. How? He focused on the positive emotions of love, hope, humor, and faith, while watching hours of Marx Brothers films. Unfortunately, the illness returned. Why? Cousins had not gotten to the root of the problem—which, according to New Thought expert Louise Hay, was a negative "mental pattern." Though Cousins was able to laugh this second sickness away as well, this incident leads us to an important element of healing disease, and in particular "C."

## CLEANSING THE MIND OF NEGATIVITY & ILLUSION

We cannot expect to permanently cure an illness with the mind if the mind is still operating under former self-negating thoughts and ideas. After all, disease starts on the mental plane. So we must embark on a rigorous program of mental cleansing, and here is how.

To purge your mind of mental darkness, it is absolutely essential that you begin by developing *a deep and abiding love for yourself*. Forgive yourself for anything and everything you have done in the past. The same for anyone who has hurt you: forgive them. Accept everyone as they are. Let everything go that is not positive, that does not make you feel good, that does not make you happy.

Do not make excuses. There are no legitimate reasons for not doing this. It is as easy to mentally purify your mind as you believe it is. Millions of people have done it, and you can too!

Set yourself free from guilt, regret, self-pity, grief, remorse, and shame, *now*. Throw them away. These are highly toxic emotions that pollute our Subconscious Minds, and put us on the well-worn road to ruin. Children do not feel these negative emotions. Why? Because they are "pure in heart,"[1926] and know innately that having been created in the image of God,[1927] that they are perfect, even as our Father in Heaven is perfect.[1928] If you have reclaimed your inner child,[1929] you have Christ Consciousness, "the mind of Christ,"[1930] and you know that this is surely true, for God is true.[1931]

Guilt separates us from God, for it stems from the autonomous "I," the conceited and unspiritual human Ego (Satan)—which is an earthly illusion. We want to strengthen our oneness with God, not weaken it. So cut self-reproach loose from your life. If you do not, due to the Law of

Attraction it will not only bring you more guilt, but more things to feel guilty about. Remember: *what you believe in becomes true for you, what you think you attract, what you say you draw, what you feel you magnetize, what you have faith in you materialize.*

Yes, it is true: due to our human nature (Satan, the Devil), we have all sinned (made mistakes) and "come short of the glory of God."[1932] However, our divine nature (God),[1933] our union with the Indwelling Christ,[1934] makes us "partakers in His holiness,"[1935] freeing us from our past mistakes,[1936] and causing us to become "new creatures" in Him.[1937] For then "old things are passed away; behold, all things are become new."[1938] According to the Great Psychologist Jesus, this wonderful spiritual cleansing of our former selves, our former lives, is available to all those who believe.[1939]

To truly experience this "newness," you must unlearn the sadomasochistic hamartiological doctrines of organized religion, manmade notions that would have you suffer a lifetime of pain over former errors in judgment. Jesus never taught these narrow-minded dogmatic ideas, and in fact, He preached against them,[1940] even saying of Himself: "I judge no man."[1941] Paul states that Jesus "was made a little lower than the angels,"[1942] and that we humans "will judge angels."[1943] Think about that for a moment! Here is more of what Jesus said in the Gospel of John:

> "And if any man hear my words, and believe not, I judge him not: for *I came not to judge the world, but to save the world.*"[1944]

In the Gospel of Luke, Jesus gives this reply to a man who has asked for His help with a family issue: "Man, who made me a judge . . . over you?"[1945]

It is obvious that far from coming to earth to condemn us, Jesus' teachings are intended to help us find happiness, as He Himself declared:

> "*These things have I spoken unto you, that my joy might remain in you, and that your joy might be full.*"[1946]

Because the concept of suffering lifelong guilt over sin (real or imagined) is anti-Jesus, it is also un-Christian; and because it is un-Christian it is unwholesome; and because it is unwholesome it must be discarded if you want to achieve perfect health.

According to the Apostle John, those who preach a gospel of guilt, blame, and condemnation preach a false gospel:

"For God sent not his Son into the world to condemn the world;
but that the world through him might be saved."[1947]

Cleanse your soul by releasing the past and all painful memories
completely. Then look ahead, knowing that you are assured of a bright
future filled with the joy of God. This is what Jesus meant when He said:
"No man, having put his hand to the plough, and looking back, is fit for the
kingdom of God."[1948]

The past is truly all behind you, and there is nothing you can do
about it except live out the residual effects created by your earlier negative
thoughts. It is these very thoughts that helped manifest "C" in your body to
begin with, so get rid of them this instant!

Here is Paul's advice on "forgiving and forgetting":

"Brethren . . . this one thing I do, forgetting those things which are
behind, and reaching forth unto those things which are before, I
press toward the mark for the prize of the high calling of God in
Christ Jesus."[1949]

## TO HEAL YOU MUST LET GO OF THE "BATTLE" MENTALITY

There is another injurious idea that needs to be discarded if you want to be
healed. We often hear the expression, "he is *battling* 'C,'" "he is *fighting*
'C,'" or "she lost her *struggle* with 'C.'" This view that the treatment of "C"
is a war, and that one must "fight" the disease to win that war, is wrong, for
it only stalls or even prevents healing.

In the opinion of the great healers and spiritual teachers across the
ages, self-created stress—produced by negative thinking and negative
lifestyle habits—is the number one and only real cause of disease, including
"C." This stress, as mentioned, can come in an almost unlimited number of
forms, from ongoing self-hatred and depression to long running anger and
grief; from an acidic heavy diet to prolonged negative beliefs.

One of the more common stress factors is overwork or
overloading, which stems from our Ego's (Satan's) atheistic belief that we
live in a godless world of Darwinian competition, where suffering is the
inherent lot of humanity, and where only the strong and brutal survive.
According to this primitive school of thought, one must "never give up," but
instead "battle," "claw," and "fight" one's way to the top of every challenge.

Because of the Law of Attraction, however, those who see life and
work as a battle will only draw in more experiences that reinforce this view.

Eventually, the accumulated stress of these acid-producing thoughts and experiences robs so much oxygen from the body's cells that they begin to ferment, helping to bring on the condition doctors call "C."

The simple solution to this issue is to stop looking at the world as a great competition for money, love, food, and space, for according to Jesus' teachings on the Law of Attraction, there is unlimited abundance, more than enough for all![1950]

Then there is the warrior-like idea that we must "never give up" on a goal, a project, a relationship. While we should never "give up" on the Law of Attraction (for it is an eternal spiritual law created by God for our benefit),[1951] in almost every other circumstance this concept can be extremely self-destructive. Indeed, many people actually create "C" in their bodies from this very type of stress.

Self-loving individuals, however, know when it is time to let go. They follow the all-wise Holy Spirit (intuition), which, if we listen carefully, will tell us if and when we need to move on. In fact, sometimes it is the smartest thing to do, for God may be trying to unlock a new door for us, one that cannot be opened until we close the present one.

As mentioned, it is extremely important that we cease viewing diseases like "C" as something we need to "fight" against. This "violent" approach actually exacerbates illnesses by attracting more reasons to "battle" them. Bear in mind that *all* negative thoughts, emotions, and actions are acidic, both physically and spiritually, and few things are more negative than the act of pushing, struggling, and contention. Here is what God said on this subject:

"Not by might, nor by power, but by my spirit, saith the Lord of hosts."[1952]

In other words, we heal, not by force, by brute strength, but by thought ("spirit"), by the Divine Mind (the "Lord of hosts").

All diseases, especially "C," need to be approached in a gentle, peaceful, loving manner. Jesus taught that love is the most important principle we can live by: love of God (Divine Mind),[1953] love of self (the Indwelling Christ), and love of one's neighbor (a spiritual extension of ourselves).[1954] Love is, He stated, "the first and greatest commandment," and upon it "hangs the entire law."[1955] This makes love the one and only true cure-all for every known sickness!

So right now, reject the "battle" mentality that society has foisted upon us; throw out the old negative ways of thinking and replace them with your new knowledge of the Law of Love and Attraction.

Treat your mind, body, and soul with respect, kindness, gentleness, and above all love. These positive principles will attract more of the same, lifting the spirit and distributing fresh oxygen throughout the body. Since ultimately unremitting long-term stress (be it from overwork, unhealthy lifestyle, or self-hatred) is the only real cause of "C," self-love is the one and only real cure.

## HEALING AFFIRMATIONS & VISUALIZATIONS

Love is indeed all-healing. Therefore to effect a cure, think loving thoughts. Create and recite affirmations of self-love, such as "I am a wonderful," "I am beautiful," "I am intelligent," "I am a valuable person," "I love and respect myself." The more self-loving affirmations you create, the better. The more often these are repeated the better.[1956] The old cycle of self-hatred must be replaced with tender, affectionate, kindly thoughts, feelings, and emotions toward the Self. This is what manifests perfect healing and health; it is the road to your personal bliss, or what Jesus called "the Kingdom of God."[1957]

According to the Master Himself, you must be "born again to enter the Kingdom of God";[1958] you must become a "new creature" in Christ,[1959] so that your old negative thoughts and habits are left behind, replaced with new positive thoughts and habits.[1960] For "new wine" (new thoughts) can only be poured into a "new bottle" (a new mind), and the old wine (old thoughts) and the old bottle (your old mind) must be disposed of.[1961]

Does this work? If you have complete faith and fully believe it, absolutely! For by the Law of Attraction, *whatever you believe to be true must be true—for you.*

Your affirmations should be combined with clear self-loving visualizations. Remember the words of those spiritually advanced pre-Christian Christians, the Gnostics: "What thou see, thou shall become."[1962] For example, imagine yourself whole and healthy, radiant with self-love, peace, and happiness. Visualize the great love of God moving through the cells of your body, cleansing, purifying, and healing. See the old toxic "C" cells dying off, being replaced by perfectly healthy new cells. Emerson explained visualization this way:

> "A vivid thought brings the power to paint it; and in proportion to the depth of its source is the force of its projection."

Visualization works because your Divine Mind does not know what is real or not real; it sees no difference between the physical and the spiritual, the visible or the invisible, the past or the present. It accepts everything you think as 100 percent fact in the present moment. As such, it merely sets to work physically manifesting what you tell it to through your most persistent thoughts, words, and emotions.[1963] This is why Jesus warned against, for example, thinking impure thoughts:

> "Ye have heard that it was said by them of old time, 'thou shalt not commit adultery': but I say unto you, that whosoever looketh on a woman to lust after her hath committed adultery with her already in his heart."[1964]

And this is precisely why you should never ever focus on the disease itself. Do not think about your "condition." Do not study your "symptoms." You do not need to know how you got it, why you got it, how the disease "works," or anything else related to it. Knowing these things does not serve you in any way, and only consumes valuable time and energy that could be devoted to the healing principles of the Law of Attraction.

Reject both the pessimistic prognosis and the hopeless diagnosis. Refuse to talk about the illness. Do not even say its name. If you have to discuss it with someone, call it "C," like I do. Strip it of all its power by diminishing and ignoring it. Behave as if you do not have the disease, and never did—believe this with all your heart! Why? Because nothing is real unless you think it is. Whatever you continuously think about, you create. Whatever you give ongoing attention to, expands. Whatever you dwell on, you summon. Whatever you talk about, you strengthen. Whatever you most strongly believe, you manifest.

So accept this fact right now: disease is not real. Only health is real. For you are an individualization of God, and God is perfect, He knows nothing about ill health. You only know about it because this false belief was instilled in you by society, by mass mind. Reject the egotistical idea of disease and believe only in perfect health.

See yourself as you want to be, not as you are.[1965] Identify yourself with the Father's infinite health-giving power within you. Claim your healing, have complete faith (no doubts!), relax, and expect a perfect outcome, knowing with every fiber of your being that God will give you your "expected end."[1966]

Your disregard of the concept of "illness" will cause it to begin to fade from your life, while redirecting your focus onto perfect health will attract it to you, allowing your true healthy nature to return, just as God intended.

This is the Lord's teaching exactly: do not concentrate on your disease, which is visible. Rather, concentrate on the image of yourself as being in perfect health, which is as of yet invisible. Here is how Paul summarized this aspect of Jesus' Law of Attraction teaching:

> " While we look not at the things which are seen, but at the things which are not seen: for the things which are seen are temporal; but the things which are not seen are eternal."[1967]

Remember, what I call "the Law of Attraction, God in action," always delivers to you what you are thinking about. So focus *only* on what you want: perfect health. Say to yourself, over and over: "I AM healed. I AM cured. I AM in perfect health. Thank you God for healing me!" These powerful words of self-love connect you with the Divine, and bring into being what you are thinking and what you believe.

You were made in God's image,[1968] and this duplication is so accurate that Paul says you reflect him as "in a mirror."[1969] Now, God is perfect.[1970] Therefore you are perfect as well.[1971] If you feel you are not, it is only because you think you are not. Think, believe, and know that you are perfect, and you will be. Let go of any doubt, fear, or apprehension. Say with the Psalmist to God, "I will fear no evil: for thou art with me."[1972]

You cannot fail to achieve your goal because God cannot fail. Here is what the book of 1 Chronicles says on this topic:

> "Be strong and of good courage, and *do it: fear not, nor be dismayed*: for the Lord God, even my *God, will be with thee; he will not fail thee, nor forsake thee.*"[1973]

The book of Joshua states it this way:

> "Have not I commanded thee? Be strong and of a good courage; be not afraid, neither be thou dismayed: for *the Lord thy God is with thee whithersoever thou goest.*"[1974]

The following comforting fact, reminding us of the Universal Indwelling Christ,[1975] our God-Self,[1976] is from the book of Psalms:

> "If I ascend up into heaven, thou art there: if I make my bed in hell, behold, thou art there. If I take the wings of the morning, and dwell in the uttermost parts of the sea; even there shall thy hand lead me, and thy right hand shall hold me."[1977]

Yes, the Father (Divine Mind) is with us at all times, wherever we go. Thus, everything done through the power of the ever triumphant God, no matter how small, is a success. For as Jesus declared, that is the Law:

> "And it is easier for heaven and earth to pass, than one tittle of the law to fail."[1978]

## THE PHYSICAL CURE FOR "C"

Having studied the mental cure for "C," now let us turn to the physical cure. Treating "C" both mentally *and* physically is an unbeatable combination that can work for anyone, in particular those who may not yet have enough faith to effect a mental healing alone.

From what we have already seen, it is obvious that if you were told that "there is no cure for "C," you have been deceived. But some might protest that mainstream medicine does not recognize mental/spiritual healing; so in that sense, mainstream doctors are indeed justified in saying that there is no cure.

To this argument I say horse-feathers! Yes, when mainstream medicine declares that there is no cure for "C," they are referring to a physical cure. But even here they are wrong once again, making this statement just another great hoax on the public.

Actually, the *physical* cure for "C" was discovered in the late 1920s by a German biochemist named Dr. Otto Heinrich Warburg. In fact, he received the 1931 Nobel Prize in Physiology and Medicine for his remarkable breakthrough. Warburg found that normal cells get their energy from oxygen (alkalinity), while "C" cells get their energy from fermentation (acidity). In essence, this means that normal cells are aerobic (thrive with oxygen), while "C" cells are anaerobic (thrive without oxygen).

This takes us back to my analogy of the human body as a pond: positive thoughts and an alkaline diet produce oxygen-enriching properties in the body, resulting in optimum health, or a "living, vital pond." Negative thoughts and acidic foods, on the other hand, produce oxygen-robbing properties in the body, resulting in poor health, or a "stagnant, fermenting pond." This is so important, let us read it again, this time highlighted:

*Positive thoughts and an alkaline diet produce oxygen-enriching properties in the body, resulting in optimum health, or a "living, vital pond." Negative thoughts and acidic foods, on the other hand, produce oxygen-robbing properties in the body, resulting in poor health, or a "stagnant, fermenting pond."*

Study this principle until you fully understand it and have memorized it. It contains the Wisdom of the Ages,[1979] "the mystery of Christ," which God revealed to us through the secret "door of utterance."[1980] It is the key, in fact, to unlocking the mystery of all manner of unwellness.[1981]

## YES YOU HOLD THE KEY TO YOUR OWN CURE!

You now know what causes "C," and because of this you are well on your way to understanding the correct holistic approach to "dissolving" it. Warburg himself maintained that "there is no disease whose prime cause is better known." In other words, the medical establishment no longer has any valid excuse for not aiding the public in the prevention and proper treatment of "C."

For those who want to prevent creating this disease, or for those who already have it and wish to rid themselves of it, "the Way of the Light" is now clear.[1982] In fact, using Jesus' teachings on faith and love, the positive power of the mind, and the Law of Attraction, in combination with a natural foods/alkaline heavy diet and a healthy lifestyle, any disease can be successfully treated!

The choice is always with the individual, for God, in His infinite wisdom and unconditional love for us, gave us complete freedom to build or destroy our own lives. This personal independence we inherited from the Indwelling Christ,[1983] for "where the Spirit of the Lord is, there is liberty."[1984] That is part of the uncompromising Law.[1985]

## A WORD ON DOCTORS

Doctors have their role, often an important one, in health and healing. So if you feel the need to see a medical practitioner for any reason whatsoever, especially if you think that you do not have enough faith yet, a high enough level of Christ Consciousness, by all means, listen to your inner voice and seek out professional care.

And keep in mind that it does not have to be all or nothing: medicine or Jesus. A doctor's scientific methods can work harmoniously in conjunction with the Master's spiritual methods to improve our well-being. Thus Jesus did not speak out against doctors—and neither do I.[1986]

What Jesus *did* speak out about, however, is that when doctors fail to effect a cure, when they give up on us, when they declare our condition "hopeless," we can always turn to God and heal ourselves by way of the Divine Mind, by having complete faith in the Law of Attraction.

This is precisely what happened to the woman who was healed by touching Jesus' robe: she had spent her last penny on doctors, and exhausted all other possibilities. Having been pronounced "incurable" by her physicians, she turned inward and healed herself by taking hold of Jesus' robe. She totally believed that merely touching the hem of the Lord's garment would heal her. And so it did! This is why Jesus said to her:

> "Daughter be of good comfort: *thy faith hath made thee whole*; go in peace."[1987]

Pertaining to doctors, what we must always keep in mind is that they do not "heal" us through medications and surgery. In most cases, drugs only hide the symptoms of disease, and removing unhealthy cells from the body with a scalpel is only taking away the materialization of negative thoughts created by the patient. This is why diseases treated using these methods are so often unsuccessful: if the patient does not change their thinking, the ailment will simply return after surgery or the medication is withdrawn.

Even when surgery and pharmaceuticals are considered necessary (and in many cases they can help us get back on the road to health), remember that it is our bodies which heal themselves. For our natural state is health and, when ill, it is the body's nature to seek to correct the imbalance, eliminate the dis-ease, and restore us to a state of ease.

We will recall that self-healing is done through the immune system, which gets its "orders" from the Subconscious Mind, which gets its thoughts from the Conscious Mind. So heed the warning I have repeatedly offered throughout this book: since *your word is always in the process of creating your world*,[1988] you must watch what you think. Keep your thoughts positive, wholesome, childlike, uplifting, and life-affirming!

It is easy enough to prove that our body always gravitates toward health and that well-being is our natural state: when we accidently cut a finger our body immediately sets about to heal it. The only thing that can slow or interrupt this healing process is negative thinking, along with an unhealthy lifestyle.

Therefore, if we align our thoughts and lifestyle choices with the Father, we can be assured of a long and healthy life. For the cellular intelligence at work in our bodies is the same intelligence that created all life, and even the Universe itself: "God is all mind,"[1989] and this, the Divine Mind, being perfect, knows nothing but perfect health!

## GOD'S HEALING POWER IS ETERNAL & UNIVERSAL

The so-called "miracles" of biblical times did not come to an end after Jesus' death on the cross, as so many people believe today. Amazing healings are still occurring everyday—as Pope John Paul II and thousands of other Christians, both well-known and unknown, have shown.

And supernatural cures do not happen only among modern Christians. Because God, Divine Mind, is "no respecter of persons,"[1990] miraculous healings were taking place in pre-Christian times, and they continue to take place all over the world, among people of every religious persuasion (as men like the great Indian saint Mahavatar Babaji have demonstrated),[1991] and even among the non-religious.

How can even the godless experience the miraculous? It is because, regardless of our beliefs, we are all products of Divine Mind, "the offspring of God," as Paul put it,[1992] each born with a piece of the Father inside of us:[1993] the Indwelling Christ, our Higher Self.[1994] And it is this divine aspect of us that contains all the healing power of God, and which can be activated by even an infinitesimally small amount of faith; belief so diminutive that it could easily fit inside of a tiny mustard seed the size of this period.[1995]

## FINAL WORDS ON HEALING

Everything starts and stops in the Divine Mind, Almighty God; "the Alpha and Omega, the beginning and the end, the first and the last."[1996] To those who believe and understand this principle, God said He will "give unto him that is athirst of the fountain of the water of life freely."[1997] Jesus also commented on this magical inner "fluid":

> "Whosoever drinketh . . . [earthly] water shall thirst again: but whosoever drinketh of the [spiritual] water that I shall give him shall never thirst; but the water that I shall give him shall be in him a well of water springing up into everlasting life."[1998]

Jesus' "water" and God's "fountain of the water of life" both refer to the same thing: the fresh, oxygen-rich stream that feeds the "pond" that is our mind and body. It is the literal life-giving, all-healing water of the Father, Divine Mind, whom Luke called the "Prince of Life,"[1999] and whose holy liquid (love) *always* succeeds when everything else fails. It is, in other words, Truth! Isaiah said:

> "And the Lord shall guide thee continually, and satisfy thy soul in drought, and make fat thy bones: and thou shalt be like a watered garden, and like a spring of water, whose waters fail not."[2000]

One aspect of God, the "Lord," is the divine power of your mind, which, when merged with the Law of Attraction, can be used to heal yourself, your loved ones, or even strangers. All that is needed is the patient's full unqualified faith, a word that is used in the Bible to mean complete "conviction," complete "belief," complete "confidence," complete "trust" in the unseen.

This idea is perfectly embodied in the official motto of the United States of America: "In God we trust." Contrary to what militant atheists think, this is not a religious slogan. It is scientific slogan, for "God" and "Nature" are identical, just as everyone from Jesus and Buddha to Albert Einstein and Luther Burbank have shown us.

The Father of all Nature Himself said that the righteous will live their lives solely by faith in the unseen.[2001] And if you are reading this book you are among the righteous, for it means you are a truth seeker,[2002] walking as a Child of Light,[2003] moving forward on the Way of Holiness[2004] to certain oneness in the Indwelling Christ.[2005] This level of faith is identical to the "faith of the Son of God"![2006]

For those who are ill, this all-trusting faith means total belief in the reality that a healing has *already* taken place within the body. Keep this belief firmly planted in your mind and do not let it go, *no matter how things appear on the physical.* For by focusing on only that which you want (healing), and believing that it has already occurred, the Law of Attraction must bring it to you. Remember: God is the creator of not only the Law of Attraction, but also of what Christian mystics call the "Universal Medicine," that is, the one and only true secret healer, and it is in this power that we must believe if we wish to become whole.

Paul said that intense, pure, unadulterated faith—100 percent belief in the reality of what is as yet unseen—is our shield against the illusion of evil, which, due to negative thinking, can manifest as ill health and disease.[2007] God certainly does not form His opinion according to the physical,[2008] and neither does Jesus, as His own words prove:

"Judge not according to the appearance [of things] . . ."[2009]

This is why serious practitioners of the Law of Attraction follow Paul's advice, and "calleth those things which be not as though they were."[2010]

Believe then in what you want rather than in what is. This is the definition of pure faith; the kind of spiritual conviction that can cure any illness no matter what your medical diagnostic report says. For, while science works in the visible (the physical bodily organs) to alter the invisible (on the cellular level), God operates in the opposite fashion—and on a much grander scale—by working in the invisible (spiritual realm) to alter the visible (material realm).

This is what is meant by "mind over matter." This is why Jesus preached an immanent God,[2011] it is why He preached an immanent Holy Spirit,[2012] and it is why Paul preached an immanent Christ,[2013] or what he revealingly referred to as "the *mind* of Christ."[2014] You see, it is all spiritual, or what scientists call "psychological," for psyche is the Greek word for the "soul" and the soul is identical to the mind.

But not just any mind. The soul is one with the true and everlasting mind: God's mind, Divine Mind!

Now a part of the Divine Mind has been placed inside you, and you can use it in any manner you wish. You are Aladdin, your thoughts are the magic lamp, and the Universal Mind is your personal genie. Believe and you will be defended from any kind of negativity; disbelieve and you open yourself up to every sort of problem and danger. The book of Proverbs gives us this promise:

"There shall no evil happen to the just [believers]: but the wicked [nonbelievers] shall be filled with mischief [troubles]."[2015]

Understand this simple principle and no illness can stand up against you.[2016] Follow it and sickness will pass you by.[2017] Practice this and you will, like Paul, "walk by faith, not by sight,"[2018] completely healed and protected from disease everyday for the rest of your life.[2019] For it is the Great I AM, your Indwelling God Presence,[2020] not science, that is the true healer.[2021] Medicine facilitates. God cures.

An angel of the Lord coming to lead an earthly soul to Heaven. Though today it has fallen out of fashion, the early Church taught that there are many levels in the Afterlife. "In my Father's house are many mansions," saith the Lord, while Paul once described his visit to the "third" of seven different heavens. Which one will you go to after you discard your material body: the highest, the lowest, or somewhere in between? According to Jesus, the level of Heaven we go to in the Hereafter will match the level of spiritual maturity we attain while on earth, and according to those who have had near-death experiences (NDEs), the spiritual maturity we achieve on earth all depends on our thoughts, words, and deeds while we are here. In order to "obtain a better resurrection" then, it is in our best interest to practice the Law of Attraction wisely by always focusing on positive, wholesome, prosperous thoughts, images, and ideas. This guarantees us a wonderful life of abundance, health, and happiness, both here and in the World Beyond. Let us heed the words of the Master from Galilee: "With what measure ye mete, it shall be measured to you: and unto you that hear shall more be given."

# 24

# JESUS, THE LAW, & THE AFTERLIFE

"The heart of the wise teaches his mouth, and
addeth learning to his lips."[2022]

## THE KINGDOM OF HEAVEN IS HERE & NOW

**JESUS DID NOT SPEND MUCH** time discussing the Afterlife; that is, what happens to us after we break the "golden bowl," sever the "silver cord,"[2023] discard our physical bodies, and ascend to the world of Spirit. He mentioned that there would be no marriage in Heaven and that when our souls arrive in the Celestial City we will live "as the angels of God."[2024]

But other than occasionally and briefly touching on such topics, His emphasis was almost always on this world, the physical plane. As the "high priest" of the good things that already exist on earth,[2025] He repeatedly told His followers: "The Kingdom of Heaven is at hand,"[2026] meaning our potential bliss is not set in the future, it is in the present moment.[2027]

When they pressed Him to teach them more about the Great Beyond, Jesus replied impatiently: "God is not the God of the dead, but of the living."[2028] And to those who showed more concern about the Afterlife than the present one he said: "Let the dead bury their dead: but go thou and preach the kingdom of God."[2029] It is clear from such statements that Jesus was mainly concerned about the earthly Kingdom, not the heavenly one. The question is why?

We have seen that the "great and boundless realm,"[2030] the Kingdom of God (or Kingdom of Heaven as it also called), is a state of consciousness that has been made available to us in the here and now;[2031] that it can only be entered by those who "crucify" their adult Egos and become as "a little child";[2032] that we must enter the gate of the Kingdom alone, as an individual (groups are banned).[2033] We have learned that once inside, all the riches from God's unlimited storehouse are made available to us,[2034] enabling us to create any kind of life we choose here on earth. For

> "there is a spirit in man: and the inspiration of the Almighty giveth them [the years we spend on the physical plane] understanding."[2035]

Yes, Jesus' teachings on the Law of Attraction, just one aspect of what He called "the Gospel of the Kingdom,"[2036] are nearly all focused on this life. But why did He seem to virtually ignore what happens to us in the next life? Just as importantly: does the Law of Attraction stop working at physical death? Does it operate from the moment we are born to the moment we die, and then simply cease?

At first glance it would seem that there is no concrete answer, for Jesus never addressed the question directly. However, He *did* address it, as He did so many subjects, mystically and indirectly, as we are about to see.

THE EVERLASTING LAW OF ATTRACTION
First, logic tells us that since the Law of Attraction is an immutable scientific-spiritual principle, that it must be eternal. And if eternal, we must have been under its operation before we were born and we will be under its operation after we die. Therefore the tentative answer to the question is yes, the Law continues to be active at all times and all places.

If true, this means that just as your thoughts, beliefs, words, and actions create your experiences in this life, they will also create your experiences after you leave here for the next one! Jesus hints at this very fact in the Lord's Prayer:

> "Our Father [Divine Mind] which art in heaven, hallowed be thy name. Thy kingdom come. Thy will be done *in earth, as it is in heaven*."[2037]

To put it another way, since what we believe becomes true for us here, it will also become true for us after death. I maintain that this is why Jesus placed so much emphasis on attaining the Kingdom of God on earth, for *the level of spiritual consciousness we achieve here will govern where we go and what happens to us after we leave here.* As Paul said to the Corinthians:

"Every man shall receive his own reward according to his own labour."[2038]

Thus, Jesus wants us to grow spiritually as much as possible during our earthly lives, so that we can go to the highest level possible when we discard the physical vehicle and ascend to our true home, the realm of Spirit.

YOUR EARTHLY LIFE DETERMINES YOUR HEAVENLY LIFE
We have all heard the doctrine of God's divine reward and punishment system following death; namely, that after our judgment before God, the righteous go to Heaven and the evil go to Hell. But these are just the outer exoteric words. What is their inner esoteric meaning?

"God" is Divine Mind, a scientific-supernatural mental power given to us when we were made in the image of God.[2039] "Righteousness" is right (positive) thinking, or what John called "the spirit of truth,"[2040] while "evil" is wrong (negative) thinking, or what he called "the spirit of error."[2041] The "judgment" is our own assessment of our earthly lives based on what our predominant thoughts were.

In short, when we pass away, what happens to us will be determined by our thoughts, beliefs, and actions while we were here. We will go, in other words, to that level of Heaven or Hell that we have earned during our time on earth. What do I mean by "level"?

SEVEN HEAVENS, SEVEN HELLS
Original Christianity taught that Heaven has seven levels and that Hell has seven levels. Paul alluded to this fact when he described a near-death experience he once had:

> "I knew a man in Christ above fourteen years ago, (whether in the body, I cannot tell; or whether out of the body, I cannot tell: God knoweth;) such an one caught up to the third heaven."[2042]

Mystically the seven degrees of Heaven[2043] and Hell[2044] accord with the seven planets of the ancient world,[2045] the seven holes in the head (two eyes, two nostrils, two ears, and mouth), the four seven-day phases of the Moon each month,[2046] the Seven Wonders of the World,[2047] the seven days of the week (each named after a Pagan god or goddess),[2048] the "seven churches" in the book of Revelation,[2049] the seven bodies of Man,[2050] the seven chakras,[2051] the seven days of Creation,[2052] and so on.[2053]

Most significantly, according to Christian numerology, seven is the mystical number of physical manifestation through thought: the Law of Attraction!

What level of Heaven or Hell will you go to after you depart from your physical body? This was one of Jesus' main concerns during His final three years on earth and, as such, it should be yours too. Let us see what the Lord had to say on this subject.

THE ROAD TO HEAVEN IS GUIDED BY THE INDWELLING CHRIST

Speaking as the Indwelling Christ, the "Christ in you,"[2054] Jesus makes the following statement in the Gospel of Matthew:

> "And every one that hath forsaken houses, or brethren, or sisters, or father, or mother, or wife, or children, or lands, for my name's sake, shall receive an hundredfold, and *shall inherit everlasting life*."[2055]

In the Gospel of Mark, Jesus elaborates on this theme:

> "Verily I say unto you, there is no man that hath left house, or brethren, or sisters, or father, or mother, or wife, or children, or lands, for my sake, and the gospel's, but he shall receive an hundredfold now in this time, houses, and brethren, and sisters, and mothers, and children, and lands, with persecutions; *and in the world to come eternal life*."[2056]

This statement is from the Gospel of Luke:

> "Verily I say unto you, there is no man that hath left house, or parents, or brethren, or wife, or children, for the kingdom of God's sake, who shall not receive manifold more in this present time, and *in the world to come life everlasting*." Then he took unto him the twelve, and said unto them, "Behold, we go up to Jerusalem, and all things that are written by the prophets concerning the Son of man shall be accomplished."[2057]

What is Jesus saying? Here is the inner meaning:

> "Anyone who takes my true Gospel of the Kingdom[2058] teachings on the Law of Attraction seriously enough to forsake his personal life, will be able to physically manifest anything he wants, not only in this world but also in the next."[2059]

Could the truth behind Jesus' statements be any clearer?

THE MIND & THE NEAR-DEATH EXPERIENCE

For both Christians and non-Christians, we have indisputable eschatological evidence that what we believe here on earth affects where we go after we "die."

To begin with, thousands of people who have had near-death experiences (NDEs) report astonishing experiences in the Spirit World, proving that the mind is the primary power in Heaven, just as it is on earth.

As they hover between life and "death" at the gates of Heaven, many meet with deceased but excited relatives and friends, while others come upon kindly strangers. Others are temporarily given the knowledge of the inner workings of the entire Universe, such as Paul, who wrote of his NDE in the "third heaven":[2060]

> "And I knew such a man, (whether in the body, or out of the body, I cannot tell: God knoweth;) how that he was caught up into paradise, and heard unspeakable words, which it is not lawful for a man to utter."[2061]

Most interestingly, some come face to face with angelic beings of light, or even Jesus-like figures: men (and sometimes women) with long hair, white robes, and compassionate expressions, ablaze in radiant pastel colors.

The messages NDEers bring back from these astonishing encounters are important to our discussion, so let us look at a few of these now.

Often the decision to "live" (stay here on earth) or "die" (pass into the Spirit World) is left solely up to the individual, and this decision is always made mentally, through mere thinking. For while they are in the realm of Spirit, NDEers are able to move about instantaneously by thought alone, create anything they like by mere desire, and communicate with other spirits mentally—that is telepathically, directly from mind to mind.

Beliefs, and the feelings, emotions, and desires that spring from them, govern all in Heaven, where everything travels at the speed of thought; that is, instantaneously. Revealingly, because thought is spiritual energy, in some cases NDEers experience themselves as "pure thought," without a body of any kind. The light beings NDEers encounter make it clear that the most important thing during our life on earth is to grow in knowledge and learn to love, which exactly matches Jesus' teachings.[2062]

It seems then that what we think of as Heaven is actually a mental realm, a psychological domain, where "God is all mind,"[2063] where mind is all God, and where everything is both all God and all mind.[2064] Consider the words of Jesus, which He uttered as His "death" on the cross approached:

> "I came forth from the Father [Divine Mind], and am come into the [physical] world: again, I leave the [physical] world, and go to the Father [Divine Mind]."[2065]

Then there is the statement He made to Mary when she tried to reach out to Him after His resurrection:

> "Touch me not; for I am not yet ascended to my Father [Divine Mind]: but go to my brethren, and say unto them, I ascend unto my Father, and your Father; and to my God, and your God."[2066]

Scientists who study NDEs also provide a wealth of information that relates to Jesus and the Law of Attraction, once again reinforcing the theory that *what we think here impacts our lives in the Afterworld*.

For example, though NDEs are a universal phenomena, numerous studies have shown that the NDE itself is *not* a one-size-fits-all experience. In fact, what people go through during their brief journey to Heaven relies almost entirely on their individual mindset, their feelings, and their expectations. Thus each NDE is different, *depending on the mind of the individual*.

After leaving their physical body, NDEers report that their mind becomes hyper alert, clear, and sensitive, far beyond the way it functions on earth. Hearing, taste, feel, smell, and sight intensify, and thinking speeds up, memory becomes perfect, and thoughts themselves become more distinct, acute, accurate, and vivid. Mind so dominates the Spirit World that some NDEers actually only encounter the minds of other people there, not the people themselves (who they feel only as a sort of "presence").

Many NDE researchers hold that while NDEs are indeed real, the experiences one has, the imagery one sees, the figures one meets, even the realm one goes to during an NDE, are all determined "entirely by the mind of the experiencer." And this is true for individuals of all ages, proving that the nature of the NDE is *not* related to physical brain development.

As NDEers pass into the Divine Light, everything around them seems to conform to what they always believed Heaven would be like. Thus, people who love Nature come upon splendiferous vistas of flowery fields, fragrant grassy meadows, endless fruit orchards, gurgling brooks, stupendous mountain ranges, multiple rainbows spilling across the brilliant but sunless blue sky, cascading waterfalls, golden valleys, giant tree groves, crystalline rivers, and evergreen forests spreading as far as the eye can see.

NDEers who prefer an urban life enter into a large and magnificent city with translucent jewel-studded walls, gates of exquisite pearl, and a river of pure liquid silver running through its center. This otherworldly metropolis contains countless breath-taking architectural wonders, such as all-glass buildings, porcelain statues, alabaster cathedrals, huge columned temples, wide flower-lined avenues, sumptuous parks with river bridges and stone walkways, sparkling fountains, colorfully bejewelled Victorian mansions filled with luxurious furnishings and surrounded by lush manicured lawns, and streets that are literally paved with gold. In a word, these particular NDEers have traveled to the self-luminescent Heavenly City of God, the "Holy Jerusalem," with its "River of Life," as described in the book of Revelation,[2067] lovingly prepared by the Father for all those who believe.[2068]

Most revealingly, NDEers who had always believed in a strict vengeful God, were most likely to have feelings of concern, panic, and dread. They were also more apt to encounter a mysterious panel of dark hooded figures, who tersely reviewed their earthly "Book of Life,"[2069] then passed a "final judgment" upon them. Some in this group were even forced to witness hellish scenarios, such as lakes of liquid fire filled with trapped screaming souls. These individuals, who described their trip to the Afterworld as "woeful," "miserable," and "regrettable," came back to earth with a lifelong fear of death.

On the other hand, those who had always held the belief that the Father is a gentle accepting God of unconditional love and forgiveness, were more apt to feel a sense of peace, joy, warmth, and unity during their journey to the World Beyond. And they were more likely to have a solitary life review in which they judged their own lives on earth using their own minds. They also had a better chance of having pleasant experiences and seeing beautiful scenarios, such as English gardens, grassy meadows, tree-lined parks, and white sandy beaches edging clear turquoise seas. These individuals, who longingly described their trip to the Afterworld as "going home," lost all fear of death and actually looked forward to "dying" one day.

THE LIFE REVIEW

The heavenly "life review" that so many NDEers experience is especially insightful. It is not a long dreary list of our sins, meant to instill guilt and shame, as mainstream religion teaches. Rather, according to those who have actually gone through it and returned to tell about it, one's life review is based on the most prominent positive and negative thoughts and feelings we had while on earth, as well as the deeds that resulted from them (good and bad). Often, NDEers report, during their life review they viscerally reexperience not only their own feelings, but *all* of the feelings they aroused in everyone else they had ever come in contact with![2070]

NDEers also tell us that our "Judgment Day" always ends with complete absolution, the main import being that we incarnate on earth in order to learn from both our successes and our failures—all in an effort to improve and develop ourselves and raise our spiritual awareness. For our purpose in coming here is to realize our divinity, develop and use our divine powers properly, and learn to love unconditionally.

From all of this data it is clear that we will "rise or sink" in the Afterlife according to, not what religion we belong to (for there is no religion in the Spirit World),[2071] but almost entirely according to the *thoughts* we have (and the resulting actions we engage in) during our earthly sojourn. In other words, as Paul said, "our end will accord with our deeds,"[2072] for,

> "we must all appear before the judgment seat of Christ; that every one may receive the things done in his body, according to that [which] he hath done, whether it be good or bad."[2073]

The inner meaning:

> "After physical death we will all have a Life Review in which the Indwelling Christ will determine what level of Heaven we are to go to based on the acts we performed while on earth. We will be assigned exactly according to the things we thought, said, and did, whether they were positive or negative."[2074]

Yes, we will "receive the due reward of our deeds,"[2075] a universal spiritual doctrine that Peter pared down to just a few words: "The Father judgeth according to every man's work."[2076] Knowing this, prepare yourself well for the day you return to Spirit by following Peter's simple instructions:

> "What manner of persons ought ye to be in all holy conversation and godliness, looking for and hasting unto the coming of the day

of God [that is, 'death'] . . . We, according to his promise, look for
new heavens and a new earth, wherein dwelleth righteousness.
Wherefore, beloved, seeing that ye look for such things, be diligent
that ye may be found of him in peace, without spot, and
blameless."[2077]

## AFTER DEATH YOU ENCOUNTER WHAT YOU BELIEVE IN

What can we learn from these scriptures and from the experiences of
NDEers?

If you believe in a God of fire and brimstone, who sends all sinners
to Hell for eternity, then this seems to be what you will experience after
death. If you believe in a God of love and forgiveness, who saves all His
children in Heaven for all eternity, then this seems to be what you will
experience after death. In short, what you think, believe, feel, and do here
determines what happens to you in the Next World. Hence, in his book
*Secrets of the Light*, my friend, three-time NDEer Dannion Brinkley, writes:

> "A belief in kindness that creates an ongoing stream of good deeds
> on behalf of others is an energy capable of reverberating far into
> Heaven. What you do in this life, based on a belief in the love and
> perfection of eternal life, decides the quality of life awaiting you in
> the Hereafter. Belief in compassion, love, and thoughtfulness
> perpetuates more of the same."[2078]

## DEFINING EVERLASTING LIFE

Let us look more closely now at what Jesus meant when he said that those
who follow His genuine Gospel, the "Gospel of the Kingdom,"[2079] will have
"everlasting life" in the "world to come."[2080]

The phrase "everlasting life" insinuates its opposite: everlasting
death. Of course, we know that there is no such thing as literal "death," for
according to both religion[2081] and science (in this case, the laws of
thermodynamics), energy cannot be created or destroyed, and everything,
including the human soul, is made up of energy. As immortal indestructible
beings, how it is possible that we could "die" then?

Everlasting life means an eternal existence in Heaven. Everlasting
death means an eternal existence in Hell. The choice is ours, for everything
is based on our thoughts! If we think positive thoughts, say positive things,
feel positive emotions, and perform positive deeds, NDE studies tell us that
we will indeed spend eternity in the Celestial City, the home of God and His
angels. However, if we think negative thoughts, say negative things, feel

negative emotions, and perform negative deeds, NDE studies tell us that we will more likely spend eternity in the Subterranean City, the home of Satan and his angels.

Yet, because the Father "will have all men to be saved, and to come unto the knowledge of the truth,"[2082] there is the possibility of release, even from this infernal region. But only if and when we change our thoughts and beliefs to accord with God and the Law of Love. "For whosoever shall call upon the name of the Lord shall be saved."[2083] Through the mercy of His unconditional love for us, the Almighty always gives us a chance—even after physical death—to improve our condition, to "obtain a better resurrection," as the Hebraist phrased it.[2084]

WE ALL RETURN TO THE DIVINE MIND
Are Heaven and Hell real places? Both Jesus and the reports of NDEers tell us that we experience what we expect to experience, that what we believe becomes real for us. Therefore, believe and expect only good, feel only good, and do only good, and your outcome after you pass and have been "carried by the angels into Abraham's bosom" will be heavenly.[2085]

According to the enlightened self-realized teachers of nearly every religion, our souls arrive in the Hereafter at the level that corresponds to the degree of spirituality we attain on earth, and the degree of spirituality we attain on earth depends on the thoughts we think.[2086] If you want to join the Lord in Paradise then,[2087] you must think paradisiacal thoughts. As below, so above!

As mentioned, just before His crucifixion Jesus told His followers that at the moment of His "death" He would "go unto the Father, for my Father is greater than I."[2088] John said it like this: ". . . his hour was come that he should depart out of this world unto the Father."[2089]

We have learned that the "Father" is Jesus' esoteric term for the Divine Mind. Thus, those who follow the path, the teachings, the Way of the Master,[2090] the Indwelling Christ,[2091] will, like Jesus, return to the Father when we "die." Here we will live in eternal harmony and unending bliss in a magical kingdom "which God hath prepared for them that love him";[2092] a place of unimaginable splendor where "all spiritual blessings" await us.[2093] To get there we need only use our mental faculties here on earth wisely. Fortunately for us, the Indwelling Christ provides us with this very wisdom![2094]

TAKE CARE WHAT YOU WRITE IN YOUR BOOK OF LIFE!
Remember: every second of each day you are literally writing your Book of
Life with your thoughts, and this is the same book that you will be judged
by in the World Beyond,[2095] the place where your "incorruptible and
undefiled inheritance" has been "reserved for you."[2096]

The moral? Take great care to guard the entrance of your mind.
Analyze every thought before sending it to your Subconscious. Allow in
only the most positive, loving, and healthful thoughts; send out
unconditional love and goodwill to all people; respect all life, from the
smallest creatures to the largest animals. Remember our Lord's Golden
Rule admonition:

> "And as ye would that men should do to you, do ye also to them
> likewise."[2097]

Follow these simple instructions and, as Zechariah noted, you will
be as happy as a man sipping wine.[2098] Comply with these easy directions
and you will end up in your own personal Garden of Eden. For according
to the changeless, boundless, ageless, timeless Law of Attraction, just as on
earth, in the Afterworld you create your own Heaven or Hell. This is what
Jesus was referring to when, speaking as the Indwelling Christ (Divine Law)
that lives within each one of us,[2099] He said:

> "And whosoever liveth and believeth in me shall never die.
> Believest thou this?"[2100]

What is your answer?

Jesus washing the feet of the Apostles after the Last Supper. According to mainstream Christian doctrine, Jesus is teaching them the lesson of humility. But this is just the outer exoteric meaning. Mystical Christianity reveals to us a much deeper and more important one. Feet are the lowest parts of our bodies. Because they merge with dirt, they symbolize the Lower Self. Water symbolizes truth. As always, Jesus here symbolizes the Universal Indwelling Christ. Thus, in mystical terms this scene actually depicts the cleansing of the Lower Self with the Living Waters (truth) of the God Within. When the Lower Self is "washed," the purification of our entire being is finally complete, for our Higher Self is already perfect. We are then made whole, freed from our past, freed from sin, freed from the fetters of the material world. This is why Jesus made this arcane statement to Peter: "He that is washed needeth not save to wash his feet, but is clean every whit." Saint Augustine referred to this occult practice as "ordering aright the path of our spiritual footsteps." What does the symbolic "washing of our feet" mean for humanity on a personal level? After He had finished the foot cleansing ritual, Jesus told the Apostles: "I have given you an example, that ye should do as I have done to you." The inner meaning here is that we are to strive to be Christlike. This purifies the Lower Self, bringing it into alignment with the Higher Self. This mystical "marriage of Cana," the merging of the masculine Lower Self with the feminine Higher Self, or what the ancients called the *Hieros Gamos* (the "Sacred Union"—mystically, of the sun-god Sol and the moon-goddess Luna), is the true wedding of the "bride" (human Ego) and the "bridegroom" (Indwelling Christ) that John the Baptist spoke of, and it is what Jesus meant by the statement: "The Father is in me, and I in him." Why is this doctrine so important to Jesus? "Washing our feet" at the doorway to the Kingdom of Heaven allows us entrance in. Here, in this sacred Holy of Holies, a psychological state known as Christ Consciousness, or what Paul called "the mind of Christ," we may use the Law of Attraction positively and productively to alter our lives and improve our conditions, health, and finances. Those who have ears to hear, let them hear!

# 25

# THINK ON THESE THINGS

A Summary of the Teachings of
Jesus & the Law of Attraction

"Whatsoever things are true, whatsoever
things are honest, whatsoever things are just,
whatsoever things are pure, whatsoever things
are lovely, whatsoever things are of good
report; if there be any virtue, and if there be
any praise, think on these things."[2101]

## FOLLOWING THE WAY OF JESUS

**E**VERYDAY YOU ARE FACED WITH a decision: to follow the path of God or follow the path of Satan. Following the path of God (Divine Mind) means thinking positive thoughts, saying positive things, and performing positive deeds. Following the path of Satan (Human Mind, or Ego), means thinking negative thoughts, saying negative things, and performing negative deeds.

If you choose God's path, the Law of Attraction will attract to you health, wealth, and happiness. If you choose Satan's path, the Law of Attraction will attract to you ill health, poverty, and unhappiness.[2102]

The wise man and woman, those at one with the incorruptible Indwelling Christ,[2103] always select the road less travelled, the one Jesus walked on: "the Way of God,"[2104] "the Way of the Light,"[2105] "the Way of Holiness";[2106] for this path naturally brings with it lifelong riches in body, mind, and spirit.[2107] This is a biblical reality that is promised by God, Jesus, and the Holy Ghost.[2108] And because it is both a spiritual and a physical principle, the Law of Attraction is also backed up by science, for throughout the entire Universe, from the infinitesimal quark to the impossibly massive galaxy supercluster, like always attracts like.

Jesus—who, in my opinion, is the most advanced soul to have ever incarnated on earth—left us with a set of simple instructions on how to live our lives to the fullest. These He embodied in what He referred to as "the Gospel of the Kingdom [of God]."[2109] What follows is the essence of these teachings. It represents the Lord's *true* Gospel, the authentic arcana of the Christ; ancient wisdom distilled from the previous chapters, comprising a complete philosophical system that I have termed:

## JESUS' GOOD NEWS FOR ALL HUMANITY

✠ You and God are one.

✠ You and Jesus are one.

✠ You and the Christ are one.

✠ You and the Holy Spirit are one.

✠ You and the Comforter (Paraclete) are one.

✠ You possess a portion of the Divine Mind and all of its infinite abilities.

✠ This is because you are an individualization, an expression, of God.

✠ Thus you too have the same divine powers possessed by Jesus.

✠ As Jesus, Paul, and John taught, the immortal Indwelling Christ is universal and exists in every individual as his or her real self, the Higher Self.

✠ All of this makes you a god or goddess in your own right.

✠ Because "God is all mind," the root of existence is mental, psychological; that is, spiritual. (Psychology means the "study of the Soul.")

✠ The Divine Mind is the combined amalgamation of the Superconscious, Conscious, and Subconscious Minds.

✠ In the Bible the Superconscious Mind is represented by "Father," the Conscious Mind is represented by the "Son," and the Subconscious Mind is represented by the "Holy Spirit."

✠ All three of these minds exist within you. They are your personal Inner Trinity, always ready to serve you—their only spiritual purpose.

✠ We communicate with God—Sovereign Mind, Divine Mind—through thought.

✠ The Divine Mind works via a well-known and demonstrable scientific principle: like attracts like. This is called the Law of Attraction.

✠ Out of His love for us, God gave the Law of Attraction to humanity as His personal gift, so that we would have unfettered freedom to write our own life stories, create our own daily experiences, and form our own circumstances.

✠ Knowledge of the Law of Attraction dates back to the very beginning of historical times, with some of the earliest known practitioners being the ancient Babylonians. We can be sure then that it was known to and used by prehistoric men and women as well.

✠ The Law of Attraction, recognized by everyone from Zoroaster, Lao Tzu, Moses, Buddha, Pythagoras, and Jesus, to Saint Augustine, Joan of Arc, Isaac Newton, Thomas Edison, Edgar Cayce, and Winston Churchill, is a self-evident, provable, and eternal scientific-spiritual principle.

✠ The Law of Attraction is immutable and cannot be violated.

✠ We live in a reciprocal psychological Universe: whatever you send out mentally, you receive back physically; or in Paul's mystical words: "Whatsoever a man soweth, that shall he also reap."

✠ Thus, you are responsible for everything that has come into your life, all the positive and all the negative. The sooner you accept this fact, the sooner you can begin to initiate positive changes.

✠ While this concept may seem like "bad news," it is actually part of the "Good News" that Jesus came to earth to teach us, for the Law of Attraction liberates us from the cumbersome restraints of the physical plane.

✠ Taking responsibility for our entire lives may seem unfair at first, but it is actually the epitome of perfect justice, which is exactly why God provided us with this amazing endowment: the Law of Attraction guarantees you absolute liberty to make of your life whatever it is you desire.

✠ The Law of Attraction can be ignored, but the ensuing results from its unceasing operation cannot be avoided.

✠ The Law of Attraction cannot be switched "off." It is always "on," working every second of every day to physically manifest your most dominant thoughts. Thus you are always automatically using it, either consciously (which creates order in your life), or unconsciously (which creates chaos in your life).

✠ To put it another way, the Law is a two-edged sword that is *always* being used by you either productively or destructively, depending on your thoughts, beliefs, feelings, and actions.

✠ Since "God is no respecter of persons," anyone can use the Law to better their lives, whether saint or sinner. This answers the age-old question: why do the righteous sometimes suffer while the evil sometimes prosper?

✠ What we think in the invisible is externalized in the visible. As above, so below.

✠ When we think positive thoughts, we attract their like to us while repelling their opposite: negativity. When we think negative thoughts, we attract their like to us while repelling their opposite: positivity. The moral? If you want to live the good life, think only good thoughts!

✠ Like the great spiritual teachers before and after Him, Jesus found it necessary to divide His followers into three different spiritual levels, degrees, or classes: the first, the lowest, was made up of the general public (the "Somatics," or spiritual beginners); the second was geared toward His Disciples (the "Psychics," or spiritual intermediates); and the third, the highest, was comprised of the Twelve Apostles (the "Perfect," or spiritually advanced). To this day the Church is still divided into these three basic levels of spiritual maturity, though most are unaware of it.

✠ As discussed by both Jesus and Paul, the Bible was written in three "spiritual" languages to match the three spiritual educational levels of its readers: the Exoteric (for the spiritually immature), the Mesoteric (for the spiritually moderate), and the Esoteric (for the spiritually enlightened).

✠ Jesus taught in parables to protect His most sacred doctrines from abuse by the unenlightened, or spiritually immature.

✠ Pertaining to the Law of Attraction specifically, however, Jesus gave us numerous formulas of varying complexity so that anyone, whatever their level of spiritual evolvement, could learn to use it.

✠ The Law of Attraction works around three basic principles: conception (of one's desires), absolute faith (in the power of the Law), and allowance (of the physical manifestation of our desires).

✠ The most efficient way to work with the Law is using affirmations, but one can also use visualization, prayer, and meditation.

✠ To get the most out of the Law of Attraction we must be "born again" and become as "little children," which allows us entrance into the Kingdom of God within. Here, in this pristine state of consciousness, the laws of the physical world have less control over us and our spiritual (divine) abilities are at their maximum power.

✠ God, Divine Mind, has no limitations. Therefore you can manifest anything you can imagine through correct use of the Law.

✠ Because God is Mind, what the Bible writers call "sin" is essentially wrong-thinking, and what they refer to as "righteousness" is simply right-thinking.

✠ Love is the first and foremost principle of the Law of Attraction.

✠ Unconditional self-love is vital if you wish to create a stable, healthy, prosperous life, for everything begins with the real you, your Higher Self, which the ancients called "the Christ."

✠ Just as Jesus and the Apostles taught, the Christ exists within each one of us, which is why it is known to Christian mystics as the Universal Indwelling Christ.

✠ The Christ, being eternal, existed before the founding of Christianity, and even before the creation of the Universe. Thus the early Church Fathers wrote that it is timeless, ageless, and unchangeable.

✠ Cultivating happiness (despite what may be currently going on around us) is essential to working positively with the Law, for happiness attracts all of the materials we need in the building of our personal Kingdom of Heaven (harmony) here on earth.

✠ We can create new relationships, heal broken ones, or maintain existing ones using the Law of Attraction.

✠ The Law of Attraction can improve your present job or manifest a new one.

✠ Abundance is the natural state of the Universe, and it is therefore the natural state of humanity.

✠ What we call "wealth" and "poverty" are both products of the mind. Thus, your current financial condition reveals your most predominant thoughts over the past few years. If you want to change your monetary situation, change your thoughts.

✠ Your current state of health is also a product of your thoughts, beliefs, and feelings. As such, you can use the Law of Attraction to prevent or heal any disease, even cancer.

✠ Disease is ignorance, therefore the cure is knowledge.

✠ The Law of Attraction, like the human soul, is eternal. Therefore, the circumstances you were born into are a product of the predominant thoughts you had before your "birth," while the circumstances you will experience after "death" (that is, where you will go in the

Afterlife) will be determined by your most persistent thoughts and beliefs during your earthly life.

✠ Nearly all of God's and Jesus' commandments are Law of Attraction principles (or are related to the Law in some way), given to us for our benefit, not theirs.

✠ Think godly thoughts, for these are God's thoughts.

✠ Desire for everyone else what you desire for yourself.

✠ Hunger, disease, crime, and poverty would all end tomorrow if everyone used the Law of Attraction consciously *and* properly.

✠ Change the entire future of the world by mentoring your children in the teachings found in this book.

✠ You were born to be wealthy!

✠ You were born to be healthy!

✠ You were born to be happy!

✠ Remember: your word is what makes your world. Thus, what you think you attract, what you believe you magnetize, what you say you invite, what you imagine you beckon, what you picture you gather, what you expect you summon, what you focus on you augment, what you project you induce, what you plant you harvest, what you sow you grow, what you envision you call forth, what you perceive you invoke, what you conceptualize you mobilize, what you feel you solicit. Therefore, always pay close attention to what is going in and out of your Conscious Mind!

## GOD IS FOR YOU

Following Jesus' teachings on the Law of Attraction is vital if you want to achieve perfect health, wealth, and happiness. But it is not mandatory. For under the Law of Attraction, God has given us total freedom[2110] (through the Indwelling Christ)[2111] to create our own lives, circumstances, environment, situations, events, experiences, and conditions, for better or for worse.[2112]

Either way we are always following the Law, though the outcome is completely different depending on which path we choose: if we control our thoughts, keep them on the positive, we are intentionally using the Law constructively. If we allow our thoughts to run wild, to accord with mass mind, we are unintentionally using the Law destructively.[2113] It is always our decision.[2114] Obviously, we always want to "bring into captivity every thought to the obedience of [the Indwelling] Christ."[2115]

Here is what Jesus, speaking as the World-Christ, the Universal Indwelling Christ,[2116] the "Christ in you,"[2117] the Universal Divine Mind, tells us:

> "Whosoever heareth these sayings of mine, and doeth them, I will liken him unto a wise man, which built his house upon a rock: and the rain descended, and the floods came, and the winds blew, and beat upon that house; and it fell not: for it was founded upon a rock.
>
> "And every one that heareth these sayings of mine, and doeth them not, shall be likened unto a foolish man, which built his house upon the sand: and the rain descended, and the floods came, and the winds blew, and beat upon that house; and it fell: and great was the fall of it."[2118]

Whether you are a believer, a skeptic, or a nonbeliever, you are wise indeed if you build your "house" (life) on "the rock" (foundation) of Jesus by following his commandments (teachings).[2119] He, the Indwelling Christ (Divine Law), is the "living stone" of God (Divine Mind) that was rejected by the Pharisees (human Ego) of the institutional Church (human law). But anyone can become a "member" of Jesus' personal "church within"[2120] by transforming himself into a "living stone," thereby becoming a building block in the Father's spiritual temple.[2121]

Jesus' "Inner Church"—the true church, "made by God, not man"[2122]—has nothing to do specifically with Christianity (for Jesus was a Jew[2123] not a Christian),[2124] nor even religion (Jesus clearly stated that He did not intend to start a religion in His own name).[2125] But it does have everything to do with your well-being ("salvation") both in this lifetime and in the Hereafter, which has always been Jesus' main concern.[2126]

Keep your mind focused on God, on all that is good, noble, and beautiful, on anything that is godly and uplifts your spirit.[2127] This raises your consciousness up from your Lower Self (Paul's "outward man") to your Higher Self (Paul's "inward man"),[2128] allowing you entrance into the sacred Kingdom of Heaven within.[2129] Here you will find permanent perfect tranquility, as well as health, prosperity, security, and happiness, just as the book of Isaiah promises:

> "Thou wilt keep him in perfect peace, whose mind is stayed on thee: because he trusteth in thee."[2130]

After attaining this exalted goal, it will truly be said of you:

> "Ye are come unto mount Sion, and unto the city of the living God, the heavenly Jerusalem, and to an innumerable company of angels."[2131]

Because "we are his workmanship,"[2132] God is not only in us,[2133] He is also for us.[2134] And with His protection no harm of any kind can befall us.[2135] By thinking only positive, harmonious, loving thoughts, we live out of our God-Selves, where we are eternally safe, guided, and watched over by the Creator.[2136] For "if God be for us, who can be against us?"[2137]

Realize your oneness with God,[2138] your innate divinity,[2139] along with the God-powers that the Father has bestowed on you.[2140] This allows you to put the Law of Attraction to work in the creation of wellness, abundance, and joy. Then you too, along with the Psalmist, will have "peace within thy walls, and prosperity within thy palaces."[2141]

The Great I AM,[2142] the Christ Within,[2143] is "the way, the truth, and the life," for no man or woman can enter the Kingdom of God except by following the commandments of Divine Law.[2144] Thus saith the Master:

> "Then shall the righteous shine forth as the sun in the kingdom of their Father. Who hath ears to hear, let him hear."[2145]

According to Jesus Himself, if we let go of fear and merely believe,[2146] we can all become "Suns" (Sons) in the Realm of Divine Mind.[2147] You may believe this with all your heart, for it is impossible for God to lie.[2148]

THE OPENING OF YOUR SPIRITUAL EYES
The teachings in this book have shown you "a more excellent way" of achieving blessedness, vitality, and affluence.[2149] They have removed the scales from your eyes,[2150] and lit your inner candle, enlightening your darkness.[2151] In reading them you have allowed the Word of God entrance into your heart, giving you divine understanding and "light."[2152] Truly, "this day is this scripture fulfilled in your ears."[2153] You have come to consciousness in "the name of the Lord," and for this you are greatly blessed.[2154]

You are now "full of joy"[2155] knowing that you can cocreate with the Father and with the Son to make any kind of life you want.[2156] "Christ hath made you free,"[2157] for you "have tasted the good word of God,"[2158] and "put on the armor of light."[2159] "The true light now shineth" in you,[2160] for "Christ has given thee light."[2161] Having "fled from the idolatry" of Pagan Christianity,[2162] you now understand why Paul called himself a "fool for

Christ,"[2163] for "you belong to Christ,"[2164] meaning you are saved:

> "Ye heard the word of truth, the gospel of your salvation: in whom also after that ye believed, ye were sealed with that holy Spirit of promise."[2165]

This is the Truth, Christ's Truth, spoken in love.[2166]

## REMOVING THE VEIL

You have "crucified" your Ego on the Holy Cross,[2167] an archetypal symbol of the Tree of Life,[2168] and so like Paul, you too "bear in your body the marks of the Lord Jesus"[2169]—that is, the Christ Within, the "Son in you."[2170] Since the Christ has revealed Himself inside you, you are now "like Him,"[2171] for "Christ is in all."[2172] You have "risen with Christ" and will "appear with him in glory,"[2173] and, like the Master, will one day "arise and go to your Father."[2174] The veil that once blinded your mind to the Truth has been removed by the Indwelling Christ,[2175] which has been "made manifest in our mortal flesh."[2176]

With the "eyes of your understanding being enlightened,"[2177] you have been turned from the Darkness to the Light, from the power of Satan (the Ego) to the power of God (the Divine).[2178] The "Morning Star has risen in your heart," and you are now "like a light that shineth in a dark place."[2179] The godly power and life force of the Christ, so perfectly personified in Jesus,[2180] has now become self-evident in your own material body.[2181]

Having heard and understood the "Word of Truth," the "gospel of your salvation," you have been authenticated and eternally stamped with the Holy Spirit,[2182] the promised Comforter.[2183] Be at peace.[2184] You are one of God's possessions, guaranteeing the divine inheritance that is rightfully yours.[2185] So "hold forth the Word of Life" and "rejoice in the Day of Christ"![2186]

## THE MYSTICAL UNION

You have been "made alive in Christ,"[2187] "baptized into the Christ,"[2188] and christed ("anointed")[2189] by the Father Himself.[2190] And as the symbolic spiritual "bride" of Christ, you have been joined in blessed "matrimony" with He who is the mystical "bridegroom."[2191]

This, the Hieros Gamos ("Sacred Union"), reconnects you to the Divine, so that you are once again capable of establishing a direct one-on-one relationship with God—the same type of relationship you originally had with Him as a child,[2192] but which you lost due to the spiritually corrosive influences of the mass mind and misguided religion.[2193]

## A PECULIAR PEOPLE

The preexistent Indwelling Christ,[2194] the "Shepherd of your soul,"[2195] has "called you out of darkness into his marvelous light."[2196] As a child of this Light,[2197] you are now an official member of the "chosen generation," the "royal priesthood," the "holy nation."[2198]

Having peered deep into the mysterious and secret "oracles of God,"[2199] and having learned from them of Jesus' true teachings on the Law of Attraction,[2200] you are now one of us: because we walk in the Light of the Divine Mind,[2201] the world calls us a "peculiar people,"[2202] a title we are proud to bear for the sake of "the Christ of God."[2203]

## A NEW AND LIVING WAY

As a metalworker hammers and burns the impurities out of unrefined gold and silver, so God's Word has forged and purified you.[2204] The Divine Logos has become a lamp for your feet and a light for your path.[2205]

Jesus' Law of Attraction doctrine is the "Holy Grail" that our souls seek. And you have discovered it: "a new and living way"![2206] And having "found the Christ,"[2207] you have become an "ambassador for Christ,"[2208] a minister in the Holy Spirit's "ministry of reconciliation."[2209] Now you need only keep your inner eyes fixed on He who has authored your faith![2210] You have planted your thought-seeds in the fertile field of the Subconscious Mind, and are now ready to harvest the rewards of your dedication, study, and hard work.[2211] Paul said:

> "It is high time to awake out of sleep [spiritual ignorance]: for now is our salvation nearer than when we believed. The night [of the Lower Self] is far spent, the day [of the Higher Self] is at hand: let us therefore cast off the works of darkness [wrong-thinking], and let us put on the armour of light [spiritual enlightenment].
>
> "Let us walk honestly, as in the day; not in rioting and drunkenness, not in chambering and wantonness, not in strife and envying. But put ye on the Lord Jesus Christ [that is, realize and focus on your oneness with the Universal Indwelling Christ]."[2212]

In other words, "stand fast in the Lord,"[2213] and pursue the Kingdom of God Within before anything else. You will then become the king of your own Inner Realm,[2214] and "all these things shall be added unto you."[2215]

PRACTICE THE LAW OF ATTRACTION WITH PURE FAITH

To reap the most benefit from this book, follow the Thirteenth Apostle's advice: continue to practice what you have learned, backed by an all-consuming faith.[2216] James the Just agreed, saying:

> "But be ye doers of the word, and not hearers only, deceiving your own selves. For if any be a hearer of the word, and not a doer, he is like unto a man beholding his natural face in a glass: for he beholdeth himself, and goeth his way, and straightway forgetteth what manner of man he was. But whoso looketh into the perfect law of liberty, and continueth therein, he being not a forgetful hearer, but a doer of the work, this man shall be blessed in his deed."[2217]

Pray, and follow these suggestions. Let God straighten out your "crooked places" (unspiritual ways), raise your "valleys" (sadness), and lower your "hills" (problems).[2218] Your sins (past mistakes) will be blotted out and "the times of refreshing [renewal] shall come from the presence of the Lord [Divine Mind]."[2219] This is one of the great mysteries of the Christ "which have been kept secret from the foundation of the world."[2220] But it has been revealed in you,[2221] and to you![2222]

Let us see now look more closely at the Gnosis ("Knowledge") and Sophia ("Wisdom") you have acquired.

YOU & GOD ARE ONE!

You have learned, along with Paul, that it is with your mind (thoughts) that you serve the Law of the Divine Mind.[2223] You have been made aware of the "deep things of God,"[2224] of the Eternal Truth that "dwelleth *with* you"[2225] and that "dwelleth *in* you."[2226] According to our Lord, that Eternal Truth is that you and God are one,[2227] making you a veritable "son of God," just like Jesus Himself.[2228]

As a believer, you not only take on the likeness of God,[2229] you literally "put on Christ,"[2230] the "Son in you";[2231] or more to the point, the "Christ is formed in you,"[2232] for you, though temporarily encased in the earthly, "bear the image of the heavenly."[2233] In the Aquarian Gospel, Jesus says:

> "Look not upon the flesh; it is not king. Look to the Christ within, who shall be formed in every one of you, as he is formed in me."[2234]

Welcome the Indwelling Christ. Accept the gift of His mystical offering, and let your oneness with Him satiate the hunger of your soul:

> "Behold, I stand at the door, and knock: if any man hear my voice, and open the door, I will come in to him, and will sup with him, and he with me."[2235]

## RECOVERING THE MEMORY OF OUR DIVINE NATURE

Though we were all given "spiritual amnesia" upon coming to earth (so that our testing in Earth School would be fair and thorough),[2236] deep inside we have always known about our divine origin. For the Father (Divine Mind) wrote about our godly nature (Divine Law) in our "hearts,"[2237] that is, in our "inward parts" (Subconscious Mind), long before we were born:[2238] we are His and He is ours, and we are all one.[2239]

Hindus call our recollection of this scientific fact, "right remembrance." And it truly is, for it has been, as Paul declares,

> "written not with ink, but with the Spirit of the living God; not in tables of stone, but in fleshy tables of the heart. And such trust have we through Christ to God-ward."[2240]

This truth is not some arcane religious concept that only a few privileged Church authorities have access to. It "is nigh thee, even in thy mouth, and in thy heart."[2241] This applies to you, me, and to everyone else.

Unfortunately, the veil that separates the spiritual from the material world[2242] closed in on most of us, and we began to "see through a glass darkly."[2243] For along the way, due to the negative concepts and beliefs of the mass mind, we had forgotten the dazzling reality of theosis.[2244] And here is the so-called "original sin" Jesus came to "save" us from! This was part of His great mission here on earth: to teach us *true* psychology (the study of the Soul) and "redeem" our minds; that is, help us recover the lost teaching concerning our divinity, our at-one-ment with the Father, Divine Mind.

## TRUE AT-ONE-MENT WITH THE FATHER

Our at-one-ment with the Universal Mind is God's promise, revealed to us, not intellectually,[2245] but spiritually—through self-knowledge (Gnosis),[2246] prayer,[2247] meditation,[2248] inspiration,[2249] imagination,[2250] visions,[2251] dreams,[2252] trances,[2253] intuition,[2254] revelations,[2255] and Christophanies,[2256] epiphanies, theophanies, and theaphanies.[2257]

Self-knowledge is how Jesus,[2258] Paul,[2259] and their ancient followers learned about the Divine,[2260] and we are to achieve our spiritual enlightenment in this same manner as well:[2261] directly from God, not Man![2262] This is why, as Paul warned, it is senseless to argue with others about religion and sacred scripture.[2263] Not only are we all at different stages of spiritual development, but true spiritual knowledge does not come from teachers, preachers, or books. It comes only from the King Within,[2264] that is, the crowned Indwelling Christ.[2265] Thus, according to our degree of spiritual maturity, the Christ Within only gives us what we are capable of absorbing, learning, and understanding—just as Jesus taught.[2266]

## YOUR KNOWLEDGE OF THE CHRIST WITHIN IS INNATE

Here, in the Father's own words, is proof that you are born with the foreknowledge of the Indwelling Christ, and that once you are reminded of this great truth—as you have throughout this book—you will never have to be taught it again:

> "For this is the covenant that I will make with the house of Israel [believers] after those days, saith the Lord; I will put my laws into their mind, and write them in their hearts: and I will be to them a God, and they shall be to me a people: and they shall not teach every man his neighbour, and every man his brother, saying, 'Know the Lord': for all shall know me, from the least to the greatest."[2267]

Everyone has a God-Self, their true self, the Universal Christ,[2268] that "dwells in the midst of thee";[2269] the eternal "high priest"[2270] of "a royal priesthood"[2271] who pastors the "church within,"[2272] the one and only authentic Church of the Lord, constructed by God, not man.[2273] But thanks to the false and misleading beliefs of our Philistinian society and our Pharisaic religions, most have forgotten about it and have split away from God (a tragic reality related in the etiological tale of Adam and Eve in the Garden of Eden).[2274] Even if they are dimly aware of the Christ Within, many have no idea how to access it.

## CONNECTING WITH YOUR GOD-SELF

To connect with your God-Self, your old limited consciousness must die[2275] and you must be "born again";[2276] that is, you must let go of your old beliefs (Paul's "old man"),[2277] and become mentally open, flexible, and innocent, like a child[2278] (Paul's "new man").[2279] Jesus put it this way: you must discard your "old wine" (former unspiritual beliefs) and your "old bottles" (former unspiritual belief systems), and pour "new wine" (fresh spiritual beliefs) into "new bottles" (fresh spiritual belief systems).[2280]

Mystically speaking (that is, psychologically), this realization—that you are the Indwelling Christ[2281]—is the "Second Coming" for you on a personal level,[2282] for it is through the Christ Within that we connect with the Divine Mind (the Father).[2283]

## KEEP LOOKING FORWARD

"Remember Lot's wife:"[2284] once you have experienced the resurrection within, the Inner Parousia,[2285] there is no looking back, no turning back.[2286] The Lord said:

> "No man, having put his hand to the plough, and looking back, is fit for the kingdom of God."[2287]

Instead, seize upon this day, this moment, for the Kingdom of Heaven is here and now.[2288] It is the "good land flowing with milk and honey,"[2289] the "better country," the "heavenly city" that the Father has personally prepared for you.[2290] To enter it, obey God, not men,[2291] and follow the Lord's true Gospel, what He referred to not as "the Gospel of Jesus" (as Mark did),[2292] but as "the Gospel of the Kingdom."[2293] Simply "abide in Him,"[2294] and the Indwelling Christ[2295] will surely "show" you the Good News of the Inner Sacred Realm.[2296]

## BE CHRISTLIKE

To achieve this high pure state of consciousness, which Paul referred to as the "mind of Christ,"[2297] you will need to "walk in love."[2298] That is, you must leave the "crooked path"[2299] and "go into the street which is called Straight,"[2300] and there follow the Way[2301] of the King of Kings: the Indwelling Christ.[2302]

You must "live godly in Christ":[2303] think Christlike thoughts,[2304] speak Christlike words,[2305] perform Christlike deeds;[2306] you need to walk in Christ;[2307] literally live the Christ-life,[2308] until "you are complete in Him" (that is, one with Him and He with you).[2309] "Strive to be like him," Ignatius wisely said.[2310] And here is the inner meaning of Peter's esoteric commandment, "honor the King":[2311] the "King" is your Higher Self (Divine Spirit),[2312] your Higher Self is the Christ (Divine Law),[2313] and the Christ is God (Divine Mind).[2314] Reread this. It is *the Secrets of Secrets!*

The Saint of Tarsus declared: "Let this mind be in you, which was also in Christ Jesus."[2315] This state of mind spiritually connects you to both the Indwelling Christ and the Father.[2316] In other words, you have now achieved total at-one-ment with Spirit,[2317] for you belong to God, and always have.[2318] You have awoken from your spiritual slumber (unenlightenment) into the full glory of Christ Consciousness (enlightenment), "beholding," as the Psalmist says, "thy face in righteousness: I shall be satisfied, when I awake, with thy likeness."[2319] This is what Paul meant by "the great mystery of godliness,"[2320] and it unveils the hidden meaning behind the often misunderstood words of Jesus:

> "If a man love me, he will keep my words: and my Father will love him, and we will come unto him, and make our abode with him."[2321]

"For he who does such things," wrote Paul's cousin and companion Barnabas, "shall be glorified in the Kingdom of God."[2322] Set your standards high, and the Father will set you on high,[2323] bearing you on eagles' wings unto Himself![2324]

## THE MASTER SECRET: GOD IN MAN!

With your union with the One Source established, by the Law of Attraction Divine Mind will then give you your heart's desire,[2325] for like always attracts like. James the Just understood this truth, which is why he made this mystical statement: "Draw nigh to God, and he will draw nigh to you."[2326] This is excellent spiritual advice, for we magnetize to our ourselves all that we think, say, and do.[2327]

Jesus' brother is speaking, of course, about your Omniscient Parent, the Supreme One who loves you more than you love yourself. He is the unitive Omnific Father that dwelleth within you,[2328] and who does everything for you based on your thoughts.[2329] *Est deus in nobis* ("God is in us"), said the astute ancient Pagan Ovid. This is the same Divine Mind that Jesus spoke of so often,[2330] and which He taught to His followers:

> ". . . the words that I speak unto you I speak not of myself: but the Father that dwelleth in me, he doeth the works."[2331]

Now you know the Master Secret, the ultimate "Secret of Life" that unenlightened Man has been futilely seeking *outside* of himself for thousands of years. Yet it has always been available to us. Why? Because it is *within* us,[2332] it is a part of us,[2333] it *is* us.[2334] Known as the doctrine of theosis, I am speaking of Man deified, or rather God in Man,[2335] the two deific cocreators[2336] who construct our lives using the "workshop of the mind,"[2337] the true laboratory of God!

Here is what the early Hellenistic Christians taught:

> "Jesus, who raised Man up, overcame his humanity to become like God. Not so that God would be brought down to Man's level, but so that Man would be brought up to God's level."[2338]

This is part of the great "revelation of the mystery, which was kept secret since the world began,"[2339] "the mystery of Christ,"[2340] the "mystery which hath been hid from ages and from generations."[2341] It is, as the Master put it, one of the "mysteries of the kingdom of God,"[2342] revealed by Jesus Himself 2,000 years ago. And this is it: due to our divinity, "*as a man thinketh in his heart, so is he.*"[2343]

## THE CORNERSTONE OF CHRIST'S TEACHINGS

Our at-one-ment with the Father, our personal Christhood, the Divine Within, is the cornerstone of Christ's Gospel of the Kingdom teachings: all believers are "changed into the image of the glory of the Lord,"[2344] and literally "bear the image of the heavenly,"[2345] flawlessly reflecting the glory of the Father "as in a mirror."[2346] For the Universal Christ Within[2347] is "the true Light which lighteth every man that cometh into the world."[2348] Indeed, those who understand this and live it, "shine as lights in the world."[2349]

Yet, this bold fact—which Jesus' enemies called "blasphemy"[2350] and "heresy,"[2351] and for which He was condemned to death[2352]—was rejected by the ancient founders of the Ecclesia, the mainstream Christian Church, and it is still being repudiated by many formalistic Christians to this day.[2353]

If only Jesus' critics had known and understood this mighty truth, which Paul called "the wisdom of God in a mystery." Then "they would not have crucified the Lord of glory"![2354]

## PAUL SAID WE ARE EQUAL WITH GOD!

But having read this book, while you may have been spiritually blind, now you see;[2355] now "ye are complete in Christ,"[2356] for you know the Eternal Truth that is "the same yesterday, and to day, and for ever."[2357] This is not my Truth, Christianity's Truth, or even Jesus' Truth. It is cosmic, eternal, unchanging Truth, which Hindus call "vidya": *what you believe becomes true for you*. So by fully believing that you are divine, one with the Father, it is so! What could be simpler? What could be grander?

What greater endowment could ever be bestowed upon us? We possess the mental ability to use the Law of Attraction to make of our lives whatever we choose. "Thanks be unto God for his unspeakable gift,"[2358] Paul said, thus "neglect not the gift that is *in* thee," for it will "save thee."[2359] This internal "gift" is the divine power of thought, as he notes in Philippians:

> "*Let this mind be in you*, which was also in Christ Jesus: who, being in the form of God, thought it not robbery *to be equal with God*."[2360]

I am going to paraphrase this spectacular statement to get at the hidden inner meaning:

> *Let this knowledge, this state of mind, be in you, which was also in Jesus: it is not wrong for you to think, believe, and know that you are one with God!*

Meditate often on this fact. If you keep to this message, it is guaranteed that you will live the rest of your life in perfect oneness with both the Indwelling Christ and with the Divine Mind. For with a sacred unction you have been christed ("anointed")[2361] by God Himself,[2362] filling you to overflowing with His divine glory, perfection, and power.[2363]

Because of this you no longer need "a schoolmaster,"[2364] that is, external teachers.[2365] From now on the Spirit of the Indwelling Christ will teach you anything you want to know,[2366] passing this "self-revealed" knowledge (Gnosis) directly from His Spirit into yours.[2367]

## WHY JESUS LAUGHED ON THE CROSS

Accept these internal teachings as factual and follow them, and you will remain in constant union with the Indwelling Christ.[2368] For "the Spirit is Truth,"[2369] and this Truth is the authentic "Gnosis of the Christ Within," which those who have been anointed to receive it, spread everywhere like a fine perfume.[2370] Paul said: "Blessed are those who understand and follow the teachings of Jesus Christ, for they shall dwell in the Light for all eternity."[2371]

Now you know why ancient Gnostic Christians portrayed Jesus laughing as He hung on the cross.[2372] He knew "the Secret" that His Roman captors and Jewish opponents could never understand; namely, the great "mystery of the Kingdom of God"[2373] that He shared with all those "who have ears to hear":[2374] our deathless souls are one with God and He with us, and we are one with everyone and everything else.[2375] And this fact provides you with the divine power to shape your life any way you wish,[2376] as the Lord tells us in the Gospel of John:

> "If ye abide in me, and my words abide in you, ye shall ask what ye will, and it shall be done unto you."[2377]

This incredible universal message, of our divine oneness with the Father and our share in His supernatural powers, is the Great Esoteric Secret taken straight from the Book of Seven Seals.[2378] It is the mystical spiritual food Jesus said He "ate," but which even His own followers "knew not of."[2379] "Eating" of this "food" yourself (that is, understanding, accepting, and practicing this truth) will set you free from your past, from sin, from wrong-thinking, from disease, unhappiness, and impoverishment of all kinds.[2380]

Fully believing in it and executing it on a daily basis will change your life forever. We can do nothing without first going through the Christ Within,[2381] so relinquish the Ego and heed the words of the Master:

> "If ye keep my commandments, ye shall abide in my love; even as I have kept my Father's commandments, and abide in his love. These things have I spoken unto you, that my joy might remain in you, and that your joy might be full."[2382]

## THE REAL GOOD NEWS!

Thanks to the Universal Eternal Indwelling Christ,[2383] the Holy One,[2384] which existed before Jesus[2385] and which will always exist,[2386] you are deific, godlike, and immortal; one with what Hindus call the "unborn, undying, indestructible Lord of all things living." This is "the gospel of the omnipotence of Man,"[2387] the true and only authentic "Gospel of Jesus Christ,"[2388] or what the Master Himself correctly called "the Gospel of the Kingdom."[2389]

It is the same "secret saying" that has so often been unfairly ridiculed, misunderstood, edited, (purposefully) mistranslated, cruelly outlawed, and finally buried by the enemies of Christ beneath the scrapheap of "ecclesiastical necessity." Only now it has been recovered for all to see. Those who are of Jesus' flock, who look to Him as their spiritual shepherd, will "hear His voice" and understand.[2390]

This, the genuine Gospel, the real "Good News," is your saving grace,[2391] which is why Paul literally called it the "gospel of your salvation."[2392] Thus it is the most important fact you will ever learn in your life: due to your Inner Divine Trinity (the Superconscious, the Conscious, and the Subconscious Minds),[2393] you can do anything through the Father Within,[2394] the Indwelling Christ,[2395] and the Inner Holy Spirit.[2396] This is, as Paul bitterly complained, "the truth of God that was changed into a lie" by the mainstream Christian Church.[2397]

## THE TRUTH OF OUR DIVINE NATURE IS IMMORTAL

This is the same so-called "blasphemous" teaching that caused fundamentalist Jews to turn against Jesus and condemn Him to death before Pilate.[2398] It is the same doctrine that fundamentalist Christians censored and banned 1,900 years ago, and which institutional Christianity continues to suppress and ignore to this day.

Though Jesus died for this Truth, men cannot slay the Truth itself.[2399] And that Truth is Jesus' esoteric Gospel of the Kingdom teaching that because our true self, our Great "I AM that I AM,"[2400] is made in the image of,[2401] and is in fact identical to, the Father,[2402] the Indwelling Christ,[2403] and the Holy Spirit,[2404] we are all deities,[2405] true "partakers in His holiness."[2406] For, even as the scriptures tell us, the Christ Himself *is* God,[2407] and "Christ is in all."[2408] *Everyone who is of the Truth will hear and understand this astounding message!*[2409]

## WHAT THINGS SOEVER YE DESIRE

Now, because we are gods, we can use the Law of Attraction to sculpt our own destinies, just as Jesus promised:

> "What things soever ye desire, when ye pray, believe that ye receive them, and ye shall have them."[2410]

The Universe itself will fade into nothingness before this statement does,[2411] for "the word of the Lord endureth for ever."[2412] In the language of the eternal Indwelling Christ Himself, "Heaven and earth shall pass away, but my words shall not pass away":[2413]

# YE ARE GODS![2414]

Jesus portrayed as the living embodiment of the Universal Indwelling Christ, which is none other than the real self, the Higher Self, the God-Self, of every human being. Whatever our religion or worldview, whatever word we choose to call God, whatever our nationality, race, or creed, whatever life we have chosen to live, according to Jesus, the Truth remains "the same yesterday, and to day, and for ever." And here is that Truth, openly revealed by our Lord:

*" I am in my Father, and ye in me, and I in you."* [2415]

*Jesus*

# Proverbs 3
To be read once a day

"My son, forget not my law; but let thine heart keep my commandments: for length of days, and long life, and peace, shall they add to thee. Let not mercy and truth forsake thee: bind them about thy neck; write them upon the table of thine heart: so shalt thou find favour and good understanding in the sight of God and man. Trust in the Lord [Divine Mind] with all thine heart; and lean not unto thine own understanding [Human Mind/Ego/Satan]. In all thy ways acknowledge him, and he shall direct thy paths. Be not wise in thine own eyes: fear [respect] the Lord, and depart from evil. It shall be health to thy navel, and marrow to thy bones. Honour the Lord with thy substance, and with the firstfruits of all thine increase: so shall thy barns be filled with plenty, and thy presses shall burst out with new wine. My son, despise not the chastening of the Lord; neither be weary of his correction [the Law of Attraction]: for whom the Lord loveth he correcteth; even as a father the son in whom he delighteth. Happy is the man that findeth wisdom [in Greece, personified by the wisdom-goddess Sophia], and the man that getteth understanding. For the merchandise of it is better than the merchandise of silver, and the gain thereof than fine gold. She [wisdom; that is, knowledge of the Law of Attraction] is more precious than rubies: and all the things thou canst desire are not to be compared unto her. Length of days is in her right hand; and in her left hand riches and honour. Her ways are ways of pleasantness, and all her paths are peace. She is a tree of life [the living connection between heaven and earth] to them that lay hold upon her: and happy is every one that retaineth her. The Lord by wisdom [the Law of Attraction] hath founded the earth; by understanding hath he established the heavens. By his knowledge [Gnosis] the depths are broken up, and the clouds drop down the dew. My son, let not them depart from thine eyes [Third Eye/inner perception]: keep sound wisdom and discretion: so shall they be life unto thy soul [Subconscious Mind], and grace to thy neck. Then shalt thou walk in thy way safely, and thy foot shall not stumble. When thou liest down, thou shalt not be afraid: yea, thou shalt lie down, and thy sleep shall be sweet. Be not afraid of sudden fear, neither of the desolation of the wicked, when it cometh. For the Lord shall be thy confidence, and shall keep thy foot from being taken [up in the trap of atheism]."[2416]

*He that hath ears to hear, let him hear.*[2417]

# ACADEMIC
# SECTION

Sapientia
Intellectus
Consilium
Fortitudo
Scientia
Pietas
Timor

Isaiah XI: 2

# GLOSSARY

## A Comparative Guide to
## Traditional Christian & Mystical Christian Doctrine

Note: As different cultures view spiritual doctrines and symbols differently in different time periods, no two schools of thought agree on every one of these definitions. As such, there is some fluidity across the various entries.

---

**ANCIENT OF DAYS:** Daniel's term for the Higher Self, the Indwelling Christ.[2418]

**ATONEMENT:** As with many other biblical doctrines, the idea of atonement too has been mistranslated (in many cases, intentionally), and thus its truly salvific power has long been denied the masses. Mainstream Christianity teaches that atonement is the reconciliation of God and humankind through the sacrificial death of Jesus Christ. This is merely the outer (exoteric) meaning, however. The inner (esoteric) meaning is that atonement is a reminder or spiritual restoration of our *at-one-ment*, our union, our complete and perfect oneness, with the Father (Superconscious Mind), the Christ (Conscious Mind), and the Holy Ghost (Subconscious Mind). Contrary to orthodox Christian teaching, Jesus never used the word atonement, and in fact, it only appears once in the entire New Testament (in Paul's letter to the Romans).[2419] Despite this, Jesus made His teachings on the topic of at-one-ment clear and available to all who have ears to hear: we are one with God, Christ, and the Holy Spirit.[2420] This is part of the "great mystery of godliness" Paul referred to.[2421]

**CHRIST:** Spiritual law, Divine Law, which includes the Law of Attraction. The Christ or *Christos* is also the Divine Self or Higher Self of each individual, idealized in Jesus, but which also exists in each one of us as a potential state of consciousness. Mystically speaking, though there was only one Jesus (a symbol of fully enlightened Man), there are many Christs, for God has personally christed ("anointed")[2422] each and every one of us Himself,[2423] lovingly forming the "Son *in* you and me."[2424] Hence, the Lord warned: "If any man shall say unto you, 'Lo, here is Christ,' or 'there'; believe it not."[2425] Known in mystical Christianity as the doctrine of theosis, that is, the deification of Man, Paul plainly and openly called our Indwelling Christ the "Christ in you,"[2426] stating that "Christ is in all."[2427] Solomon described it more mystically: "The spirit of man is the candle of the Lord."[2428] The Universal Indwelling Christ, also known as the World-Christ, has always existed and always will.[2429] For it is "without father, without mother, without descent, having neither beginning of days, nor end of life; but made like unto the Son of God."[2430] Being unborn, immortal, eternal, undying, changeless, incorporeal, immanent, indestructible, and timeless, the Christ Within existed, of course, before Jesus (as He Himself acknowledged),[2431] and lives on in each one of us as what Hindus call the Supreme Self and what Emerson called the Oversoul. Holy Scripture asserts that the Indwelling Christ is indeed "everlasting,"[2432] for He "abideth for ever."[2433] Hence, speaking as the Indwelling Christ, Jesus said: "Before Abraham was I am,"[2434] and "Lo, I am with you alway[s], even unto the end of the world."[2435] When we realize our oneness, that is, our at-one-ment, with God, we attain what mystical Christians refer to as Christ Consciousness or Cosmic Consciousness, or what Paul named "the mind of Christ."[2436] "Let this mind be in you, which was also in Christ Jesus," said the Thirteenth Apostle.[2437] According to Jesus, those who follow His teachings are those who love the Indwelling Christ, and it is to these individuals that the Indwelling Christ reveals Himself.[2438] Though He was the perfect embodiment of the Christ Within, Jesus did not want attention focused on His physical being (that is, Jesus the man, the human son of Joseph and Mary),[2439] but on the Father (Divine Mind) and the Indwelling Christ (Divine Law). Thus He said: "But be not ye called Rabbi ["teacher"]: for one is your Master, even Christ; and all ye are brethren. And call no man your father upon the earth: for one is your Father, which is in heaven. Neither be ye called masters: for one is your Master, even Christ."[2440]

**COMFORTER:** Same as Holy Spirit or Holy Ghost,[2441] yet with a specific meaning of its own: spiritual understanding, the inner light, gives us peace of mind and a sense of security; of being taken care of, comforted, and loved unconditionally by God. Jesus referred to this sensation, this elevated spiritual level of consciousness, as the Comforter; in Greek, *Parakletos*, "helper," "assistant."[2442] The Lord promised that after His physical life ended, the Comforter, the Christ Within,[2443] would take care of us and guide us, just as He had while here fulfilling His earthly mission: to reestablish within humanity the doctrine of theosis; the concept of the Indwelling Christ, God in Man,[2444] that had been suppressed by Pharisaic religion.[2445] Thus, Jesus said, after I am gone, "the Comforter, which is the Holy Ghost, whom the Father will send in my name, he shall teach you all things, and bring all things to your remembrance, whatsoever I have said unto you."[2446] Like the Father, the Christ, and the Holy Ghost, the Comforter also dwells within us, not outside of us.[2447]

**CONSCIOUS MIND:** I call the Conscious Mind "The Thinker." It is a symbol of wisdom, and is related to the physical plane and the material body. Thoughts and ideas are generated here and sent onto the Subconscious Mind. In patriarchal religions the Conscious Mind is known as the "Son"; in matriarchal religions it is the "Sun." In mystical religions it is the "Christ" or "Higher Self." The Conscious Mind plays a vital role in working with the Law of Attraction. As the "Master," it conveys thoughts to the Subconscious Mind (the "Servant"), which stores our most dominant thoughts as beliefs. The Subconscious then passes these beliefs onto the Superconscious Mind, which manifests them in the physical plane as our experiences and circumstances. Thus, learning to control the thoughts coming out of the Conscious Mind is imperative if we wish to achieve health, wealth, and happiness. The Conscious Mind correlates with the left side of the brain, which operates the right (male) side of the body. Keywords: logical, sequential, analytical, objective, masculine, daytime, knowledge, earthly, ideas, facts, science.

**DEVIL, THE:** Same as Satan and Lucifer, differing in Indo-European etymology only: the word devil derives from one of the names of the Hindu word for God, *deva* ("divine"), which is related to the English word deity, which comes from the Latin word *divus*, meaning a "god" or "goddess." The Devil's traditional horns, cloven hooves, and pointed tail were borrowed by early Christian mythographers from the Greek nature-god Pan (a satyr identical to the ancient Roman nature-god Faunus, who gives us our modern word fauna). As a Law of Attraction teacher and practitioner, Jesus utterly rejected the idea of evil and the alleged existence of the Devil/Lucifer/Satan, and he asked us to do the same.[2448] The biblical Devil is, of course, an ancient personification of the human Ego, which, due to its self-centered atheistic nature, sees itself as separate and distinct from God. The Ego will stop at nothing to get us to take our focus off the Spiritual and put it on the Material. With this new understanding, the allegorical nature of Matthew's story of the "temptation of Christ" by the Devil (Ego) is now more comprehensible and meaningful.[2449] See Satan and Lucifer.

**DIVINE MIND:** Same as God.

**EARS:** When Jesus uses the word "ears," he is often referring not to the physical ones, but to the Inner Ear, or the "Third Ear," meaning spiritual or inner perception (intuition) as opposed to intellectual or outer perception (the two physical ears).[2450]

**ECCLESIA:** A Greek word meaning "assembly," but translated by King James' English scribes as "church."[2451] In this book I use the term Ecclesia to indicate the mainstream (institutionalized) Christian Church as opposed to the many less conventional, unorthodox, independent, and even so-called "heterodox" Christian denominations, sects, and cults. The Ecclesia, whether it be Catholic or Protestant, has ruled Christianity (politically, often ruthlessly) since it began to take form shortly after Jesus' Ascension. The great irony is that Jesus Christ, after whom the ecclesiastical Christian Church was named, espoused a decidedly unconventional, unecclesiastical spirituality,[2452] one He called "the Gospel of the Kingdom,"[2453] a creed that was in stark contrast to what the Church would later teach in His name, and which they referred to as "the Gospel of Jesus Christ."[2454] Indeed, not only were Jesus' esoteric teachings considered iconoclastic by contemporary orthodox Jewish authorities (and later by posthumous orthodox Christian authorities—who labeled them "heresy"),[2455] but His "heterodoxical" doctrines concerning the oneness of God and Man[2456] were actually what led to His execution on the cross,[2457] for in Mosaic Law, this concept, theosis or "God in Man,"[2458] was considered blasphemy,[2459] and was punishable by death.[2460]

**EGO:** From the Latin word *ego*, meaning "I." In mystical Christianity (as opposed to the meaning used in modern psychology) the Ego is identical to the biblical Satan/the Devil/Lucifer. Occultly, the "Crucifixion" is meant to be that of the Ego, which is attached to the physical body: the dissolving of our Lower Self, the godless, self-centered aspect of human nature, which either ignores or disdains God, and believes that we are separate from Him. Sadly, the latter idea, which goes completely contrary to Jesus' teachings on the at-one-ment of God and Man, is still very much alive in many Ego-centered Christian denominations. By "crucifying" the atheistic Ego, or what Paul called "our old man," we are "born again" and realize our oneness with God.[2461] We are then free to live out of the Higher Self, the Indwelling Christ,[2462] the Great I AM,[2463] where happiness, health, and prosperity reign.[2464] See Satan, the Devil, and Lucifer.

**ENLIGHTENMENT:** The realization that we are an individualization, an expression, a manifestation, a differentiation, an extension of God, that we are one with all things, and in particular with God, and that our Higher Self, the Supreme Self, the Indwelling Christ,[2465] is in fact God, the Father, Divine Mind.[2466] In other words, when you realize in your soul that you are a god, as Jesus taught, you have attained enlightenment.[2467] Enlightenment is the opposite of spiritual darkness, ignorance, and immaturity, as well as scientific atheism. The only thing that can block us from enlightenment is the Ego (Satan), which being vain and dualistic, sees "you" as being separate from God. Throughout the Bible enlightenment is variously symbolized as light, a flame, fire, candles, and more generally the ever constant, ever circling, ever present Sun. Thus in Psalms, God is called "my light and my salvation,"[2468] while in Malachi the Indwelling Christ is referred to as the "Sun of Righteousness."[2469] Psalms also gives us this beautiful passage: "For thou wilt light my candle: the Lord my God will enlighten my darkness."[2470] As enlightenment takes place in the mind, ancient artists portrayed enlightened individuals with nimbuses, halos, or bright auras around their heads, Christian symbols of what Hindus know as the "Crown Chakra,"[2471] and what Peter referred to as the "crown of glory."[2472] Paul called attaining enlightenment "having the mind of Christ,"[2473] and also "the helmet of salvation."[2474] The mainstream Christian word for enlightenment is indeed "salvation," the mystical Christian term is "gnosis."[2475] Both are identical or similar in meaning to the related words: nirvana, satori, epiphany, bodhi, theophany, theaphany, mar'eh, hierophany, tapas, kensho, Abraham Consciousness, Moses Consciousness, Krishna Consciousness, Krishnahood, Buddha Consciousness, Buddhahood, Christ Consciousness, Christhood, Cosmic Consciousness, self-realization, ananda, sat-chit-ananda, moksa, hazon, kaivalya, christophany, mukti, yogasema, apavarga, darshan, sukha, fana, illumination, turiya, and samadhi. In very general terms, all indicate the same thing: the realization that our Higher Self, the omnipresent indestructible Indwelling Christ, is one with God. Jesus not only said that we are one with God,[2476] but that we literally are gods.[2477] Understanding this, knowing this with full undeviating faith, is enlightenment.

**EVIL:** From the Old English word *yfel*, meaning "the antithesis of good" (that is, God), and thus connoting the "Evil One," that is, the "Devil." According to what is known as "the Ancient Wisdom," evil is the absence of God, or separation from God, Divine Mind. Yet, there is nothing evil outside of us. The Devil (or Satan) himself is merely the biblical personification of our Lower Self. Evil in fact is created by wrong-thinking, and is therefore a product of the human mind (Ego).[2478] Thus, due to the Law of Attraction, if we believe in evil, we attract it. If we do not believe in evil, it cannot harm us. The only things that can come into our lives are those which we invite through prolonged and persistent thought.[2479] Jesus wisely taught: "Resist not evil."[2480] Resistance is recognizing evil as a reality, which draws more of it to you. By not resisting evil, it disappears as the manmade illusion that it is.

**EYES:** When Jesus, Paul, and other enlightened biblical figures use the word "'eyes," in many cases they are referring not to our two physical ones, but to our Inner Eye, or "Third Eye," meaning spiritual or inner perception (intuition) as opposed to intellectual or outer perception (tuition).[2481] Paul knew the Third Eye as "the eyes of your understanding."[2482] Jesus liked to contrast two-eyed physical vision (intellectual perception) with single-eyed spiritual vision: "The light of the body is the [Third] eye: if therefore thine eye be single [spiritual], thy whole body shall be full of light [enlightenment]. But if thine eye be evil [double, physical], thy whole body shall be full of darkness [spiritual ignorance]. If therefore the light that is in thee be darkness, how great is that darkness!"[2483] The following mystical passage from Ephesians is now understandable: "For ye were sometimes darkness, but now are ye light in the Lord: walk as children of light."[2484] The Third Eye goes by many other names as well, depending on the religion, for example: the Eye of Shiva, the Inner Eye, the Star of the East, Ajna, the Dove Descending From Heaven, and the Eye of Intuition. The Third Eye is associated with the Brow (sixth) Chakra and sometimes the Crown (seventh) Chakra, as well as shamanic sight or clairvoyance.

**FATHER:** Jesus' esoteric code word for the Divine Mind. In patriarchal religions the same as "God." In matriarchal religions the Supreme Being was (and still is) known as "Mother" or "Goddess." Since earliest times it has been the practice of enlightened spiritual teachers, like Jesus, to depict the Divine Mind as a parent, in order to make the concept more accessible to the spiritually immature and the metaphysically undeveloped masses. Thus in male-based religions (theology) the Divine Mind has always been imaged as a masculine parent, in female-based religions (thealogy) as a feminine one.

**GNOSIS:** The Greek word for "knowledge"; used by certain early Christians to refer to inner self-knowledge (Higher Knowledge, the unchangeable Truth that Hindus refer to as *vidya*) as opposed to outer academic-knowledge (Lower Knowledge, the relative Truth that Hindus refer to as *avidya*). The entire catalog of universal knowledge (Gnosis) and wisdom (Sophia) is contained within us, but it cannot be accessed through the intellect (tuition). Only through the Spirit (intuition). In Hinduism this great mass of inner Gnosis is known as the "Divine Library Within," thus Thomas Paine said: "My mind is my own church." Self-revealed knowledge is necessary because we are all at different degrees of spiritual awareness, each one of us requiring a different level of teaching. Thus, as it should be, each individual interprets the Bible differently. This is why God made it impossible for us to use human knowledge to either understand sacred scripture[2485] or know Him.[2486] Only through self-revealed Gnosis, via the wisdom of the Indwelling Christ,[2487] can we attain the faith to discover the God Within.[2488] An entire branch of early Christianity takes its name from the word Gnosis (divine inner knowledge): the pre-Christian Gnostics (many who later became Christians) held that a true understanding of God can only come from self-revelation, which includes prayer, intuition, epiphanies, inspiration, visions, imagination, dreams, and the like. Many of these freethinking Christian sects also taught the true Gospel, "the Gospel of the Kingdom,"[2489] or rather "the Gospel of the Kingdom of God,"[2490] which included Jesus' doctrines on the Sacred Christ Within,[2491] our innate oneness with the Father,[2492] and His creed on the Law of Attraction.[2493] "For what thou see, thou shall become," taught the Gnostics.[2494] Because of this very teaching, Gnostic Christianity was considered a threat to the Ecclesiastics (the hierarchy of the Catholic Church), and so Gnostic Christians were persecuted, tortured, and murdered, and their sacred books put to the torch. As a result, much of Jesus' authentic teachings concerning Gnosis were lost. Yet, evidence of the Master's belief in self-revealed knowledge, and that of some of His followers, can still be found in the canonical Bible,[2495] and in numerous recently discovered Gnostic Christian texts.[2496]

**GOD:** A religious word for the ultimate and supreme reality; mystically it is the sum total of all three minds: the Superconscious, the Conscious, and the Subconscious, which together form the Divine Mind. Ideas and thoughts are generated in the Conscious Mind (the "Son"); these are sent to the Subconscious Mind ("Holy Spirit"), where they become beliefs; these are then communicated to the Superconscious Mind (the "Father"), where they are generated into material reality. God is thus the Creator, the One, the Source of All. In some metaphysical schools God is the Superconscious Mind alone, while scientists refer to Him as the "Unified Field," "the laws of physics," or simply "Nature"—for God is everything and everything is God.[2497] In matriarchal religions God is a "she" who "is known in her palaces" as Goddess or Mother-Goddess.[2498] Actually, as the Old Testament plural word Elohim (meaning "God/Goddess") reveals,[2499] "God" actually embodies both the Male Principle and the Female Principle,[2500] and is therefore called by some, such as the ancient Gnostic Christians, the "Mother-Father," the "Androgynous One,"[2501] or the "Androgynous Father."[2502] There is nothing that is not God, so true pure atheism is impossible. We dwell, breath, swim in God. Paul said that in Him/Her/It "we live, and move, and have our being."[2503] The Hindus call God "Brahman," the Creator-God of the Hindu Holy Trinity, Trimurti. According to the ancient Christian doctrine of theosis (embraced by the early Church Fathers), like Christ[2504] and the Holy Spirit,[2505] God also dwells within us,[2506] making up our Divine Inner Trinity.[2507] Thus Jesus said: "Ye are gods."[2508] See Jehovah and Yahweh.

**GODDESS:** In prehistoric matriarchal religions (pre-6000 B.C.), during what has been called the Matriarchate (the nearly worldwide phenomenon of female-headed, though largely egalitarian, societies), Goddess was the name for the Supreme Being, who, at that time, was imaged as purely female. Later, after the rise of the idea of a male Supreme Being (post-6000 B.C.), the word Goddess was used to denote the feminine aspect of God, at which time she became God's "wife" or "consort." As patriarchy spread across the West and Near East during the early historic period, mainstream Christianity and Judaism eventually totally suppressed her worship. In the former religion she was metamorphisized into the figure of the Virgin Mary, the Holy Spirit, and various fictitious female saints,[2509] while in the latter she continues to be venerated among Jewish mystics in her old Hebrew form as Asherah or Ashtoreth.[2510] The first known artistic portrayals of the Great Mother-Goddess date from the Acheulian Period of the Lower Paleolithic Age, some 500,000 years ago, at which time *Homo erectus* was carving crude female figures in her honor. Both the Neanderthal and Cro-Magnon peoples also produced a panoply of beautiful artistic representations of Goddess, the second group creating, most notably, the renowned but misnamed "Venus" figurines. See God, Holy Spirit, Holy Trinity, and I AM.[2511]

**GOSPEL:** Contrary to popular thought, there are two completely different Gospels presented in the New Testament: the first preached by Jesus during His ministry, which He called "the Gospel of the Kingdom,"[2512] and the second preached by His followers after His death, which they referred to as "the Gospel of Jesus Christ."[2513] The former, Jesus' Gospel, included His doctrines on the divinity of Man,[2514] the Law of Attraction,[2515] and our at-one-ment with the Father and the Indwelling Christ.[2516] The latter, created by His posthumous followers, was constructed around a Paganistic-Jewish-Catholic Christology centering on Jesus as the messianic Savior of Mankind.[2517] Because Jesus' Gospel, the Gospel of the Kingdom, threatened both Catholic hegemony and the priesthood, over many centuries it was gradually suppressed and replaced by the Gospel of Jesus Christ, the one still followed by mainstream Christianity to this day. While the institutional Church has ousted the original "Good News" for its own manmade one, interest in Jesus' Gospel continues among the spiritually mature. Peter said that the topic of the true Gospel, the Gospel of the Kingdom, is so enthralling that even "the angels desire to look into it."[2518]

**HEAVEN:** A literal place or a state of consciousness here and in the Afterlife, depending on one's beliefs. This is due to the fact that the Law of Attraction makes real what we believe to be real. Thus Jesus declared that the "Kingdom of God [Heaven] is within you."[2519]

**HELL:** In institutional Christianity a physical place of punishment and anguish located in the Christian Underworld, the destination of all sinners in the Afterlife. In Jesus' original language (Aramaic), however, Hell means "mental torment"; in other words, when you sin ("miss the mark"), that is, when you do something that is unspiritual, the Law of Attraction brings immediate suffering by drawing more disharmony to you. In the New Testament the word "Hell" is written in three ways. The first is *Hades*, which is not Hell but rather the personal name of the Greek god of the Underworld (as such he is identical to the Roman underworld god Orcus).[2520] The second word, the Hebrew *Geenna*, also has nothing to do with the Hell of mainstream Christianity. *Geenna* refers to a real geographical site in ancient Israel: the Valley of Hinnom, just south of Jerusalem, which once served as a landfill for the town's refuse.[2521] The third reference to Hell uses the Greek word *Tartaroo* (in English, Tartarus), which like Hades, is the name of both an ancient Grecian god and sometimes the Greek Underworld itself. In this case, Tartarus is the lowest, darkest level of Hell.[2522] According to both early Christians[2523] and modern mainstream Christians,[2524] Jesus briefly visited Hell after His burial in the tomb, a belief intimated by Paul in his letter to the Ephesians.[2525]

**HIDDEN MAN OF THE HEART:** One of Peter's terms for the Higher Self.[2526]
**HIGHER SELF:** Same as Christ.

**HOLY GHOST:** Same as Holy Spirit.

**HOLY SPIRIT:** The ancient biblical coded name for the Subconscious Mind, it is feminine in nature. The idea of the Holy Spirit began in ancient matriarchal religions as Goddess, the Great Mother, one of whose sacred animals was the dove ("peace"), which is why "the spirit of God" descended on Jesus "like a dove" at His baptism.[2527] De-feminized, marginalized, masculinized, and Christianized in the 1st and 2nd Centuries, the great Mother-Goddess was gradually absorbed as the Holy Spirit or Holy Ghost into the Catholic Church's Holy Trinity.[2528] Her true origins, however, are still evident in the New Testament. Here both the words ghost and spirit are written *pneuma* in Greek, which means "breath," "wind," or "movement of air," making the true translation of Holy Ghost, the "Holy Breath." This is why Jesus ordained His Disciples by breathing on them, a ritual known as insufflation: this implanted them with the Holy Spirit.[2529] The Holy Breath (Subconscious Mind) is, of course, connected to the Word or Logos (Conscious Mind), that is, the divine power of thought,[2530] and was used by God in the creation of our species, *homo sapiens*.[2531] The Holy Spirit is identical to the Comforter or Paraclete who "dwelleth with you, and shall be in you."[2532] Paul tells us that the Holy Spirit is a gift from God,[2533] one that He intentionally planted "in our hearts."[2534] Thus like the Father (Divine Mind)[2535] and the Son (the Indwelling Christ),[2536] the Holy Spirit dwells within us.[2537] See Goddess and I AM.

**HOLY TRINITY:** Threefold symbol of the great triune God, known to Christian mystics as the Divine Mind.[2538] Mainstream Christianity did not adopt the idea of the Trinity until the 12th Century, after which it proclaimed that while the Father is God,[2539] the Son is God,[2540] and the Holy Spirit is God,[2541] all are in fact one.[2542] To help canonize the idea of the Holy Trinity and firmly establish it among the Catholic masses, early on the Church forged 1 John 5:7, artificially adding it to John's letter sometime after the mid 4th Century (as with so many other well-known Bible scriptures, this one too is absent from our earliest complete and original Bible manuscripts, such as the Codex Sinaiticus). In some mystical Christian schools the Father is "Mind" (Thought) the Son is "Idea" (Word) and the female Holy Spirit is "Expression" (Action), which correlates with the threefold nature of man: Spirit (Superconscious Mind, the "Father," the great "I AM"), Body (Conscious Mind, the "Son"), and Soul (Subconscious Mind, the "Holy Spirit"). Hence, ancient Gnostic Christians referred to the Trinity as "the Father, the Mother, and the Son, the perfect power."[2543] The Apostle John described our Cosmic Inner Trinity like this: "For there are three that bear record in heaven [enlightenment, harmony, nirvana, samadhi], the Father [Superconscious Mind], the Word [Conscious Mind], and the Holy Ghost [Subconscious Mind]: and these three are one."[2544] The idea of the Holy Trinity did not originate with Christianity of course. Rather, it is a universal concept found worldwide in countless Pagan religions, dating back to the dawn of history. In India, for example, individuals venerate Trimurti, the Hindu Holy Trinity, made up of Brahma the Creator, Vishnu the Preserver, and Shiva the Destroyer. Hindu scriptures refer to what we Christians call the Father as "Sat," the Son as "Tat," and the Holy Ghost as "Aum" (identical to Om, I AM, and amen). The archetypal religious triad first sprang from out of early matriarchal societies, where it was imaged as an all-female trinity known as the Triple-Goddess. This is due to the fact that paternity, the male's role in reproduction, was unknown in prehistoric times.

Thus, the female was worshiped as a magical parthenogenic goddess, with men playing a subservient (or sometimes an equal) role in society and religion (for example, the Minoans of ancient Crete). Naturally then, as the archaeological record confirms, the first artistic depictions of a Supreme Being were female, which gave rise to the worship of the Great Mother-Goddess, or Universal Earth-Mother. And indeed, artistic portrayals of male deities, such as statues and cave etchings of male gods, do not appear until much later—*after* paternity was discovered through the domestication of wild animals (circa 10,000-6,000 B.C.). Thus the Divine Feminine and the all-female trinity were the forerunners of the Great Father-God, or Heavenly Father, and the gender-mixed trinity that we find in Christianity today: God the Father (male), the Son (male), and the Holy Spirit (female). As an archetype found in one form or another in the majority of pre-Christian societies around the world, the Triple-Goddess is known far and wide, from, for instance, ancient Ireland[2545] and Norway,[2546] to ancient Rome[2547] and Greece.[2548] The Triple-Goddess symbolizes the three-fold nature of humanity (body, mind, and spirit), the three phases of the moon (waxing, full, waning), and the three ages of Man and Woman: childhood (the "maiden" or "prince"), adulthood (the "mother" or "father"), and seniorhood (the "crone" or "grandfather"). As ancient goddesses in general, and in particular the Great Mother-Goddess, were associated with the ocean (the maternal "amniotic fluid" from which all life sprang), their names were often comprised of the *ma* ("mother") and *mar* ("sea") elements, meaning "Mother-Sea." For example, we have the early goddess names: Ma Ma, Maerin, Maid Marian, Mar, Mara, Marah, Mari, Maria, Mariam, Marie, Marratu, Mary, Maya, and Meri, to name but a few. To this day Jesus' mother Mary is still widely known by the ancient Pagan title that the Catholic Church "borrowed" from the Greek love-goddess Aphrodite:[2549] Stella Maris ("Star of the Sea"). Like nearly all mythological Pagan figures, the Triple-Goddess too was eventually Christianized, absorbed into Christian myth[2550] as the "Three Marys" who "stood by the cross of Jesus" during His crucifixion.[2551] As the first spiritual triad to appear in the archeological record (the earliest and most rudimentary depictions of the Triple-Goddess are roughly made triangular-shaped stones, made by Neanderthals between 100,000 and 40,000 years ago), it is clear that the prehistoric Triple-Goddess served as prototype not only for the Christian Holy Trinity of the 12th Century, but for all historic religious trinities. See Goddess and I AM.

**I AM:** The secret and sacred name of God, revealed to Moses by God Himself.[2552] It means self-generating "Being," and is personified in ancient religion and myth as the archetypal Virgin-Mother-Goddess, who reproduces parthenogenically; that is, creates life alone, without the aid of a male partner. Since we are one with God,[2553] we also contain the I AM, or what I refer to as the Great I AM Within.[2554] It is our real self, our Higher Self, our Divine Self, and is identical to the Indwelling Christ,[2555] or what Hindus call the Atman. Our realization of our oneness with God, our at-one-ment with Divine Mind, is one of the most important steps we can achieve in life, which is why the Hindu sage Ramana Maharshi called it "self-realization," and it is why Jesus called it "salvation."[2556] In Hinduism the I AM is written "AUM" or "OM," and is often used as a mantra or spiritual chant. In Hebrew it is "Amam," in Tibet it is "Hum," in ancient Egypt it was "Amon," and in traditional Christianity it is "Amen," yet another symbolic manifestation of the ever creative Word, known as the "Logos" in Gnostic

Christianity.[2557] Pliny called the I AM: *Artifex Omnium Natura*, the "Creator of All Nature." Descartes said: "I think, therefore I AM." The Apostle John was well versed in the Gnosis of the Great I AM or OM: he used it occultly as the Greek word "OM-ega" (Omega),[2558] and also as "the Amen, the faithful and true witness, the beginning of the creation of God."[2559] Having long ago rejected Jesus' secret teachings on the Great I AM, institutional Christianity does not recognize it, even though it is clearly revealed in the Bible, not only in God's statement, "I AM that I AM,"[2560] and Jesus' statement "before Abraham was, I AM,"[2561] but also as the book of Revelation's "voice of many waters."[2562] In mystical Christianity the I AM is used in various ways by those on the path toward spiritual enlightenment. As noted earlier in this book, one example is the Law of Attraction: affirmations for specific desires should start off with "I AM" in order to form a magnetic union between the thought and God. This increases the vibrational intensity of the affirmation, speeding it on its way from the Conscious Mind (the Son), to the Subconscious Mind (the Holy Spirit), and from there onto the Superconscious Mind (the Father, Divine Mind). According to mystical Christian doctrine, whenever Jesus used the Great I AM in a sentence, it is always in reference to the Indwelling Christ that we all possess. This is not surprising, as Jesus had obliterated his personal Ego, becoming completely merged with the Universal Christ.[2563] For example, mystically (psychologically) speaking, His statement, "I AM the way, the truth, and the life: no man cometh unto the Father, but by me,"[2564] actually means "no one can connect to the Divine Mind except by way of the Christ Within."[2565] Jesus confirmed that the Great I AM is eternal, unborn, timeless, and unchanging: "Lo, I AM with you alway[s], even unto the end of the world."[2566]

**INDWELLING CHRIST:** Cosmic Man, same as Christ.[2567]

**INNER MAN:** One of Paul's terms for the Higher Self.[2568]

**INWARD MAN:** One of Paul's terms for the Higher Self.[2569]

**ISRAEL:** A Hebrew word meaning "God prevails." Thus, in mystical religion ancient Israel symbolizes the Spirit, perfection, monotheism, and enlightened Man, which was at odds with Egypt, a mystical symbol of materialism, imperfection, polytheism, and unenlightened Man.[2570] The word Israel derives from the names of three ancient Pagan deities: the Egyptian Mother-Goddess Isis, the Egyptian Father-God Ra, and the Canaanite Father-God El, giving Isis-Ra-El, or IsRaEl.

**JEHOVAH:** Same as God. The word Jehovah is a creation of Medieval English priests, who combined the Tetragrammaton, JHVH—the Hebrew name of God (without vowels), and also spelled YHWH, that is, Yahweh—with the vowels of the word Adonai (a, o, a), resulting in the word J-a-H-o-V-a-H, or in English, Jehovah.[2571] Adonai is the plural form of Adon, the name of a Canaanite fertility-god, known more familiarly as the Greek love-god Adonis. See God and Yahweh.

**JESUS:** In mainstream Christianity the Messiah, the Savior of All Mankind, born of the Virgin Mary, and whose death on the cross is humanity's salvation from original sin. In mystical Christianity Jesus is a great and enlightened teacher, healer, and prophet, the human son of Joseph and Mary,[2572] a mortal personification of the Christ, and the earthly representative of the ideal man/woman, the "pattern for the sons of men,"[2573] who "cometh down from heaven, and giveth life unto the world";[2574] that is, to show us, by example, how we too can attain Christhood.[2575] Esoterically Jesus is "the love of God made manifest to men."[2576]   Born a "son of man" (that is, a human being), His Transfiguration into a "son of God" (enlightened human being) after His baptism by John[2577] was so that "the men of earth might see the possibilities of man;"[2578] while as the Christ He "came to manifest the power of God."[2579]  In the Aquarian Gospel, Jesus says: "I come to manifest the Christ to men . . .[2580] what I am, all men will be . . .[2581] what I have done all men can do . . . for every man is God made flesh."[2582]  To those with "the mind of Christ," both the mainstream and the mystical definitions have the same meaning.[2583]  As the embodiment of the Christ, Jesus is Divine Law incarnate.  This is why I refer to him, in Greek, as *Iesous Trismegistus*: "Thrice-Greatest Jesus."  He was, after all—how ever else one might view him—the world's most enlightened teacher, most powerful healer, and most sagacious prophet.

**KINGDOM OF GOD:** Jesus' arcane term for what I call the "Realm of Divine Mind," a spiritual state of consciousness available to everyone right now, here on earth.[2584]  This concept is so potentially powerful, so religiously radical, and so politically explosive, that Jesus never openly and clearly defined the Kingdom of God, except secretly to His closest Disciples—the 120 initiates who gathered together after His death in the secret "upper room" (private temple) at Jerusalem.[2585]  As such, it was never taught to the masses, and these mysterious teachings were either never included in the books of the New Testament, or more likely (as I outline in Appendix B), they were removed and concealed by the Catholic Church in the first few centuries A.D.  Today we know the Kingdom of God as each individual's idea of bliss, harmony, the perfect life on the material plane.  In other words, it is a state of mind, one that is ruled over by the Indwelling Christ (Divine Law)[2586] and facilitated by the Father (Divine Mind).[2587]  Thus it exists *within* us, which is precisely what Jesus taught.[2588]  The celebrated spiritual teacher Paramahansa Yogananda called the Kingdom of God the "portable paradise." We enter the Kingdom by being "born again"[2589] and reviving and nurturing our "inner child," two of the primary prerequisites for entrance.[2590]  This, just one aspect of the authentic Gospel, which the Lord called "the Gospel of the Kingdom"[2591] (not "the Gospel of Jesus Christ"),[2592] was the true focus of His entire three-year ministry—as the Bible explicitly illustrates.[2593]  Tragically, the Master's teachings on the here-and-now Kingdom of God were long ago suppressed by the institutional Church, and in the process it was transformed into a mystical, unknowable, unattainable realm relegated strictly to the Afterlife.  The term Kingdom of God was also sometimes used by the ancients to refer to what we now call the Superconscious Mind, or what modern scientists call "Nature" or the "Unified Field."

**KINGDOM OF HEAVEN:** Same as Kingdom of God.

**LOGOS:** The Word, the active, creative, mental power of God in Man.[2594]  Also sometimes the thought of God.  In mainstream Christianity the term was appended to Jesus as the symbol of the ideal (that is, completely enlightened) man/woman.  As such, the Logos represents the Conscious Mind, the mental aspect of the Divine Mind.  In mystical Christianity the Logos or Word is thought.  Because our predominate thoughts always manifest as physical reality, we now have the inner meaning of the phrase: "the Word was made flesh."[2595]  Word of Faith theology holds that we can alter physical reality through dwelling on and repeating the Word (that is, sacred scripture).  This accords exactly with Jesus' teachings on the Law of Attraction (what we believe becomes real for us), as the Bible itself shows.[2596] Despite this fact, many mainstream Christian authorities continue to deny the power of the Logos in individual Man, much to the detriment of the laity.

**LOWER SELF:** Same as the Ego, known in the Bible as "Satan," "Lucifer," or the "Devil." It is part of our human nature and dies with our physical body. The Lower Self, false self, or Human Self is opposed by the Higher Self, real self, or Divine Self, also known as the Indwelling Christ.[2597] Paul referred to the Lower Self as the "outward man,"[2598] while the always mystical Apostle John called it "the beast that was, and is not, and yet is."[2599]

**LUCIFER:** Identical to Satan and the Devil. Like them, Lucifer too is the *Demon est Deus Inversus* (the "Devil is God Inverted"), as the etymology of his name reveals: the word Lucifer is Latin for "bringer of light," and derives from the bright "Morning Star," which is none other than the figure of the Roman goddess of love, Venus, who, as the brilliantly luminous planet of the same name, appears with the sun in the morning sky, and who was thus known to the ancients as the "bringer of light." The book of Isaiah corroborates this, identifying Lucifer as the "son of the morning,"[2600] while Paul complained that "Satan himself is transformed into an angel of light."[2601] In mystical Christianity the word Lucifer is an allusion to the fact that it is through our sins (mistakes) that we become enlightened (that is, "walk in the light").[2602] In other words, through overcoming the "temptations" of Satan/the Devil (the human Ego), we gradually raise our consciousness, bringing ourselves ever closer to realizing our oneness with the Divine Mind, or God—which is enlightenment. Furthermore, Jesus is "the light [enlightenment] of the world"[2603] and, as the greatest teacher of the Law of Love,[2604] is Himself love incarnate.[2605] Occultly speaking then, Jesus and the "bringer of light"—the love-goddess Venus, the bright "morning star"—are one and the same, as Jesus Himself states in the book of Revelation: "I am the root and the offspring of David, and the bright and morning star."[2606] Indeed, this was part of Jesus' great mission here on earth: to reinvest religion with the Feminine Principle (love), which had been lost over time due to the patriarchal intellectualization of spirituality.[2607] See Satan and the Devil.

**MASS MIND:** The everyday thoughts, concepts, and beliefs of society, of the human race, and so is sometimes also called "race mind." Some of these beliefs are positive (e.g., "the best things in life are free"), but most are negative (e.g., "making money is difficult"), and thus have a destructive impact on the spiritual evolution of humanity.

**OUTWARD MAN:** One of Paul's terms for the Lower Self.[2608]

**PARACLETE:** Same as Comforter.

**RACE MIND:** Same as Mass Mind.

**RIGHTEOUSNESS:** Because the Law of Attraction is scientifically precise, there is a right and a wrong way of thinking. Righteousness is right-thinking.[2609]

**SATAN:** The evil god of Judeo-Christian mythology, Satan is, along with the Devil and Lucifer, an arcane symbol of the atheistic, ever self-serving human Ego, which is why Paul calls him "the god of this [earthly] world."[2610] Satan's name and figure were borrowed from the ancient Egyptian serpent-god Sata, an underworld expression of the Egyptian father-god Ra, whose Jewish equivalent was the father-god Yahweh, in English, Jehovah (the Father, the Lord, God). Indeed, to this day most mystery schools view God and Satan not as two separate, opposing beings, but rather as two sides of the same coin, one known as the *Demon est Deus Inversus*, Latin for the "Devil is God Inverted." Thus Mormons believe that Satan and Jesus (God) are brothers,[2611] while Kabbalists maintain that the true name of Satan is (numerologically speaking) God's name in reverse. Likewise, in the book of Isaiah, God says: "I form the light, and create darkness: I make peace, and create evil: I the Lord do all these things."[2612] According to ancient Law of Attraction doctrine, God is Divine Mind, individualized in each one of us as our Superconscious, Conscious, and Subconscious Minds (our inner "Holy Trinity").[2613] The most powerful force in the Universe, Divine Mind is equally capable of creating both good and evil, as we have all repeatedly proven to ourselves.[2614] Only when we learn to think positive thoughts can we use Divine Mind constructively, for good (God), instead of destructively, for evil (Devil). Jesus taught that Satan, the evil aspect of God or Divine Mind, is an illusion, and so should be ignored and denied. For if we respond to it, we become one with it. By the Law of Attraction, reacting to something only attracts more of it. Thus the Master said: "Resist not evil."[2615] See the Devil and Lucifer.

**SIN:** From the Old English archer's word, *synne*, meaning "to miss the mark [bull's-eye]." In other words, originally a sin was a "mistake," an error against the Spirit,"[2616] an unspiritual thought, word, or deed, which, as Jesus taught, could be canceled by simply asking God for forgiveness;[2617] that is, by renewing one's faith in God.[2618] Jesus indeed spent little time discussing the cause and nature of sin,[2619] but focused almost exclusively on the forgiveness of sin, most poignantly illustrated in the wonderful parable of the Prodigal Son.[2620] Unfortunately, the true meaning of the word sin was recast by the early Catholic Church, in part, into the regrettable manmade concept of "original sin," which appears nowhere in the Bible, and which was, in fact, repudiated by Paul.[2621]

**SON OF GOD:** In traditional Christianity Jesus was the Son of God from birth. In mystical Christianity, however, He adopted this title only *after* His baptism in the Holy Spirit. Now enlightened, He became a true Son of God. As noted in the next entry, the historical Jesus never referred to Himself as the "Son of God."[2622] This phrase then must have been appended to His biblical biography by the Ecclesia after His death. But since we are all Sons of God, this fact is not spiritually important (though it is theologically important). Indeed, the Bible tells us that whoever "receives Jesus," whoever is "led by the spirit of God," becomes and is to be called a "Son of God," just as Jesus was,[2623] for we are all born with the "Son in me," as Paul put it.[2624] Thus, Jesus told Mary that His Father was her Father, and that His God was her God.[2625] Esoterically, the Son of God is our Higher Self, the Indwelling Christ,[2626] the perfected soul of each individual. The outer meaning of Son of God is "Child of God"; the inner meaning is "One with God." While the word "Son" is used in institutional Christianity, in the mystery religions, including the occult branches of Paganism, Christianity, and Judaism, it is spelled "Sun." Hence, in the book of Malachi, Jesus is referred to as the "Sun of Righteousness";[2627] His birthday was placed on December 25, the Winter Solstice birthday of the Pagan sun- and savior-gods Mithras, Adonis, and Sol; the Christian Sabbath was moved from Saturn's Day (Saturday) to Sun's Day (Sunday);[2628] and early mystical Christians artistically portrayed the Lord as a literal sun-god, identical to the Greek solar-deity

Helios. In my book *Christmas Before Christianity: How the Birthday of the "Sun" Became the Birthday of the "Son,"* I detail the development of the ecclesiastical Christian concept of the son-god from out of the pre-Christian Pagan idea of the sun-god.

**SON OF MAN:** An ancient everyday Aramaic expression, also written the "son of adam,"[2629] meaning a mortal human: "man" in Greek is *anthropos*, "man" in Hebrew is *adam*. As is clear from the Gospel of Q (the earliest known record of Jesus' teachings, and mentioned by both Bishop Papias of Hierapolis[2630] and Paul),[2631] the historical Jesus never once used the phrase "Son of God" in regard to Himself.[2632] Only the "Son of Man," that is, the "son of a man."[2633] This was due to the fact that He wanted to stress the divinity of *all* human beings, not just Himself—for we all possess the Universal Inner Christ,[2634] the Indwelling Christ (Divine Law).[2635] According to objective scholarly studies of the development of the New Testament and the Church, it seems clear that during the Paganization and apotheosization process of Jesus (late 1ˢᵗ Century A.D. to the 5ᵗʰ Century), the Church gave Him the title "Son of God" in order to deemphasize His humanity and emphasize His divinity. Indeed, He was not formally declared a Savior-God until the year 325, at the Council of Nicaea. Up until then, His mostly Jewish followers considered Him nothing more than a great teacher, healer, and prophet, just as Jews do to this very day. Evidence for the Paganization of Jesus is abundant. Not only are all references to Jesus as the "Son of God" completely absent from the Gospel of Q, but we have canonical proof as well. Acts 8:37 (in which Jesus is referred to as the "Son of God"), for example, is an obvious interpolation, since it is not found in the earliest known New Testament texts (such as the Codex Sinaiticus). In mystical Christianity the "Son of Man" is exemplified in the pre-baptized Jesus, who had not yet realized His own divinity, that is, His oneness with God (Divine Mind), until the Holy Spirit descended on Him in the form of a dove (enlightenment). Mystically, the Son of Man is the Conscious Mind, the unperfected soul. Thus we are all "Sons of Man" until we understand and accept our oneness with the Universal Divine Mind, after which we become "Sons of God."[2636] The outer meaning of Son of Man is "Child of Humanity," that is, one born of mortal parents, as the Bible clearly states Jesus was.[2637] The inner meaning then is "a mortal human being." In the Gnostic Christian Gospel of Mary (Magdalene), Jesus tells the Apostles that "the Son of Man is inside of you. Those who earnestly seek oneness with him shall locate him."[2638] In other words, in order to use the Law of Attraction properly, we must seek to have a "pure" Conscious Mind.

**SUBCONSCIOUS MIND:** I call the Subconscious Mind "the Communicator." It is a symbol of love, the soul, and all that is spiritual. The Subconscious Mind (female) receives thoughts and ideas from the Conscious Mind (male), which it communicates to the Superconscious Mind (androgynous) as beliefs. In patriarchal religions the Subconscious is identical to the "Holy Spirit." In matriarchal religions it is identical to the "moon." The Subconscious Mind never tires, never sleeps, and never dies. It is the spiritual aspect of our mental system, passing with us into the World Beyond after so-called "death." While we are here on earth, it acts as our obedient personal assistant and attendant, always ready to help turn our dominant thoughts and beliefs into physical reality. Thus, it is also occultly known as "the Servant," unquestioningly operating under the auspices of "the Master," the Conscious Mind (personified in Jesus).[2639] The Subconscious not only regulates many of our body's involuntary functions and cellular processes (such as our circulation, digestion, breathing, and immune system), but it also records and stores all of our thoughts, beliefs, experiences, and memories. Proof of the Subconscious Mind's tremendous spiritual and physical powers can be seen in, for example, the commonplace healing of cuts, burns, and broken bones, the unassisted "miraculous" curing of nearly every known disease, the placebo effect, and hypnosis. Additional evidence comes from the so-called "occult arts," such as divination, telepathy, clairaudience, levitation, intuition, remote viewing, clairvoyance, retrocognition, clairsentience, bilocation, automatic writing, and channeling, all which take place in and through the Subconscious Mind. It is also via the Subconscious that we experience night "dreams," during which time our souls temporarily return to the world of Spirit to rest and reenergize themselves. This is only possible because the Subconscious is a spiritual instrument that links the earthly to the heavenly. Learning how to work with the Law of Attraction and the Subconscious Mind to establish health, wealth, and happiness in our lives is to truly possess one of the Keys to the Kingdom of Heaven.[2640] Correlates with the right side of the brain, which operates the left (female) side of the body. Keywords: emotional, random, intuitive, subjective, feminine, nighttime, belief, heavenly, expression, symbols, spirituality.

**SUN:** Mystically, the same as Christ: revealed knowledge of Divine Law. The sun is a common solar symbol in ancient Pagan and Christian literature and art, one representing enlightenment, the lucent Higher Self, the incandescent Divine Self, the luminescent Indwelling Christ of each individual.[2641] A modern remnant of the early Christian connection between the *Son* of God and the *Sun* of God is found in the German word for the sun: *sonne*, in English "son." (The German word for son is *sohn*.) The book of Malachi refers to Jesus as the "Sun of Righteousness,"[2642] John says "his countenance was as the sun,"[2643] while Jesus referred to Himself as "the Light of the world."[2644] Speaking as the Christ Within, He describes His mission this way: "I am come a light [enlightenment] into the world, that whosoever believeth on me should not abide in darkness [spiritual ignorance]."[2645] Thus, all those who believe in Him, that is, who recognize the Indwelling Christ, become "children of light."[2646] This is why ancient Christian writers associated Jesus with the astrological star-sign Leo the Lion, ruled by the sun;[2647] early Christian artists portrayed Jesus as the Greek solar-god Helios, riding across the sky each day in his fiery chariot; the Lord's birthday was assigned to the birthday of the Roman sun-god Mithras on December 25; the Christian Sabbath was changed from Saturday (Saturn's Day) to Sunday (the Sun's Day);[2648] the Church gave Jesus the Pagan title *Sol Justitiae*, the "Just Sun"; the Twelve Apostles were identified with the twelve astrological star-signs (orbiting Jesus "the Sun"); Jesus' mother, the Virgin Mary, was portrayed as being "clothed with the sun . . . and upon her head a crown of twelve stars";[2649] and under Constantine the Great, 4th-Century Christians famously worshiped Jesus as the Roman solar-deity *Sol Invictus*, the "Unconquered Sun." Revealingly, while Matthew identifies Jesus' paternal grandfather as Jacob,[2650] Luke says his name was Heli,[2651] a variation of the name Helios—yet another mystical allusion to Jesus' association with the sun, the ever effulgent Indwelling Christ.[2652] See Son of God.

**SUN OF RIGHTEOUSNESS:** Malachi's name for the Indwelling Christ.[2653] See also Sun and Son of God.

**SUPERCONSCIOUS MIND:** I call the Superconscious Mind "the Creator." It is the

Source, the Divine One, the Ultimate Mind, and is related to the mental plane and all-encompassing universal power. It receives beliefs (strong predominant thoughts) from the Subconscious Mind, which it then manifests as physical reality. In patriarchal religions the Superconscious Mind is the "Father" or "God." In matriarchal religions it is the "Mother" or "Goddess." In mystical religions it is the "I AM,"[2654] "Divine Mind," the "Akashic Record," and the "Book of Life."[2655] In science it is the "Unified Field," "Nature," or the "laws of physics." Along with the Conscious Mind (the Son) and the Subconscious Mind (the Holy Spirit), the Superconscious Mind (the Father) forms our Inner Holy Trinity.[2656] Keywords: androgynous, light, perfection, omnipresent, omnipotent, omniscient, omniactive, manifestation, materialization, universal, infinite, eternal.

**THEALOGY:** From the Greek word *thea* ("goddess") and the Latin word *logia* ("sayings"), thus the "study of Goddess," or more generally the study of female-based religions and spiritual practices.

**THEOLOGY:** From the Greek word *theo* ("god") and the Latin word *logia* ("sayings"), thus the "study of God," or more generally the study of male-based religions and spiritual practices.

**THIRD EYE:** See Eyes.

**THIRD EAR:** See Ears.

**UNRIGHTEOUSNESS:** Because the Law of Attraction is scientifically precise, there is a right and a wrong way of thinking. Unrighteousness ("sin") is wrong-thinking.[2657]

**WORD, THE:** Same as Logos.

**YAHWEH:** Same as God. The name Yahweh (or without vowels, YHWH or JHVH) is a Hebrew word whose mystical meaning is the "Immortal Masculine and Feminine Principles." Thus, from an arcane viewpoint God is an androgyne made up of both male and female energies. This corresponds loosely with the multi-god "Elohim" of the Old Testament (the godly "us" of Genesis),[2658] the seven (some say twelve) deities who make up the Jewish godhead, and who "created man in his own image, in the image of God created he him; *male and female created he them.*"[2659] The English name for Yahweh is Jehovah, fabricated from combining a, o, a, the vowels of a Pagan god-name (Adonai, that is Adon or Adonis), and the sacred Tetragrammaton, JHVH, thus giving JaHoVaH. King James' scribes routinely translated the Tetragrammaton as "Lord,"[2660] though "Jehovah" is used four times in the Old Testament.[2661] See God and Jehovah.

*"Fear Not. Believe Only. For all things are possible to him that believeth."*[2662]

*Jesus*

# APPENDIX A
Past Well-known Teachers &
Practitioners of the Law of Attraction

Abraham
Akhoy Kumar Mozumdar
Albert Einstein
Aldous Huxley
Alethea Brooks Small
Alexander Graham Bell
Alfred G. Moses
Alfred North Whitehead
Alfred Tennyson
Amos Bronson Alcott
Andrew Carnegie
Anna Kingsford
Annie Besant
Annie Rix Militz
Arthur Schopenhauer
Audrey Hepburn
Augustine "Og" Mandino II
Baruch Spinoza
Beatrice of Nazareth
Benjamin Disraeli
Buddha
Carl Jung
Charles Brodie Patterson
Charles F. Haanel
Charles Fillmore
Christian D. Larson
Christian Nestell Bovee
Clara Beranger
Comte de Saint Germaine
Confucius
Dag Hammarskjöld
Dale Carnegie
Dante
Dorothea Brande
Edgar Cayce
Edward Walker
Elizabeth Towne
Ella Wheeler Wilcox
Emanuel Swedenborg
Emma Curtis Hopkins
Emmet Fox
Ernest Holmes
Fannie Brooks James
Fenwicke Holmes
Florence Scovel Shinn
Francis Bacon
Francis Larimer Warner
Frank Bruce Robinson
Frank Channing Haddock
Gandhi
Genevieve Behrend
George Augustus Henry Sala
George Burns
George Wharton James
Georg W. Friedrich Hegel
Giordano Bruno

Harriet Emilie Cady
Helen Wilmans
Henry David Thoreau
Henry Drummond
Henry Ford
Henry Thomas Hamblin
Henry Ward Beecher
Henry Wood
Horatio Bonar
Horatio Dresser
Ignatius of Loyola
Isaac Newton
James Allen
James Dillet Freeman
Jerry Hicks
Jesus
Jiddu Krishnamurti
Joan of Arc
Joel S. Goldsmith
Johann Heinrich Pestalozzi
Johann Wolfgang von Goethe
John Herman Randall Jr.
John Milton
Joseph Murphy
Julian of Norwich
Kate Atkinson Boehme
Kenneth G. Mills
Krishna
Lao Tzu
Leonardo da Vinci
Lilian Whiting
Ludwig van Beethoven
Luther Burbank
Malinda Cramer
Marcus Aurelius
Margery Kempe
Marguerite Porete
Mary Baker Eddy
Masaharu Taniguchi
Max Freedom Long
Meher Baba
Meister Eckhart
Mildred Mann
Morris Lichtenstein
Moses
Mother Teresa
Myrtle Fillmore
Napoleon Hill
Neville Goddard
Nona Lovell Brooks
Norman Vincent Peale
Orison Swett Marden
Paracelsus
Paramahansa Yogananda
Pascal
Perry Joseph Green

Phineas Park Quimby
Pierre Teilhard de Chardin
Plato
Plotinus
Pope John Paul II
Pope Urban
Prentice Mulford
Pythagoras
R. Buckminster Fuller
Ralph Waldo Emerson
Ralph Waldo Trine
Raymond Charles Barker
René Descartes
Richard Maurice Bucke
Robert Browning
Robert Collier
Rumi
Russell Conwell
Saint Augustine
Saint Bernadette
Saint Catherine of Sienna
Saint Clelia Barbieri
Saint Francis of Assisi
Saint Gemma Galgani
Saint Hildegard of Bingen
Saint John
Saint Joseph of Cupertino
Saint Padre Pio of Pietrelcina
Saint Paul of Tarsus
Saint Teresa of Avila
Saint Vincent Ferrer
Samuel Smiles
Socrates
Sri Mahavatar Babaji
Stuart Grayson
Swami Narayanananda
Swami Sri Yukteswar
Thaddeus Golas
Therese Neumann
The Twelve Apostles
Thomas Edison
Thomas Troward
Uell Stanley Andersen
Victor Hugo
Wallace D. Wattles
Walter Clemow Lanyon
Walt Whitman
Warren Felt Evans
William Blake
William Clement Stone
William Ellery Channing
William James
William Temple Hornaday
William Walker Atkinson
Winston Churchill
Zoroaster

# THE CHRISTIAN TETRAMORPH
The Four Evangelists as Pagan Astrological Sun-Signs

In the late 2ⁿᵈ Century the Church Father Irenaeus assigned personal names to four anonymous Jewish-Christian books that he had selected for placement in the New Testament. These names, "John," "Mark," "Matthew," and "Luke" were mystically associated with the Cherubim, the "four living creatures" of the book of Ezekiel, which the Old Testament prophet in turn borrowed from the Pagans' four Compass-Gods: Aquila (later to become Scorpio), Leo, Aquarius, and Taurus—known collectively to the ancient Egyptians as the "Fathers." In Pagan astrology these equate with the four basic elements of Nature, as spelled out in the Hebrew of mystical Judaism: *Iammin*, "water"; *Nour*, "fire"; *Rouach*, "air"; and *Iebeschah*, "earth." The first letter of each Hebrew word spells INRI, an acronym, according to mainstream Christianity, representing the Latin: *Iesus Nazarenus, Rex Iudaeorum* ("Jesus of Nazareth, King of the Jews"), the sign on Jesus' cross. Mystically speaking, however, in my opinion INRI is an acronym for the Latin: *In Nobis Regnat Iesus* ("Within Us Jesus Reigns"). These four fixed astrological sun-signs, which form the Galactic Cross in the natal horoscope, can still be seen in the iconography of ancient Christian structures all over Europe, such as France's famous Chartres Cathedral. This same Paganization process was used by the orthodox Church to apotheosize the "Son of Man" (the title Jesus used for Himself), transforming Him, after His death, into the "Son of God." Though the overt connection between Paganism and Christianity has long been known to Church authorities, it, along with Jesus' secret teachings on the Law of Attraction, has been skillfully hidden from the laity for nearly 2,000 years.

MATTHEW AS AQUARIUS
THE WATERMAN (AIR/NORTH)

MARK AS LEO
THE LION (FIRE/SOUTH)

LUKE AS TAURUS
THE BULL (EARTH/EAST)

JOHN AS AQUILA
THE EAGLE (WATER/WEST)

(From the author's book: *Christmas Before Christianity*)

# APPENDIX B

How the Church Lost Jesus'
Teachings on the Law of Attraction

𝕴𝖔𝖈𝖍𝖑𝖆𝖎𝖓𝖓 𝕾𝖊𝖆𝖇𝖗𝖔𝖔𝖐

Jesus preached what He referred to as the *Gospel of the Kingdom*.[2663] Modern Christians, however, preach what they call the *Gospel of Jesus Christ*.[2664] Why? In the earliest records of Jesus' sayings, He refers to Himself only as the *Son of Man*.[2665] Modern Christians, however, call Him the *Son of God*.[2666] What happened to Jesus' original teachings and title? Why the dramatic religion-altering changeover after the Lord's death? In this essay I will explore these topics and their connection to the simultaneous disappearance of the Master's teachings on the Law of Attraction.

## THE RISE OF THE ORTHODOX CHURCH

**A**FTER ROMAN EMPEROR CONSTANTINE THE Great's pseudo conversion to Christianity in the 4th Century, the Catholic Church (the Ecclesia) became the official state religion, imbuing it with nearly unlimited theocratic power. In an effort to secure political and religious control across the Empire, one of the first things the Church did with its newfound authority was to label itself "orthodox" and all other branches of Christianity "heterodox."

Over the following centuries it mercilessly stamped out any religious ideas that it did not agree with, pronouncing them "heretical." As I will show, in the process, the books that would become the New Testament were heavily revised, edited, and redacted, with the end result that today these twenty-seven books contain countless alterations, modifications, additions, subtractions, intercalations, emendations, and interpolations, as well as so-called "restorations" and "improvements," not found in the earliest known biblical manuscripts.

NEW TESTAMENT TAMPERING

Two of the latter, the Codex Sinaiticus (written around A.D. 340) and the Codex Vaticanus (written about the same time), confirm this, revealing numerous intentionally edited passages. The Codex Sinaiticus alone, which contains the oldest complete copy of the New Testament, bears some 23,000 scholia, textual notes, and modifications, penned by early Catholic authorities who sought to "correct" various biblical passages.

According to the Church, the changes resulting from these were either simply the products of dittography (the accidental duplication of letters) or haplography (the accidental omission of similar letters). However, as we are about to see, these modifications were far from "accidental." In fact, most were quite intentional. The question is why?

The real motivation behind all of this scriptural doctoring was both *theological* (the desire to rid Jesus of His all too human qualities,[2667] while transforming Him from a master teacher, healer, and prophet, into a literal messianic political god),[2668] and *doctrinal* (the need to biblically establish so-called "Apostolic Succession"). In the latter case, this essentially anti-Gnostic doctrine states that there is a "chain" of Church authority that can be traced from Jesus, Peter, and the other Apostles,[2669] in a continual line up to the present pope.

Evidence of priestly New Testament tampering is ubiquitous and overt. To start with, some ancient sacred texts, such as the Book of Enoch (cited by Jesus' brother Jude),[2670] were so lethal to the Ecclesia's agenda (to promote a divine Jesus and institute apostolic authority), that they were never even allowed into that infamous group of banned intertestamental works[2671] known as the Apocrypha.[2672]

Nonetheless, many of those that originally made it past this critical barrier and into the biblical canon were later purposefully removed by orthodox priests. Texts revealing that many of the so-called "words and ideas of Jesus" were not original to Him, but came from posthumous works, for example, had to be expunged, for they themselves were evidence of priestly interference.

Two of these, the Epistle of Barnabas (written circa A.D. 70 to 117) and the Shepherd of Hermas (written circa A.D. 150), were excised from the original New Testament sometime after the 4th Century. How do we know this? Because they were included in the New Testament of the Codex Sinaiticus, but are missing from today's Bibles. This brazen removal was done despite the fact that both Barnabas and Hermas were accepted as canonical documents by many of the early Church Fathers, including Clement of Alexandria, Origen, and Irenaeus.

## REARRANGING THE OLD TESTAMENT

The Old Testament did not remain unscathed either. In an effort to move the focus away from the Lord's human nature and onto His divine nature, its ancient pre-Christian prophecies concerning the coming Messiah, the Son of God, had to be more directly tied to the New Testament.

This was done by reordering a number of books so that the Old Testament ended not with Job (as in the 4th-Century Codex Sinaiticus), but with Malachi (the eighth from the last book in the Codex Sinaiticus), who, according to newly issued Catholic doctrine, predicted the coming of John the Baptist as the reincarnated "Elijah"[2673] and Jesus as the "Sun of Righteousness."[2674]

## SCRIBAL EDITING & SCRIPTURE TWISTING

Rearranging the order of the Bible's books, and even the deletion of entire books that revealed too much of the natural Jesus and not enough of the supernatural Jesus, was only the beginning, however.[2675]

To further highlight the Lord's celestial character, scribal priests not only added what I call "divinity passages" that did not exist in the original Bible (such as Acts 8:37 and 1 John 5:7, both which are absent from the Codex Sinaiticus),[2676] they also emended and retranslated many of the New Testament writers' authentic statements, striking out what I call "humanity passages."

For example, in the book of Acts the original Greek word *pais*, meaning "servant," was replaced with the Greek words *huios* ("son") or *paidion* ("child"). In this way Jesus went from what Luke had originally called a human "servant of God," to what the Church renamed the divine "Son of God"[2677] or "child of God."[2678]

## THE APOSTLES EMPHASIZED JESUS' HUMANITY

In contrast to the orthodox Church, Paul, who understood that the Christ was not only in Jesus,[2679] but in all men and women,[2680] never hesitated to focus on the human Jesus, stating that He

> "took upon him the form of a servant, and was *made in the likeness of men*; and being found in fashion *as a man*, he humbled himself, and became obedient unto death, even the death of the cross."[2681]

In his letter to his followers at Rome, Paul wrote:

> "For what the law could not do, in that it was weak through the flesh, *God sending his own Son in the likeness of sinful flesh*, and for sin, condemned sin in the flesh."[2682]

In his letter to the Corinthians, Paul calls Jesus "the last Adam,"[2683] another overt reference to Jesus' humanity: *adam* is Hebrew for "man," or more precisely, a "human being."[2684]

Just as the Hebraist, the writer of the book of Hebrews, repeatedly refers to Jesus as "this man,"[2685] Mark—who "chose" to leave out the Master's miraculous nativity story and resurrection appearances—also emphasized Jesus' humanity, depicting Him as a repentant human sinner who became the Son of God only *after* His baptism by John,[2686] or perhaps *after* His resurrection,[2687] after which He was adopted by God—a "problem" (known as Adoptionism) that was later "corrected" by unknown scribal hands in the books of Matthew,[2688] Luke,[2689] and John (who avoids the issue by eliminating Jesus' baptism altogether).[2690]

Luke shows Jesus openly calling himself the "Son of Man" (a common Aramaic term for a mortal human being)[2691] before the Jewish authorities, while simultaneously spurning the title "Son of God."[2692] Mark even has Jesus denying that He descends from David,[2693] contravening one of the Old Testament requirements for Messiahship.[2694] This "difficulty" too was later remedied in other New Testament books, with mixed, confusing, contradictory, and often irreconcilable results.[2695]

The Ecclesia, of course, wanting to present Jesus purely as a god, or as God the Father Himself, fought back against Adoptionism. Church officials, like the 3rd-Century Antioch Bishop Paul of Samosata, who held that Jesus was a man who later became God after He was "instilled" with the Indwelling Christ,[2696] were summarily deposed or even excommunicated.[2697]

Yet, what is revealing is that Adoptionism (also known as Dynamic Monarchianism) was the doctrine embraced by Jesus' earliest followers, not its opposite, Tritheism, the tenet developed and held much later by the orthodox Church.[2698] Hence, the Lucan passage found in current Bibles, "Thou art my beloved Son; in thee I am well pleased,"[2699] is missing from a number of ancient New Testament manuscripts, such as the Codex Bezae (written perhaps about the year 400). In its place we find this scripture: "Thou art my Son; today I have begotten thee,"[2700] confirming the original Adoptionist stance of Jesus' first followers who, according to the Bible, viewed the Lord as "a man," albeit a great one, but still "a man."[2701]

If this evidence is not convincing enough, we need only look to Jesus, who, as mentioned, often referred to Himself as the "Son of Adam," or in modern English, the "Son of Man" (from the Greek *anthropos*, "man," a human being).[2702] On at least one occasion he very straightforwardly referred to Himself simply as "a man."[2703]

Was this the only time Jesus used this phrase? It is highly doubtful. What happened to the other occurrences then? Only the discovery of a *complete* copy of the *original* New Testament will reveal the answer.

## "ECCLESIASTICAL NECESSITY" & "CANONICAL CONSENSUS"
Though the Catholic Church is responsible for what I call the Great Bible Purging that peaked during the 4th-Century reign of the Roman Empire's "first Christian emperor," the sun-worshiping Constantine, this was not the only Christian institution to engage in biblical meddling. Later, in 1881, the Protestants took their own flagrant liberties with the Good Book, issuing the Revised (English) New Testament, with some 6,000 textural modifications, at least 25 percent which altered the meaning of those scriptures involved.

Then, in 1885, Protestants went on to remove fourteen important holy texts (today known as the "Apocrypha") from the King James Version that did not meet with their approval. This despite the fact that Jesus Himself quotes a number of these "forbidden" works, and therefore endorsed them![2704]

It is probable that the *original* primitive Christian "Bible" contained between 500 and 600 books. Today, however, the King James Version contains a mere sixty-six: thirty-nine in the Old Testament, twenty-seven in the New Testament. This means that nearly 90 percent of the first "Bible" (that is, those sacred texts that were sanctioned and read by early Christians) has been censored and discarded, with much of the remaining 10 percent so diluted through redaction, interpolation, and emendation that it would be virtually unrecognizable to Jesus.

The Church's reasoning behind its blatant manipulation of sacred scripture, as well as its invention of thousands of arbitrary rules, regulations, rituals, superstitions, and doctrines that were all unknown to Jesus (and which He would never have condoned), has always been based on what it terms "ecclesiastical necessity," but which I maintain should more correctly be called "political necessity." Either way, much has been lost due to "canonical consensus," in essence a centuries-long program of biblical literary genocide, and we are all the poorer for it.

## WHAT WAS LOST?
The extent of Jesus' missing doctrines will never be fully known, but it is clear that much if not most of what He said and taught is absent from the Bible: over two dozen surviving canonical scriptures themselves tell us so.[2705] Not even Jesus' post-resurrection teachings are recorded in the New Testament. Only that He spoke of "things pertaining to the kingdom of God."[2706]

How can this be? How can such an important corpus of information simply be missing? Was there something about Jesus' pre-ascension teachings that was not as significant to the four Gospelers as His pre-crucifixion ones? And where are the Master's "lost years," the all important eighteen missing years of His life between the ages of twelve and thirty?[2707]

There can only be one answer to these questions: it is apparent that there was something the early orthodox Church Fathers truly did not like about Jesus' teachings, in particular those concerning the "kingdom"![2708]

## BONFIRES OF RELIGIOUS SUPPRESSION

As part of the Catholic Church's often violent and bloody expurgation of these "unorthodox" tenets, countless Christian sects, such as the Nicolaitans,[2709] were censured, their members persecuted and scattered, their leaders ruthlessly tortured and slaughtered, and their holy books, including hundreds of rare Gospels, burned, all pitilessly excoriated by orthodox heresiologists. With the suppression of these early Christians, among them the Gnostics[2710] (from the Greek word *gnosis*, that is, self "knowledge"),[2711] we lost even more of Jesus' authentic words and deeds—a fact which even the Apostle John hints at.[2712]

We will note that the Catholic Church continued to persecute, arrest, torture, and kill members of Christian sects that it considered "heretical" right into the Medieval period. Such groups included the noble and courageous Knights Templar (officially "dissolved" by Pope Clement V in 1312 for "heresy"), who managed to survive endless pogroms, then went underground, taking their knowledge of Jesus' actual words with them.[2713]

What were these teachings, and why were they so aggressively targeted by the orthodox priesthood?

## THE SECRET SAYINGS OF JESUS

What angered the Church were Jesus' "secret sayings," that is, His esoteric doctrines. In the mystical Christian tradition this body of inner teachings is called "the Gospel of the Kingdom,"[2714] or more fully, "the Gospel of the Kingdom of God,"[2715] a spiritual belief system that includes the Lord's tenets concerning the Indwelling Christ or God-Self, the power of Divine Thought, and the Law of Attraction, all which He spent His last few years fervently preaching across the Near East.[2716] The ancient Ecclesia did its best to suppress these ideas, or simply ignore them, strategies still employed by both Catholic and Protestant authorities to this very day. Fortunately for us, they have been only partially successful.[2717]

From the early Church's point of view, this politically based censorship is understandable: how could orthodox Christian authorities compete with Jesus' teaching that each one of us is a manifestation of God—a literal god in our own right, as He put it[2718]—with the supernatural ability to shape and control our own daily lives, even our own destinies?[2719]

To counter this "dissentient doctrine," the Church began deemphasizing Jesus' humanity as the ordinary mortal "son of Joseph,"[2720] while emphasizing His divinity as the "Only Begotten Son of God."[2721] As we are about to see, this was just the beginning of a long and nefarious deification process, cleverly copied by the Church from the Pagans' millennia-old tradition of apotheosization: giving human leaders—such as kings, queens, emperors, and emporesses—divine status by elevating them to the level of gods and goddesses.

EARLY CHRISTIAN WRITINGS LOST & FOUND

Much to the benefit of Christians everywhere, fragments and even entire texts of ancient Jewish, Jewish Christian, and Gnostic Christian writings, such as the Dead Sea Scrolls and the Nag Hammadi Library, have been found recently, allowing us to piece back together many of Jesus' original teachings concerning the Law of Attraction, as well as many other fascinating spiritual mysteries.[2722] One of the hundreds of these texts, the Book of Thomas the Contender, begins with this enigmatic statement:

> "The secret words that Jesus related to His brother Judas Thomas
> . . ."[2723]

The celebrated Gnostic Christian Gospel of Thomas, also begins with a cryptic comment:

> "These are the esoteric sayings which Jesus taught, and which His brother Didymos Judas Thomas chronicled. And He [Jesus] said, 'Whoever figures out the true meaning of these hidden sayings will never experience death.'"[2724]

These are provocative words indeed, particularly because, having been written as early as the year A.D. 50 (or even earlier), Thomas is older than the four canonical Gospels. It is easy to see then why Thomas' Gospel was one of the first "heterodoxical" books to be thrown into the fire.

Even more propitious for us, ecclesiastical authorities failed to completely "cleanse" the Bible of Jesus' macarisms; that is, His diamond-like aphoristic observations or "secret sayings"; and in fact, like the Old Testament, the New Testament still contains dozens of Law of Attraction statements, most of them straight from the mouth of the Lord Himself—as this book, *Jesus and the Law of Attraction*, amply attests.

CONCEALING BOTH THE HUMAN JESUS & DIVINE MAN

There is one great tragedy in all of this, however. As mentioned, mainstream Christianity continues to disregard or even hide these amazing teachings, the latter method often employed through "modern" translations of the Bible that purposefully obliterate the true meaning of Jesus' original words—another attempt to try and prevent His "divinity" from being scrutinized and questioned.[2725]

Even the mere discussion of pre-Christian Jewish sects whose teachings were similar to those of Jesus has been discouraged, and early on the names of these groups were expunged by the Church from texts under consideration for inclusion in the New Testament canon. One of these sects was the sun-worshiping Essenes (the "Saints"), whose mysterious leader, the "Teacher of Righteousness," shares numerous commonalities with Jesus.[2726] As a result, one of the 1st Century's most important, best known, and most prevalent Jewish communities (one that had a demonstrable influence on the Lord and His teachings), is not mentioned anywhere in either the Old Testament or the New Testament.[2727]

From the very beginning, this conspicuous fact alone has caused every objective Bible scholar to question the orthodox doctrine of the "inerrancy" and "infallibility" of biblical scripture. For Josephus named the Essenes one of the three primary Jewish sects of that period (the other two were the Pharisees and the Sadducees). If their name was left out or even removed from the Bible's original texts, what else might have been blacklisted, expurgated, and bowdlerized?[2728]

Moreover, why the nearly wholesale disregard for and overt hostility toward the Master's original sayings?

It is for the very same reason the early Catholic Church tried so diligently to destroy them: Jesus' simple spiritual teachings about our oneness with both the Christ and God were deemed "dangerous" because they threaten and undermine the Church's complex manmade religious tenets, along with her apostolic authority, political power, and missionary program.

Thus, Jesus' immortal declaration, "the kingdom of God is within you," was retranslated as "the kingdom of God is among you," or even less accurate and more misleading, "the reign of God is already in your midst."[2729] Such linguistic subterfuge is just another tragic result of "ecclesiastical necessity," intentionally invented to suppress the Lord's true teachings on the Indwelling Christ,[2730] the Kingdom Within[2731] (or what He called "the Gospel of the Kingdom"),[2732] and the Law of Attraction.[2733]

## CENSORING JESUS IN ANCIENT & MODERN TIMES

Of this villainous backroom effort to conceal both the human Jesus and divine Man, Ralph Waldo Emerson bitterly noted:

> ". . . what a distortion did his doctrine and memory suffer in the same, in the next, and the following ages."

Yes, the religiously insincere, whose "minds are blinded"[2734] by the god of this world (that is, "Satan," the human Ego),[2735] have thoroughly "corrupted the word of God"[2736] through their lingual treachery, irresponsible behavior, sacrilegious meddling, and "violence to the Law."[2737] In the process, they have violated the Father's own injunction against biblical tampering[2738]—and the apathetic, unenlightened, and spiritually lazy in our churches have been paying the price ever since.[2739]

How ironic that during His life, Jesus' secret teachings were suppressed because they opposed traditional Judaism.[2740] Yet 2,000 years later they are still being suppressed, now because they oppose traditional Christianity, the very faith that took its name from him!

## THE TRUTH HAS BEEN KEPT FROM THE CHRISTIAN LAITY

Since nearly all mainstream religious teachers are either ignorant of these "hidden" Jesuine teachings, or are aware of them but have simply refused to publicly acknowledge them, it is little wonder that the arcanum of Christ's sacred doctrines regarding the Law of Attraction are unfamiliar to much of the Christian laity. The matter is made worse by many Church members themselves, a large percentage which do not actually read and study the Bible on their own, but instead merely accept (and parrot) what they hear from the pulpit each Sunday.

Even less are aware of how Christianity was formed (out of Essenic Judaism and Gnostic Paganism),[2741] and how the Christian Bible was created and arranged (by questionable human hands from often purposefully altered, highly edited, error-filled copies of copies).[2742] One historian, Arthur Findlay, has found some 36,191 mistranslations in the King James Version alone.

If the Christian masses were more knowledgeable on these topics, there would be an almighty uproar, the likes of which have never been heard in the halls of Christendom before.[2743] The clergy would then have no choice but to answer and admit the truth: a divine Jesus came to earth, in great part, to remind us of our own divinity, and to teach us how to create our own reality using the Law of Attraction. This knowledge, Jesus' true teaching, has been stolen from us and we deserve to have it returned. For the Lord originally gave these doctrines to us, His followers, not the clergy![2744]

## RESUSCITATING THE GOOD NEWS ABOUT THE DIVINE MIND

What a spiritual catastrophe this has been for humanity, for the Law of Attraction is one of the greatest gifts God (Divine Mind) has ever given Man, one that He intended for us to use for our benefit everyday of our lives. Jesus certainly believed so, which is why He called it "the Good News about the Realm of Divine Mind"; or in the psychological language of the day, "the Gospel of the Kingdom [of God]."[2745]

I believe that Jesus' teaching on the Divine Mind and the Law of Attraction should have never been banned from the Church, and because the need for it is now greater than ever, it should be resuscitated and reinstated as part of orthodox Christian doctrine. Since this is not likely to happen any time soon, I felt it was time to make Christ's Law of Attraction doctrines directly available to the public, both Christian believers and skeptical nonbelievers. This book, *Jesus and the Law of Attraction*, is the result.

## A SPIRITUAL EXPLORATION REQUIRING AN OPEN MIND
Unlike many other books on the Law of Attraction, not only is this one constructed specifically around the Good Book, but it concerns a profound scientific principle that Jesus took so seriously he devoted his entire adult life to it. That principle is the reality of the power of the Divine Mind (God), that hidden aspect of each individual, which Jesus referred to, in the coded arcane language of His day, as the "Father which is in secret."[2746]

To gain a true understanding of this suppressed concept has required us to delve into some of Christianity's deepest spiritual mysteries, which, in turn, requires an open and enquiring mind—like that of a little child, as Jesus put it, for "such is the Kingdom of God."[2747]

## WHY THE LAW OF ATTRACTION IS NOT PREACHED TODAY
Unfortunately, there are those who derogatorily dismiss anything they have never heard in church or do not understand, as "New Age,"[2748] particularly those who are members of Christianity's formalistic, fundamentalist, orthodox, and traditional schools of thought. This judgment is often made without any investigation, however. New concepts are never considered by such individuals, questions are never asked, and "unauthorized" books are never opened. As Jesus' brother Jude aptly expressed it, such people always "speak evil of those things which they know not."[2749]

Is it any wonder then, given the tradition of dogmatism, authoritarianism, intolerance, and political correctness of much of orthodox Christianity, that so many modern Christians are unaware of the Law of Attraction, that it has never been preached in their church, and that if it is mentioned by their pastor or priest at all, it is denigrated, equated with syncretistic spiritual teachings that were long ago anathematized by the Ecclesia, institutional Christianity?

## THE KINGDOM OF GOD: THE TRUE & ORIGINAL GOSPEL
Yet the "Good News of the Kingdom of God"[2750] is literally the foundation upon which all of Jesus's teachings are constructed! Indeed, based on overwhelming

evidence (much of it presented in this book), we can be sure that this doctrine was Jesus' true and original Gospel, which is why He literally called it not "the Gospel of Jesus," but "the Gospel of the Kingdom."[2751] Not surprisingly, the Kingdom of God, or what I call the "Realm of Divine Mind," is referred to by name fifty-four times in Matthew, nineteen times in Mark, forty-three times in Luke, three times in John, and thirty-one times in the other twenty-three books of the New Testament.

Furthermore, it is alluded to in dozens of other Gospel passages, while nearly every one of Jesus' parables is directly concerned with "the Kingdom." Matthew devotes entire sections to this topic, including Chapters Five, Six, Seven, Thirteen, Twenty-four, and Twenty-five. According to Luke, the "kingdom" was Jesus major preoccupation between ages thirty and thirty-three,[2752] and after His Resurrection the Lord returned to earth and appeared before His apostles, where, for forty days, the only thing He discussed with them was "the Kingdom of God"![2753]

After reading this book you will understand why Jesus placed so much emphasis on the Divine Mind and the Law of Attraction, to the exclusion of almost every other spiritual topic. It is one of God's most amazing endowments to us, and certainly humanity's most wonderful discovery: the ability to fashion our own circumstances.

## JESUS & ORIGINAL SIN, SALVATION & ATONEMENT

The great irony is that while mainstream Christianity completely disregards one of the Lord's most important doctrines—that our oneness with God makes us gods ourselves (with unlimited spiritual powers to sculpt our own fortunes)[2754]—words were put in His mouth (figuratively and literally) that He never uttered.

Contrary to what many have been taught, for example, Jesus never once mentions anything about "original sin" (the idea that human nature, even that of newborns, is innately "corrupt" due to the Fall of Adam in the Garden of Eden). In fact, not only does the phrase "original sin" itself appear nowhere in the Bible, but, from a mystical Christian standpoint, all of the scriptures that allegedly refer to it have been grossly misinterpreted by ecclesiastical apologists.[2755]

Let us look at it from Jesus' point of view: if we are one with God (as He taught),[2756] we are each a god in our own right (as He also taught).[2757] If original sin is to be accepted as real then, in condemning and punishing us, God would also be condemning and punishing Himself. Obviously, God, who is universal love,[2758] would never do such a thing. For Jesus showed us that both God and the human entity He created in His own image[2759] are both already spiritually perfect.[2760]

Another problem for the institutional Church: Jesus uses the word "salvation" (according to the mainstream definition: deliverance from the power and effects of sin through Jesus' crucifixion) only once in the entire New Testament (in Luke); and even then He does not in any way connect the word to his own execution or resurrection.[2761] This is quite odd considering that the Ecclesia teaches that Jesus' salvific death on the cross was the "central theme of His life's mission" on earth, and hence the "foundational doctrine of the entire Church." Furthermore, the word here is more accurately translated from Aramaic (the language Jesus actually used) as "life," not "salvation," completely altering the meaning of this particular Lucan passage.[2762]

Jesus also never uses the word "atonement" (the mainstream Christian idea that we are reconciled with God by the redemptive life and death of Jesus). The word appears only once in the New Testament, in Paul's letter to the Romans.[2763] Jesus did not speak of atonement for the same reason he did not speak of original sin or salvation: according to mystical Christian tradition, since we are of divine origin, our real selves, our souls or Higher Selves, are beyond sinfulness.[2764]

Or, to put it another way, because our incorporeal true self, the Indwelling Christ, is inherently pure, we are inherently pure. And it always has been and it always will be. This secret knowledge is built into the name of our Lord: Jesus means "God is salvation," or in mystical parlance, "the Indwelling Christ redeems you from sin."

This being true, the earliest Christians taught that we need not be "saved" from anything. Indeed, to the contrary, they taught the doctrine of Universal Salvation, just as Jesus' Disciples did. Here is how one of them, Luke, put it: "*All* flesh shall see the salvation of God,"[2765] for, Paul declared, the Father wants each and every one of His children to be delivered: "God will have *all* men to be saved, and to come unto the knowledge of the truth."[2766] The Father Himself said: "In the end I will bestow my Spirit on *all* people,"[2767] for I am "not willing that any should perish, but that *all* should come to repentance [that is, see the error of wrong-thinking and be saved]."[2768]

Yes, each of us will be saved. How could it be otherwise? As Jesus revealed to the world, we are endowed with all of the power, perfection, and divinity of the Almighty, as His great and irrevocable gift[2769] to humanity, the Law of Attraction, amply confirms.[2770]

God tells us that we were made in His image.[2771] Was God "born in sin"? Of course not. And because of this neither were we. Yes, we all make mistakes, and indeed figuratively, as Isaiah wrote, "we are all as an unclean thing, and all our righteousnesses [that is, even our so-called "righteous acts"] are as filthy rags."[2772] But this is only because we have a *human nature* (the Lower Self)—something God the Father does not possess.

THE TRUE MEANING OF SIN

And here we have the actual meaning of "sin": it stems from our humanness. Fortunately, like Jesus, being dyophysitical (dual-natured),[2773] we also have a *divine nature*,[2774] making us "partakers in His holiness."[2775] This, the "Inner Christ,"[2776] is our real self, the eternal "high priest"[2777] of the one and only true church,[2778] the God-made "church within."[2779] And it is this divinity which completely counterbalances our errors, forever freeing us from sin.[2780]

Consider this. Without a law there is no crime, which, according to the mainstream Church, is exactly what occurred with Jesus' death on the cross. His sacrifice put an end to the Law of Moses,[2781] as the writer of Hebrews confirms:

> "For Christ is not entered into the holy places made with hands, which are the figures of the true; but into heaven itself, now to appear in the presence of God for us: Nor yet that he should offer himself often, as the high priest entereth into the holy place every year with blood of others; for then must he often have suffered since the foundation of the world: but now once [just one time] in the end of the world hath he appeared [at exactly the right moment in history] to put away sin by the sacrifice of himself."[2782]

Thus, we can no longer be called "sinners," because the original law that outlined the nature of sin was terminated,[2783]

> "blotting out the handwriting of ordinances that was against us, which was contrary to us, and [Jesus] took it out of the way, nailing it to his cross.[2784] . . . For he [God] hath made him to be sin for us, who knew no sin; that we might be made the righteousness of God in him [that is, purified by the Divine Mind through the Indwelling Christ]."[2785]

In this way, when Jesus cried "it is finished" on the cross,[2786] the Law of Moses was nullified,[2787] and the Devil (that is, the concept of evil) was finally destroyed.[2788] God has truly

> "delivered us from the power of darkness, and hath translated us into the kingdom of his dear Son."[2789]

In short, all true believers are now "dead to sin,"[2790] and "perfected forever."[2791]

> "For as by one man's disobedience many were made sinners, so by

the obedience of one shall many be made righteous."[2792]

It is true that despite our saving grace in the Christ, our Lower Self can continue to sin. And it is also true that, according to the Law of Attraction, we will one day have to "pay" for these errors in the form of the chaos and unhappiness that we will have invited into our lives.[2793] Yet, as for our Higher Self, the God in us, it is indeed perfect,[2794] and is therefore incapable of sinning.[2795]

The Lord well understood this truth. In the Gospel of the Nazoreans, when His mother and brothers encourage Jesus to go with them to have their sins redeemed by John the Baptist, Jesus replies:

> "In what way have I sinned? I have not. Why then should I be baptized by him?"[2796]

## EVERYONE IS WELCOME AT GOD'S FEAST

These are just a few of the great secret teachings of Jesus; which is why, being esoteric, they were distorted and even covered up by early Church officials to begin with, and it is why they are still being twisted and concealed to this day.

But you have a right to know about them and learn about them, to join in the wonderful feast celebrating the mystical union between God and Man—and in reading this book, you have! This is, after all, one of Jesus' greatest desires; one that, as He usually did, He expressed in highly cryptic, and thus often overlooked, terms:

> "'Go ye therefore into the highways, and as many as ye shall find, bid to the marriage.' So those servants went out into the highways, and gathered together all as many as they found, both bad and good: and the wedding was furnished with guests."[2797]

## MAN'S SALVATION OR THE CHURCH'S PRESERVATION?

In the Aquarian Gospel we find these words:

> "The priesthood cannot be reformed; it is already dead; its greatest needs are graves and funeral chants. The new age [of the Indwelling Christ] calls for liberty; the kind that makes each man a priest, enables him to go alone, and lay his offerings on the shrine of God."[2798]

In the same work, the anti-formalistic Jesus makes these remarks:

> "When men become afraid of God, and take him for a foe, they

dress up other men in fancy garbs and call them priests, and charge them to restrain the wrath of God by prayers; and when they fail to win his favor by their prayers, to buy him off with sacrifice of animal, or bird, when man sees God as one with him, as Father-God, he needs no middle man, no priest to intercede; he goes straight up to him and says, 'My Father-God!' and then he lays his hand in God's own hand, and all is well. And this is God. You are, each one, a priest, just for yourself; and sacrifice of blood God does not want. Just give your life in sacrificial service to the all of life, and God is pleased."[2799]

Paul, who based his doctrines not on what he learned from religious teachers, but directly from the resurrected Jesus,[2800] was also against manmade, formal, organized religion,[2801] as he notes in his letter to the Colossians:

"Wherefore if ye [your Lower Self] be dead with [the Indwelling] Christ from the rudiments [empty religious tenets and rituals] of the world, why, as though living in the world, are ye subject to ordinances, (touch not; taste not; handle not; which all are to perish with the using;) after the [religious] commandments and doctrines of men? Which things have indeed a shew of wisdom in will worship, and humility, and neglecting of the body; not in any honour to the satisfying of the flesh [that is, they are spiritually useless].

"If ye then be risen with Christ [if you are spiritual rather than religious], seek those things which are above [in the Higher Self], where Christ sitteth on the right hand of God [Divine Mind]. Set your affection on things above, not on things on the earth. For ye are dead [your Lower Self has been overcome by your Higher Self], and your life is hid [now merged] with Christ in God. When [the Indwelling] Christ, who is our life, shall appear [to you], then shall ye also appear with him in glory [that is, share in His divine powers]."[2802]

Paul is correct: when we become one with the Christ Within, we come to realize our innate godliness, our oneness with God Himself.

So yes, it is understandable that if the laity were to learn Jesus' "secret," it would subvert the clergy's spiritual authority and political power within the Church. But does this make suppressing the truth about Man's divinity and staggering celestial powers morally right? Which is more important, humanity's salvation or the Church's preservation?[2803]

## JESUS DENOUNCED THOSE WHO WITHHELD "THE SECRET"

In 1st-Century Rome, those religious instructors and spiritual leaders who withheld the teachings of the Law of Attraction (embedded within Christianity's first and authentic Gospel, Jesus' "Gospel of the Kingdom")[2804] from the masses were harshly denounced by the Lord, who angrily declared that they "make the word of God of none effect through their tradition" by "teaching for doctrines the commandments of men."[2805]

Paul said such individuals were filled with "cunning craftiness, whereby they lie in wait to deceive."[2806] And deceive they did. Being ignorant of the Truth, they disregarded the Way of God (Divine Mind),[2807] and instead tried to establish the Way of Man (human mind).[2808] Here is how the Gospel of Luke phrases Jesus' condemnation:

> "Woe unto you, lawyers [religious teachers]! for ye have taken away the key of knowledge [Gnosis]: ye entered not in yourselves, and them that were entering in ye hindered."[2809]

Here is how it appears in the Gospel of Matthew:

> "But woe unto you, scribes and Pharisees, hypocrites! for ye shut up the kingdom of heaven against men: for ye neither go in yourselves, neither suffer ye them that are entering to go in."[2810]

The inner meaning of these two scriptures is this:

> "Judgment Day will be a harsh one for many of you formalistic religious teachers, for you conceal the key of knowledge [gnosis] concerning the Law of Attraction. Not only do you not embrace it yourselves, but you prevent those who are interested in it from even hearing about it, let alone practicing it."[2811]

How tragic. Especially knowing that, according to Jesus, the main purpose of the Law of Attraction is to allow us to create our ideal lives right now, right here on earth. The book of Hebrews, for example, states that Jesus came to show us the good things that are *already* here, not in the Afterlife.[2812] As He Himself often declared, "the kingdom of heaven *is* at hand."[2813] Truly blessed are those humble individuals who understand this, "for theirs *is* the kingdom of heaven."[2814] Jesus always speaks of the Kingdom of Heaven, of God, in the *present* tense, not the future tense!

Knowing how Jesus felt about those who hide the teaching of the Law of Attraction, it is little wonder that he said "the Law" would be unavailable to us unless we raise our spiritual consciousness above that of these same types of unenlightened strict religious teachers. Here is how he stated it:

> "For I say unto you, that except your righteousness shall exceed the righteousness of the scribes and Pharisees, ye shall in no case enter into the kingdom of heaven."[2815]

Based on these and numerous other biblical passages, is it not immoral, a veritable sin, for church officials to keep the Law of Attraction from the laity?

As the Bible clearly illustrates, and as my own book has shown, revealing the "Gospel of the Kingdom"[2816] to humanity—along with reinstating the Female Principle (love) back into what had become an essentially devitalized, patriarchalized (male dominant) form of spirituality[2817]—was one of the primary reasons Jesus came to earth to begin with. The goal for us then should be to teach this doctrine in every church, for it is an integral aspect of Jesus' salvific plan. Failing in this we have failed to follow the admonition of the Lord:

> "Go ye into all the world, and preach *the gospel* to every creature."[2818]

## JESUS & HIS FOLLOWERS WERE NOT CHRISTIANS

Just what did Jesus mean by "the gospel"? Certainly not what is meant by it today!

Since His Gospel and the Law of Attraction are integrally connected, and because we cannot truly understand either without knowing how Jesus saw Himself and His earthly mission, let us examine this topic for a moment. To do this we will look at the statements Jesus and His followers actually made, not the Paganized manmade words and purposeful mistranslations that now surround them—and which He, along with Paul, repeatedly warned us about.[2819]

While today it is universally assumed that Jesus was the founder of Christianity and that the Gospel concerns our salvation through His death and resurrection, a careful reading of the New Testament (KJV) discloses a very different story.

Contrary to what many Christians have been taught, Jesus was a Jew, which is exactly what the Three Wise Men (astrologers) called Him[2820]—just one reason the Lord never called Himself, His Apostles, or His followers "Christians." Not even the Apostles ever referred to themselves using this term.

It is a fact that having rejected organized Judaism (for by then, Jesus had overturned the old Law of Moses and instituted a "new covenant"),[2821] neither the Master or His followers considered themselves Jews in a strictly orthodox sense.[2822]  However, they had undergone Jewish religious rituals as children,[2823] and as adults often made reference to their Jewish background,[2824] continued to follow Jewish customs,[2825] acknowledged the Jewish Sabbath (Saturday),[2826] celebrated Jewish holy days,[2827] and met and taught in synagogues and in the Jewish temple at Jerusalem—practices that were continued by Jesus' followers even well after His Ascension.[2828]  They were all certainly viewed as Jews by others.[2829]

Paul, who was widely known as a "leader of the Nazarenes," a Judaizing Christian sect,[2830] often used his Jewishness to his advantage when he saw fit.[2831]  He even publicly admitted that he was an Israelite,[2832] a Hebrew, a descendant of Abraham,[2833] of the "Jews' religion,"[2834] and more specifically, a Jew[2835] of the rigorous sect of the Pharisees.[2836]  Peter was another Apostle who did not try to hide his Jewish background.[2837]

Even the Last Supper, purposefully held during the Jewish Passover, was not in any way Christian, nor did Jesus intend it to be.[2838]  It was a form of a bread and wine communal meal or sacrament,[2839] borrowed from the Nazarenes, the Qumranians, and the Essenes—Jewish sects[2840] who had adopted Melchizedek's custom from the Old Testament.[2841]

## WHAT JESUS' FOLLOWERS ACTUALLY CALLED THEMSELVES

What religion did Jesus belong to then?  We know it was not the Christian religion, because the word "Christian" had not been coined yet.  It was not until after His death that it was invented by the anti-Jesus Pagans at Antioch, probably about the year A.D. 65.[2842]

Even then, the Lord's followers did not use this term for themselves, for originally the word "Christian" was applied to them by their enemies as a term of disrespect and ridicule.[2843]  This is why this designation does not appear anywhere in the four canonical Gospels, and why it appears only three times in the New Testament outside of them.[2844]  This is why, in fact, the word Christian was never used by Jesus' followers until well after the year 65.

What then did the first followers of Jesus call themselves?  They used various terms, such as: the "saints,"[2845] the "faithful,"[2846] "servants,"[2847] the "elect,"[2848] "apostles,"[2849] the "called,"[2850] "followers,"[2851] the "church" (assembly),[2852] the "brethren,"[2853] "believers,"[2854] and a "peculiar people."[2855] Jesus Himself referred to His followers as "disciples,"[2856] as His followers themselves occasionally did as well.[2857]  Some referred to them as "this sect,"[2858] or "the sect of the Nazarenes,"[2859] based on the fact that Jesus was known as a Nazarene[2860] (someone from the city of Nazareth).[2861]

The point is that no one, neither Jesus or His earliest followers, referred to their particular group as Christians, for they did not consider themselves Christians.

The Gospel of Q (alluded to by Paul,[2862] and also by Bishop Papias of 2nd-Century Turkey),[2863] substantiates this: the earliest known collection of Jesus' teachings, the first "layer" (known as Q1) was written in the early 30s A.D., shortly after Jesus' death. Yet, nowhere does Q mention a "church," Christianity, or even religion.[2864] And as the book of Acts attests, even with the birth of the institutional Church (the Ecclesia) on the day of the first Pentecost after Jesus' Ascension,[2865] there is no mention of Christianity. Instead, as noted, these so-called "first Christians" continued to meet and teach at the local Jewish Temple[2866] and honor Jewish holy days.[2867]

## JESUS SAID HE DID NOT INTEND TO FOUND A NEW RELIGION

While the first biblical mention of the word "Christian" would not come until many decades later, even if it had been in existence during Jesus' life, He would not have used the term. Why?

Because, according to His own words, He did not intend to overturn the old religion (Judaism), nor did He intend to create a new faith in His name—not Christianity or any other religion:[2868]

> "Think not that I am come to destroy the law [of Moses], or the [Jewish] prophets: I am not come to destroy, but to fulfil."[2869]

Indeed, as the Sermon on the Mount patently illustrates,[2870] the Lord's intention rather was to initiate a return to a more mystical form of spirituality, one free of the pseudorighteousness, dogmatic formalism, pathological creeds, empty ceremonialism, censorious diatribes, and imperious fundamentalism of the religious Pharisees,[2871] militaristic Herodians,[2872] and political Sadducees,[2873] whom Jesus is shown repeatedly cursing, damning, and vilifying.[2874]

## CHRISTIANITY & THE CHRIST HAVE ALWAYS EXISTED

We must also ask ourselves this question: if God's Truth, being "the same yesterday, and to day, and for ever,"[2875] is immortal and unchanging, how then could Jesus have been the originator of it? Being enlightened, He well understood that you cannot "found" a religion that has always existed and that will never perish. This is why Voltaire said that Plato—who was born four centuries *before* Jesus—was "one of the greatest teachers of Christianity."[2876]

Here is how the venerable Church Father Saint Augustine expressed this same idea.

> "That which is known as the Christian religion existed among the ancients, and never did not exist; from the beginning of the human race until the time when Christ came in the flesh, at which time the

true religion, which already existed began to be called Christianity."

Eusebius, the well-known ancient Roman Christian historian and the bishop of Caesarea in the early 4th Century, made a similar statement:

"The names of Jesus and Christ were both known and honored by the ancients [that is, pre-Christian peoples]. . . . That which is called the Christian religion is neither new nor strange, but—if it be lawful to testify the truth—was known to the ancients."

Early Gnostic Christians preached the identical doctrine. In their work entitled the Tripartite Tractate, we read:

"Not only did the Christ exist from the very beginning [of time], but so did the Church."[2877]

We have canonical evidence for these views as well. Paul, for example, acknowledged that the Indwelling Christ, and therefore Christianity, were both known to his own henotheistic ancestors, the Israelites, who, according to Jewish tradition, crossed the Red Sea some 1,500 years before the birth of Jesus:

"Moreover, brethren, I would not that ye should be ignorant, how that all our fathers were under the cloud, and all passed through the sea; and were all baptized unto Moses in the cloud and in the sea; and did all eat the same spiritual meat; and did all drink the same spiritual drink: for they drank of that spiritual Rock that followed them: and *that Rock was Christ.*"[2878]

In his letter to the Ephesians, Paul asserts that Jesus (the Indwelling Christ) chose us to be His "adopted children" even prior to the earth being formed:

"According as he hath chosen us in him *before the foundation of the world,* that we should be holy and without blame before him in love: having predestinated us unto the adoption of children by Jesus Christ to himself, according to the good pleasure of his will . . ."[2879]

In his letter to the Colossians, Paul makes this cosmic statement about the Indwelling Christ,

". . . who is the image of the invisible God, the firstborn of every creature: for by him were all things created, that are in heaven, and that are in earth, visible and invisible, whether they be thrones, or dominions, or principalities, or powers: all things were created by him, and for him: and *he is before all things*, and by him all things consist."[2880]

The Apostle Peter wrote that the Christ has always been recognized, but for the benefit of humanity, was made known physically in the form of Jesus some 2,000 years ago:

"Who verily was foreordained *before the foundation of the world*, but was manifest in these last times for you . . ."[2881]

The prophet Daniel, who lived some 600 years before the birth of the Lord, was well aware of the World-Christ and His "everlasting" church:

"I saw in the night visions, and, behold, one like the Son of man came with the clouds of heaven, and came to the Ancient of days, and they brought him near before him. And there was given him dominion, and glory, and a kingdom, that all people, nations, and languages, should serve him: his dominion is an everlasting dominion, which shall not pass away, and his kingdom that which shall not be destroyed."[2882]

The Hebraist noted that because the Christ "continueth forever, he hath an unchangeable priesthood,"[2883] while Jesus Himself had this to say on the subject of the eternalness of the Christ Within:

"I am Alpha and Omega, the beginning and the ending," saith the Lord, "which is, and which was, and which is to come, the Almighty."[2884]

Again, speaking as the indwelling Christ, Jesus once commented on "the glory which I had with God *before the world was*,"[2885] openly declaring: "*Before Abraham was, I AM.*"[2886] The universal unfading omnipresence of the Christ Within is also mentioned by Jesus in these pantheistic passages from the Gospel of Thomas:

"If you are alone, fear not, I am with you. Lift up any rock and there I AM. Cut open any piece of wood, and you will find me."[2887]

## THE TRUE "RELIGION" OF JESUS

It is plain from these statements that Jesus did not come to found a *new* truth, an impossibility to begin with. For truth is eternal, imperishable, deathless, and perpetual. Instead, He incarnated on earth to reestablish the *original* truth, saying: "Ye shall know the truth, and the truth shall make you free."[2888] Why was this necessary? Because the Truth about humanity and God had been forgotten by most people in His day—just as it has by the majority of people in our day.

According to mystical Christian hermeneutics, Jesus' "religion" was indeed not a religion at all, but rather a simple informal belief system,[2889] a unitive spirituality that stressed a personal relationship with the Divine,[2890] and which was therefore based on the individual (rather than the group),[2891] unconditional love for ourselves and others,[2892] unqualified forgiveness,[2893] knowledge of our oneness with God,[2894] a universal spirituality or "church within"[2895]—that is, the "true tabernacle,"[2896] headed by our Higher Self, the everlasting "high priest" (Christ Within),[2897] love of the Universal Brotherhood of Man (for all souls are equal),[2898] the unconditional love, mercy, and kindness of God for us (whether merited or not),[2899] and complete faith in the Father (Divine Mind).[2900]

At the time, all that was required to join the Lord's group was belief;[2901] not in a particular religion, but belief in the Great I AM within;[2902] that is, the Inner God,[2903] the Indwelling Christ,[2904] and the Holy Ghost Within[2905]—all three which existed before Jesus and which exist in each one of us now, for they are immortal, timeless, ineffable, ageless, changeless, exhaustless, incorruptible, and universal.[2906] This is the same Inner Triune God that Hindus refer to as the "unborn, undying, indestructible Lord of all things living."

Jesus' spirituality, His "religion," as some incorrectly call it, was actually all-inclusive, and incorporated even those who did not follow Him: "He that is not against us is for us," said the all-wise Teacher and Healer.[2907] This story from the Aquarian Gospel aptly illustrates my point:

> And John said, "Master, who may seek and save the lost? and who may heal the sick, and cast the demons out of those obsessed? When we were on the way we saw a man who was not one of us, cast demons out and heal the sick. He did it by the sacred Word and in the name of Christ; but we forbade him, for he did not walk with us."
>
> And Jesus said, "You sons of men, do you imagine that you own the powers of God? And do you think that all the world must wait for you to do the works of God? God is not man that he should have a special care for any man, and give him special gifts.

Forbid not any man to do the works of God.

> "There is no man who can pronounce the sacred Word, and in the name of Christ restore the sick, and cast the unclean spirits out, who is not [a] child of God. The man of whom you speak is one with us. Whoever gathers in the grain of heaven is one with us. Whoever gives a cup of water in the name of Christ is one with us; so God shall judge."[2908]

Thus, the severe religiocentrism that burgeoned among a number of early Jewish groups,[2909] and later among some of Jesus' followers after His Ascension[2910] (and which is still very much alive today in many Christian communities), completely opposes the Lord's true and original teachings on religious tolerance.[2911]

Furthermore, Jesus' goal for every person is the attainment of the "Kingdom of God,"[2912] entrance into which requires the innocence, humility, faith, and mental flexibility of "little children."[2913] Being manmade, religious rituals, creeds, philosophies, rules, ceremonies, tenets, theologies, and doctrinal beliefs do not fill the heart of those who truly hunger after God. It is how you live that is important, how you treat others; it is the motivation behind your thoughts, words, and actions that count to God.[2914] Thus saith the Christ.[2915] And his half-brother James the Just agreed:

> "Pure religion and undefiled before God and the Father is this, to visit the fatherless and widows in their affliction, and to keep himself unspotted from the world."[2916]

Now you know why Paul, as just one example, never addressed the topic of religion specifically. Instead, he urged all of us to live a life of gentleness, humility, and patience, with charity toward everyone.[2917]

In short, the "religion" of Jesus is not a religion at all. It is simply love, mercy, and forgiveness; that is right-thinking, or what the ancients called righteousness.[2918]

## "THE WAY"

This makes the Lord's "faith" identical to what Hindus call Sanatana Dharma, or the "Eternal Way." This is the One Universal Religion that is known by hundreds of thousands of different names around the world. For at the core of Sanatana Dharma lies those three immortal and timeless spiritual truths upon which all religions are ultimately founded: love, compassion, and wisdom. Thus, if we were to give a name to Jesus' "religion," it would be "The Way"—which is exactly what He[2919] and His followers called it![2920]

But the name is not original to Jesus. He was simply borrowing a title that was commonplace among many of the great spiritual teachers throughout pre-Christian history, from the Old Testament authors, such as Moses,[2921] Jeremiah,[2922] Job,[2923] and the Psalmist,[2924] to the ancient philosopher-priest Hermes Trismegistus[2925] and the famed Chinese teacher Lao Tzu, the founder of the religion literally known as "The Way": Tao (that is, Taoism).[2926]

## MICAH & THOMAS PAINE ON THE "RELIGION" OF JESUS
Some 750 years before Jesus' birth, Micah articulated the Lord's spiritual belief system, the Way, perfectly:

> "What doth the Lord require of thee, but to do justly, and to love mercy, and to walk humbly with thy God?"[2927]

This is the exact same "religion" that Deist and American Founding Father Thomas Paine wrote about in his famous pamphlet, *The Age of Reason*:

> "I believe in one God, and no more; and I hope for happiness beyond this life. I believe in the equality of man, and I believe that religious duties consist in doing justice, loving mercy, and endeavoring to make our fellow-creatures happy."

Sadly, many of those who had the privilege of hearing Jesus teach His "religion" in person "understood not the things which he spake unto them." To this very day many Christians still do not understand.[2928]

## JESUS WAS VIEWED AS A TEACHER BY HIS EARLIEST FOLLOWERS
From numerous New Testament passages, it is clear that the anti-fundamentalist Jesus—who vigorously opposed formalized, organized, institutionalized religion at nearly every opportunity[2929]—purposefully set out to abolish ceremonial religious law, "even the law of commandments contained in ordinances."[2930] As we have seen, our Lord accomplished this, according to Paul, by

> "blotting out the handwriting of ordinances that was against us [that is, the Law of Moses], which was contrary to us, and took it out of the way, nailing it to his cross."[2931]

Not surprisingly, Jesus, the world's most notable religious nonconformist, regarded Himself as a type of cosmic mystic, a spiritual philosopher, an aphoristic teacher with a radical message (God and Man are one);[2932] a wandering transcendental sage who, as Luke perfectly described

Him, simply "went about doing good."[2933]

Hence, Jesus was repeatedly addressed by His original followers, not as Messiah (a word that does not appear in the New Testament), but as *Rabbi* ("scholar"),[2934] *Rabboni* ("my scholar"),[2935] *Kurios* ("philosopher"),[2936] and *Didaskalos* ("teacher," "doctor").[2937] Likewise, He spoke of Himself (the Christ) as *Kathegetes* ("instructor," "guide").[2938] So central was His role as a spiritual mentor that it is referred to some sixty times throughout the four Gospels,[2939] "for he *taught* them as one having [divine] authority, and not as the [book educated] scribes."[2940] Even the spiritually unenlightened Pharisees recognized Him as a superlative metaphysical educator:

> There was a man of the Pharisees, named Nicodemus, a ruler of the Jews: the same came to Jesus by night, and said unto him, "*Rabbi* [teacher], we know that *thou art a teacher come from God*: for no man can do these miracles that thou doest, except God be with him."[2941]

Yes, Jesus was known far and wide, even by His critics, as "a teacher come from God."

Yet, just as He did not want His Disciples to allow themselves to be called "teachers," Jesus did not want the term applied to Himself either. Not because He was not a teacher of course, but because He wanted our focus to remain on the "True Teacher of us all," the Indwelling Christ:

> "But be not ye called 'Rabbi': for one is your Master [teacher], even Christ; and all ye are brethren. . . . Neither be ye called masters [teachers]: for one is your Master, even Christ."[2942]

Naturally, as one who perfectly fit the mold of a roving guru-like educator, the Lord shunned allegiance to any single religion, faith, or sect. In other words, *Jesus was philosophic, not theologic; spiritual, not religious.*

## JESUS' FOCUS WAS THE "FATHER," NOT HIMSELF

Seen as a "miracle worker" by the multitudes,[2943] when the Lord was not healing the sick, mad, deaf, blind, and lame, or preaching His personal Gospel, "the Gospel of the Kingdom"[2944] (that is, our oneness with the Father,[2945] our divine nature,[2946] the Inner Kingdom,[2947] and the Law of Attraction),[2948] He often found Himself trying to discourage the growth of a personalty cult in His name.

Thus, when the Pharisees sought to stone Him to death, Jesus appealed for His life by saying that the "doctrine" He preached was not His own, but "his that sent me." Here is the story as it appears in the Gospel of John:

Now about the midst of the feast Jesus went up into the temple, and taught. And the Jews marvelled, saying, "How knoweth this man letters, having never learned?" Jesus answered them, and said, "*My doctrine is not mine, but his that sent me. If any man will do his will, he shall know of the doctrine, whether it be of God, or whether I speak of myself. He that speaketh of himself seeketh his own glory: but he that seeketh his glory that sent him, the same is true, and no unrighteousness is in him.*

"Did not Moses give you the law, and yet none of you keepeth the law? Why go ye about to kill me?" . . . Then cried Jesus in the temple as he taught, saying, "Ye both know me, and ye know whence I am: and *I am not come of myself*, but he that sent me is true, whom ye know not. But I know him: for I am from him, and he hath sent me."[2949]

When the Jewish authorities picked up stones and began to threateningly close in on Jesus, He defended Himself even more forcefully, clearly stating that He was not seeking His own glory:

"*I do nothing of myself*; but as my Father hath taught me, I speak these things. And he that sent me is with me: the Father hath not left me alone; for I do always those things that please him. . . . But now ye seek to kill me, a man that hath told you the truth, which I have heard of God. . . . If God were your Father, ye would love me: for I proceeded forth and came from God; *neither came I of myself, but he [that] sent me. . . . I seek not mine own glory*: there is [only] one that seeketh and judgeth. . . . *If I honour myself, my honour is nothing* . . ."[2950]

If this is not clear enough, Jesus later restates this fact even more plainly:

". . . *the word which ye hear [me preach] is not mine*, but the Father's which sent me."[2951]

And why does Jesus speak the words of the Father instead of His own? The Master answered this question as well: "My Father is greater than I."[2952] For, as He enigmatically states in the Apocryphon of James:

"The Father does not need me, for fathers do not need sons. Instead it is always sons who need fathers."[2953]

During one particular incident in the Gospel of Mark, when the Lord and His Apostles come upon a fig tree that He had cursed earlier, they notice that it has since withered and died. As they look to Him for an explanation, He is quick to reply. But Jesus does not tell them: "See what I have done, have faith in me." He says: "Have faith in God,"[2954] again keeping the attention on the Father rather than on Himself.

In the Gospel of John, Jesus speaks of God and His "sheep" this way:

> "*My Father*, which gave them [to] me, *is greater than all*; and no man is able to pluck them out of my Father's hand."[2955]

Jesus makes numerous other self-deflecting statements in John, such as:

> "Verily, verily, I say unto you, *the Son can do nothing of himself*, but what he seeth the Father do: for what things soever he doeth, these also doeth the Son likewise."[2956]

> "*I can of mine own self do nothing* . . . *because I seek not mine own will, but the will of the Father which hath sent me. If I bear witness of myself, my witness is not true.*"[2957]

> ". . . the works which the Father hath given me to finish, the same works that I do, bear witness of me, that *the Father hath sent me*."[2958]

> "For I came down from heaven, *not to do mine own will*, but the will of him that sent me."[2959]

And, as mentioned:

> "*I seek not my own glory* . . ."[2960]

Here are two of the most revealing and little discussed statements Jesus makes regarding how He wanted to be perceived:

> I *receive not honour from men.*"[2961]

> "*I am come in my Father's name* . . ."[2962]

Think about what Jesus is saying here! "I do not seek out, need, or want human praise. I have come to earth on behalf of the Divine Mind, not on behalf of myself."

From these statements is it not crystal clear that the Lord did not want us to focus on Him, the human Jesus? He wanted our attention centered on

God, on the "Father," the Master's occult word for the Divine Mind. This is why both early Gnostic Christians and orthodox Christians referred to the Gospel not as "the Gospel of Jesus," but as "the Gospel of God."[2963]

This is also why, in the Gospel of Thomas, Jesus calls the Inner Kingdom not the "Kingdom of Jesus" or the "Kingdom of Christ," but the "Kingdom of the Father."[2964] And it is why the book of Hebrews calls Jesus an "Apostle"—not of Himself (an impossibility), but of God the Father.[2965] Consider the statement Jesus makes in Matthew:

> "And call no man your father upon the earth: for one is your Father, which is in heaven."[2966]

The inner mystical (psychological) meaning:

> "You only have one true parent, and it is the Divine Mind, which is an elevated state of consciousness."[2967]

This advanced high level of spiritual consciousness, called by Hindus and Buddhists "samadhi," was occultly known to Jesus and the Apostles as the "upper room."[2968] Of it Paul wrote mystically:

> "The first man [that is, the Lower Self] is of the earth, earthy: the second man [that is, the Higher Self] is the Lord from heaven. As is the earthy, such are they also that are earthy [unenlightened]: and as is the heavenly, such are they also that are heavenly [enlightened]. And as we have borne the image of the earthy [in body], we shall also bear the image of the heavenly [in spirit]."[2969]

Jesus said truly: "My Kingdom is not of this world,"[2970] meaning that it is not physical, but spiritual—that is, it is mental in nature.[2971] For our Universe, having been created by the mental (Logos) power of the Divine Mind,[2972] operates on thought and thought alone![2973]

The ancient Hebrew prophets, whose sayings Jesus was so familiar with, also understood that the Divine Mind, not human teachers and leaders, was meant to be the true center of religious worship. Hence, they continually referred to the Father as the one and only "Savior,"[2974] the one and only "Redeemer,"[2975] the one and only "Lord."[2976]

Both the Psalmist and Isaiah believed that our salvation, our savior, is the Divine Mind (God)—and they clearly said so,[2977] as did the Virgin Mary.[2978] And as Israelite kings (and in some cases even high priests) were considered deities, and so were called the "anointed" (that is, "messiahs" or "christs"),[2979] it is not surprising that in many biblical passages Jesus downplays Himself and His kingly role as Messiah and Savior as well, another effort to keep the focus on the Father, the Divine Mind.[2980]

Thus in an attempt to discourage the adoration of His followers and put the focus back on "he that sent me,"[2981] Jesus would often make comments such as: "the Son of man came not to be ministered unto, but to minister."[2982] He did not even consider Himself to be inherently good, as Mark relates:

> And when he was gone forth into the way, there came one running, and kneeled to him, and asked him, "Good Master, what shall I do that I may inherit eternal life?" And Jesus said unto him, "*Why callest thou me good? there is none good but one, that is, God.*"[2983]

## JESUS CONSISTENTLY SHUNNED PERSONAL ATTENTION

An unbiased reading of the four Gospels tells us that, like other egoless spiritual teachers from time immemorial, Jesus too eschewed personal attention. Once, when a woman in the crowd yelled out to Him, "blessed [happy] is the woman who gave birth to you and nursed you!,"[2984] Jesus immediately took the focus off Himself and put it back on Sovereign Mind, Divine Mind, replying:

> "Yea rather, blessed [happy] are they that hear the word of God, and keep it."[2985]

After His healing sessions Jesus frequently asked those in attendance *not* to tell anyone that He was involved,[2986] and He would not allow the Apostles to discuss the private experiences and visions they shared with Him with others.[2987] Often He tried to hide both His identity and His whereabouts,[2988] and in some cases He even "charged his disciples that they should tell no man that he was Jesus the Christ."[2989] Once, when Peter observed that Jesus was "the Christ of God," the Lord immediately reprimanded the Apostle, commanding him to "tell no man that thing."[2990]

## JESUS DID NOT SPEAK OF THE GOSPEL IN RELATION TO HIMSELF

Most revealingly, Jesus never spoke of the Gospel, the "Good News," as being about Himself. Instead He openly referred to it as "the Gospel of the Kingdom,"[2991] avowing that the true Gospel is about "he that sent me,"[2992] that is, the "Father":

> "For *I have not spoken of myself*; but the Father which sent me, he gave me a commandment, what I should say, and what I should speak."[2993]

Why this overwhelming emphasis on God?

Again, as Jesus attested, the Father "is greater than I."[2994] And why is the Father "greater"? Because "God is all mind";[2995] He is, as Hermes Trismegistus referred to Him, the "All-Father Mind," the "Mind of All," the Divine Mind, the thought-creator of the Universe and all life.[2996]

Neither did the Lord ever claim that it was He who healed the sick, raised the dead, or performed His other miracles ("works").[2997] As always, He attributes all these things to the "Father," the Divine Mind that exists within each one of us:[2998]

> ". . . the words that I speak unto you *I speak not of myself*: but *the Father that dwelleth in me, he doeth the works*."[2999]

In fact, Jesus repeatedly asserted that there was absolutely nothing He did or said that came from Himself. Rather, it was all from the "Father":

> Then said Jesus unto them, "When ye have lifted up the Son of man, then shall ye know that I am he, and that *I do nothing of myself*; but as my Father hath taught me, I speak these things."[3000]

And again:

> "*I can of mine own self do nothing*: as I hear, I judge: and my judgment is just; because *I seek not mine own will*, but the will of the Father which hath sent me. *If I bear witness of myself, my witness is not true*."[3001]

At this point we should not be shocked to learn that at times Jesus openly resisted the messianic role that some of His followers ascribed to Him. Mark, for example, relates the following strange event in which Jesus' messiahship is announced for the first time by a group of demoniacs:

> And unclean spirits, when they saw him, fell down before him, and cried, saying, "Thou art the Son of God." And he straitly charged them that they should not make him known.[3002]

Luke tells the story like this:

> Now when the sun was setting, all they that had any sick with divers diseases brought them unto him; and he laid his hands on every one of them, and healed them. And devils also came out of many, crying out, and saying, "Thou art Christ the Son of God."

And he rebuking them suffered them not to speak: for they knew
that he was Christ. [3003]

John the Apostle recorded this emotional outburst, in which Jesus
deemphasizes Himself, trying to deflect attention back onto what He believed
was most important:

Jesus cried and said, "*He that believeth on me, believeth not on me, but
on him that sent me.* And he that seeth me seeth him that sent
me."[3004]

This declaration is so important to our discussion, that we will repeat it!

"*He that believeth on me, believeth not on me, but on him that sent me.*"

The inner meaning:

"If you follow me, trust in me, are committed to me, or believe in
me, it is really not me you are following, trusting, committed to,
or believe in. It is the one who sent me."[3005]

As we have noted, the "one who sent me" is the "Father," Jesus' occult term for
the Universal Divine Mind. [3006]

## EMPHASIZING THE HUMAN JESUS

Like the Lord, Paul too often emphasized the divine Father over the man Jesus,
as is clear from this comment in Ephesians: "Be ye therefore followers of
God."[3007]

The Gospel of John goes on to reinforce Jesus' self-diverting words by
describing Him, not as the heavenly Son of God, but as the earthly son of the
very human Joseph,[3008] while the book of Hebrews insinuates that Jesus was not
born perfect, but grew in perfection throughout His human lifetime.[3009]

Here we are dealing not with apocryphal myth, but with canonical
facts, available in the King James Bible for all to see, read, and ponder for
themselves.

## THE TRUE NATURE OF THE GOSPEL

Little wonder then that in the entire New Testament it is not Jesus but Mark
who is the only individual to specifically speak of "the gospel of Jesus Christ,"
and even then he does this only once.[3010] What does Mark mean by the word
"gospel"?

Since he could not have been speaking of the then nonexistent canonical books we now call the four Gospels (Matthew, Mark, Luke, and John), it is clear that he must have meant something else entirely—and indeed he did.

In modern terminology, when Mark says "the Gospel of Jesus Christ," he is referring to the "*teachings* of Jesus Christ," and in fact Webster defines the word gospel as "the *teachings* of a religious teacher." In the very same chapter, Mark also uses Jesus' much earlier phrase for the Gospel, referring to it as "the gospel of the Kingdom of God";[3011] that is, "the sacred teachings on how to create a life of perfect happiness here on earth and in the hereafter, in accordance with the laws of the Divine Mind."

As for the ancient New Testament use of the word gospel (in Greek, *euaggelion*), language authorities translate it variously as: "good tidings," "the glad tidings concerning the Kingdom of God," "the glad tidings of salvation through Jesus," and "the announcement of the grace of God," all which are clearly cabalistic references to both the redemptive power of Jesus (that is, the Indwelling Christ)[3012] and Jesus' teachings on the Laws of Love[3013] and Attraction.[3014]

## THE TRANSFORMATION OF THE GOSPEL

It was only after Jesus' death that what had begun as His Gospel ("the Gospel of the Kingdom")[3015] concerning the Divine Mind,[3016] the Inner Kingdom,[3017] and the Law of Attraction,[3018] came to be associated with His personal birth, life, deeds, demise on the cross, resurrection, transfiguration, and ascension.[3019] Along with this development, these elements began to be gathered into the four eponymous books, whose unknown authors were based on the four astrological quarter-signs of mystical Christianity, Judaism, and Paganism (representing the two yearly solstices and two yearly equinoxes).[3020]

Using the "four living creatures" from the book of Ezekiel as a Zodiacal guide,[3021] the Catholic Church Father Irenaeus artificially attributed the four books to John (the "eagle," the *water* symbol of the star-sign Aquila),[3022] Mark (the "lion," the *fire* symbol of the star-sign Leo),[3023] Matthew (the "man," the *air* symbol of the star-sign Aquarius),[3024] and Luke (the "ox," the *earth* symbol of the star-sign Taurus).[3025]

Ezekiel's four beasts were borrowed, of course, from the four ancient Compass-Gods of Paganism, who in turn represented the four basic elements. In mystical Hebrew these were written: *Iammin*, "water"; *Nour*, "fire"; *Rouach*, "air"; and *Iebeschah*, "earth." The first letters of these four Hebrew words form the acronym INRI, to the institutional Church symbolizing the Latin: *Iesus Nazarenus, Rex Iudaeorum* ("Jesus of Nazareth, King of the Jews"), the sign placed above Jesus' head as He hung on the cross,[3026] and to the mystical Church representing the Latin: *In Nobis Regnat Iesus* ("Within Us Reigns Jesus").[3027]

Thus, from the very beginning, the four canonical Gospels were steeped not merely in the doctrines of Jesus, but in the doctrines of His Jewish and Pagan critics as well—an ill omen of things to come!

## THE PAGANIZATION OF JESUS

Tragically, it was during this same post-resurrection period that the Lord Himself began to be Paganized. According to mystical Christianity, Gnostic Christianity, ancient historians, paleographic research, and modern form criticism, here is how it occurred.

As I note in my book, *Jesus and the Gospel of Q*, the original Gospel of Q (known as Q1)—the earliest known book of Jesus' teachings—lacks any references to the Master's divinity, virgin birth, baptism, miracles, messiahship, violent debates with the Pharisees, last supper, trial, death, resurrection, transfiguration, or ascension, nor does it name any of the Twelve Apostles, or use the Pagan title "Son of God" for Jesus. In fact, throughout Q, Jesus refers to Himself only as the "Son of Man" (that is, a human being). Since Q was merely a collection of His wisdom sayings, it is patently clear from these facts that His original followers viewed Him, not as the prophesied Jewish Messiah, but rather as an enlightened spiritual teacher, healer, and prophet.

However, after the Ecclesia (the Catholic Church) was established as Rome's official state religion under Constantine the Great in the early 4th Century, it sought to congeal its newly won political, social, and religious power. To do this it needed to stamp out Pagan religion[3028] while simultaneously converting the Empire's enormous Pagan population.[3029] To more easily attract non-Christian converts and quickly grow its membership, it was decided that the human figure of Jesus would have to undergo the traditional Pagan ritual of apotheosization (god-making).[3030]

During this sweeping process, despite His repeated insistence that "there is none good but God,"[3031] the human Jesus was deified, fetishized, idolatrized, mythologized, dogmatized, and politicized[3032] by those whose "understanding had become darkened" (that is, the unenlightened).[3033] Along the way, the "Son of Man" (as He was genuinely known to His original followers),[3034] was dehumanized and replaced with the "Son of God"[3035] (a title that Jesus only uses directly for Himself once—in an overtly spurious comment—in all four of the canonical Gospels).[3036]

Then, at the First Council of Nicaea in 325, it was officially announced and confirmed for the first time that Jesus was a Savior-God, a Paganesque proclamation that would have shocked His earliest followers and thoroughly enraged Jesus—who taught that we are all gods in our own right.[3037]

Worse still, Malachi's mystical description of Jesus as the "Sun of

Righteousness"[3038] was taken literally by the Church Fathers, prompting a number of scandalous alterations to the figure and biography of Jesus between the 2nd and 5th Centuries.

For example, the Lord's birthday was designated as December 25, the Winter Solstice birthday of the Roman sun-god Sol; the Christian Sabbath was moved from the Jewish Sabbath, Saturday (Saturn's Day), to the Pagan holy day devoted to the sun-god Mithras, Sunday (the Sun's Day);[3039] Christian artists began depicting Jesus as one of the various Pagan solar-gods, such as Helios, Apollo, Sol, or Phoebus, hurtling across the vault of the heavens each day in a fiery chariot; Jesus was given the Pagan god title *Sol Justitiae*, the "Sun of Justice"; Christian worshipers began facing east each morning before sunrise to honor His daily nativity; under Constantine the Great, the Church began venerating Jesus as the mighty Pagan solar-deity *Sol Invictus*, the "Unconquered Sun"; and as the book of Revelation shows, Jesus became strongly associated with the astrological star-sign Leo the Lion, which is ruled by the sun.[3040]

Subsequently, the religion created by Man in the Lord's name went from one focused on the *teachings of* Jesus the human spiritual educator (as He was regarded by His first followers), to one *about* Jesus the divine religious Messiah (as He is regarded by today's mainstream Christians). In succinct terms, *Christianity went from focusing on the message to focusing on the messenger!*

What was behind this appalling transformation, one that so negligently violated the doctrines of Jesus Himself? And why was it allowed to occur in the first place?

The always sagacious mystic John the Apostle answered the question this way: those in control "loved the praise of men more than the praise of God."[3041] Or as Paul put it, the authorities of the institutional Church, who, opposing the truth,[3042] and seeing godliness as a means for financial gain,[3043] acted out of personal ambition, jealousy, and rivalry, rather than out of love and good will.[3044]

Simply put, under Catholicism, Christianity reverted back to religious formalism, ceremonialism, fundamentalism, and Judeo-Pagan myth-making, many of the very things Jesus came to earth to combat. As Paul complained to Titus: "The Church ended up giving heed to fables and to the commandments of men that turn from the truth."[3045]

## THE THEOLOGIZATION OF THE GOSPELS

Jesus' teachings themselves underwent much abuse as well: to the small book of Jesus' wisdom sayings (the Gospel of Q) were appended a complicated set of theological creeds, stories, and doctrines pertaining not to His teachings, but to supporting the claim of the "apostolic chain of succession," so vital to the running of the new institutionalized Church. The result?

The four—and in some cases, overtly contradictory—astrologically-named canonical Gospels: "Matthew" (Aquarius), "Mark" (Leo), "Luke" (Taurus), and "John" (Aquila), artistically portrayed as the Pagan Christian Tetramorph, which can still be seen in the iconography of Christian structures around the world, such as France's celebrated Chartres Cathedral.

Critiqued, modified, redacted, and expurgated by strict orthodox eisegetes and often careless interpolators, numberless unnamed Catholic apologists, priests, editors, catechists, ecclesiastics, scribes, and copyists finally stripped much of Jesus' sacred doctrines of their cosmic beauty, elegant simplicity, and mystical wonder. This was done through a harsh "cleansing" process of distortion, systematization, ritualization, secularization, Romanization, theologization, modernization, and finally Catholicization.[3046] In effect, any theology, liturgy, ontology, or Christotelicism that did not support the Ecclesia's orthodox views was either rewritten or bowdlerized, eventually to be suppressed under the label "heresy."

The Church's politically oriented ecclesiology (to fully dominate the Roman Empire) had to somehow be tied to the early Bible's Christology, an impossible task as the Good Book existed at the time. To solve this problem, Jesus' childlike guru-like doctrines were turned from fluid, cosmic, universal, interreligious, transdenominational, numinous, supernal, ecumenical, spiritual teachings about the "Father which is in secret,"[3047] the "Gospel of the Kingdom,"[3048] the "mysteries of the Kingdom of God,"[3049] and the "Indwelling Christ,"[3050] into concretized, self-reflexive, soteriological, kerygmatic Christian creeds concerning the divine aspects of Jesus Himself.[3051]

In short, Jesus' simple aphoristic sayings, known as gnomologia ("small [that is, concise] words"), were overlaid with a mass of complex theological dogma, and the focus went from His teaching on the Kingdom of God[3052] to the Church's teaching on the "King" of the Kingdom of God.[3053]

Along the way, humanity was stripped of its innate divinity then imbued with "original sin," while Jesus was made the exclusive possessor ("the *only* begotten Son")[3054] of what He and Paul had taught was the *Universal* Inner Christ, present in *all* men and women.[3055] The *spiritual* authority of Jesus was also diminished, replaced by the *religious* authority of the Church at Rome—transformations clearly evident if one not only studies the Gospel of Q, but also reads the New Testament books in the order in which they were written instead of the order in which they appear today.[3056]

Honest Christians, who well understood both "the Truth of God"[3057] and "the Truth of Christ,"[3058] were not happy, and many openly expressed their displeasure. Several centuries later, one of them, English Christian mystic and poet William Blake wrote:

The vision of Christ that thou dost see
Is my vision's greatest enemy. . . .
Thine loves the same world that mine hates;
Thy Heaven-doors are my Hell-Gates. . . .
Both read the Bible day and night;
But thou read'st black where I read white.[3059]

## PAUL & THE DOCETIC CHRIST

Like Blake and thousands of other early Christians, Paul too was greatly upset with the Ecclesia and its constant meddling with authentic Church history and doctrine. Indeed, by claiming that Jesus was the only person in human evolution who possessed a divine nature, the Church at Rome had violated the Lord's own teaching on the catholicity of the Indwelling Christ,[3060] as well as the teachings of the Apostles![3061]

Not only this, but, so Paul claimed, he himself had personally encountered the Universal Indwelling Christ[3062] (in a spectral form known in Gnostic circles as a "phantasm") on the road to Damascus.[3063] Thus, he strongly warned his followers to avoid being seduced by the Church's false beliefs regarding the Master.

In the following passages from 2 Corinthians, surely two of the most sensational scriptures in the entire Bible, Paul reemphasizes the universality[3064] and invisibility of the Christ Within,[3065] reasserting the Docetic idea that though Jesus was indeed the Christ (that is, He, like all humans, possessed the Indwelling Christ), the two are, in fact, separate entities:[3066]

> ". . . though *we have known Christ after the flesh*, yet now henceforth *know we him no more.* Therefore *if any man be in Christ*, he is a new creature: old things are passed away; behold, all things are become new."[3067]

## THE TRUTH OF GOD BECAME "A LIE"

The inevitable consequences of all this have been spiritually catastrophic for Christianity: Jesus preached what he called "the Gospel of the Kingdom,"[3068] yet those who came after Him began preaching what they called "the Gospel of Jesus Christ"[3069]—entirely destroying and suppressing the Master's primary message: we are all one with the Indwelling Christ[3070] and with God.[3071]

Thus, as Paul states, they began to "pervert the Gospel of [the Indwelling] Christ"[3072] and "preacheth another Jesus,"[3073] and "the truth of God" was transformed "into a lie"[3074] and a "fable."[3075]

> "For such are false apostles, deceitful workers, transforming themselves into the apostles of Christ."[3076]

In addition, having "changed the glory of the uncorruptible God into an image made like to corruptible man, and to birds, and fourfooted beasts, and creeping things," Christians began to worship a "dead" physical image of God rather than the "living" invisible God Himself,[3077] which went completely contrary to Jesus' teachings.[3078]

In the Gnostic Christian work entitled the Apocalypse of Peter, the author complains about those "empty rivers" who "mislead," who are "without [inner] perception," who "oppose and blaspheme the truth," who "do not understand the Mystery," and who serve only as "messengers of error." Who are these individuals? According to this particular Christian document, they are those unqualified men and women who have presumptuously assumed leadership of the institutional church, "as if they have gotten their authority from the Father."[3079]

The manmade changes created by these spiritually blind individuals were already well underway in the late 60s of the 1st Century, when the canonical Peter referred to them as "damnable heresies," "evil spoken against the Way of Truth,"[3080] and "cunningly devised fables"![3081]  In his letter to the Colossians, Paul wrote:

> "Beware lest any man spoil you through philosophy and vain deceit, after *the tradition of men*, after the rudiments of the world [mass mind], and *not after [the Indwelling] Christ.*"[3082]

In the midst of the Church's massive assault on the Lord and his sacred teachings, Paul urged his followers to hold

> "fast the faithful word as he hath been taught, that he may be able by sound doctrine both to exhort and to convince the gainsayers. For there are many unruly and vain talkers and deceivers . . . who subvert whole houses, teaching things which they ought not, for filthy lucre's [money's] sake. . . . [Beware of them;] not giving heed to *Jewish fables*, and *commandments of men*, that turn from the truth."[3083]

On April 11, 1823, America's third president, Thomas Jefferson, wrote a letter to our second president, John Adams, discussing his views on the Paganization of Jesus and the wholesale distortion of His sacred words by the organized branch of Christianity:

> "The truth is, that the greatest enemies to the doctrines of Jesus are those, calling themselves the expositors of them, who have perverted them for the structure of a system of fancy absolutely

incomprehensible, and without any foundation in His genuine words. And the day will come, when the mystical generation of Jesus, by the Supreme Being as His Father, in the womb of a virgin, will be classed with the fable of the generation of Minerva in the brain of Jupiter. But we may hope that the dawn of reason, and freedom of thought in these United States, will do away all this artificial scaffolding, and restore to us the primitive and genuine doctrines of this the most venerated Reformer of human errors."

Jefferson is right, of course, and yet how unfortunate for the world. Jesus taught that we are to personally worship an impersonal God, while the modern Church teaches the opposite: that we are to impersonally worship a personal God!

Among those Jesuine doctrines to suffer the most revision was the Master's one and only true Gospel, "the Gospel of the Kingdom."[3084] To turn it from one about His teachings into one about He Himself required major editing, for as we have seen, Jesus never once referred to the Gospel as "my Gospel," the "Gospel about me," the "Gospel of Jesus," or the "Gospel of Christ."

## THE GOSPEL & THE LAW OF ATTRACTION

If the Gospel was not originally about Jesus, who or what was it about? Why did both Jesus and Matthew call it "the Gospel of the Kingdom"[3085] instead of "the Gospel of Jesus"? Why does Mark start off referring to it as "the Gospel of Jesus Christ,"[3086] then a few lines later begins calling it "the Gospel of the Kingdom of God"?[3087] And why did Luke only call it "the Gospel,"[3088] while John makes no mention of it at all?

All of these questions can be resolved by looking at the second Gospeler.

Mark's mention of "the Gospel of the Kingdom of God"[3089] was in reference to the year A.D. 30, when Jesus began His earthly ministry, while his mention of "the Gospel of Jesus Christ"[3090] was what Mark himself was calling it at the time he was writing, about the year A.D. 60, some twenty-seven years after Jesus' death.

The answer to this seeming conundrum then is obvious. It is overt proof that Jesus preached the "the Gospel of the Kingdom [of God]," which is exactly what He called it,[3091] not "the Gospel of Jesus Christ." Though modern clergymen and women like to merge these two Gospels into one, in all actuality they are entirely separate philosophies. This is why the latter one was preached *only* by Jesus' posthumous followers, "making the word of God of none effect"![3092] The question is why the world-shaking, religion-altering switchover?

Jesus never viewed the Gospel as pertaining to Himself. As we have discussed, to the Master of Galilee the "Good News" was always about the Kingdom of God (the Father), which included His doctrines on the Law of Attraction.

Besides His own words, additional proof for this view comes from the fact that He did not specifically direct the Gospel to healthy, wealthy, free, and happy people. Only to the sick, the poor, the imprisoned, and the wretched. Why? Because healthy prosperous individuals are already properly using the Law of Attraction (whether consciously or unconsciously), and therefore do not need it to be taught to them. As the Lord said to His Apostles:

> "They that are whole need not a physician; but they that are sick."[3093]

There is a deeper meaning here than what first appears, however. Psychologically, Jesus is saying:

> "Those who are enlightened ('whole') do not need spiritual assistance; only those who have not yet discovered their oneness with God (the 'sick')."[3094]

The "whole" of course are "whole" because they know about and correctly use the Law of Attraction, while the "sick" are "sick" because they are still completely unaware of it, or they know of it but are using it incorrectly. This is why Jesus focused His attention almost exclusively on the latter group.

Thus, in illustrating the purpose of the Gospel, Jesus mystically paraphrased the book of Isaiah:[3095]

> "The Spirit of the Lord is upon me, because he hath anointed me to preach *the gospel* to the poor [materially impoverished]; he hath sent me to heal the brokenhearted [those subjugated by Satan], to preach deliverance [the Law of Attraction] to the captives [those bound in a self-made hell], and recovering of sight to the blind [the spiritually ignorant], to set at liberty them that are bruised [those who have created difficult lives for themselves]. . ."[3096]

Now we have a better understanding of what Jesus actually meant when He sent out the Twelve Apostles to preach "the Gospel of the Kingdom." He did not tell them to go to the fit (successful) and able-bodied (spiritually enlightened). Instead, He gave them this command:

> "Heal the sick, cleanse the lepers, raise the dead, cast out devils:

freely ye have received, freely give."[3097]

In Luke the connection between Jesus, the Gospel of the Kingdom of God, the Law of Attraction, and the unenlightened of society is even more striking:

> "Then he called his twelve disciples together, and gave them power and authority over all devils [psychosomatic illnesses], and to cure diseases [physical ailments]. And he sent them to preach *the kingdom of God* [Divine Mind], and to heal the sick [unenlightened]. . . . And they departed, and went through the towns, preaching *the gospel*, and healing every where."[3098]

The Gospel of Matthew gives us this astonishing passage:

> "And Jesus went about all the cities and villages, teaching in their synagogues, and preaching *the gospel of the kingdom*, and healing every [spiritual] sickness and every [physical] disease among the people."[3099]

Again, let us note that Matthew does not say Jesus went out and preached "the Gospel of Jesus Christ." He states that Jesus preached "the gospel of the kingdom," the same phrase the Lord uses for the Gospel.[3100] This, the one and only true *original* Gospel, contains His principles on the Law of Attraction and what I call "the Realm of Divine Mind." These authentic "principles of the doctrine of Christ"[3101] are corroborated by several other passages in Luke:

> "And the people . . . followed him [Jesus]: and he received them, and spake unto them of *the kingdom of God*, and healed them that had need of healing."[3102]

> [Jesus said:] "And into whatsoever city ye enter, and they receive you, eat such things as are set before you: and heal the sick that are therein, and say unto them, '*The kingdom of God* is come nigh unto you [that is, it is inside of you right now].'"[3103]

Other accounts connected with Jesus offer further supporting evidence. Once, when He was resting in the desert, the multitudes followed Him there and implored Him not to leave. He could not stay, however, for He had an important mission—but it was not to preach the *Gospel of Jesus Christ*. As He Himself said:

> "I must preach the *Kingdom of God* to other cities also: for therefore am I sent."[3104]

Again, Jesus' focus is not on Himself, it is on God, Divine Mind. This is why Paul referred to it not as the "kingdom of Jesus," but as "the kingdom of [the Indwelling] Christ and of God."[3105]

## THE GOSPEL IN THE REST OF THE NEW TESTAMENT BOOKS

The writers of the Apostolic history, Pauline epistles, Petrine epistles, general epistles, and the Johannine material (including the Apocalypse) well understood the true meaning of the Gospel Jesus preached. This is why, after all, they also never use the specific phrase "the Gospel of Jesus Christ."[3106] Instead, they call it: "the gospel of the grace of God,"[3107] "the gospel of God,"[3108] "the gospel of peace,"[3109] "the gospel of your salvation,"[3110] "the gospel of the blessed God,"[3111] or simply "the gospel."[3112]

Paul never uses the phrase "Gospel of Jesus Christ" either, but instead makes reference to his own personal teachings, telling the "believers" at Rome that they will one day be judged "by Jesus Christ according to *my* gospel."[3113]

Paul does make mention of the "gospel of his Son"[3114] and the "gospel of Christ."[3115] But this term, "Christ's gospel,"[3116] is the same as calling it "the Gospel of the Divine Self"—Christ and Son being the mystical Christian words for "the Higher Self of each individual,"[3117] something the enlightened Apostle knew as "the mystery of the gospel."[3118]

It was Paul too who came closest to labeling the Gospel what it really is when he called it the "gospel according to the power of God."[3119] This "power of God" is that great spiritual force that lies within all believers.[3120] It is the power of thought of the Universal Divine Mind, the combined elements of our inner psychological trinity: the Superconscious Mind (the "Father," or God), the Conscious Mind (the "Son," or the Word), and the Subconscious Mind (the "Holy Ghost," or Holy Spirit).[3121] It is the same thought-power that Jesus displayed when he taught the multitudes,[3122] and of which Luke spoke·

> "And they were astonished at his doctrine: for his word was with power."[3123]

Now it is clear why Paul preferred referring to the Glad Tidings not as "the gospel of Jesus," but as "the gospel of God," or in modern parlance, "the Good News of Divine Mind."[3124]

## PROOF OF THE SUPPRESSION OF JESUS' ORIGINAL GOSPEL

How calamitous and egregious it is that the modern day Christian Church, the

Ecclesia, no longer teaches the authentic Gospel of our Lord, what He Himself called "the Gospel of the Kingdom."[3125]  In fact, what He labeled the all-important "mysteries of the Kingdom of God,"[3126] is completely absent from mainstream Christianity today.

No wonder the Church no longer "heals the sick, cleanses the lepers, raises the dead, casts out devils,"[3127] or performs any other "miracles": with the purposeful concealment of His true Gospel (that Man and God are one),[3128] Jesus' teachings on the Law of Attraction (which include His health, happiness, and prosperity doctrines) have also virtually disappeared.

I, along with millions of other Christians, consider these facts irrefutable proof that the Master's most important teachings, His mystical messages, have been suppressed by the Church, much to the spiritual and physical impoverishment of both the laity and the clergy.

Despite the loss of much of Jesus' genuine teachings, however, there is still much that can be learned about His Law of Attraction doctrines from surviving texts, as this very book abundantly attests.  Blessed be His Holy Name forever and ever![3129]

# NOTES

1. Because Jesus purposefully neglected to clearly define the "Kingdom of God," Bible scholars have never been able to agree on exactly what it is, and to this day there is no consensus among orthodox Christian authorities as to its theological meaning. Among mystical Christian authorities, however, no such problem exists, for, as I show, the genuine interpretation of the "Kingdom of God" is actually well-known, having been passed down through numerous secret Christian societies and brotherhoods into the present day.

2. See e.g., Matthew 13:1-53.

3. See e.g., Matthew 15:15-17; 16:5-12; Mark 7:17-18; Luke 2:50; John 10:6.

4. See Eusebius' *History of the Church*, 3:39.

5. For Paul's reference, see Acts 20:35, where he cites a saying by Jesus that is not found in the canonical Bible.

6. In the minds of the Q people, once Q was absorbed into Matthew, Luke, and Mark (not to mention numerous other noncanonical Gospels and works), they probably saw little reason to preserve it. Thus, it gradually fell out of use and eventually vanished. After all, it was considered a theological document, not a historical one. At the time then, little or no importance was attached to it. Examples of the Gospel of Q that were used in the Gospel of Matthew: 5:3-4, 6, 39, 42, 44-47; 6:9-13; 7:7-11, 12; 10:26-31, 39; 8:20-22; 16:25.

7. For more on Jesus and Q, see my book, *Jesus and the Gospel of Q*.

8. At least 35 percent of the words in the Gospel of Thomas parallel those in Q.

9. The Gospel of Thomas (and its 114 sayings, or doctrines of Jesus) was discovered at Nag Hammadi, Egypt, in 1945, with the first English translation coming out in 1959. This particular (physical) document has been dated to around the year A.D. 340, although earlier corroborating finds at Oxyrhynchus, Egypt, date back to at least A.D. 130. Due to the style, wording, and tone of the Gospel of Thomas, the Nag Hammadi and Oxyrhynchus fragments must have been based on a scroll containing the core sayings of Jesus that was composed as early as the 30s or 40s A.D., that is, the Gospel of Q. Thus, the original Gospel of Thomas was probably written sometime between A.D. 50 and 75. This makes the Gospel of Thomas—which may actually turn out to be a version of the Gospel of Q— of particular importance to those who are interested in learning about the pre-Paganized, pre-politicized, pre-Catholicized figure of Jesus, His original teachings, and His original followers, the Jesus community of Q.

10. Matthew 18:3.

11. Matthew 13:45-46.

12. Romans 16:25.

13. John 1:38, 49; 6:25.

14. Isaiah 9:6.

15. Matthew 8:14-18; 9:1-8, 35; Luke 4:23.

16. Matthew 7:20.

17. Proverbs 23:7; the Gospel of Philip, Logion 48; Matthew 7:12; 9:22, 29.

18. Hebrews 4:12.

19. I cover this topic at length in my science-based book, *UFOs and Aliens: The Complete Guidebook*, which has been endorsed by numerous scientists.

20. See e.g., Matthew 23.

21. Einstein also made these two statements: "I maintain that the cosmic religious feeling is the strongest and noblest motive for scientific research." "Science without religion is lame; Religion without science is blind."

22. Emerson's exact quote: "All science is transcendental or else passes away. Botany is now acquiring the right theory—the avatars of Brahma [God] will presently be the textbooks of natural history."

23. Psalms 91:1-16.

24. 1 Corinthians 15:51.

25. Mark 10:27; Revelation 3:8.

26. 1 Corinthians 2:10.

27. Acts 9:18.

28. John 9:25.

29. Matthew 11:15.

30. 1 John 1:5.

31. Matthew 13:35.

32. Revelation 14:6.

33. 1 Corinthians 2:7.

**34.** Acts 17:27-28; Romans 8:11; 1 Corinthians 3:16; 1 John 3:24; 4:12, 15-16.

**35.** Mark 16:15.

**36.** Ephesians 5:14.

**37.** Matthew 16:19.

**38.** Mark 9:23; 10:27.

**39.** Colossians 2:2-3.

**40.** Romans 8:14.

**41.** Matthew 16:17.

**42.** AGJC, 9:11.

**43.** 1 Thessalonians 5:6; Proverbs 10:5.

**44.** Romans 13:11.

**45.** Mark 12:34.

**46.** Matthew 18:3.

**47.** Matthew 4:23; 9:35; 24:14; Mark 1:14.

**48.** Matthew 6:6, 18.

**49.** Luke 17:20-21.

**50.** Matthew 25:34.

**51.** Ephesians 1:17.

**52.** Colossians 1:12.

**53.** John 16:24.

**54.** 2 Corinthians 4:15.

**55.** Philippians 2:13.

**56.** Revelation 4:11.

**57.** Luke 12:32.

**58.** 1 Corinthians 3:21-22.

**59.** 1 Peter 1:4.

**60.** Proverbs 18:21.

**61.** Exodus 3:8.

**62.** John 10:34.

**63.** John 14:12. In the Gnostic Christian work, the Apocryphon of James (also known as the Secret Book of James), 6:17-20, Jesus tells His Twelve Apostles: "Become better than I; make yourselves like the son of the Holy Spirit."

**64.** Genesis 3:22.

**65.** Psalms 82:6.

**66.** Isaiah 41:23.

**67.** See e.g., John 17:21; Hebrews 12:10; 2 Peter 1:4.

**68.** See e.g., Mark 3:21; John 10:19-20.

**69.** See e.g., Matthew 26:65; Mark 14:64; John 10:33.

**70.** Philippians 2:6.

**71.** John 10:34.

**72.** John 10:22-40.

**73.** My paraphrasal.

**74.** Pertaining to John 10:34: here the KJV has long used the singular Greek word *theos* (θεος), meaning a "god" or "God" (the singular Greek word for "goddess" is *thea*). Taking *theos* then, if we translate Jesus' statement literally, He is actually saying: "you are god," or even "you are God." This meaning, of course, correlates exactly with the metaphysical teachings of mystical Christianity, that we are not just merely gods and goddesses in our own right, but, being extensions or individualizations of the Divine, we are each a piece of God the Father Himself. Thus, the esoteric (inner) meaning of "you are gods" is "you are God." It is intriguing to note that the scripture Jesus is quoting, Psalms 82:6, uses the Hebrew word *elohim*, which, depending on various factors, can be either plural, meaning "gods" or "goddesses," or plural intensive-singular, meaning "god" or "goddess," or also "God." Additionally we will note that the earliest (currently) known Greek word used in John 10:34 is the plural word *theoi* (θεοι), meaning "gods" (the plural Greek for "goddesses" is *theai*). If the *original* and *complete* Gospel of John is ever found, it will be of great scholarly and theological interest to see what word was actually used in this particular scripture: *theoi* ("gods") or *theos* "god"). Mystically, however, it will make little difference, for both words have the same spiritual meaning and significance.

**75.** John 17:21; Hebrews 12:10; 2 Peter 1:4.

**76.** John 17:20-23.

**77.** Galatians 4:7.

**78.** Galatians 4:19.

**79.** Colossians 3:10-11. For more on this topic, see my book, *Christ Is All and In All.*

**80.** See e.g., Acts 17:7, where both Caesar and Jesus are referred to as a "king." In Acts 26:28, during his conversation with Paul, King Herod Agrippa uses the word "Christian" derogatorily, for as a royal he has been christed ("anointed") and is therefore already a "Christ."

**81.** See e.g., Leviticus 4:3; 1 Samuel 2:10; 2 Samuel 1:21; 1 Chronicles 16:22; Psalms 18:50; Isaiah 45:1; Lamentations 4:20; Daniel 9:25-26; Habakkuk 3:13.

**82.** See e.g., Matthew 1:1, 18.

**83.** See e.g., Matthew 16:16, 20; 26:63; John 1:41; 4:29, 42; 7:41; 11:27; 20:31; 1 John 5:1.

**84.** 2 Corinthians 13:5.

**85.** Colossians 1:27. See also Romans 8:10; 1 Corinthians 6:15, 17; 2 Corinthians 5:16; 13:3, 5.

**86.** Philippians 2:5.

**87.** John 1:9.

**88.** Daniel 7:13-14.

**89.** Matthew 22:41-46. See also Daniel 7:13-14; Micah 5:2; Matthew 28:20; John 8:58; Hebrews 7:3; Revelation 22:13.

**90.** See the Gnostic Christian work, the Prayer of the Apostle Paul.

**91.** Proverbs 20:27.

**92.** Revelation 1:16.

**93.** Malachi 4:2.

**94.** As I point out in my book *Christmas Before Christianity* (pp. 68, 77), Jesus' title, Christ, derives from the old Babylonian word for the Chaldean sun-god, *Chris*; in Hebrew, *hrs*, or with vowels, *heres*. The Greeks later borrowed *Chris* for their word for anointing, *christos*, which became Christ, "the anointed," in English.

**95.** Revelation 5:5.

**96.** John 12:36.

**97.** Ephesians 5:14.

**98.** My paraphrasal.

**99.** Colossians 1:25-27.

**100.** My paraphrasal.

**101.** 1 John 3:2.

**102.** 1 John 3:1.

**103.** Romans 8:14.

**104.** Genesis 1:27.

**105.** Galatians 4:3-7. See also Romans 8:15.

**106.** The Acts of Paul and Thecla, 1:19. My paraphrasal.

**107.** AGJC, 92:11-12.

**108.** Matthew 1:1.

**109.** John 1:12.

**110.** Psalms 45:7.

**111.** Galatians 2:20; 2 Corinthians 13:5.

**112.** 2 Corinthians 1:21.

**113.** Due to their close companion in the book of Hebrews (7:3, 21), some early Christian mystery schools taught that Jesus was a reincarnation of Melchizedek, as did the ancient Gnostic Christians. See e.g., the Gnostic Christian Jewish document entitled, Melchizedek. My mainstream Christian copy of the King James Bible lists Melchizedek as a "type of Christ." See also Psalms 110:4; Revelation 22:13.

**114.** Hebrews 7:3. Hindus preach the same doctrine: all who attain at-one-ment with God (Christhood) become a Melchizedek or Christ. Thus the enlightened ancient Hindu teacher and philosopher Sri Adi Shankara wrote: "Mind, nor intellect, nor ego, feeling . . . I am He, I am He, Blessed Spirit, I am He! No birth, no death, no caste have I; Father, mother, have I none. . . ."

**115.** Daniel 7:13-14.

**116.** Besides Jesus and Melchizedek, many other enlightened souls have been described in this manner. One modern example is the great Indian Saint Sri Mahavatar Babaji, who is known as the "deathless sage." The miracle-working holy man, who has "no birthday, parents, or family," is at least hundreds of years old, a fact attested to by the many individuals who have encountered him over the centuries. Despite this, the "ageless and immortal" Babaji, who, like Jesus, can levitate, biolocate, perform instant healings, and raise the dead (among many other "miracles"), is said to still be walking the earth to this day, usually—though he can take on any physical form—appearing to startled eyewitnesses as a radiant young man.

117. Matthew 24:14. See also Matthew 4:23; 9:35; Luke 4:43.

118. Revelation 14:6.

119. Genesis 1:26-27.

120. 2 Corinthians 1:21.

121. 2 Corinthians 11:10.

122. Galatians 1:16.

123. 1 John 2:20.

124. Galatians 4:19.

125. 2 Corinthians 4:4.

126. Genesis 1:26-27.

127. 2 Corinthians 3:18.

128. Matthew 24:23.

129. Daniel 7:13-14.

130. John 12:32; 14:20; 15:4; 17:21-23, 26; Colossians 1:27; 3:10-11; Romans 8:10; 1 Corinthians 6:15, 17; 2 Corinthians 5:16; 13:3, 5; Galatians 1:16; 2:20; 4:19; Ephesians 3:14-17; Philippians 1:20; 2:5; 1 Peter 1:11; 1 John 2:27; 3:24; 4:4.

131. John 14:8-11.

132. See Isaiah 64:8.

133. 2 Corinthians 4:7.

134. 2 Corinthians 4:11.

135. Matthew 23:10. See also Colossians 4:1; 2 Corinthians 13:5.

136. Psalms 8:5. Here, the KJV uses the word "angel," a seemingly purposeful mistranslation of the original *elohim*, a Hebrew masculine word whose traditional meaning is usually defined as "a plurality of male deities," but is usually written, misleadingly, as simply "God." In some mystical Christian schools, however, the Elohim is a group of seven female deities, the daughters of the enigmatic priest Melchizedek. In others the Elohim is comprised of seven pairs of male and female couples: 1) Hercules and Amazonia, 2) Apollo and Lumina, 3) Heros and Amora, 4) Astrea and Purity, 5) Cyclopea and Virginia, 6) Peace and Aloha, and 7) Arcturus and Victoria. In the Bible the Elohim are known occultly as "the seven spirits of God" (see e.g., Revelation 3:1; 4:5; 5:6) and the "morning stars" that "sang together" (Job 38:7). In traditional mainstream Christianity the Elohim are the creators of the Universe, Man, and all life on earth, as the Bible itself attests. While the first chapter of Genesis mistranslates the plural elohim as the singular "God," the device is given away in verse 26: "And God said, 'Let *us* make man in *our* image, after *our* likeness.' (Note: the feminine singular of elohim is *eloah*, "goddess," which derives from the divine name-title, El, the name of the Canaanite Supreme male god and father of Baal. The name-title El was absorbed by the ancient Hebrews, becoming a generic name for God. See e.g., Psalms 18:31; 33, 48; 68:21; Job 8:3. El is also used by the Old Testament writers as a prefix fronting other various names of God. See e.g., Genesis 14:18; 17:1; Joshua 3:10. Sometimes the biblical Father is referred to as "El, the God [Elohim]," as in Genesis 33:20.)

137. 1 Corinthians 6:3.

138. Jeremiah 23:6; 33:16.

139. John 17:21; Hebrews 12:10; 2 Peter 1:4.

140. Colossians 1:27.

141. 1 Corinthians 6:15, 17; 2 Corinthians 5:16; 13:3, 5.

142. Daniel 7:13-14.

143. Romans 6:6; Galatians 2:20.

144. Colossians 3:1-3.

145. Galatians 1:16. My paraphrasal.

146. Daniel 7:13-14.

147. Matthew 22:41-46. See also Daniel 7:13-14; Micah 5:2; Matthew 28:20; John 8:58; Hebrews 7:3; Revelation 22:13.

148. Psalms 46:10.

149. Exodus 3:14.

150. John 17:21; Hebrews 12:10; 2 Peter 1:4.

151. Exodus 3:4.

152. 1 Corinthians 15:10.

153. Galatians 4:12.

**154.** Just as Christians teach that Jesus is the Logos or the Word, Hindus teach that God is the Aum or Om, the "Creative Word."

**155.** The name Solomon (Sol-Om-On), meaning the "Sun-God of On," indicates that he was an ancient Hebrew rendition of the archetypal sun-god, known in Egypt as Ra, in Greece as Apollo, in Persia as Mitra or Mithra (later Mithras), and in Mesopotamia as Shamash (Chemosh of the Bible). See e.g., 1 Kings 11:7, 33. Thus mystically Solomon and his 1,000 "wives, princesses, and concubines" (1 Kings 11:3) symbolize the Solar System, with the women representing the planets and various other celestial bodies. Solomon's "black" lover (see e.g., Song of Solomon 1:1-4, 5-8) is none other than the Egyptian Isis, Supreme Mother-Goddess and personification of the earth (that is, black topsoil).

**156.** Revelation 1:8, 11; 21:6.

**157.** Revelation 3:14. For John's corresponding Gospel text, see John 1:1-3.

**158.** 2 Corinthians 3:18.

**159.** Isaiah 40:6.

**160.** Galatians 4:19.

**161.** Colossians 3:11.

**162.** Genesis 1:27.

**163.** Ephesians 3:16.

**164.** Romans 7:22.

**165.** 1 Peter 3:4.

**166.** Acts 3:14.

**167.** Daniel 7:9, 13, 22.

**168.** Hebrews 13:8.

**169.** John 12:34.

**170.** John 12:32; 14:20; 15:4; 17:21-23, 26; Colossians 1:27; 3:10-11; Romans 8:10; 1 Corinthians 6:15, 17; 2 Corinthians 5:16; 13:3, 5; Galatians 1:16; 2:20; 4:19; Ephesians 3:14-17; Philippians 1:20; 2:5; 1 Peter 1:11; 1 John 2:27; 3:24; 4:4.

**171.** John 18:5-6.

**172.** Mark 14:61-62.

**173.** John 8:23.

**174.** John 6:35.

**175.** John 10:7. In Hinduism, this cosmic "door" is viewed as a spiritual portal through which trained yogis can leave and reenter their physical bodies at will. Thus Jesus, speaking as the Indwelling Christ, said: " I am the door: by me if any man enter in, he shall be saved, and shall go in and out, and find pasture." John 10:9.

**176.** John 10:11.

**177.** John 8:12.

**178.** Revelation 1:18.

**179.** John 13:13.

**180.** Matthew 11:29.

**181.** John 18:37.

**182.** John 14:6.

**183.** John 15:1.

**184.** Mark 14:61-62.

**185.** Daniel 7:13-14.

**186.** Colossians 3:11.

**187.** See Mark 14:63-64.

**188.** Acts 24:14.

**189.** John 1:14.

**190.** Matthew 22:41-46. See also Daniel 7:13-14; Micah 5:2; Matthew 28:20; John 8:58; Colossians 1:17; Hebrews 7:3; Revelation 22:13.

**191.** John 8:58.

**192.** Genesis 11:26.

**193.** Genesis 17:5.

**194.** Ephesians 4:6.

**195.** John 8:23-24; 27-28.

**196.** My paraphrasal.

**197.** Daniel 7:13-14.

198. Genesis 17:1; Exodus 3:14-15; Psalms 46:10; Mark 8:29; 14:61-62; Luke 22:70; John 6:35; 8:12, 23, 58; 9:5; 10:7-11, 30-39; 11:25; 12:26, 46; 13:13; 14:3, 6, 10-11, 20; 15:1; 17:10, 16.
199. John 13:19.
200. Colossians 1:19; 2:9.
201. John 10:30. Zen Buddhists have a similar saying. *Namu Dai Butsu*: "I am one with the great Buddha."
202. John 17:23; Galatians 3:28.
203. Colossians 1:27.
204. Ephesians 2:6, 13.
205. John 17:11.
206. John 17:21-22.
207. See e.g., Isaiah 9:6; Matthew 22:41-45; John 1:1; 14:9; 1 Timothy 3:16; Titus 1:3. Indeed, many mainstream Christian churches today teach that the Jehovah of the Old Testament "became" the man known as Jesus in the New Testament, and even translate the name of Jesus (meaning "Jehovah the Savior") as "He is Jehovah the Savior."
208. Romans 3:29-30.
209. Deuteronomy 6:4; Mark 12:29. See also AGJC, 96:3-7.
210. Isaiah 42:8.
211. Romans 9:26; 2 Corinthians 6:16.
212. John 12:32; 14:20; 15:4; 17:21-23, 26; Colossians 1:27; 3:10-11; Romans 8:10; 1 Corinthians 6:15, 17; 2 Corinthians 5:16; 13:3, 5; Galatians 1:16; 2:20; 4:19; Ephesians 3:14-17; Philippians 1:20; 2:5; 1 Peter 1:11; 1 John 2:27; 3:24; 4:4.
213. Colossians 1:15-17.
214. John 1:1-14. See also John 8:58; Psalms 90:2; 1 Timothy 1:17; Colossians 1:17; Hebrews 9:14; Matthew 22:41-46; Mark 12:35-37.
215. Psalms 82:6.
216. John 10:34.
217. Romans 8:14. See also John 1:12; 1 John 3:1-2.
218. Galatians 3:28.
219. Genesis 1:26-27; 3:5, 22.
220. John 14:9.
221. My paraphrasal.
222. Philippians 3:8.
223. Hebrews 12:10.
224. Leviticus 11:44-45.
225. Psalms 86:2.
226. The doctrine of the hypostatic union—as pertaining only to Jesus—is a late creation of the Catholic Church, which did not formally adopt the concept until the 6th Century, at the Fifth General Council of Constantinople held in A.D. 533. Before that Christians held a myriad of different beliefs on the subject. Among them were those forwarded by such doctrinal authorities as Eutyches, Arius, Apollinaris, and Nestorius.
227. Colossians 2:9-10.
228. Galatians 3:20.
229. See Genesis 17:1; Exodus 3:14-15; Psalms 46:10; Mark 8:29; 14:61-62; Luke 22:70; John 6:35; 8:12, 23, 58; 9:5; 10:7-11, 30-39; 11:25; 12:26, 46; 13:13; 14:3, 6, 10-11, 20; 15:1; 17:10, 16.
230. John 14:20.
231. *Refutation of All Heresies*, Book 10, Chapter 30.
232. *City of God*, Book 11, Chapter 26.
233. From a letter to Adelphos.
234. John 10:34.
235. *Summa Theologica*, Part 3, Question 16, Article 7.
236. From the poem, *Song of Myself*.
237. I have paraphrased John 17:10.
238. Romans 8:16-17.
239. John 10:34. See my book, *Christ Is All and In All.*
240. Luke 6:45.
241. John 15:5.

242. Dr. Sagan's original statement was: "The cosmos is also within us. We're made of star stuff. We are a way for the cosmos to know itself." Powerful and wonderful words from one of the world's greatest skeptical scientists.

243. From Emerson's essay, "Compensation."

244. John 17:21; Hebrews 12:10; 2 Peter 1:4.

245. The Sophia of Jesus Christ, 96:3-4.

246. Job 42:2.

247. John 1:1. The Hindu Vedas, written long before the Bible, possess nearly identical passages, for example: "In the beginning was the Lord of Creatures; second to him was the Word . . . the Word was verily Brahman." In Hinduism, as in mystical Christianity, each individual is seen as possessing the Word, or Divine Logos Within. This idea, which was connected to one of Jesus' original Law of Attraction teachings, was long ago suppressed by the Ecclesia (the mainstream Christian Church).

248. 1 John 1:1.

249. Hebrews 11:3.

250. Hebrews 1:3.

251. My paraphrasal.

252. 1 John 2:14.

253. Revelation 19:13.

254. John 12:32; 14:20; 15:4; 17:21-23, 26; Colossians 1:27; 3:10-11; Romans 8:10; 1 Corinthians 6:15, 17; 2 Corinthians 5:16; 13:3, 5; Galatians 1:16; 2:20; 4:19; Ephesians 3:14-17; Philippians 1:20; 2:5; 1 Peter 1:11; 1 John 2:27; 3:24; 4:4.

255. John 1:3.

256. Hebrews 1:3.

257. Psalms 33:9; John 6:63.

258. The Dialogue of the Savior, Logion 8.

259. John 14:20.

260. John 17:21.

261. 2 Peter 1:2-4.

262. Hebrews 12:10.

263. John 12:32; 14:20; 15:4; 17:21-23, 26; Colossians 1:27; 3:10-11; Romans 8:10; 1 Corinthians 6:15, 17; 2 Corinthians 5:16; 13:3, 5; Galatians 1:16; 2:20; 4:19; Ephesians 3:14-17; Philippians 1:20; 2:5; 1 Peter 1:11; 1 John 2:27; 3:24; 4:4.

264. Genesis 1:26, 28.

265. John 12:26.

266. 2 Corinthians 13:14.

267. 1 John 5:7.

268. Romans 1:20.

269. 1 Corinthians 11:3.

270. 1 Corinthians 8:6.

271. My paraphrasal.

272. See e.g., Luke 17:13.

273. See e.g., John 13:13.

274. See e.g., Matthew 16:20.

275. See e.g., Malachi 4:2.

276. John 14:6.

277. John 1:14.

278. Ephesians 2:18; Romans 5:1-2; 8:10; 1 Corinthians 6:15, 17; 2 Corinthians 5:16; 13:3, 5.

279. 2 Peter 3:8.

280. See e.g., Luke 11:13; 1 Thessalonians 4:8.

281. See e.g., Matthew 3:16; Mark 1:10; Luke 3:22; John 1:32; Revelation 12:1.

282. See e.g., Genesis 2:7.

283. See e.g., John 20:19-22. See also, e.g., AGJC, 9:15-18; 22:10, 13; 26:9; 75:11-12; 95:29; 135:4; 142:3; 145:24; 179:15-16; 180:22, 28.

284. See e.g., Luke 12:12.

285. See e.g., Luke 14:26.

286. See e.g., Matthew 20:27; 23:11; 24:45-51; Mark 9:35; Luke 16:13; John 13:16.

287. Romans 1:1.
288. 2 Timothy 2:24.
289. Titus 1:1.
290. John 14:16-17; 1 Corinthians 6:19; 2 Timothy 1:14.
291. Isaiah 45:11.
292. Matthew 6:10.
293. Matthew 11:27.
294. Ephesians 1:3.
295. Revelation 22:13.
296. Acts 17:28. Paul is quoting the noted Greek poet Aratus of Cilicia, who lived in the 4th and 3rd Centuries B.C. A crater on our moon was named after Aratus.
297. John 3:27.
298. AGJC, 129:18.
299. Mark 12:31.
300. Ephesians 4:25.
301. Romans 12:5.
302. See e.g., Philippians 4:3; Revelation 3:5; 20:12-15.
303. Akasha is more commonly known as the Akashic Records.
304. John 4:24. The KJV has "God is *a* Spirit," which is a mistranslation. The original text is: "God is Spirit." See also Romans 1:20; 1 Timothy 1:17.
305. John 12:32; 14:20; 15:4; 17:21-23, 26; Colossians 1:27; 3:10-11; Romans 8:10; 1 Corinthians 6:15, 17; 2 Corinthians 5:16; 13:3, 5; Galatians 1:16; 2:20; 4:19; Ephesians 3:14-17; Philippians 1:20; 2:5; 1 Peter 1:11; 1 John 2:27; 3:24; 4:4.
306. Hebrews 5:5-6; 6:20. See also Hebrews 7:3. We believers are all members of a very special spiritual community, "a royal priesthood," as Peter called it. 1 Peter 2:9.
307. AGJC, 15:22; Hebrews 9:24.
308. Hebrews 8:2. My paraphrasal. See also Hebrews 9:11.
309. Matthew 22:41-46. See also Daniel 7:13-14; Micah 5:2; Matthew 28:20; John 8:58; Colossians 1:17; Hebrews 7:3; Revelation 22:13.
310. Exodus 3:14; Ezekiel 37:14; John 14:10-11; Romans 8:9, 11; 1 Corinthians 3:16; 6:17; 14:25; 2 Corinthians 6:16; 9:14; Ephesians 2:22; 4:6; Philemon 2:13; 1 John 3:24; 4:4, 12-13, 16; Zechariah 2:10.
311. AGJC, 163:37.
312. Luke 10:16.
313. 2 Corinthians 3:18.
314. 2 Corinthians 1:21.
315. Genesis 1:27.
316. 1 John 4:12. See also John 1:18.
317. John 10:38; 14:8-13.
318. 1 Corinthians 2:16.
319. 1 Peter 4:1.
320. Ancient Gnostic Christians, as they continue to do today, taught the doctrine of "spiritual resurrection" (the spirit leaves the body and ascends into Heaven) as opposed to "physical resurrection" (the spirit and the body remain intact and ascend into Heaven together). For more on the Gnostic Christian view of resurrection see the following works: the Treatise on the Resurrection, the Gospel of Philip, the Testimony of Truth, the Exegesis On the Soul, and the Gospel of Thomas. Some of the canonical works also contain Gnostic elements regarding the resurrection. See e.g., 1 Corinthians 15:50; Romans 6:5; 2 Timothy 2:18; 1 John 2:28; John 11:25.
321. Mark 13:32.
322. John 1:12; Romans 8:14, 19; Philippians 2:15; 1 John 3:2.
323. Job 22:28.
324. 1 Corinthians 6:17; 2 Corinthians 6:16, 18; Ephesians 4:6. See also 2 Samuel 7:14; 1 Chronicles 17:13; Isaiah 43:6; Jeremiah 31:9.
325. Daniel 7:13-14.
326. Colossians 2:9.
327. John 12:32; 14:20; 15:4; 17:21-23, 26; Colossians 1:27; 3:10-11; Romans 8:10; 1 Corinthians 6:15, 17; 2 Corinthians 5:16; 13:3, 5; Galatians 1:16; 2:20; 4:19; Ephesians 3:14-17; Philippians 1:20; 2:5; 1 Peter 1:11; 1 John 2:27; 3:24; 4:4.

328. John 14:23.
329. Colossians 2:10.
330. Philippians 2:5-6.
331. AGJC, 91:35-36, 38-41.
332. Luke 10:22.
333. See 1 Chronicles 28:20.
334. Some of these disciplines and phenomena are merely different words for the same thing.
335. Romans 13:1.
336. Deuteronomy 6:4; Isaiah 42:8; Mark 12:29.
337. See AGJC, 8:2.
338. Romans 11:36.
339. Matthew 22:32.
340. John 14:20.
341. Luke 11:13.
342. John 14:26.
343. John 17:21.
344. 2 Peter 1:3-4.
345. The Epistle of Paul to the Laodiceans, 1:11.
346. Hebrews 12:10.
347. Job 22:28.
348. Romans 16:25.
349. Isaiah 40:22.
350. Ephesians 4:6.
351. Zechariah 1:3.
352. See Colossians 1:12-17.
353. Zechariah 12:1.
354. Genesis 1:1.
355. Proverbs 18:7.
356. Compare Genesis 1:1 with John 1:1.
357. See Romans 11:29.
358. John 18:38.
359. Luke 11:2.
360. My paraphrasal.
361. Matthew 18:18-19.
362. Matthew 16:19.
363. Proverbs 23:7.
364. My paraphrasal.
365. Matthew 16:19.
366. Proverbs 16:9.
367. Isaiah 45:7. See also Proverbs 16:4.
368. AGJC, 73:20.
369. James 3:5-18.
370. The Testament of Levi, 4:6-7.
371. Hebrews 4:12.
372. Revelation 1:16.
373. Isaiah 45:21.
374. Galatians 5:1.
375. Galatians 2:4.
376. 2 Corinthians 3:17.
377. Romans 9:1.
378. John 8:32. See also the Bhagavad Gita 4:16.
379. Matthew 2:23.
380. The Gospel of Philip, Logion 51.
381. Ephesians 2:18; Romans 5:1-2; 8:10; 1 Corinthians 6:15, 17; 2 Corinthians 5:16; 13:3, 5.
382. Genesis 1:28.
383. Deuteronomy 11:26-28.

384. Isaiah 45:7. See also Proverbs 16:4.

385. See Isaiah 45:7.

386. Romans 8:9, 11.

387. 1 John 3:20.

388. AGJC, 20:13.

389. Exodus 3:14; Ezekiel 37:14; John 14:10-11; Romans 8:9, 11; 1 Corinthians 3:16; 6:17; 14:25; 2 Corinthians 6:16; 9:14; Ephesians 2:22; 4:6; Philemon 2:13; 1 John 3:24; 4:4, 12-13, 16; Zechariah 2:10.

390. Proverbs 4:23.

391. Romans 16:25.

392. AGJC, 145:31.

393. Canonical Mark appears to be the "public" version of the original, Secret Mark, which was reserved for Jesus' most advanced students, the Twelve Apostles.

394. Clement referred to Jesus' mysterious teachings in the Secret Gospel of Mark as "that truth hidden by seven veils."

395. Luke 8:10.

396. Clement's comment is from his work *Stromata*.

397. Mark 4:34.

398. AGJC, 115:10-14.

399. John 16:12.

400. Luke 8:10.

401. The belief that "Christ" is Jesus' surname is still current in many parts of the world.

402. See Luke 3:23; John 1:45; 6:42; Hebrews 3:3; 7:24; 10:12.

403. Matthew 16:20.

404. John 12:32; 14:20; 15:4; 17:21-23, 26; Colossians 1:27; 3:10-11; Romans 8:10; 1 Corinthians 6:15, 17; 2 Corinthians 5:16; 13:3, 5; Galatians 1:16; 2:20; 4:19; Ephesians 3:14-17; Philippians 1:20; 2:5; 1 Peter 1:11; 1 John 2:27; 3:24; 4:4.

405. 1 Corinthians 3:16.

406. Matthew 3:2; 4:17; 5:3, 10; 10:7.

407. Colossians 1:27. See also Ephesians 2:13-18.

408. Matthew 5:48.

409. Colossians 2:10.

410. Genesis 1:27.

411. AGJC, 127:6.

412. 2 Peter 1:4.

413. John 17:21,

414. See John 14:12.

415. John 12:32; 14:20; 15:4; 17:21-23, 26; Colossians 1:27; 3:10-11; Romans 8:10; 1 Corinthians 6:15, 17; 2 Corinthians 5:16; 13:3, 5; Galatians 1:16; 2:20; 4:19; Ephesians 3:14-17; Philippians 1:20; 2:5; 1 Peter 1:11; 1 John 2:27; 3:24; 4:4.

416. Romans 8:14; John 1:12.

417. See e.g., Galatians 4:19; 2 Corinthians 1:21.

418. Daniel 7:13-14.

419. See the Gnostic text entitled, the Prayer of the Apostle Paul.

420. See Psalms 110:1.

421. Matthew 22:41-46. See also Daniel 7:13-14; Micah 5:2; Matthew 28:20; John 8:58; Hebrews 7:3; Revelation 22:13.

422. One of the Hindu prayers goes like this: "They call you by so many names. They divide you, as it were, by different names; yet in each one of these is to be found your omnipotence. You can be reached through any of these."

423. These three "essential types of mankind" are also discussed at length in numerous Gnostic Christian texts. See e.g., the document known as the Tripartite Tractate, Part 3, Chapter 14.

424. The orthodox Church was not the only branch that divided its members into three classes. The so-called "heterodox" branch did as well, including the following Christian sects: the Basilideans, the Simonians, the Valentinians, the Marcosians, Manicheans, and the Ophites. As illustrated in the Bhagavad-Gita, Hinduism also teaches that Man must go through three distinct stages of spiritual development before attaining the ultimate goal of self-realization or enlightenment.

**425.** 1 Corinthians 4:1.

**426.** 1 Corinthians 15:41.

**427.** 1 Corinthians 2:7.

**428.** 1 Corinthians 2:10.

**429.** 1 Corinthians 14:2. What was this "hidden wisdom," in Greek, literally the "*Mistikos Sophia*"? From the name itself we know that it was related, in part, to the mysteries of the Sacred Feminine, for Sophia was the great Greek wisdom-goddess (known as Sapientia in Rome, and as Shekina in mystical Judaism), worshiped widely across the Roman world.

**430.** 1 Corinthians 4:1.

**431.** 1 Corinthians 2:6-16; 3:1-3.

**432.** 1 Corinthians 4:8, 14-21.

**433.** Matthew 5:48.

**434.** Matthew 19:21.

**435.** John 17:23.

**436.** Luke 6:40.

**437.** My paraphrasal.

**438.** The Gospel of Thomas, Logion 114. Paul often used this same occult symbolism to denote spiritual immaturity (females) and spiritual maturity (males). See e.g., 1 Corinthians 14:34; 1 Timothy 2:11-12.

**439.** The Gospel of Thomas the Contender, 140:9-11. My paraphrasal. (Some translations have "for" instead of "of.")

**440.** 2 Corinthians 13:9, 11.

**441.** Ephesians 4:13.

**442.** Philippians 3:12.

**443.** Philippians 3:15.

**444.** Colossians 1:28.

**445.** Colossians 4:12.

**446.** 2 Timothy 3:17.

**447.** Hebrews 11:40.

**448.** James 1:4.

**449.** James 3:2.

**450.** 1 Peter 5:10.

**451.** Hebrews 6:1-6.

**452.** 1 Corinthians 2:7.

**453.** Colossians 2:2-3.

**454.** Romans 1:16-17.

**455.** Colossians 1:26.

**456.** The Genesaic cosmogony, or Hebrew creation story, is an obvious apologue: not only are there two separate versions in Genesis (the first, the Priestly Account—which contains no Adam and Eve/Garden of Eden legend—runs from Genesis 1:1-31 through 2:1-3; while the much older second version, the Jehovistic Account, runs from Genesis 2:4-25 through 3:1-24), but earth scientists can find no trace of a worldwide flood during the period it was supposed to have occurred, or at any other time in our planet's history for that matter. Additionally, numerous nearly identical Creation myths were in existence long before the writing of Genesis. Notable examples of pre-biblical cosmologies include the Babylonian creation story, the Sumerian creation story, and the Mesopotamian creation story, all which heavily influenced the writer(s) of Genesis. Other elements were borrowed from older creation myths as well: the Pagans' "First Man" Adamu or Adapa became "Adam," while the Pagans' "First Woman" Hawwah, Hebat, Heba, or Hebe was transformed into "Eve."

**457.** Titus 1:14.

**458.** See e.g., Galatians 4:21-24.

**459.** 1 Peter 3:20-21.

**460.** 1 Corinthians 1:10-12; 4:6, 16.

**461.** Romans 2:16; 16:25; 2 Timothy 2:8.

**462.** 2 Corinthians 3:6.

**463.** Romans 2:29.

**464.** Romans 7:6.

**465.** See e.g., Matthew 13:3, 34; Mark 4:33; 12:1.

**466.** See Matthew 5:1-2.

467. Matthew 13:38.

468. Mark 4:33.

469. See Romans 3:2; Hebrews 5:12; 1 Peter 4:11.

470. Ephesians 2:18; Romans 5:1-2; 8:10; 1 Corinthians 6:15, 17; 2 Corinthians 5:16; 13:3, 5.

471. See Ephesians 2:18.

472. Hebrews 5:11-14; 6:1.

473. Mark 4:10-12.

474. See Isaiah 6:9-10.

475. Matthew 13:10-17.

476. Matthew 13:18-23.

477. My paraphrasal.

478. See John 19:38.

479. Note: Some scholars believe that The Thunder: Perfect Mind is Gnostic, while others do not. I fall in with the former group.

480. Matthew 24:14. See also Matthew 4:23; 9:35; Luke 4:43.

481. 1 Peter 1:12.

482. See e.g., Matthew 17:1; Mark 9:2; 14:33; Luke 8:51; 9:28.

483. My paraphrasal.

484. AGJC, 58:6-9.

485. Matthew 5:48.

486. Romans 1:17; Galatians 3:11; Hebrews 10:38.

487. John 7:24; 2 Corinthians 10:7.

488. 1 Timothy 1:17.

489. Paul repeatedly preached against the anthropomorphic Paganesque God that is embraced in so many Christian churches today. See e.g., 2 Corinthians 6:16; 1 Thessalonians 1:9. See also 1 Corinthians 12:2; Revelation 9:20.

490. Matthew 19:28; Luke 22:30; 2 Timothy 2:12; Revelation 3:12, 21; 5:10; 20:6; 22:5.

491. Luke 17:20-21.

492. Matthew 24:14. See also Matthew 4:23; 9:35; Luke 4:43.

493. Proverbs 18:20.

494. 1 Timothy 1:17.

495. Genesis 1:27.

496. 2 Corinthians 3:18.

497. John 10:34; Psalms 82:6.

498. 2 Peter 1:3. My paraphrasal.

499. Isaiah 55:11.

500. My paraphrasal.

501. Proverbs 16:3.

502. Matthew 11:15.

503. Matthew 16:19.

504. Revelation 10:7.

505. John 16:24.

506. 1 Corinthians 2:7.

507. Luke 8:10.

508. 1 Timothy 3:9.

509. Colossians 2:2-3.

510. Romans 11:33. My paraphrasal.

511. Ephesians 1:9.

512. Ephesians 3:4.

513. Ephesians 5:32.

514. Ephesians 3:3.

515. Ephesians 3:9.

516. Colossians 4:3.

517. John 17:21.

518. 1 John 5:13-15.

519. Jeremiah 33:3.

**520**. Haggai 1:13; 2:5.
**521**. John 8:29; 16:32.
**522**. See e.g., Psalms 66:19-20.
**523**. John 16:23.
**524**. Zechariah 10:6.
**525**. John 4:35.
**526**. See e.g., 2 Samuel 22:7-16.
**527**. Hosea 2:16. The name Baal means "Father" or "Lord."
**528**. Genesis 14:18-20. In these passages El Elyon's name has been mistranslated as the "most high."
**529**. Genesis 17:1; Ruth 1:20. The name Israel itself comes from Paganism: *Is* derives from the name of the Egyptian Mother-Goddess Isis; *Ra* derives from the name of the Egyptian Father-God Ra; and *El* derives from the Canaanite Father-God El. Thus Isis-Ra-El, or Is-Ra-El.
**530**. See e.g., Psalms 2:4-12.
**531**. Exodus 15:3.
**532**. Numbers 11:32-36.
**533**. Exodus 35:2-3.
**534**. Exodus 12:15.
**535**. Deuteronomy 22:20-21; Leviticus 21:9.
**536**. Leviticus 24:16.
**537**. Deuteronomy 18:20.
**538**. See e.g., Numbers 31:1-18; Deuteronomy 2:30-34; 3:6; 7:1-6; 20:16-17; Joshua 6:17-21; 7:10-26; 8:26; 10:28-40; 11:10-21; Judges 18:6, 27; 1 Samuel 6:19; 15:1-8, 33; 18:27; 2 Samuel 8:4; 1 Chronicles 21:1-15; 1 Kings 18:40; 2 Kings 19:35.
**539**. Exodus 34:14.
**540**. There are numerous other biblical scriptures illustrating the capricious barbarity of the Paganized Old Testament "Lord of Lords," the Pagan-styled Hebrew sky-god that Jesus did away with. See e.g., Lamentations 2:21; 3:10-11; Hosea 13:7-8; Ezekiel 6:12-13; 8:17-18; Isaiah 13:6-18; Micah 6:9-16; Nahum 1:2-6; Habakkuk 3:5; Zephaniah 1:2-3.
**541**. See e.g., 2 Maccabees 6:2.
**542**. John 4:24. The KJV has "God is *a* Spirit," a mistranslation. The original is: "God is Spirit." See also Romans 1:20; 1 Timothy 1:17.
**543**. John 5:37.
**544**. John 1:18.
**545**. John 6:46.
**546**. 1 John 4:12.
**547**. The Apocryphon of John, 2:34. My paraphrasal.
**548**. Deuteronomy 5:8.
**549**. AGJC, 8:19-20.
**550**. Luke 20:38.
**551**. Mark 12:18-27.
**552**. John 4:24. The KJV has "God is *a* Spirit." This is a mistranslation. The original text is: "God is Spirit." See also Romans 1:20; 1 Timothy 1:17.
**553**. Romans 8:9, 11; Ezekiel 36:27.
**554**. Colossians 1:15. See also 1 Timothy 1:17.
**555**. 1 Timothy 6:16.
**556**. Acts 7:48. See also Acts 17:24.
**557**. AGJC, 15:22.
**558**. Hebrews 8:2. My paraphrasal. See also Hebrews 9:11.
**559**. John 4:24. The KJV has "God is *a* Spirit," which is a mistranslation. The original is: "God is Spirit." See also Romans 1:20; 1 Timothy 1:17.
**560**. John 12:32; 14:20; 15:4; 17:21-23, 26; Colossians 1:27; 3:10-11; Romans 8:10; 1 Corinthians 6:15, 17; 2 Corinthians 5:16; 13:3, 5; Galatians 1:16; 2:20; 4:19; Ephesians 3:14-17; Philippians 1:20; 2:5; 1 Peter 1:11; 1 John 2:27; 3:24; 4:4.
**561**. Matthew 24:24; Mark 13:22.
**562**. Luke 17:21.
**563**. AGJC, 61:15.

**564**. John 17:21; Hebrews 12:10; 2 Peter 1:4.

**565**. John 4:23.

**566**. Acts 17:22-29.

**567**. 1 Corinthians 11:12.

**568**. 1 John 4:12; Ezekiel 36:27.

**569**. Colossians 1:27; Romans 8:10; 1 John 4:12; 1 Corinthians 6:15, 17; 2 Corinthians 5:16; 13:3, 5.

**570**. John 1:9.

**571**. 2 Corinthians 3:18.

**572**. 1 Corinthians 15:49.

**573**. 2 Corinthians 3:18.

**574**. Matthew 19:28; Luke 22:30; 2 Timothy 2:12; Revelation 3:12, 21; 5:10; 20:6; 22:5.

**575**. Luke 17:20-21.

**576**. Romans 14:17.

**577**. The Gospel of Thomas, Logion 3.

**578**. The Gospel of Thomas, Logion 113.

**579**. *Refutation of All Heresies*, Book 5, Chapter 2.

**580**. Luke 17:20-21.

**581**. Exodus 3:14; Ezekiel 37:14; John 14:10-11; Romans 8:9, 11; 1 Corinthians 3:16; 6:17; 14:25; 2 Corinthians 6:16; 9:14; Ephesians 2:22; 4:6; Philemon 2:13; 1 John 3:24; 4:4, 12-13, 16; Zechariah 2:10.

**582**. John 1:14.

**583**. Proverbs 16:3.

**584**. 1 John 5:19.

**585**. 1 John 2:15-17.

**586**. My paraphrasal.

**587**. The biblical allegory of this account can found here: Matthew 4:1-11.

**588**. See John 16:33.

**589**. Matthew 5:37. See also James 5:12.

**590**. Matthew 24:28.

**591**. John 3:3.

**592**. Matthew 18:3.

**593**. 1 Corinthians 2:16. See also Philippians 2:5.

**594**. 2 Peter 1:11.

**595**. Matthew 18:3.

**596**. The Hindu calls this type of bliss *ananda*.

**597**. Matthew 11:29-30.

**598**. Ezekiel 36:26.

**599**. John 15:7.

**600**. Psalms 30:2.

**601**. Daniel 7:9, 13, 22.

**602**. Malachi 4:2.

**603**. John 12:32; 14:20; 15:4; 17:21-23, 26; Colossians 1:27; 3:10-11; Romans 8:10; 1 Corinthians 6:15, 17; 2 Corinthians 5:16; 13:3, 5; Galatians 1:16; 2:20; 4:19; Ephesians 3:14-17; Philippians 1:20; 2:5; 1 Peter 1:11; 1 John 2:27; 3:24; 4:4.

**604**. 1 Corinthians 2:16.

**605**. Isaiah 45:7.

**606**. Matthew 16:27.

**607**. Colossians 3:25.

**608**. Galatians 6:5.

**609**. Acts 8:9-11. Simon Magus (that is, Simon the Magician) was the founder of the Gnostic Christian sect known as the Simonites or Simonians, and was worshiped by his followers as a god-man comparable to Jesus. From him the word "simony" is derived—though the New Testament story connected with this fact is an obvious fictitious interpolation. See Acts 8:18-25.

**610**. Matthew 5:45.

**611**. My paraphrasal.

**612**. Psalms 91:1.

**613**. My paraphrasal.

**614.** Malachi 3:6.

**615.** Hebrews 13:8.

**616.** 1 Peter 4:19.

**617.** John 12:32; 14:20; 15:4; 17:21-23, 26; Colossians 1:27; 3:10-11; Romans 8:10; 1 Corinthians 6:15, 17; 2 Corinthians 5:16; 13:3, 5; Galatians 1:16; 2:20; 4:19; Ephesians 3:14-17; Philippians 1:20; 2:5; 1 Peter 1:11; 1 John 2:27; 3:24; 4:4.

**618.** Genesis 17:1; Exodus 3:14-15; Psalms 46:10; Mark 8:29; 14:61-62; Luke 22:70; John 6:35; 8:12, 23, 58; 9:5; 10:7-11, 30-39; 11:25; 12:26, 46; 13:13; 14:3, 6, 10-11, 20; 15:1; 17:10, 16.

**619.** Psalms 30:10; 1 Corinthians 3:9; 2 Corinthians 6:1; Ephesians 2:19-22; Hebrews 13:6.

**620.** Hebrews 6:19.

**621.** Galatians 4:28.

**622.** Hebrews 6:17.

**623.** Galatians 3:29.

**624.** My paraphrasal.

**625.** 1 Timothy 3:16.

**626.** The Shepherd of Hermas, 1:3.

**627.** Romans 8:14.

**628.** Galatians 4:1-7.

**629.** Romans 8:16-17.

**630.** Romans 9:22.

**631.** John 12:32; 14:20; 15:4; 17:21-23, 26; Colossians 1:27; 3:10-11; Romans 8:10; 1 Corinthians 6:15, 17; 2 Corinthians 5:16; 13:3, 5; Galatians 1:16; 2:20; 4:19; Ephesians 3:14-17; Philippians 1:20; 2:5; 1 Peter 1:11; 1 John 2:27; 3:24; 4:4.

**632.** Exodus 3:14; Ezekiel 37:14; John 14:10-11; Romans 8:9, 11; 1 Corinthians 3:16; 6:17; 14:25; 2 Corinthians 6:16; 9:14; Ephesians 2:22; 4:6; Philemon 2:13; 1 John 3:24; 4:4, 12-13, 16; Zechariah 2:10.

**633.** 1 Corinthians 3:23.

**634.** John 1:1-14. See also John 8:58; Psalms 90:2; 1 Timothy 1:17; Hebrews 9:14; Matthew 22:41-46; Mark 12:35-37.

**635.** Ephesians 1:11.

**636.** See Genesis 17:1-14.

**637.** Acts 3:25.

**638.** Zechariah 8:8. One of the etymologies of Jerusalem is "abode of peace."

**639.** Isaiah 40:3-4.

**640.** My paraphrasal.

**641.** Joshua 24:15.

**642.** James 1:8.

**643.** Deuteronomy 6:4; Mark 12:29; 1 Timothy 2:5; James 2:19.

**644.** Romans 7:25; 8:6.

**645.** Matthew 6:24.

**646.** 2 Corinthians 6:14-15.

**647.** Galatians 5:17.

**648.** Isaiah 41:18.

**649.** Philippians 4:8.

**650.** Matthew 13:46.

**651.** Psalms 121:1.

**652.** 1 Thessalonians 5:12-23.

**653.** Psalms 33:9; John 6:63.

**654.** Matthew 11:29-30. It is interesting to note that in English the Greek word *zeugos* can be spelled either "yoke" or "yoga." Furthermore, both of these words mean "balance" or "union." Is Jesus actually saying, "my yoga is easy" in this scripture? Many think so. If true, it lends credence to the ancient tradition that during his eighteen "silent" years, our Lord spent some of His time studying in India. According to the Aquarian Gospel of Jesus the Christ, as just one example, this is exactly what He did. See AQJC, Sections Six and Seven.

**655.** Galatians 6:7-8.

**656.** My paraphrasal.

**657.** Ephesians 6:8.

**658.** Galatians 5:22-23.

659. My paraphrasal.

660. Luke 9:56.

661. Romans 15:4.

662. Matthew 6:14-15.

663. Matthew 18:35.

664. Mark 11:25-26.

665. Luke 6:37.

666. Daniel 7:13-14.

667. Genesis 17:1; Exodus 3:14-15; Psalms 46:10; Mark 8:29; 14:61-62; Luke 22:70; John 6:35; 8:12, 23, 58; 9:5; 10:7-11, 30-39; 11:25; 12:26, 46; 13:13; 14:3, 6, 10-11, 20; 15:1; 17:10, 16.

668. Matthew 7:2.

669. Mark 4:24.

670. Luke 6:38.

671. Colossians 3:23-25.

672. Luke 12:2.

673. Romans 15:4.

674. Isaiah 41:13.

675. 2 Timothy 2:7.

676. Genesis 17:1; Exodus 3:14-15; Psalms 46:10; Mark 8:29; 14:61-62; Luke 22:70; John 6:35; 8:12, 23, 58; 9:5; 10:7-11, 30-39; 11:25; 12:26, 46; 13:13; 14:3, 6, 10-11, 20; 15:1; 17:10, 16.

677. John 12:32; 14:20; 15:4; 17:21-23, 26; Colossians 1:27; 3:10-11; Romans 8:10; 1 Corinthians 6:15, 17; 2 Corinthians 5:16; 13:3, 5; Galatians 1:16; 2:20; 4:19; Ephesians 3:14-17; Philippians 1:20; 2:5; 1 Peter 1:11; 1 John 2:27; 3:24; 4:4.

678. Deuteronomy 6:4.

679. Exodus 20:2-3.

680. 2 Corinthians 3:18.

681. Exodus 20:4. See also John 4:24 (note: the KJV has "God is a Spirit," which is a mistranslation); Romans 1:20; 1 Timothy 1:17.

682. Exodus 20:7.

683. Exodus 20:8.

684. Exodus 20:12.

685. Mark 10:29-30. See also Luke 14:26.

686. Psalms 37:14-15.

687. Exodus 20:13.

688. AGJC, 95:26-27.

689. Exodus 20:14. See also Hebrews 13:4.

690. Exodus 20:15.

691. Exodus 20:16.

692. Exodus 20:17.

693. Psalms 107:19-20.

694. Matthew 24:14. See also Matthew 4:23; 9:35; Luke 4:43.

695. See Romans 11:29.

696. Isaiah 42:8; 44:8; Deuteronomy 6:4.

697. 1 Corinthians 8:6.

698. See John 14:20.

699. 2 Corinthians 10:5.

700. Luke 2:49.

701. 2 Corinthians 11:3.

702. See e.g., Matthew 13:55; Mark 6:3; Luke 3:23; 4:22; John 1:45; 6:42.

703. Daniel 7:13-14.

704. John 12:32; 14:20; 15:4; 17:21-23, 26; Colossians 1:27; 3:10-11; Romans 8:10; 1 Corinthians 6:15, 17; 2 Corinthians 5:16; 13:3, 5; Galatians 1:16; 2:20; 4:19; Ephesians 3:14-17; Philippians 1:20; 2:5; 1 Peter 1:11; 1 John 2:27; 3:24; 4:4.

705. Ephesians 3:16.

706. Romans 7:22.

707. 1 Peter 3:4.

**708**. John 1:9.

**709**. Daniel 7:9, 13, 22.

**710**. Genesis 17:1; Exodus 3:14-15; Psalms 46:10; Mark 8:29; 14:61-62; Luke 22:70; John 6:35; 8:12, 23, 58; 9:5; 10:7-11, 30-39; 11:25; 12:26, 46; 13:13; 14:3, 6, 10-11, 20; 15:1; 17:10, 16.

**711**. Hebrews 5:5-6; 6:20. See also Hebrews 7:3; 1 Peter 2:9.

**712**. AGJC, 15:22; Hebrews 9:24.

**713**. Hebrews 8:2. See also Hebrews 9:11.

**714**. These are: 1) love, 2) faith, 3) strength, 4) judgement, 5) understanding, 6) self-control, 7) power, 8) the will, 9) imagination, 10) fervor, 11) orderliness, and 12) acquisitiveness.

**715**. Daniel 7:13-14.

**716**. Matthew 28:18, 20.

**717**. John 16:24.

**718**. My paraphrasal.

**719**. John 16:23.

**720**. My paraphrasal.

**721**. Luke 9-13.

**722**. My paraphrasal.

**723**. John 14:13-14.

**724**. My paraphrasal.

**725**. John 12:32; 14:20; 15:4; 17:21-23, 26; Colossians 1:27; 3:10-11; Romans 8:10; 1 Corinthians 6:15, 17; 2 Corinthians 5:16; 13:3, 5; Galatians 1:16; 2:20; 4:19; Ephesians 3:14-17; Philippians 1:20; 2:5; 1 Peter 1:11; 1 John 2:27; 3:24; 4:4.

**726**. John 15:16.

**727**. My paraphrasal.

**728**. John 15:7.

**729**. My paraphrasal.

**730**. Matthew 21:18-22.

**731**. Matthew 17:20.

**732**. 1 Timothy 3:9.

**733**. Galatians 2:16; 3:14.

**734**. John 15:1-7.

**735**. My paraphrasal.

**736**. Matthew 18:18-19.

**737**. My paraphrasal.

**738**. Matthew 6:31-33.

**739**. My paraphrasal.

**740**. Mark 11:24.

**741**. My paraphrasal.

**742**. Matthew 21:42.

**743**. Matthew 24:14. See also Matthew 4:23; 9:35; Luke 4:43.

**744**. 1 John 3:22.

**745**. 1 John 5:13-15.

**746**. James 1:5-7.

**747**. James 4:3.

**748**. My paraphrasal.

**749**. Galatians 6:7.

**750**. My paraphrasal.

**751**. 2 Corinthians 9:6-12.

**752**. The Epistle of Ignatius to Polycarp, 1:10.

**753**. Numbers 14:28.

**754**. Deuteronomy 30:2, 3, 5.

**755**. Psalms 37:2-8, 11, 18, 22-29.

**756**. Proverbs 23:7.

**757**. Proverbs 21:23.

**758**. 1 John 5:7.

**759.** Genesis 17:1; Exodus 3:14-15; Psalms 46:10; Mark 8:29; 14:61-62; Luke 22:70; John 6:35; 8:12, 23, 58; 9:5; 10:7-11, 30-39; 11:25; 12:26, 46; 13:13; 14:3, 6, 10-11, 20; 15:1; 17:10, 16.

**760.** The Sophia of Jesus Christ, 96:3-4.

**761.** John 12:32; 14:20; 15:4; 17:21-23, 26; Colossians 1:27; 3:10-11; Romans 8:10; 1 Corinthians 6:15, 17; 2 Corinthians 5:16; 13:3, 5; Galatians 1:16; 2:20; 4:19; Ephesians 3:14-17; Philippians 1:20; 2:5; 1 Peter 1:11; 1 John 2:27; 3:24; 4:4.

**762.** John 12:32; 14:20; Galatians 3:20, 28.

**763.** John 1:18. See also 1 John 4:12.

**764.** 1 Corinthians 3:16; 1 John 4:16; Romans 8:11.

**765.** 1 John 2:27; 3:24; 4:4.

**766.** Romans 10:8.

**767.** 2 Timothy 1:14; 1 Corinthians 6:19; 1 Corinthians 6:19; 2 Corinthians 1:22. Also 1 Thessalonians 4:8.

**768.** John 14:16-17.

**769.** Paul acknowledges that God (Divine Mind) is keeping track of everything we think, including our "secret" innermost thoughts. See Romans 2:16.

**770.** AGJC, 28:4-6.

**771.** John 1:14.

**772.** John 8:32.

**773.** Job 11:6.

**774.** Matthew 13:35.

**775.** 1 Peter 1:13.

**776.** Proverbs 29:18.

**777.** Proverbs 16:3.

**778.** Matthew 6:6.

**779.** See e.g., Matthew 9:2; 14:27; Mark 6:50; John 16:33; Acts 23:11; 27:22, 25, 36.

**780.** Ephesians 4:26-27, 29, 31-32; 5:1-2.

**781.** Romans 12:11.

**782.** John 12:32; 14:20; 15:4; 17:21-23, 26; Colossians 1:27; 3:10-11; Romans 8:10; 1 Corinthians 6:15, 17; 2 Corinthians 5:16; 13:3, 5; Galatians 1:16; 2:20; 4:19; Ephesians 3:14-17; Philippians 1:20; 2:5; 1 Peter 1:11; 1 John 2:27; 3:24; 4:4.

**783.** Matthew 5:18.

**784.** Isaiah 45:11.

**785.** Matthew 6:31-33.

**786.** 1 Corinthians 4:20.

**787.** Colossians 1:15.

**788.** Mark 11:22.

**789.** Colossians 2:12.

**790.** 1 Timothy 3:9.

**791.** Hebrews 11:1, 3.

**792.** Our true self, the Christ Within, sees all things spiritually, not materially. Thus, it is from the Indwelling Christ (not teachers or books) that we learn of the many mysteries of the Kingdom of God. See e.g., Galatians 1:11-12; 2 Corinthians 12:1-4; Ephesians 3:1-5. See also Matthew 16:17; Luke 2:26; Romans 1:17; Galatians 1:1; 1 Peter 1:12.

**793.** John 12:32; 14:20; 15:4; 17:21-23, 26; Colossians 1:27; 3:10-11; Romans 8:10; 1 Corinthians 6:15, 17; 2 Corinthians 5:16; 13:3, 5; Galatians 1:16; 2:20; 4:19; Ephesians 3:14-17; Philippians 1:20; 2:5; 1 Peter 1:11; 1 John 2:27; 3:24; 4:4.

**794.** Galatians 2:6.

**795.** 2 Corinthians 10:7.

**796.** John 7:24.

**797.** Galatians 5:6.

**798.** 1 Peter 1:7.

**799.** John 11:40.

**800.** Mark 9:23; 10:27.

**801.** For the full story, see Mark 9:14-27.

**802.** Matthew 14:25-31.

**803.** See Luke 8:22-25.

804. Proverbs 16:3.
805. See Matthew 16:19; Luke 11:2.
806. Hebrews 11:1.
807. Romans 4:17.
808. John 6:35.
809. See Matthew 6:34.
810. Mark 9:24.
811. Hebrews 2:4. See also Galatians 5:22-23.
812. Proverbs 3:5-6.
813. See Matthew 10:8.
814. Luke 12:32. See also Philippians 2:13.
815. See Isaiah 45:9-12; 55:8-9.
816. Romans 16:27.
817. John 1:14.
818. Daniel 1:17.
819. Joel 2:28.
820. Numbers 12:6.
821. Ephesians 5:20.
822. Philippians 4:11.
823. Hebrews 13:5. See also Deuteronomy 31:6.
824. 1 Thessalonians 5:18.
825. Psalms 95:2.
826. 2 Corinthians 9:11.
827. Psalms 30:10; 1 Corinthians 3:9; 2 Corinthians 6:1; Ephesians 2:19-22; Hebrews 13:6.
828. Philippians 4:6.
829. 2 Timothy 2:24.
830. Hebrews 6:12.
831. Jeremiah 29:11.
832. Deuteronomy 31:8.
833. Daniel 7:13-14.
834. Luke 11:33.
835. 1 Corinthians 16:13.
836. Romans 15:5. See also Luke 21:19; Romans 2:7; 12:12; James 5:8; 2 Peter 1:6; Revelation 1:9.
837. Jeremiah 29:11.
838. Matthew 24:13.
839. Matthew 9:29.
840. Luke 22:47-51.
841. Matthew 17:24-27. There is some debate as to whether Jesus caused the coin to manifest in the fish's mouth, or whether He merely caused Peter to catch a fish that had already swallowed a coin. Either way, if we are to take this account literally, it is a "miracle," an awesome demonstration of the power of faith and the Law of Attraction.
842. Mark 6:47-51.
843. Matthew 26:53.
844. AGIC 70:16.
845. Matthew 14:14-21.
846. Matthew 14:25.
847. See e.g., Matthew 8:27; Luke 8:23-25.
848. Matthew 28:18.
849. The Dialogue of the Savior, 9:3. My paraphrasal.
850. Proverbs 16:3.
851. John 14:12.
852. A Gnostic Christian text also known as the Secret Book of James.
853. John 12:32; 14:20; 15:4; 17:21-23, 26; Colossians 1:27; 3:10-11; Romans 8:10; 1 Corinthians 6:15, 17; 2 Corinthians 5:16; 13:3, 5; Galatians 1:16; 2:20; 4:19; Ephesians 3:14-17; Philippians 1:20; 2:5; 1 Peter 1:11; 1 John 2:27; 3:24; 4:4.
854. Galatians 3:26-28.

855. Psalms 27:1.
856. My paraphrasal.
857. John 10:34; 14:12.
858. Matthew 6:8.
859. Isaiah 65:24.
860. See e.g., Romans 2:6-7.
861. Festus accused Paul of this very thing. See Acts 26:24.
862. 2 Timothy 3:7.
863. See e.g., Matthew 15:15-17; 16:6-12; 26:34-35; Mark 14:3-8; John 14:8-9.
864. Hebrews 6:15.
865. Ecclesiastes 3:1. See also Ecclesiastes 3:2-8.
866. Proverbs 10:11.
867. See e.g., Romans 2:6-7.
868. See Romans 11:29.
869. 2 Corinthians 9:15.
870. Galatians 5:1.
871. Isaiah 45:21.
872. Galatians 2:4.
873. 2 Corinthians 3:17.
874. See Deuteronomy 11:26-28. The Book of Life, or Akashic Record, as it is also known, is real. See e.g., Revelation 3:5; 20:12-15.
875. Exodus 3:14; Ezekiel 37:14; John 14:10-11; Romans 8:9, 11; 1 Corinthians 3:16; 6:17; 14:25; 2 Corinthians 6:16; 9:14; Ephesians 2:22; 4:6; Philemon 2:13; 1 John 3:24; 4:4, 12-13, 16; Zechariah 2:10.
876. Sleep deprivation and dream studies show that the real purpose of nightly sleep is dreaming, not bodily rest. The physical tiredness or exhaustion we experience each night before going to bed is merely our soul's method of forcing us to sleep so that we will dream. It is the spirit that is renewed by so-called "sleep" and "dreams," not the body. Our spiritual "batteries" seem to last about sixteen hours a day, after which they require eight hours of "recharging," which is done through dreaming—that is, temporarily visiting the Spirit World, the true home of the soul.
877. Psalms 82:6.
878. John 10:34.
879. Hebrews 5:5-6; 6:20. See also Hebrews 7:3; 1 Peter 2:9.
880. AGJC, 15:22; Hebrews 9:24.
881. 1 John 3:1.
882. Matthew 12:50.
883. Romans 8:38-39.
884. See Luke 15:11-32.
885. Matthew 7:14.
886. AGJC, 12:11.
887. Genesis 28:12; Luke 12:8; John 1:51; Revelation 1:20.
888. Matthew 10:7.
889. Matthew 5:3, 10.
890. Philippians 4:5.
891. John 4:35.
892. Deuteronomy 30:8-18.
893. Proverbs 13:12.
894. See e.g., Genesis 2:9; 3:22; Proverbs 3:18; 11:30; Revelation 2:7; 22:2, 14.
895. Exodus 3:14.
896. Psalms 82:6; John 10:34.
897. Exodus 3:15.
898. John 8:58.
899. Matthew 11:5; Mark, 7:37; John 1:12.
900. Romans 8:14.
901. Ephesians 2:18; Romans 5:1-2; 8:10; 1 Corinthians 6:15, 17; 2 Corinthians 5:16; 13:3, 5.
902. Galatians 5:6.
903. See Romans 4:17.

**904.** See John 7:24; 2 Corinthians 10:7.

**905.** Galatians 2:6.

**906.** John 10:34.

**907.** See Genesis 17:1; Exodus 3:14-15; Psalms 46:10; Mark 8:29; 14:61-62; Luke 22:70; John 6:35; 8:12, 23, 58; 9:5; 10:7-11, 30-39; 11:25; 12:26, 46; 13:13; 14:3, 6, 10-11, 20; 15:1; 17:10, 16.

**908.** See e.g., Revelation 16:17; 21:6. Similarly, on the cross Jesus said: "It is finished." John 19:30.

**909.** See e.g., 1 Chronicles 16:36; Nehemiah 5:13; Psalms 41:13; Matthew 6:13; Luke 25:53; John 21:25; Romans 11:36; Ephesians 3:21; 1 Timothy 1:17; Hebrews 13:21; 1 Peter 5:11; Jude 1:25; Revelation 1:6.

**910.** See Ephesians 5:18-19.

**911.** John 12:35.

**912.** John 1:9.

**913.** Colossians 1:27.

**914.** Genesis 17:1; Exodus 3:14-15; Psalms 46:10; Mark 8:29; 14:61-62; Luke 22:70; John 6:35; 8:12, 23, 58; 9:5; 10:7-11, 30-39; 11:25; 12:26, 46; 13:13; 14:3, 6, 10-11, 20; 15:1; 17:10, 16.

**915.** Genesis 1:27. See also 2 Corinthians 3:18.

**916.** John 12:36. See also 1 Thessalonians 5:5.

**917.** The Gospel of Philip, Logion 48.

**918.** Matthew 18:19.

**919.** See e.g., Romans 2:6-7.

**920.** Psalms 66:19-20.

**921.** Jeremiah 23:36.

**922.** Luke 18:27; Revelation 3:8.

**923.** Luke 8:50.

**924.** Genesis 1:26-27; 2 Corinthians 3:18.

**925.** Matthew 19:26.

**926.** Romans 12:21.

**927.** Psalms 138:8.

**928.** Luke 8:1.

**929.** Matthew 6:6.

**930.** My paraphrasal.

**931.** Philippians 3:20.

**932.** My paraphrasal.

**933.** 1 Corinthians 6:17; 2 Corinthians 6:16; Ephesians 4:6.

**934.** Matthew 6:4.

**935.** Matthew 6:18.

**936.** My paraphrasal.

**937.** Ezekiel 44:13.

**938.** Approaching Spirit from the intellect does not work, for spiritual things are only revealed to Man by way of the Holy Spirit. See e.g., 1 Corinthians 1:17-31; 2:1-16.

**939.** Luke 8:50.

**940.** 1 Corinthians 5:13.

**941.** Matthew 7:6.

**942.** Luke 12:53.

**943.** Matthew 10:37. Hinduism also preaches against over attachment to the biological family, particularly if it impedes one's path to enlightenment, or what we Christians call Christ Consciousness or "the mind of Christ." 1 Corinthians 2:16.

**944.** The Thunder: Perfect Mind, 20:23-25. My paraphrasal.

**945.** The Teachings of Silvanus, 111:8-13. My paraphrasal.

**946.** 1 Thessalonians 5:17.

**947.** Ephesians 6:18.

**948.** Luke 18:1.

**949.** Romans 10:12.

**950.** 1 Peter 3:12.

**951.** John 4:24. The KJV has "God is *a* Spirit," which is a mistranslation. The original text is: "God is Spirit." See also Romans 1:20; 1 Timothy 1:17.

**952.** Acts 17:22-29.

953. 2 Corinthians 1:3.
954. Exodus 3:14; Ezekiel 37:14; John 14:10-11; Romans 8:9, 11; 1 Corinthians 3:16; 6:17; 14:25; 2 Corinthians 6:16; 9:14; Ephesians 2:22; 4:6; Philemon 2:13; 1 John 3:24; 4:4, 12-13, 16; Zechariah 2:10.
955. 1 Corinthians 2:16; Philippians 2:5.
956. The Sophia of Jesus Christ, 96:3-4.
957. Galatians 6:7.
958. John 11:41-42.
959. John 12:32; 14:20; 17:20-23.
960. Psalms 37:4-5.
961. Isaiah 65:24.
962. Isaiah 30:19.
963. 2 Chronicles 7:14.
964. Job 22:27.
965. Jeremiah 29:11-13.
966. Jeremiah 33:2-3.
967. 1 John 5:14-15.
968. Genesis 17:1; Exodus 3:14-15; Psalms 46:10; Mark 8:29; 14:61-62; Luke 22:70; John 6:35; 8:12, 23, 58; 9:5; 10:7-11, 30-39; 11:25; 12:26, 46; 13:13; 14:3, 6, 10-11, 20; 15:1; 17:10, 16.
969. Isaiah 58:9.
970. Philippians 4:6.
971. AGJC, 137:8-9, 14-18.
972. 2 Corinthians 10:5.
973. See e.g., Romans 2:6-7.
974. See Matthew 16:24; Luke 14:26-27, 33; John 8:31-32.
975. See e.g., Mark 1:3; 10:52; Luke 3:4; John 1:23; 14:4; Acts 9:2; 18:25-26; 19:9, 23; 22:4; 24:14, 22.
976. John 12:32; 14:20; 15:4; 17:21-23, 26; Colossians 1:27; 3:10-11; Romans 8:10; 1 Corinthians 6:15, 17; 2 Corinthians 5:16; 13:3, 5; Galatians 1:16; 2:20; 4:19; Ephesians 3:14-17; Philippians 1:20; 2:5; 1 Peter 1:11; 1 John 2:27; 3:24; 4:4.
977. John 14:6. Long before the rise of Christianity, Pagan religions were teaching this same concept. Speaking, as Jesus did, as the Indwelling Christ, Buddha, for instance, said: "You are my children, I am your father. Through me you have been released from your sufferings. I myself, having reached the other shore, help others to cross the stream. I myself having attained salvation, am a savior of others. Being comforted, I comfort others and lead them to the place of refuge. . . . My thoughts are always in the Truth. For lo, my self has become the Truth. Whoever comprehends the Truth will see the Blessed One." Likewise, the Hindu God Krishna declared: "I am the goal of the wise man, and I am the Way. . . . I am the end of the path, the witness, the Lord, the sustainer. I am the place of abode, the beginning, the friend and the refuge."
978. John 3:18. See also 1 John 4:9.
979. Matthew 3:3; Mark 1:3; Luke 3:4; John 1:23; Acts 18:25.
980. Neither the Conscious Mind (the physical/male) nor the Subconscious Mind (the spiritual/female) should ever dominate the other. Finding the ideal equilibrium between the two—known as self-actualization in psychology, and self-realization in Hinduism—should be one of the great goals of every individual. This hypostatic fusion, this symbolic "marriage" of our human and our divine natures (see John 17:21; Hebrews 12:10; 2 Peter 1:4), is known in mystical Christianity as the Hieros Gamos, or "Sacred Union." The physical ritual of the Hieros Gamos was practiced by some early Gnostic Christians (much to the dismay of the Apostles; see e.g., Revelation 2:6-15), but was eventually adopted by the Ecclesia as a metaphor of the union between Christ (the "groom") and His followers (the "bride"). See e.g., 2 Corinthians 11:2; Ephesians 5:25; Revelation 19:7-9; 21:2.
981. Luke 17:20-21.
982. 2 Corinthians 10:5.
983. The Epistle of Barnabas, 14:5.
984. 2 Timothy 1:7.
985. Matthew 10:16.
986. My paraphrasal. See also Romans 16:19.
987. Job 3:25.
988. Hebrews 4:12.
989. Deuteronomy 11:26-28.
990. Ephesians 4:27.
991. Matthew 5:18.

**992**. Matthew 7:12. The Golden Rule, or the Law of Reciprocity, is found in one form or another in all of the major and minor religions, dating from the earliest known societies, including Judaism (see e.g., Leviticus 19:18, and the Testament of Levi, 4:6-7). Some 500 years before the time of Jesus, for example, Confucius said: "What you do not wish for yourself, do not do to others." In the pre-Christian *Mahabharata*, as another example, we find this Hindu passage: "Treat others as thou wouldst thyself be treated. Do nothing to thy neighbor which hereafter thou wouldst not have they neighbor do to thee." Taoism, Islam, Buddhism, Jainism, and Wicca, among many other worldwide religions, have also long taught the Golden Rule.

**993**. Psalms 45:7.

**994**. Proverbs 12:6.

**995**. Ephesians 2:18; Romans 5:1-2; 8:10; 1 Corinthians 6:15, 17; 2 Corinthians 5:16; 13:3, 5.

**996**. Acts 10:34. See also Romans 2:11; Ephesians 6:9; Colossians 3:25; 1 Peter 1:17.

**997**. Ephesians 2:18.

**998**. See e.g., Matthew 19:24.

**999**. Matthew 22:9.

**1000**. Matthew 8:11.

**1001**. 1 Thessalonians 2:12.

**1002**. 1 Peter 5:7.

**1003**. Psalms 91:1, 10.

**1004**. Psalms 23:1-6.

**1005**. 2 Timothy 1:7.

**1006**. Matthew 6:25-33.

**1007**. John 12:32; 14:20; 15:4; 17:21-23, 26; Colossians 1:27; 3:10-11; Romans 8:10; 1 Corinthians 6:15, 17; 2 Corinthians 5:16; 13:3, 5; Galatians 1:16; 2:20; 4:19; Ephesians 3:14-17; Philippians 1:20; 2:5; 1 Peter 1:11; 1 John 2:27; 3:24; 4:4.

**1008**. Matthew 19:28; Luke 22:30; 2 Timothy 2:12; Revelation 3:12, 21; 5:10; 20:6; 22:5.

**1009**. Luke 17:20-21.

**1010**. Matthew 24:14. See also Matthew 4:23; 9:35; Luke 4:43.

**1011**. Mark 1:1.

**1012**. John 7:16.

**1013**. Mark 9:41; John 17:3.

**1014**. John 8:28-29, 40, 42, 50, 54.

**1015**. John 12:26.

**1016**. Matthew 3:2; 4:17; 5:3, 10; 10:7.

**1017**. Matthew 19:26; Revelation 3:8.

**1018**. 2 Peter 1:10-11.

**1019**. 1 Corinthians 1:4-5.

**1020**. AGJC, 71:3-7.

**1021**. Matthew 22:14.

**1022**. Matthew 7:21-23.

**1023**. Matthew 8:11.

**1024**. Matthew 21:31.

**1025**. Acts 14:22.

**1026**. 2 Thessalonians 1:5.

**1027**. The Sermon on the Mount for example (which Jesus partially patterned on a group of exhortatory scriptures known as the Testaments of the Twelve Patriarchs—fragments of which were recently found among the Dead Sea Scrolls), is essentially the Master's entire teaching on the Kingdom of God, which includes many of His Law of Attraction doctrines. See Matthew 5:1-48; 6:1-34; 7:1-29.

**1028**. Genesis 17:1; Exodus 3:14-15; Psalms 46:10; Mark 8:29; 14:61-62; Luke 22:70; John 6:35; 8:12, 23, 58; 9:5; 10:7-11, 30-39; 11:25; 12:26, 46; 13:13; 14:3, 6, 10-11, 20; 15:1; 17:10, 16.

**1029**. Galatians 5:24.

**1030**. Mark 8:35.

**1031**. John 12:32; 14:20; 15:4; 17:21-23, 26; Colossians 1:27; 3:10-11; Romans 8:10; 1 Corinthians 6:15, 17; 2 Corinthians 5:16; 13:3, 5; Galatians 1:16; 2:20; 4:19; Ephesians 3:14-17; Philippians 1:20; 2:5; 1 Peter 1:11; 1 John 2:27; 3:24; 4:4.

**1032**. Ecclesiastes 12:8.

**1033**. 2 Peter 1:5-11.

1034. 1 Corinthians 2:16.
1035. Daniel 7:13-14.
1036. Psalms 27:1.
1037. Hebrews 12:2.
1038. Galatians 5:24.
1039. See Colossians 2:13-14. Here Paul refers to the Lower Self as the "flesh" and the Higher Self as the "Christ."
1040. Galatians 2:20.
1041. Philippians 1:21.
1042. My paraphrasal.
1043. Romans 6:6; Ephesians 4:22; Colossians 3:9.
1044. Ephesians 2:15; 4:24; Colossians 3:10.
1045. Romans 12:2.
1046. 1 John 2:13.
1047. The Epistle of Barnabas, 10:11.
1048. Colossians 3:1-3.
1049. Isaiah 55:6-8.
1050. See e.g., Romans 2:6-7.
1051. This is the same reason hypnosis must be repeated periodically on individuals seeking to rid their minds of negative beliefs, ideas, and concepts.
1052. Enlightened Hindus rightly call death, that is, the shedding of the physical body, "kicking the frame."
1053. Ephesians 2:18; Romans 5:1-2; 8:10; 1 Corinthians 6:15, 17; 2 Corinthians 5:16; 13:3, 5.
1054. Romans 6:23.
1055. My paraphrasal.
1056. See 2 Corinthians 4:16.
1057. Romans 7:18-25.
1058. 1 Peter 5:8.
1059. 1 Corinthians 15:31.
1060. Romans 8:36.
1061. 2 Corinthians 4:16.
1062. Ephesians 4:22-24.
1063. Genesis 1:26-27.
1064. Matthew 10:32-40.
1065. Matthew 11:12.
1066. Matthew 9:16-17.
1067. My paraphrasal.
1068. AGJC, 120:8-11.
1069. 1 Corinthians 2:9; 2 Epistle of Clement, 4:14.
1070. Matthew 26:29.
1071. Romans 12:2.
1072. John 10:34.
1073. John 14:12.
1074. See e.g., Mark 3:21; John 10:20.
1075. See e.g., Matthew 5:1; 14:23; Mark 1:12-13, 35; 6:46-47; Luke 4:1; 5:15-16; 6:12; John 6:15.
1076. Matthew 7:13-14. Pre-Christian religions have long taught this same spiritual concept. The Katha Upanishad of the Hindus, for instance, possesses this scripture: "Like the sharp edge of a razor, the sages say, is the path. Narrow it is, and difficult to tread."
1077. My paraphrasal.
1078. Matthew 5:3, 10.
1079. Matthew 21:31.
1080. Matthew 19:30.
1081. Psalms 119:89-90.
1082. Galatians 5:20-21.
1083. See e.g., 1 Corinthians 1:17-31; 2:1-16.
1084. Luke 17:21.
1085. 1 Timothy 1:17.

**1086.** Luke 13:18-21.

**1087.** Matthew 6:33.

**1088.** Luke 18:29-30.

**1089.** John 3:3.

**1090.** Matthew 18:3.

**1091.** See Appendix B.

**1092.** Jesus warned His followers to be careful of false Christians; that is, those who preach manmade doctrines as if they come from the Master. See e.g., Matthew 15:9.

**1093.** Galatians 4:22-25. Jesus' use of allegory, symbolism, and parables is also well-known. See e.g., Matthew 12:40; 16:5-12; Luke 8:10; John 2:18-21. To prove that the modern practice of literalizing holy scripture is quite absurd, let us consider an example from the book of Revelation, where Jesus is described as a lamb with "seven horns and seven eyes" (Revelation 5:6). Taken literally, this is grotesque, misleading, and nonsensical. Taken symbolically, however, the veil is removed: seven is the number of completion and perfection, horns are symbols of power and strength, eyes are archetypal symbols of knowledge and enlightenment, and the lamb represents purity and innocence.

**1094.** Matthew 24:14. See also Matthew 4:23; 9:35; Luke 4:43.

**1095.** Galatians 2:16.

**1096.** Romans 13:11.

**1097.** Matthew 15:6-9.

**1098.** Romans 10:3. See also Romans 10:1-2.

**1099.** Matthew 15:14.

**1100.** See e.g., Luke 11:42.

**1101.** John 5:17. My paraphrasal.

**1102.** Matthew 12:1-8.

**1103.** Matthew 23:23.

**1104.** AGJC, 95:39-40, 42-43.

**1105.** AGJC, 126:1-19.

**1106.** Matthew 23:1-22, 24-38.

**1107.** AGJC, 126:28-31.

**1108.** 1 Corinthians 10:14.

**1109.** Psalms 2:1.

**1110.** Habakkuk 2:18; 1 Corinthians 12:2.

**1111.** AGJC, 43:13.

**1112.** John 4:24. The KJV has "God is *a* Spirit," which is a mistranslation. The original text is: "God is Spirit." See also Romans 1:20; 1 Timothy 1:17.

**1113.** Philippians 3:3.

**1114.** Acts 17:29.

**1115.** 2 Corinthians 3:6.

**1116.** See Matthew 12:26.

**1117.** 1 Corinthians 9:27.

**1118.** 1 John 3:10.

**1119.** 2 Peter 2:14, 17.

**1120.** See e.g., Matthew 23:1-39; John 8:44.

**1121.** Ephesians 4:18.

**1122.** AGJC, 109:2-11.

**1123.** Galatians 5:17-26.

**1124.** Matthew 5:20.

**1125.** My paraphrasal.

**1126.** Luke 10:21.

**1127.** Luke 12:15.

**1128.** Mark 10:25. The original Aramaic translation of this scripture is: "My sons, how hard it is for those who trust in their wealth to enter into the kingdom of God! It is easier for a rope to pass through the eye of a needle than for a rich man to enter into the kingdom of God."

**1129.** Matthew 18:3.

**1130.** John 12:32; 14:20; 15:4; 17:21-23, 26; Colossians 1:27; 3:10-11; Romans 8:10; 1 Corinthians 6:15, 17; 2 Corinthians 5:16; 13:3, 5; Galatians 1:16; 2:20; 4:19; Ephesians 3:14-17; Philippians 1:20; 2:5; 1 Peter 1:11; 1 John 2:27; 3:24; 4:4.

**1131.** Acts 3:14.

**1132.** Acts 11:26. See Appendix B.

**1133.** See e.g., Matthew 12:49; Mark 6:1; Luke 6:13; John 4:1.

**1134.** Mark 10:15.

**1135.** AGJC, 131:8-15.

**1136.** 2 Corinthians 4:16.

**1137.** Revelation 17:8.

**1138.** 1 Peter 2:1-3.

**1139.** My paraphrasal.

**1140.** AGJC, 126:24.

**1141.** Titus 1:15.

**1142.** 1 Corinthians 2:16.

**1143.** AGJC, 44:22-25.

**1144.** Matthew 18:1-6; 10-14.

**1145.** Ephesians 2:18; Romans 5:1-2; 8:10; 1 Corinthians 6:15, 17; 2 Corinthians 5:16; 13:3, 5.

**1146.** Matthew 7:14.

**1147.** Psalms 30:10; 1 Corinthians 3:9; 2 Corinthians 6:1; Ephesians 2:19-22; Hebrews 13:6.

**1148.** John 10:34. See also Genesis 1:27; Psalms 82:6; Isaiah 41:23.

**1149.** Colossians 1:27; Romans 8:10.

**1150.** Ephesians 2:18; Romans 5:1-2; 8:10; 1 Corinthians 6:15, 17; 2 Corinthians 5:16; 13:3, 5.

**1151.** John 17:21; Hebrews 12:10; 2 Peter 1:4.

**1152.** See e.g., John 14:16-17. See also John 14:26.

**1153.** Matthew 12:31-32.

**1154.** This is particularly true for those who blaspheme due to ignorance in spiritual unbelief. See e.g., 1 Timothy 1:13.

**1155.** John 17:21; Hebrews 12:10; 2 Peter 1:4.

**1156.** John 17:21; Hebrews 12:10; 2 Peter 1:4.

**1157.** Isaiah 53:6.

**1158.** Colossians 3:11.

**1159.** Exodus 3:14; Ezekiel 37:14; John 14:10-11; Romans 8:9, 11; 1 Corinthians 3:16; 6:17; 14:25; 2 Corinthians 6:16; 9:14; Ephesians 2:22; 4:6; Philemon 2:13; 1 John 3:24; 4:4, 12-13, 16; Zechariah 2:10.

**1160.** See e.g., Deuteronomy 6:13; Psalms 115:11, 13.

**1161.** Ecclesiastes 12:13; 1 Peter 2:17; Revelation 14:7.

**1162.** Luke 14:26.

**1163.** My paraphrasal.

**1164.** The Gospel of Thomas, Logion 75. My paraphrasal.

**1165.** Luke 8:10. See also Matthew 13:11.

**1166.** 1 Corinthians 13:12.

**1167.** Luke 17:21.

**1168.** Early Christians, both Gnostic and Ecclesiastic, taught that we cannot know God through the intellect, only through the "heart" (that is, intuition). As such, as Jesus taught, knowledge of God must come from within, from "my Father which is in heaven," not from without. See e.g., Matthew 16:17. See also Luke 2:26; 10:21; 1 Corinthians 1:17-31; 2:1-16; Galatians 1:11-12; Ephesians 3:1-5; 1 Peter 1:12.

**1169.** Ephesians 3:19.

**1170.** See e.g., John 7:14-17.

**1171.** Philippians 2:12. See also AGJC, 100:17. Buddha made a similar comment: "Work out your salvation with diligence."

**1172.** 1 Corinthians 1:17-31; 2:1-16. Thus, one enlightened soul, Socrates, once said: "As for me, all I know is that I know nothing."

**1173.** See Romans 2:28-29.

**1174.** Galatians 6:4.

**1175.** John 3:3.

**1176.** My paraphrasal.

1177. My paraphrasal.

1178. John 12:32; 14:20; 15:4; 17:21-23, 26; Colossians 1:27; 3:10-11; Romans 8:10; 1 Corinthians 6:15, 17; 2 Corinthians 5:16; 13:3, 5; Galatians 1:16; 2:20; 4:19; Ephesians 3:14-17; Philippians 1:20; 2:5; 1 Peter 1:11; 1 John 2:27; 3:24; 4:4.

1179. Matthew 22:41-46. See also Daniel 7:13-14; Micah 5:2; Matthew 28:20; John 8:58; Hebrews 7:3; Revelation 22:13.

1180. John 1:9.

1181. 1 Peter 3:4.

1182. Daniel 7:9, 13, 22.

1183. Ephesians 3:16.

1184. Romans 7:22.

1185. 1 Corinthians 9:25. Early Christians also referred to the Crown Chakra (a symbol of spiritual enlightenment) as the "Crown of Rejoicing" (1 Thessalonians 2:19), "Crown of Righteousness" (2 Timothy 4:8), "Crown of Life" (James 1:12; Revelation 2:10; AGJC, 95:17), "Crown of Glory" (1 Peter 5:4), and the "Golden Crown" (Revelation 14:14). The New Testament portrays the Virgin Mary "clothed with the sun," wearing a similar coronate symbol: a "crown of twelve stars" (Revelation 12:1), an obvious borrowing from the much older Hindu sun-goddess Aditi, who wore a crown of twelve stars representing the twelve signs of the Zodiac.

1186. 1 Peter 5:4.

1187. Luke 11:2.

1188. Genesis 17:1; Exodus 3:14-15; Psalms 46:10; Mark 8:29; 14:61-62; Luke 22:70; John 6:35; 8:12, 23, 58; 9:5; 10:7-11, 30-39; 11:25; 12:26, 46; 13:13; 14:3, 6, 10-11, 20; 15:1; 17:10, 16.

1189. See e.g., Acts 6:4; Ephesians 6:18; Colossians 4:2.

1190. See e.g., Titus 3:8.

1191. See e.g., Psalms 5:1; 19:14; 49:3; 104:34; 119:97, 99.

1192. See e.g., Acts 14:23; 1 Corinthians 7:5.

1193. See e.g., 2 Timothy 3:14-17.

1194. See e.g., Exodus 15:1; Judges 5:3; 2 Samuel 22:50; 1 Chronicles 15:28; 16:7-11, 23-25; 2 Chronicles 20:18-21; 29:25-30; Isaiah 12:4-5; Psalms 57:7-11; 98:4-6; 146:1.

1195. See e.g., Jeremiah 31:3; Luke 6:27; Romans 12:9-10; 1 Corinthians 13:1-13; 1 John 4:7-11, 16-18.

1196. See e.g., 1 Corinthians 13:4, 8, 13.

1197. See e.g., Matthew 5:21-22; 18:3; 22:40; 38-41; 43-46; Luke 6:27-38; John 14:22.

1198. See e.g., John 8:7; Acts 10:28; Ephesians 4:2; Romans 14:1-4; 1 Peter 3:8-11.

1199. See e.g., Psalms 37:26; Proverbs 11:24-25; 19:17; Luke 6:38; 12:33; Acts 20:35; 2 Corinthians 9:6.

1200. Some 500 years before Christ, Buddha laid out his own eight-part guideline for attaining Self-Godhood. It is known as the Noble Eightfold Path: 1) Right View; 2) Right Intention; 3) Right Speech; 4) Right Action; 5) Right Livelihood; 6) Right Effort; 7) Right Mindfulness; and 8) Right Concentration. As all of the world's most enlightened individuals tap into the same universal consciousness, it is probable, or at least possible, that Jesus' eight Beatitudes are loosely based on Buddha's eight "Beatitudes." See Matthew 5:3-10.

1201. Matthew 7:12.

1202. Acts 20:35.

1203. Colossians 2:10.

1204. Luke 19:9.

1205. Luke 3:6; Romans 10:13; Acts 2:17; 2 Peter 3:9.

1206. For more on these topics, see Appendix A and Appendix B.

1207. Matthew 24:14. Jesus publicly uttered this phrase one or two years *before* His death, sometime in A.D. 32 or 33. See also Luke 4:43.

1208. Mark 1:1. This passage was written about the year A.D. 60, some twenty-seven years (a generation) *after* Jesus' death. See Appendix B.

1209. 1 Peter 1:12.

1210. Proverbs 12:14.

1211. Daniel 7:13-14.

1212. John 12:32; 14:20; 15:4; 17:21-23, 26; Colossians 1:27; 3:10-11; Romans 8:10; 1 Corinthians 6:15, 17; 2 Corinthians 5:16; 13:3, 5; Galatians 1:16; 2:20; 4:19; Ephesians 3:14-17; Philippians 1:20; 2:5; 1 Peter 1:11; 1 John 2:27; 3:24; 4:4.

1213. Genesis 17:1; Exodus 3:14-15; Psalms 46:10; Mark 8:29; 14:61-62; Luke 22:70; John 6:35; 8:12, 23, 58; 9:5; 10:7-11, 30-39; 11:25; 12:26, 46; 13:13; 14:3, 6, 10-11, 20; 15:1; 17:10, 16.

1214. 1 John 4:8, 16.

1215. Colossians 1:27.

1216. AGJC, 68:11.

1217. Romans 11:25.

1218. Colossians 4:3.

1219. Colossians 1:19.

1220. John 12:32; 14:20; 15:4; 17:21, 23.

1221. AGJC, 15:22.

1222. Colossians 1:27.

1223. John 1:9.

1224. Colossians 2:3.

1225. John 4:32.

1226. 1 Corinthians 10:3-4.

1227. Acts 17:28.

1228. See e.g., 1 John 3:11.

1229. Evidence for the marriage between Yahweh (Jehovah) and Ashtoreth (Asherah) is plentiful in both the archaeological record (e.g., inscriptions on pottery found in the Sinai Desert from the 8ᵗʰ Century B.C., seek the blessing of Yahweh *and* Ashtoreth) as well as in the Bible. As one example of the latter: the Old Testament clearly states that at one time a statue of Ashtoreth was worshiped in Yahweh's Temple at Jerusalem (2 Kings 23:12-14). Adoration of the Hebrew Mother-goddess was widespread, as the Bible also attests: early Jewish women wore crescent moon amulets in Ashtoreth's honor (Isaiah 3:18), and wove hangings for her sacred grove (2 Kings 23:7), for like many ancient deities she was often worshiped in special sacralized forests (see e.g., 1 Kings 15:13).

1230. 1 Kings 11:1-5.

1231. The fossil record indicates that the Patriarchal Takeover got its start in the region of the Black Sea around the year 4300 B.C., then spread west into Europe and south into the Near and Middle Eastern regions.

1232. See e.g., 1 Kings 16: 31-34; 18:1-46; 19:1-21; 2 Kings 9:22-37. See also Jeremiah 44:1-30.

1233. 1 Kings 15:10-16.

1234. See 2 Kings 9:29-37. Jezebel further courted her own demise by violently attacking and killing a number of Israel's patriarchal (God-worshiping) priests. See 1 Kings 18:4, 13; 19:1-2; 21:5-15.

1235. 2 Kings 11:1-21. As with Jezebel, Athaliah's murderers' had other reasons for taking her life as well: after her son Ahaziah was killed by Jehu, the female Judean monarch (who ruled for six years) murdered the entire sitting royal family (except the infant Joash).

1236. 2 Kings 5:15.

1237. See 2 Kings 23:1-37.

1238. The study of, belief in, and even worship of Ashtoreth (Asherah) survives into the present day in mystical (feminine) Judaism.

1239. Goddess-worship was still considered a "problem" by some early Christian leaders well into the 1ˢᵗ Century A.D. Paul, for example, bitterly complained about the "worldwide" veneration of the Roman moon-goddess Diana, and even called for the destruction of her temples. See Acts 19:24-35. For more information on the Patriarchal Takeover, goddess-worship, and the Female Principle, see my books, *Christmas Before Christianity: How the Birthday of the "Sun" Became the Birthday of the "Son"*; *Britannia Rules: Goddess-worship in Ancient Anglo-Celtic Society*; *The Book of Kelle: An Introduction to Goddess-worship and the Great Celtic Mother-Goddess Kelle*; and *The Goddess Dictionary of Words and Phrases*.

1240. My division of "male" and "female" traits is meant to be general. After all, just as there are today, in ancient times there were ancient female patriarchalists (god-worshipers) and male matriarchalists (goddess-worshipers). Nonetheless, based on everything from anthropological, archaeological, and religiomythological studies, to modern psychological, sociological, and criminological studies, I feel that such gender traits hold accurate for the average individual.

1241. Luke 3:21-22.

1242. See e.g., Matthew 5:1-48.

1243. See Appendix B.

1244. Despite the violent efforts of ancient religious patriarchalists, they were not able to completely stamp out goddess-worship. Not even the persecution of the Great Mother's followers, as well as the destruction of thousands of goddess temples (later built over with synagogues and churches) could totally eradicate her religion. Indeed, goddess-worship continued to be extremely popular all across the Near and Middle East, even centuries after Jesus' death. See e.g., Acts 19:27. Christian goddess-worship, of course, continues to this day in a thousand different forms (chiefly via the figure of the Virgin Mary, commonly known by her Pagan goddess title, Stella Maris, "Star of the Sea"). But it is found most openly, as in Judaism, in its mystical branches and sects.

**1245.** Matthew 22:35-40.

**1246.** Ephesians 4:25.

**1247.** Mark 12:28-34.

**1248.** Colossians 3:14.

**1249.** Genesis 17:1; Exodus 3:14-15; Psalms 46:10; Mark 8:29; 14:61-62; Luke 22:70; John 6:35; 8:12, 23, 58; 9:5; 10:7-11, 30-39; 11:25; 12:26, 46; 13:13; 14:3, 6, 10-11, 20; 15:1; 17:10, 16.

**1250.** Matthew 22:41-46; Colossians 1:27. See also Daniel 7:13-14; Micah 5:2; Matthew 28:20; John 8:58; Hebrews 7:3; Revelation 22:13.

**1251.** AGJC, 8:5-16.

**1252.** The Gospel of Thomas, Logion 82. My paraphrasal.

**1253.** Matthew 5:48.

**1254.** John 17:21; Hebrews 12:10; 2 Peter 1:4.

**1255.** Romans 11:16; 1 Corinthians 3:17; 6:19; 1 Peter 1:16.

**1256.** Matthew 13:46.

**1257.** Matthew 7:6.

**1258.** John 14:23.

**1259.** Ephesians 4:32.

**1260.** Mainstream Christianity teaches that self-forgiveness is not biblical. This is incorrect. In Colossians 3:13 we find the following Pauline commandment on forgiveness: "Forbearing one another, and forgiving *one another* . . ." The Greek root word for the two italicized words, "one another," is *heautou*, which means "themselves," but also "*ourselves*" and "*yourselves*." Thus, this scripture actually means: "Forbearing one another, and forgiving one another *as well as ourselves* (or *yourselves*)." Also see Philippians 3:13-14.

**1261.** 1 John 4:16.

**1262.** John 10:34.

**1263.** John 12:32; 14:20; 15:4; 17:21-23, 26; Colossians 1:27; 3:10-11; Romans 8:10; 1 Corinthians 6:15, 17; 2 Corinthians 5:16; 13:3, 5; Galatians 1:16; 2:20; 4:19; Ephesians 3:14-17; Philippians 1:20; 2:5; 1 Peter 1:11; 1 John 2:27; 3:24; 4:4.

**1264.** Matthew 19:28; Luke 22:30; 2 Timothy 2:12; Revelation 3:12, 21; 5:10; 20:6; 22:5.

**1265.** Luke 17:21.

**1266.** Matthew 22:41-46. See also Daniel 7:13-14; Micah 5:2; Matthew 28:20; John 8:58; Hebrews 7:3; Revelation 22:13.

**1267.** Romans 15:5-6.

**1268.** 1 Corinthians 2:16.

**1269.** 1 Timothy 3:16.

**1270.** 1 Corinthians 3:16-17; 6:19-20.

**1271.** 1 Corinthians 6:17; 2 Corinthians 6:16; Ephesians 4:6.

**1272.** John 14:20. See also Malachi 3:1.

**1273.** Zechariah 10:6.

**1274.** Galatians 6:7.

**1275.** Romans 13:10.

**1276.** Galatians 6:10.

**1277.** See Matthew 18:21-35.

**1278.** See Romans 12:18.

**1279.** John 1:9.

**1280.** Titus 3:2.

**1281.** Romans 14:1-13; 1 Thessalonians 5:14.

**1282.** Philippians 4:8.

**1283.** See e.g., Ephesians 4:29-32.

**1284.** Matthew 5:44.

**1285.** Matthew 7:12.

**1286.** 1 Peter 1:22.

**1287.** Luke 17:20-21.

**1288.** See e.g., 1 Peter 3:8-12; James 4:11; 5:9.

**1289.** 1 Peter 2:1.

**1290.** See e.g., Titus 3:2.

**1291.** Isaiah 5:11; 1 Corinthians 9:25; 1 Thessalonians 5:4-8.

1292. Proverbs 6:34; 14:30; Ephesians 4:31.

1293. 1 Peter 2:23.

1294. Matthew 5:44. See also 1 Peter 3:8-11.

1295. Luke 6:37.

1296. Philippians 1:28; 1 Peter 3:13-17.

1297. See 2 Corinthians 7:2; Zechariah 8:17.

1298. 2 Timothy 2:14, 16, 23; Titus 3:9.

1299. Matthew 5:39.

1300. See James 2:1-4, 8-9. Spiritually speaking there is only one race, the human race, which is why Jesus commanded us to love the Brotherhood of Man. 1 Peter 2:17. Paul states that God "hath made of one blood all nations of men for to dwell on all the face of the earth." Acts 17:26. All who use the Law of Attraction for good are spiritually related, are "family." Matthew 12:48-50; Luke 8:19-21. We are "all one in Christ Jesus." Galatians 3:28. All people are "one body in Christ, and every one members one of another." Romans 12:5. "There is no difference between the Jew and the Greek." Romans 10:12. See also AGJC, 24:27.

1301. The Epistle of Ignatius to the Philadelphians, 2:16.

1302. Leviticus 19:2.

1303. James 2:1-26.

1304. Romans 2:11.

1305. 1 Peter 2:17.

1306. Galatians 3:28.

1307. See Matthew 5:3-11.

1308. Zechariah 8:19.

1309. See Isaiah 9:6.

1310. 1 Thessalonians 5:23.

1311. Jeremiah 10:10.

1312. 1 John 4:16.

1313. AGJC, 94:13.

1314. See AGJC, 97:9.

1315. Matthew 5:18.

1316. Proverbs 25:11.

1317. Matthew 7:1-5.

1318. Psalms 66:19-20.

1319. Proverbs 16:3.

1320. John 16:23.

1321. Leviticus 19:4. See also Revelation 9:20.

1322. Habakkuk 2:18; 1 Corinthians 12:2.

1323. Exodus 20:4; Leviticus 26:1; Deuteronomy 4:16, 23; Jeremiah 10:14.

1324. Psalms 2:1.

1325. See Appendix A and Appendix B.

1326. John 4:24. The KJV has "God is a Spirit," which is a mistranslation. The original text is: "God is Spirit." See also Romans 1:20; 1 Timothy 1:17.

1327. Acts 14:15.

1328. 2 Corinthians 6:16; Ephesians 4:6. See also John 12:32; 14:20; 1 Corinthians 6:17.

1329. See e.g., Acts 7:48; 17:24-25; Hebrews 9:11, 24. In mystical Christianity, the worship of the traditional Christian anthropomorphic God is considered a violation of God's own commandment against the worship of Him as a "graven image." See e.g., Exodus 20:4; Leviticus 26:1; Deuteronomy 4:16.

1330. 1 Peter 2:25.

1331. Matthew 7:9-11.

1332. For more on this topic, see my book *Christmas Before Christianity*. See also 2 Maccabees 6:2.

1333. Matthew 5:43-47. Some 500 years earlier, Buddha made a similar statement, and for the same reason as Jesus: "Cleanse your heart of malice and cherish no hatred, not even against your enemies; but embrace all living beings with kindness."

1334. John 14:20-24.

1335. John 15:9-17.

1336. 1 Corinthians 13:1-8, 13.

1337. Galatians 5:14.

**1338**. John 4:24. The KJV has "God is *a* Spirit," which is a mistranslation. The original text is: "God is Spirit." See also Romans 1:20; 1 Timothy 1:17.

**1339**. John 12:32; 14:20; 15:4; 17:21-23, 26; Colossians 1:27; 3:10-11; Romans 8:10; 1 Corinthians 6:15, 17; 2 Corinthians 5:16; 13:3, 5; Galatians 1:16; 2:20; 4:19; Ephesians 3:14-17; Philippians 1:20; 2:5; 1 Peter 1:11; 1 John 2:27; 3:24; 4:4.

**1340**. Genesis 17:1; Exodus 3:14-15; Psalms 46:10; Mark 8:29; 14:61-62; Luke 22:70; John 6:35; 8:12, 23, 58; 9:5; 10:7-11, 30-39; 11:25; 12:26, 46; 13:13; 14:3, 6, 10-11, 20; 15:1; 17:10, 16.

**1341**. Numbers 23:19.

**1342**. 1 Corinthians 10:26.

**1343**. See Hosea 11:9.

**1344**. Mark 12:30.

**1345**. Mark 12:31.

**1346**. Matthew 25:31-46.

**1347**. Romans 13:8-10.

**1348**. John 15:16.

**1349**. Jeremiah 29:11.

**1350**. 1 Thessalonians 4:8.

**1351**. See e.g., 1 Corinthians 11:28. See also 2 Corinthians 13:5.

**1352**. John 12:32; 14:20; 15:4; 17:21-23, 26; Colossians 1:27; 3:10-11; Romans 8:10; 1 Corinthians 6:15, 17; 2 Corinthians 5:16; 13:3, 5; Galatians 1:16; 2:20; 4:19; Ephesians 3:14-17; Philippians 1:20; 2:5; 1 Peter 1:11; 1 John 2:27; 3:24; 4:4.

**1353**. Proverbs 16:9.

**1354**. Luke 12:4-7.

**1355**. Isaiah 9:6.

**1356**. 1 Corinthians 3:21-22.

**1357**. 2 Corinthians 4:15.

**1358**. The Gospel of Philip, Logion 48.

**1359**. The Gospel of Thomas, Logion 6.

**1360**. Matthew 6:33.

**1361**. 1 John 4:8, 16.

**1362**. Jeremiah 33:6; James 5:15.

**1363**. 1 Corinthians 2:16.

**1364**. Revelation 3:8.

**1365**. My interpretation. The orthodox Church maintains that INRI stands for: *Iesus Nazarenus, Rex Iudaeorum* ("Jesus the Nazarene, King of the Jews").

**1366**. Ephesians 3:20.

**1367**. 1 John 3:20.

**1368**. Philippians 4:13.

**1369**. Proverbs 23:7.

**1370**. Hebrews 5:9.

**1371**. Daniel 7:13-14.

**1372**. John 12:32; 14:20; 15:4; 17:21-23, 26; Colossians 1:27; 3:10-11; Romans 8:10; 1 Corinthians 6:15, 17; 2 Corinthians 5:16; 13:3, 5; Galatians 1:16; 2:20; 4:19; Ephesians 3:14-17; Philippians 1:20; 2:5; 1 Peter 1:11; 1 John 2:27; 3:24; 4:4.

**1373**. 1 Peter 5:10.

**1374**. Hebrews 10:14.

**1375**. Matthew 5:48.

**1376**. Genesis 17:1; Exodus 3:14-15; Psalms 46:10; Mark 8:29; 14:61-62; Luke 22:70; John 6:35; 8:12, 23, 58; 9:5; 10:7-11, 30-39; 11:25; 12:26, 46; 13:13; 14:3, 6, 10-11, 20; 15:1; 17:10, 16.

**1377**. 2 Samuel 22:31.

**1378**. Colossians 2:10.

**1379**. John 17:21. See also John 14:20.

**1380**. Exodus 3:14; Ezekiel 37:14; John 14:10-11; Romans 8:9, 11; 1 Corinthians 3:16; 6:17; 14:25; 2 Corinthians 6:16; 9:14; Ephesians 2:22; 4:6; Philemon 2:13; 1 John 3:24; 4:4, 12-13, 16; Zechariah 2:10.

**1381**. 2 Corinthians 3:18.

**1382**. Genesis 1:27.

1383. AGJC, 163:37.

1384. Luke 10:37.

1385. John 17:23.

1386. 2 Thessalonians 2:17.

1387. AGJC, 122:41.

1388. Ephesians 4:15.

1389. 1 Corinthians 16:14.

1390. Proverbs 13:3.

1391. 1 John 4:16.

1392. Psalms 144:15; 146:5; Proverbs 16:20.

1393. Proverbs 3:13.

1394. Proverbs 29:18.

1395. Psalms 2:1. See also Appendix B.

1396. Matthew 16:16; Acts 14:15; 2 Corinthians 3:3; 6:16; 1 Timothy 4:10; 6:17; Hebrews 3:12; Revelation 7:2.

1397. John 4:24. The KJV has "God is *a* Spirit," which is a mistranslation. The original text is: "God is Spirit." See also Romans 1:20; 1 Timothy 1:17.

1398. See Genesis 17:1; Exodus 3:14-15; Psalms 46:10; Mark 8:29; 14:61-62; Luke 22:70; John 6:35; 8:12, 23, 58; 9:5; 10:7-11, 30-39; 11:25; 12:26, 46; 13:13; 14:3, 6, 10-11, 20; 15:1; 17:10, 16.

1399. Romans 2:6. See also 1 Corinthians 3:8.

1400. My paraphrasal.

1401. 2 Corinthians 10:5.

1402. Ephesians 6:10-18.

1403. AGJC, 39:18.

1404. It is not known where the symbol of the "Three Wise Monkeys" originated, although speculation surrounds Asia and Africa. In Japan the individual monkeys are called: Mizaru (see no evil), Kikazaru (hear no evil), and Iwazaru (speak no evil). The country's most famous depiction of the Three Wise Monkeys is at Nikko, on the "Sacred Stable" at the city's 400 year old Shinto shrine known as Nikko Toshogu.

1405. Romans 16:19.

1406. See e.g., John 12:31; Hebrews 2:14.

1407. Romans 10:4.

1408. Romans 6:2.

1409. Romans 5:19.

1410. Hebrews 9:26.

1411. Romans 6:6; Ephesians 4:22; Colossians 3:9.

1412. 1 Corinthians 10:13.

1413. James 1:12-14.

1414. See e.g., Philippians 1:28; 1 Peter 3:13-14.

1415. Proverbs 3:6.

1416. Matthew 5:39.

1417. Matthew 26:52.

1418. 1 Corinthians 14:20.

1419. My paraphrasal.

1420. Isaiah 35:4; Romans 12:19.

1421. Hebrews 12:29; Proverbs 15:26.

1422. Matthew 5:38-48.

1423. AGJC, 8:17-23.

1424. 1 Corinthians 13:5.

1425. John 12:32; 14:20; 15:4; 17:21-23, 26; Colossians 1:27; 3:10-11; Romans 8:10; 1 Corinthians 6:15, 17; 2 Corinthians 5:16; 13:3, 5; Galatians 1:16; 2:20; 4:19; Ephesians 3:14-17; Philippians 1:20; 2:5; 1 Peter 1:11; 1 John 2:27; 3:24; 4:4.

1426. Matthew 5:48.

1427. Habakkuk 1:13.

1428. AGJC, 52:8.

1429. John 1:12.

**1430.** John 12:32; 14:20; 15:4; 17:21-23, 26; Colossians 1:27; 3:10-11; Romans 8:10; 1 Corinthians 6:15, 17; 2 Corinthians 5:16; 13:3, 5; Galatians 1:16; 2:20; 4:19; Ephesians 3:14-17; Philippians 1:20; 2:5; 1 Peter 1:11; 1 John 2:27; 3:24; 4:4.
**1431.** Ephesians 2:18; Romans 16:27.
**1432.** Proverbs 15:15.
**1433.** See e.g., Matthew 9:2; 14:27; Mark 6:50; John 16:33; Acts 23:11; 27:22, 25, 36.
**1434.** 1 Thessalonians 5:16.
**1435.** Proverbs 15:13.
**1436.** John 13:17.
**1437.** Proverbs 14:3.
**1438.** Mark 10:27; Revelation 3:8.
**1439.** 2 Corinthians 7:6.
**1440.** Colossians 3:13.
**1441.** Philippians 3:13-14.
**1442.** Romans 2:11.
**1443.** Ecclesiastes 5:2; Matthew 7:1-5.
**1444.** In the case of abusive or extremely unhealthy (toxic) relationships, this, of course, is not realistic or advised.
**1445.** See e.g., Romans 2:6-7.
**1446.** Matthew 6:6.
**1447.** See e.g., Proverbs 23:7.
**1448.** Mark 11:24.
**1449.** Matthew 17:20; 21:21.
**1450.** 1 Corinthians 4:10.
**1451.** John 16:24.
**1452.** 1 Corinthians 2:9; Ephesians 3:20; 2 Epistle of Clement, 4:14.
**1453.** Proverbs 3:5.
**1454.** Proverbs 15:4.
**1455.** Acts 10:34; Romans 2:11; Ephesians 6:9; Colossians 3:25; 1 Peter 1:17.
**1456.** Romans 10:12; Galatians 3:28; Colossians 3:11.
**1457.** Romans 12:5; Ephesians 4:4.
**1458.** See Isaiah 45:11.
**1459.** Hebrews 3:14.
**1460.** Psalms 30:10; 1 Corinthians 3:9; 2 Corinthians 6:1; Ephesians 2:19-22; Hebrews 13:6.
**1461.** Hebrews 12:10.
**1462.** John 1:14.
**1463.** Proverbs 16:3.
**1464.** Jeremiah 29:11.
**1465.** Hebrews 10:35-36.
**1466.** See e.g., Romans 2:6-7.
**1467.** John 12:32.
**1468.** Proverbs 15:2.
**1469.** Colossians 1:19.
**1470.** Ephesians 3;8.
**1471.** 1 Timothy 6:17.
**1472.** Some Christian groups incorrectly teach that "there is no such thing as evolution." Webster defines evolution as "a process of change in a certain direction." Thus, as the offspring of two parents, we are all products of evolution. This in no way contradicts the Bible, for what we Christians call "God," scientists call "Nature." Thus Deists, like U.S. President Thomas Jefferson, believe that God Himself set evolution in motion.
**1473.** Genesis 1:20-21.
**1474.** Matthew 13:16.
**1475.** See e.g., Romans 9:30-32.
**1476.** Ephesians 2:18; Romans 5:1-2; 8:10; 1 Corinthians 6:15, 17; 2 Corinthians 5:16; 13:3, 5.
**1477.** John 6:37.
**1478.** John 16:15.
**1479.** Romans 8:31-32.

1480. Psalms 37:4-5.
1481. John 16:27.
1482. Luke 15:31.
1483. See e.g., John 4:35.
1484. Luke 12:32.
1485. Matthew 5:3, 10; 10:7.
1486. Hebrews 11:9.
1487. Exodus 3:8; Leviticus 20:24; Numbers 14:8; Deuteronomy 6:3; 11:9; 26:15; 27:3; Jeremiah 11:5; 32:22; Ezekiel 20:6.
1488. Galatians 4:7.
1489. AGJC, 33:8-10.
1490. Luke 12:32. See also Philippians 2:13.
1491. John 10:10.
1492. Zechariah 2:8.
1493. 3 John 1:2.
1494. Matthew 2:23.
1495. 1 John 1:1-3.
1496. Mark 1:1.
1497. Matthew 24:14. See also Matthew 4:23; 9:35; Luke 4:43. For more on this topic, see Appendix B.
1498. Mark 6:3; Matthew 13:55.
1499. Matthew 14:15-21; Mark 6:35-44.
1500. Matthew 17:24-27.
1501. John 13:29.
1502. Matthew 17:24-27.
1503. See e.g., 1 Corinthians 9:5-6.
1504. See e.g., Matthew 9:14; Mark 1:29; 10:10; Luke 4:38.
1505. Matthew 10:8.
1506. Matthew 24:14. See also Matthew 4:23; 9:35; Luke 4:43. For more on this topic, see Appendix B.
1507. See e.g., Matthew 9:18-26; Mark 2:14-15; 5:38; Luke 7:1-10; 7:36; 8:41; 14:1; 19:5.
1508. See e.g., John 11:48; Acts 18:2.
1509. Matthew 8:20.
1510. John 17:21; Hebrews 12:10; 2 Peter 1:4.
1511. Luke 17:20-21.
1512. My paraphrasal.
1513. Revelation 21:2, 22.
1514. Ancient Gnostic Christians held that Jesus and Mary Magdalene were lovers. See e.g., the Gospel of Philip, Logion 59. Early Mormon leaders, such as Orson Hyde, Orson Pratt, and Joseph Fielding Smith, taught that Jesus was married to Mary (and as a "polygamist," to several other women as well).
1515. Luke 8:1-3. See also the Gospel of Mary [Magdalene], 5:5.
1516. John 19:38.
1517. See Mark 15:43.
1518. Matthew 27:57.
1519. 2 Corinthians 8:9.
1520. Philippians 4:19.
1521. See e.g., Mark 2:1; 9:33.
1522. John 14:2.
1523. AGJC, 87:11-12; 103:1. See also 90:16; 102:1; 119:1; 174:9.
1524. For more on this subject see Appendix B.
1525. 2 Corinthians 9:8.
1526. James 2:5.
1527. Colossians 3:11.
1528. Numbers 23:19; Hebrews 6:18.
1529. See Genesis 3:19.
1530. Deuteronomy 8:18.
1531. Deuteronomy 28:12.
1532. 1 Chronicles 29:12.

1533. Hosea 2:8.
1534. Psalms 35:27.
1535. Ecclesiastes 3:13.
1536. Ecclesiastes 5:19.
1537. 1 Chronicles 29:12.
1538. Haggai 2:8.
1539. Romans 8:16-17.
1540. 1 Corinthians 3:21-22.
1541. 1 Timothy 6:10.
1542. Mark 10:25. The original Aramaic translation of this scripture is: "My sons, how hard it is for those who trust in their wealth to enter into the kingdom of God! It is easier for a rope to pass through the eye of a needle than for a rich man to enter into the kingdom of God."
1543. 1 John 2:15-16.
1544. Deuteronomy 8:13-14.
1545. Psalms 62:10.
1546. Ephesians 3:8.
1547. Ephesians 3:16.
1548. Genesis 13:2.
1549. Genesis 26:12-14.
1550. Genesis 30:43. See also Genesis 32:5.
1551. Genesis 36:6-7.
1552. 2 Samuel 19:31-32.
1553. 1 Chronicles 29:26-28.
1554. 2 Chronicles 1:13-15.
1555. 2 Chronicles 17:3, 5.
1556. 2 Chronicles 32:27.
1557. Job 1:1-3.
1558. Proverbs 10:22.
1559. Psalms 122:6-7.
1560. Mark 15:43.
1561. Luke 19:2-8.
1562. Luke 18:18-23.
1563. Luke 8:2-3; 23:55-56; 24:10; Mark 15:40-41; 16:1.
1564. 1 Corinthians 16:19.
1565. Romans 16:11.
1566. Acts 8:27-39.
1567. Colossians 4:15.
1568. Acts 10:1-33.
1569. Romans 16:10.
1570. Acts 16:14-15, 40.
1571. 3 John 1:1-8.
1572. 2 Timothy 1:16-18; 4:19.
1573. 1 Corinthians 1:16.
1574. Acts 5:1-10,
1575. Acts 4:36-37.
1576. Philemon 1:1-2.
1577. See e.g., James 2:1-3.
1578. Philippians 4:15-18.
1579. Acts 4:34.
1580. The Gospel of Mary, 10:15-16. My paraphrasal.
1581. Deuteronomy 8:18.
1582. Colossians 1:12.
1583. Proverbs 3:9-10.
1584. Luke 9:44.
1585. Joel 2:24.
1586. Isaiah 54:17.

1587. Zechariah 4:6-7.
1588. 1 Timothy 6:17.
1589. 1 Samuel 2:7.
1590. Acts 10:34; Romans 2:11; Ephesians 6:9; Colossians 3:25; 1 Peter 1:17.
1591. Ephesians 6:9.
1592. Isaiah 55:10-11.
1593. Psalms 33:9; John 6:63.
1594. See e.g., 1 Timothy 3:3, 8; Titus 1:7, 11; 1 Peter 5:2.
1595. See e.g., Ecclesiastes 10:19.
1596. Proverbs 16:3.
1597. Ephesians 2:18; Romans 5:1-2; 8:10; 1 Corinthians 6:15, 17; 2 Corinthians 5:16; 13:3, 5.
1598. Psalms 30:10; 1 Corinthians 3:9; 2 Corinthians 6:1; Ephesians 2:19-22; Hebrews 13:6.
1599. Philippians 2:13.
1600. Psalms 35-27-28.
1601. Matthew 6:19-21.
1602. 1 Timothy 6:10.
1603. My paraphrasal.
1604. John 10:10.
1605. My paraphrasal.
1606. John 3:27.
1607. Genesis 17:1; Exodus 3:14-15; Psalms 46:10; Mark 8:29; 14:61-62; Luke 22:70; John 6:35; 8:12, 23, 58; 9:5; 10:7-11, 30-39; 11:25; 12:26, 46; 13:13; 14:3, 6, 10-11, 20; 15:1; 17:10, 16.
1608. John 12:32; 14:20; 15:4; 17:21-23, 26; Colossians 1:27; 3:10-11; Romans 8:10; 1 Corinthians 6:15, 17; 2 Corinthians 5:16; 13:3, 5; Galatians 1:16; 2:20; 4:19; Ephesians 3:14-17; Philippians 1:20; 2:5; 1 Peter 1:11; 1 John 2:27; 3:24; 4:4.
1609. John 6:27, 31-35, 48-51.
1610. Daniel 7:13-14.
1611. Luke 11:2.
1612. John 6:37.
1613. Colossians 1:19.
1614. Genesis 1:26-27.
1615. Galatians 4:7.
1616. 1 Corinthians 3:21-22.
1617. Psalms 23:1.
1618. Psalms 23:5.
1619. 1 Corinthians 10:26.
1620. Malachi 3:10.
1621. John 16:24.
1622. Revelation 1:18.
1623. Mark 11:24.
1624. Mark 11:24.
1625. 1 Corinthians 3:6.
1626. My paraphrasal.
1627. Luke 17:21.
1628. John 14:10.
1629. The Sophia of Jesus Christ, 96:3-4.
1630. Genesis 3:19.
1631. Psalms 30:10; 1 Corinthians 3:9; 2 Corinthians 6:1; Ephesians 2:19-22; Hebrews 13:6.
1632. Philippians 4:19.
1633. Matthew 6:33.
1634. 2 Corinthians 8:5.
1635. Luke 8:50.
1636. 1 Thessalonians 5:18.
1637. 1 Corinthians 2:9; Ephesians 3:20; 2 Epistle of Clement, 4:14.
1638. Colossians 3:24.
1639. Colossians 1:12.

**1640.** John 14:10.

**1641.** Psalms 1:1-3.

**1642.** Proverbs 16:24.

**1643.** Hebrews 4:12.

**1644.** See e.g., 1 Timothy 4:7-9.

**1645.** Matthew 22:32.

**1646.** Matthew 15:11.

**1647.** Matthew 15:1-3, 7-20.

**1648.** AGJC, 126:22-27.

**1649.** My paraphrasal.

**1650.** 1 Timothy 4:1-5.

**1651.** Romans 14:20.

**1652.** My paraphrasal.

**1653.** 1 Corinthians 8:8.

**1654.** My paraphrasal.

**1655.** Matthew 4:4.

**1656.** 1 Timothy 4:6.

**1657.** Hebrews 13:9.

**1658.** Mark 16:18.

**1659.** Mark 16:16.

**1660.** Matthew 5:48.

**1661.** Romans 3:23.

**1662.** Romans 14:2, 14.

**1663.** My paraphrasal.

**1664.** 2 Corinthians 9:15.

**1665.** Genesis 1:26-27; 17:1; Exodus 3:14-15; Psalms 46:10; Mark 8:29; 14:61-62; Luke 22:70; John 6:35; 8:12, 23, 58; 9:5; 10:7-11, 30-39; 11:25; 12:26, 46; 13:13; 14:3, 6, 10-11, 20; 15:1; 17:10, 16.

**1666.** 1 Corinthians 3:16-17.

**1667.** My paraphrasal.

**1668.** 1 Corinthians 6:17; 2 Corinthians 6:16; Ephesians 4:6.

**1669.** Malachi 3:1.

**1670.** John 14:16-17; 1 Corinthians 6:19-20; 2 Timothy 1:14.

**1671.** Isaiah 9:6.

**1672.** Jeremiah 10:10.

**1673.** Isaiah 60:19.

**1674.** Daniel 7:14.

**1675.** 2 Peter 1:11.

**1676.** Genesis 21:33.

**1677.** Genesis 9:16.

**1678.** Proverbs 10:25.

**1679.** John 3:16.

**1680.** Jeremiah 31:3.

**1681.** Isaiah 35:10.

**1682.** Isaiah 45:17,

**1683.** Revelation 14:6.

**1684.** Psalms 30:10; 1 Corinthians 3:9; 2 Corinthians 6:1; Ephesians 2:19-22; Hebrews 13:6.

**1685.** 1 Corinthians 12:27.

**1686.** See Romans 14:2-5.

**1687.** Ironically, the word oxygen derives from the Greek words oxys, "acid," and genes, "generate," thus meaning "acid-forming." At the time the word oxygen was coined in the late 1700s, it was wrongly believed that the newly discovered chemical was a prerequisite for the formation of acids.

**1688.** Genesis 1:29.

**1689.** Proverbs 15:17.

**1690.** See e.g., Matthew 3:4; Mark 1:6.

**1691.** Romans 14:2.

**1692.** Luke 24:41-43. See also Matthew 11:19. As with so many of the stories surrounding Jesus, this one too is more properly read and understood as an allegory hiding a profound spiritual truth.

**1693.** Like most biblical topics, this one too provides numerous scriptural contradictions. For example, in the book of Acts, Peter experiences the following vision three times, in which God commands him to kill certain animals and eat them. This is the description of the second occurrence: ". . . he fell into a trance, and saw heaven opened, and a certain vessel descending unto him, as it had been a great sheet knit at the four corners, and let down to the earth: wherein were all manner of fourfooted beasts of the earth, and wild beasts, and creeping things, and fowls of the air. And there came a voice to him, 'Rise, Peter; kill, and eat.' But Peter said, 'Not so, Lord; for I have never eaten any thing that is common or unclean.' And the voice spake unto him again the second time, 'What God hath cleansed, that call not thou common.' This was done thrice: and the vessel was received up again into heaven." Acts 10:11-16. See also Acts 11:5-10.

**1694.** Ezekiel 47:12.

**1695.** AGJC, 20:13.

**1696.** Matthew 21:22.

**1697.** Matthew 15:11.

**1698.** John 10:30.

**1699.** Galatians 6:7-8.

**1700.** More specifically, since each bodily organ is controlled by the Subconscious Mind (spiritual consciousness), when we are not spiritually attuned in the mental area that correlates with a specific organ, that organ may become weakened, opening it up to illness. For example, negative emotions and ideas such as unforgiveness, vengefulness, and racism cut one off from love, which governs the physical heart. This can lead to problems connected to the cardiovascular system. The physical remedy is the spiritual cure, and the spiritual cure is the physical remedy: one must develop a consciousness of unconditional love (harmony) for everyone. According to Jesus' teachings on the Law of Attraction, the Father (Divine Mind) will then automatically begin attracting like vibrations to the diseased (disharmonious) area, and a healing will take place. Every organ, even every cell, of the body will respond in identical fashion to its spiritual correlate.

**1701.** Proverbs 15:26.

**1702.** Malachi 4:2.

**1703.** My paraphrasal.

**1704.** John 17:21; Hebrews 12:10; 2 Peter 1:4.

**1705.** John 12:32; 14:20; 15:4; 17:21-23, 26; Colossians 1:27; 3:10-11; Romans 8:10; 1 Corinthians 6:15, 17; 2 Corinthians 5:16; 13:3, 5; Galatians 1:16; 2:20; 4:19; Ephesians 3:14-17; Philippians 1:20; 2:5; 1 Peter 1:11; 1 John 2:27; 3:24; 4:4.

**1706.** Hebrews 12:10.

**1707.** Romans 2:6-7; Proverbs 12:5.

**1708.** Matthew 13:43.

**1709.** 1 John 2:29.

**1710.** 2 Corinthians 10:5.

**1711.** AGJC, 89:20.

**1712.** Matthew 5:48.

**1713.** Philippians 4:8.

**1714.** 1 Timothy 4:7-9.

**1715.** 1 Corinthians 2:16.

**1716.** Isaiah 57:19.

**1717.** AGJC, 84:19-24.

**1718.** 1 Corinthians 12:27.

**1719.** Matthew 5:48.

**1720.** 1 Corinthians 2:16. See also Philippians 2:5.

**1721.** Colossians 1:15; Hebrews 11:27; 1 Timothy 1:17.

**1722.** Deuteronomy 33:27.

**1723.** John 4:24 (the KJV has "God is *a* Spirit," which is a mistranslation of "God is Spirit"); 2 Corinthians 3:17.

**1724.** Job 33:4.

**1725.** John 20:19-22. The word ghost here (in Greek *pneuma*) is mystically translated as "breath," "wind," or a "movement of air." Thus the Holy Ghost is actually the life-giving Holy Breath, which is why Jesus breathed on His Disciples in order to imbue (ordain) them with the Holy Spirit. Occultly, the Holy Breath (Subconscious Mind) is spiritually tied to the Word or Logos (Conscious Mind), that is, the power of thought. John 1:1. As we have seen, the Holy Breath was used by God in the creation of mankind. Genesis 2:7.

1726. Jeremiah 30:17.
1727. This is assuming that she does not to do anything that specifically harms her liver physically, such as drink alcohol. Of course, one can override even the damage from alcohol if he or she has enough faith.
1728. Revelation 21:5.
1729. John 17:2.
1730. John 17:21; 2 Peter 1:4.
1731. Hebrews 12:10.
1732. Luke 8:50.
1733. The Epistles of Jesus Christ and Abgarus King of Edessa, 1:2.
1734. Acts 26:8.
1735. John 14:12.
1736. Matthew 11:11.
1737. Matthew 11:13-14; 17:10-13.
1738. John 10:34; 14:12.
1739. In his *History of the Church* (3:39), Eusebius cites the following statement by Papias: "Matthew arranged in order the sayings [known as *logia*] in the Hebrew [i.e., Aramaic] language, and each one interpreted as he was able." In my opinion, as well as the opinion of many others, Papias could have only been referring to the lost Gospel of Q.
1740. In Acts 20:35, Paul cites a saying by Jesus that is not found anywhere in the canonical Bible. Thus, it could have only come from a pre-New Testament document (based on common oral tradition), one that has been labeled the Gospel of Q by modern theological scholars.
1741. Mark 16:17-20.
1742. Romans 10:8.
1743. See Mark 11:22-23.
1744. Mark 16:19-20.
1745. Acts 1:1-3.
1746. Luke 17:20-21.
1747. Matthew 19:28; Luke 22:30; 2 Timothy 2:12; Revelation 3:12, 21; 5:10; 20:6; 22:5.
1748. 1 Corinthians 2:16.
1749. Daniel 7:13-14.
1750. Mark 11:24.
1751. Mark 10:27; Revelation 3:8.
1752. 1 Corinthians 3:9. See also Psalms 30:10; 2 Corinthians 6:1; Ephesians 2:19-22; Hebrews 13:6.
1753. The Higher Self was known to Daniel as the "Ancient of Days." See Daniel 7:9, 13, 22.
1754. Romans 8:10; 1 Corinthians 6:15, 17; 2 Corinthians 5:16; 13:3, 5.
1755. 1 Corinthians 2:16.
1756. Matthew 12:28.
1757. Philippians 4:13.
1758. Matthew 11:27.
1759. Galatians 5:6.
1760. AGJC, 23:5-13.
1761. See Acts 17:22-28.
1762. Jeremiah 33:6.
1763. See Jeremiah 8:22.
1764. See 1 Maccabees 6:2.
1765. Colossians 1:15.
1766. Matthew 5:16.
1767. Exodus 3:14; Romans 8:9, 11; 1 Corinthians 3:16; 6:17; 14:25; 2 Corinthians 6:16; 9:14; Ephesians 2:22; 4:6; Philemon 2:13; 1 John 3:24; 4:4, 12-13, 16; Zechariah 2:10.
1768. John 14:20.
1769. Ezekiel 37:14.
1770. Peter, for example, ascribed Jesus' healings to God. See Acts 2:22.
1771. Matthew 9:27-30.
1772. Matthew 15:22-28.
1773. My paraphrasal.
1774. Mark 5:25-34.

1775. Colossians 1:15. See also 1 Timothy 1:17.
1776. Luke 8:40-42, 49-56.
1777. Mark 10:46-52.
1778. Luke 17:12-19.
1779. Matthew 8:5-10, 13.
1780. Acts 10:34; Romans 2:11; Ephesians 6:9; Colossians 3:25; 1 Peter 1:17.
1781. Matthew 13:54-58.
1782. Mark 6:5-6.
1783. Hebrews 4:2.
1784. Hebrews 11:6.
1785. Mark 9:14-27.
1786. Acts 14:8:11.
1787. Matthew 21:18-22.
1788. My paraphrasal.
1789. John 12:32; 14:20; 15:4; 17:21-23, 26; Colossians 1:27; 3:10-11; Romans 8:10; 1 Corinthians 6:15, 17; 2 Corinthians 5:16; 13:3, 5; Galatians 1:16; 2:20; 4:19; Ephesians 3:14-17; Philippians 1:20; 2:5; 1 Peter 1:11; 1 John 2:27; 3:24; 4:4.
1790. Matthew 8:16-17.
1791. Isaiah 53:5.
1792. John 12:32; 14:20; 15:4; 17:21-23, 26; Colossians 1:27; 3:10-11; Romans 8:10; 1 Corinthians 6:15, 17; 2 Corinthians 5:16; 13:3, 5; Galatians 1:16; 2:20; 4:19; Ephesians 3:14-17; Philippians 1:20; 2:5; 1 Peter 1:11; 1 John 2:27; 3:24; 4:4.
1793. 1 John 3:1.
1794. Galatians 4:7.
1795. 1 Corinthians 3:21-22.
1796. John 5:1-15.
1797. See e.g., Hebrews 9:22. This ancient Judaic doctrine was, in fact, copied from the sacrificial blood rites of Paganism. Hebrews 10:4 correctly identifies some of the animals that were used; in this example, "bulls" and "goats."
1798. See Appendix B.
1799. Genesis 1:26-27; Matthew 5:48.
1800. The unknown forger of 2 Thessalonians (written after Paul's death) certainly believed this doctrine. See e.g., 2 Thessalonians 2:11-12.
1801. Psalms 2:1.
1802. AGJC, 43:13.
1803. See e.g., Luke 18:9-14.
1804. See e.g., John 5:14; 8:11; Luke 18:42.
1805. James 5:15.
1806. AGJC, 41:1-24.
1807. Luke 7:36-50.
1808. Mark 2:7; Luke 5:21.
1809. See AGJC, 90:16-26.
1810. Isaiah 45:7.
1811. Luke 15:7.
1812. Romans 3:27; 9:32; Galatians 2:16.
1813. Romans 6:11-22; 8:2.
1814. Romans 10:13.
1815. Proverbs 10:12. Peter taught a similar doctrine. See 1 Peter 4:8.
1816. Luke 7:47.
1817. 1 John 4:8, 16.
1818. Exodus 3:14; Ezekiel 37:14; John 14:10-11; Romans 8:9, 11; 1 Corinthians 3:16; 6:17; 14:25; 2 Corinthians 6:16; 9:14; Ephesians 2:22; 4:6; Philemon 2:13; 1 John 3:24; 4:4, 12-13, 16; Zechariah 2:10.
1819. Matthew 6:6, 18. See also John 14:20.
1820. Colossians 1:27-28; Romans 8:9.
1821. See also Galatians 4:19.
1822. See e.g., Romans 1:7; John 20:28; Acts 5:3-4; Deuteronomy 6:4.

1823. AGJC, 13:16.
1824. AGJC, 15:18.
1825. See Luke 15:11-32.
1826. Luke 18:9-14.
1827. Acts 15:8-9.
1828. Matthew 24:14. See also Matthew 4:23; 9:35; Luke 4:43.
1829. Titus 3:11.
1830. 1 John 1:7.
1831. Luke 18:35-43.
1832. Luke 10:25-27.
1833. Genesis 1:27.
1834. John 17:21.
1835. 2 Corinthians 3:18.
1836. AGJC, 22:24.
1837. Luke 3:6; Romans 10:13; Acts 2:17; 2 Peter 3:9.
1838. See Romans 11:29.
1839. Ephesians 2:4, 8.
1840. Titus 3:5.
1841. 2 Corinthians 12:9.
1842. James 5:19.
1843. John 5:14.
1844. 1 John 4:16. See also 1 John 3:1.
1845. See Romans 12:21.
1846. Romans 15:4.
1847. Romans 15:6; 1 Corinthians 6:20; 1 Peter 4:16.
1848. See Isaiah 40:3-4.
1849. Acts 18:25; John 14:6.
1850. 2 Corinthians 7:10.
1851. Psalms 119:130.
1852. John 12:32; 14:20; 15:4; 17:21-23, 26; Colossians 1:27; 3:10-11; Romans 8:10; 1 Corinthians 6:15, 17; 2 Corinthians 5:16; 13:3, 5; Galatians 1:16; 2:20; 4:19; Ephesians 3:14-17; Philippians 1:20; 2:5; 1 Peter 1:11; 1 John 2:27; 3:24; 4:4.
1853. See the Apocryphon of James, 6:7.
1854. Matthew 5:48.
1855. Romans 8:2.
1856. John 12:32; 14:20; 15:4; 17:21-23, 26; Colossians 1:27; 3:10-11; Romans 8:10; 1 Corinthians 6:15, 17; 2 Corinthians 5:16; 13:3, 5; Galatians 1:16; 2:20; 4:19; Ephesians 3:14-17; Philippians 1:20; 2:5; 1 Peter 1:11; 1 John 2:27; 3:24; 4:4.
1857. Romans 6:18; 8:2.
1858. Luke 5:20.
1859. Luke 7:50; 18:42.
1860. Matthew 9:2.
1861. John 8:3-5.
1862. John 8:7-9.
1863. John 8:10-11.
1864. Matthew 11:29-30.
1865. John 10:10.
1866. Leviticus 19:18; Matthew 22:39; Mark 12:31; Galatians 5:14; James 2:8.
1867. Matthew 6:24.
1868. James 1:8.
1869. Matthew 7:14.
1870. Isaiah 55:7.
1871. Isaiah 35:8.
1872. Romans 2:6-7; Proverbs 12:5.
1873. Hebrews 12:9-10.
1874. AGJC, 130:21.

**1875.** Luke 12:10.

**1876.** John 12:32; 14:20; 15:4; 17:21-23, 26; Colossians 1:27; 3:10-11; Romans 8:10; 1 Corinthians 6:15, 17; 2 Corinthians 5:16; 13:3, 5; Galatians 1:16; 2:20; 4:19; Ephesians 3:14-17; Philippians 1:20; 2:5; 1 Peter 1:11; 1 John 2:27; 3:24; 4:4.

**1877.** 1 Peter 3:4.

**1878.** Daniel 7:9, 13, 22.

**1879.** Romans 7:22.

**1880.** Colossians 1:27.

**1881.** Proverbs 3:11-12.

**1882.** 1 John 4:16.

**1883.** Acts 17:27-28.

**1884.** Luke 3:6; Romans 10:13; Acts 2:17; 2 Peter 3:9.

**1885.** AGJC, 22:31.

**1886.** John 14:20.

**1887.** John 17:21; Hebrews 12:10; 2 Peter 1:4.

**1888.** Romans 6:6-7. See also Galatians 5:24.

**1889.** Romans 6:11.

**1890.** James 5:14, 15-16.

**1891.** See 1 Corinthians 12:9, 11.

**1892.** Mark 9:23.

**1893.** John 4:48.

**1894.** Hebrews 11:1, 3.

**1895.** My paraphrasal.

**1896.** Proverbs 17:22.

**1897.** Proverbs 12:18.

**1898.** Job 22:28.

**1899.** Matthew 9:27-30.

**1900.** AGJC, 91:14-15.

**1901.** Exodus 15:26.

**1902.** Genesis 17:1; Exodus 3:14-15; Psalms 46:10; Mark 8:29; 14:61-62; Luke 22:70; John 6:35; 8:12, 23, 58; 9:5; 10:7-11, 30-39; 11:25; 12:26, 46; 13:13; 14:3, 6, 10-11, 20; 15:1; 17:10, 16.

**1903.** Galatians 5:22-23.

**1904.** Proverbs 3:7-8.

**1905.** My paraphrasal.

**1906.** Mark 4:20.

**1907.** Isaiah 58:8.

**1908.** See e.g., Matthew 8:14-18; 9:1-8, 35; Luke 4:23.

**1909.** Job 22:28; John 1:12; Romans 8:14, 19; Philippians 2:15; 1 John 3:2.

**1910.** John 1:14.

**1911.** Matthew 24:14. See also Matthew 4:23; 9:35; Luke 4:43.

**1912.** 2 Corinthians 9:15.

**1913.** Psalms 30:10; 1 Corinthians 3:9; 2 Corinthians 6:1; Ephesians 2:19-22; Hebrews 13:6.

**1914.** 1 John 5:7.

**1915.** Psalms 46:10.

**1916.** James 4:8.

**1917.** Philippians 4:5.

**1918.** Job 22:21-22.

**1919.** Habakkuk 2:20.

**1920.** Zechariah 2:13.

**1921.** AGJC, 40:3, 5-14.

**1922.** Isaiah 26:3.

**1923.** Philippians 4:7.

**1924.** John 14:27.

**1925.** Mark 1:12-13.

**1926.** Matthew 5:8.

**1927.** Genesis 1:27. See also 2 Corinthians 3:18.

1928. Matthew 5:48.
1929. Matthew 18:3; 19:13-14.
1930. 1 Corinthians 2:16.
1931. John 3:33.
1932. Romans 3:23.
1933. John 17:21; Hebrews 12:10; 2 Peter 1:4.
1934. John 12:32; 14:20; 15:4; 17:21-23, 26; Colossians 1:27; 3:10-11; Romans 8:10; 1 Corinthians 6:15, 17; 2 Corinthians 5:16; 13:3, 5; Galatians 1:16; 2:20; 4:19; Ephesians 3:14-17; Philippians 1:20; 2:5; 1 Peter 1:11; 1 John 2:27; 3:24; 4:4.
1935. Hebrews 12:10.
1936. Romans 6:18.
1937. Galatians 6:15.
1938. 2 Corinthians 5:17.
1939. John 15:3. See also Luke 5:12-13.
1940. Matthew 5:48.
1941. John 8:15.
1942. Hebrews 2:9.
1943. 1 Corinthians 6:3.
1944. John 12:47.
1945. Luke 12:14.
1946. John 15:11.
1947. John 3:17.
1948. Luke 9:62.
1949. Philippians 3:13-14.
1950. John 10:10.
1951. See Matthew 10:22.
1952. Zechariah 4:6.
1953. Matthew 22:37.
1954. Mark 12:31.
1955. Matthew 22:36-40.
1956. See e.g., Romans 2:6-7.
1957. Matthew 6:33.
1958. John 3:3, 5.
1959. Galatians 6:15.
1960. 2 Corinthians 5:17.
1961. Mark 2:22.
1962. The Gospel of Philip, Logion 48.
1963. See e.g., Romans 2:6-7.
1964. Matthew 5:27-28.
1965. John 7:24; 2 Corinthians 10:7.
1966. Jeremiah 29:11.
1967. 2 Corinthians 4:18.
1968. Genesis 1:27.
1969. 2 Corinthians 3:18
1970. Psalms 18:30.
1971. Matthew 5:48.
1972. Psalms 23:4.
1973. 1 Chronicles 28:20.
1974. Joshua 1:9.
1975. Daniel 7:13-14.
1976. John 12:32; 14:20; 15:4; 17:21-23, 26; Colossians 1:27; 3:10-11; Romans 8:10; 1 Corinthians 6:15, 17; 2 Corinthians 5:16; 13:3, 5; Galatians 1:16; 2:20; 4:19; Ephesians 3:14-17; Philippians 1:20; 2:5; 1 Peter 1:11; 1 John 2:27; 3:24; 4:4.
1977. Psalms 139:8-10.
1978. Luke 16:17.
1979. Proverbs 4:7.

**1980.** Colossians 4:3.

**1981.** In conjunction with exercise and an alkaline-heavy diet (as well as limiting acid-producing activities and foods), there are numerous other methods of supercharging the body with oxygen. Deep-breathing exercises, oxygen therapy, ozone therapy, baking soda, and hydrogen peroxide, to mention just a few, have all been known to aid in the successful treatment (elimination) of "C." Entire schools of thought have been formed around these remedies, and dozens of books have been written about them. Though still controversial among most mainstream medical experts, oxygen-enhancing treatments continue to produce positive results when they are used correctly and safely. Concerning food, one should, as mentioned, focus on alkaline foods, most of which are high in oxygen. A friend recently told me of an individual he knew who cured himself of "C" by simply drinking large quantities of freshly made organic carrot juice everyday—no doctors, no medication, no radiation, no surgery. Taking copious amounts of food-based (as opposed to synthetic) nutritional supplements has been known to produce similar results. The list of cures for "C" is nearly endless, and each has its own success stories and supporters, a growing number of which come from the mainstream medical community.

**1982.** The Epistle of Barnabas, 14:5.

**1983.** Galatians 2:4.

**1984.** 2 Corinthians 3:17.

**1985.** Galatians 5:1.

**1986.** Luke 5:31.

**1987.** Luke 8:43.

**1988.** Psalms 33:9; John 6:63.

**1989.** The Sophia of Jesus Christ, 96:3-4.

**1990.** Acts 10:34; Romans 2:11; Ephesians 6:9; Colossians 3:25; 1 Peter 1:17.

**1991.** Babaji, as he is more popularly known, performed many of the same miracles as Jesus, including raising the dead. Such acts accord with Jesus' own prophecy. See e.g., John 14:12.

**1992.** Acts 17:29.

**1993.** 1 Corinthians 6:17; 2 Corinthians 6:16; Ephesians 4:6.

**1994.** John 12:32; 14:20; 15:4; 17:21-23, 26; Colossians 1:27; 3:10-11; Romans 8:10; 1 Corinthians 6:15, 17; 2 Corinthians 5:16; 13:3, 5; Galatians 1:16; 2:20; 4:19; Ephesians 3:14-17; Philippians 1:20; 2:5; 1 Peter 1:11; 1 John 2:27; 3:24; 4:4.

**1995.** Matthew 17:20.

**1996.** Revelation 22:13.

**1997.** Revelation 21:6.

**1998.** John 4:13-14.

**1999.** Acts 3:15.

**2000.** Isaiah 58:11.

**2001.** Habakkuk 2:4.

**2002.** Jeremiah 5:1.

**2003.** Ephesians 5:8.

**2004.** Isaiah 35:8.

**2005.** Galatians 3:28.

**2006.** Galatians 2:20.

**2007.** Ephesians 6:16; 1 Thessalonians 5:8. See also 2 Corinthians 10:7.

**2008.** Galatians 2:6.

**2009.** John 7:24.

**2010.** Romans 4:17.

**2011.** John 4:24. The KJV has "God is *a* Spirit," which is a mistranslation. The original text is: "God is Spirit." See also Romans 1:20; 1 Timothy 1:17.

**2012.** John 14:16-17; 1 Corinthians 6:19; 2 Timothy 1:14.

**2013.** 2 Corinthians 5:16; Colossians 1:27.

**2014.** 1 Corinthians 2:16.

**2015.** Proverbs 12:21.

**2016.** Exodus 23:25.

**2017.** Deuteronomy 28:1-2.

**2018.** 2 Corinthians 5:7.

**2019.** Proverbs 4:20-23.

**2020.** Genesis 17:1; Exodus 3:14-15; Psalms 46:10; Mark 8:29; 14:61-62; Luke 22:70; John 6:35; 8:12, 23, 58; 9:5; 10:7-11, 30-39; 11:25; 12:26, 46; 13:13; 14:3, 6, 10-11, 20; 15:1; 17:10, 16; Ephesians 4:6.

**2021**. Exodus 15:26. Thus, the noted Victorian physician Dr. James Johnson, editor of *The Medico-Chirurgical Review*, once said: "I declare, as my conscientious conviction, founded on long experience and reflection, that if there was not a single physician, surgeon, man-midwife, chemist, apothecary, druggist, nor drug on the face of the earth, there would be less sickness and less mortality than now prevails."

**2022**. Proverbs 16:23.

**2023**. The biblical "golden bowl" is an ancient symbol of the human skull. "Breaking" the golden bowl is a mystical allusion to the death of the physical body. The biblical "silver cord" is a non-physical rope, ribbon, or band that ties our spirit to our physical body. It is often seen by individuals during NDEs, who state that it is attached between the shoulder blades, or sometimes at the stomach, back of the neck, or top of the head. When the silver cord is cut, or "loosened," as the Bible says, the spiritual body and the physical body are permanently separated and "death" quickly follows. The spiritual body is then freed to ascend into Heaven, while the physical body "returns to the earth" from whence it came. See Ecclesiastes 12:6-7.

**2024**. Matthew 22:30. Jesus made a more detailed comment on this topic in *The Aquarian Gospel of Jesus the Christ*: "Behold, men recognize their mothers, fathers, sisters, brothers here in flesh; but when the veil is rent and men walk in the realms of soul, the tender lines of love that bind the groups of fleshy kin in families will fade away. Not that the love for anyone will be the less; but men will see in all the motherhood, the fatherhood, the sisterhood, the brotherhood of man. The family groups of earth will all be lost in universal love and fellowship divine." Then to the multitudes he said, "Whoever lives the life and does the will of God is child of God and is my mother, father, sister, friend." AGJC, 106:17-21. See also Matthew 12:48-50. Following Jesus' teaching on the Universal Brotherhood of Man (1 Peter 2:17; Romans 10:12; 15:7; Colossians 3:11; 1 Timothy 2:1-5), Paul also says that there will be no gender division in the Afterlife; and since there is also no need for physical reproduction in the Spirit Realm, there is no marriage there. Galatians 3:28.

**2025**. Hebrews 9:11.

**2026**. Matthew 4:17; 10:7. See also Matthew 5:3, 10.

**2027**. During the Sermon on the Mount Jesus also spoke of the Kingdom in the present tense. See e.g., Matthew 5:3, 10.

**2028**. Matthew 22:32. See also Luke 20:38.

**2029**. Luke 9:60.

**2030**. This is how Jesus described the Kingdom of God in the Gospel of Judas.

**2031**. Matthew 3:2; 4:17; 5:3, 10; 10:7.

**2032**. Mark 10:15.

**2033**. Matthew 7:13-14.

**2034**. John 10:10; Colossians 1:19, 26-27; 2:2-3.

**2035**. Job 32:8.

**2036**. Matthew 24:14. See also Matthew 4:23; 9:35; Luke 4:43.

**2037**. Matthew 6:10.

**2038**. 1 Corinthians 3:8.

**2039**. Genesis 1:27.

**2040**. 1 John 4:6.

**2041**. 1 John 4:6.

**2042**. 2 Corinthians 12:2.

**2043**. See e.g., Genesis 2:1; 1 Chronicles 16:26; Psalms 68:33; Ephesians 3:10; 4:9-10; Hebrews 1:10; 2 Peter 3:13; Revelation 12:12. See also the Gnostic Christian documents, On the Origin of the World and also the Apocalypse of Paul, in which the Seven Heavens are frequently and overtly referred to.

**2044**. See e.g., Philippians 2:10. Paul may be alluding to the seven levels of Hell here.

**2045**. In ancient times the furthermost outer planets had not been discovered yet, and the Sun and the Moon were considered planets. Thus, the seven "planets" of the ancient world were: the Sun, the Moon, Mercury, Mars, Jupiter, Venus, and Saturn, all which were later appended to the names of our seven weekdays (in the same order, Sunday through Saturday).

**2046**. Ancient Hebrew women wore crescent Moon amulets in honor of the great Hebrew Mother-Goddess Ashtoreth (Asherah). See e.g., Isaiah 3:18.

**2047**. One of these, the great Temple of the Pagan goddess Diana (Artemis) at Ephesus, is alluded to in Acts 19:27, 35.

**2048**. Our weekdays were named after the seven planets of the ancient world: Sunday was named after the Pagan Sun-god (the Sun's day), Monday after the Pagan Moon-goddess (the Moon's Day), Tuesday after the Pagan god Tiw/Mercury (Tiw's Day), Wednesday after the Saxon god Woden/Mars (Woden's Day), Thursday after the Pagan god Thor/Jupiter (Thor's Day), Friday after the Pagan goddess Fri, Frey, or Frigg/Venus (Fri's Day), and

Saturday after the Pagan god Saturn (Saturn's Day).

**2049.** Revelation 1:4, 11, 20. In mystical Christianity the "seven churches" of Revelation are considered an allegory of the seven chakras found along the human spine, referred to in Eastern literature as the "seven lotuses of light."

**2050.** In mystical Christianity the seven bodies, from the densest to the lightest, are: 1) the Physical Body; 2) the Ethereal Body; 3) the Astral Body; 4) the Mental Body; 5) the Casual Body; 6) the Spiritual Body; 7) the Divine Body. These seven bodies correlate with the seven chakras. See following note.

**2051.** In mystical Christianity the seven chakras ("wheels"), from lowest to highest, are: 1) Root Chakra, tailbone area. 2) Sacral Chakra, lower abdomen. 3) Solar Plexus Chakra, upper abdomen. 4) Heart Chakra, center of chest. 5) Throat Chakra, throat area. 6) Third Eye Chakra, forehead. 7) Crown Chakra, top of head (symbolized by the royal crown, or the "crown of glory" as Peter called it, 1 Peter 5:4; or the "incorruptible crown," as Paul referred to it, 1 Corinthians 9:25).

**2052.** Genesis 2:2-3; Hebrews 4:4.

**2053.** In accordance with ancient Jewish and Christian numerology, the number seven, along with its numerological corollaries (e.g., 70, 77, 70,000, etc.), appears over 500 times in the Bible. Jesus, as just one example, appointed 70 additional Disciples (Luke 10:1, 17), and taught that we are to forgive someone not seven times, but "seventy times seven." (Matthew 18:22.)

**2054.** John 12:32; 14:20; 15:4; 17:21-23, 26; Colossians 1:27; 3:10-11; Romans 8:10; 1 Corinthians 6:15, 17; 2 Corinthians 5:16; 13:3, 5; Galatians 1:16; 2:20; 4:19; Ephesians 3:14-17; Philippians 1:20; 2:5; 1 Peter 1:11; 1 John 2:27; 3:24; 4:4.

**2055.** Matthew 19:29.

**2056.** Mark 10:29-30.

**2057.** Luke 18:29-31.

**2058.** Matthew 24:14. See also Matthew 4:23; 9:35; Luke 4:43.

**2059.** My paraphrasal.

**2060.** 2 Corinthians 12:2.

**2061.** 2 Corinthians 12:3-4.

**2062.** Luke 11:52; Matthew 22:36-40. See also 1 Corinthians 1:5; 2 Corinthians 4:6; Ephesians 1:17; 3:4; 4:13; Colossians 2:2-3; 3:10; 1 Timothy 2:4; 2 Timothy 3:7; 2 Peter 1:2-3, 8; 3:18.

**2063.** The Sophia of Jesus Christ, 96:3-4.

**2064.** 1 Corinthians 8:6.

**2065.** John 16:28.

**2066.** John 20:17.

**2067.** Revelation 21:10-27; 22:1-5.

**2068.** Hebrews 11:16.

**2069.** See e.g., Revelation 3:5; 20:12-15.

**2070.** This means that when you make someone happy here on earth, you will feel their happiness during that part of your life review. Conversely, if you caused someone to suffer during your earthly lifetime, you will experience the same pain they felt when you hurt them. It should be noted that the Life Review lasts only for a brief second, for there is no time in heaven as we know it on earth.

**2071.** We will not need religion when we are living in the very presence of God—which is why John the Revelator saw "no temple" in the Celestial City during his ecstatic vision of the Afterlife. See Revelation 21:22. Gandhi is famous for his statement: "Thank God there is no religion in Heaven!"

**2072.** 2 Corinthians 11:15.

**2073.** 2 Corinthians 5:10.

**2074.** My paraphrasal.

**2075.** Luke 23:41.

**2076.** 1 Peter 1:17.

**2077.** 2 Peter 3:11-14.

**2078.** After being struck by lightning in 1975, Dannion was clinically dead for twenty-eight minutes, during which time he had one of the most complete near-death experiences ever recorded. The life-changing event, chronicled in his New York Times bestselling book, *Saved by the Light*, was dramatized in the 1995 hit TV movie (of the same name) starring Eric Roberts.

**2079.** Matthew 24:14. See also Matthew 4:23; 9:35; Luke 4:43.

**2080.** Luke 18:30.

**2081.** See e.g., Proverbs 12:28.

**2082.** 1 Timothy 2:4.

2083. Romans 10:13.
2084. Hebrews 11:35.
2085. Luke 16:22.
2086. See e.g., 1 Peter 1:17.
2087. Luke 23:43.
2088. John 14:28. See also John 14:12; 16:10, 16.
2089. John 13:1.
2090. Mark 1:3; 10:52; Luke 3:4; John 1:23; 14:4; Acts 9:2; 18:25-26; 19:9, 23; 22:4; 24:14, 22.
2091. Romans 8:10; 1 Corinthians 6:15, 17; 2 Corinthians 5:16; 13:3, 5.
2092. 1 Corinthians 2:9; 2 Epistle of Clement, 4:14.
2093. Ephesians 1:3.
2094. 1 Corinthians 4:10.
2095. Revelation 3:5; 20:12-15.
2096. 1 Peter 1:4.
2097. Luke 6:31. See also Matthew 7:12.
2098. Zechariah 10:7.
2099. John 12:32; 14:20; 15:4; 17:21-23, 26; Colossians 1:27; 3:10-11; Romans 8:10; 1 Corinthians 6:15, 17; 2 Corinthians 5:16; 13:3, 5; Galatians 1:16; 2:20; 4:19; Ephesians 3:14-17; Philippians 1:20; 2:5; 1 Peter 1:11; 1 John 2:27; 3:24; 4:4.
2100. John 11:26.
2101. Philippians 4:8.
2102. Deuteronomy 11:26-28.
2103. 1 Corinthians 4:10; Galatians 3:28.
2104. John 14:5-6. See also Matthew 7:14; 21:32; 22:16; Mark 1:3; 12:14; Luke 1:79; 3:4; 20:21; John 1:23.
2105. The Epistle of Barnabas, 14:5.
2106. Isaiah 35:8.
2107. 1 Kings 3:13; 1 Chronicles 29:12; 2 Chronicles 1:12; Psalms 104:24; 112:3; Proverbs 8:18; 19:14; Ecclesiastes 5:19; Isaiah 45:3; Ephesians 1:18; 2:7; 3:8; Philippians 4:19.
2108. 1 Kings 8:56; Galatians 3:29; Hebrews 9:15; 10:36; 2 Peter 3:13; 1 John 2:25.
2109. Matthew 24:14.
2110. 2 Corinthians 3:17.
2111. Galatians 2:4.
2112. Deuteronomy 11:26-28.
2113. Deuteronomy 11:26-28.
2114. Joshua 24:15.
2115. 2 Corinthians 10:5.
2116. Daniel 7:13-14.
2117. John 12:32; 14:20; 15:4; 17:21-23, 26; Colossians 1:27; 3:10-11; Romans 8:10; 1 Corinthians 6:15, 17; 2 Corinthians 5:16; 13:3, 5; Galatians 1:16; 2:20; 4:19; Ephesians 3:14-17; Philippians 1:20; 2:5; 1 Peter 1:11; 1 John 2:27; 3:24; 4:4.
2118. Matthew 7:24-27.
2119. 1 Corinthians 10:4.
2120. AGJC, 15:22; Hebrews 9:24.
2121. 1 Peter 2:4-5.
2122. Hebrews 8:2. My paraphrasal. See also Hebrews 9:11.
2123. See e.g., Luke 4:16. See also John 18:20.
2124. The term "Christian" was invented by Pagans, particularly at Antioch, as a derogatory term for the followers of Jesus. This is one reason Jesus never referred to Himself, the Apostles, or His followers as "Christians," and it is why the Apostles never called each other "Christians." The word, in fact, appears only three times in the entire Bible (Acts 11:26; 26:28; 1 Peter 4:16), and was only accepted as a legitimate appellation for Jesus' followers long after His death.
2125. John 7:16. See also Appendix B.
2126. John 10:10.
2127. 1 Timothy 1:4; Titus 2:12.
2128. 2 Corinthians 4:16.
2129. Luke 17:20-21.

2130. Isaiah 26:3.
2131. Hebrews 12:22.
2132. Ephesians 2:10.
2133. John 14:20.
2134. Genesis 21:22; Joshua 1:5-9.
2135. Isaiah 41:10.
2136. Psalms 23:4.
2137. Romans 8:31.
2138. John 14:20.
2139. John 17:21; Hebrews 12:10; 2 Peter 1:4.
2140. John 14:12.
2141. Psalms 122:7.
2142. Genesis 17:1; Exodus 3:14-15; Psalms 46:10; Mark 8:29; 14:61-62; Luke 22:70; John 6:35; 8:12, 23, 58; 9:5; 10:7-11, 30-39; 11:25; 12:26, 46; 13:13; 14:3, 6, 10-11, 20; 15:1; 17:10, 16.
2143. John 12:32; 14:20; 15:4; 17:21-23, 26; Colossians 1:27; 3:10-11; Romans 8:10; 1 Corinthians 6:15, 17; 2 Corinthians 5:16; 13:3, 5; Galatians 1:16; 2:20; 4:19; Ephesians 3:14-17; Philippians 1:20; 2:5; 1 Peter 1:11; 1 John 2:27; 3:24; 4:4.
2144. John 14:6.
2145. Matthew 13:43.
2146. Luke 8:50.
2147. John 1:12; Romans 8:14; Philippians 2:15; 1 John 3:1-2.
2148. Hebrews 6:18.
2149. 1 Corinthians 12:31.
2150. Acts 9:18.
2151. Psalms 18:28.
2152. Psalms 119:130.
2153. Luke 4:21.
2154. Psalms 118:26.
2155. Acts 2:28.
2156. Psalms 30:10; 1 Corinthians 3:9; 2 Corinthians 6:1; Ephesians 2:19-22; Hebrews 13:6.
2157. Galatians 5:1.
2158. Hebrews 6:5.
2159. Romans 13:12.
2160. 1 John 1:8.
2161. Ephesians 5:14.
2162. 1 Corinthians 10:14.
2163. 1 Corinthians 4:10.
2164. Galatians 3:29.
2165. Ephesians 1:13.
2166. Ephesians 4:15.
2167. Colossians 2:13-14.
2168. Christianity's earliest crucifixion stories speak of Jesus being nailed to, or "hanged" on, a tree (the "Tree of Life" or "World Tree"), not a cross. This ancient tradition is still evident in the New Testament. See e.g., Acts 5:30; 10:39; 13:29; Galatians 3:13; 1 Peter 2:24. Due to its numerous bounteous "gifts" (e.g., wood, shade, bark, sap, foliage, branches, logs, kindling, fruits, and sheer beauty) and human-like shape, the tree, and in turn the Tree of Life (mentioned in Genesis 2:9; 3:22, 24; Revelation 2:7; 22:2, 14), became a symbol of the All-Giving, Life-Bearing Mother-Goddess, whose unending love, protection, and nourishment is freely given out to all her earthly children . Tree crucifixion—which was eventually replaced by cross crucifixion for the sake of convenience—was a popular element in pre-Christian myths concerning Pagan gods. Such deities included the Phrygian savior Attis, the Greek savior Prometheus, the Nordic savior Odin, and the Hindu savior Krishna (or Chrishna). All were hanged on trees while wearing the foliage crown of each tree's respective deity. Jesus too was shown wearing a tree crown during His crucifixion. See e.g., Matthew 27:29; Mark 15:17; John 19:2. For more on this topic, see my book *Christmas Before Christianity*.
2169. Galatians 6:17.
2170. Galatians 1:16.
2171. 1 John 3:2.

2172. Colossians 3:11.
2173. Colossians 3:1, 4.
2174. Luke 15:18.
2175. 2 Corinthians 3:14-16.
2176. 2 Corinthians 4:7, 11.
2177. Ephesians 1:18.
2178. Acts 26:18.
2179. 2 Peter 1:19.
2180. Colossians 2:9.
2181. 2 Corinthians 4:10.
2182. Ephesians 1:13.
2183. John 14:16, 26; 15:26; 16:7.
2184. Job 22:21.
2185. Ephesians 1:14.
2186. Philippians 2:16.
2187. 1 Corinthians 15:22.
2188. Romans 6:3.
2189. 1 John 2:20.
2190. 2 Corinthians 1:21.
2191. See e.g., Matthew 9:15; Mark 2:19-20; Luke 5:35; John 3:29; Romans 7:4; 2 Corinthians 11:2; Ephesians 5:31-32; Revelation 19:6-9; 21:2-9.
2192. Matthew 18:2-5.
2193. Romans 12:2.
2194. See the Gnostic work the Prayer of the Apostle Paul.
2195. 1 Peter 2:25.
2196. 1 Peter 2:9.
2197. John 12:36; Ephesians 5:8; 1 Thessalonians 5:5.
2198. 1 Peter 2:9.
2199. Romans 3:2; Hebrews 5:12; 1 Peter 4:11.
2200. Mark 11:24.
2201. Psalms 89:15; Isaiah 2:5; 1 John 1:7; Revelation 21:24.
2202. 1 Peter 2:9.
2203. Luke 9:20.
2204. Malachi 3:3.
2205. Psalms 119:105.
2206. Hebrews 10:20.
2207. John 1:41.
2208. 2 Corinthians 5:20.
2209. 2 Corinthians 5:18.
2210. Hebrews 12:2.
2211. John 4:35.
2212. Romans 13:11-14.
2213. 1 Thessalonians 3:8.
2214. Matthew 19:28; Luke 22:30; 2 Timothy 2:12; Revelation 3:12, 21; 5:10; 20:6; 22:5.
2215. Matthew 6:33.
2216. 2 Timothy 3:14.
2217. James 1:22-25.
2218. Isaiah 40:4.
2219. Acts 3:19.
2220. Matthew 13:35.
2221. Galatians 1:16.
2222. 1 John 2:27.
2223. Romans 7:25.
2224. 1 Corinthians 2:10.
2225. John 14:17.
2226. 2 John 1:2.

2227. John 17:21.

2228. John 1:12.

2229. Psalms 17:15.

2230. Galatians 3:27.

2231. Galatians 1:16.

2232. Galatians 4:19.

2233. 1 Corinthians 15:49.

2234. AGJC, 68:13.

2235. Revelation 3:20.

2236. If we came to the material plane with full memories of all that we knew in the Spirit Realm, we could not be properly tested, for our "test score" (life review) would be unfairly skewed in our favor. Thus, in Earth School we "enroll" (are born) spiritually "nonliterate" (unconscious), then strive to become "literate" (come to consciousness) during the process of our "education" (lifetime). In other words, as with any regular school, we can only be tested on that which we learn while "attending" a particular school, in this case, Earth School. To be tested on our pre-earthly knowledge would be useless since we already possess it, which is why this information is blocked from us just before birth. In order to pass the "exam of life," we must discover "the mystery of Christ" for ourselves while our spirits are here, encased in physical bodies. Our final "graduation" from Earth School (our enlightenment) allows us entry into the highest level of Heaven.

2237. Psalms 37:31.

2238. Jeremiah 31:33.

2239. John 17:21.

2240. 2 Corinthians 3:3-4.

2241. Romans 10:8.

2242. See e.g., Hebrews 6:19; 10:20.

2243. 1 Corinthians 13:12.

2244. See my book, Christ Is All and In All.

2245. See e.g., 1 Corinthians 1:17-31; 2:1-16.

2246. See e.g., Matthew 16:17; Luke 2:26; 10:21; 1 Corinthians 2:10; Galatians 1:11-12; Ephesians 3:1-5; 1 Peter 1:12.

2247. See e.g., Psalms 5:3; 6:9; Proverbs 15:29; Isaiah 56:7; Daniel 9:17; Jonah 2:7; Matthew 21:22; Luke 6:12; Acts 1:14; Philippians 1:19; James 5:15; 1 Peter 4:7.

2248. See e.g., Psalms 5:1; 19:14; 49:3; 104:34; 119:97, 99.

2249. See e.g., Job 32:8; 2 Timothy 3:16.

2250. See e.g., 1 Chronicles 29:18.

2251. See e.g., Genesis 15:1; 46:2; Numbers 12:6; Psalms 89:19; Isaiah 1:1; Job 7:14; Ezekiel 1:1; 8:4; Daniel 2:19; Joel 2:28; Matthew 17:9; Luke 1:22; Acts 2:17; 9:10; 10:3, 17, 19; 16:9; 2 Corinthians 12:1; Revelation 9:17.

2252. See e.g., Genesis 42:9; Deuteronomy 13:1; Daniel 1:17; 2:1-2; 5:12; Joel 2:28; Acts 2:17.

2253. See Numbers 24:4, 16; Acts 10:10; 11:5; 22:17.

2254. 1 Corinthians 2:10.

2255. 2 Corinthians 12:1, 7; Galatians 1:11-12; Ephesians 1:17; 3:3; 1 Peter 1:13; Revelation 1:1.

2256. Acts 9:1-9.

2257. See e.g., Genesis 3:9-19; Exodus 3:1-6; 13:21-22; Isaiah 6:1-5; Amos 7:1-4; Jeremiah 1:11-13; Zechariah 1:5; Psalms 18:8-16; Acts 27:23-24.

2258. John 7:14-17.

2259. Galatians 1:11-12; 2 Corinthians 12:1-4; Ephesians 3:1-5.

2260. See e.g., Matthew 16:17; Luke 2:26; Romans 1:17; Galatians 1:1; 1 Peter 1:12.

2261. John 14:26; Philippians 2:12. See also AGJC, 100:17.

2262. See e.g., 1 Thessalonians 4:9.

2263. 2 Timothy 2:14, 16, 23.

2264. Luke 17:20-21.

2265. 1 Thessalonians 2:19.

2266. Matthew 13:10-13.

2267. Hebrews 8:10-11.

2268. Daniel 7:13-14.

2269. Zechariah 2:10-11.

2270. Hebrews 5:5-6; 6:20. See also Hebrews 7:3.

2271. 1 Peter 2:9.

2272. AGJC, 15:22; Hebrews 9:24.

2273. Hebrews 8:2. See also Hebrews 9:11.

2274. In the book of Genesis, Adam and Eve (archetypal Man and Woman) are shown being made as divine beings in the image of God (1:27), after which they are tempted by the serpent (the human Ego) to eat the forbidden fruit (that is, to participate in the base activities of the Lower Self). Having lost the childlike spiritual nature of the Higher Self, they forget about their oneness with the Father, and are banished from the Garden of Eden (the world of Spirit) to the world of the physical (earth). See Genesis 3:1-24. According to mystical Christianity, Jesus, like the saviors and messiahs of other religions, came to earth to remind us of our unity, our at-one-ment with God, first lost in the Garden of Eden.

2275. 1 Corinthians 15:31.

2276. John 3:3.

2277. Romans 6:6; Ephesians 4:22; Colossians 3:9.

2278. Matthew 18:3; 19:13-14.

2279. Ephesians 4:24; Colossians 3:10.

2280. Luke 5:37-38.

2281. John 12:32; 14:20; 15:4; 17:21-23, 26; Colossians 1:27; 3:10-11; Romans 8:10; 1 Corinthians 6:15, 17; 2 Corinthians 5:16; 13:3, 5; Galatians 1:16; 2:20; 4:19; Ephesians 3:14-17; Philippians 1:20; 2:5; 1 Peter 1:11; 1 John 2:27; 3:24; 4:4.

2282. 1 John 2:28.

2283. Ephesians 2:18.

2284. Luke 17:32.

2285. In one Gnostic Christian document, Jesus tells His Disciples that "the resurrection you're waiting for has already occurred, but you haven't recognized it yet." The Gospel of Thomas, Logion 51.

2286. Genesis 19:26.

2287. Luke 9:62.

2288. Matthew 3:2; 4:17; 5:3, 10; 10:7.

2289. Exodus 3:8.

2290. Hebrews 11:16.

2291. Acts 5:29.

2292. Mark 1:1.

2293. Matthew 24:14. See also Matthew 4:23; 9:35; Luke 4:43.

2294. 1 John 2:28.

2295. John 12:32; 14:20; 15:4; 17:21-23, 26; Colossians 1:27; 3:10-11; Romans 8:10; 1 Corinthians 6:15, 17; 2 Corinthians 5:16; 13:3, 5; Galatians 1:16; 2:20; 4:19; Ephesians 3:14-17; Philippians 1:20; 2:5; 1 Peter 1:11; 1 John 2:27; 3:24; 4:4.

2296. Luke 8:1.

2297. 1 Corinthians 2:16.

2298. Ephesians 5:2.

2299. Isaiah 59:8.

2300. Acts 9:11.

2301. John 14:6; Acts 24:14.

2302. 1 Timothy 6:15.

2303. 2 Timothy 3:12.

2304. Romans 8:27.

2305. Romans 15:5-6.

2306. John 13:15; 14:15; 1 John 2:6; 3:2; Romans 8:29; 1 Corinthians 11:1; Ephesians 5:1-2; James 5:10; 1 Peter 2:21.

2307. Colossians 2:6.

2308. AGJC, 107:6.

2309. Colossians 2:10.

2310. The Epistle of Ignatius to the Ephesians, 1:5.

2311. 1 Peter 2:17.

2312. 1 Timothy 1:17.

**2313.** John 15:4; 17:21-23, 26; Colossians 1:27; 3:10-11; Romans 8:10; 1 Corinthians 6:15, 17; 2 Corinthians 5:16; 13:3, 5; Galatians 1:16; 2:20; 4:19; Ephesians 3:14-17; Philippians 1:20; 2:5; 1 Peter 1:11; 1 John 2:27; 3:24; 4:4.

**2314.** John 14:20. See also Exodus 3:14; Ezekiel 37:14; John 14:10-11; Romans 8:9, 11; 1 Corinthians 6:17; 2 Corinthians 6:16; Ephesians 2:22; 4:6.

**2315.** Philippians 2:5.

**2316.** 2 John 2:19.

**2317.** Romans 5:11.

**2318.** Acts 27:23.

**2319.** Psalms 17:15.

**2320.** 1 Timothy 3:16.

**2321.** John 14:23.

**2322.** The Epistle of Barnabas, 15:7.

**2323.** Deuteronomy 28:1. See also Job 5:11; Psalms 69:29; 91:14.

**2324.** Exodus 19:4.

**2325.** Matthew 6:33; Psalms 37:4-5.

**2326.** James 4:8.

**2327.** Isaiah 55:11.

**2328.** 1 Corinthians 6:17; 2 Corinthians 6:16; Ephesians 4:6.

**2329.** Psalms 139:23; Proverbs 16:3.

**2330.** John 14:20.

**2331.** John 14:10.

**2332.** Luke 17:21.

**2333.** John 14:16-17.

**2334.** John 17:21.

**2335.** Exodus 3:14; Ezekiel 37:14; John 14:10-11; Romans 8:9, 11; 1 Corinthians 3:16; 6:17; 14:25; 2 Corinthians 6:16; 9:14; Ephesians 2:22; 4:6; Philemon 2:13; 1 John 3:24; 4:4, 12-13, 16; Zechariah 2:10.

**2336.** Psalms 30:10; 1 Corinthians 3:9; 2 Corinthians 6:1; Ephesians 2:19-22; Hebrews 13:6.

**2337.** AGJC, 20:13.

**2338.** The Teachings of Silvanus, 111:1-4. My paraphrasal.

**2339.** Romans 16:25.

**2340.** Colossians 4:3.

**2341.** Colossians 1:26.

**2342.** Luke 8:10.

**2343.** Proverbs 23:7.

**2344.** 2 Corinthians 3:18.

**2345.** 1 Corinthians 15:49.

**2346.** 2 Corinthians 3:18.

**2347.** Daniel 7:13-14.

**2348.** John 1:9.

**2349.** Philippians 2:15.

**2350.** John 10:33.

**2351.** Acts 24:14.

**2352.** See e.g., Matthew 26:65; Mark 14:64; John 5:18; 19:7. Jesus was not the first to be persecuted by members of His own faith (in His case, Judaism) for espousing unorthodox teachings. In 5th-Century China the Zen master Tao-sheng was pronounced a "heretic" and forcibly thrown out of his Buddhist community for teaching that everyone has a Buddha nature. Years later it was discovered that Buddha himself had preached this same doctrine. Jesus taught that we all have a Buddha nature as well, though He used the term "the Christ" (that is, Christ nature), while His followers used the term "Divine Nature." See Matthew 16:20; 2 Peter 1:4.

**2353.** Matthew 21:42; Mark 8:31; Luke 7:30. See also Psalms 118:22; Acts 4:11; Ephesians 2:20; 1 Peter 2:6.

**2354.** 1 Corinthians 2:7-8.

**2355.** John 9:25.

**2356.** Colossians 2:10.

**2357.** Hebrews 13:8.

**2358.** 2 Corinthians 9:15.

**2359.** 1 Timothy 4:14, 16.

**2360.** Philippians 2:5-6.

**2361.** 1 John 2:20.

**2362.** 2 Corinthians 1:21.

**2363.** Psalms 23:5.

**2364.** Galatians 3:25.

**2365.** 1 John 2:27.

**2366.** Matthew 7:7; Luke 11:9.

**2367.** Spiritual knowledge can only be gained spiritually, not intellectually. See 1 Corinthians 1:17-31; 2:1-16.

**2368.** 1 John 2:24-25.

**2369.** 1 John 5:6.

**2370.** 2 Corinthians 2:14.

**2371.** The Acts of Paul and Thecla, 1:20. My paraphrasal.

**2372.** See e.g., the Gnostic Christian work, the Apocalypse of Peter.

**2373.** Mark 4:11.

**2374.** Mark 4:23

**2375.** John 14:20.

**2376.** Mark 11:24.

**2377.** John 15:7.

**2378.** Revelation 5:1, 5.

**2379.** John 4:32.

**2380.** John 8:32.

**2381.** John 15:5.

**2382.** John 15:10-11.

**2383.** Daniel 7:13-14.

**2384.** Acts 3:14.

**2385.** See the Gnostic work, the Prayer of the Apostle Paul.

**2386.** Matthew 22:41-46. See also Daniel 7:13-14; Micah 5:2; Matthew 28:20; John 8:58; Hebrews 7:3; Revelation 22:13.

**2387.** AGJC, 178:14.

**2388.** Mark 1:1.

**2389.** Matthew 24:14. See also Matthew 4:23; 9:35; Luke 4:43.

**2390.** John 10:27.

**2391.** 1 Corinthians 15:1-2.

**2392.** Ephesians 1:13.

**2393.** 1 John 5:7.

**2394.** John 10:30; 17:22; 1 Corinthians 6:17; 12:12; 2 Corinthians 6:16; Ephesians 4:6.

**2395.** Philippians 4:13.

**2396.** John 14:16-17; 1 Corinthians 6:19; 2 Corinthians 1:22; 2 Timothy 1:14.

**2397.** Romans 1:25.

**2398.** See e.g., Matthew 26:65; Mark 14:64; John 5:18; 10:30-40; Acts 13:28.

**2399.** AGJC, 60:13.

**2400.** Exodus 3:14.

**2401.** Genesis 1:26-27

**2402.** John 14:20.

**2403.** Galatians 3:28.

**2404.** John 14:16-17; 1 Corinthians 6:19; 2 Corinthians 1:22; 2 Timothy 1:14.

**2405.** John 10:34; Genesis 3:22; Psalms 82:6; Isaiah 41:23.

**2406.** Hebrews 12:10.

**2407.** See e.g., Isaiah 9:6; Matthew 22:41-45; John 1:1-4, 14; 10:30; 14:9; 1 Corinthians 8:6; 2 Corinthians 4:4; Colossians 1:15, 19; 1 Timothy 3:16; Titus 1:3. Indeed, many mainstream Christian churches today teach that the Jehovah of the Old Testament "became" the man known as Jesus in the New Testament, and even translate the name of Jesus (meaning "Jehovah the Savior") as "He is Jehovah the Savior."

**2408.** Colossians 3:11.

**2409.** John 18:37.

**2410.** Mark 11:24.

2411. Matthew 24:35. See also Jeremiah 31:36.

2412. 1 Peter 1:25.

2413. Luke 21:33.

2414. John 10:34; Genesis 3:22; Psalms 82:6; Isaiah 41:23.

2415. John 14:20.

2416. Proverbs 3:1-26.

2417. Matthew 11:15.

2418. Daniel 7:9, 13, 22.

2419. Romans 5:11.

2420. John 14:20.

2421. 1 Timothy 3:16.

2422. 1 John 2:20.

2423. 2 Corinthians 1:21.

2424. Galatians 1:16.

2425. Matthew 24:23.

2426. John 12:32; 14:20; 15:4; 17:21-23, 26; Colossians 1:27; 3:10-11; Romans 8:10; 1 Corinthians 6:15, 17; 2 Corinthians 5:16; 13:3, 5; Galatians 1:16; 2:20; 4:19; Ephesians 3:14-17; Philippians 1:20; 2:5; 1 Peter 1:11; 1 John 2:27; 3:24; 4:4.

2427. Colossians 3:11.

2428. Proverbs 20:27.

2429. Daniel 7:13-14. See also John 17:5, 24; Revelation 22:13.

2430. Hebrews 7:3.

2431. Matthew 22:41-46. See also Micah 5:2; Matthew 28:20; John 8:58; Hebrews 7:3.

2432. Micah 5:2.

2433. John 12:34.

2434. John 8:58.

2435. Matthew 28:20.

2436. 1 Corinthians 2:16. See also Philippians 2:5.

2437. Philippians 2:5.

2438. John 14:21.

2439. See e.g., Matthew 13:55; Mark 6:3; Luke 3:23; 4:22; John 1:45; 6:42.

2440. Matthew 23:8-10.

2441. John 14:26.

2442. John 14:16; 15:26; 16:7.

2443. John 12:32; 14:20; 15:4; 17:21-23, 26; Colossians 1:27; 3:10-11; Romans 8:10; 1 Corinthians 6:15, 17; 2 Corinthians 5:16; 13:3, 5; Galatians 1:16; 2:20; 4:19; Ephesians 3:14-17; Philippians 1:20; 2:5; 1 Peter 1:11; 1 John 2:27; 3:24; 4:4.

2444. Exodus 3:14; Ezekiel 37:14; John 14:10-11; Romans 8:9, 11; 1 Corinthians 3:16; 6:17; 14:25; 2 Corinthians 6:16; 9:14; Ephesians 2:22; 4:6; Philemon 2:13; 1 John 3:24; 4:4, 12-13, 16; Zechariah 2:10.

2445. Romans 1:25.

2446. John 14:26.

2447. John 14:17, 20; 1 Corinthians 6:19.

2448. Matthew 5:39.

2449. Matthew 4:1-11.

2450. See e.g., Matthew 11:15; 13:9, 15-16, 43; Mark 4:9, 23; 7:16; 8:18; Luke 8:8; 9:44; 14:35; 1 Corinthians 1:17-31; 2:1-16.

2451. See e.g., Matthew 16:18; Acts 11:26.

2452. See Appendix B.

2453. Matthew 24:14. See also Matthew 4:23; 9:35; Luke 4:43.

2454. Mark 1:1.

2455. Acts 24:14.

2456. John 10:34; 14:20.

2457. See Matthew 26:65; Mark 14:63-64; John 5:18; 10:30-40.

2458. Philippians 2:6.

2459. Exodus 20:3.

2460. The manner of execution was stoning. Leviticus 24:16.

**2461**. Romans 6:6; Galatians 2:20.
**2462**. John 12:32; 14:20; 15:4; 17:21-23, 26; Colossians 1:27; 3:10-11; Romans 8:10; 1 Corinthians 6:15, 17; 2 Corinthians 5:16; 13:3, 5; Galatians 1:16; 2:20; 4:19; Ephesians 3:14-17; Philippians 1:20; 2:5; 1 Peter 1:11; 1 John 2:27; 3:24; 4:4.
**2463**. Genesis 17:1; Exodus 3:14-15; Psalms 46:10; Mark 8:29; 14:61-62; Luke 22:70; John 6:35; 8:12, 23, 58; 9:5; 10:7-11, 30-39; 11:25; 12:26, 46; 13:13; 14:3, 6, 10-11, 20; 15:1; 17:10, 16.
**2464**. Psalms 122:7.
**2465**. John 12:32; 14:20; 15:4; 17:21-23, 26; Colossians 1:27; 3:10-11; Romans 8:10; 1 Corinthians 6:15, 17; 2 Corinthians 5:16; 13:3, 5; Galatians 1:16; 2:20; 4:19; Ephesians 3:14-17; Philippians 1:20; 2:5; 1 Peter 1:11; 1 John 2:27; 3:24; 4:4.
**2466**. See e.g., Isaiah 9:6; Matthew 22:41-45; John 1:1; 14:9; 1 Timothy 3:16; Titus 1:3. We will note that a number of modern mainstream Christian churches believe that the Jehovah of the Old Testament "became" the man known as Jesus in the New Testament. Thus they translate the name of Jesus (meaning "Jehovah the Savior") as "He is Jehovah the Savior."
**2467**. John 10:34.
**2468**. Psalms 27:1.
**2469**. Malachi 4:2.
**2470**. Psalms 18:28.
**2471**. Early Christians had their own names for the Crown Chakra, including the "Incorruptible Crown" (1 Corinthians 9:25), "Crown of Rejoicing" (1 Thessalonians 2:19), "Crown of Righteousness" (2 Timothy 4:8), "Crown of Life" (James 1:12; Revelation 2:10), "Crown of Glory" (1 Peter 5:4), and the "Golden Crown" (Revelation 14:14).
**2472**. 1 Peter 5:4.
**2473**. 1 Corinthians 2:16. See also Philippians 2:5.
**2474**. Ephesians 6:17.
**2475**. See e.g., Matthew 16:17; Luke 2:26; 10:21; 1 Corinthians 2:10; Galatians 1:11-12; Ephesians 3:1-5; 1 Peter 1:12.
**2476**. John 14:20.
**2477**. John 10:34. See also Psalms 82:6.
**2478**. See Proverbs 15:26.
**2479**. See e.g., Romans 2:6-7.
**2480**. Matthew 5:39.
**2481**. See e.g., Matthew 13:15-16; Mark 8:18; Luke 10:23; 19:42; 24:16, 31; John 12:40; 1 Corinthians 1:17-31; 2:1-16.
**2482**. Ephesians 1:18.
**2483**. Matthew 6:22-23.
**2484**. Ephesians 5:8.
**2485**. See e.g., John 5:39.
**2486**. 1 Corinthians 1:17-31; 2:1-16.
**2487**. 1 Corinthians 1:30.
**2488**. 1 Corinthians 2:5; 1 Corinthians 6:17; 2 Corinthians 6:16; Ephesians 4:6; Zechariah 2:10.
**2489**. Matthew 24:14. See also Matthew 4:23; 9:35; Luke 4:43.
**2490**. Mark 1:14.
**2491**. John 12:32; 14:20; 15:4; 17:21-23, 26; Colossians 1:27; 3:10-11; Romans 8:10; 1 Corinthians 6:15, 17; 2 Corinthians 5:16; 13:3, 5; Galatians 1:16; 2:20; 4:19; Ephesians 3:14-17; Philippians 1:20; 2:5; 1 Peter 1:11; 1 John 2:27; 3:24; 4:4.
**2492**. John 14:20.
**2493**. Mark 11:24.
**2494**. The Gospel of Philip, Logion 48.
**2495**. See e.g., Matthew 16:17; Luke 2:26; 10:21; 1 Corinthians 2:10; Galatians 1:11-12; Ephesians 3:1-5; 1 Peter 1:12.
**2496**. See e.g., the Gospel of Thomas.
**2497**. 1 Corinthians 10:26.
**2498**. See e.g., Psalms 48:3.
**2499**. The singular of the plural Elohim is Eloah, "Goddess," from El, "God."
**2500**. Genesis 1:27; 5:2.

**2501**. See e.g., the Apocryphon of John. Also, as just one of thousands of biblical examples, see e.g., the Hebrew word for "God" (Elohim) in Genesis 1:1. See also Galatians 3:28.

**2502**. See e.g., the Gospel of the Egyptians, 3:10-11.

**2503**. Acts 17:28.

**2504**. John 12:32; 14:20; 15:4; 17:21-23, 26; Colossians 1:27; 3:10-11; Romans 8:10; 1 Corinthians 6:15, 17; 2 Corinthians 5:16; 13:3, 5; Galatians 1:16; 2:20; 4:19; Ephesians 3:14-17; Philippians 1:20; 2:5; 1 Peter 1:11; 1 John 2:27; 3:24; 4:4.

**2505**. John 14:16-17; 1 Corinthians 6:19; 2 Timothy 1:14.

**2506**. Exodus 3:14; Ezekiel 37:14; John 14:10-11; Romans 8:9, 11; 1 Corinthians 3:16; 6:17; 14:25; 2 Corinthians 6:16; 9:14; Ephesians 2:22; 4:6; Philemon 2:13; 1 John 3:24; 4:4, 12-13, 16; Zechariah 2:10.

**2507**. 1 John 5:7; 2 Corinthians 13:14.

**2508**. John 10:34.

**2509**. The Church Christianized then transmogrified the Pagan Mother-Goddess (and her many minor manifestations) into countless fabricated saints, after which hagiographers and mythologists heavily embellished their so-called "biographies." Among them were: the Three Marys (John 19:25), Brigid, Marina, Sophia, Eugenia, Irene, Felicity, Lucy, Philomena, Euphrosyne, Margaret, Agape, Faith, Ursula, Thecla of Iconium, Pelagia of Tarsus, Chionia, Tatiana, Agatha, Veronica, Febronia, Barbara, Thais, Ann, Euphemia, Agnes, Viviana, Afra, Christine, and Anastasia. Many, if not all of these figures, will be found to have well-known Pagan goddess antecedents around whom they were originally based.

**2510**. 1 Kings 11:5, 33; 2 Kings 23:13.

**2511**. For more information on Goddess, thealogy, and the Divine Feminine, see my books, *Christmas Before Christianity: How the Birthday of the "Sun" Became the Birthday of the "Son"; Britannia Rules: Goddess-worship in Ancient Anglo-Celtic Society; The Book of Kelle: An Introduction to Goddess-worship and the Great Celtic Mother-Goddess Kelle;* and *The Goddess Dictionary of Words and Phrases.*

**2512**. Matthew 24:14. See also Matthew 4:23; 9:35; Luke 4:43.

**2513**. Mark 1:1.

**2514**. John 17:21; Hebrews 12:10; 2 Peter 1:4.

**2515**. Mark 11:24.

**2516**. John 14:20.

**2517**. Luke 2:11; John 4:42.

**2518**. 1 Peter 1:12.

**2519**. Luke 17:20-21.

**2520**. See e.g., Luke 16:23.

**2521**. See e.g., Matthew 23:15. According to the Old Testament, early Jews performed human sacrifice (including children) in the Valley of Gehenna, adding to its "hellish" ambiance and reputation. The site, then known as Tophet ("place of fire"), was the location of the Shrine of Molech, a Tyrian fire-god. See e.g., Leviticus 18:21; 20:2-5; 1 Kings 11:7; 2 Kings 23:10; 2 Chronicles 28:3; 33:6; Jeremiah 7:31-32; 19:2-14; 32:35. See also Isaiah 30:33.

**2522**. See e.g., 2 Peter 2:4.

**2523**. See the Book of the Resurrection of Christ.

**2524**. See the Apostles' Creed.

**2525**. See Ephesians 4:9.

**2526**. 1 Peter 3:4.

**2527**. Matthew 3:16.

**2528**. 1 John 5:7; 2 Corinthians 13:14.

**2529**. John 20:19-22.

**2530**. John 1:1.

**2531**. Genesis 2:7.

**2532**. See John 14:16-17.

**2533**. 1 Thessalonians 4:8.

**2534**. 1 Corinthians 6:19; 2 Corinthians 1:22.

**2535**. Exodus 3:14; Ezekiel 37:14; John 14:10-11; Romans 8:9, 11; 1 Corinthians 3:16; 6:17; 14:25; 2 Corinthians 6:16; 9:14; Ephesians 2:22; 4:6; Philemon 2:13; 1 John 3:24; 4:4, 12-13, 16; Zechariah 2:10.

**2536**. John 12:32; 14:20; 15:4; 17:21-23, 26; Colossians 1:27; 3:10-11; Romans 8:10; 1 Corinthians 6:15, 17; 2 Corinthians 5:16; 13:3, 5; Galatians 1:16; 2:20; 4:19; Ephesians 3:14-17; Philippians 1:20; 2:5; 1 Peter 1:11; 1 John 2:27; 3:24; 4:4.

**2537**. 1 Corinthians 6:19; 2 Timothy 1:14.

**2538.** Matthew 28:19.

**2539.** Romans 1:7.

**2540.** John 20:28.

**2541.** Acts 5:3-4.

**2542.** Deuteronomy 6:4.

**2543.** See e.g., the Apocryphon of John.

**2544.** 1 John 5:7.

**2545.** In Ireland the Triple-Goddess is known as the Morrigan, and is made up of the goddesses Éire (from whom the name Ireland, "Éire's Land," derives), Banba, and Fódla.

**2546.** In Norse mythology the Triple-Goddess is called the Norns, and is made up of the goddesses Urðr, Verðandi, and Skuld (known in the British Isles as Scotia, she gave her name to Scotland).

**2547.** The ancient Romans called their Triple-Goddess the Matres, "the [three] Mothers."

**2548.** The ancient Greeks referred to their Triple-Goddess as the Moirai, made up of the goddesses Clotho, Lachesis, and Atropos.

**2549.** Aphrodite's name means "born of sea-foam." She is the Greek version of the Roman love-goddess Venus.

**2550.** By the use of the word myth here I do not mean "imaginary" or "fictitious," but rather "the collective traditional stories of the Christian Church."

**2551.** John 19:25. The "Three Marys" were the Virgin Mary (Jesus' mother), Mary Magdalene (according to many early traditions, Jesus' wife), and Mary the wife of Cleophas (Jesus' aunt).

**2552.** Exodus 3:14.

**2553.** Romans 8:9, 11.

**2554.** See Genesis 17:1; Exodus 3:14-15; Psalms 46:10; Mark 8:29; 14:61-62; Luke 22:70; John 6:35; 8:12, 23, 58; 9:5; 10:7-11, 30-39; 11:25; 12:26, 46; 13:13; 14:3, 6, 10-11, 20; 15:1; 17:10, 16.

**2555.** John 12:32; 14:20; 15:4; 17:21-23, 26; Colossians 1:27; 3:10-11; Romans 8:10; 1 Corinthians 6:15, 17; 2 Corinthians 5:16; 13:3, 5; Galatians 1:16; 2:20; 4:19; Ephesians 3:14-17; Philippians 1:20; 2:5; 1 Peter 1:11; 1 John 2:27; 3:24; 4:4.

**2556.** Luke 19:9.

**2557.** Hinduism teaches that God is the Aum or Om, the "Creative Word," while Christianity teaches that Jesus is the Word or the Logos.

**2558.** Revelation 1:8, 11; 21:6.

**2559.** Revelation 3:14. For John's corresponding Gospel text, see John 1:1-3.

**2560.** Exodus 3:14.

**2561.** John 8:58.

**2562.** Revelation 14:2; 19:6.

**2563.** Daniel 7:13-14.

**2564.** John 14:6.

**2565.** My paraphrasal. See John 12:32; 14:20; 15:4; 17:21-23, 26; Colossians 1:27; 3:10-11; Romans 8:10; 1 Corinthians 6:15, 17; 2 Corinthians 5:16; 13:3, 5; Galatians 1:16; 2:20; 4:19; Ephesians 3:14-17; Philippians 1:20; 2:5; 1 Peter 1:11; 1 John 2:27; 3:24; 4:4.

**2566.** Matthew 28:20.

**2567.** John 12:32; 14:20; 15:4; 17:21-23, 26; Colossians 1:27; 3:10-11; Romans 8:10; 1 Corinthians 6:15, 17; 2 Corinthians 5:16; 13:3, 5; Galatians 1:16; 2:20; 4:19; Ephesians 3:14-17; Philippians 1:20; 2:5; 1 Peter 1:11; 1 John 2:27; 3:24; 4:4.

**2568.** Ephesians 3:16.

**2569.** Romans 7:22, 1 Corinthians 4:16.

**2570.** We will note here that monotheism actually got its start in ancient Egypt, under the reign of the Pharaoh Akhenaten (circa 1380 B.C.-1334), also known as Amenhotep IV. The one God venerated by Akhenaten was none other than Ra the sun-god, one of the many solar-deities that would be later assimilated into the figures of both the Christian "Father," whom Isaiah called "the Everlasting Light" (Isaiah 60:19; see also Revelation 21:23; 22:5), and the Christian "Son," whom Malachi called "the Sun of Righteousness" (Malachi 4:2).

**2571.** Exodus 6:3; Psalms 83:13; Isaiah 12:2; 26:4.

**2572.** See e.g., Matthew 13:55; Mark 6:3; Luke 3:23; 4:22; John 1:45; 6:42.

**2573.** AGJC, 127:6, 26.

**2574.** John 6:33.

**2575.** Colossians 1:27.

**2576.** AGJC, 128:31.

**2577.** See e.g., Mark 1:4-11.

**2578.** AGJC, 129:13-14.

**2579.** AGJC, 138:41.

**2580.** AGJC, 135:15.

**2581.** AGJC, 176:30.

**2582.** AGJC, 163:36, 37.

**2583.** 1 Corinthians 2:16. See also Philippians 2:5.

**2584.** Matthew 3:2; 4:17; 5:3, 10; 10:7.

**2585.** See Acts 1:12-15.

**2586.** John 12:32; 14:20; 15:4; 17:21-23, 26; Colossians 1:27; 3:10-11; Romans 8:10; 1 Corinthians 6:15, 17; 2 Corinthians 5:16; 13:3, 5; Galatians 1:16; 2:20; 4:19; Ephesians 3:14-17; Philippians 1:20; 2:5; 1 Peter 1:11; 1 John 2:27; 3:24; 4:4.

**2587.** John 10:38; 14:6, 10-13.

**2588.** Luke 17:20-21.

**2589.** John 3:3.

**2590.** Matthew 18:3; 19:14.

**2591.** Matthew 24:14. See also Matthew 4:23; 9:35; Luke 4:43.

**2592.** Mark 1:14-15.

**2593.** See e.g., Luke 4:43; 8:1; Acts 1:1-3.

**2594.** Exodus 3:14; Ezekiel 37:14; John 14:10-11; Romans 8:9, 11; 1 Corinthians 3:16; 6:17; 14:25; 2 Corinthians 6:16; 9:14; Ephesians 2:22; 4:6; Philemon 2:13; 1 John 3:24; 4:4, 12-13, 16; Zechariah 2:10.

**2595.** John 1:14.

**2596.** See e.g., Matthew 8:8, 16; Mark 2:2; Luke 4:32; 8:11; John 2:22; 15:3; 1 John 2:5.

**2597.** John 12:32; 14:20; 15:4; 17:21-23, 26; Colossians 1:27; 3:10-11; Romans 8:10; 1 Corinthians 6:15, 17; 2 Corinthians 5:16; 13:3, 5; Galatians 1:16; 2:20; 4:19; Ephesians 3:14-17; Philippians 1:20; 2:5; 1 Peter 1:11; 1 John 2:27; 3:24; 4:4.

**2598.** 2 Corinthians 4:16.

**2599.** Revelation 17:8.

**2600.** Isaiah 14:12.

**2601.** 2 Corinthians 11:14.

**2602.** Isaiah 2:5; 1 John 1:7; Revelation 21:24.

**2603.** John 8:12; 9:5.

**2604.** Matthew 5:43-44; 22:36-40.

**2605.** 1 John 4:7-8.

**2606.** Revelation 22:16.

**2607.** Paul complained about this same problem in his day. See e.g., 1 Corinthians 1:17-31; 2:1-16.

**2608.** 2 Corinthians 4:16.

**2609.** Proverbs 12:5.

**2610.** 2 Corinthians 4:4.

**2611.** The centuries old LDS doctrine of the brotherhood of Jesus and Satan has been preached since the Church's founding, as the official writings of numerous Mormon authorities reveal. Among them: Brigham Young, Spencer W. Kimball, George Q. Cannon, John A. Widtsoe, James E. Talmage, Neal A. Maxwell, and Bruce R. McConkie, to name but a few.

**2612.** Isaiah 45:7.

**2613.** See 1 John 5:7.

**2614.** Romans 3:23.

**2615.** Matthew 5:39.

**2616.** 1 John 4:6.

**2617.** See e.g., Luke 18:9-14.

**2618.** See e.g., John 5:14; 8:11; Luke 18:42.

**2619.** One exception to this is Matthew 15:18-19.

**2620.** See Luke 15:11-32.

**2621.** See e.g., Romans 5:6-9. The doctrine of "original sin" was founded by the Catholic Church upon a "misreading" of Genesis 3:1-24, and also upon Paul's infamous comment: "Wherefore, as by one man [namely Adam] sin entered into the world, and death by sin; and so death passed upon all men, for that all have sinned" (Romans 5:12). Actually, the original meaning here has been greatly perverted over the centuries. What Paul is saying in this particular passage is merely that because "sin is death" (Romans 6:23), and because both sin

(Romans 3:23) and death are universal (Isaiah 40:6), then all people must be sinners, nothing more. In fact, in Romans 5:10, Paul wholly contradicts what would later become the idea of "original sin," which states that we must "pay" for the sins of Adam and Eve: "For if, when we were enemies, we were reconciled to God by the death of his Son, much more, being reconciled, we shall be saved by his life."

**2622.** See e.g., Matthew 27:54 (this scripture is, of course, absent from the Gospel of Q). According to this theory, other "Son of God" passages, such as John 10:36 (also missing from Q), must be late interpolations as well, added after Jesus' death, but before the writing of the Codex Sinaiticus in the middle of the 4ᵗʰ Century.

**2623.** John 1:12; Romans 8:14; Philippians 2:15; 1 John 3:1-2.

**2624.** Galatians 1:16.

**2625.** John 20:17.

**2626.** John 12:32; 14:20; 15:4; 17:21-23, 26; Colossians 1:27; 3:10-11; Romans 8:10; 1 Corinthians 6:15, 17; 2 Corinthians 5:16; 13:3, 5; Galatians 1:16; 2:20; 4:19; Ephesians 3:14-17; Philippians 1:20; 2:5; 1 Peter 1:11; 1 John 2:27; 3:24; 4:4.

**2627.** Malachi 4:2.

**2628.** See Acts 20:7.

**2629.** See e.g., Ezekiel 2:1, passim.

**2630.** See Eusebius' *History of the Church*, 3:39.

**2631.** See Acts 20:35.

**2632.** The one known reference Jesus makes to this phrase, John 10:36, is an obvious late priestly interpolation, for in all actuality, He never makes this statement anywhere else in the New Testament. Thus, we have yet another example of a self-reflexive passage artificially inserted by the Catholic Church to emphasize the divinity of Jesus.

**2633.** See Matthew 8:20 (from the first layer, known as Q1, of the Gospel of Q).

**2634.** Daniel 7:13-14.

**2635.** John 12:32; 14:20; 15:4; 17:21-23, 26; Colossians 1:27; 3:10-11; Romans 8:10; 1 Corinthians 6:15, 17; 2 Corinthians 5:16; 13:3, 5; Galatians 1:16; 2:20; 4:19; Ephesians 3:14-17; Philippians 1:20; 2:5; 1 Peter 1:11; 1 John 2:27; 3:24; 4:4.

**2636.** John 1:12; Romans 8:14; Philippians 2:15; 1 John 3:1-2.

**2637.** See e.g., Luke 3:23; John 1:45; 6:42.

**2638.** The Gospel of Mary, 8:15-21. My paraphrasal.

**2639.** Matthew 10:24.

**2640.** See Matthew 16:19; Revelation 1:18.

**2641.** John 12:32; 14:20; 15:4; 17:21-23, 26; Colossians 1:27; 3:10-11; Romans 8:10; 1 Corinthians 6:15, 17; 2 Corinthians 5:16; 13:3, 5; Galatians 1:16; 2:20; 4:19; Ephesians 3:14-17; Philippians 1:20; 2:5; 1 Peter 1:11; 1 John 2:27; 3:24; 4:4.

**2642.** Malachi 4:2.

**2643.** Revelation 1:16.

**2644.** John 8:12.

**2645.** John 12:46.

**2646.** John 12:36.

**2647.** See Revelation 5:5.

**2648.** See Acts 20:7.

**2649.** Revelation 12:1. This overtly Pagan depiction of Mary was borrowed by the Revelator from ancient images of the Hindu sun-goddess Aditi, who tenderly governed her twelve children, the twelve star-signs.

**2650.** Matthew 1:10.

**2651.** Luke 3:23.

**2652.** John 12:32; 14:20; 15:4; 17:21-23, 26; Colossians 1:27; 3:10-11; Romans 8:10; 1 Corinthians 6:15, 17; 2 Corinthians 5:16; 13:3, 5; Galatians 1:16; 2:20; 4:19; Ephesians 3:14-17; Philippians 1:20; 2:5; 1 Peter 1:11; 1 John 2:27; 3:24; 4:4.

**2653.** Malachi 4:2.

**2654.** Genesis 17:1; Exodus 3:14-15; Psalms 46:10; Mark 8:29; 14:61-62; Luke 22:70; John 6:35; 8:12, 23, 58; 9:5; 10:7-11, 30-39; 11:25; 12:26, 46; 13:13; 14:3, 6, 10-11, 20; 15:1; 17:10, 16.

**2655.** See e.g., Philippians 4:3; Revelation 3:5; 20:12-15.

**2656.** 1 John 5:7.

**2657.** Proverbs 15:26.

**2658.** Genesis 1:26; 3:22.

**2659.** Genesis 1:27.

**2660**. See e.g., Genesis 2:4.

**2661**. Exodus 6:3; Psalms 83:13; Isaiah 12:2; 26:4.

**2662**. Luke 8:50; Mark 9:23.

**2663**. Matthew 24:14. See also Matthew 4:23; 9:35; Luke 4:43.

**2664**. Mark 1:1. See also Acts 5:42.

**2665**. Matthew 8:20. This "Son of Man" passage is found in Q1 (the earliest layer) of the Gospel of Q.

**2666**. Matthew 27:54. This "Son of God" passage is not found in any of the three layers (Q1, Q2, Q3) of the Gospel of Q.

**2667**. One example: in the Codex Sinaiticus' version of the Gospel of Matthew 24:36, it reads: "But of that day and hour knoweth no man, not the angels of heaven, neither the Son, but the Father only." In later versions of Matthew, such as the King James Version, the phrase "neither the Son" was removed, completely altering the meaning of Jesus' statement to correlate with the theological and political agenda of the early Ecclesia (Catholic Church): to institute a "chain of tradition" establishing apostolic authority, stretching from Peter (the first pope) to the present one. Proof that this was not merely scribe's error but an intentional deletion by Catholic priests, is that the phrase "neither the Son" was retained in the Gospel of Mark (see Mark 13:32).

**2668**. Did Jesus see Himself as the political Messiah ("Christ") of Israel, the literal "King of the Jews"? Based on the evidence at hand, it is doubtful. For one thing, since there are no political messianic references in either the Gospel of Q or the Gospel of Thomas (our two earliest known Gospels), we can only conclude that the many eschatological elements of the four canonical Gospels are artificial emendations and interpolations. If this theory is correct, these would have been intentionally added by priestly scribes to support the political messianic expectations of the people and the developing orthodox Church. This view is supported by the synoptic Gospels themselves: nowhere in Matthew, Mark, or Luke does Jesus explicitly, publicly, or unambiguously state or even admit that He is Israel's long-awaited political Messiah. Instead, in several instances He virtually denies it by commanding His Disciples to "tell no man that he was Jesus the Christ" (that is, the Messiah). See Matthew 16:20, and also Mark 1:34; 8:30; Luke 4:41; 9:21. Those passages which appear to show Jesus acknowledging a messianic mission actually reaffirm what the Gospel of Q tells us: Jesus thought of Himself as the Son of Man, not the Son of God. See e.g., Matthew 26:63-64; Mark 14:61-62; Luke 22:67-70. When asked directly by Pilate if He was the Messiah, Jesus evades the question by replying, "Thou sayest [that I am]." See Matthew 27:11; Mark 15:2; Luke 23:3. Even the Gospel of John, which breaks from the synoptics by openly proclaiming Jesus' messiahship (see e.g., John 4:25-26; 17:3), contains this account. See John 18:33-37. The meaning of this preponderance of evidence I will leave to the reader to decide.

**2669**. See Matthew 16:18-19; John 20:19-22; Acts 8:14-17.

**2670**. Jude 1:14-15. The original text for Jude's quote, confirmed by the finding of the Book of Enoch among Qumran's Essenic Dead Sea Scrolls, is 1 Enoch 1:9.

**2671**. The intertestamental works (e.g., Esdras, Tobit, Judith, Bel and the Dragon, Maccabees, Baruch, Enoch, Story of Susanna, Prayer of Manasseh, Jubilees) are extremely significant, for they tell us what was occurring in the Near East and what people (such as the Essenes, Gnostics, Nazoreans, Iessaeans, Therapeutae, Pharisees, Sadducees, and Zealots) were thinking during the all-important (incorrectly called) "400 Silent Years," roughly between 400 B.C. and A.D. 0. For it was during this fruitful and dynamic four-century period that many of the Jewish, Gnostic, and Pagan doctrines, creeds, ideas, beliefs, and rituals that would one day become part of Christianity were developed. Of course, this is precisely why the intertestamental books were banned by the Church.

**2672**. Like many other unaffiliated and unbiased religious scholars, I believe that the Book of Enoch (theorized to have been authored by the Essenes) is a significant work that should be given its rightful place in the canonical Bible. It was not only a favorite work of Jesus and the Apostles (like Paul and Jude), and was endorsed as authentic scripture by numerous early Church authorities (among them Athenagoras, Barnabas, Clement of Alexandria, Tertullian, and Irenaeus), but it is an important historical record of the pre-Christian beginnings of Christianity. Of course, it is this last fact that got it into trouble: the Book of Enoch not only shows the enormous and overt manipulation of biblical documents by early orthodox Christian priests (for Enoch contains the original wording of many scriptures later used and redacted by the Church), it also reveals that much of what we consider original to Jesus and Christianity actually derives from that small group of pre-Christian sun-worshiping Jews known as the Essenes ("the Saints"). Enoch uncovers the authentic history of the formation of Christianity for all the world to see: it is primarily a product of Essenic Judaism! Thus, the Book of Enoch was permanently banned in the 4th Century A.D. by, among others, Hillary (bishop of Poitiers), Augustine (bishop of Hippo), and Jerome (papal secretary to Pope Damasus I).

**2673**. Malachi 4:5. See also Malachi 3:1; Luke 1:13-17; Matthew 11:11-15; 17:10-13.

**2674**. Malachi 4:2. See also Malachi 3:1.

**2675**. Numerous missing biblical books are mentioned in the Bible itself. Some are entitled, some are not. The list of these "lost" or censored books numbers in the hundreds. See e.g., Esther 2:23; 6:1; 10:2; 1 Chronicles 27:4; 29:29; 2 Chronicles 9:29; 12:15; 13:22; 20:34; 26:22; 33:19; Numbers 21:14; Exodus 24:7; 1 Kings 11:41; 1 Samuel 10:25; 2 Samuel 1:18; Joshua 10:13; Matthew 2:23; 1 Corinthians 5:9; Ephesians 3:3; Colossians 4:16; Jude 1:3.

**2676**. Acts 8:37 also does not appear in any of our other earliest Greek New Testaments, such as the Codex Vaticanus, Codex Alexandrinus, and Codex Ephraemi. The passage was artificially appended to the 8th Chapter of Acts in order to emphasize the divinity of Jesus over His humanity. Thus, the famed statement of the Ethiopian eunuch here, "I believe that Jesus Christ is the Son of God," entered the biblical canon both illicitly and unhistorically. As for 1 John 5:7, this was also added by the orthodox Church to John's letter after the writing of the Codex Sinaiticus (in the mid 4th Century). The reason? To further emphasize the divinity of Jesus, *and* to help establish Catholicism's new doctrine of the Holy Trinity—which Jesus never discusses in His earliest known teachings (the Gospel of Q), and which is otherwise entirely absent from the authentic (that is, earliest) New Testament texts.

**2677**. See e.g., Acts 3:13, 26.

**2678**. See e.g., Acts 4:27, 30.

**2679**. See e.g., Matthew 16:16; John 1:41; 1 John 5:1.

**2680**. Colossians 1:27. See also Romans 8:10; 1 Corinthians 6:15, 17; 2 Corinthians 5:16; 13:3, 5.

**2681**. Philippians 2:7-8.

**2682**. Romans 8:3.

**2683**. 1 Corinthians 15:45.

**2684**. See the Hebrew "Adam" in Genesis 2:19.

**2685**. See Hebrews 3:3; 7:24; 10:12.

**2686**. See Mark 1:4-5, 9-11.

**2687**. See Acts 13:33.

**2688**. See Matthew 3:13-17. An obvious interpolation occurs here in Matthew concerning John the Baptist and Jesus' baptism. After acknowledging Jesus early on in Chapter 3, much later, in Chapter 11, John does not recognize Jesus and asks Him to identify Himself. Matthew 11:1-4. The unknown author(s) of Matthew confused their various sources then failed to recheck their work.

**2689**. See Luke 3:16-17, 21-22.

**2690**. See John 1:19-34.

**2691**. See e.g., Ezekiel 2:1, passim. The phrase Son of Man should actually be written, "Son of Adam," or even more correctly, "son of adam," for here *adam* is used as a Hebrew noun for "man" (related to the Hebrew *damah*, "soil," "dust," "earth"). In the New Testament "man" is from the Greek word *anthropos*. Thus throughout the four Gospels we find the phrase *huios* ("son") *tou* ("of") *anthropos* ("man"), literally meaning, I am the "son of a mortal man." Jesus, of course, used this phrase in its metaphysical sense: "I represent the ideal man, God perfected in humanity."

**2692**. Luke 22:66-70.

**2693**. Mark 12:35-37. Some non-Marcan scriptures corroborate this view. While Mary did not descend from David, her husband Joseph did. According to Matthew and Luke, however, Joseph was not Jesus' biological father. See e.g., the contradiction in Matthew 1:1, 20. Some early Christians sought to correct this idea, stating that Mary too, like Joseph, descended from David. See e.g., the Gospel of the Birth of Mary, 1:1.

**2694**. See e.g., 2 Samuel 7:12-13; Isaiah 9:7. See also Luke 1:32-33; Romans 1:3.

**2695**. Compare, e.g., Matthew 1:1-17 with Luke 3:23-38.

**2696**. Again, see Matthew 3:13-17, where many believe we have overt biblical proof of Adoptionism.

**2697**. Throughout the centuries, countless Christians besides Paul of Samosata, many of them of high authority, have embraced Adoptionism, among them: Lucian, Theodotus of Byzantium, Arius, Artemon, Elipandus of Toledo, Bishop Felix of Urgel, Abelard, Folmar, and Luitolph. One Christian sect in particular, the 1st-Century Ebionites, were strong supporters of Adoptionism.

**2698**. Tritheism holds that God, Jesus, and the Holy Spirit are gods, each one distinct from the other.

**2699**. Luke 3:22.

**2700**. As noted, this Adoptionist passage in the Codex Bezae is from Luke 3:22, but the original is from Psalms 2:7 (cited in Hebrews 1:5; 5:5). See also Isaiah 42:1. In the Gospel of the Ebionites, 4:3-4, we find the same sentiment: "You are my beloved Son, in you I am well pleased. . . . I have this day begotten you." Adding to its validity as an original canonical saying, this specific wording, or something close to it, was quoted by a number of early Church Fathers as well, including Augustine, Clement, Origen, Epiphanius, and Justin.

**2701.** See e.g., Matthew 8:27; 26:72, 74; Mark 14:71; John 4:29; 9:11. Jesus' critics and enemies also viewed Him as a mortal human being. See e.g., Luke 23:4, 6, 14, 47; John 7:46; 9:16; 10:33; 11:47; 18:17, 29; 19:5.

**2702.** See e.g., Matthew 8:20, 9:6; 10:23; 12:8; 18:11; 25:13; Mark 2:10, 28; 10:45; 13:26; 14:62; Luke 6:5; 9:22; 11:30; 17:30; 19:10; 24:7; John 1:51; 3:14; 6:27; 8:28; 12:23; 13:31.

**2703.** See e.g., John 8:40.

**2704.** Clearly Jesus authorized the Apocrypha for He cited or alluded to scriptures from the following books: Sirach, Judith, Tobit, 1 Maccabees, 2 Maccabees, and Wisdom. Compare e.g., Matthew 6:7 with Sirach 7:14; Luke 6:31 with Tobit 4:15; and Luke 14:13 with Tobit 4:7. Paul also relied on the books of the Apocrypha. Compare e.g., Romans 9:21 with Wisdom 15:7; Romans 11:34 with Wisdom 9:13; and 2 Corinthians 9:7 with Sirach 35:9. Jesus also borrowed heavily from the apocryphal work known as the Testaments of the Twelve Patriarchs for His celebrated Sermon on the Mount.

**2705.** The following scriptures clearly show evidence of Jesus' missing teachings. In some instances entire passages have been edited out; in others only remnants of His words remain. In many cases it is obvious that the flow of the text has been interrupted by what appear to be deletions, intercalations, emendations, and interpolations—all the unscrupulous work of ancient orthodox Catholic priests and scribes: Matthew 4:17, 23; 9:10, 13, 35; 10:7, 27; 13:54; 16:21; 21:23; Mark 1:14-15, 21, 39; 2:2, 13, 15, 17; 4:33-34; 6:2, 6, 35; 8:31; 10:1; Luke 2:46-47; 4:15, 31, 44; 5:3, 17, 29, 32; 6:6; 9:11; 10:39; 13:10-35; 20:1; 24:27; John 4:40-42; 7:14; 8:2.

**2706.** Acts 1:3.

**2707.** To this day Buddhists claim that Jesus spent these missing eighteen "silent years" traveling through Asia (e.g., Tibet and India), where he studied under various spiritual masters. There is evidence to back up this claim: a Buddhist monastery on the island of Sri Lanka (earlier known as Ceylon) possesses documents recording Jesus' visit; early Christian texts have been found among ancient Tibetan chronicles; and in India a 1ˢᵗ-Century coin was discovered bearing the image of Jesus. Others have suggested that the Lord also visited Egypt, Iran, and Greece for the same educational purposes. The Bible itself may support such claims. Some of Jesus' own words suggest that at one time He traveled the world. See e.g., Matthew 24:14; Mark 13:10; Luke 24: 47; John 9:5.

**2708.** Most of Jesus' life story is indeed missing: his entire childhood, from shortly after birth to age twelve, and from ages twelve to thirty. In fact, the only portions of Jesus' life the Bible portrays are His birth and the three years between ages thirty and thirty-three. How can it be that the Bible records so little biographical information on the world's most amazing, beloved, and popular religious figure, the eponymous Messiah of the world's largest religion? If we are to believe that Jesus was an authentic historical figure who lived and died, then the only explanation is that this material was deleted by hostile ecclesiastical hands in an attempt to dehumanize then deify Him.

**2709.** Revelation 2:6. The Nicolaitans, who took their name from their leader Nicolas (Acts 6:5), syncretized various Pagan and Jewish elements in the formation of their particular Christian sect. They were eventually branded "heretical" by Catholic authorities, sealing their fate. Particularly offensive to the Ecclesia were the Gnostic sect's wild feasts and orgies, which they held in the name of Christ. See Revelation 2:14-15.

**2710.** Some deny that the Gnostics were Christians. If this is true, why then did the Catholic Church spend centuries trying to stamp them out, and why to this day are they still being branded "heretical" by the mainstream Christian Church? The fact is that though Gnosticism existed long before the rise of Christianity, it embraced various aspects of the "new" religion after its emergence in the 1ˢᵗ Century, becoming in every way Christian. Indeed, in many aspects, in my opinion, the early Gnostics were more Christian than were their more orthodox Christian counterparts, who eventually veered completely off course from the Gospel as it was taught by Jesus.

**2711.** See e.g., Matthew 16:17; Luke 2:26; 10:21; 1 Corinthians 2:10; Galatians 1:11-12; Ephesians 3:1-5; 1 Peter 1:12.

**2712.** See e.g., John 20:30; 21:25.

**2713.** Despite the Catholic Church's centuries-old quest to destroy them, the Knights Templar flourish into the present day. The largest order in the world is the *Ordo Supremus Militaris Templi Hierosolymitani* ("The Sovereign Military Order of the Temple of Jerusalem"), or as they are more commonly known, Knights Templar International.

**2714.** Matthew 24:14. See also Matthew 4:23; 9:35; Luke 4:43.

**2715.** Mark 1:14.

**2716.** See e.g., Luke 4:43; 8:1.

**2717.** In fact, Gnostic Christianity thrives to this day, more popular than ever, while the teaching of Jesus' suppressed esoteric doctrines is being carried on in a variety of public organizations, secret societies, underground fraternities, and mystery schools. These include the Order of the Rosy Cross (Rosicrucians), Knights Templar International, Freemasonry, the Great White Brotherhood, the Self-Realization Fellowship, Martinism, Christian Science, the Scottish Knights Templar, Unitarianism, the Universalist Church, New Thought Theology, the

Theosophical Society, Religious Science, the Unity Church, the Association for Research and Enlightenment, and Anthroposophy, among many others.

**2718.** John 10:34. See also Psalms 82:6; Isaiah 41:23.

**2719.** John 14:12.

**2720.** See e.g., Matthew 13:55; Mark 6:3; Luke 3:23; 4:22; John 1:45; 6:42.

**2721.** See e.g., John 3:18.

**2722.** Luke mentions that there were "many" other gospels, or what he calls "declarations" (Luke 1:1). These would have included both Church-approved gospels, now lost, and the "heretical" Gnostic Gospels that were later suppressed by the Church. Paul also makes reference to the Gnostic Gospels (2 Corinthians 11:4; Galatians 1:6-9).

**2723.** The Book of Thomas the Contender, Logion 1. My paraphrasal.

**2724.** The Gospel of Thomas, Introduction and Logion 1. My paraphrasal.

**2725.** Many translations of the Bible only accidently change the intent of Jesus' words. However, the end result is the same: the true meaning of the Lord's original teaching is lost, becoming more remote with each new translation.

**2726.** The possible link between Jesus and the Essenes (flourished $2^{nd}$ Century B.C. to $1^{st}$ Century A.D.) is sharply debated among religious scholars. Did Jesus study under or actually join the Essenes during His "silent years," the eighteen years between ages twelve and thirty? Some evidence, such as the Essenic Book of Enoch, suggests so: the Lord paraphrases this work on numerous occasions. Thus, many believe, for example, that Jesus may have derived some of His teachings, and even patterned His own mission, around the cryptic Essenic figure, the "Teacher of Righteousness," who was venerated as the sect's messiah, came into conflict with orthodox Jewish authorities, and was eventually murdered by them due to his radical teachings. There are other tantalizing pieces of circumstantial evidence, such as the fact that the Last Supper took place in what was then considered the "Essene Quarter" of Jerusalem. Jesus could have called this gathering anywhere. Why did He choose to meet his Apostles for the last time in this specific location? The debate on the possible connections between Jesus, the Essenes, and the Dead Sea Scrolls continues.

**2727.** The Essenes were discussed by numerous early important Church Fathers and historians, including Saint Epiphanius, Josephus, Philo, and Pliny the Elder.

**2728.** It is clear to me that because Jesus opposed the Pharisees and the Sadducees, their names were left in the New Testament. Conversely, because He borrowed so heavily from the Essenes (with whom He had much in common), they were left out of the New Testament. The reason? In part, because the Church needed Jesus' primary teachings to appear to be original, not borrowed from pre-Christian religious sects—as in fact we now know many of them obviously were.

**2729.** Luke 17:21. This is only one of thousands of examples of biblical meddling that could be given, calling into question the Church's doctrines of biblical inerrancy and scriptural infallibility. To accept these creeds, one must ignore, for instance, the overt facts that there are countless scriptures missing (e.g., Mark 16: 9-20; John 21:25; Acts 8:37; 1 John 5:7) from the Codex Sinaiticus (our oldest known *complete* Bible) that are found in today's Bibles (obvious additions), and that there are a number of books included in the Codex Sinaiticus (e.g., the Epistle of Barnabas, the Shepherd of Hermas) that are missing from today's Bibles (obvious deletions).

**2730.** John 14:20.

**2731.** One of the most flagrant and consequential editorial abuses in the Bible occurs in the Gospel of Matthew (1:20-23), where an interfering scribe intentionally mistranslates Isaiah's original Hebrew word *almah* ("young woman") from the faulty Septuagint as *parthenos* (an actual "virgin"). This greatly aided in the Paganization of Jesus, forever and drastically altering the doctrinal foundation of Christianity itself

**2732.** Matthew 24:14. See also Matthew 1:21, 5:33; Luke 4:43.

**2733.** Mark 11:24.

**2734.** 2 Corinthians 3:14.

**2735.** 2 Corinthians 4:4.

**2736.** 2 Corinthians 2:17.

**2737.** See Zephaniah 3:4.

**2738.** Revelation 22:18-19.

**2739.** Romans 13:11; 1 Thessalonians 5:5-6.

**2740.** See e.g., Matthew 26:65; Mark 14:64; John 10:33.

**2741.** Christianity is without question the world's most syncretistic religion. Though it began as a direct outgrowth of Essenic Judaism, it also borrowed heavily from Gnosticism and Paganism. The early Church, for instance, adopted the sun-worshiping Essenes' sacrament, the Gnostics' doctrine of the "Word" or "Logos," and the Pagans' Sabbath day in honor of the sun-god: Sun's Day, or Sunday (prior to this the Church had celebrated its Sabbath on Saturn's Day, or Saturday, the Jewish holy day honoring the agricultural-god Saturn). See Acts 20:7. Hundreds of other examples of this type of overt religious fusion could be given.

**2742.** As of now there are still no known *original* and *complete* biblical texts for us to study or compare with our present day Bibles.

**2743.** For example, there are entire sections of the Vatican Library in Rome that are off limits, even to the Church's most respected scholars. What is so "dangerous" about these particular "secret" ancient scrolls, documents, and books, that not even Catholicism's top academics and theologians are allowed to view them? Is it possible that they contain original and complete New Testament texts showing Jesus' authentic esoteric teachings about the divinity of mankind and the Law of Attraction? If not, why have they been so thoroughly suppressed for the past 2,000 years?

**2744.** Matthew 20:28.

**2745.** Matthew 24:14. See also Matthew 4:23; 9:35; Luke 4:43.

**2746.** Matthew 6:6, 18.

**2747.** Luke 18:16.

**2748.** Because they are based on the core beliefs of numerous religions, many mainstream Christians haughtily denounce New Age teachings as a "syncretistic" belief system. However, Christianity itself is, as noted above, the most syncretistic religious belief system in the world, one that has adopted or absorbed thousands of doctrines, rituals, concepts, traditions, symbols, myths, and even figures, from countless pre-Christian Jewish and Pagan religions. For more on this topic, see my book *Christmas Before Christianity*.

**2749.** Jude 1:10.

**2750.** Luke 8:1.

**2751.** Matthew 24:14. See also Matthew 4:23; 9:35; Luke 4:43.

**2752.** See e.g., Luke 4:43; 9:2, 60.

**2753.** Acts 1:1-3.

**2754.** Colossians 1:19, 26-27; 2:2-3.

**2755.** See e.g., Genesis 8:21; Job 15:14; Psalms 14:2-3; 51:5; Proverbs 22:15; Ecclesiastes 9:3; Jeremiah 17:9; Romans 5:12; 6:23; 1 Corinthians 15:22; Ephesians 2:1-3. Some Christian groups attribute original sin to a pre-Adamic event in which angelic beings rebelled against God. See e.g., 2 Peter 2:4; Jude 6. Despite all the modern day scripture-twisting and unenlightened translating that has gone on, none of these passages actually say anything about the doctrine of "original sin." Indeed, the concept of hereditary sin being transmitted genetically to the entire human race is completely absent from both the Old and the New Testaments. Why? Because the idea was invented by the early Catholic Church out of "ecclesiastical necessity" hundreds of years after the writing of the New Testament. It was then later artificially linked to the above scriptures.

**2756.** John 17:20-23.

**2757.** John 10:34.

**2758.** 1 John 4:8, 16.

**2759.** Genesis 1:27.

**2760.** Matthew 5:48.

**2761.** Luke 19:9. This is not to say that Jesus did not have a plan of salvation. He certainly did, and He preached almost nothing else but this plan—which He called "the mystery of Kingdom of God" (Mark 4:11)—during his final years.

**2762.** The Aramaic version of Luke 19:9 reads: "Jesus said to him, 'Today *life* has come to this house, because he also is a son of Abraham.'"

**2763.** Romans 5:11.

**2764.** Note that this does not mean that our Lower Selves cannot sin. Only that our Higher Selves are not "born in sin"; that they are not "tainted" with the "sin of Adam." The Higher Self is, in other words, eternally pure and unsullied, even by life on earth.

**2765.** Luke 3:6. See also Romans 10:13; Acts 2:17; 2 Peter 3:9.

**2766.** 1 Timothy 2:4.

**2767.** My paraphrasal of Acts 2:17.

**2768.** 2 Peter 3:9.

**2769.** See Romans 11:29.

**2770.** Mark 11:24.

**2771.** Genesis 1:26-27. See also 2 Corinthians 3:18.

**2772.** Isaiah 64:6.

**2773.** Some, the monophysitics, argue that Jesus has only one nature, half divine, half human.

**2774.** John 17:21; 2 Peter 1:4.

**2775.** Hebrews 12:10.

**2776.** John 12:32; 14:20; 15:4; 17:21-23, 26; Colossians 1:27; 3:10-11; Romans 8:10; 1 Corinthians 6:15, 17; 2 Corinthians 5:16; 13:3, 5; Galatians 1:16; 2:20; 4:19; Ephesians 3:14-17; Philippians 1:20; 2:5; 1 Peter 1:11; 1 John 2:27; 3:24; 4:4.

**2777.** Hebrews 5:5-6; 6:20. See also Hebrews 7:3; 1 Peter 2:9.

**2778.** Hebrews 8:2. See also Hebrews 9:11.

**2779.** AGJC, 15:22; Hebrews 9:24.

**2780.** Romans 6:1-18.

**2781.** Romans 10:4.

**2782.** Hebrews 9:24-26.

**2783.** Romans 5:13.

**2784.** Colossians 2:14.

**2785.** 2 Corinthians 5:21.

**2786.** John 19:30.

**2787.** Hebrews 7:18-19.

**2788.** See e.g., John 12:31; Colossians 2:15; Hebrews 2:14.

**2789.** Colossians 1:13.

**2790.** Romans 6:2.

**2791.** Hebrews 10:14.

**2792.** Romans 5:19.

**2793.** Hebrews 10:26-27.

**2794.** Colossians 2:10.

**2795.** Colossians 2:13.

**2796.** The Gospel of the Nazoreans, 2:2. My paraphrasal.

**2797.** See e.g., Matthew 22:9-10.

**2798.** AGJC, 56:17-18.

**2799.** AGJC, 28:22-25.

**2800.** Galatians 1:11-12; 2 Corinthians 12:1-4; Ephesians 3:1-5.

**2801.** See e.g., Colossians 2:11-23.

**2802.** Colossians 2:20-23; 3:1-4.

**2803.** Personally, I am not worried about the survival of the institutionalized Church. There will always be a need for organized religion, and that is as it should be.

**2804.** Matthew 24:14. See also Matthew 4:23; 9:35; Luke 4:43.

**2805.** Matthew 15:6, 9.

**2806.** Ephesians 4:14.

**2807.** See e.g., Luke 20:21; Acts 18:26.

**2808.** See Romans 10:1-4.

**2809.** Luke 11:52.

**2810.** Matthew 23:13.

**2811.** My paraphrasal.

**2812.** Hebrews 9:11.

**2813.** Matthew 10:7.

**2814.** Matthew 5:3. See also Matthew 5:10.

**2815.** Matthew 5:20.

**2816.** Matthew 24:14. See also Matthew 4:23; 9:35; Luke 4:43.

**2817.** For more information on Jesus and the Divine Feminine, see my books, *Christmas Before Christianity: How the Birthday of the "Sun" Became the Birthday of the "Son"*; *Britannia Rules: Goddess-worship in Ancient Anglo-Celtic Society*; *The Book of Kelle: An Introduction to Goddess-worship and the Great Celtic Mother-Goddess Kelle*; and *The Goddess Dictionary of Words and Phrases*.

**2818.** Mark 16:15.

**2819.** See e.g., Matthew 15:9; Ephesians 4:14; Colossians 2:8.

**2820.** Matthew 2:2.

**2821.** See e.g., Hebrews 7:18-19, 22; 8:1-13; 9:1-28; 10:1-20; Romans 3:20; Galatians 3:22-29. See also Jeremiah 31:31-34; Psalms 110:4; Zechariah 6:12-13; Haggai 2:6.

**2822.** See e.g., Ephesians 2:15; Titus 1:14.

**2823.** As Jewish infants, both Jesus and Paul were circumcised, according to Hebrew custom (Genesis 17:10-12), eight days after birth. Luke 2:21; Philemon 3:5. Since he was the son of a Jewish mother, the adult Timothy was circumcised by order of Paul. Acts 16:3. Non-Jews, like Titus, were not required to undergo the operation. Galatians 2:3.

**2824.** See e.g., Acts 19:34; 21:29; 22:3; Romans 2:28-29; 9:3-4; Galatians 2:14.

**2825.** See e.g., Acts 21:26. Also see Acts 18:18, where Paul is following a well-known Nazirite religious custom (Numbers 6:2-21).

**2826.** See e.g., Mark 1:21; 6:2; Luke 4:16, 31; 6:6; 13:10; 23:54-56; Acts 13:14, 44; 15:21; 16:13; 17:2; 18:4.

**2827.** See e.g., Matthew 26:17-19; Luke 22:1-15; John 2:13-23; 10:22-23; Acts 2:1; 18:21; 20:16; 1 Corinthians 5:7-8; 16:8.

**2828.** See e.g., Matthew 12:29; 13:54; 21:14-15, 23; 24:1; 26:55; Mark 1:21-29; 3:1; 6:2; 11:11, 15-16, 27, 35; 13:1; 14:49; Luke 2:40-46; 4:16-38, 44; 6:6, 59; 19:47; 20:1; 21:37-38; 22:53; John 7:14, 28; 8:2, 20, 59; 10:23; 18:20; Acts 2:46; 3:1, 3; 5:21, 25, 42; 13:14-42; 14:1; 17:1-17; 18:4, 19, 26; 19:8; 21:26-27, 29-30; 22:17; 24:12, 18.

**2829.** See e.g., Acts 16:19-20; 19:34.

**2830.** Acts 24:5.

**2831.** See e.g., 1 Corinthians 9:20. See also Acts 28:17, 20; Romans 2:17, 28-29.

**2832.** Romans 11:1.

**2833.** 2 Corinthians 11:22.

**2834.** Galatians 1:13-14.

**2835.** See e.g., Acts 21:39; 22:3; Galatians 2:15.

**2836.** Acts 23:6; 26:4-5.

**2837.** Galatians 2:14.

**2838.** See Luke 22:15.

**2839.** See Acts 20:7.

**2840.** See e.g., Matthew 26:17-30.

**2841.** See e.g., Genesis 14:18. Many believe that the Last Supper was a Seder, a Jewish ceremonial meal held on the first night of Passover. It is worth noting that the use of "bread and wine" type sacraments in the New Testament is of Pagan origins. The primary difference was that ancient Pagans used ritually sacrificed animals, such as bulls and goats, partaking of their meat and blood (a practice referred to, e.g., in Hebrews 10:4). Among the Nazarenes and Essenes, and later, Christians, bread and wine were substituted for meat and blood. One pre-Christian Roman faith, Mithraism, the most popular religion at the time of Jesus, also used bread in its sacrament: small buns with crosses etched on top. Early Gnostic Christians taught that Jesus' "flesh" (symbolized by bread) is the Word (Logos), while His "blood" (symbolized by wine or water) is the Holy Spirit. See e.g., the Gospel of Philip, Logion 25.

**2842.** The earliest biblical use of the word "Christian" is from 1 Peter (4:16), which was written about A.D. 65, over three decades *after* Jesus' death. As is clear from this particular passage, it was coined around this time by Pagans as a term of shame and derision for Jesus' followers. This is why the word was not used by the early church, and why it appears nowhere in any of the New Testament books that followed the writing of 1 Peter, except Acts (written about the year A.D. 67). These include, in order of writing: Matthew, Luke, Hebrews, 2 Peter, Jude, John, 1 John, 2 John, 3 John, and Revelation. (Naturally, the word is not in Mark, which was written around A.D. 61, four years prior to 1 Peter.) In neither of the two instances in which the word Christian appears in Acts (11:26; 26:28) is it shown being used by Jesus' followers as a name for themselves. In the latter passage, the Judean monarch Herod Agrippa says to Paul: "You have almost persuaded me to be a Christian." However, this was said sarcastically and mockingly, for Herod, being a king ("anointed"), was already considered a christ, since ancient peoples considered their leaders to be literal deities. This was done through the process of "christing," anointing the head with sacred (olive) oil later known as chrism. See e.g., 1 Samuel 15:17; 2 Samuel 2:4, 7; 3:39; 5:3, 17; 12:7; 23:1; 1 Kings 1:45; 5:1; 2 Kings 9:3, 6, 12; 11:12; 23:30; 1 Chronicles 11:3; 14:8; 29:22; 2 Chronicles 23:11; Psalms 18:50.

**2843.** Acts 11:26.

**2844.** See Acts 11:26; 26:28; 1 Peter 4:16.

**2845.** Romans 16:15. Note: the name of the Essenes, believed by many to be the Jewish sect from which Christianity emerged, also means the "Saints" or the "Holy Ones."

**2846.** Ephesians 1:1.

**2847.** Philippians 1:1.

**2848.** Colossians 3:12.

**2849.** 2 Peter 3:2.

2850. Romans 1:6.
2851. 1 Thessalonians 2:14.
2852. Acts 2:47. In Jesus' day the word church did not refer to a physical structure, but rather to a group of believers.
2853. Galatians 1:2.
2854. Acts 5:14.
2855. 1 Peter 2:9.
2856. See e.g., Matthew 12:49; Mark 6:1; Luke 6:13; John 4:1.
2857. Acts 6:7.
2858. Acts 28:22.
2859. Acts 24:5.
2860. Matthew 2:23. It is worth noting that a sect bearing this name, the Nazarenes, was later declared "heretical" by the orthodox Church, the same institution that suppressed the "secret sayings" of Jesus. Also worthy of mention: though Matthew quotes a prophecy, "He shall be called a Nazarene" (Matthew 2:23), the Bible contains no such prediction. Indeed, the word Nazareth appears nowhere in the thirty-nine books of the Old Testament. Nazareth has been identified in modern times with the town of en-Nasira.
2861. From a modern academic viewpoint, it would be entirely appropriate to refer to these individuals collectively as the Jesus group, the Jesus people, or the Jesus movement.
2862. See Acts 20:35, where Paul cites a non-canonical saying by Jesus, one that could have only come from a primitive pre-New Testament document.
2863. See Eusebius' *History of the Church*, 3:39.
2864. For more on Q, see my book, *Jesus and the Gospel of Q*.
2865. Acts 2:1, 41-45, 47.
2866. See e.g., Acts 2:46; 3:1-3; 5:42; 21:26-30; 26:21.
2867. See e.g., Acts 2:1; 18:21; 20:16.
2868. John 7:16. Further evidence that Jesus did not invent a new religion is that He left no detailed instructions on how to organize his followers into a fully operational church. He did not even once clearly define "the Kingdom of God (or Heaven)", the very foundation of His life teachings.
2869. Matthew 5:17.
2870. See Matthew 5:1-11.
2871. See e.g., Matthew 3:7; 23:27; Luke 11:39.
2872. See e.g., Matthew 22:15-22; Mark 3:6; 12:13-17.
2873. See e.g., Matthew 3:7; 16:1-12; 22:23-34.
2874. See e.g., Matthew 23:1-39.
2875. Hebrews 13:8.
2876. My paraphrasal.
2877. The Tripartite Tractate, 3:34-35. My paraphrasal.
2878. 1 Corinthians 10:1-4.
2879. Ephesians 1:4-5. See also Philippians 2:13.
2880. Colossians 1:15-17.
2881. 1 Peter 1:20.
2882. Daniel 7:13-14.
2883. Hebrews 7:24. My paraphrasal.
2884. Revelation 1:8.
2885. John 1:15.
2886. John 8:58.
2887. The Gospel of Thomas, Logion 77. My paraphrasal.
2888. John 8:32.
2889. See e.g., John 8:1-15.
2890. Matthew 6:6.
2891. See e.g., Matthew 6:1-6; 23:9.
2892. See e.g., Matthew 22:37-39.
2893. See e.g., Jeremiah 31:34; Matthew 6:14-15; Mark 11:25-26; Luke 17:3-4; 24:57; 1 John 1:9.
2894. John 14:20.
2895. Romans 12:5; AGJC, 15:22; Hebrews 9:24.
2896. Hebrews 8:2. See also Hebrews 9:11.

**2897.** Hebrews 5:5; 6:20; 1 Peter 2:9.

**2898.** See e.g., Matthew 12:48-50; Luke 8:19-21; Romans 10:12; 15:7; Colossians 3:11; 1 Timothy 2:1-5; 1 Peter 2:17; AGJC, 24:27. Paul rightly said: "There is neither Jew nor Greek, there is neither bond nor free, there is neither male nor female: for ye are all one in Christ Jesus." Galatians 3:28. Truly, God "hath made of one blood all nations of men for to dwell on all the face of the earth." Acts 17:26.

**2899.** 2 Corinthians 12:9; Ephesians 2:4, 8.

**2900.** See e.g., Matthew 17:20; Mark 11:22; Luke 22:32. There is scriptural evidence that Jesus also seems to have taught more occultic doctrines, such as the Laws of Metempsychosis and Reincarnation. See e.g., Matthew 11:11-15; 16:13-14; 17:10-13; 26:52. See also Luke 1:13-17; John 1:6; 3:3-8; 8:56-58; 9:1-3, 34; 10:9; 14:1-3, 12; Romans 9:10-14; Ephesians 1:4; Hebrews 2:2-3; Revelation 3:12. The Old Testament too brims with passages that can only be interpreted as palingenetic or reincarnational doctrines, all also closely tied to the Law of Attraction. See e.g., Genesis 9:6; Deuteronomy 31:2; Jeremiah 1:5-6; Job 33:27-30; Proverbs 8:22-31; Obadiah 1:15. Naturally, many mainstream Christian authorities today refute the claim that Jesus and the prophets taught reincarnation. Yet, I invite my readers to study the above scriptures and decide for themselves—with this one important caveat: bear in mind that according to the Law of Attraction, *what we believe becomes true for us.* One must also consider the extrabiblical evidence. Many Gnostic Christian groups are known to have taught the preexistence of the soul and reincarnation, evidence for which maybe found in such sacred Gnostic texts as Pistis Sophia ("Faith Wisdom"). Not only did many early Christian sects formally embrace these doctrines (for example, the Priscillians, Simonists, Manicheans, Marcionists, Basilidians, Valentinians, Cathari, Albigenses, Waldensians, Bogomiles, and Paulicians), but for a time the institutional Church itself did as well, for, as the above passages surely reveal in my opinion, they were taught by none other than Jesus Himself. And based on their writings, many believe that numerous Church Fathers and authorities, such as Saint Augustine, Saint Clement of Alexandria, Bishop Synesius, Justin Martyr, Saint Gregory, Origen, Arnobius, Basilides, Lactantius, and Saint Jerome, also accepted these concepts, and in some cases even taught them. Eventually, of course, because the idea of palingenesis or metempsychosis did not suit the "ecclesiastical necessity" of the Catholic Church, it (and by implication, reincarnation) was condemned, and attempts began to be made to rid the canonical books of all traces of it. The chief orthodox cleansing of the canonical Bible seems to have occurred in the year 553 after the Second Ecumenical Council at Constantinople. It was here that the Byzantine Christian Emperor Justinian I (the Great) decided that the idea of the preexistence of the souls was a threat to the institutional Church, and that it therefore must be declared a "heresy" and struck from the Bible. His famous anti-metempsychosis edict reads: "If anyone asserts the fabulous preexistence of souls, and shall assert the monstrous restoration which follows from it [that is, reincarnation]: let him be anathema." Despite the Church's issuance of execrations against the doctrine of the transmigration of souls, numerous Catholic authorities have supported the idea of reincarnation right into modern times, among them Belgian Cardinal Mercier, Archbishop Passavalli, and the noted European priest Edward Dunski.

**2901.** Romans 10:1-4.

**2902.** Genesis 17:1; Exodus 3:14-15; Psalms 46:10; Mark 8:29; 14:61-62; Luke 22:70; John 6:35; 8:12, 23, 58; 9:5; 10:7-11, 30-39; 11:25; 12:26, 46; 13:13; 14:3, 6, 10-11, 20; 15:1; 17:10, 16.

**2903.** Exodus 3:14; Ezekiel 37:14; John 14:10-11; Romans 8:9, 11; 1 Corinthians 6:17; 2 Corinthians 6:16; Ephesians 2:22; 4:6.

**2904.** John 12:32; 14:20; 15:4; 17:21-23, 26; Colossians 1:27; 3:10-11; Romans 8:10; 1 Corinthians 6:15, 17; 2 Corinthians 5:16; 13:3, 5; Galatians 1:16; 2:20; 4:19; Ephesians 3:14-17; Philippians 1:20; 2:5; 1 Peter 1:11; 1 John 2:27; 3:24; 4:4..

**2905.** John 14:16-17; 1 Corinthians 6:19; 2 Timothy 1:14.

**2906.** The Great I AM has always existed: John 8:58. The Inner God has always existed: Psalms 90:2; 1 Timothy 1:17. The Indwelling Christ has always existed: John 1:1-14. The Holy Spirit has always existed: Hebrews 9:14. Thus all four predate Jesus, as the Master Himself acknowledged: Matthew 22:41-46; Mark 12:35-37. See also Daniel 7:13-14; Micah 5:2; Matthew 28:20; Hebrews 7:3; Revelation 22:13.

**2907.** Luke 9:50. See also Romans 8:31.

**2908.** AGJC, 131:31-40. For the canonical version of this account, see Mark 9:38-41.

**2909.** Religio-facism and spiritual intolerance began early among the Israelites. See e.g., 2 Kings 5:15; Isaiah 45:5; Psalms 135:5.

**2910.** See e.g., Acts 4:10-12.

**2911.** Jesus, like all enlightened souls, understands that it is not religion but spirituality that is important, and spirituality, by its very nature, cannot be categorized, collectivized, or organized. It is an individual journey, which is why Paul enjoined religious tolerance to his followers in Rome. See Romans 14:1-10. It is interesting to note that amid the narrow-mindedness of many of the ancient Jews, there were also signs of religious tolerance. See e.g., the words of Trito-Isaiah in Isaiah 56:1-8.

2912. Matthew 24:14. See also Matthew 4:23; 9:35; Luke 4:43.

2913. Matthew 18:3.

2914. 1 Corinthians 3:8.

2915. See e.g., Matthew 7:16-24.

2916. James 1:27.

2917. See e.g., Ephesians 4 and 5.

2918. Proverbs 12:5.

2919. See e.g., Matthew 7:13-14; 21:32; John 14:6.

2920. See e.g., Mark 1:3; 10:52; Luke 3:4; John 1:23; 14:4; Acts 9:2; 18:25-26; 19:9, 23; 22:4; 24:14, 22. Barnabas, an early disciple and a companion of Paul (Acts 13:43), more aptly called Jesus' "religion" the "Way of the Light." The Epistle of Barnabas, 14:5.

2921. See e.g., Genesis 18:19; Exodus 32:8; Deuteronomy 9:16.

2922. See e.g., 2 Kings 21:22.

2923. See e.g., Job 31:7.

2924. See e.g., Psalms 25:8.

2925. Hermes Trismegistus, a mysterious ancient figure, is said to have founded the religion of Hermeticism and authored the wonderful mystic writings known as the *Corpus Hermeticum*.

2926. Lao Tzu is the probable author of the ancient Chinese work entitled *Tao Te Ching*, "The Way of Virtue."

2927. Micah 6:8. See also Deuteronomy 10:12.

2928. See e.g., Mark 7:17-18; Luke 2:50; John 10:6.

2929. See e.g., Matthew 12:1-8; 15:1-20; 23:1-39; Mark 2:23-28; 12:33.

2930. Ephesians 2:15.

2931. Colossians 2:14. See also Hebrews 7:18-19.

2932. That Jesus, according to the Gospel of Q, saw himself as a teacher of spiritual maxims rather than the world altering Jewish Messiah or the Christian Savior, is clear from numerous canonical Gospel passages that derive from Q. See e.g., the following Q-based scriptures: Luke 4:46-49; 10:3; 12:14.

2933. Acts 10:38.

2934. See e.g., John 1:38, 49; 6:25.

2935. See e.g., John 20:16. See also Mark 10:51, where Rabboni is translated "Lord."

2936. See e.g., Matthew 8:21; John 20:28.

2937. See e.g., Matthew 8:19; Mark 9:5; Luke 8:24; John 9:2.

2938. See e.g., Matthew 23:8, 10.

2939. See e.g., Matthew 5:2; 13:54; Mark 1:21; 2:13; 4:2; 9:31; 10:1; 11:17; 12:35; Luke 4:15, 31; 5:3; 6:6; 11:1; 19:47; 20:1; John 6:59; 7:14, 28; 8:2, 20; 18:20.

2940. Matthew 7:29.

2941. John 3:1-2.

2942. Matthew 23:8-10.

2943. See e.g., John 2:23; 6:2, 26; 7:31; 9:16; 11:47; Acts 2:22.

2944. Matthew 24:14. See also Matthew 4:23; 9:35; Luke 4:43.

2945. John 14:20.

2946. John 17:21.

2947. Luke 17:20-21.

2948. Mark 11:24.

2949. John 7:14-19, 28-29. Paul held the same belief. See 1 Corinthians 4:4.

2950. John 8:28-29, 40, 42, 50, 54.

2951. John 14:24.

2952. John 14:28.

2953. My paraphrasal.

2954. Mark 11:22.

2955. John 10:29.

2956. John 5:19.

2957. John 5:30-31.

2958. John 5:36.

2959. John 6:38.

2960. John 8:50.

2961. John 5:41.

2962. John 5:43.
2963. See e.g., the Sophia of Jesus Christ, 119:15, and also Romans 1:1; 15:16; 2 Corinthians 11:7; 1 Thessalonians 2:2, 8-9; 1 Peter 4:17.
2964. The Gospel of Thomas, Logion 57.
2965. Hebrews 3:1.
2966. Matthew 23:9.
2967. My paraphrasal.
2968. See e.g., Mark 14:15; Luke 22:12; Acts 1:13.
2969. 1 Corinthians 15:47-49.
2970. John 18:36.
2971. Luke 17:20-21.
2972. Hebrews 11:3.
2973. John 1:1-4.
2974. See e.g., Hosea 13:4; Isaiah 43:3, 11; 45:15, 21; Psalms 106:21.
2975. See e.g., Isaiah 47:4; 49:26; 54:8; 60:16; Jeremiah 50:34.
2976. See e.g., Psalms 118:27; 140:6; Isaiah 36:7; Ezekiel 28:26; Haggai 1:12.
2977. See e.g., Psalms 62:7; Isaiah 12:2.
2978. See e.g., Luke 1:46-47.
2979. See e.g., Leviticus 4:3; 6:22; 1 Samuel 2:10; 12:3; 2 Samuel 1:14; 22:51; 1 Chronicles 16:22; Psalms 18:50; 20:6; 28:8; 84:9; Isaiah 45:1; Lamentations 4:20.
2980. See e.g., Matthew 26:63-64; John 18:37.
2981. John 7:28; 8:26, 29.
2982. Mark 10:45.
2983. Mark 10:17-18.
2984. Luke 11:27.
2985. Luke 11:28.
2986. See e.g., Matthew 8:4; 9:30; 12:15-16; Mark 3:12; 5:43; 7:36; 8:30; Luke 5:14; 8:56.
2987. Matthew 17:9; Mark 9:9; Luke 9:36.
2988. Mark 7:24.
2989. Matthew 16:20.
2990. Luke 9:20-21.
2991. Matthew 24:14.
2992. John 7:28; 8:26, 29.
2993. John 12:49.
2994. John 14:28.
2995. The Sophia of Jesus Christ, 96:3-4.
2996. Ephesians 3:9.
2997. See e.g., Mark 10:52; Luke 8:48; 17:19.
2998. Exodus 3:14; Ezekiel 37:14; John 14:10-11; Romans 8:9, 11; 1 Corinthians 3:16; 6:17; 14:25; 2 Corinthians 6:16; 9:14; Ephesians 2:22; 4:6; Philemon 2:13; 1 John 3:24; 4:4, 12-13, 16; Zechariah 2:10.
2999. John 14:10.
3000. John 8:28.
3001. John 5:30-31.
3002. Mark 3:11-12.
3003. Luke 4:40-41.
3004. John 12:44-45.
3005. My paraphrasal.
3006. Psalms 30:10; 1 Corinthians 3:9; 2 Corinthians 6:1; Ephesians 2:19-22; Hebrews 13:6.
3007. Ephesians 5:1.
3008. John 1:45. See also John 6:42. These passages, of course, contradict Matthew 1:18, 20, which states that Jesus' father was the Holy Ghost.
3009. Hebrews 5:8-9.
3010. Mark 1:1.
3011. Mark 1:14. Jesus used the phrase the "gospel of the kingdom," which means the same thing. Matthew 24:14.

**3012.** John 12:32; 14:20; 15:4; 17:21-23, 26; Colossians 1:27; 3:10-11; Romans 8:10; 1 Corinthians 6:15, 17; 2 Corinthians 5:16; 13:3, 5; Galatians 1:16; 2:20; 4:19; Ephesians 3:14-17; Philippians 1:20; 2:5; 1 Peter 1:11; 1 John 2:27; 3:24; 4:4.

**3013.** Matthew 22:36-40.

**3014.** Mark 11:24.

**3015.** Matthew 24:14. See also Matthew 4:23; 9:35; Luke 4:43.

**3016.** John 12:44-45.

**3017.** Luke 17:20-21.

**3018.** Mark 11:24.

**3019.** See e.g., Mark 1:1.

**3020.** Contrary to today's teachings of the Ecclesia (the organized institutionalized Christian Church), ancient Jews and Christians were well versed in astrology and its twelve star signs, as is clear from the following biblical passages. See e.g., Genesis 1:14-15; 37:9-11; Deuteronomy 4:19, 24; Job 3:1-10; 9:7; 38:4-7, 32; Psalms 19:1-4; 84:11; Ecclesiastes 3:1-8; Isaiah 14:12-14; Jeremiah 8:1-2; Ezekiel 1:10; Malachi 4:2; Matthew 2:1-10; 12:32; 13:39-40; 17:2; 24:3; 28:20; Luke 1:78; 18:29-30; 21:25; John 1:4-9; 8:12; 12:46; 1 Corinthians 3:6-8; 10:11; Ephesians 1:21; 5:14; Hebrews 6:5; 9:26; 2 Peter 1:19; Revelation 1:7, 16; 2:27-29; 4:6-7; 8:16; 12:1; 15:3; 22:16. Additionally, Jesus, born in the Age of Aries (the Ram), was at first called "the Lamb of God" (John 1:29, 36; Revelation 5:6). Later, because His ministry began during the Age of Pisces (the Two Fishes), His sacred symbol became the fish, *ichthys* (Greek for "fish") being an acronym for "Jesus, Christ, of God, Son, Savior." Note: The fish is a universal savior symbol due to the fact that it lives in the primordial ocean, the salvific "life-giving" sea, the archetypal amniotic fluid of the Great Mother-Goddess. The fish is thus linked to salvation, fertility, and to female deities in general. Hence, many goddesses have names comprised of the ancient elements *ma* ("mother") or *mar* ("sea"), e.g., Ma Ma, Maerin, Maid Marian, Mar, Mara, Marah, Mari, Maria, Mariam, Marie, Marratu, Mary, Maya, Meri, etc. Other associations: the Greek goddess Aphrodite's name means "born of the (sea) foam," the Canaanite goddess Astarte was known as "Lady of the Sea," and the Virgin Mary was given the Pagan goddess title Stella Maris, "Star of the Sea." Rivers all over Europe retain the names of the goddesses they were once associated with (such as Ireland's Rivers Boyne, Shannon, Lagan, and Bride). Cities, regions, and even countries and continents, also take their names from goddesses: Scotland, Ireland, Italy, Albania, Scandinavia, Crete, Britain, Venice, Athens, Rome, Greece, Holland, Africa, Romania, Denmark, etc. Other ancient links between Jesus, fish, the sea, salvation, and goddesses: early Christian converts were known as *pisciculi*, "little fish." Jesus Himself became an emblem of the Pagan fish-man, a symbol of the Life Principle Within (the Mother-Goddess' amniotic ocean), even comparing Himself to another celebrated fish-man, Jonah, who spent three nights in the "whale's belly" (Matthew 12:40; Luke 11:30). Jesus was a "fisher of men" (Matthew 4:19; Mark 1:17), while the Virgin Mary is often portrayed with the *Vesica Piscis* ("fish bladder"), with its double crescent moons and sacred Yoni, a mystical Christian symbol of the procreative power of the Divine Feminine (the Hindu Mother-Goddess Aditi was often depicted standing on a crescent moon wearing a crown of twelve Zodiacal stars, imagery later appended to Mary; see e.g., Revelation 12:1). Even the Twelve Apostles—patterned on such pre-Christian Pagan deities as the Twelve Titans of Greek mythology, the Twelve Aesirs of Scandinavian mythology, the Twelve Aditya of Hindu mythology, and the Twelve Helpers of Egyptian mythology—became associated with the twelve star-signs of astrology, who annually "orbited" their Divine Father Jesus, known to 4th-Century Christians as the great Pagan sun-god *Sol Invictus*. In chronological order we have what I call the Twelve Apostolic Powers of Man as emblemized in the twelve star-signs: James, Aries the Ram (judgement); Andrew, Taurus the Bull (strength); Thomas, Gemini the Twins (understanding); Nathaniel, Cancer the Crab (imagination); Judas, Leo the Lion (acquisitiveness); James the Just, Virgo the Virgin (self-denial); Jude, Libra the Scales (orderliness); John, Scorpio the Scorpion (love); Philip, Sagittarius the Archer (power); Simon, Capricorn the Goat (emotion); Matthew, Aquarius the Water Bearer (the will); and Peter, Pisces the Two Fishes (faith). The "Twelve Days of Christmas" were also modeled on these ancient Pagan-Christian connections, beginning with James (Aries) on December 26, ending with Peter (Pisces) on January 6. In mystical Christianity the Twelve Apostles are also connected to the Twelve Mental Faculties (closely related to the Twelve Apostolic Powers above). There are many interpretations, including: 1) Peter, the deductive mind; 2) Andrew, faith; 3) James, hope; 4) Philip, love; 5) Bartholomew, perseverance; 6) Thomas, truth-seeking; 8) James Alpheus, modesty; 9) Simon, gentleness; 10) Judas (brother of James), compassion; 11) Matthew, critical thinking; and 12) Judas Iscariot, prudence. In Hinduism the Sacred Twelve are symbolic of Cosmic Man, and are thus associated with the Sahasrara (seventh) Chakra (the Christ, the Sun, the Son, or Crown Chakra) and the six lower spinal "wheels," which owing to their dual positive and negative energies, equal twelve: the sixth, Ajna Chakra; fifth, Vishudda Chakra; fourth, Anahata Chakra; third, Manipura Chakra; second, Svadhishthana Chakra; and first, the Muladhara Chakra. Here, the human body—along with its millions of "subjects" (cells)—is considered a "kingdom," ruled over by a king, the Indwelling Christ, who exists (as the Crown Chakra) in the skull (behind the Third Eye), symbolized in Christian legend as Golgotha (the "place of the skull"), the skullcap shaped hill at Jerusalem where Jesus was crucified. See Matthew 27:3; Mark 15:22; John 19:17. Luke calls Golgotha *kranion* in Greek, which is cranium in English. King James' scribes translated *kranion* as "Calvary." See Luke 23:33. The English word Calvary derives from *calvariae locus*, the Latin translation of the Greek *kraniou topos* (the "location of the cranium"). According to Eusebius, the Romans later built a temple honoring the goddess Aphrodite over Golgotha. This was long ago torn down, however, and replaced with a Christian church, the first construction which was begun by the Crusaders in the 12th Century.

**3021.** Ezekiel 1:5, 10; Revelation 4:6-7. Ezekiel borrowed his "four living creatures" from the Greeks' Four Compass-Deities, an astrological Pantheon that had already existed in various forms for thousands of years. The Zodiac of the ancient Egyptians, for example, possessed only four constellations, known as "the Four Sons of Horus": 1) Amset, the man-god who ruled Winter and the north. 2) Hapi, the ape-god who ruled Summer and the south. 3) Tuamutef, the jackal-god who ruled Spring and the east. 4) Gebhsennuf, the hawk-god who ruled Autumn and the west.

**3022.** Aquila (later changed to Scorpio, symbolized by the scorpion) rules the Autumnal Equinox and the compass direction west.

**3023.** Leo rules the Summer Solstice and the compass direction south.

**3024.** Aquarius rules the Winter Solstice and the compass direction north.

**3025.** Taurus rules the Vernal Equinox and the compass direction east.

**3026.** Matthew 27:37; John 19:19.

**3027.** My interpretation.

**3028.** During the early 6th Century, under the Christian Emperor Justinian's "Corpus Juris Civilis," numerous laws were passed banning Paganism, and "apostasy," that is, embracing any faith but Catholicism, was punishable by death.

**3029.** Paul, as just one example, acknowledged that many of his followers were former Pagans. See 1 Corinthians 12:1-2.

**3030.** According to paleographic, biblical, mythological, and historical evidence, including that which has been uncovered by the form critic school, it was at this time that Jesus began to be portrayed as a sort of dying-and-rising god, modeled on the likes of such earlier Pagan messiah- and savior-deities as the Greek Adonis, the Phrygian Attis, the Hindu Krishna, the Chaldean Criti, the Greek Dionysus, the Egyptian Horus, the Greek Ieoud, the Jewish Jesus ben Pandira, the Essenic Teacher of Righteousness (or Son of Man), the Babylonian Marduk, the Indian Mitra, the Graeco-Roman Mithras, the Graeco-Roman Prometheus, the Hebrew Shemesh, the Gnostic Jewish Son of Righteousness, and the Babylonian Tammuz. For more on this topic, see my book *Christmas Before Christianity*.

**3031.** Matthew 19:17; Mark 10:18.

**3032.** See e.g., Matthew 2:2; 27:37; Mark 15:18; Luke 23:38; John 12:13; 19:19; Acts 1:6; Revelation 5:13.

**3033.** Ephesians 4:18.

**3034.** The Lord never once calls Himself the "Son of God" in any of the three layers of the Gospel of Q, the earliest known record of Jesus' teachings. He does, however, call Himself the "Son of Man" on numerous occasions throughout Q, just as He does in the canonical Gospels. See e.g., Matthew 16:13; Luke 22:48; John 8:28.

**3035.** As we have seen, scriptures such as Acts 8:37 (referring to Jesus as the "Son of God") were added to the New Testament after the mid 4th Century A.D., the time period in which the Codex Sinaiticus—in which this particular passage is absent—was written.

**3036.** See John 10:36. This scripture—in which Jesus refers back to an *earlier* statement of His ("because I said 'I am the Son of God'")—must be an interpolation, because there is no other canonical Gospel passage in which He *openly* and *directly* refers to Himself by this title. The interpolator failed to cross check the scriptures before putting this obviously out-of-place comment in the Lord's mouth.

**3037.** John 10:34.

**3038.** Malachi 4:2.

**3039.** See Acts 20:7.

**3040.** See Revelation 5:5. For more on these changes to the figure of Jesus, see my book *Christmas Before Christianity: How the Birthday of the "Sun" Became the Birthday of the "Son."*

**3041.** John 12:43.

**3042.** 2 Timothy 3:8.

**3043.** 1 Timothy 6:5.

**3044.** Philippians 1:15-17.

**3045.** Titus 1:14. My paraphrasal.

**3046.** Of the thousands of examples of biblical tampering and redacting that could be given, here are a few well-known examples from the four Gospels. 1) Originally Matthew started with Chapter 3. Chapters 1 and 2 were appended later. 2) The Matthean birth story is jumbled, a result of later emendations and interpolations. For example, a) 1:25 repeats 1:21; b) 1:18, 20 contradict 1:23; c) 1:16 contradicts Luke 3:23. Other signs of overt manipulation in Matthew: a) the words "except it be for fornication" were added later to 19:9; b) 19:19 contradicts Luke 14:26; c) in Matthew (and Luke) the Resurrection occurs in one day, but in John it takes over a week. 3) Matthew 18:11 is an interpolation missing from the Codex Sinaiticus. 4) Matthew 23:14 is an interpolation missing from the Codex Sinaiticus. 5) The phrase "Son of God" in Mark 1:1 is an interpolation, for it is not found in many early manuscripts, including the Codex Sinaiticus. 6) Mark 9:44, 46 are late interpolations that are also missing from many early manuscripts, including the Codex Sinaiticus. 7) Mark 11:26, an interpolation, is missing from the Codex Sinaiticus. 8) Mark 15:28, an interpolation missing from the Codex Sinaiticus. 9) The last twelve verses of Mark 16 were added much later (in the 2nd Century), allegedly by a man named Aristion. This (i.e., verses 9-20), the so-called "longer version," though known to some of the early Church Fathers (e.g., Justin Martyr, Tatian, and Irenaeus), was not declared "canonical" until the year 1545, at the Council of Trent. 10) Like Matthew, the first two chapters of Luke were added later. Originally it began with what is now Chapter 3. 11) Luke 17:36 is an interpolation missing from the Codex Sinaiticus. 12) Luke 23:17 is an interpolation missing from the Codex Sinaiticus. 13) John contains no parables, no nativity story, no genealogy of Jesus, no agony in the Garden of Gethsemane, and no mention of Judas' kiss or the Mount of Olives. Why? In fact, John portrays a Jesus so entirely different from Matthew, Mark, and Luke, that his Gospel was placed in its own category (the Johannine literature, which includes John's three letters), separate from the triple tradition of the Synoptic Gospels. 14) John 5:4 is an obvious interpolation, one that is missing from the Codex Sinaiticus. 15) John 17:3 is also an overt addition, for Jesus would have never referred to Himself "Jesus Christ." 16) John 7:5 contradicts historical fact, for Jesus' brother James the Just later became head of the Church at Jerusalem (see e.g., Acts 12:17; 15:13; 21:18; 1 Corinthians 15:7; Galatians 2:9). 17) John 7:53-8:11 are late additions, as they are missing from the oldest known manuscripts, such as the Codex Sinaiticus. 18) John 19:19 reads: "Jesus of Nazareth," a mistranslation of the original: "Jesus the Nazarene." 19) John's prologue (1:1-18) is not original. A common Graeco-Roman hymn concerning the Holy Breath (the "Word") descending into the material plane as light, it was later added to the main text to serve as the book's preface. 20) John 21 is a late addition to the Gospel, which originally ended with Chapter 20. 21) John 6:62 is an unfinished sentence. 22) John 7:53 through 8:1-11 is a late addition, for it is missing from early New Testament manuscripts, such as the Codex Sinaiticus. 23) John 12:34 claims that Mosaic Law stipulates that the "Christ abideth for ever," yet no such passage exists in the Old Testament. 24) The editors and redactors of John garbled Jesus' words at the Last Supper, providing two different endings to His discourse (see John 14:31; 18:1). The original text terminated at the close of Chapter 14, with Chapters 15, 16, and 17 (which contain some duplications of Chapter 14) being appended by an unknown interpolator. As mentioned, the Bible contains thousands of such examples. Matthew and Mark, for instance, tell us that Jesus' last words were different than those according to Luke, and Luke tells us that they were different than those according to John. See Matthew 27:46; Mark 15:34 (both are copies of Psalms 22:1); Luke 23:46; John 19:30. Then there are the two different versions of the death of Judas. See Matthew 27:5; Acts 1:18. John says that Jesus ascended to Heaven on the same day as His resurrection (John 20:17), while Luke tells us that Jesus did not ascend for forty days (Acts 1:3). There are three slightly different accounts of Paul's conversion, even within the same book. See Acts 9:1-19; 22:3-16; 26:2-18. Like so many other New Testament books, Acts contains a number of late interpolations, for example, 15:34; 24:7; 28:29, none of which appear in the Codex Sinaiticus. The list goes on. The many "irreconcilable differences" between the canonical Gospels call into question both the accuracy and the historicity of all four books. Of course, these issues mattered little to the original unknown authors, who wrote for theological purposes not historical ones. And it is true that the countless internal problems of the four Gospels need not affect one's faith. However, what they do touch on is the creed of Bible inerrancy and scriptural infallibility. Mainstream Christianity's ongoing doctrinal retranslations, mistranslations, additions, subtractions, and overall rewriting and reinterpreting, all which continue unabated into the present day, have only added to the scriptural confusion spawned by the early Church.

**3047.** Matthew 6:6.

**3048.** Matthew 24;14

**3049.** Luke 8:10.

**3050.** John 12:32; 14:20; 15:4; 17:21-23, 26; Colossians 1:27; 3:10-11; Romans 8:10; 1 Corinthians 6:15, 17; 2 Corinthians 5:16; 13:3, 5; Galatians 1:16; 2:20; 4:19; Ephesians 3:14-17; Philippians 1:20; 2:5; 1 Peter 1:11; 1 John 2:27; 3:24; 4:4.

**3051.** As mentioned, by repeatedly contradicting one another, it is obvious that the four canonical Gospels call into question each other's veracity. As just one example, Jesus' final words on the cross differ in all four books: see Matthew 27:46 (who uses Hebrew based text); Mark 15:34-35 (who uses Aramaic based text); Luke 23:46; and John 19:30 (who both use Greek). Only one can be authentic. Which one is it? Because of this problem, redaction and form critics view all four passages as fictional Catholic embellishments. The hundreds of differences between the four Gospels also reveal the enormous editing processes they have each been subjected to over the centuries. This biblical manipulation continues into the present day, with each new "translation" veering further and further away from the original meaning of Jesus' words.

**3052.** Matthew 24:14.

**3053.** Mark 1:1.

**3054.** John 3:16.

**3055.** Daniel 7:13-14; John 10:34.

**3056.** According to majority opinion, the twenty-seven books of the New Testament were written in the following chronological order, from the most undeveloped Christology in James to the most sophisticated Christology in Revelation. The estimated year(s) in which each document is believed to have been written follows in parentheses: 1) James (A.D. 35-50s); 2) Galatians (48-58); 3) Titus (50s); 4) Mark (50s-60s); 5) Matthew (50s-60s); 6) 1 Thessalonians (51); 7) 2 Thessalonians (51); 8) 1 Corinthians (55); 9) 2 Corinthians (56); 10) Romans (57); 11) Colossians (60); 12) Philemon (60); 13) Ephesians (60); 14) Philippians (61); 15) Luke (early 60s); 16) Acts (62-64); 17) 1 Timothy (62-64); 18) 1 Peter (65); 19) 2 Timothy (64-68); 20) 2 Peter (67-68); 21) Hebrews (68); 22) Jude (69); 23) John (85); 24) 1 John (89); 25); 3 John (89); 26) 2 John (90); 27) Revelation (95-96). As no complete original manuscript of any of the New Testament books has ever been found, none of these dates are certain. If, for example, the "Theophilus" Luke addresses (Luke 1:3; see also Acts 1:1) is Theophilus of Antioch, a church patriarch who died around the year 183, the Gospel of Luke may have actually been written as late as the early 180s. Note: elements of the transformation of Jesus from a counterculture philosopher and teacher to a mythological apocalyptic visionary can also be traced in the three layers of the Gospel of Q: Q1 (probably composed in the early A.D. 30s), Q2 (possibly composed in the 40s or 50s), and Q3 (possibly composed as late as the year 75).

**3057.** Romans 15:8.

**3058.** 2 Corinthians 11:10.

**3059.** From Blake's poem, "The Everlasting Gospel," 4:1-2, 7-8, 13-14.

**3060.** Daniel 7:13-14; John 10:34.

**3061.** John 17:21; Hebrews 12:10; 2 Peter 1:4.

**3062.** Daniel 7:13-14.

**3063.** See e.g., Acts 9:1-9; 22:6-11.

**3064.** See Daniel 7:13-14.

**3065.** Colossians 1:12-15.

**3066.** One school of Docetism holds that Jesus, though a Son of God, was a human being, who did not fully recognize his own Indwelling Christ until he received this revelation in the form of a dove at the time of His baptism (enlightenment). Another school of Docetism maintains that Jesus' body was not actually physical, but was rather a "phantasm" made of "spiritual" (non-physical) flesh. Thus, He did not suffer on the cross. Though Paul seems to have preached a form of Gnostic Docetism in the 1st Century (see the foregoing and the following two notes), the Catholic Church pronounced the doctrine heretical at the First Council of Nicaea in the year 325.

**3067.** 2 Corinthians 5:16-17.

**3068.** Matthew 24:14.

**3069.** Mark 1:1.

**3070.** John 12:32; 14:20; 15:4; 17:21-23, 26; Colossians 1:27; 3:10-11; Romans 8:10; 1 Corinthians 6:15, 17; 2 Corinthians 5:16; 13:3, 5; Galatians 1:16; 2:20; 4:19; Ephesians 3:14-17; Philippians 1:20; 2:5; 1 Peter 1:11; 1 John 2:27; 3:24; 4:4.

**3071.** Exodus 3:14; Ezekiel 37:14; John 14:10-11; Romans 8:9, 11; 1 Corinthians 3:16; 6:17; 14:25; 2 Corinthians 6:16; 9:14; Ephesians 2:22; 4:6; Philemon 2:13; 1 John 3:24; 4:4, 12-13, 16; Zechariah 2:10.

**3072.** Galatians 1:7.

**3073.** 2 Corinthians 11:4.

**3074.** Romans 1:25.

**3075.** 2 Timothy 4:4.

**3076.** 2 Corinthians 11:13.

**3077.** Romans 1:23.

**3078.** Mark 12:27.

3079. My paraphrasal of various passages from the Apocalypse of Peter.
3080. 2 Peter 2:1-2.
3081. 2 Peter 1:16.
3082. Colossians 2:8.
3083. Titus 1:9-11, 14.
3084. Matthew 24:14.
3085. See e.g., Matthew 4:23; 9:35; 24:14.
3086. Mark 1:1.
3087. Mark 1:14.
3088. See e.g., Luke 4:18; 7:22; 9:6; 20:1.
3089. Mark 1:14.
3090. Mark 1:1.
3091. Matthew 24:14.
3092. Mark 7:13.
3093. Luke 5:31.
3094. My paraphrasal.
3095. Isaiah 61:1.
3096. Luke 4:18.
3097. Matthew 10:8.
3098. Luke 9:1-2, 6.
3099. Matthew 9:35.
3100. Matthew 24:14.
3101. Hebrews 6:1.
3102. Luke 9:11.
3103. Luke 10:8-9.
3104. Luke 4:42-43.
3105. Ephesians 5:5.
3106. There is one near exception: 2 Thessalonians 1:8.
3107. Acts 20:24.
3108. Romans 1:1.
3109. Romans 10:15.
3110. Ephesians 1:13.
3111. 1 Timothy 1:11.
3112. Acts 8:25.
3113. Romans 2:16; 16:25.
3114. Romans 1:9.
3115. Romans 1:16.
3116. 2 Corinthians 2:12.
3117. Colossians 1:27.
3118. Ephesians 6:19.
3119. 2 Timothy 1:8.
3120. Ephesians 1:19.
3121. See 1 John 5:7.
3122. See e.g., Mark 1:27.
3123. Luke 4:32.
3124. 2 Corinthians 11:7. My paraphrasal.
3125. Matthew 24:14.
3126. Luke 8:10.
3127. Matthew 10:8.
3128. John 14:20.
3129. Psalms 145:21.

# MEET THE AUTHOR

ochlainn Seabrook, winner of the prestigious Jefferson Davis Historical Gold Medal for his "masterpiece," *A Rebel Born: A Defense of Nathan Bedford Forrest*, is an unreconstructed Southern historian, award-winning author, Civil War scholar, and traditional Southern Agrarian of Scottish, English, Irish, Welsh, German, and Italian extraction. An encyclopedist, lexicographer, musician, artist, graphic designer, genealogist, and photographer, as well as an award-winning poet, songwriter, and screenwriter, he has a 40 year background in historical nonfiction writing and is a member of the Sons of Confederate Veterans, the Civil War Trust, and the National Grange.

Due to similarities in their writing styles, ideas, and literary works, Seabrook is often referred to as the "new Shelby Foote," the "Southern Joseph Campbell," and the "American Robert Graves" (his English cousin).

The grandson of an Appalachian coal-mining family, Seabrook is a seventh-generation Kentuckian, co-chair of the Jent/Gent Family Committee (Kentucky), founder and director of the Blakeney Family Tree Project, and a board member of the Friends of Colonel Benjamin E. Caudill. Seabrook's literary works have been endorsed by leading authorities, museum curators, award-winning historians, bestselling authors, celebrities, noted scientists, well respected educators, TV show hosts and producers, renowned military artists, esteemed Southern organizations, and distinguished academicians from around the world.

Lochlainn Seabrook, award-winning Civil War scholar, unreconstructed Southern historian, and Bible authority, is America's most popular and prolific pro-South author. He holds the world's record for the most Nathan Bedford Forrest books written by a single author: nine.

Seabrook has authored over 45 popular adult books on the American Civil War, American and international slavery, the U.S. Confederacy (1781), the Southern Confederacy (1861), religion, theology and thealogy, Jesus, the Bible, the Apocrypha, the Law of Attraction, alternative health, spirituality, ghost stories, the paranormal, ufology, social issues, and cross-cultural studies of the family and marriage. His Confederate biographies, pro-South studies, genealogical monographs, family histories, military encyclopedias, self-help guides, and etymological dictionaries have received wide acclaim.

Seabrook's eight children's books include a Southern guide to the Civil War, a biography of Nathan Bedford Forrest, a dictionary of religion and myth, a rewriting of the King Arthur legend (which reinstates the original pre-Christian motifs), two bedtime stories for preschoolers, a naturalist's guidebook to owls, a worldwide look at the family, and an examination of the Near-Death Experience.

Of blue-blooded Southern stock through his Kentucky, Tennessee, Virginia, West Virginia, and North Carolina ancestors, he is a direct descendant of European royalty via his 6th great-grandfather, the Earl of Oxford, after which London's famous Harley Street is named. Among his celebrated male Celtic ancestors is Robert the Bruce, King of Scotland, Seabrook's 22nd great-grandfather. The 21st great-grandson of Edward I "Longshanks" Plantagenet), King of England, Seabrook is a thirteenth-generation Southerner through his descent from the colonists of Jamestown, Virginia (1607).

The 2nd, 3rd, and 4th great-grandson of dozens of Confederate soldiers, one of his closest connections to the War for Southern Independence is through his 3rd great-grandfather, Elias Jent, Sr., who fought for the Confederacy in the Thirteenth Cavalry Kentucky under Seabrook's 2nd cousin, Colonel Benjamin E. Caudill. The Thirteenth, also known as "Caudill's Army," fought in numerous conflicts, including the Battles of Saltville, Gladsville, Mill Cliff, Poor Fork, Whitesburg, and Leatherwood.

Seabrook is a descendant of the families of Alexander H. Stephens, John Singleton Mosby, and Edmund Winchester Rucker, and is related to the following Confederates and other 19th-Century luminaries: Robert E. Lee, Stephen Dill Lee, Stonewall Jackson, Nathan Bedford Forrest, James Longstreet, John Hunt Morgan, Jeb Stuart, P. G. T. Beauregard (designed the Confederate Battle Flag), George W. Gordon, John Bell Hood, Alexander Peter Stewart, Arthur M. Manigault, Joseph Manigault, Charles Scott Venable, Thornton A. Washington, John A. Washington, Abraham Buford, Edmund W. Pettus, Theodrick "Tod" Carter, John B. Womack, John H. Winder, Gideon J. Pillow, States Rights Gist, Henry R. Jackson, John Lawton Seabrook, John C. Breckinridge, Leonidas Polk, Zachary Taylor, Sarah Knox Taylor (first wife of Jefferson Davis), Richard Taylor, Davy Crockett, Daniel Boone, Meriwether Lewis (of the Lewis and Clark Expedition) Andrew Jackson, James K. Polk, Abram Poindexter Maury (founder of Franklin, TN), William Giles Harding, Zebulon Vance, Thomas Jefferson, George Wythe Randolph (grandson of Jefferson), Felix K. Zollicoffer, Fitzhugh Lee, Nathaniel F. Cheairs, Jesse James, Frank James, Robert Brank Vance, Charles Sidney Winder, John W. McGavock, Caroline E. (Winder) McGavock, David Harding McGavock, Lysander McGavock, James Randal McGavock, Randal William McGavock, Francis McGavock, Emily McGavock, William Henry F. Lee, Lucius E. Polk, Minor Meriwether (husband of noted pro-South author Elizabeth Avery Meriwether), Ellen Bourne Tynes (wife of Forrest's chief of artillery, Captain John W. Morton), South Carolina Senators Preston Smith Brooks and Andrew Pickens Butler, and famed South Carolina diarist Mary Chesnut.

Seabrook's modern day cousins include: Patrick J. Buchanan (conservative author), Cindy Crawford (model), Shelby Lee Adams (Letcher County, Kentucky, portrait photographer), Bertram Thomas Combs (Kentucky's fiftieth governor), Edith Bolling (wife of President Woodrow Wilson), and actors Robert Duvall, Reese Witherspoon, Lee Marvin, Rebecca Gayheart, Andy Griffith, and Tom Cruise.

Seabrook's screenplay, *A Rebel Born*, based on his book of the same name, has been signed with acclaimed filmmaker Christopher Forbes (of Forbes Film). It is now in pre-production, and is set for release in 2016 as a full-length feature film. This will be the first movie ever made of Nathan Bedford Forrest's life story, and as a historically accurate project written from the Southern perspective, is destined to be one of the most talked about Civil War films of all time.

Born with music in his blood, Seabrook is an award-winning, multi-genre, BMI-Nashville songwriter and lyricist who has composed some 3,000 songs (250 albums), and whose original music has been heard in film (*A Rebel Born, Cowgirls 'n Angels, Confederate Cavalry, Billy the Kid: Showdown in Lincoln County, Vengeance Without Mercy, Last Step, County Line, The Mark*) and on TV and radio worldwide. A musician, producer, multi-instrumentalist, and renown performer—whose keyboard work has been variously compared to pianists from Hargus Robbins and Vince Guaraldi to Elton John and Leonard Bernstein—Seabrook has opened for groups such as the Earl Scruggs Review, Ted Nugent, and Bob Seger, and has performed privately for such public figures as President Ronald Reagan, Burt Reynolds, Loni Anderson, and Senator Edward W. Brooke. Seabrook's cousins in the music business include: Johnny Cash, Elvis Presley, Billy Ray and Miley Cyrus, Patty Loveless, Tim McGraw, Lee Ann Womack, Dolly Parton, Pat Boone, Naomi, Wynonna, and Ashley Judd, Ricky Skaggs, the Sunshine Sisters, Martha Carson, and Chet Atkins.

Seabrook, a libertarian, lives with his wife and family in historic Middle Tennessee, the heart of Forrest country and the Confederacy, where his conservative Southern ancestors fought valiantly against Liberal Lincoln and the progressive North in defense of Jeffersonianism, constitutional government, and personal liberty.

LOCHLAINNSEABROOK.COM

If you enjoyed this book, you will be interested in Mr. Seabrook's other popular Jesus-related titles:

☞ THE BIBLE & THE LAW OF ATTRACTION: 99 TEACHINGS OF JESUS, THE APOSTLES, & THE PROPHETS
☞ JESUS & THE GOSPEL OF Q: CHRIST'S PRE-CHRISTIAN TEACHINGS AS RECORDED IN THE NEW TESTAMENT
☞ CHRIST IS ALL & IN ALL: REDISCOVERING YOUR DIVINE NATURE & THE KINGDOM WITHIN
☞ CHRISTMAS BEFORE CHRISTIANITY: HOW THE BIRTHDAY OF THE "SUN" BECAME THE BIRTHDAY OF THE "SON"

*Available from Sea Raven Press and wherever fine books are sold*

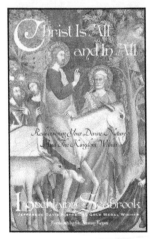
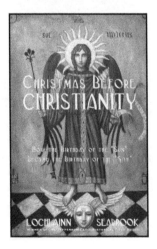

ALL OF OUR BOOK COVERS ARE AVAILABLE AS 11" X 17" POSTERS, SUITABLE FOR FRAMING.

# SeaRavenPress.com

# SOW GOOD THOUGHTS!